THE HUMAN RECORD

Sources of Global History

VOLUME I: *To 1700*

ALFRED J. ANDREA
University of Vermont

JAMES H. OVERFIELD
University of Vermont

HOUGHTON MIFFLIN COMPANY BOSTON
Dallas Geneva, Illinois Palo Alto Princeton, New Jersey

CREDITS

Cover

World Map by al-Idrisi (twelfth century); MS. Pococke 375, folios 3v.–4v., Bodleian Library, Oxford.

Chapter-Opening Illustrations

Chapter 1: Courtesy of the Trustees of the British Museum. Chapter 2: Erich Lessing Culture and Fine Arts Archive. Chapter 3: Antonello Perissinotto, Padua. Chapter 4: R. B. Fleming. Chapter 5: Ministry of Information and Broadcasting, Government of India. Chapter 6: Museum fuer Indische Kunst Berlin/Staatliche Museen Preussischer Kulturbesitz. Chapter 7: Erich Lessing Culture and Fine Arts Archive. Chapter 8: Oronoz Photographic Archives, Madrid. Chapter 9: Bradley Smith Collection/Laurie Platt Winfrey, Inc. Chapter 10: Adam Woolfitt/Woodfin Camp & Associates. Chapter 11: 45.32 Chinese Painting: Yüan dynasty, corr. with A.D. 1347. Chao Yung, by. A horse and a groom in a red coat. Paper makimono: 31.7 × 73.5 cm (12-1/2 × 28-15/16″). Courtesy of the Freer Gallery of Art, Smithsonian Institution, Washington, D.C. Chapter 12: Courtesy of the Trustees of the British Museum. Chapter 13: The Bettmann Archive.

Source credits appear on page 451.

Printed in the U.S.A.

Library of Congress Catalog Card Number: 89-80909

ISBN: 0-395-48399-9

ABCDEFGHIJ-B-9543210-89

We Dedicate This Book with Love and Thanks to
Juanita B. Andrea and Susan L. Overfield

CONTENTS

PART III *Continuity, Change, and Interchange, 500–1500*

CHAPTER 9 Asia ... 264

CHAPTER 10 Western Europe ... 305

GEOGRAPHIC CONTENTS

Africa

The Americas

The Ancient Mediterranean

Central Asia

China

India

Japan

Medieval and Early Modern Europe

Southeast Asia

Southwest Asia

TOPICAL CONTENTS

PREFACE

Many goals and principles have guided our work on *The Human Record.* We are committed to the proposition that students of history at all levels need to meet the challenge of analyzing primary sources. Involvement with the evidence of the past enables students to see that historical scholarship is primarily a process of drawing inferences from incomplete and often ambiguous clues, not of collecting, cataloguing, and memorizing immutable facts. Analysis of primary sources is also the basis for historical understanding; to discover what people thought and did and to organize this into a record of the human past, historians must search for evidence—for the sources of history. For the student of world history, who attempts to understand the development over time of human institutions and ways of thought, this search is essential to determine periods of significant historical change, as well as lines of continuity.

For these reasons, we have compiled a collection of sources that emphasizes the long and intricate course of human history and that reveals the differences and affinities among the world's cultures. Volume I follows the evolution of the cultures that most significantly influenced world history from 3500 B.C. to A.D. 1700, with particular emphasis on the major religious, social, and intellectual traditions of the Afro-Eurasian ecumene. It concurrently develops the theme of the growing interconnectedness of human societies down to the early modern age. Volume II traces the gradual emergence of the West to a position of global hegemony, the simultaneous historical development of other civilizations and societies around the world, the eventual anticolonial revolts of the twentieth century, and the emergence of today's "one world." We have taken care to group selections thematically, avoiding isolated sources that provide a "taste" of some culture or age but, by their dissociation, shed no light on the dual phenomena of historical change and continuity. Our objective is to present an overview of global history in mosaic form.

In selecting and placing the various pieces of our mosaic, we aimed to create a balanced picture of human history and to craft a book that reveals the contributions of all major geographic areas. In a similar vein, we attempted to give our readers a collection of sources representing a wide variety of perspectives and experiences. Believing that the study of history properly concerns every aspect of past human behavior, we sought sources that mirror the concerns and practices of all manner of persons and groups.

At the same time, most of the sources that appear in these two volumes reflect the actions and thoughts of history's great and near great. It cannot be otherwise in a book that seeks to cover the highpoints of over five millennia of history.

Our quest for historical balance also led us into the arena of nonverbal evidence. Although most historians center their research on documentary sources, the discipline obligates us to consider all of the clues surrendered by the past, and these include its artifacts. Moreover, we have discovered that students enjoy analyzing pictures of artifacts and seem to remember vividly the conclusions they draw from them. For these reasons, we have included a number of illustrations of works of art that we ask the users of this book to analyze as historical sources. We also took special care in selecting the artwork that opens each chapter. Each piece of art illustrates an important theme developed in the chapter, and we urge our readers to study these pictures as additional sources. All are identified at the rear of the volume.

For the introductory student, source analysis is often a daunting exercise. Therefore, to make these selections as accessible as possible, we have provided our readers with a variety of aids. First there is the Prologue, in which we explain, initially in a theoretical manner and then through concrete examples, how a student of history goes about the task of interpreting written and artifactual sources. Next we offer part, chapter, subchapter, and individual source introductions, all to help the reader place each selection into a meaningful context and to understand its historical role and significance.

Suggested questions for analysis also precede each source. The questions fall into three categories. Some are quite specific and are intended to assist the reader in picking out important pieces of information or in noticing something we consider especially suggestive. Answering concrete questions of this sort prepares the student researcher for the next, more significant level of analysis, drawing general inferences. Questions that demand such conclusions invariably follow. Finally, we offer questions that challenge the student to compare the individual or society that produced a particular source with an individual, group, or culture encountered earlier in the volume. We believe such comparisons help students fix more firmly in their minds the distinguishing cultural characteristics of the various societies they encounter in their brief survey of world history.

Another form of help we proffer is to gloss the sources, explaining in full those words and allusions that a first-year college student cannot reasonably be expected to know. To facilitate reading, these footnotes appear at the bottom of the page on which they are cited. Some documents also contain italicized interlinear notes that serve as transitions and suggest the main themes of the passages that follow. Used primarily in lengthier sources from the great thinkers, these notes help to guide students through the readings.

By virtues of its comprehensiveness, organization, and pedagologic features, some instructors may choose to use *The Human Record* as a replacement for a standard textbook. Most of our colleagues, however, will probably use it as a supplement to a standard text, and many will decide not to require their students to analyze every entry. To assist professors (and students) in selecting documents and artifacts that best suit their interests and needs, we have prepared two analytical tables of contents for each volume. The first lists readings and artifacts by geographic and cultural area, the second by topic. The two tables suggest to instructor and student alike the rich variety of material available within these pages, particularly for research papers in comparative history.

Specific suggestions for assignments and classroom activities are offered in the Instructor's Manual that accompanies *The Human Record*. In this manual, prepared by the editors, we also explain our reasons for choosing the sources that appear in these volumes and the insights we believe students should be capable of drawing from them. Further, we describe classroom strategies for eliciting thought and discussion on the various sources and offer bibliographic suggestions and a pronunciation guide. Much of the advice we present is the fruit of our own use of these sources in the classroom.

Our final duty is to thank the many professionals who offered their expert advice and assistance during the preparation of this book. Among our friends and colleagues at the University of Vermont, we must acknowledge the cheerful and competent help of Bridget M. Butler, the Department of History's Administrative Assistant, and the invaluable support of the entire Reference Department of Bailey-Howe Library, particularly Nancy Crane, its director, and Bonnie Ryan, head of interlibrary loan services. Scholars at UVM who generously shared their expertise with us include Robert V. Daniels, Constance McGovern, Kristin M. Peterson-Ishaq, Abubaker Saad, Wolfe W. Schmokel, Peter Seybolt, John W. Seyller, Marshall True, and Denise Youngblood. We wish to thank especially Peter D. Andrea, who drew the prototype for map 2 in Volume I.

We wish also to acknowledge the following instructors who read and commented on all or portions of our manuscript in its various stages of preparation. Their comments and suggestions helped us to see more clearly what we were doing and where we were headed. They forced us to rethink a number of our conclusions and general statements, and in several instances we deleted or added a particular text in response to excellent advice. Even on those occasions when we disagreed with their interpretations and suggestions, we benefited from the exchange of ideas.

Jerry Bentley, *University of Hawaii, Manoa*
Dan Binkley, *Hawaii Pacific College*
Robert Carlisle, *St. Lawrence University*

James Casada, *Winthrop College*
Allen Cronenberg, *Auburn University*
Stephen Englehart, *California Polytechnic State University, Pomona*
Lorraine Gesick, *University of Nebraska at Omaha*
Marc Gilbert, *North Georgia College*
Robert Gowen, *East Carolina University*
William Hamblin, *University of Southern Mississippi*
Craig Lockard, *University of Wisconsin—Green Bay*
Peter Mellini, *Sonoma State University*
Bruce Mouser, *University of Wisconsin—La Crosse*
Richard Porterfield, *Glassboro State College*
Kerry Spiers, *University of Louisville*

Special thanks are owed to the editors and staff of Houghton Mifflin. It has been a pleasure to work with a publishing firm that takes such pride in its professionalism.

Finally, our debt to our spouses is beyond payment, but the dedication of this book to them reflects in some small way how deeply we appreciate their support.

A. J. A.

J. H. O.

PROLOGUE: HOW TO READ THE EVIDENCE

1. What Is History?

Many students believe that studying history simply involves memorizing dates, names, battles, treaties, and countless similar facts. After all, so the argument goes, the past is over and done with. Historians know what has happened, and all students have to do is absorb that body of knowledge. But this notion is wrong. History, as is true of all branches of human understanding, involves discovery and interpretation. Historians are continually learning more about the past and shedding fresh light on its meaning. As you become involved in interpreting historical evidence, you will come to understand and appreciate the creative process that takes place as we explore the past.

The drive to understand what has gone before us is innately human and springs from our need to know who we are. History serves this function of self-discovery in a variety of ways. Its subject matter is universal, dealing with all aspects of past human activity and belief. Among the many issues historians face in interpreting our complex and variegated past, two are fundamental: continuity and change. How and why do things change over time, and how and why do certain values and practices endure throughout a society's history? Answers to these questions, no matter how partial or tentative, reveal the dynamics of a culture. When applied to the global community, historical perspective enables us to appreciate the richness of human experience and expression and the factors underlying the striking similarities and differences that exist among the world's peoples.

The collection of sources in this book will help you discover some of the principal lines of development within world history and understand the major cultural traditions and forces that have shaped history around the globe. We will not hand you answers, however: you will have to work for them, for hard work lies at the heart of historical study. The word *history,* which is Greek in origin, means "learning through inquiry," and that is precisely what historians do. They discover and interpet the past by asking questions and conducting research. Their inquiry revolves around an examination of evidence left by the past. For lack of a better term, historians call that evidence "primary source material."

2. Primary Sources: Their Value and Limitations

Primary sources for the most part are records that have been passed on in written form, thereby preserving the memory of past events. These written sources include, but are not limited to, official records, private correspondence, literature, religious texts, memoirs — the list goes on and on. None of these sources by itself contains unadulterated truth or the whole picture. Each gives us only a glimpse of reality, and it is the historian's task to fit these fragments of the past into a coherent picture.

Imagine for a moment that some historian in the late twenty-first century decides to write a history of your college class. Think about the primary sources that researcher would seek out: the school catalogue, the registrar's class lists, academic transcripts, and similar official documents; class lecture notes, course syllabi, exams, term papers, and textbooks; diaries and private letters; the school newspaper, yearbooks, and sports programs; handbills, posters, and even photographs of graffiti; recollections recorded by some of your classmates long after they have graduated. With some more thought you can add other items to the list, among them some important nonwritten sources, such as recordings of popular music and photographs and videotapes of student life and activity. But let us confine ourselves, for the moment, to written records. What do all these documentary sources have in common?

As we examine this list of sources, we realize that, though numerous, these records do not and cannot present the past in its entirety. Where do we see among them the long telephone calls home, the all-night study groups, the afternoons spent at the student union? Someone may have recorded memories of some of these events, but how complete and trustworthy is that evidence? Also keep in mind that all the documents available to our twenty-first-century historian will be fortunate survivors. They will represent only a small percentage of the vast bulk of written material generated during your college career. Thanks to the wastebasket, the delete key, the disintegration of materials, and the inevitable loss of life's memorabilia as years slip by, the evidence available to the future historian will be fragmentary. This is always the case with historical evidence. We cannot preserve the records of the past in their totality, nor do we wish to. Clearly, the more remote the past, the more fragmentary our documentary evidence. Imagine the feeble chance any particular document from the twelfth century had of surviving the wars, wastebaskets, and worms of the past 800 years.

Now let us consider those many individual pieces of documentary evidence relating to your class's history that have survived. As we review the list, we see that not one of those primary sources gives us a pure, unvarnished, and complete picture. Each has its perspective, value, and limitations.

You certainly know that every college catalogue presents an idealized picture of campus life. Despite its flaws, however, that catalogue can be an important piece of evidence because it reflects the values of the faculty and administrators who composed it and provides useful information by listing rules and regulations, courses, instructors, school organizations, and similar items. That information, however, is the raw material of history, not history itself, and certainly it does not reflect the full historical reality of your class.

What is true of the catalogue is equally true of the student newspaper and every other piece of evidence generated by or pertinent to your class. Each primary source is a part of a larger whole but, as we have already seen, we do not have all the pieces. Think of your historical evidence in terms of a jigsaw puzzle. Many of the pieces are missing, but it is possible to put most, though probably not all, of the remaining pieces together in a reasonable fashion to form a fairly accurate and coherent picture. The picture that emerges may not be complete, but it is useful and valid. The keys to fitting these pieces together are hard work and imagination. Each is absolutely necessary.

3. Examining the Sources

Hard work speaks for itself, but students are often unaware that a historian also needs an imagination to reconstruct the past. After all, many students ask, doesn't history consist of strictly defined and irrefutable dates, names, and facts? Where does imagination enter into the process of learning these facts? Again, let us consider your class's history and its documentary sources. Many of those documents provide factual data — dates, names, grades, statistics — and these data are important, but individually and collectively they have no historical meaning until they are interpreted. Your college class is not a collection of statistics and facts. It is a group of individuals who, despite their differences, share and help mold a collective experience. It is a community evolving within a particular time and space. Influenced by the larger environment in which it finds itself, it is, in turn, an influence on that world. Any valid or useful history must reach beyond a mere list of dates, names, and facts to interpret the historical characteristics and role of your class. What were its values? How did it change and why? What impact did it have? These are some of the important questions a historian asks of the evidence.

In order to arrive at answers, the historian must examine each and every piece of evidence as fully as possible and wring from that evidence as many *inferences* as possible. Facts may be the foundation stones of history, but inferences are its edifices. An inference is a logical conclusion drawn from evidence, and it is the inference that is the heart and soul of historical inquiry.

Every American schoolchild learns that Christopher Columbus "sailed the ocean blue in 1492." That fact is worthless, however, unless the student understands the motives, causes, and significance of this late fifteenth-century voyage. Certainly a historian must know when Columbus sailed west. After all, time is history's framework. Yet the questions historians ask go beyond simple chronology. Why did Columbus sail west? What factors made possible and almost inevitable Spain's involvement in such enterprises at this time? Why was Europe willing and able to exploit the "New World"? These are some of the significant questions whose inferential answers historians seek, and those answers can be found only in the evidence.

One noted historian, Robin Winks, has written a book entitled *The Historian as Detective*, and the image is appropriate, although inexact. Like the detective, the historian examines clues in order to reconstruct events. However, the detective is essentially interested in discovering what happened, who did it, and why, while the historian goes one step further and asks what it all means.

Like the detective interrogating witnesses, the historian also examines the testimony of sources, and both researchers ask similar questions. First and foremost, the historian must evaluate the *validity* of the source. Is it what it purports to be? Artful forgeries have misled many historians. Even if the source is authentic, and most are, it can still draw the historian into significant error. The possibility always exists that the source's author is lying or otherwise deliberately misrepresenting reality. Even if this is not the case, the historian can easily be led astray by not fully understanding the *perspective* reflected in the document. As any detective who has examined a number of eyewitnesses to an event knows, viewpoints differ radically due to a number of factors. The police detective has the opportunity to reexamine witnesses and offer them the opportunity to change their testimony in the light of new evidence and deeper reflection. The historical researcher is usually not so fortunate. Even when the historian attempts to establish a creative interchange with documentary evidence by studying it in a probing manner and comparing it with other evidence, there is no way to cross-examine it in detail. What is written is written. Given this fact, it is absolutely necessary for the historian to understand, as fully as possible, the source's perspective. Thus, the historian must ask several key questions. *What* kind of document is this? *Who* wrote it? For *whom* and *why*? *Where* was it composed and *when*?

The *what* is important, because understanding the nature of the particular source can save the historian a great deal of frustration. Many historical sources simply do not directly address the questions a historian would like to ask of them. That twenty-first-century historian would be foolish to try to learn much about the academic quality of your school's courses from a study of the registrar's class lists and grade sheets. Student and faculty class notes, copies of old syllabi, exams, papers, and textbooks would be far more fruitful sources.

Who, for whom, and *why* are equally important questions. The official school catalogue undoubtedly addresses some issues pertaining to student social life. But should this document, designed to attract potential students and to place the school in the best possible light, be read and accepted uncritically? Obviously not. It should be tested against student testimony, discovered in such sources as private letters, memoirs, posters, the student newspaper, and the yearbook.

Where and *when* are also important questions to ask of a primary source. As a general rule, distance in space and time from an event colors perceptions and can adversely affect the validity of a source's testimony. The recollections of a person celebrating a twenty-fifth class reunion may prove quite insightful and valuable. Conceivably this graduate now has a perspective and even information that were absent a quarter of a century earlier. Just as conceivably this person's memory might be playing tricks. It is possible for a source to be so close to or so distant from the event it deals with that its view is distorted or totally erroneous. Even so, the source is not necessarily worthless. Often the blind spots and misinformation within a source reveal to the researcher much about the author's attitudes and sources of information.

The historical detective's task is not easy. In addition to constantly questioning the validity and perspectives of available sources, the historical researcher must often use whatever evidence is available in imaginative ways. He or she must interpret these fragmentary and flawed glimpses of the past and piece together the resultant inferences as best as possible. While realizing that a complete picture of the past is never possible, the historian assumes the responsibility of re-creating a past that is valid and has meaning for the present.

4. You and the Sources

This book will involve you actively in the work of historical inquiry by asking you to draw inferences based on your careful analysis of primary-source evidence. This is not an easy task, especially at first, but it is well within your capability, and we will help you all along the way.

You will analyze two types of evidence, documents and artifacts. Each source will be authentic, so you will not need to worry about validating it. We will supply you with the information necessary to place each piece of evidence in its proper context, and we will suggest questions you legitimately can and should ask of each source. If you carefully read the introductions and notes, the questions, and the sources — and think about what you are doing — solid inferences will follow.

To illustrate how you should go about this task and what is expected of you, we have prepared a sample exercise, which we will take you through step by step. The exercise consists of a document written by Christopher Columbus and a reproduction of an early sixteenth-century woodcut. First we present the document just as it would appear in any of the chapters of this book: introduction, suggested analytical questions, and the source itself, with explanatory notes. Then we show you how to read that document. The exercise will not draw every possible insight and inference from the document, but it will demonstrate how to set about answering several of the more important questions you should ask of that source.

Following that, we introduce you to the art of "reading" a nonwritten piece of historical evidence. After a few general words on how a historian uses artifacts as evidence, we present the piece of evidence just as it would appear in the book. Then we show you what we read in this picture. By the end of this exercise, if you have worked closely with us, you should be ready to begin interpreting sources on your own.

Christopher Columbus

A LETTER CONCERNING RECENTLY DISCOVERED ISLANDS

There is no need to recount in detail the story of Christopher Columbus (1451–1506), a Genoese sea captain in the service of Isabella of Castile and Ferdinand of Aragon, who sailed westward over the Atlantic Ocean seeking a new route to the empires of East Asia. On October 12, 1492, his fleet of three ships dropped anchor at a small Bahamian island, which Columbus claimed for Spain, naming it San Salvador. The fleet then sailed to the major islands of Cuba, which he named Juana, and Hispaniola (where the modern nations of Haiti and the Dominican Republic are located), which he named Española. After exploring the two islands and establishing the post of Navidad del Señor on Española, Columbus departed for Spain in January 1493. On his way home, Columbus prepared a public account of his expedition to the "Indies" and posted it from Lisbon, Portugal, where he landed in early March. As intended, the letter preceded Columbus to the Spanish royal court, which he entered in triumph in April.

As you analyze the document, you should be aware of several facts. The admiral was returning with only two of his vessels. He had lost his flagship, the *Santa Maria,* when it was wrecked on a reef off present-day Haiti on Christmas Day. Also, many of Columbus's facts and figures reflect more his enthusiasm than dispassionate analysis. His estimate of the dimensions of the two main islands he explored exaggerates their sizes. His optimistic report of the wide availability of such riches as gold, spices, cotton, and mastic, an eastern Mediterranean aromatic gum, was not borne out by subsequent explorations and colonization. Gold was rare in the islands; the only indigenous "spice" proved to be the fiery chili pepper; the wild cotton was excellent but not plentiful; and mastic was nonexistent in the Caribbean.

Questions for Analysis

1. What evidence is there in the letter that allows us to judge Columbus's reliability as an objective reporter? To what extent can we trust his account?

2. What do the admiral's admitted actions regarding the natives and the ways in which he describes these people allow us to conclude about his attitudes toward these "Indians" and his plans for them?
3. What does Columbus's description of the physical attributes of the islands he explored suggest about some of the motives that underlay his voyage?
4. What does this letter tell us about the culture of the people of the Caribbean on the eve of European expansion into that region?

Knowing that it will afford you pleasure to learn that I have brought my undertaking to a successful termination, I have decided upon writing you this letter to acquaint you with all the events which have occurred in my voyage, and the discoveries which have resulted from it.

Thirty-three days after my departure . . . I reached the Indian sea, where I discovered many islands, thickly peopled, of which I took possession without resistance in the name of our most illustrious Monarch, by public proclamation and with unfurled banners. To the first of these islands, which is called by the Indians Guanahani, I gave the name of the blessed Savior[1] (San Salvador), relying upon whose protection I had reached this as well as the other islands; to each of these I also gave a name, ordering that one should be called Santa Maria de la Concepcion, another Fernandina, the third Isabella, the fourth Juana,[2] and so with all the rest respectively. As soon as we arrived at that, which as I have said was named Juana, I proceeded along its coast a short distance westward, and found it to be so large and apparently without termination, that I could not suppose it to be an island, but the continental province of Cathay.[3] . . .

In the meantime I had learned from some Indians whom I had seized, that that country was certainly an island: and therefore I sailed towards the east, coasting to the distance of three hundred and twenty-two miles, which brought us to the extremity of it; from this point I saw lying eastwards another island, fifty-four miles distant from Juana, to which I gave the name of Española. . . .

In Española there are mountains of very great size and beauty, vast plains, groves, and very fruitful fields, admirably adapted for tillage, pasture, and habitation. The convenience and excellence of the harbors in this island, and the abundance of the rivers, so indispensable to the health of man, surpass anything that would be believed by one who had not seen it. The trees, herbage, and fruits of Española are very different from those of

1. Jesus Christ.

2. Named for the daughter and heiress of Isabella and Ferdinand.

3. Technically, Cathay was that area of northern China ruled by the Khitan Mongols from 907 to 1101. Columbus understood Cathay to be the entire Chinese empire of the Great Khan, not realizing that the Chinese had expelled the Mongol khans in the mid-fourteenth century.

Juana, and moreover it abounds in various kinds of spices, gold, and other metals.

The inhabitants of both sexes in this island, and in all the others which I have seen, or of which I have received information, go always naked as they were born,[4] with the exception of some of the women, who use the covering of a leaf, or small bough, or an apron of cotton which they prepare for that purpose. None of them . . . are possessed of any iron, neither have they weapons, being unacquainted with, and indeed incompetent to use them, not from any deformity of body (for they are well-formed), but because they are timid and full of fear. They carry however in lieu of arms, canes dried in the sun, on the ends of which they fix heads of dried wood sharpened to a point, and even these they dare not use habitually; for it has often occurred when I have sent two or three of my men to any of the villages to speak with the natives, that they have come out in a disorderly troop, and have fled in such haste at the approach of our men, that the fathers forsook their children and the children their fathers. This timidity did not arise from any loss or injury that they had received from us; for, on the contrary, I gave to all I approached whatever articles I had about me, such as cloth and many other things, taking nothing of theirs in return: but they are naturally timid and fearful. As soon however as they see that they are safe, and have laid aside all fear, they are very simple and honest, and exceedingly liberal with all they have; none of them refusing any thing he may possess when he is asked for it, but on the contrary inviting us to ask them.

They exhibit great love towards all others in preference to themselves: they also give objects of great value for trifles, and content themselves with very little or nothing in return. I however forbad that these trifles and articles of no value (such as pieces of dishes, plates, and glass, keys, and leather straps) should be given to them, although if they could obtain them, they imagined themselves to be possessed of the most beautiful trinkets in the world. It even happened that a sailor received for a leather strap as much gold as was worth three golden nobles, and for things of more trifling value offered by our men, especially newly coined blancas, or any gold coins, the Indians would give whatever the seller required; as, for instance, an ounce and a half or two ounces of gold, or thirty or forty pounds of cotton. . . . Thus they bartered, like idiots, cotton and gold for fragments of bows, glasses, bottles, and jars; which I forbad as being unjust, and myself gave them many beautiful and acceptable articles which I had brought with me, taking nothing from them in return; I did this in order that I might the more easily conciliate them, that they might be led to become Christians, and be inclined to entertain a regard for the King and Queen, our Princes and all Spaniards, and that I might induce them to take an interest in seeking out, and collecting, and delivering to us such things as they possessed in abundance, but which we greatly needed.

They practice no kind of idolatry, but have a firm belief that all strength and

4. Marco Polo, whom Columbus had read, described a number of island folk in South Asia who went naked.

power, and indeed all good things, are in heaven, and that I had descended from thence with these ships and sailors, and under this impression was I received after they had thrown aside their fears. Nor are they slow or stupid, but of very clear understanding; and those men who have crossed to the neighboring islands give an admirable description of everything they observed; but they never saw any people clothed, nor any ships like ours. On my arrival at that sea, I had taken some Indians by force from the first island that I came to, in order that they might learn our language, and communicate to us what they knew respecting the country; which plan succeeded excellently, and was a great advantage to us, for in a short time, either by gestures and signs, or by words, we were enabled to understand each other. These men are still traveling with me, and although they have been with us now a long time, they continue to entertain the idea that I have descended from heaven; and on our arrival at any new place they published this, crying out immediately with a loud voice to the other Indians, "Come, come and look upon beings of a celestial race": upon which both women and men, children and adults, young men and old, when they got rid of the fear they at first entertained, would come out in throngs, crowding the roads to see us, some bringing food, others drink, with astonishing affection and kindness.

Each of these islands has a great number of canoes, built of solid wood, narrow and not unlike our double-banked boats in length and shape, but swifter in their motion: they steer them only by the oar. These canoes are of various sizes, but the greater number are constructed with eighteen banks of oars, and with these they cross to the other islands, which are of countless number, to carry on traffic with the people. I saw some of these canoes that held as many as seventy-eight rowers. In all these islands there is no difference of physiognomy, of manners, or of language, but they all clearly understand each other, a circumstance very propitious for the realization of what I conceive to be the principal wish of our most serene King, namely, the conversion of these people to the holy faith of Christ, to which indeed, as far as I can judge, they are very favorable and well-disposed. . . .

Juana . . . I can assert . . . is larger than England and Scotland united; . . . there are in the western part of the island two provinces which I did not visit; one of these is called by the Indians Anam,[5] and its inhabitants are born with tails.[6]. . . But the extent of Española is greater than all Spain from Catalonia to Fontarabia, which is easily proved, because one of its four sides which I myself coasted in a direct line, from west to east, measures five hundred and forty miles. This island is to be regarded with especial interest, and not to be slighted; for although as I have said I took possession of all these islands in the name of our invincible King, and the government of them is unreservedly committed to his said Majesty, yet there was one large town in Española of which especially I took possession, situated in a remark-

---

5. Havana.

6. Marco Polo reported the existence of tailed humans (possibly orangutans) in the islands of Southeast Asia.

ably favorable spot, and in every way convenient for the purposes of gain and commerce.

To this town I gave the name of Navidad del Señor,[7] and ordered a fortress to be built there, which must by this time be completed, in which I left as many men as I thought necessary, with all sorts of arms, and enough provisions for more than a year. I also left them one caravel,[8] and skillful workmen both in ship-building and other arts, and engaged the favor and friendship of the King of the island in their behalf, to a degree that would not be believed, for these people are so amiable and friendly that even the King took a pride in calling me his brother. But supposing their feelings should become changed, and they should wish to injure those who have remained in the fortress, they could not do so, for they have no arms, they go naked, and are moreover too cowardly; so that those who hold the said fortress, can easily keep the whole island in check, without any pressing danger to themselves, provided they do not transgress the directions and regulations which I have given them.[9]

As far as I have learned, every man throughout these islands is united to but one wife, with the exception of the kings and princes, who are allowed to have twenty:[10] the women seem to work more than the men. I could not clearly understand whether the people possess any private property, for I observed that one man had the charge of distributing various things to the rest, but especially meat and provisions and the like. I did not find, as some of us had expected, any cannibals amongst them,[11] but on the contrary men of great deference and kindness. Neither are they black, like the Ethiopians: their hair is smooth and straight: for they do not dwell where the rays of the sun strike most vividly. . . . Thus, as I have already said, I saw no cannibals, nor did I hear of any, except in a certain island called Charis, which is the second from Española on the side towards India, where dwell a people who are considered by the neighboring islanders as most ferocious: and these feed upon human flesh.[12] The same people have many kinds of canoes, in which they cross to all the surrounding islands and rob and plunder wherever they can; they are not different from the other islanders, except that they wear their hair long, like women, and make use of the bows and javelins of cane, with sharpened spear-points fixed on the thickest end, which I have before described, and therefore they are looked upon as ferocious, and regarded by the other Indians with unbounded fear; but I think no more of them than of the rest. These are

7. The Lord's Nativity (Christmas).

8. The wreck of the *Santa Maria,* which was totally useless to the garrison.

9. When Columbus returned in November 1493, he discovered that the entire garrison had been killed by the native inhabitants in reaction to intolerable abuses.

10. Marco Polo had described a number of polygamous customs in his Asiatic memoirs.

11. Both Polo's late thirteenth-century travelogue and the equally popular late fourteenth-century *Travels* of John Mandeville reported numerous instances of cannibalism.

12. These would be the Caribs, who shortly before the arrival of Columbus began to displace the peaceful Arawak people of the Lesser Antilles, the archipelago to the east and south of Hispaniola. Sixteenth-century Spanish writers unanimously agreed that the Caribs were cannibals. At least one modern historian has cast doubt on the Caribs' alleged cannibalism, but most accept the basic veracity of the Spanish accounts.

the men who form unions with certain women, who dwell alone in the island Matenin, which lies next to Española on the side towards India; these latter employ themselves in no labor suitable to their own sex, for they use bows and javelins as I have already described their paramours as doing, and for defensive armor have plates of brass, of which metal they possess great abundance.[13] They assure me that there is another island larger than Española, whose inhabitants have no hair,[14] and which abounds in gold more than any of the rest. I bring with me individuals of this island and of the others that I have seen, who are proofs of the facts which I state.

Finally, to compress into few words the entire summary of my voyage and speedy return, and of the advantages derivable therefrom, I promise, that with a little assistance afforded me by our most invincible sovereigns, I will procure them as much gold as they need, as great a quantity of spices, of cotton, and of mastic (which is only found in Chios),[15] and as many slaves for the service of the navy as their Majesties may require. I promise also rhubarb and other sorts of drugs, which I am persuaded the men whom I have left in the aforesaid fortress have found already and will continue to find. . . .

Although all I have related may appear to be wonderful and unheard of, yet the results of my voyage would have been more astonishing if I had had at my disposal such ships as I required. But these great and marvelous results are not to be attributed to any merit of mine, but to the holy Christian faith, and to the piety and religion of our Sovereigns; for that which the unaided intellect of man could not compass, the spirit of God has granted to human exertions, for God is wont to hear the prayers of his servants who love his precepts even to the performance of apparent impossibilities. Thus it has happened to me in the present instance, who have accomplished a task to which the powers of mortal men had never hitherto attained; for if there have been those who have anywhere written or spoken of these islands, they have done so with doubts and conjectures, and no one has ever asserted that he has seen them, on which account their writings have been looked upon as little else than fables.

Therefore let the king and queen, our princes and their most happy kingdoms, and all the other provinces of Christendom, render thanks to our Lord and Savior Jesus Christ, who has granted us so great a victory and such prosperity. Let processions be made, and sacred feasts be held, and the temples be adorned with festive boughs. Let Christ rejoice on earth, as he rejoices in heaven in the prospect of the salvation of the souls of so many nations hitherto lost. Let us also rejoice, as well on account of the exaltation of our faith, as on account of the increase in our temporal prosperity, of which not only Spain, but all Christendom will be partakers.

---

13. Columbus had read in Marco Polo of two islands, one inhabited solely by women, another exclusively by men. Mandeville, who probably never traveled to most of the Asiatic lands he so vividly described, wrote of the land of Amazonia, populated totally by warrior women. There is no evidence that this female society reported by Columbus ever existed in the Caribbean. Neither is there any evidence that the Caribbean Amerindians used metal to any significant degree.

14. John Mandeville described people with little body hair, and Marco Polo told of Buddhist monks whose heads and faces were shaved.

15. An island in the Aegean Sea (an arm of the Mediterranean, between Greece and Turkey).

5. Interpreting Columbus's Letter

This letter contains a number of interesting and potentially important facts. For example, the natives whom Columbus encountered on these islands were apparently homogeneous, were skilled sailors, and initially offered no resistance. Yet as fascinating as these facts are, knowing them does not make a person a historian. Similarly, garnering such isolated items from a source does not constitute analysis. Historical analysis consists of drawing as much inferential insight as possible from a source and trying to answer, at least in part, the central question of historical study: what does it all mean? This document allows us to do just that.

The historian uses no secret method or magic formula to draw historical insights from documentary evidence. All she or he needs are attention to detail, thoroughness, common sense, and a willingness to enter imaginatively into the mind of the document's author as fully and honestly as possible while trying to set aside momentarily personal values and perspectives. Anyone who is willing to work can profitably interpret written primary sources. To prove that point, let us answer the first three questions for analysis on pages P-6 and P-7.

The first question — What evidence is there in the letter that allows us to judge Columbus's reliability as an objective reporter? — strikes at the heart of historical inquiry. The researcher always has to evaluate the worth of each source, and this means understanding its point of view and reliability. In this letter, several points are obvious. Columbus believes he has discovered Asian islands. Marco Polo's *Travels* and other accounts of Asia have provided a number of reference points by which he can recognize the Orient, and he believes he has found many of them. Equally obvious is the fact that Columbus is trying to present his discoveries in the best possible light. He is sending this letter ahead to the court of Ferdinand and Isabella to ensure that he will be received on arrival with due honor.

His account contains exaggeration and error. As the introduction informs us, Columbus overestimates the size of several islands and, except for chilies, the spices he claims to have discovered proved eventually to be mirages.

We also find Columbus deliberately trying to mislead his reader. The *Santa Maria* has been lost, yet the admiral wants the reader to believe that he left the ship in seaworthy condition with the sailors who remained in the garrison at Navidad del Señor. Still, this is the only outright falsehood that we can discover in the letter. Generally, despite Columbus's enthusiasm and understandable tendency to exaggerate and to see what he wants to see, he seems to want to present a factual account.

Although he was prepared to encounter every sort of human monstrosity and undoubtedly would have enjoyed reporting such contacts, Columbus honestly notes that all the natives he has met are quite unmonstrous in appearance and temperament. He does report stories of people with tails, cannibals, and warlike women who live apart from men, but there is no good reason to believe that the admiral is deliberately misleading anyone. The fierce Caribs were real enough, although Columbus did not encounter any on his first voyage. Rumors of tailed people and latter-day Amazons might have been the result of the natives' efforts to please Columbus. It is not difficult to imagine the admiral inquiring after the location of those various human curiosities whom Polo and others had placed in the islands of the Indian Ocean, and the Amerindian natives agreeably pointing across the waters to other islands. All things considered, Columbus's letter may be accepted as a generally honest, if not totally accurate, account of his discoveries and experiences.

That basic honesty, tempered by an understandable enthusiasm and desire to present his accomplishments in a positive and attractive manner, comes through in his attempt to describe both the islands' physical qualities and the people he has encountered. The picture that emerges tells us a lot about the complex motives underlying his great adventure. Let us consider the second and third questions for analysis together, as they are closely related.

We notice that Columbus has matter-of-factly taken possession of these lands in the names of the monarchs of Spain and has even renamed the islands without once giving thought to anyone else's claims. Also, despite his avowed interest in protecting and winning over these native peoples, whom he apparently likes and admires, he thinks nothing of seizing some natives as soon as he arrives and of carrying several "Indians" back to Spain. Moreover, he remarks toward the end of his letter that he will procure from these islands as many slaves to serve in the navy as the monarchs of Spain desire. At the same time, and this may strike the modern student as curious, Columbus notes that he has acted kindly toward these natives so that they might become both Christians and loyal subjects of Ferdinand and Isabella. According to the admiral, the Indians' intelligence, timidity, naiveté, ignorance, sense of wonder at the Europeans, and ability to communicate freely among themselves make them prime candidates for conversion and subjugation. Is Columbus concerned with these people as humans, and is he interested in helping them achieve salvation through conversion? The tone of this letter suggests that he is, but there is a contrary note, which points up the tension that would exist within the entire Spanish colonial experience: Columbus believes it to be his and Catholic Spain's right and duty to rule and exploit these people.

Conquest of these people and their lands involved more than just a sense of divine mission and Christian altruism — as real as these motives were. Columbus, his royal patrons, and most others who joined overseas adventures expected to gain in earthly wealth as well. Even a superficial reading of his letter shows us the admiral's preoccupation with the riches of these islands. Gold, spices, cotton, aromatic mastic, and, of course, slaves are the material rewards that await Christian Europeans, and Columbus is fully interested in them.

Is he being cynical or hypocritical when, in his closing words, Columbus claims that Jesus Christ has provided this great victory to the Spanish monarchs, and, indeed, to all Christians, and from it will flow the dual benefits of worldly riches and the conversion of many people? It does not seem likely. Here was a man who saw no contradiction between spreading the faith and benefiting materially from that action, even if doing so meant exploiting those he had converted. He and most of his contemporaries generally perceived no inconsistency in converting a people to the freedom of an otherworldly faith and enslaving them in this world.

There are other questions we can ask of this source and other insights we can gather from it. Certainly it tells us a lot about this Amerindian culture, the issue raised in question 4 on page P-7. Despite his cultural blinders, his naiveté, and his tendency at times to see what he wanted to see, Columbus was an accurate and perceptive observer, and anyone interested in the culture of the Caribbean peoples, before Europeans had much chance to influence it, must necessarily look to this and similar accounts of first contacts. It would be good practice for you to try to answer question 4, which we have only briefly considered.

We trust that you now have a good idea of how a student of history should examine and mine a documentary source. Let us next look at an artifact.

6. Unwritten Sources

Historians distinguish between the prehistorical and historical past, and the chief characteristic of any historical culture is that it provides written records from which we can reconstruct its past. Without a large volume and variety of documentary sources it is impossible to write any society's history in detail. This is not to say that the unwritten relics of the past are worthless. The art and science of archeology proves the contrary, and historians, as we shall see, use such sources. As a rule of thumb, however, no matter how extensive its physical remains may be, if a culture has not left us records we can read, its history largely remains a closed book. The ancient civilizations of Harappan India and Minoan Crete, for example, knew and practiced the art of writing, but until we learn how to decipher their texts, we can draw only vague pictures of their respective histories.

Given the central role documents play in our reconstruction of the past, it should surprise no one to learn that most historians concentrate their research almost exclusively on written sources. Yet historians would be foolish to overlook *any* piece of evidence from the past. As we suggested earlier, photographs can be a rich source for anyone researching the history of your class. Our future historian might even want to study all the extant souvenirs and supplies sold in your school's bookstore. Examined properly, they probably could help fill in some gaps in the story of your class's cultural history.

Artifacts can be illuminating, particularly when used in conjunction with records. Coins tell us a lot about a society's ideals or its leaders' programs. Art in its many forms reveals the interests, attitudes, and modes of perception of various segments of society. More down-to-earth items, such as domestic utensils and tools, allow us to infer much about the lives of common individuals. In this book we concentrate on written sources, for reasons already outlined, but we also include some examples of important artifactual evidence. Let us look at an example and proceed to "read" it.

AN ANONYMOUS WOODCUT OF 1511

Columbus arrived in Barcelona in April 1493 to discover not only had his letter arrived, but it had already been published and publicly circulated. Within months the letter was translated into several languages, and the Latin translation alone went through nine editions, several of which were lavishly illustrated, before the end of 1494. Printers discovered that educated Europeans had an almost insatiable desire to learn about the peoples and lands Columbus and other explorers were "discovering," and they catered to that interest.

Their clientele wanted not only to read about the fascinating peoples, flora, and

fauna of these lands — they wanted also to see them. Consequently, as books proliferated on the new explorations, so did the number of printed illustrations, many of which are quite fanciful and tell us more about the Europeans who created them than the peoples and regions they supposedly portrayed. The woodcut print we have chosen appeared in a popular English pamphlet of 1511.

Questions for Analysis

1. What scene has the artist set? What do each person's actions, dress, and demeanor tell us about her or him? What has the artist placed to the immediate right of the standing man, and what function does it have in this scene?
2. What does this illustration tell us about popular European notions concerning the natives of the New World?

7. Interpreting the Woodcut

What a charming, even idyllic domestic scene. An attractive mother nurses an infant at her breast while amusing an older child with a feather. A well-muscled, equally attractive and proud father stands nearby, holding the tools of his trade while next to him the family's dinner is slowly cooking. Dinner, of course, may strike us as macabre, as these are cannibals, and it looks like roast European is on the menu. The tools of the father's trade are weapons. Both children are naked, and the parents are virtually nude, save for what appear to be leaves that cover their loins, decorative necklaces, armbands and anklets of some indeterminate material, and feathers in their hair.

What is the message? What we have is a reprise of the image provided by Columbus in his letter of 1493 — the "noble savage." These are fully human beings with human bonds and affections. Yet they are still "savages," as their clothing (or lack of it), decorations, weapons, and choice of food would have suggested to most sixteenth-century Europeans. Here, as Columbus and many of those who followed agreed, were a people who could become Christians but who also, by virtue of their backwardness, were to be subjugated. There is something appealing about their innocent savagery, but what of that poor fellow whose severed members are slowly roasting?

Have we read too much into the woodcut? It is arguable that we may have. The historian always faces this problem when trying to analyze an isolated piece of evidence, particularly when it is a nonverbal source. Yet this artifact is not completely isolated, for we brought to its analysis insight gained from documentary evidence — Columbus's letter. That is how we generally read the artifacts of historical cultures. We attempt to place them in the context of what we have already learned or inferred from documentary sources. Documents illuminate artifacts, and artifacts make more vivid and tangible the often shadowy world of words.

As you attempt to interpret the unwritten sources in this book, keep in mind what you have learned from the documents you have already read, your textbook, and class lectures. Remember that we have chosen these artifacts to illustrate broad themes and general trends. You should not find their messages overly subtle. As with the documents, always try to place each piece of nonverbal evidence into its proper context, and, in that regard, read the introductions and questions for analysis very carefully. We will do our best to provide you with all the information and clues you need.

Good luck and have fun!

The Human Record

PART I

The Ancient World

The term *ancient world* defies simple definition. In its broadest sense, it encompasses a variety of societies that ranged from isolated tribes of hunter-gatherers living in the Old Stone Age to empires ruling over vast regions of the earth and existing well into the first millennium A.D. More narrowly defined, it includes all the civilizations that rose, flourished, and in some cases collapsed between approximately 3500 B.C. and A.D. 500. We shall confine ourselves to the narrower meaning, the first 4,000 years of human civilization.

The story of human civilization during these four millennia begins in the river valleys of Mesopotamia, Egypt, northwest India, and northern China, and along the Pacific coast of South America and the gulf coast of Mexico. The various Amerindian civilizations developed in isolation from the rest of the world, but all the original civilizations of Eurasia and Africa responded, in varying degrees, to external influences. Of the four original nuclei of Afro-Eurasian civilization, only Harappan India eventually passed away. The others expanded in this atmosphere of cross-fertilization and, in the process, introduced the modes of civilization to their neighbors. The result was the emergence of distinctive regional cultures in portions of Eurasia and Africa.

By 300 B.C. the eastern hemisphere of the globe had four dominant cultural pools — China, India, the Middle East, and the Greco-Mediterranean world. Of these, geography dictated that the culture of China would be the one least influenced by foreign stimuli because of the region's relative isolation at the eastern end of the Eurasian land mass. Conversely, the culture of the Middle East — the crossroads of this Afro-Eurasian world of civilized peoples — was the most eclectic.

During the last centuries B.C. and the early centuries A.D., the cultures at either end of this great expanse of land, China and the Greco-Roman world, achieved political unity and expanded at the expense of their less civilized neighbors, such as Koreans and Southeast Asians in the East and Celts in the West. The result was two great empires, Han China and Rome, linked by East African, Middle Eastern, Indian, and Central Asiatic intermediaries, several of which were massive, well-organized empires in their own right. Consequently, goods and ideas were exchanged throughout Eurasia and parts of Africa more freely and quickly than ever before.

By A.D. 500 internal and external pressures had precipitated the political collapse of the Chinese and Roman empires, and with those disasters the first age of Afro-Eurasian unification was at an end. The world that followed was, for several centuries to come, far more fragmented and localized. The ancient world had spent itself.

C H A P T E R

1

The First Civilizations

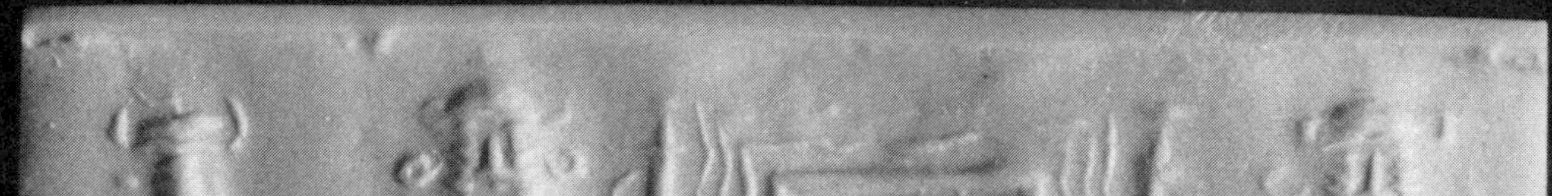

The word *civilization* is derived from the Latin adjective *civilis*, which means "relating to a state." No matter how else one defines civilization, an organized state stands at the center of every society we call civilized, and the world's first civilizations were organized around sacred states. That is, each early civilization produced a ruling class that governed by divine mandate. Religious beliefs and political and social forms varied, according to time and place, but ultimately all legitimate power was perceived as descending from the gods.

Those who ruled were a minority and maintained power by exploiting the many. This was a fact of early civilized life largely because, until modern times, states could produce only severely limited surpluses due to the narrow agrarian basis of their economies. That surplus, which is so necessary for the creation of a state, could be channeled into state-building activities only if rulers kept the majority of their subjects at a fairly low level of subsistence by exacting from them a major portion of the surplus through taxes, labor services, and military conscription. Thus, the more agreeable benefits of civilization, such as literature and the other arts, were principally the exclusive property and tools of the few.

Each of the world's first civilizations eventually evolved a system of writing, and in each case the art of writing served, at least initially, to strengthen the authority of its rulers. Whether writing was used to record temple possessions or taxes due, to give permanence to laws, or to provide priests with a coherent body of sacred texts, writing set apart those who exercised power from those who were powerless.

Not all the records left behind by these first civilizations are open to us. We still cannot decipher the texts of Harappan India, Minoan Crete, or the kingdom of Kush. Happily, this is not the case with Mesopotamia, Egypt, and China. The written sources left behind by these three civilizations reveal societies that were strikingly different in perspective and structure, even as they shared certain characteristics common to all early civilizations.

Mesopotamia: The Land of Two Rivers

According to one eminent historian, "History begins at Sumer," a judgment with a good deal of truth if one accepts the notion that without the records of civilization there is no history. It is in Sumer, which lies just to the north of the Persian Gulf in an area encompassed by the southern regions of modern-day Iraq, that we discover the first evidence of human civilization. By 3500 B.C. a number of Sumerian city-states had emerged, and humanity was embarked on the adventure of civilization.

Generally we call the Sumerians, and the other peoples who succeeded them in this region of the Middle East, "Mesopotamians." The term, which means "those who dwell between the rivers," acknowledges the origin of the world's first known civilization in the valley created by the Tigris and Euphrates rivers.

By approximately 1800 B.C. the Sumerians had been absorbed by waves of infiltrators and invaders and ceased to exist as an identifiable people. Moreover, the cultural center of gravity within Mesopotamia had shifted northward to the regions of middle Mesopotamia, centering on the city of Babylon and elsewhere.

Despite their disappearance as a people, the Sumerians laid the framework for what proved to be a dynamic Mesopotamian civilization that exercised profound cultural influence throughout the Middle East and beyond for about 3,000 years. Between roughly 3500 and 500 B.C., Mesopotamia was where much of the action was, so far as the history of Middle Eastern civilization was concerned.

That action was both constructive and destructive. The Mesopotamians have been credited with such "firsts" as the world's first governments, schools, codes of law, ethical systems, and epic literature. Just as prominent in Mesopotamian life were disasters, both natural and human-generated.

The geography of Mesopotamia provided its people with the challenge of harnessing the waters of its two great rivers, and from the necessary cooperative effort that resulted, civilization arose. Yet those rivers also threatened to destroy the fragile fabric of civilized society, insofar as they were unpredictable and could easily turn into uncontrollable torrents. Moreover, most of southern Mesopotamia was covered by either arid wasteland or marsh. Consequently, Sumerian civilization was built upon heroic labor in the midst of a hostile environment.

Another significant geographical aspect of Mesopotamian life, which also proved to be an important factor throughout its history, is the land's openness to incursions. To the north and east lie the hills and mountains of Iran and Armenia, from which wave after wave of invaders descended into the inviting valley of cities. To the south and west lies the desert of Arabia, out of which came countless nomads century after century. In many instances these invaders toppled a preexisting state and then settled down to become, in turn, Mesopotamians.

Whether they came from the desert fringes, as did the Amorites, who established the first Babylonian Empire around 1800 B.C., or were mountain folk, such as the

Kassites, whose chariots toppled Babylon soon after 1700, they all eventually became part of a Mesopotamian cultural complex whose modes of life and thought the Sumerians had set in place at the dawn of human civilization.

THE EPIC OF GILGAMESH

The two basic concerns shared by all human beings are finding meaning in life and confronting the reality of death. In Mesopotamia, where life and human fortune were so precarious, people deeply probed these issues, which became the subjects of numerous myths. Eventually, Mesopotamia evolved its classic answer to these questions in the form of its greatest work of literature, *The Epic of Gilgamesh*.

A myth is not a deliberate piece of fiction or simply a story told to amuse an audience. It represents an attempt by a prescientific society to make sense out of the universe. Where the scientist objectifies nature, seeing the world as an "it," the myth-maker lives in a world where everything has a soul, a personality, and its own story. A raging river is not a body of water responding to physical laws but an angry or capricious god. In the same manner, the fortunes of human society are not the consequences of chance, history, or any laws discoverable by social scientists. Rather, the gods and other supernatural spirits intervene directly in human affairs, punishing and rewarding as they wish. The insight thus gained into the ways of the gods largely satisfies the emotional and intellectual needs of the myth-maker.

Most of our extant texts of *The Epic of Gilgamesh* were discovered in the ruins of the late-seventh-century B.C. library of the Assyrian king Ashurbanipal. Strong evidence shows, however, that the story, at least in its basic outline, is Sumerian in origin and goes back to the third millennium (2000s) B.C. The hero, Gilgamesh, was a historic figure, who probably ruled the city-state of Uruk around 2750 B.C. We know virtually nothing about his life, but he obviously impressed contemporaries enough to become the focal point of a series of oral sagas that, over the centuries, coalesced into the epic that bears his name.

The story contains a profound theme, the conflict between humanity's talents and aspirations and its mortal limitations. Gilgamesh, "two-thirds a god and one-third human," is a man of heroic proportions and appetites who must still face the inevitability of death.

In the early sections of this epic, Gilgamesh and his companion Enkidu engage in a series of spectacular exploits out of the conviction that if a person must accept death and inferiority to the gods, it is still possible to win a form of immortality in everlasting fame. They soon learn, however, how tenuous life is and how empty the victory of posthumous fame.

In the course of one of those heroic deeds, the slaying of the Bull of Heaven, they commit sacrilege against Ishtar, goddess of love and fertility, and for this one of them must die. The one chosen is Enkidu. As our selection opens, Enkidu, after having cursed the heroic past that has brought him to this fate, tells Gilgamesh of a vision he has had.

Questions for Analysis

1. What was the Mesopotamian view of the afterlife?
2. Consider the story of Utnapishtim. What do the various actions of the gods and goddesses allow us to infer about how the Mesopotamians viewed their deities? Consider especially Ea's treatment of the truth. According to the epic, what are the respective roles of the gods and humans? What do the Mesopotamian deities require of humanity? What do humans expect of their gods?
3. What is the moral of *The Epic of Gilgamesh*?
4. Historians often characterize the Mesopotamian view of life as pessimistic. Does this judgment seem correct in light of the message of the epic? If not, then how would you characterize the Mesopotamian philosophy of life?

As Enkidu slept alone in his sickness, in bitterness of spirit he poured out his heart to his friend. "It was I who cut down the cedar, I who levelled the forest, I who slew Humbaba[1] and now see what has become of me. Listen, my friend, this is the dream I dreamed last night. The heavens roared, and earth rumbled back an answer; between them stood I before an awful being, the sombre-faced man-bird; he had directed on me his purpose. His was a vampire face, his foot was a lion's foot, his hand was an eagle's talon. He fell on me and his claws were in my hair, he held me fast and I smothered; then he transformed me so that my arms became wings covered with feathers. He turned his stare towards me, and he led me away to the palace of Irkalla, the Queen of Darkness,[2] to the house from which none who enters ever returns, down the road from which there is no coming back.

"There is the house whose people sit in darkness; dust is their food and clay their meat. They are clothed like birds with wings for covering, they see no light, they sit in darkness. I entered the house of dust and I saw the kings of the earth, their crowns put away for ever; rulers and princes, all those who once wore kingly crowns and ruled the world in the days of

1. The giant who guarded the cedar forest and was slain by Enkidu and Gilgamesh.

2. Goddess of the Underworld.

old. They who had stood in the place of the gods like Anu and Enlil,[3] stood now like servants to fetch baked meats in the house of dust, to carry cooked meat and cold water from the water-skin. In the house of dust which I entered were high priests and acolytes, priests of the incantation and of ecstasy; there were servers of the temple, and there was Etana, that king of Kish whom the eagle carried to heaven in the days of old.[4] There was Ereshkigal[5] the Queen of the Underworld; and Belit-Sheri squatted in front of her, she who is recorder of the gods and keeps the book of death. She held a tablet from which she read. She raised her head, she saw me and spoke: 'Who has brought this one here?' Then I awoke like a man drained of blood who wanders alone in a waste of rushes; like one whom the bailiff has seized and his heart pounds with terror."

Enkidu dies, and Gilgamesh now realizes that fame is no substitute for life. Facing the reality of his own death, he begins a desperate search for immortality. In the course of his search, he meets Siduri, a goddess of wine, who advises him:

"Gilgamesh, where are you hurrying to? You will never find that life for which you are looking. When the gods created man they allotted to him death, but life they retained in their own keeping. As for you, Gilgamesh, fill your belly with good things; day and night, night and day, dance and be merry, feast and rejoice. Let your clothes be fresh, bathe yourself in water, cherish the little child that holds your hand, and make your wife happy in your embrace; for this too is the lot of man."

Gilgamesh, however, refuses to be deflected from his quest. After a series of harrowing experiences, he finally reaches Utnapishtim, a former mortal whom the gods had placed in an eternal paradise, and addresses him.

"Oh, father Utnapishtim, you who have entered the assembly of the gods, I wish to question you concerning the living and the dead, how shall I find the life for which I am searching?"

Utnapishtim said, "There is no permanence. Do we build a house to stand for ever, do we seal a contract to hold for all time? Do brothers divide an inheritance to keep for ever, does the flood-time of rivers endure? It is only the nymph of the dragon-fly who sheds her larva and sees the sun in his glory. From the days of old there is no permanence. The sleeping and the dead, how alike they are, they are like a painted death. What is there between the master and the servant when both have fulfilled their doom? When the Annunaki,[6] the judges, come together, and

3. Dead earthly kings. Anu was the supreme king of the gods and the source of all order and government, and Enlil was the storm god, who supported royal authority.

4. A legendary king of the Sumerian city of Kish.

5. Another name for Irkalla.

6. Gods of the Underworld who judge the dead.

Mammetun[7] the mother of destinies, together they decree the fates of men. Life and death they allot but the day of death they do not disclose."

Then Gilgamesh said to Utnapishtim the Faraway, "I look at you now, Utnapishtim, and your appearance is no different from mine; there is nothing strange in your features. I thought I should find you like a hero prepared for battle, but you lie here taking your ease on your back. Tell me truly, how was it that you came to enter the company of the gods and to possess everlasting life?" Utnapishtim said to Gilgamesh, "I will reveal to you a mystery, I will tell you a secret of the gods."

"You know the city Shurrupak, it stands on the banks of Euphrates? That city grew old and the gods that were in it were old. There was Anu, lord of the firmament, their father, and warrior Enlil their counsellor, Ninurta[8] the helper, and Ennugi[9] watcher over canals; and with them also was Ea.[10] In those days the world teemed, the people multiplied, the world bellowed like a wild bull, and the great god was aroused by the clamor. Enlil heard the clamor and he said to the gods in council, 'The uproar of mankind is intolerable and sleep is no longer possible by reason of the babel.' So the gods agreed to exterminate mankind. Enlil did this, but Ea because of his oath[11] warned me in a dream. He whispered their words to my house of reeds, 'Reed-house, reed-house! Wall, O wall, hearken reed-house, wall reflect; O man of Shurrupak, son of Ubara-Tutu; tear down your house and build a boat, abandon possessions and look for life, despise worldly goods and save your soul alive. Tear down your house, I say, and build a boat. These are the measurements of the barque as you shall build her: let her beam equal her length, let her deck be roofed like the vault that covers the abyss; then take up into the boat the seed of all living creatures.'

"When I had understood I said to my lord, 'Behold, what you have commanded I will honor and perform, but how shall I answer the people, the city, the elders?' Then Ea opened his mouth and said to me, his servant, 'Tell them this: I have learnt that Enlil is wrathful against me, I dare no longer walk in his land nor live in his city; I will go down to the Gulf to dwell with Ea my lord. But on you he will rain down abundance, rare fish and shy wildfowl, a rich harvest-tide. In the evening the rider of the storm will bring you wheat in torrents.'. . .

"On the seventh day the boat was complete. . . .

"I loaded into her all that I had of gold and of living things, my family, my kin, the beast of the field both wild and tame, and all the craftsmen. I sent them on board. . . . The time was fulfilled, the evening came, the rider of the storm sent down the rain. I looked out at the weather and it was terrible, so I too boarded the boat and battened her down. . . .

"For six days and six nights the winds blew, torrent and tempest and flood overwhelmed the world, tempest and flood raged together like warring hosts. When the seventh day dawned the storm from the south subsided, the sea grew calm, the flood was stilled; I looked at the

7. Goddess of fate.

8. God of war.

9. God of irrigation.

10. God of wisdom and providence.

11. Apparently an oath to protect humanity, because Ea was the god of life-giving water and good fortune.

face of the world and there was silence, all mankind was turned to clay. The surface of the sea stretched as flat as a roof-top; I opened a hatch and the light fell on my face. Then I bowed low, I sat down and I wept, the tears streamed down my face, for on every side was the waste of water. I looked for land in vain, but fourteen leagues distant there appeared a mountain, and there the boat grounded; on the mountain of Nisir the boat held fast, she held fast and did not budge. One day she held, and a second day on the mountain of Nisir she held fast and did not budge. A third day, and a fourth day she held fast on the mountain and did not budge; a fifth day and a sixth day she held fast on the mountain. When the seventh day dawned I loosed a dove and let her go. She flew away, but finding no resting-place she returned. Then I loosed a swallow, and she flew away but finding no resting-place she returned. I loosed a raven, she saw that the waters had retreated, she ate, she flew around, she cawed, and she did not come back. Then I threw everything open to the four winds, I made a sacrifice and poured out a libation[12] on the mountain top. Seven and again seven cauldrons I set up on their stands, I heaped up wood and cane and cedar and myrtle. When the gods smelled the sweet savor, they gathered like flies over the sacrifice.[13] Then, at last, Ishtar also came, she lifted her necklace with the jewels of heaven that once Anu had made to please her. 'O you gods here present, by the lapis lazuli round my neck I shall remember these days as I remember the jewels of my throat; these last days I shall not forget.[14] Let all the gods gather round the sacrifice, except Enlil. He shall not approach this offering, for without reflection he brought the flood; he consigned my people to destruction.'

"When Enlil had come, when he saw the boat, he was wrath and swelled with anger at the gods, the host of heaven, 'Has any of these mortals escaped? Not one was to have survived the destruction.' Then the god of the wells and canals Ninurta opened his mouth and said to the warrior Enlil, 'Who is there of the gods that can devise without Ea? It is Ea alone who knows all things.' Then Ea opened his mouth and spoke to warrior Enlil, 'Wisest of gods, hero Enlil, how could you so senselessly bring down the flood? . . .

It was not I that revealed the secret of the gods; the wise man learned it in a dream. Now take your counsel what shall be done with him.

"Then Enlil went up into the boat, he took me by the hand and my wife and made us enter the boat and kneel down on either side, he standing between us. He touched our foreheads to bless us saying, 'In time past Utnapishtim was a mortal man; henceforth he and his wife shall live in the distance at the mouth of the rivers.' Thus it was that the gods took me and placed me here to live in the distance, at the mouth of the rivers."

Utnapishtim said, "As for you, Gilgamesh, who will assemble the gods for your sake, so that you may find that life for which you are searching?"

After telling his story, Utnapishtim challenges Gilgamesh to resist sleep for six days and seven

12. Poured out wine or some other beverage as an offering to the gods.

13. Many myth-making people believe that the gods gain nourishment from the greasy smoke of burnt sacrifices.

14. She presents a rainbow.

nights. When Gilgamesh fails the test, Utnapishtim points out how preposterous it is to search for immortality when one cannot even resist sleep. Out of kindness, Utnapishtim does tell Gilgamesh where he can find a submarine plant that will, at least, rejuvenate him. Consequently, the hero dives to the bottom of the sea and plucks it. However, humanity is to be denied even the blessing of forestalling old age and decrepitude, since the plant is stolen from Gilgamesh by a serpent. His mission a failure, Gilgamesh returns to Uruk.

The destiny was fulfilled which the father of the gods, Enlil of the mountain, had decreed for Gilgamesh: "In nether-earth the darkness will show him a light: of mankind, all that are known, none will leave a monument for generations to come to compare with his. The heroes, the wise men, like the new moon have their waxing and waning. Men will say, 'Who has ever ruled with might and with power like him?' As in the dark month, the month of shadows, so without him there is no light. O Gilgamesh, this was the meaning of your dream. You were given the kingship, such was your destiny, everlasting life was not your destiny. Because of this do not be sad at heart, do not be grieved or oppressed; he has given you power to bind and to loose, to be the darkness and the light of mankind. He has given unexampled supremacy over the people, victory in battle from which no fugitive returns, in forays and assaults from which there is no going back. But do not abuse this power, deal justly with your servants in the palace, deal justly before the face of the Sun." . . .

Gilgamesh, the son of Ninsun, lies in the tomb. At the place of offerings he weighed the bread-offering, at the place of libation he poured out the wine. In those days the lord Gilgamesh departed, the son of Ninsun, the king, peerless, without an equal among men, who did not neglect Enlil his master. O Gilgamesh, lord of Kullab,[15] great is thy praise.

THE CODE OF HAMMURABI

Mesopotamia's characteristic sense of insecurity resulted in its producing not only great philosophical literature but also detailed codes of law. *The Code of Hammurabi* is the most famous but certainly not the earliest of the many collections of law that were produced throughout the first 3,000 years of Mesopotamian civilization.

Whether these codes were Sumerian, Babylonian, Assyrian, or Chaldean, a number of common elements unite them, chief of which is the expressed purpose, as the prologue to Hammurabi's code declares, "to promote the welfare of the people . . . to cause justice to prevail in the land, to destroy the wicked and the evil, that the strong might not oppress the weak." There is no good reason to doubt that even

15. Part of Uruk.

conquerors such as Hammurabi (1792–1750 B.C.), who briefly united Mesopotamia and transformed Babylon into the capital of an empire, sought to promote justice through law.

Questions for Analysis

1. In some cases guilt or innocence is determined by recourse to divine intervention or judgment (laws 2, 131, 132), whereas in others it is determined by examination of physical evidence or witnesses (laws 122, 123). How do you explain this disparity, and what does it suggest about Mesopotamian society?
2. Mesopotamian society has been characterized as patriarchal (dominated by male heads of households). Does the evidence in this code of law tend to support or refute that judgment? What does the code reveal about the status of women in this society? Do you find any evidence that women had any protections or liberties?
3. What evidence is there of class discrimination in Babylon?
4. How does the code protect commerce and property?
5. How does Hammurabi seek to provide for the basic welfare of his subjects and to protect them from the effects of crime?
6. How are all members of this society made responsible for its good order?
7. The principle of "an eye for an eye and a tooth for a tooth" usually means in modern idiom a philosophy of retribution noted for its severity and lack of compassion. Does such a characterization do justice to the spirit behind this code?

[*Prologue*]
When Marduk[1] commissioned me to guide the people aright,
to direct the land,
I established law and justice in the language of the land,
thereby promoting the welfare of the people.
At that time (I decreed):

[*Trials*]

2. If a seignior[2] brought a charge of sorcery against a(nother) seignior, but has not proved it, the one against whom the charge of sorcery was brought, upon going to the river, shall throw himself into the river, and if the river has then overpowered him,[3] his accuser shall take over his estate; if the river has shown that

1. The chief god of Babylon.

2. A free person who has significant social standing.

3. If the person drowns in the Euphrates.

seignior to be innocent and he has accordingly come forth safe, the one who brought the charge of sorcery against him shall be put to death, while the one who threw himself into the river shall take over the estate of his accuser.

3. If a seignior came forward with false testimony in a case, and has not proved the word which he spoke, if that case was a case involving life, that seignior shall be put to death. . . .

[*Victim Rights*]

23. If . . . [a][4] robber has not been caught, the robbed seignior shall set forth the particulars regarding his lost property in the presence of god,[5] and the city and governor, in whose territory and district the robbery was committed, shall make good to him his lost property.

24. If it was a life (that was lost), the city and governor shall pay one mina[6] of silver to his people.[7] . . .

[*Business and Contracts*]

98. If a seignior gave money to a(nother) seignior for a partnership, they shall divide equally in the presence of god[8] the profit or loss which was incurred. . . .

107. When a merchant entrusted (something) to a trader[9] and the trader has returned to his merchant whatever the merchant gave him, if the merchant has then disputed with him whatever the trader gave him, that trader shall prove it against the merchant in the presence of god and witnesses and the merchant shall pay to the trader sixfold whatever he received because he had a dispute with his trader. . . .

109. If outlaws have congregated in the establishment of a woman wine seller and she has not arrested those outlaws and did not take them to the palace, that wine seller shall be put to death. . . .

122. If a seignior wishes to give silver, gold, or any sort of thing to a(nother) seignior for safekeeping, he shall show to witnesses the full amount that he wishes to give, arrange the contracts, and then commit (it) to safekeeping.

123. If he gave (it) for safekeeping without witnesses and contracts and they have denied (its receipt) to him at the place where he made the deposit, that case is not subject to claim. . . .

229. If a builder constructed a house for a seignior, but did not make his work strong, with the result that the house which he built collapsed and so has caused the death of the owner of the house, that builder shall be put to death.

230. If it has caused the death of a son of the owner of the house, they shall put the son of that builder to death.

231. If it has caused the death of a slave of the owner of the house, he shall give slave for slave to the owner of the house. . . .

4. Throughout the text, words in brackets have been added as glosses by the editors. Brackets around glosses from the original sources have been changed to parentheses to distinguish them.

5. Will take an oath before Marduk.

6. About 500 grams of silver. A mina was divided into 60 shekels.

7. The victim's family.

8. At the temple of Marduk.

9. The trader is a traveling salesperson.

245. If a seignior hired an ox and has caused its death through carelessness or through beating, he shall make good ox for ox to the owner of the ox. . . .

249. If a seignior hired an ox and god struck it and it has died, the seignior who hired the ox shall (so) affirm by god and then he shall go free.

[*Women*]

131. If a seignior's wife was accused by her husband, but she was not caught while lying with another man, she shall make affirmation by god and return to her house.

132. If the finger was pointed at the wife of a seignior because of another man, but she has not been caught while lying with the other man, she shall throw herself into the river for the sake of her husband.[10] . . .

138. If a seignior wishes to divorce his wife who did not bear him children, he shall give her money to the full amount of her marriage-price[11] and he shall also make good to her the dowry[12] which she brought from her father's house and then he may divorce her.

139. If there was no marriage-price, he shall give her one mina of silver as the divorce-settlement.

140. If he is a peasant, he shall give her one-third mina of silver.

141. If a seignior's wife, who was living in the house of the seignior, has made up her mind to leave in order that she may engage in business, thus neglecting her house (and) humiliating her husband, they shall prove it against her; and if her husband has then decided on her divorce, he may divorce her, with nothing to be given her as her divorce-settlement upon her departure. If her husband has not decided on her divorce, her husband may marry another woman, with the former woman living in the house of her husband like a maidservant.

142. If a woman so hated her husband that she has declared, "You may not have me," her record shall be investigated at her city council, and if she was careful and was not at fault, even though her husband has been going out and disparaging her greatly, that woman, without incurring any blame at all, may take her dowry and go off to her father's house.

143. If she was not careful, but was a gadabout, thus neglecting her house (and) humiliating her husband, they shall throw that woman into the water. . . .

148. When a seignior married a woman and a fever has then seized her, if he has made up his mind to marry another, he may marry (her), without divorcing his wife whom the fever seized; she shall live in the house which he built and he shall continue to support her as long as she lives.

149. If that woman has refused to live in her husband's house, he shall make good her dowry to her which she brought from her father's house and then she may leave.

150. If a seignior, upon presenting a field, orchard, house, or goods to his

10. Subject herself to a trial by the river. See law 2.

11. The price he paid her family in order to marry her.

12. The required money or goods she brought to the marriage.

wife, left a sealed document with her, her children may not enter a claim against her after (the death of) her husband, since the mother may give her inheritance to that son of hers whom she likes, (but) she may not give (it) to an outsider. . . .

[*Assault*]

195. If a son has struck his father, they shall cut off his hand.

196. If a seignior has destroyed the eye of a member of the aristocracy, they shall destroy his eye.

197. If he has broken a(nother) seignior's bone, they shall break his bone.

198. If he has destroyed the eye of a commoner or broken the bone of a commoner, he shall pay one mina of silver.

199. If he has destroyed the eye of a seignior's slave or broken the bone of a seignior's slave, he shall pay one-half his value.

200. If a seignior has knocked out a tooth of a seignior of his own rank, they shall knock out his tooth.

201. If he has knocked out a commoner's tooth, he shall pay one-third mina of silver.

202. If a seignior has struck the cheek of a seignior who is superior to him, he shall be beaten sixty (times) with an oxtail whip in the assembly.

203. If a member of the aristocracy has struck the cheek of a(nother) member of the aristocracy who is of the same rank as himself, he shall pay one mina of silver.

204. If a commoner has struck the cheek of a(nother) commoner, he shall pay ten shekels of silver.

205. If a seignior's slave has struck the cheek of a member of the aristocracy, they shall cut off his ear.

206. If a seignior has struck a(nother) seignior in a brawl and has inflicted an injury on him, that seignior shall swear, "I did not strike him deliberately"; and he shall also pay for the physician.

207. If he has died because of his blow, he shall swear (as before), and if it was a member of the aristocracy, he shall pay one-half mina of silver.

208. If it was a member of the commonalty, he shall pay one-third mina of silver.

209. If a seignior struck a(nother) seignior's daughter and has caused her to have a miscarriage, he shall pay ten shekels of silver for her fetus.

210. If that woman has died, they shall put his daughter to death. . . .

213. If he struck a seignior's female slave and has caused her to have a miscarriage, he shall pay two shekels of silver.

214. If that female slave has died, he shall pay one-third mina of silver.

[*Physicians' Fees*]

215. If a physician performed a major operation on a seignior with a bronze lancet and has saved the seignior's life, or he opened up the eye-socket of a seignior with a bronze lancet and has saved the seignior's eye, he shall receive ten shekels of silver.

216. If it was a member of the commonalty, he shall receive five shekels.

217. If it was a seignior's slave, the owner of the slave shall give two shekels of silver to the physician.

218. If a physician performed a major operation on a seignior with a bronze lancet and has caused the seignior's death, or he opened up the eye-socket of a seignior and has destroyed the seignior's eye, they shall cut off his hand.

Egypt: The Land of Two Lands

Civilization seems to have arisen in Egypt shortly after it first appeared in Sumer. Although there is evidence of early Sumerian contact with the Egyptians, Egypt's civilization was probably largely self-generated, and its history and cultural patterns followed courses that differed substantially from those of Mesopotamia. Egyptians, however, shared the same myth-making way of perceiving reality.

An integral element of Egyptian myth was the belief that Egypt was the land of divine harmony ruled by a living god-king or pharaoh who balanced all conflicting cosmic forces. Around 3100 B.C. the land of the Nile was unified into a single state, although culturally it remained two distinctive lands: the rich delta region of the north, known as Lower Egypt (because the Nile flows northward), and the long but narrow strip of green land that borders the Nile to the south, known as Upper Egypt. Prior to their unification, Lower and Upper Egypt had been separate kingdoms. As far as Egyptians were concerned, they were two antithetical yet complementary lands that were brought into harmony by a unifying king who was a god on earth.

The state that resulted from this union enjoyed about 3,000 years of historically unparalleled prosperity and stability. Between approximately 3100 and 343 B.C. Egypt experienced only a handful of relatively short-lived periods of either major internal turmoil and the consequent breakdown of central authority or domination by foreign powers. This long history of centralized monarchy and native rule was due in large part to the blessings of geography. Egypt was fairly secure behind its barriers of sea and desert, and the Nile's annual flooding was predictable and beneficial.

The sense of security that followed from these geographic and historical circumstances was reflected in the life-affirming spirit that pervaded Egyptian religion and philosophy. It also left its imprint on Egypt's arts. Whether painting charming scenes of everyday activities or composing tender love poems, Egyptian artists celebrated the joys of life. At the same time, codes of law, which figure so prominently in the historical records of Mesopotamia, are not to be found in the literature of ancient Egypt. Though Egyptians were equally concerned with maintaining a well-ordered society, their avenue to this goal differed greatly from that of Mesopotamians.

INSCRIPTIONS FROM THE TOMB OF KING UNIS

Unis ruled around 2400 B.C. in that age of Egyptian history known as the Old Kingdom (ca 2700–2200 B.C.), and when he died his body was placed in a pyramid at

Sakkarah. Egyptians would continue to bury their dead with great ceremony for thousands of years to come, but it was essentially only in the period of the Old Kingdom that they constructed pyramids to house the mummified remains of kings, members of their families, and select royal servants.

The following two inscriptions were carved within King Unis's pyramid and probably served as magical incantations to speed the king's body to its final resting place "in the West" (the place of afterlife where the sun set). As you read them, note that the king is identified with a number of deities, chief of whom is Osiris.

According to Egyptian mythology, Osiris was a beneficent god who, upon being granted rule over humanity, introduced to his subjects knowledge of agriculture and the arts. In jealousy, his evil brother Seth killed Osiris and dismembered his body. Isis, Osiris's wife, proceeded to search throughout the land until she recovered the scattered remains. With the help of other deities, she put the pieces back together, thereby creating the first mummified corpse. Miraculously, she conceived a son, Horus, from her dead husband. In time Horus set out to avenge his father by engaging Seth in battle. In the course of the fight, Horus lost his left eye but dealt Seth a debilitating blow. The gods intervened, restored Horus's eye, and divided the universe between Horus and Seth. Seth became the god of Upper Egypt; Horus claimed Lower Egypt. Meanwhile, Horus presented his restored eye to his father's corpse, thus effecting Osiris's resurrection. Osiris then retired to the kingdom of the blessed to serve as god of resurrection and transferred his earthly rule over humanity to his son.

Keep this myth in mind as you analyze these texts. Also be aware that a living king of Egypt was identified with Horus; in death he became Osiris.

Questions for Analysis

1. How is King Unis presented as the harmonizer of the two lands of Egypt and, therefore, all contradictory elements in the universe?
2. Compare Unis and Gilgamesh. How do their destinies and roles differ? Does your answer suggest any reasons why we fail to find among the records of Egypt codes of law similar to those of Mesopotamia?

O King Unis, thou hast not at all departed dead, thou hast departed living! For thou sittest upon the throne of Osiris,[1] with the scepter in thy hand, that thou mightest give command to the living, and with the grip of thy wand in thy hand,

1. The throne inherited by Horus.

that thou mightest give command to those secret of place.[2] Thy arm is Atum,[3] thy shoulders are Atum, thy belly is Atum, thy back is Atum, thy rear is Atum, thy legs are Atum, and thy face is Anubis.[4] The regions of Horus serve thee, and the regions of Seth serve thee.

. . .

O Atum, the one here is that son of thine, Osiris, whom thou hast caused to survive and to live on.[5] He lives — (so also) this King Unis lives. He does not die — (so also) this King Unis does not die. He does not perish — (so also) this King Unis does not perish. He is not judged — (so also) this King Unis is not judged. (But) he judges — (so also) this King Unis judges. . . .

What thou hast eaten is an eye.[6] Thy belly is rounded out with it. Thy son Horus leaves it for thee, that thou mayest live on it. He lives — this King Unis lives. He does not die — this King Unis does not die. He does not perish — this King Unis does not perish. He is not judged — this King Unis is not judged. He judges — this King Unis judges.

Thy[7] body is the body of this King Unis. Thy flesh is the flesh of this King Unis. Thy bones are the bones of this King Unis. When thou departest, this King Unis departs. When this King Unis departs, thou departest.

THE PERSON WHO WAS TIRED OF LIFE

The brilliant reign of Pepi II (ca 2275–2185 B.C.) marked the end of the Old Kingdom. Shortly after Pepi's death, pharaonic power collapsed and Egypt was plunged into a period of internal turmoil known as the First Intermediate Period (ca 2185–2050 B.C.). Eventually, this age of local rule and social upheaval gave way to the Middle Kingdom (ca 2050–1800 B.C.), an era of revived central authority but one characterized by a deepened awareness of social justice. Moreover, eternal life, which in the Old Kingdom had largely been seen as the preserve of the divine pharaoh, the royal family, and certain favored servants of the king, was now viewed as available to all Egyptians through the grace and power of the god-king who dwelt among them.

Before Egyptians attained the new optimism of the Middle Kingdom, however, they had to suffer through the political and social conflicts of the First Intermediate Period. In the following document from that troubled age, we read an unusual dialogue between an individual and his soul. Although the first portion of the dialogue is missing from the sole papyrus copy that has survived, it is clear that this person,

2. The dead.
3. A creator god.
4. The jackel-headed god of the dead.
5. Osiris was the great-grandson of Atum.
6. The eye of Horus.
7. Refers to Osiris.

alone in the world and friendless, is weary of life and contemplates suicide yet wonders if death will be any better.

As you read this dialogue, keep in mind that in the Old Kingdom it was generally believed that a deceased person could achieve eternal life with Osiris only if the person's survivors arranged to have the body embalmed and entombed with the proper accompanying rituals.

Questions for Analysis

1. What evidence strongly suggests that this dialogue was composed in the First Intermediate Period?
2. Why do we infer that this person was alone in the world?
3. Does being alone in the world cause this person ultimately to despair of achieving eternal life? What does your answer to this question suggest?
4. Consider the soul's advice, "Follow the happy day and forget care." Does the troubled person accept this notion? Compare this with the advice Siduri gives Gilgamesh. Does Gilgamesh ultimately accept it? What do the different resolutions of the psychological crises faced by these two people tell us about their respective civilizations?

O my soul, too stupid to (ease) misery in life and yet holding me back from death ere I come to it,[1] sweeten the West[2] for me. Is it (too much) trouble? Yet life is a transitory state, and even trees fall. Trample on wrong, for my misery endures. May Thoth[3] who pacifies the gods judge me; may Khons[4] defend me, even he who writes truly; may Re hear my plaint, even he who (commands) the solar bark;[5] may Isdes[6] defend me in the Holy Chamber[7] (because the needy one is weighed down with the burden) which he has lifted up from me; it is pleasant that the gods should ward off the secret (thoughts) of my body.[8]

What my soul said to me: Are you not a man? Indeed you are alive, but what do you profit? Yet you yearn for life like a man of wealth.[9]

---

1. The complaint is that the person's soul is unable to relieve the pain of life but restrains the sufferer from ending it all by suicide.

2. Make death easy.

3. The god of wisdom, who settled the dispute between Horus and Seth.

4. The god of the moon.

5. The sun-god who daily traveled in a solar boat across the sky.

6. A god associated with Thoth.

7. The Hall of Judgment for the dead.

8. Apparently the gods will protect the person from either his or her sins or worst fears.

9. The person greedily holds on to life.

I said: I have not gone (even though) that is on the ground.[10] . . . Yonder is a resting place (attractive) to the heart; the West is a dwelling place. . . . If my guiltless soul listens to me and its heart is in accord with me, it will be fortunate, for I will cause it to attain the West, like one who is in his pyramid, to whose burial a survivor attended.[11] . . . If you hold me back from death in this manner,[12] you will find nowhere you can rest in the West. Be so kind, my soul, my brother, as to become my heir who shall make offering and stand at the tomb on the day of burial, that he may (prepare) a bier for the necropolis.[13]

My soul opened its mouth to me that it might answer what I had said: If you think of burial, it is a sad matter; it is a bringer of weeping through making a man miserable; it is taking a man from his house, he being cast on the high ground;[14] never again will you go up that you may see the sun. Those who built in granite and constructed (halls) in goodly pyramids with fine work, when the builders became gods their stelae were destroyed,[15] like the weary ones who died on the riverbank through lack of a survivor,[16] the flood having taken its toll and the sun likewise, to whom talk the fishes of the banks of the water. Listen to me; behold it is good for men to hear. Follow the happy day and forget care. . . .

I opened my mouth to my soul that I might answer what it had said:

Behold, my name is detested,
Behold, more than the smell of vultures
On a summer's day when the sky is
  hot. . . .
Behold, my name is detested,
Behold (more than) a town belonging to
  the monarch
Which mutters sedition when his back is
  turned.

To whom can I speak today?
Brothers are evil
And the friends of today unlovable.

To whom can I speak today?
Hearts are rapacious
And everyone takes his neighbor's
  goods.

(To whom can I speak today?)
Gentleness has perished
And the violent man has come down on
  everyone.

To whom can I speak today?
Men are contented with evil
And goodness is neglected everywhere.

To whom can I speak today?
He who should enrage a man by his ill
  deeds,
He makes everyone laugh (by) his wicked
  wrongdoing.

To whom can I speak today?
Men plunder
And every man robs his neighbor. . . .

10. "Even though I have lost everything, I have not yet killed myself."

11. If the soul does not desert its owner, it will achieve eternal life.

12. "If you prevent my suicide."

13. The soul will take the place of the suicide's survivors and prepare a resting place in the necropolis, where the dead are buried.

14. Necropolises were often situated on plateaus.

15. The monuments (stelae) and graves of the dead builders (the kings of the Old Kingdom who in death have become gods) have been ransacked.

16. Even the kings of old now lie like unburied victims of a flood.

To whom can I speak today?
There are no just persons
And the land is left over to the doers of wrong. . . .

To whom can I speak today?
The wrong which roams the earth,
There is no end to it.

Death is in my sight today
(As when) a sick man becomes well,
Like going out-of-doors after detention.

Death is in my sight today
Like the smell of myrrh,
Like sitting under an awning on a windy day. . . .

Death is in my sight today
As when a man desires to see home
When he has spent many years in captivity.

Verily, he who is yonder[17] will be a living god,
Averting the ill of him who does it.

Verily, he who is yonder will be one who stands in the Bark of the Sun,[18]
Causing choice things to be given therefrom for the temples.

Verily, he who is yonder will be a sage
Who will not be prevented from appealing to Re when he speaks.

What my soul said to me: Cast complaint upon (the peg),[19] my comrade and brother; make offering on the brazier[20] and cleave to life, according as (I) have said. Desire me here, thrust the West aside,[21] but desire that you may attain the West when your body goes to earth, that I may alight after you are weary; then will we make an abode together.

HYMN TO AMON-RE

Between approximately 1730 and 1570 B.C., a group of hated foreign conquerors, known as the Hyksos, ruled Lower Egypt. Their expulsion was spearheaded by princes of Thebes who eventually instituted the eighteenth royal dynasty of Egypt and launched the Age of Empire or New Kingdom (ca 1570–1100). During that period Egypt became a major power in East Africa and the Middle East, driving south into Nubia, a region the conquerors termed "the land of the blacks," and battling the Hittites of Asia Minor for control of Syria-Palestine. Imperial adventure and expan-

17. In the realm of the dead.

18. Re's celestial boat.

19. "Hang up your cares as you would a garment on a peg."

20. "Sacrifice to the gods."

21. "Give up the idea of premature death."

sion produced temporary prosperity and growth at home, especially in the fifteenth century. The art and literature of the Eighteenth Dynasty reveal a world of opulence and a society whose elites enjoyed the good life to the fullest.

Over this society presided pharaoh, a god-king on earth, and over pharaoh ruled Amon-Re, a heavenly father. By the sixteenth century, the chief god of Egypt was clearly Amon-Re, a composite of Amon (or Amun or Amen), a god of wind, and Re (or Ra), a sun deity and one of Egypt's oldest and most revered gods. Amon originally had been an obscure local god of Thebes, but the rise to power in the Middle Kingdom of a new ruling family from Thebes brought him to prominence and resulted in his identification with Re. The hymn to Amon-Re that follows was composed between 1550 and 1350 B.C., at the height of Egypt's imperial greatness.

Questions for Analysis

1. In what ways does this hymn reveal a society that sees the world as harmonious and the gods as beneficent?
2. In what ways is Amon-Re distinguished from other gods?
3. Where is there evidence of Egypt's new imperialism in this hymn?
4. Compare this Egyptian view of the world with that of Mesopotamia.

Adoration of Amon-Re, the Bull Residing in Heliopolis,[1] chief of all gods, the good god, the beloved who gives life to all that is warm and to all good cattle.

Hail to thee, Amon-Re,
Lord of the Thrones of the Two Lands, Presiding over Karnak,[2]
Bull of His Mother,[3] Presiding over His Fields!
Far-reaching of stride, presiding over Upper Egypt,
The Lord of the Madjoi and ruler of Punt,[4]
Eldest of heaven, first-born of earth,
Lord of what is, enduring in all things, enduring in all things.
Unique in his nature like the fluid of the gods,[5]

---

1. The "city of the sun." This city, sacred to Re, was located near Memphis, the ancient capital of the Old Kingdom.

2. The great temple of Amon at Karnak was located across the Nile from Thebes. It is one of the world's most extensive religious complexes.

3. As sun-god, Amon-Re re-created himself daily.

4. Regions of the south and southeast.

5. According to one Egyptian creation myth, Re created the gods with his spittle.

The goodly bull of the Ennead,[6] chief of all gods,
The lord of truth and father of the gods.
Who made mankind and created the beasts,
Lord of what is, who created the fruit tree,
Made herbage, and gave life to cattle.
The goodly daemon[7] whom Ptah[8] made,

The goodly beloved youth to whom the gods give praise,
Who made what is below and what is above,
Who illuminates the Two Lands
And crosses the heavens in peace:[9]
The King of Upper and Lower Egypt: Re, the triumphant,
Chief of the Two Lands,
Great of strength, lord of reverence,
The chief one, who made the entire earth.
More distinguished in nature than any (other) god,
In whose beauty the gods rejoice,
To whom is given jubilation in the Per-wer,[10]
Who is given ceremonial appearance in the Per-nezer.[11]
Whose fragrance the gods love, when he comes from Punt,
Rich in perfume, when he comes down (from) Madjoi,
The Beautiful of Face who comes (from) God's Land.[12]
The gods fawn (at) his feet,
According as they recognize his majesty as their lord,
The lord of fear, great of dread,
Rich in might, terrible of appearances,
Flourishing in offerings and making provisions.
Jubilation to thee who made the gods,
Raised the heavens and laid down the ground!

---

6. The nine chief deities of Heliopolis.

7. God or spirit.

8. The creator god of Memphis.

9. Daily Re sails across the heavens.

10. Literally, the "Great House." This was the religious capital of Upper Egypt, where the god-king presided as priest. The word *pharaoh* is derived from this term.

11. Lower Egypt's counterpart to the Per-wer. Both lands retained their separate identities. Hence, the king had two official palaces, one in each land, and there were elaborate ceremonies for his coronation and death held in each land, each with its own ritual and insignia.

12. The East, land of the rising sun.

LOVE SONGS OF A WOMAN FROM THE NEW KINGDOM

Religion in its various forms — the belief that a loving god-king dwelt in their midst, the hope of eternal life after death, the practice of magic as protection from malevolent spirits — was central to Egyptian life. We would be mistaken, however, if we envisioned the ancient Egyptians as a people who were not concerned with more mundane realities. Life, at least for the privileged, was good, and they enjoyed it. Perhaps the very sweetness of life was a major factor in the evolution of the Egyptian notion that death is not an end to life.

The literature and art of Egypt, especially that of the New Kingdom, present glimpses of a world that gloried in the beauty of nature and the joys of sensual love. The three songs that appear here date from the later New Kingdom and illustrate the Egyptian celebration of these basic pleasures.

Question for Analysis

1. Obviously these poems were meant to be sung by a woman and may have been composed by a woman. What might we infer from them about the status and freedom enjoyed by this female lover?

My brother,[1] my beloved,
My heart pursues the love of thee,
All that thou hast brought into being.
I say to thee: "See what I am doing!"
I have come from setting my trap with
  my (own) hand;
In my hand are my bait and my snare.
All the birds of Punt, they alight in Egypt,
Anointed with myrrh.[2]
The first one comes and takes my worm.
Its fragrance is brought from Punt,
And its talons are full of resin.
My wish for thee is that we loose them
  together,
When I am alone with thee,
That I might let thee hear the cry
Of the one anointed with myrrh.
How good it would be
If thou wert there with me
When I set the trap!

1. The terms *brother* and *sister* do not necessarily refer to blood siblings; it was the fashion to speak of one's beloved as brother or sister. Pharaohs did frequently marry their sisters, however.

2. Punt, the land of Yemen or southern Arabia, was famous for its perfumes and resins, such as myrrh. Perfume was highly valued in Egyptian society and widely used by its elites.

The best is to go to the fields,
To the one who is beloved!

. . .

The voice of the swallow speaks and
  says:
"The land has brightened — What is thy
  road?"[3]
Thou shalt not, O bird, disturb me!
I have found my brother in his bed,
And my heart is still more glad,
(When he) said to me:
"I shall not go afar off.
My hand is in thy hand,
I shall stroll about,
And I shall be with thee in every pleasant
  place."

He makes me the foremost of maidens.
He injures not my heart.

. . .

Would that thou wouldst come (to the
  sister speedily),
Like a horse of the king,
Picked from a thousand of all steeds,
The foremost of the stables!
It is distinguished in its food,
And its master knows its paces.
If it hears the sound of the whip,
It knows no delay,
And there is no foremost of the
  chasseurs[4]
Who can stay before it (to hold it).
How well the sister's heart knows
That he is not far from the sister!

China: The Age of Shang and Western Chou

The study of history has been one of China's most revered and continuous traditions for well over 2,000 years. By the time of their greatest historian, Ssu-ma Ch'ien (ca 145–90 B.C.), the Chinese had evolved a chronology for Chinese civilization that reached back into the early third millennium. Yet much of this "history" was more the stuff of legend than historical research, and modern archeology has yet to discover any compelling evidence to indicate the existence of a civilized state in China before about 1800 B.C. Despite the unanimous assertion of classical Chinese historians, such as Ssu-ma Ch'ien, that royal rule in China stretched back to about 2850 B.C., the earliest royal dynasty today's scholars can identify with certainty is that of the Shang (also known, in its later stages, as the Yin). Traditional Chinese histories provide two different sets of dates for Shang rule: 1766 to 1122 and 1523 to 1028 B.C. Recent archeological evidence strongly supports the earlier sets of dates.

3. "Where are you going?"
4. Chariot-warriors.

Much of our knowledge of the Shang, whose kingdom was centered on the middle portions of the Yellow River in northern China, is due to the discoveries of archeologists over the past half century. They have unearthed magnificent bronze ceremonial vessels, an entire capital city, and an early form of Chinese ideographic writing on what are known as oracle bones. Although scholars can read them, these oracle bones provide little detail about the social and political history of the Shang, for they served one purpose, magical divination of the future. China's earliest extant literary and political documents date from the subsequent Chou Dynasty.

The Shang Dynasty fell to the Chou, a Chinese frontier people from the West, around 1100 B.C. The era of Chou rule, which lasted approximately nine hundred years, falls into two periods: Western and Eastern Chou. The age of Western Chou witnessed a fairly strong feudal monarchy ruling over a number of dependent vassal states. This ended when King Yu was killed and the capital city, Hao, was overrun in 771 B.C. In 770 the royal heir and those members of the court who survived fled eastward to the auxiliary capital, Loyang, where the Chou continued to reside as kings until 256 B.C. The kings of Eastern Chou never enjoyed the power of their western forebearers, and for the next five hundred years they reigned over but did not rule a kingdom where all real power resided in the hands of local lords.

THE BOOK OF HISTORY

The *Shu Ching* or *Book of History* is the oldest complete work among what are known as the five Confucian classics. The five classics were canonized as the basic elements of the Confucian educational system only during the second century B.C., when the books were reconstructed by order of several emperors of the Han Dynasty (202 B.C.–A.D. 220). Although Han scholars probably refashioned elements of the *Shu Ching*, the work was already ancient in Confucius's day, and the book, as we have received it, is probably essentially the same text that Confucius (551–479 B.C.) knew, studied, and accepted as an authentic record of Chinese civilization.

Despite its title, the *Book of History* is not a work of historical interpretation or narration. Rather, it is a collection of documents spanning some 1,700 years of Chinese history and legend, from 2357 to 631 B.C. Many of the documents, however, are spurious: they are the creations of much later periods and reflect, therefore, the attitudes of these later eras.

The document that appears here was composed in the age of Chou but purports to be the advice given by the faithful I Yin to King T'ai Chia, second of the Shang kings. According to the story behind this document, when the first Shang king,

T'ang, died around 1753 B.C., his chief minister I Yin took it upon himself to instruct the new, young king in the ways and duties of kingship and the workings of the Mandate of Heaven.

The Mandate of Heaven was a political-social philosophy that served as the basic Chinese explanation for the success and failure of monarchs and states for centuries, until the end of the empire in A.D. 1912. Whenever dynasties fell, the reason invariably offered by China's sages was that they had lost the moral right to rule, which is given by Heaven alone. In this context, Heaven did not mean a personal god but a cosmic, all-pervading power. Most scholars believe that the theory of the Mandate of Heaven was an invention of the Chou to justify their overthrow of the Shang. The king, after all, was the father of his people, and paternal authority was the basic cement of Chinese society from earliest times. Rebellion against a father, therefore, needed extraordinary justification.

Questions for Analysis

1. What evidence do you find of the Chinese cult of reverence for the ancestors?
2. What evidence do you find that suggests classical Chinese political philosophy perceived the state as an extended family?
3. What sort of harmony does the monarch maintain?
4. How does a monarch lose the Mandate of Heaven, and what are the consequences of this loss?
5. Politicians in the United States often promise "innovative answers to the challenges of tomorrow." What would I Yin think about such an approach to statecraft? What would I Yin think about modern politicians who attempt to appear youthful?
6. Would I Yin accept the notion that one must distinguish between a ruler's private morality and public policies?
7. What does the theory of the Mandate of Heaven suggest about the nature of Chinese society?
8. Compare the Chinese vision of its ideal monarch with Egyptian and Mesopotamian views of kingship. Despite all their obvious cultural differences, did each of these societies expect its king to perform essentially the same task? If so, what was that task?

In the twelfth month of the first year . . . I Yin sacrificed to the former king, and presented the heir-king reverently before the shrine of his grandfather. All the princes from the domain of the nobles and the royal domain were present; all the officers (also), each continuing to discharge his particular duties, were there to receive the orders of the chief minister. I Yin then clearly described the complete virtue of the Meritorious Ancestor for the instruction of the young king.

He said, "Oh! of old the former kings of Hsia cultivated earnestly their virtue, and then there were no calamities from Heaven. The spirits of the hills and rivers likewise were all in tranquillity; and the birds and beasts, the fishes and tortoises, all enjoyed their existence according to their nature. But their descendant did not follow their example, and great Heaven sent down calamities, employing the agency of our ruler[1] who was in possession of its favoring appointment. The attack on Hsia may be traced to the orgies in Ming-t'iao.[2] . . . Our king of Shang brilliantly displayed his sagely prowess; for oppression he substituted his generous gentleness; and the millions of the people gave him their hearts. Now your Majesty is entering on the inheritance of his virtue; — all depends on how you commence your reign. To set up love, it is for you to love your relations; to set up respect, it is for you to respect your elders. The commencement is in the family and the state. . . .

"Oh! the former king began with careful attention to the bonds that hold men together. He listened to expostulation, and did not seek to resist it; he conformed to the wisdom of the ancients; occupying the highest position, he displayed intelligence; occupying an inferior position, he displayed his loyalty; he allowed the good qualities of the men whom he employed and did not seek that they should have every talent. . . .

"He extensively sought out wise men, who should be helpful to you, his descendant and heir. He laid down the punishments for officers, and warned those who were in authority, saying, 'If you dare to have constant dancing in your palaces, and drunken singing in your chambers, — that is called the fashion of sorcerers; if you dare to set your hearts on wealth and women, and abandon yourselves to wandering about or to the chase, — that is called the fashion of extravagance; if you dare to despise sage words, to resist the loyal and upright, to put far from you the aged and virtuous, and to seek the company of . . . youths, — that is called the fashion of disorder. Now if a high noble or officer be addicted to one of these three fashions with their ten evil ways, his family will surely come to ruin; if the prince of a country be so addicted, his state will surely come to ruin. The minister who does not try to correct such vices in the sovereign shall be punished with branding.' . . .

"Oh! do you, who now succeed to the throne, revere these warnings in your person. Think of them! — sacred counsels of vast importance, admirable words forcibly set forth! The ways of Heaven are not invariable: — on the good-doer it sends down all blessings, and on the evil-doer it sends down all miseries. Do you but be virtuous, be it in small things or in large, and the myriad regions will have cause for rejoicing. If you be not virtuous, be it in large things or in small, it will bring the ruin of your ancestral temple."

1. T'ang, founder of the Shang Dynasty.

2. According to legend, Chieh, the last Hsia king, held notorious orgies at Ming-t'iao.

THE BOOK OF SONGS

The *Shih Ching* or *Book of Songs* is another of the five Confucian classics that served as the basic texts of an educational system that molded China's leaders for over 2,000 years. The work consists of 305 poetic songs, covering a variety of topics from love to war, whose dates of composition largely fall between about 900 and 600 B.C. The book ultimately became "Confucian" because Confucius and his disciples for the next two and a half millennia used the songs as texts for moral instruction. No good reason exists to believe that Confucius had a hand in crafting any of the poems or even in assembling the collection.

The following ballad celebrates the virtues of Chung Shan Fu, ninth-century chief minister to King Hsuan. A careful reading of the song reveals not only the Chou Dynasty's vision of itself but also its philosophy of what constituted good government and personal virtue.

Questions for Analysis

1. Does the poet believe that one can distinguish between Chung Shan Fu's personal qualities and his abilities as a leader?
2. The first four lines of the poem neatly sum up the classical Chinese self-image. What was it?
3. According to this song, what is good government, and how does one achieve it?
4. Scholars often characterize traditional Chinese social and political philosophy as conservative. Is there any evidence in this song to support that judgment?
5. What is the meaning of the proverb, "Inward power is light as a feather; yet too heavy for common people to raise"? What does it tell us about China's political-social philosophy?

The people of our race were created by Heaven
Having from the beginning distinctions and rules.
Our people cling to customs,
And what they admire is seemly behavior.
Heaven, looking upon the land of Chou,
Sent a radiance to earth beneath.
To guard this Son of Heaven[1]
It created Chung Shan Fu.

In his nature Chung Shan Fu
Is a pattern of mildness and blessedness.
Good is his every attitude and air,
So cautious, so composed!

1. The king.

Following none but ancient teachings,
Striving only for dignity and good
deportment,
Obedient to the Son of Heaven,
Whose glorious commands he spreads
abroad.

The king commanded Chung Shan Fu:
"Be a pattern to all the officers of Court,
Continue the work of your ancestors,
Protect the royal person,
Go out and in with the royal commands,
Be the king's throat and tongue,
Spread his edicts abroad
That through all the land men may be
stirred."

With due awe of the king's command
Did Chung Shan Fu effect it.
If in the land anything was darkened
Chung Shan Fu shed light upon it.
Very clear-sighted was he and wise.
He assured his own safety;[2]
But day and night never slackened
In the service of the One Man.[3]

There is a saying among men:
"If soft, chew it;
If hard, spit it out."
But Chung Shan Fu
Neither chews the soft,
Nor spits out the hard;
He neither oppresses the solitary and the
widow,
Nor fears the truculent and strong.

There is a saying among men:
"Inward power is light as a feather;
Yet too heavy for common people to
raise."
Thinking it over,
I find none but Chung Shan Fu that could
raise it;
For alas! none helped him.
When the robe of state was in holes
It was he alone who mended it.

THE BOOK OF SONGS

The great lords of Western Chou believed their rule was virtuous and their wars glorious, but that was not necessarily the view from other quarters. The first song is the commentary of a person from China's eastern region on the ways of these western lords. The second song could be the lament of any rank-and-file soldier in virtually any army at any time in recorded history.

Questions for Analysis

1. In the first poem the author compares the lords of Western Chou to certain heavenly constellations. What message does the poet intend to convey through this image?

2. By pleasing his ancestors.

3. The king.

2. What dichotomy does this poet draw between the people of Chou and the people of the east whom they have conquered?
3. According to the second poet, what aspects of life has soldiering disrupted?
4. Was this soldier a volunteer or a conscript?
5. How does the second poet portray the life of the common soldier?

Messy is the stew in the pot;
Bent is the thornwood spoon.
But the ways of Chou are smooth as a
grindstone,
Their straightness is like an arrow;
Ways that are for gentlemen to walk
And for commoners to behold.
Full of longing I look for them;
In a flood my tears flow.

In the Lesser East and the Greater East[1]
Shuttle and spool are idle.
"Fibre-shoes tightly woven
Are good for walking upon the dew."[2]
Foppishly mincing the young lords
Walk there upon the road.
They go away, they come back again;
It makes me ill to look at them!

That spraying fountain so cold
Does not soak firewood that is gathered
and bundled.
Heigh-ho! I lie awake and sigh.
Woe is me that am all alone!
Firewood that is gathered firewood
May still be put away.
Woe is me that am all alone!
I too could do with rest.

The men of the East, their sons
Get all the work and none of the pay.
The men of the West, their sons,
Oh, so smart are their clothes!
The men of Chou, their sons
Wear furs of bearskin, black and brown.
The sons of their vassals
For every appointment are chosen.

Fancy taking the wine
And leaving the sauce,
Having a belt-pendant so fine
And not using its full length!

In Heaven there is a River Han[3]
Looking down upon us so bright.
By it sits the Weaving Lady[4] astride her
stool,
Seven times a day she rolls up her
sleeves.
But though seven times she rolls her
sleeves
She never makes wrap or skirt.
Bright shines that Draught Ox,[5]
But can't be used for yoking to a cart.

. . .

What plant is not faded?
What day do we not march?
What man is not taken
To defend the four bounds?[6]

1. West of the coastal province of Shantung, the terminus of the Hwang Ho or Yellow River, and central Shantung, respectively.

2. That is, the shoes of a dandy.

3. The Milky Way.

4. A heavenly constellation.

5. Another constellation.

6. The frontiers.

What plant is not wilting?
What man is not taken from his wife?
Alas for us soldiers,
Treated as though we were not fellow-
men!

Are we buffaloes, are we tigers
That our home should be these desolate
wilds?

Alas for us soldiers,
Neither by day nor night can we rest!

The fox bumps and drags
Through the tall, thick grass.
Inch by inch move our barrows
As we push them along the track.

THE BOOK OF SONGS

Traditional Chinese society revolved around the family to the point that all larger social and political units were viewed as its extensions. In any society where family ties are the primary bond, courtship and marriage assume great significance.

As far back as the record goes, the Chinese have exhibited a preoccupation with stable marriage, and their practices in regard to this institution have remained fairly constant from earliest times to our own century. The following songs reveal several important customs and attitudes relating to courtship and marriage in early China.

The first song describes the courtship of a woman from the state of Ch'i, one of Eastern Chou's virtually autonomous feudal states, by a man from the state of Lu. The second song is the lament of a young married woman. The last song celebrates a happier situation.

Questions for Analysis

1. How does one initiate a courtship?
2. What obligations does the man incur upon entering into a courtship?
3. What role does love play in courtship? Did the Chinese believe love was possible within an arranged marriage?
4. Once married, to whose family does the woman belong? What role does she play in that family?
5. Compare the situation of these Chinese women with that of the Egyptian woman who composed the love songs you read earlier. What strikes you as more significant, their similarities or their differences?

Over the southern hill so deep
The male fox drags along,
But the way to Lu is easy and broad
For this Ch'i lady on her wedding-way.
Yet once she has made the journey,
Never again must her fancy roam.

Fibre shoes, five pairs;
Cap ribbons, a couple.[1]
The way to Lu is easy and broad
For this lady of Ch'i to use.
But once she has used it,
No way else must she ever go.

When we plant hemp, how do we do it?
Across and along we put the rows.
When one takes a wife, how is it done?
The man must talk with her father and
mother.
And once he has talked with them,
No one else must he court.

When we cut firewood, how do we do it?
Without an axe it would not be possible.
When one takes a wife, how is it done?
Without a match-maker he cannot get her.
But once he has got her,
No one else must he ever approach.[2]

. . .

Close the cloth-plant spreads its fibres
Along the banks of the river.
Far from big brothers, from little brothers
I must call a stranger "Father,"
Must call a stranger "Father";
But he does not heed me.

Close the cloth-plant spreads its fibres
Along the margin of the river.
Far from big brothers, from little brothers
I must call a stranger "Mother,"
Must call a stranger "Mother,"[3]
But she does not own me.

Close the cloth-plant spreads its fibres
Along the lips of the river.
Far from big brothers, from little brothers
I must call strangers kinsmen,
Must call strangers kinsmen;
But they do not listen to me.

. . .

Anxiously chirps the cicada,
Restlessly skips the grasshopper.
Before I saw my lord
My heart was ill at ease.
But now that I have seen him,
Now that I have met him,
My heart is at rest.

I climbed that southern hill
To pluck the fern-shoots.
Before I saw my lord
My heart was sad.
But now that I have seen him,
Now that I have met him,
My heart is still.

I climbed that southern hill
To pluck the bracken-shoots.
Before I saw my lord
My heart was sore distressed.
But now that I have seen him,
Now that I have met him,
My heart is at peace.

Mute Testimony

Several of the world's earliest civilizations have left written records that we cannot yet decipher and may never be able to read. These include India's Harappan civili-

1. Marriage gifts given by the bridegroom.
2. He could, however, keep concubines.
3. The theme of the young wife who is abused by her in-laws, especially her mother-in-law, is quite common in Chinese literature.

zation, which was centered in the Indus valley from before 2500 to some time after 1700 B.C.; The Minoan civilization of the Aegean island of Crete, which flourished from about 2500 to 1450 B.C.; and the black African civilization of Kush, located directly south of Egypt, which reached its age of greatness after 800 B.C. but whose origins as a state go back much earlier. For many other civilizations and cultures we have, as yet, uncovered no written records. This is true of the Olmec Amerindian civilization of Mexico, which attained its heights between 1200 and 600 B.C. before giving way to other Meso-American (Central American) civilizations, such as the Maya, whom it profoundly influenced. The Olmec did leave behind calendars that we can read, but apparently they did not create a full system of writing. The list also includes the largely mysterious Nok culture, which flourished between approximately 900 B.C. and A.D. 200 in an area encompassed today by the nation of Nigeria. These apparently preliterate people were the first known smelters of iron in sub-Saharan West Africa and may have started to practice that skill before 400 B.C.

The following pieces of artifactual evidence provide glimpses into the cultures of these often forgotten societies. As is always the case when dealing with nonverbal sources, however, the historian discovers that such clues from the past raise more questions than they answer.

MOHENJO-DARO

Both artifacts date from approximately 2100 to 1750 B.C. and were discovered at the site of the long-dead city of Mohenjo-Daro in modern Pakistan. The *Bearded Man* is a 7½-inch limestone bust of an individual wearing a garment draped over one shoulder and a headband. The *Dancing Girl* is a 4½-inch bronze statuette depicting an adolescent female who is nude except for a necklace and numerous bangles on her arms. The size of both pieces is consistent with every other sculpture unearthed at Harappan sites.

Questions for Analysis

1. In later Indian civilization, an off-shoulder garment was normally associated with holy persons, and turbans and similar headgear were a mark of high status. Consider the apparel and also the facial expression of the *Bearded Man*. What do these factors seem to tell us about this man? What function might he have served in his society?
2. Consider the size of each piece, the artistry with which each was created, and the different spirits which each seems to represent. What do these two works of art seem to tell us about the values of Harappan civilization?

Two Sculptures from Mohenjo-Daro

CRETE

This statuette, discovered at the royal palace at Knossos on Crete, measures about a foot in height and dates from around 1700–1600 B.C., a period of special brilliance in Minoan history. It represents a woman dressed in an elaborate costume and holding two snakes. The snake, such as the serpent who stole the plant of rejuvenation from Gilgamesh, was revered in the eastern Mediterranean and elsewhere as a divine creature. Among its attributes were eternal life (regularly shedding one skin for another) and the power of healing.

Questions for Analysis

1. Consider the expression on the woman's face. Do you perceive any indication of trance or possession by a magical power?

Minoan Snake Woman

2. Compare her expression, dress, and bearing with those of the *Bearded Man* and the *Dancing Girl*. Can you see why many art historians refer to him as *The Priest* but why scholars generally do not believe that the Harappan girl was a priestess?
3. No one can say with certainty whether this Minoan sculpture represents a goddess or a priestess. Do you see any evidence that suggests it was fashioned by a people who worshiped a mother goddess of the earth?
4. As is the case with ancient Harappa, all the art and other physical remains of Minoan civilization are human-sized or smaller. There are no structures or statues that rival the monumentality of Egyptian or Mesopotamian creations. What might we infer from this?

LA VENTA

We know very little about the Olmec who inhabited the region comprising the modern provinces of Vera Cruz and Tabasco along Mexico's gulf coast. As far as we know, they constructed Meso-America's first civilization. Shortly after 1200 B.C. they were building large ceremonial centers, and between approximately 900 and 600 B.C. they concentrated on the river island of La Venta.

The complex at La Venta extended over a space of more than three square miles and consisted of mounds, platforms, pyramids, and plazas. Archeologists have also unearthed at La Venta four colossal heads, each measuring eight to nine feet in height. The source for the basalt rock from which the Olmec artisans carved these heads lies over sixty miles away.

A number of similar heads, all sharing the same general facial features and wearing the same type of helmetlike headgear, have been discovered at other Olmec sites. Scholars have variously characterized these faces as "menacing," "sneering," "infantile and sexless," "powerful but gentle," and "majestic and disciplined." Who or what these sculptures represented is anyone's guess, but most experts believe they were actual Olmec leaders.

Questions for Analysis

1. What does the size of this sculpture suggest about the political, religious, and social organization of Olmec civilization? What sort of power did its leaders probably wield? What kind of labor force did they command?
2. What do you read in this face, and what does it tell you about the nature of authority in Olmec society?
3. Compare this sculpture with the *Bearded Man* and the Minoan snake woman. Do the three pieces have anything in common? Where and how do they differ? What are more significant, their differences or similarities?

The Colossal Head of La Venta

THE NILE

We are not certain whether the Minoan and Olmec sculptures we have studied portray humans or deities, but this is not the case with regard to these two temple reliefs (a raised carving on a flat background). The first piece is Egyptian and dates from the thirteenth century B.C., when Egypt's New Kingdom exercised considerable influence on its southern neighbors. Located at the temple of King Seti I at Abydos in Upper Egypt, it portrays, from right to left, the falcon-god Horus, Seti, and the goddess Isis. We will use it solely for comparison with the second relief. This piece of religious art is Kushite and dates from after 300 B.C. It is a small fragment (6-½″) of a temple tablet from Meroë, a Nubian city considerably distant from Abydos. It portrays a Nubian king of Kush and the lion-god Apedemak.

The Nubians, who were black Africans inhabiting the region directly south of Egypt, were drawn into the orbit of their powerful neighbor to the north at an early date. Yet, though they borrowed quite a bit from the Egyptians, the Nubians managed to retain their indigenous culture. Around 800 B.C. the Nubians created the

Two Temple Reliefs from the Nile

independent kingdom of Kush and around 730 B.C. were strong enough to conquer Egypt, which Kushite pharaohs ruled for close to a century. After being driven out of Egypt by the Assyrians, the Kushites eventually established a new capital for their kingdom at Meroë on the Middle Nile. Between about 350 B.C. and the early fourth century A.D., Kush was a major economic power in East Africa, largely because of Meroë's rich iron deposits.

In the relief below, one of those mighty monarchs of Kush stands face to face with the Nubians' most powerful deity. Unfortunately, we cannot decipher the writing above each figure, so we can only guess at the meaning of this scene. Perhaps the relief of Seti I provides a vital clue. There Horus, the divine son of Isis and Osiris, is handing the scepter of power to Seti, who, as long as he lives on earth, will be

identified with Horus, upon whose throne he sits. Note that the Meroitic tablet also portrays both god and king with what appear to be scepters.

Questions for Analysis

1. Do these two artifactual clues allow us to infer anything about the nature of royal power in Kush?
2. What do they tell us about the balance which the Kushites struck between accepting Egyptian influences and retaining traditional Nubian ways?

NOK

One of the major characteristics of Nok society was its production of sculpted human heads in terra cotta (baked clay). The sculpture of a woman's head represented here dates from about 200 B.C. and is considered one of the many masterpieces of Nok art. At the very least, it demonstrates the highly refined artistic techniques and sensibilities of this culture. Without any written records, it is difficult for us to say much about the Nok people, but it is clear that with these sculptures we are in the presence of artistic genius.

Questions for Analysis

1. Why do we conclude that the Nok were a Negroid people?
2. Why have many archeologists inferred that the Nok believed the head to be the center of the "life force"?
3. Some art historians have suggested that these sculptures evolved from an artistic tradition of woodcarving. What do you think is their evidence for this theory?
4. Compare this head with the sculptures from Mohenjo-Daro, Crete, and La Venta. Which pieces does it most closely resemble and why? What do you conclude from these similarities?

A Nok Woman

C H A P T E R

2

New Peoples

The oldest town yet excavated by archeologists is Jericho, which has been inhabited, almost continuously, for the past 11,000 years. Around 8000 B.C. this site, immediately west of the River Jordan in lands today occupied by the state of Israel, covered more than eight acres and supported a population of over 3,000. Most impressive of all are the town's massive watchtower, walls, and encircling ditch, which serve as silent evidence of the residents' fear of outsiders.

That fear was well based. Archeological evidence shows that Jericho suffered destruction on several occasions, and it is not too difficult to imagine that some of those catastrophes were the handiwork of invading nomads, attracted by the city's wealth.

The tension between wandering pastoral people, tending herds of domesticated animals, and settled farmers, who became the backbone of civilization, is as old as agriculture itself, and it continued to be a major factor in global history into the fifteenth century A.D. To be sure, there were many mutually beneficial relationships between civilized communities and the pastoralists who wandered their borders. However, fringe peoples who served as mercenary soldiers, traders, and carriers of new ideas could also be formidable foes, threatening the very existence of some civilizations.

Afro-Eurasian civilizations were subjected to two periods of especially intense pressure from nomadic outsiders prior to 1000 B.C. Around 1800 B.C. nomads living on the Iranian plateau perfected the two-wheeled chariot. Within the relatively short span of several centuries, groups of pastoralists used this new master weapon to establish a number of warrior kingdoms as far west as Greece and at least as far east as northern India. These peoples included the Greeks of Mycenae, the Hittites of Asia Minor, the Kassites and Mitanni of Mesopotamia, the Hyksos of Egypt, and the Aryans of India.

The second age of major nomadic disturbance took place around 1200 B.C. as an expanding knowledge of iron metallurgy made it possible for new fringe groups to challenge seriously many of the now old and tired chariot kingdoms. With plentiful and therefore cheap weapons available to both their external and internal enemies, a number of these civilized societies found themselves fighting for their very survival, and several succumbed. Mycenaean Greece slipped back into a precivilized state, as it was overwhelmed by waves of ruder Greek cousins; the mighty Hittite empire was wiped out and soon became a faded memory. Other regions rode out these invasions with greater resilience. Egypt successfully fought off the invaders but only at great cost. The land of Syria-Palestine experienced invasion and settlement by Philistines, Hebrews, and others, but in the end it managed to absorb all without losing the essential elements of civilization.

Geographic isolation protected China from these Iron Age migrations. Iron would not arrive in China until the sixth century B.C. Around 1200 B.C., however, the chariot made its appearance in China and was used to great effect by the Chou in their toppling of the Shang.

Around 1000 B.C. the general level of nomadic violence subsided for a while across Eurasia and North Africa, but the previous eight centuries had seen successive waves of nomads challenge, at times overwhelm, and in a few isolated instances eradicate the world's centers of civilization.

The Indo-Europeans

Sometime around 2000 B.C. pastoral people living on the steppes of western Asia, roughly in the area that lies north of the Caucasus Mountains, between the Black and Caspian seas, began to migrate out of their traditional grazing lands and, in successive waves, wandered into Europe, Asia Minor, Mesopotamia, Iran, and India. These bronze-armed nomads spoke a variety of related languages that shared a common origin in a prehistoric tongue scholars call "proto-Indo-European." Through their migrations, these people eventually spread their family of languages from northern India to the British Isles. The fact that *Aryan, Eire* (the Gaelic name for the Republic of Ireland), and *Iran* derive from the common archaic root word *aryo,* which means "lord," eloquently attests to the extent of the ancient Indo-European wanderings and settlements.

Among the many significant waves of Indo-European newcomers, there were those whose tongue was Sanskrit and those who spoke an early form of Greek. The Sanskrit speakers moved eastward across the Hindu Kush mountain range and into the fertile Indus valley, where they encountered Harappan civilization. The Greek speakers moved westward into the Balkans, absorbing or displacing the native agricultural people whom they encountered.

RIG VEDA

It is not totally clear if the Aryans conquered and destroyed a vigorous Harappan civilization or, what seems more likely, took over a society that was in eclipse. Whatever the case, by 1500 B.C. the Aryans were ruling northwest India as an illiterate warrior aristocracy and the Harappan arts of writing and statecraft had disappeared. India would not reemerge into the light of history until around 600 B.C.

Because the early Aryans were a preliterate people, what little we know about them we derive from their oral tradition, which survives chiefly in four great collections of priestly hymns, chants, incantations, and ritual formulas known as the *Vedas*. Veda means "wisdom" or "knowledge," and the Aryans accepted these collections of sacred poetry as the eternal word of the gods.

The most celebrated and earliest of the four is the *Rig Veda,* a collection of 1,028 songs, which probably was compiled, for the most part, in the form we know it between 1200 and 900 B.C., although it contains many elements that stretch back to a time long before the Aryans arrived in India. This Sanskrit masterpiece remains, even today, one of the sacred books of Hinduism. It is also the earliest extant major work of literature in an Indo-European tongue, predating by several centuries the Homeric Greek epics.

As is common in precivilized societies, Aryan priests, known as *brahmins*, were trained to perform prodigious feats of memory. Generation after generation, they sang these songs and passed them on to those who followed. As a result, although the Vedas would not be written down until long after 1000 B.C., many of their songs reflect the religious, social, and political realities of Aryan life around 1500 or earlier. Conversely, other Vedic hymns were the products of much later centuries and mirror the more sophisticated culture of an emerging Indo-Aryan civilization.

The following two poems illustrate this dichotomy. The first celebrates the victory over Vritra, the dragon of drought, by Indra, the most prominent god in the *Rig Veda*. The second, which certainly is one of the latest hymns in the *Rig Veda*, explains how all forms of life were generated when Purusha, the all-pervading universal spirit, was sacrificed to himself.

Questions for Analysis

1. What did Indra accomplish by slaying Vritra?
2. What sort of god is Indra, and how would you characterize the society that worshiped him as its chief deity?
3. What does the use of cattle imagery suggest about the values and economic structure of Aryan society?
4. How does the theme of the first hymn hint that the Aryans were becoming a settled, agrarian people?
5. How does the second hymn's reference to other Vedic collections help us to date the poem? Is it an early or late composition?
6. If Purusha brings forth all life by self-sacrifice, what does this suggest about the Indo-Aryan view of life and death? Is death a negation of life? Are they mutually exclusive?
7. Can you find in the hymn to Purusha any evidence of an emerging Hindu concept of the unity of all being?
8. What evidence is there in the hymn to Purusha for the emergence of what would become the Hindu caste system, and how does the author of the hymn explain and justify that system?

[*To Indra*]

I will declare the manly deeds of Indra, the first that he achieved, the thunder-wielder.

He slew the dragon,[1] then disclosed the waters, and cleft the channels of the mountain torrents.

He slew the dragon lying on the mountain: his heavenly bolt of thunder Twashtar[2] fashioned.

Like lowing kine[3] in rapid flow descending the waters glided downward to the ocean.

Impetuous as a bull, he chose the Soma,[4] and quaffed in threefold sacrifice the juices.

Maghavan[5] grasped the thunder for his weapon, and smote to death this firstborn of the dragons.

When, Indra, thou hadst slain the dragons' firstborn, and overcome the charms of the enchanters,

Then, giving life to sun and dawn and heaven, thou foundest not one foe to stand against thee.

Indra with his own great and deadly thunder smote into pieces Vritra worst of Vritras.[6]

As trunks of trees, what time the axe hath felled them, low on the earth so lies the prostrate dragon.

He, like a mad weak warrior, challenged Indra, the great impetuous many-slaying hero.

He, brooking not the clashing of the weapons, crushed — Indra's foe — the shattered forts in falling,[7]

Footless and handless still[8] he challenged Indra, who smote him with his bolt between the shoulders.

Emasculate yet claiming manly vigor, thus Vritra lay with scattered limbs dissevered. . . .

Nothing availed him lightning, nothing thunder, hailstorm or mist which he had spread around him:[9]

When Indra and the dragon strove in battle, Maghavan gained the victory for ever.

Whom sawest thou to avenge the dragon, Indra, that fear possessed thy heart when thou hadst slain him;

That, like a hawk affrighted through the regions, thou crossedst nine-and-ninety flowing rivers?

Indra is king of all that moves and moves not, of creatures tame and horned, the thunder-wielder.

Over all living men he rules as sovereign, containing all as spokes within the felly.[10]

1. Vritra. By slaying the dragon (clouds), Indra releases the waters that fall down as rain.

2. The artisan of the gods.

3. Cows.

4. An intoxicating drink reserved for the gods.

5. Lord Bountiful — another name for Indra.

6. Or dragon, worst of dragons.

7. The clouds are here pictured as forts imprisoning moisture.

8. Vritra is serpentlike, lacking feet and hands.

9. Vritra used magic to surround himself with storms and mist, but these failed him.

10. The rim of a spoked wheel.

[*To Purusha*]

A thousand heads had Purusha,[11] a thousand eyes, a thousand feet.

He covered earth on every side, and spread ten fingers' breadth beyond.

This Purusha is all that yet hath been and all that is to be;

The lord of immortality which waxes greater still by food.

So mighty is his greatness; yea, greater than this is Purusha.

All creatures are one-fourth of him, three-fourths eternal life in heaven.[12]

With three-fourths Purusha went up: one-fourth of him again was here.

Thence he strode out to every side over what eats not and what eats.

From him Viraj[13] was born; again Purusha from Viraj was born.

As soon as he was born he spread eastward and westward o'er the earth.

When gods prepared the sacrifice with Purusha as their offering,

Its oil was spring, the holy gift was autumn; summer was the wood.

They balmed as victim on the grass[14] Purusha born in earliest time.

With him the deities and all Sadhyas[15] and Rishis[16] sacrificed.

From that great general sacrifice the dripping fat was gathered up.

He formed the creatures of the air, and animals both wild and tame.

From that great general sacrifice Richas and Samahymns[17] were born:

Therefrom the metres were produced,[18] the Yajus[19] had its birth from it.

From it were horses born, from it all creatures with two rows of teeth:

From it were generated kine, from it the goats and sheep were born.

When they divided Purusha how many portions did they make?

What do they call his mouth, his arms? What do they call his thighs and feet?

The Brahmin[20] was his mouth, of both his arms was the Rajanya[21] made.

---

11. Purusha, the all-pervading universal spirit and the source of all life, is conceived as a god with countless eyes, hands, and feet. Purusha is both limitless and able to be enclosed in the smallest of spaces. In this poem, Purusha acts as both sacrifice and sacrificer.

12. One-quarter of Purusha is found in all mortal creation; three-fourths of Purusha is divine and eternal.

13. The female creative germ.

14. Special grasses laid out during Vedic sacrifices for the gods to sit upon.

15. A class of demigods.

16. Sages.

17. The constituent elements of the *Rig Veda*.

18. The verses of the *Sama Veda*. The *Sama Veda* is mostly a collection of elements from the *Rig Veda,* arranged for religious ceremonial use.

19. The ritual formulas of the *Yajur Veda*. This veda was compiled a century or two after the *Rig Veda* and served as a collection of sacrificial chants.

20. Aryan priests.

21. The Rajanya, or Kshatriyas, comprised the ruling or warrior class.

His thighs became the Vaisya,[22] from his feet the Sudra[23] was produced.

The Moon was gendered from his mind, and from his eye the Sun had birth;

Indra and Agni[24] from his mouth were born, and Vayu[25] from his breath.

Forth from his navel came mid-air; the sky was fashioned from his head;

Earth from his feet, and from his ear the regions. Thus they formed the worlds.

Seven fencing-logs had he, thrice seven layers of fuel were prepared,[26]

When the gods, offering sacrifice, bound, as their victim, Purusha.

Gods, sacrificing, sacrificed the victim: these were the earliest holy ordinances.

The mighty ones attained the height of heaven, there where the Sadhyas, gods of old, are dwelling.

Homer

ODYSSEY

History's first identifiable Greeks called themselves Achaeans. By 1600 B.C. they had created a decentralized, warrior civilization, which we term Mycenaean, after Mycenae, a city that exercised a loose leadership over the petty principalities of southern and central Greece. Around 1450 B.C. the Achaeans were masters of the island civilization of Crete and a major force in the eastern Mediterranean. It is against this background that we must place the Achaean expedition against Troy, a city in Asia Minor, which took place around 1260.

The sack of rival Troy was the high-water mark for the Achaeans. Within a century, Mycenaean civilization was collapsing due to internecine wars among the various Achaean principalities and the weight of migrations of unlettered Greek cousins from the north. These ruder kinfolk, whom we collectively call the Dorians (after the *Doric* Greek dialect, which many of them spoke), effectively smothered whatever of this fragile civilization the Achaeans themselves had failed to destroy in their post–Trojan War conflicts. By 1100 B.C. Greek society was again illiterate and stateless. When Greek literacy and civilization reemerged around 750 B.C., it was centered

22. Free herders and farmers, traders and artisans.

23. Slaves and servants. The term was generally applied to the native, dark-skinned people whom the Aryans conquered and subjugated when they entered India.

24. The god of fire and sacrifice. This Sanskrit word is cognate with *ignis,* the Latin word for "fire" (hence, "ignite" in English).

25. The wind.

26. For a sacrificial fire.

along the western shores of Asia Minor in a region know as Ionia. These Greek settlements across the Aegean had largely sprung up in the period of the so-called Dark Ages following the Dorian migrations. Here Greek colonists, benefiting from their contact with the far more developed civilizations of Southwest Asia and Egypt, produced the first Greek literature known to us (as opposed to the bureaucratic lists left behind by Mycenaean civilization). Of all this early literature, the most significant are two poems, the *Iliad* and the *Odyssey,* both ascribed to a bard called Homer.

The ancients had no doubt that Homer had lived and created both works. Modern scholars are less certain. The weight of academic opinion today is that two eighth-century Asiatic Greeks, living a generation or more apart, orally composed the epics. Each poet crafted a single, coherent work of art but, in so doing, drew heavily from a long tradition of poetic stories preserved in the memories of wandering professional bards. A century or more later, that is, after 650 and possibly closer to 550 B.C., the two poems were finally written down in basically the forms we know them today.

Despite their late composition and even later transcription, when used judiciously, they do tell us a good deal about life in the thirteenth century — the age of the Trojan War. At the same time, they reveal a lot of the values and modes of perception of later "Dark Age" society, especially that of the ninth and eighth centuries.

On one level both poems celebrate such warrior virtues as personal honor, bravery, and loyalty to one's comrades, and on a deeper level they probe the hidden recesses of human motivation and emotion. On a third level the poems address the issue of the meaning of human suffering. Why do humans experience pain and sorrow? Are they captive to the whims of the gods? Arc they and the gods subject to an overarching destiny which neither can avoid?

More to human scale than the *Iliad,* the *Odyssey* tells two intertwined stories. One traces the ten-year-long homeward voyage, after the sack of Troy, of the Achaean hero Odysseus. This clever adventurer has to battle, with cunning and skill, the enmity of Poseidon, god of the sea, and a variety of superhuman opponents before finally arriving home. The second story details the attempts of Odysseus's wife and son, Penelope and Telemachus, who, with equal cunning and skill, attempt to stall indefinitely the advances of a group of suitors who seek to marry the presumed widow. As the suitors impatiently wait to see whom she will marry, they despoil Odysseus and Penelope's home and waste Telemachus's patrimony. The two story lines merge when Odysseus returns and, with the aid of his son and several loyal servants, wreaks vengeance on the suitors by killing them all. Unlike most epics, the story ends happily with Penelope and Odysseus reunited and Telemachus assured of his inheritance.

The following selection describes one of Odysseus's most daring adventures on his troubled homeward journey– a visit to the land of the dead. Here he consults Teiresias, the blind Theban seer, and meets the shades of many famous women and men, including his old comrade in arms Achilles, the Achaeans' greatest warrior and the central character in the *Iliad*, who was killed prior to the fall of Troy.

Questions for Analysis

1. How does Homer address the issue of human responsibility for ill fortune?
2. Is there a destiny humans cannot escape?
3. What role do the gods play in this destiny?
4. Compare Achilles's sentiment toward the land of the dead with Enkidu's vision in *The Epic of Gilgamesh*. What might one infer from this parallelism?
5. It is often stated that the Greeks focused on human beings and human concerns. Does this selection seem to support or contradict that judgment?

And the soul of the Theban prophet now came up, with a gold rod in his hand, saw who I was, and saluted me.

"Royal son of Laertes, Odysseus of the nimble wits, what has brought you, the man of misfortune, to forsake the sunlight and to visit the dead in this mirthless place? Step back now from the trench and hold your sword aside, so that I can drink the blood[1] and prophesy the truth to you."

I backed away, driving my sword home in its silver scabbard. And when Teiresias spoke, after drinking the dark blood, it was the voice of the authentic seer that I heard.

"My lord Odysseus," he began, "you are in search of some easy way to reach your home. But the powers above are going to make your journey hard. For I cannot think that you will slip through the hands of the Earthshaker,[2] who has by no means forgotten his resentment against you for blinding his beloved son.[3] Notwithstanding that, you and your friends may yet reach Ithaca,[4] though not without mishap, if only you determine to keep a tight hand on yourself and your men from the moment when your good ship leaves the deep blue seas and approaches the Isle of Thrinacie, and you see there at their pasture the cattle and the fat sheep of the Sun-god, whose eye and ear miss nothing in the world. If you leave them untouched and fix your mind on getting home, there is some chance that all of you may yet reach Ithaca, though not in comfort. But if you hurt them, then I warrant you that your ship and company will be destroyed, and if you yourself do manage to escape, you will come home late, in evil plight, upon a foreign ship, with all your com-

1. The shades can communicate with Odysseus only after drinking blood from animals he has sacrificed.

2. Poseidon, god of the sea and of earthquakes.

3. Polyphemus, the Cyclops.

4. Odysseus's island kingdom.

rades dead.[5] You will find trouble too in your house — a set of scoundrels eating up your stores, making love to your royal consort, and offering wedding gifts. It is true that you will pay out these men for their misdeeds when you reach home. But whichever way you choose to kill them, whether by stratagem or in a straight fight with the naked sword, when you have cleared your palace of these Suitors, you must then set out once more upon your travels. You must take a well-cut oar and go on till you reach a people who know nothing of the sea and never use salt with their food, so that our crimson-painted ships and the long oars that serve those ships as wings are quite beyond their ken. And this will be your cue — a very clear one, which you cannot miss. When you fall in with some other traveller who speaks of the 'winnowing-fan' you are carrying on your shoulder,[6] the time will have come for you to plant your shapely oar in the earth and offer Lord Poseidon the rich sacrifice of a ram, a bull, and a breeding-boar. Then go back home and make ceremonial offerings to the immortal gods who live in the broad heavens, to all of them, this time, in due precedence.

As for your own end, Death will come to you out of the sea, Death in his gentlest guise. When he takes you, you will be worn out after an easy old age and surrounded by a prosperous people. This is the truth that I have told you.". . .

And now there came the souls of Peleus' son Achilles, of Patroclus,[7] of the noble Antilochus,[8] and of Aias,[9] who in stature and in manly grace was second to none of the Danaans[10] but the flawless son of Peleus.[11] It was the soul of Achilles, the great runner, who recognized me. In mournful, measured tones he greeted me by my titles, and went on: "What next, Odysseus, dauntless heart? What greater exploit can you plan to cap your voyage here? How did you dare to come below to Hades'[12] realm, where the dead live on without their wits as disembodied ghosts?"

"Achilles," I answered him, "son of Peleus and flower of Achaean chivalry, I came to consult with Teiresias in the hope of finding out from him how I could reach my rocky Ithaca. For I have not managed to come near Achaea yet, nor set foot on my own island, but have been dogged by misfortune. How different from you, Achilles, the most fortunate man that ever was or will be! For in the old days when you were on earth, we Argives honored you as though you were a god; and now, down here, you are a mighty prince among the dead. For you, Achilles, Death should have lost his sting."

"My lord Odysseus," he replied, "spare me your praise of Death. Put me on earth again, and I would rather be a serf in the house of some landless man, with little enough for himself to live on, than king of all these dead men that have done with life. But enough. Tell me what news there

5. The crew will kill and eat the sheep, and all will die as a result.

6. That is, where no one knows the function of an oar.

7. Achilles' best friend, who also died at Troy.

8. An Achaean hero who fell at Troy while defending his father, King Nestor of Pylos.

9. The Achaeans' second greatest warrior; he committed suicide at Troy.

10. Another name for the Achaeans or Greeks.

11. Achilles.

12. The god of the dead.

is of that fine son of mine. Did he follow me to the war and play a leading part or not? And tell me anything you have heard of the noble Peleus. . . . For I am not up there in the sunlight to protect him with the mighty arms that once did battle for the Argives[13] and laid the champions of the enemy low on the broad plains of Troy. If I could return for a single hour to my father's house with the strength I then enjoyed, I would make those who injure him and rob him of his rights shrink in dismay before my might and my unconquerable hands."

"Of the noble Peleus," I answered Achilles, "I have heard nothing. But of your dear son Neoptolemus I will give you all the news you ask for, since it was I who brought him from Scyros in my own fine ship to join the Achaean army. And there in front of the city of Troy, when we used to discuss our plans, he was always the first to speak and no words of his ever missed their mark. King Nestor and I were his only betters in debate. Nor, when we Achaeans gave battle on the Trojan plain, was he ever content to linger in the ranks or with the crowd. That impetuous spirit of his gave place to none, and he would sally out beyond the foremost. Many was the man he brought down in mortal combat. I could not tell you of all the people he killed in battle for the Argives, nor give you their names. . . . Then again, when we Argive captains took our places in the wooden horse Epeius made, and it rested solely with me to throw our ambush open or to keep it shut, all the other Danaan chieftains and officers were wiping the tears from their eyes and every man's legs were trembling beneath him, but not once did I see your son's fine color change to pallor nor catch him brushing a tear from his cheek. On the contrary he begged me time and again to let him sally from the Horse and kept fumbling eagerly at his sword-hilt and his heavy spear in his keenness to fall on the Trojans. And when we had brought Priam's[14] city tumbling down in ruins, he took his share of the booty and his special prize, and embarked safe and sound on his ship without a single wound either from a flying dart or from a sword at close quarters. The War-god in his fury is no respecter of persons, but the mischances of battle had touched your son not at all."

When I had done, the soul of Achilles, whose feet had been so fleet on earth, passed with great strides down the meadow of asphodel,[15] rejoicing in the news I had given him of his son's renown.

The Hebrews and Their Neighbors

Recent excavations at the site of the long-forgotten city of Ebla in the modern nation of Syria reveal that the land of Syria-Palestine, which serves as a land bridge between Egypt and Mesopotamia, has known civilization since about 3000 B.C. As is

13. Another name for the Achaeans.

14. The last king of Troy.

15. A flower that was said to carpet the Elysian fields, where the shades of heroes, such as Achilles, resided.

the fate of most small lands that lie next to more powerful neighbors, the region has historically been prey to invaders. Its earliest known conqueror was Sargon the Great of Akkad in Mesopotamia, who sacked Ebla sometime before 2300 B.C.

Around 1200 B.C., in the midst of the great nomadic upheavals that were testing all the civilizations of the Middle East, several different invaders penetrated the lands of Syria-Palestine and established themselves at the expense of the indigenous Canaanite population. One of these was a mixed group of invaders from the Mediterranean, who settled down in cities along the coast of what is today the state of Israel. These people, who included a large percentage of uprooted Greeks and Cretans, became known as the Philistines. A second major wave was comprised of another hybrid mass of people who spoke a language that belongs to a family of tongues we term "Semitic." These people, whom history identifies as the Hebrews, infiltrated into the region out of the southern and eastern deserts and settled the inland high ground overlooking the Philistine cities.

Prior to the waves of nomadic invaders of around 1200, the Hittite and Egyptian empires had fought one another for mastery over Syria-Palestine. With the destruction of Hittite civilization and the concurrent severe weakening of the Egyptian empire, a momentary power vacuum occurred along the eastern rim of the Mediterranean. In the absence of any outside imperial power, the various cultural groups of Syria-Palestine had several centuries of relative freedom in which to struggle with one another and to amalgamate.

For the Hebrews, amalgamation was both seductively easy and potentially disastrous. The vast majority of the various peoples who already inhabited this land known as Canaan were, like the Hebrews, Semites. Hebrews and Canaanites spoke related languages that had a common place of origin (probably the Arabian peninsula before 3000 B.C.), and they shared many other cultural similarities. As the Hebrews coalesced as a people, however, they evolved the idea that they enjoyed the special protection of a god whom they called "Yahweh." In return for that protection, this deity demanded their sole devotion. A corollary of that belief was the conviction that if the Hebrews were to prosper in Canaan, which Yahweh had promised them, they had to maintain religious (and, therefore, cultural) distance from all other people.

THE BOOK OF GENESIS

One of the chief documentary sources for both the process of cultural fusion and the fierce struggles that were taking place among the various groups of settlers in Syria-

Palestine is a collection of sacred Hebrew writings known as the Bible (from the Greek word *biblos*, which means "book"). The exclusively Hebrew, or Jewish, portion of the Bible (as opposed to the later Christian "New Testament") consists of a wide variety of different types of literature, which were mainly composed, edited, and reedited from about 1000 B.C. to possibly as late as the second century B.C., although Jewish authorities did not fix the final *canon* or accepted form of the "Old Testament" until after A.D. 100. This means that biblical accounts of early Hebrew history are, in many cases, centuries removed from the events they narrate. It is nevertheless clear that these later authors often used early written and oral sources that are now lost to us. Moreover, although these same authors primarily wrote history from a theological perspective and consequently clothed their stories in myth, independent archeological evidence has often confirmed the basic historical outline of many of the biblical stories concerning the fortunes of the Hebrews in Canaan, the Promised Land.

The first book of the Bible is known as Genesis (the "beginning") and recounts the story of humanity's relationship with Yahweh from Creation through the settlement of the Hebrew people, known as the Children of Israel, in Egypt. Tradition ascribes its authorship to Moses, who lived during the thirteenth century B.C., but within the context of the culture of ancient Israel this did not necessarily mean that Moses actually wrote or dictated the book. Rather, he was the one who provided the initial and pervading spirit behind the work. In all likelihood, a number of different authors composed and reworked Genesis over the period from before 900 to after 721 B.C.

The following selection recounts a popular Middle Eastern theme that we saw in Chapter 1 — the Flood. As you read it, be aware not only of the striking similarities between it and the story told by Utnapishtim but of the even more significant differences. Remember that the author is making a religious statement.

Questions for Analysis

1. Why does Yahweh destroy all humanity except Noah and his family? How does this reason compare with the Mesopotamian gods' reason for wanting to destroy humans and Ea's decision to warn Utnapishtim?
2. Compare Yahweh's treatment of Noah and his descendants following the Flood with the Mesopotamian gods' treatment of Utnapishtim after the waters had receded.
3. What do the Mesopotamian gods demand of humans? What does Noah's god demand?
4. From these several comparisons, what picture emerges of the god of the Hebrews? In what ways is their deity similiar to the gods of the Mesopotamians? In what ways does their god differ?

5. How might we explain the fact that both the Mesopotamians and the Hebrews had a Flood story as part of their mythology? Does the Hebrews' belief that Abraham, the father of all of Yahweh's people, was born in the Sumerian city of Ur provide a clue?
6. God establishes a covenant or agreement with all of humanity and, indeed, with all living creation, through Noah. What is that agreement?
7. Consider the story of Noah's curse on Canaan. What has Ham done to deserve such anger, and why is it his son who receives the curse? Do your answers tell us anything about the nature of Hebrew society at this time?
8. How does the story of this curse justify the Hebrews' settlement in the Promised Land? What does this suggest about the story's date of composition? How does this illustrate the Hebrews' use of myth to explain and justify historical events?

When the LORD saw how wicked everyone on earth was and how evil their thoughts were all the time, he was sorry that he had ever made them and put them on the earth. He was so filled with regret that he said "I will wipe out these people I have created, and also the animals and the birds, because I am sorry that I made any of them." But the LORD was pleased with Noah. . . .

This is the story of Noah. He had three sons, Shem,[1] Ham, and Japheth. Noah had no faults and was the only good man of his time. He lived in fellowship with God, but everyone else was evil in God's sight, and violence had spread everywhere. God looked at the world and saw that it was evil, for the people were all living evil lives.

God said to Noah, "I have decided to put an end to all mankind. I will destroy them completely, because the world is full of their violent deeds. Build a boat for yourself. . . . I am going to send a flood on the earth to destroy every living being. Everything on the earth will die, but I will make a covenant with you. Go into the boat with your wife, your sons, and their wives. Take into the boat with you a male and a female of every kind of animal and of every kind of bird, in order to keep them alive. Take along all kinds of food for you and for them." Noah did everything that God commanded.

The LORD said to Noah, "Go into the boat with your whole family; I have found that you are the only one in all the world who does what is right. Take with you seven pairs of each kind of ritually clean animal,[2] but only one pair of each kind of unclean animal. Take also seven pairs of each kind of bird. Do this so that every

1. Shem was the eldest of Noah's sons and the one from whom the Hebrews claimed direct descent. The term *Semite* (one who speaks any Semitic language, such as Hebrew, Assyrian, and Arabic) is derived from the name.

2. A ritually clean animal, such as a sheep, was one worthy of sacrifice to Yahweh. An unclean animal, such as a predator or a scavenger, would never be offered in sacrifice.

kind of animal and bird will be kept alive to reproduce again on the earth. Seven days from now I am going to send rain that will fall for forty days and nights, in order to destroy all the living beings that I have made." And Noah did everything that the LORD commanded.

Noah was six hundred years old when the flood came on the earth. He and his wife, and his sons and their wives, went into the boat to escape the flood. A male and a female of every kind of animal and bird, whether ritually clean or unclean, went into the boat with Noah, as God had commanded. Seven days later the flood came.

When Noah was six hundred years old, on the seventeenth day of the second month all the outlets of the vast body of water beneath the earth burst open, all the floodgates of the sky were opened, and rain fell on the earth for forty days and nights. On that same day Noah and his wife went into the boat with their three sons, Shem, Ham, and Japheth, and their wives. With them went every kind of animal, domestic and wild, large and small, and every kind of bird. A male and a female of each kind of living being went into the boat with Noah, as God had commanded. Then the LORD shut the door behind Noah.

The flood continued for forty days, and the water became deep enough for the boat to float. The water became deeper, and the boat drifted on the surface. It became so deep that it covered the highest mountains; it went on rising until it was twenty-five feet above the tops of the mountains. Every living being on the earth died — every bird, every animal, and every person. Everything on earth that breathed died. The LORD destroyed all living beings on the earth — human beings, animals, and birds. The only ones left were Noah and those who were with him in the boat. The water did not start going down for a hundred and fifty days.

God had not forgotten Noah and all the animals with him in the boat; he caused a wind to blow, and the water started going down. The outlets of the water beneath the earth and the floodgates of the sky were closed. The rain stopped, and the water gradually went down for 150 days. On the seventeenth day of the seventh month the boat came to rest on a mountain in the Ararat range. The water kept going down, and on the first day of the tenth month the tops of the mountains appeared.

After forty days Noah opened a window and sent out a raven. It did not come back, but kept flying around until the water was completely gone. Meanwhile, Noah sent out a dove to see if the water had gone down, but since the water still covered all the land, the dove did not find a place to light. It flew back to the boat, and Noah reached out and took it in. He waited another seven days and sent out the dove again. It returned to him in the evening with a fresh olive leaf in its beak. So Noah knew that the water had gone down. Then he waited another seven days and sent out the dove once more; this time it did not come back.

When Noah was 601 years old, on the first day of the first month, the water was gone. Noah removed the covering of the boat, looked around, and saw that the ground was getting dry. By the twenty-seventh day of the second month the earth was completely dry.

God said to Noah, "Go out of the boat with your wife, your sons, and their wives. Take all the birds and animals out with you, so that they may reproduce and spread over all the earth." So Noah went out of the boat with his wife, his sons, and their wives. All the animals and birds went out of the boat in groups of their own kind.

Noah built an altar to the LORD; he took one of each kind of ritually clean animal and bird, and burned them whole as a sacrifice on the alter. The odor of the sacrifice pleased the LORD, and he said to himself, "Never again will I put the earth under a curse because of what man does; I know that from the time he is young his thoughts are evil. Never again will I destroy all living beings, as I have done this time. As long as the world exists, there will be a time for planting and a time for harvest. There will always be cold and heat, summer and winter, day and night."

God blessed Noah and his sons and said, "Have many children, so that your descendants will live all over the earth. All the animals, birds, and fish will live in fear of you. They are all placed under your power. Now you can eat them, as well as green plants; I give them all to you for food. The one thing you must not eat is meat with blood still in it; I forbid this because the life is in the blood. If anyone takes human life, he will be punished. I will punish with death any animal that takes a human life. Man was made like God, so whoever murders a man will himself be killed by his fellow-man.

"You must have many children, so that your descendants will live all over the earth."

God said to Noah and his sons, "I am now making my covenant with you and with your descendants, and with all living beings — all birds and all animals — everything that came out of the boat with you. With these words I make my covenant with you: I promise that never again will all living beings be destroyed by a flood; never again will a flood destroy the earth. As a sign of this everlasting covenant which I am making with you and with all living beings, I am putting my bow in the clouds. It will be the sign of my covenant with the world. Whenever I cover the sky with clouds and the rainbow appears, I will remember my promise to you and to all the animals that a flood will never again destroy all living beings. When the rainbow appears in the clouds, I will see it and remember the everlasting covenant between me and all living beings on earth. That is the sign of the promise which I am making to all living beings."

The sons of Noah who went out of the boat were Shem, Ham, and Japheth. (Ham was the father of Canaan.)[3] These three sons of Noah were the ancestors of all the people on earth.

Noah, who was a farmer, was the first man to plant a vineyard. After he drank some of the wine, he became drunk, took off his clothes, and lay naked in his tent. When Ham, the father of Canaan, saw that his father was naked, he went out and told his two brothers. Then Shem and Japheth took a robe and held it behind them on their shoulders. They walked backward into the tent and covered their father, keeping their faces turned away so as not to see him naked. When Noah sobered up and learned what his youngest son had done to him, he said,

"A curse on Canaan!

---

3. According to Hebrew legend, Ham and Canaan were the direct ancestors of the Canaanites.

He will be a slave to his brothers.
Give praise to the LORD, the God of
Shem!
Canaan will be the slave of Shem.
May God cause Japheth to increase!
May his descendants live with the people
of Shem!
Canaan will be the slave of Japheth."

After the flood Noah lived 350 years and died at the age of 950.

THE BOOK OF DEUTERONOMY

The story of Noah tells of Yahweh's post-Deluge covenant with all living creatures; the story of the Hebrews' *exodus* (flight) from Egypt tells of their special covenant with this god and their becoming a Chosen People with a new identity. The Hebrews had probably entered Egypt in the time of the Hyksos' conquest of that land. With the overthrow of the Hyksos and the reestablishment of native Egyptian rule around 1570 B.C., significant numbers of Hebrews were enslaved. Probably during the reign of Ramesses the Great (1279–1213 B.C.), a charismatic leader known as Moses led a band of these Hebrews out of Egypt into Canaan. In the process of this migration, he molded them into a people and wedded them to his god Yahweh. No longer a loose band of nomads, they were now the Israelites — descendants of the patriarchs Abraham, Isaac, and Jacob (also called Israel).

The story of this thirteenth-century transformation is told in several books of the Bible. This selection comes from Deuteronomy, which, in its present form, dates from the reign of King Josiah of Jerusalem (640–609 B.C.). It was composed or, more likely, recast at a time of religious reformation, when Josiah was attempting to abolish all forms of pagan worship in his kingdom, especially the practices of the Assyrians. Although Deuteronomy, as we know it, is essentially a seventh-century creation, it is doubtlessly based on sources that date from the time of Moses.

The setting of our excerpt is the frontier of Canaan, which, according to the story of the Exodus, the Israelites reached after forty years of wandering in the desert. Moses, realizing he will die before his people cross the Jordan River into the Promised Land, delivers a final message to them.

Questions for Analysis

1. What is the covenant between Yahweh and the people of Israel? What does God promise and demand in return?

2. Compare this covenant with that given after the Flood. How, if at all, do they differ, and what do those differences suggest?
3. What elements of Moses' message would the religious reformers of seventh-century Jerusalem wish to emphasize?

Moses called together all the people of Israel[1] and said to them, "People of Israel, listen to all the laws that I am giving you today. Learn them and be sure that you obey them. At Mount Sinai[2] the LORD our God made a covenant, not only with our fathers, but with all of us who are living today. There on the mountain the LORD spoke to you face-to-face from the fire. I stood between you and the LORD at that time to tell you what he said, because you were afraid of the fire and would not go up the mountain.

"The LORD said 'I am the LORD your God, who rescued you from Egypt, where you were slaves.

"'Worship no god but me.

"'Do not make for yourselves images of anything in heaven or on earth or in the water under the earth. Do not bow down to any idol or worship it, for I am the LORD your God and I tolerate no rivals. I bring punishment on those who hate me and on their descendants down to the third and fourth generation. But I show my love to thousands of generations of those who love me and obey my laws.

"'Do not use my name for evil purposes, for I, the LORD your God, will punish anyone who misuses my name.

"'Observe the Sabbath and keep it holy, as I, the LORD your God, have commanded you. You have six days in which to do your work, but the seventh day is a day of rest dedicated to me. On that day no one is to work — neither you, your children, your slaves, your animals, nor the foreigners who live in your country. Your slaves must rest just as you do. Remember that you were slaves in Egypt, and that I, the LORD your God, rescued you by my great power and strength. That is why I command you to observe the Sabbath.

"'Respect your father and your mother, as I, the LORD your God, command you, so that all may go well with you and so that you may live a long time in the land that I am giving you.

"'Do not commit murder.

"'Do not commit adultery.

"'Do not steal.

"'Do not accuse anyone falsely.

"'Do not desire another man's wife; do not desire his house, his land, his slaves, his cattle, his donkeys, or anything else that he owns.'

"These are the commandments the LORD gave to all of you when you were gathered at the mountain. When he spoke with a mighty voice from the fire and from the thick clouds, he gave these com-

1. The Hebrews were the Children of Israel, or the Israelites, because they traced their lineage to Jacob, whose name God had changed to Israel ("one who has striven"). Jacob, the grandson of Abraham and the son of Isaac, had twelve sons, each of whom became the patriarch of one of the twelve tribes of Israel.

2. Mount Sinai was where Moses had first received the Law from Yahweh, during the period of desert wandering.

mandments and no others. Then he wrote them on two stone tablets and gave them to me. . . .

"These are all the laws that the LORD your God commanded me to teach you. Obey them in the land that you are about to enter and occupy. As long as you live, you and your descendants are to have reverence for the LORD your God and obey all his laws that I am giving you, so that you may live in that land a long time. Listen to them, people of Israel, and obey them! Then all will go well with you, and you will become a mighty nation and live in that rich and fertile land, just as the LORD, the God of our ancestors, has promised.

"Israel, remember this! The LORD — and the LORD alone — is our God. Love the LORD your God with all your heart, with all your soul, and with all your strength. Never forget these commands that I am giving you today. Teach them to your children. Repeat them when you are at home and when you are away, when you are resting and when you are working. Tie them on your arms and wear them on your foreheads as a reminder. Write them on the doorposts of your houses and on your gates.

"Just as the LORD your God promised your ancestors, Abraham, Isaac, and Jacob, he will give you a land with large and prosperous cities which you did not build. The houses will be full of good things which you did not put in them, and there will be wells that you did not dig, and vineyards and olive orchards that you did not plant. When the LORD brings you into this land and you have all you want to eat, make certain that you do not forget the LORD who rescued you from Egypt, where you were slaves. Have reverence for the LORD your God, worship only him, and make your promises in his name alone. Do not worship other gods, any of the gods of the peoples around you. If you do worship other gods, the LORD's anger will come against you like fire and will destroy you completely, because the LORD your God, who is present with you, tolerates no rivals. . . .

"The LORD your God will bring you into the land that you are going to occupy, and he will drive many nations out of it. As you advance, he will drive out seven nations larger and more powerful than you: the Hittites, the Girgashites, the Amorites, the Canaanites, the Perizzites, the Hivites, and the Jebusites.[3] When the LORD your God places these people in your power and you defeat them, you must put them all to death. Do not make an alliance with them or show them any mercy. Do not marry any of them, and do not let your children marry any of them, because then they would lead your children away from the LORD to worship other gods. If that happens, the LORD will be angry with you and destroy you at once. So then, tear down their altars, break their sacred stone pillars in pieces, cut down their symbols of the goddess Asherah,[4] and burn their idols. Do this because you belong to the LORD your God. From all the peoples on earth he chose you to be his own special people. . . .

"If you listen to these commands and obey them faithfully, then the LORD your God will continue to keep his covenant

3. With the exception of the Hittites, whose rulers were Indo-European, all of the seven peoples were Semites residing in the region of modern-day Israel, Syria, Lebanon, and Jordan.

4. Sacred poles raised to Astarte, or Asherah, the Canaanite counterpart of Ishtar, the Mesopotamian goddess of fertility and love.

with you and will show you his constant love, as he promised your ancestors. He will love you and bless you, so that you will increase in number and have many children; he will bless your fields, so that you will have grain, wine, and olive oil; and he will bless you by giving you many cattle and sheep. He will give you all these blessings in the land that he promised your ancestors he would give to you. No people in the world will be as richly blessed as you. None of you nor any of your livestock will be sterile. The LORD will protect you from all sickness, and he will not bring on you any of the dreadful diseases that you experienced in Egypt, but he will bring them on all your enemies. Destroy every nation that the LORD your God places in your power, and do not show them any mercy. Do not worship their gods, for that would be fatal."

THE BOOK OF JUDGES

Following Moses' death, Joshua led the Israelites into Canaan. Unable to wipe out or displace all the indigenous peoples, the Israelites settled in the hills and became one of several major cultural groups in the region. Between Joshua's death, which took place around 1150 B.C., and the rise of the kingdom of Israel around 1050 B.C., various leaders, known as judges, arose to lead the Israelites in times of crisis. These were not judges in a narrow juridical or institutional sense but men and women who were defenders of Yahweh's law and justice.

The following story from The Book of Judges tells why the first of the major judges, Othniel, was called to lead Israel. The book, which is based on a cycle of written epics that date to around 1000 B.C., was probably put into its final form by the same group of seventh-century reformers in Jerusalem who were recasting Deuteronomy.

Questions for Analysis

1. In what ways did the Israelites break faith with their God, and what were the consequences?
2. What is the message or lesson to be learned from this experience?

Joshua sent the people of Israel on their way, and each man went to take possession of his own share of the land. As long as Joshua lived, the people of Israel served the LORD and even after his death they continued to do so as long as the leaders were alive who had seen for themselves all the great things that the LORD had done for Israel. The LORD's servant Joshua son of Nun died at the age of a hundred and ten. He was buried in his own part of the land at Timnath Serah in the hill country of Ephraim north of Mount Gaash. That whole generation also died, and the next generation forgot the LORD and what he had done for Israel.

Then the people of Israel sinned against the LORD and began to serve the Baals.[1] They stopped worshiping the LORD, the God of their ancestors, the God who had brought them out of Egypt, and they began to worship other gods, and gods of the peoples around them. They bowed down to them and made the LORD angry. They stopped worshiping the LORD and served the Baals and the Astartes.[2] And so the LORD became furious with Israel and let raiders attack and rob them. He let the enemies all around overpower them, and the Israelites could no longer protect themselves. Every time they would go into battle, the LORD was against them, just as he had said he would be. They were in great distress.

Then the LORD gave the Israelites leaders who saved them from the raiders. But the Israelites paid no attention to their leaders. Israel was unfaithful to the LORD and worshiped other gods. Their fathers had obeyed the LORD's commands, but this new generation soon stopped doing so. Whenever the LORD gave Israel a leader, the LORD would help him and would save the people from their enemies as long as that leader lived. The LORD would have mercy on them because they groaned under their suffering and oppression. But when the leader died, the people would return to the old ways and behave worse than the previous generation. They would serve and worship other gods, and stubbornly continue their own evil ways. Then the LORD would become furious with Israel and say, "This nation has broken the covenant that I commanded their ancestors to keep. Because they have not obeyed me, I will no longer drive out any of the nations that were still in the land when Joshua died. I will use them to find out whether or not these Israelites will follow my ways as their ancestors did." So the LORD allowed these nations to remain in the land; he did not give Joshua victory over them, nor did he drive them out soon after Joshua's death.

So then, the LORD left some nations in the land to test the Israelites who had not been through the wars in Canaan. He did this only in order to teach each generation of Israelites about war, especially those who had never been in battle before. Those left in the land were the five Philistine cities, all the Canaanites, the Sidonians, and the Hivites who lived in the Lebanon Mountains from Mount Baal Hermon as far as Hamath Pass. They were to be a test for Israel, to find out whether or not the Israelites would obey the commands that the LORD had given their ancestors through Moses. And so the people of Israel settled down among the Canaanites, the Hittites, the Amorites, the Perizzites, the Hivites, and the Jebusites. They intermarried with them and worshiped their gods.

The people of Israel forgot the LORD their God; they sinned against him and worshiped the idols of Baal and Asherah.

1. Baal was the chief Canaanite god, hence, the gods of the native people.

2. All the native gods, not just Baal and Astarte.

So the LORD became angry with Israel and let King Cushan Rishathaim[3] of Mesopotamia conquer them. They were subject to him for eight years. Then the Israelites cried out to the LORD, and he sent a man who freed them. This was Othniel, the son of Caleb's younger brother Kenaz. The spirit of the LORD came upon him, and he became Israel's leader. Othniel went to war, and the LORD gave him the victory over the king of Mesopotamia. There was peace in the land for forty years, and then Othniel died.

3. A king who held major portions of Syria.

C H A P T E R

3

Development of the Religious Traditions of India and the Middle East, 800–200 B.C.

Between about 800 and 200 B.C., profound changes in thought, belief, and organization took place in China, India, the Middle East, and Hellas (the land of the Greeks). During these six centuries, the Chinese, Indians, Middle Easterners, and Greeks formulated distinctive traditions and institutions that became essential characteristics of their civilizations and the many societies they later influenced.

These developments became especially pronounced by the sixth century. It is no coincidence that Confucius, the Buddha, the Mahavira, several of the authors of the *Upanishads*, Zarathustra, Second Isaiah, and Thales all lived during or around the sixth century. Moreover, the caste system, the Persian empire, and the Greek city-states were thriving by the end of this century.

To what might we ascribe these parallel evolutions? The Age of Iron witnessed the development of considerably larger, more complex, and more competitive political and economic entities that challenged older social systems and values. This disruption of life was unsettling and led to the search for answers to some fundamental questions: What is the meaning and goal of life? How does one relate to the natural world? How does one relate to other humans?

The historical environments of the various civilizations posing such questions often differed radically. Their respective answers consequently varied significantly. In one way, however, they displayed a striking similarity. Each emerging tradition, in its own way, challenged the myth-making notion that humankind is held hostage by a capricious, god-infested nature.

India did this by denying the ultimate reality and importance of the world of observable nature. China witnessed several other approaches. One school of thought sought mystical union with nature, and two other schools sought to control nature by imposing human discipline upon it. One of the latter schools saw a solution in a moral order of virtuous behavior; the other in the order of strict and dispassionately applied human law. In the Middle East freedom from myth-laden nature was partially achieved through worship of and obedience to a totally spiritual yet personal God of the universe, who stood completely outside nature and yet imposed moral and historical order upon it. In Greece the attempt to master nature took the form of rational philosophy and science. Here certain thinkers sought to control nature by studying it objectively, thereby discovering laws that would enable humans to define more surely their place in the universe. In this manner, four major world traditions emerged: Indian transcendental religion; China's distinctive blend of practical worldliness with a mystical appreciation of nature; the Middle East's preoccupation with ethical monotheism; and Greek rationalism, with its special focus on the human condition.

In this chapter we shall explore the religious traditions that took shape in India and the Middle East.

The Emergence of Hinduism

The *Rig-Veda*'s hymn to Purusha, which appears in Chapter 2, illustrates the emergence of what eventually became one of Hinduism's major beliefs, the unity of all being. During the period spanning the tenth through fourth centuries B.C., most of the other elements of classical Hindu thought and practice took shape.

It is wrong to think of Hinduism, either modern or ancient, as a single set of beliefs and practices. To the contrary, it is a fluid mass of religious and social expressions, which collectively encompass the living faiths of all the diverse people of India who call themselves Hindu. Hinduism comfortably includes folk rituals and beliefs, which have changed little over many millennia, and the most abstract and speculative thought on the nature of God. It is polytheistic and monotheistic; it is simultaneously earthy and metaphysical. Indeed, Hindus can choose from a variety of beliefs and modes of worship dizzying to the Western observer, because ultimately the basic religious insight of Hinduism is that there are an infinite number of paths to and manifestations of the One. Thus Hindus, unlike Christians, for example, do not believe that the fullness of religious truth can be summed up in a neat package of doctrinal statements, nor do they believe that religion consists of a clear-cut struggle of truth versus error. The Western notion that something either is or is not, but cannot be both, has no place in a Hindu world, where countless apparent contradictions exist comfortably alongside one another.

Hinduism is also more than just a family of often seemingly contradictory beliefs and religious rituals. It involves all the ways in which Hindus live and relate to one another. Therefore, as one studies Hinduism's historical evolution, it is necessary to put aside the modern Western notion of a meaningful dichotomy between religion and social organization. Hinduism is a total way of life, and this is best seen in the caste system.

Not all Hindus are members of a caste, but most are, which suggests that beneath the variety of beliefs and rituals we term Hindu, there are some fairly common elements. These include the notion of the oneness of the universe; a belief in the ultimate reality of the spiritual and the nonreality of the corporeal world; the caste system; and *dharma* (caste law), reincarnation, and *karma* (the fruits of action in a previous life).

UPANISHADS

Between about 700 and 500 B.C., Indo-Aryan religious teachers brought the Vedic age to a close in a most spectacular intellectual manner. Taking certain concepts that were implied in the later Vedic hymns, these teachers developed a vision of an all-inclusive Being or Ultimate Reality called *Brahman* and enunciated that theological breakthrough in a number of speculative treatises known as *Upanishads*.

Upanishad means "additional sitting near a teacher," and these texts often take the form of a dialogue between a teacher and a pupil who seek to go beyond the Vedas in their search for ultimate wisdom. As one might expect, there is a good deal of contradiction among the many Upanishadic texts, yet a fundamental message binds them: not only is there a Universal Soul or Brahman, but the innermost essence of a person, the *atman*, or spiritual self, is one with Brahman, the Self. Humans, therefore, are not outside Divine Reality; they are part of it.

The first selection, which comes from the early and especially revered *Chandogya Upanishad*, presents two analogies to explain this theological message. The second excerpt, taken from the later but equally important *Brihadaranyaka Upanishad*, deals with the issue of how that spark of Brahman, the Self, which is contained within each mortal body, finally achieves release and rejoins the One. Here we see an early enunciation of what will become two essential elements of Hindu religious thought: reincarnation and the law of karma.

The third selection, also from the *Brihadaranyaka*, describes the state of consciousness of a person who is on the verge of attaining release from the cycle of rebirth and union with Brahman.

Questions for Analysis

1. What sort of truth does Uddalaka offer his son when he instructs him in "that . . . by which we know what cannot be known"?
2. What does the father mean when he states, "thou, O Svetaketu, art it"?
3. How is the Upanishadic view of Brahman a logical development from the message of the hymn to Purusha?
4. Why are souls reincarnated?
5. What is the law of karma?
6. How does one end the cycle of rebirth?
7. How important or real is this world to the soul that is returning to Brahman?
8. Do good and evil have meaning to the soul that has found Brahman? Why?

There lived once Svetaketu. . . . To him his father Uddalaka . . . said: "Svetaketu, go to school; for there is none belonging to our race, darling, who, not having studied, is, as it were, a Brahmin[1] by birth only."

Having begun his apprenticeship when he was twelve years of age, Svetaketu returned to his father, when he was twenty-four, having then studied all the Vedas, — conceited, considering himself well-read, and stern.

His father said to him: "Svetaketu, as you are so conceited, considering yourself

1. A member of the priestly class; "Brahmin" is a male gender variation of the neuter "Brahman."

so well-read, and so stern, my dear, have you ever asked for that instruction by which we hear what cannot be heard, by which we perceive what cannot be perceived, by which we know what cannot be known?"

"What is that instruction, Sir?" he asked. . . .

"Fetch me from thence a fruit of the Nyagrodha tree."

"Here is one, Sir."

"Break it."

"It is broken, Sir."

"What do you see there?"

"These seeds, almost infinitesimal."

"Break one of them."

"It is broken, Sir."

"What do you see there?"

"Not anything, Sir."

The father said: "My son, that subtle essence which you do not perceive there, of that very essence this great Nyagrodha tree exists.

"Believe it, my son. That which is the subtle essence, in it all that exists has its self. It is the True. It is the Self, and thou, O Svetaketu, art it."

"Please, Sir, inform me still more," said the son.

"Be it so, my child," the father replied.

"Place this salt in water, and then wait on me in the morning."

The son did as he was commanded.

The father said to him: "Bring me the salt, which you placed in the water last night."

The son having looked for it, found it not, for, of course, it was melted.

The father said: "Taste it from the surface of the water. How is it?"

The son replied: "It is salt."

"Taste it from the middle. How is it?"

The son replied: "It is salt."

"Taste it from the bottom. How is it?"

The son replied: "It is salt."

The father said: "Throw it away and then wait on me."

He did so; but salt exists for ever.[2]

Then the father said: "Here also, in this body,[3] forsooth, you do not perceive the True, my son; but there indeed it is.

"That which is the subtle essence, in it all that exists has its self. It is the True. It is the Self, and thou, O Svetaketu, art it."

. . .

"And when the body grows weak through old age, or becomes weak through illness, at that time that person, after separating himself from his members, as a mango, or fig, or Pippala-fruit is separated from the stalk,[4] hastens back again as he came, to the place from which he started, to (new) life. . . .

"Then both his knowledge and his work take hold of him,[5] and his acquaintance with former things.[6]

"And as a caterpillar, after having reached the end of a blade of grass, and after having made another approach (to another blade), draws itself together towards it, thus does this Self, after having thrown off this body and dispelled all ignorance, and after making another approach (to another body), draw himself together towards it.

"And as a goldsmith, taking a piece of gold, turns it into another, newer and more beautiful shape, so does this Self, after having thrown off this body and

2. The salt, although unperceived, remains forever in the water.

3. The human body.

4. The image is of a fruit that carries the seed of new life, even as it decays.

5. The law of karma, which is defined more fully later in the excerpt.

6. One's acquaintance with things in a former life explains the peculiar talents and deficiencies evident in a child.

dispelled all ignorance, make unto himself another, newer and more beautiful shape. . . .

"Now as a man is like this or like that, according as he acts and according as he behaves, so will he be: — a man of good acts will become good, a man of bad acts, bad. He becomes pure by pure deeds, bad by bad deeds.

"And here they say that a person consists of desires. And as is his desire, so is his will; and as is his will, so is his deed; and whatever deed he does, that he will reap.

"And here there is this verse: 'To whatever object a man's own mind is attached, to that he goes strenuously together with his deed; and having obtained the end [the consequences] of whatever deed he does here on earth, he returns again from that world . . . to this world of action.'[7]

"So much for the man who desires. But as to the man who does not desire, who, not desiring, freed from desires, is satisfied in his desires, or desires the Self only, his vital spirits do not depart elsewhere, — being Brahman, he goes to Brahman.

"On this there is this verse: 'When all desires which once entered his heart are undone, then does the mortal become immortal, then he obtains Brahman.'"

. . .

"Now as a man, when embraced by a beloved wife, knows nothing that is without, nothing that is within, thus this person, when embraced by the intelligent Self, knows nothing that is without, nothing that is within. This indeed is his (true) form, in which his wishes are fulfilled, in which the Self (only) is his wish, in which no wish is left, — free from any sorrow.

"Then a father is not a father, a mother not a mother, the worlds not worlds, the gods not gods, the Vedas not Vedas. Then a thief is not a thief, a murderer not a murderer, a Kandala not a Kandala,[8] a Sramana not a Sramana[9], a Tapasa not a Tapasa.[10] He is not followed by good, not followed by evil, for he has then overcome all the sorrows of the heart."

BHAGAVAD GITA

The *Bhagavad Gita* (*Song of the Blessed Lord*) is Hinduism's most beloved sacred text. The poem appears in its present form as an episode in the *Mahabharata* (*The Great Deeds of the Bharata Clan*), the world's longest epic, which was composed over a period from perhaps 500 B.C. to possibly A.D. 400 but which certainly drew from much earlier Aryan oral traditions. Like the Homeric Greek epics, the *Mahabharata* deals on one level with the clash of armies and the combat of individual heroes, and simultaneously on a higher plane it expounds theological and philosophical insights. Among all these spiritual interjections, the *Bhagavad Gita* is the most profound.

---

7. This, in essence, is the law of karma.

8. The offspring of a mixed-caste marriage, whose father was a Sudra (the lowest of the four great Hindu castes) and mother a Brahmin. Kandalas were treated as the lowest and most "unclean" of all casteless persons. See pages 160–161.

9. A holy beggar.

10. A person performing penance.

The *Gita*'s date of final composition is uncertain; scholars fix it anywhere between 300 B.C. and A.D. 300. What is certain is that Hindu commentators have consistently considered the song to be the last and greatest of the Upanishadic texts, for they see it as the crystallization of all that was expressed and implied in the Upanishadic tradition.

The core question addressed in the *Bhagavad Gita* is how can a person become one with Brahman while still functioning in this world? The answer comes from Lord Krishna, the incarnation of Vishnu, the Divine Preserver. In this particular corporeal form, or *avatara*, Krishna/Vishnu serves as charioteer to the warrior-hero Arjuna. Arjuna, a brave soldier, shrinks from entering battle when he realizes that he must fight close relatives. The hero-god Krishna then proceeds to resolve Arjuna's quandary by explaining to him the moral imperative of caste-duty, or dharma.

Questions for Analysis

1. Why should Arjuna not grieve for those whom he might kill?
2. According to Krishna, how "real" is the corporeal world?
3. Why should one perform one's caste-duty in a totally disinterested fashion?
4. According to Krishna, what constitutes sin? What is evil?
5. What hope, if any, does Krishna's theological message hold for the lowest elements of Hindu society?
6. The Hindu caste system is based on several elemental religious beliefs. What are they?

The deity said, you have grieved for those who deserve no grief. . . . Learned men grieve not for the living nor the dead. Never did I not exist, nor you, nor these rulers of men; nor will any one of us ever hereafter cease to be. As in this body, infancy and youth and old age come to the embodied self, so does the acquisition of another body; a sensible man is not deceived about that. The contacts of the senses, O son of Kunti! which produce cold and heat, pleasure and pain, are not permanent, they are ever coming and going. Bear them, O descendant of Bharata! For, O chief of men! that sensible man whom they (pain and pleasure being alike to him) afflict not, he merits immortality. There is no existence for that which is unreal; there is no non-existence for that which is real. And the correct conclusion about both is perceived by those who perceive the truth. Know that to be indestructible which pervades all this. . . . He who thinks it[1] to be the killer and he who thinks it to be killed, both know nothing. It kills not, is not killed. It is not born, nor does it ever die, nor, having existed, does it exist no more. Unborn, everlasting, unchangeable, and primeval, it is not killed when the body is killed. O son of Pritha!

1. The atman, or individual soul, and Brahman, which are one and the same.

how can that man who knows it thus to be indestructible, everlasting, unborn, and inexhaustible, how and whom can he kill, whom can he cause to be killed? As a man, casting off old clothes, puts on others and new ones, so the embodied self casting off old bodies, goes to others and new ones. . . . It is everlasting, all-pervading, stable, firm, and eternal. It is said to be unperceived, to be unthinkable, to be unchangeable. Therefore knowing it to be such, you ought not to grieve. But even if you think that it is constantly born, and constantly dies, still, O you of mighty arms! you ought not to grieve thus. For to one that is born, death is certain; and to one that dies, birth is certain. . . . This embodied self, O descendant of Bharata! within every one's body is ever indestructible. Therefore you ought not to grieve for any being. Having regard to your own duty also, you ought not to falter, for there is nothing better for a Kshatriya[2] than a righteous battle. Happy those Kshatriyas, O son of Pritha! who can find such a battle . . . an open door to heaven! But if you will not fight this righteous battle, then you will have abandoned your own duty and your fame, and you will incur sin. . . . Your business is with action alone; not by any means with fruit. Let not the fruit of action be your motive to action. Let not your attachment be fixed on inaction. Having recourse to devotion . . . perform actions, casting off all attachment, and being equable in success or ill-success; such equability is called devotion. . . . The wise who have obtained devotion cast off the fruit of action;[3] and released from the shackles of repeated births, repair to that seat where there is no unhappiness. . . . The man who, casting off all desires, lives free from attachments, who is free from egoism, and from the feeling that this or that is mine, obtains tranquility. This, O son of Pritha! is the Brahmic state; attaining to this, one is never deluded; and remaining in it in one's last moments, one attains the Brahmic bliss.[4]. . .

I have passed through many births, O Arjuna! and you also. I know them all, but you, O terror of your foes! do not know them. Even though I am unborn and inexhaustible in my essence, even though I am lord of all beings, still I am born by means of my delusive power. Whensoever, O descendant of Bharata! piety languishes, and impiety is in the ascendant, I create myself. I am born age after age, for the protection of the good, for the destruction of evil-doers, and the establishment of piety. . . . The fourfold division of castes was created by me according to the appointment of qualities and duties. . . . The duties of Brahmins, Kshatriyas, and Vaisyas, and of Sudras, too, O terror of your foes! are distinguished according to the qualities born of nature.[5] Tranquillity, restraint of the senses, penance, purity, forgiveness, straightforwardness, also knowledge, experience, and belief in a future world, this is the natural duty of Brahmins. Valor, glory, courage, dexterity, not slinking away from battle, gifts, exercise of lordly power, this is the natural duty of Kshatriyas. Agriculture, tending cattle, trade, this is the natural duty of Vaisyas. And the natural duty of Sudras, too, consists in service. Every

2. A member of the ruling warrior caste.

3. Do not concern themselves with the earthly consequences of their actions and develop no attachments to the corporeal rewards (fame, wealth, children) which might result from those actions.

4. Brahma-nirvana, or merging with Brahman and release from the cycle of rebirth.

5. Each caste consists of persons born to that station by virtue of their nature. Each person's karma has made that person's nature suitable for a particular caste.

man intent on his own respective duties obtains perfection. Listen, now, how one intent on one's own duty obtains perfection. Worshipping, by the performance of his own duty, him from whom all things proceed, and by whom all this is permeated, a man obtains perfection. One's duty, though defective, is better than another's duty well performed. Performing the duty prescribed by nature, one does not incur sin. O son of Kunti! one should not abandon a natural duty though tainted with evil; for all actions are enveloped by evil, as fire by smoke. One who is self-restrained, whose understanding is unattached everywhere, from whom affections have departed, obtains the supreme perfection of freedom from action by renunciation. Learn from me, only in brief, O son of Kunti! how one who has obtained perfection attains the Brahman, which is the highest culmination of knowledge. A man possessed of a pure understanding, controlling his self by courage, discarding sound and other objects of sense, casting off affection and aversion; who frequents clean places, who eats little, whose speech, body, and mind are restrained, who is always intent on meditation and mental abstraction, and has recourse to unconcern, who abandoning egoism, stubbornness, arrogance, desire, anger, and all belongings, has no thought that this or that is mine, and who is tranquil, becomes fit for assimilation with the Brahman.

Challenges to the Caste System: The Mahavira and the Buddha

By 600 B.C. the central spiritual question in Indian society was how does one find liberation from karma and the cycle of rebirth? As we have seen, the Upanishadic teachers offered their answers. The eventual result by about 300 B.C. was establishment of the caste system throughout most of Indian society and fairly general acceptance of the notion that dharma (the law) meant caste-duty. This was not, however, the only answer.

Even as the brahmin, or priestly, class was in the process of turning itself into the dominant Hindu caste, several teachers emerged from the *kshatriya*, or warrior, class to offer alternatives to the caste system. One of these was Nataputta Vardhamana (ca 599–527 B.C.), known to history as the Mahavira (the Great Hero). The other was Siddhartha Gautama (ca 563–483 B.C.), better known as the Buddha (the Enlightened One).

Each teacher and his doctrine is understandable only within the context of an Indo-Aryan cosmology. Although both formulated philosophies that denied certain concepts basic to what was emerging as classical Hinduism, the questions each of them asked and the answers they offered were predicated upon the same world-denying assumptions underlying Hinduism.

Ironically, although both doctrines began as philosophies in which divinities played no role, they became in time theistic (god-centered) religions. Jainism, which developed out of the Mahavira's teachings, would win adherents only in India, but it has survived to the present. Half a millennium after the Buddha's release from the bonds of matter, his teachings had been transformed into a family of related religions, many of which worshiped the Buddha himself as a divine being. For well over 2,000 years, Buddhism in its various forms has profoundly shaped the lives of countless devotees throughout South and East Asia and remains a vital force today, but not in India, its original home.

BOOK OF GOOD CONDUCT

Our picture of the Mahavira and his teachings is hazy because even the Jains acknowledge that the earliest written sources for the Great Hero's life and doctrine date no earlier than two centuries after his death. One of these sources is the *Acaranga Sutra* (*Book of Good Conduct*), which Jains revere as the first of their eleven major sacred texts.

Here we encounter reincarnation, karma, and dharma, but with a Jain twist, and we discover Jain *ahimsa,* or absolute nonviolence toward all life. The first excerpt defines dharma, the second tells how Mahavira conquered karma, and the third outlines the five great Jain vows.

Questions for Analysis

1. What is dharma according to Jainism, and how does it differ from and parallel conventional Hindu dharma?
2. What is the Jain definition of karma?
3. Mahavira was acknowledged as the *Jina,* or Conqueror. Consequently, his followers are Jains. What do Jains seek to conquer?
4. What sort of "heroic" life does the Great Hero challenge his followers to lead?

The Arhats[1] . . . of the past, present, and future, all say thus, speak thus, declare thus, explain thus: all breathing, existing, living, sentient creatures[2] should not be slain, nor treated with violence, nor abused, nor tormented, nor driven away.

1. Perfect souls, or saints.

2. Not only the "higher forms" of sentient life, such as humans and animals, but also insects, plants, seeds, lichens, and even beings known as "earth-bodies," "wind-bodies," "water-bodies," and "fire-bodies."

This is the pure, unchangeable, eternal law [dharma], which the clever ones, who understand the world, have declared: among the zealous and the not zealous, among the faithful and the not faithful, among the not cruel and the cruel, among those who have worldly weakness and those who have not, among those who like social bonds and those who do not: "that is the truth, that is so, that is proclaimed in this."

Having adopted [the law], one should not hide it, nor forsake it. Correctly understanding the law, one should arrive at indifference for the impressions of the senses, and "not act on the motives of the world." "He who is not of this mind, how should he come to the other?"[3]

. . .

Beings which are born in all states become individually sinners by their actions.[4]

The Venerable One[5] understands thus: he who is under the conditions of existence, that fool suffers pain. Thoroughly knowing karma, the Venerable One avoids sin.

The sage, perceiving the double karma,[6] proclaims the incomparable activity,[7] he, the knowing one; knowing the current of worldliness, the current of sinfulness, and the impulse.

Practicing the sinless abstinence from killing, he[8] did no acts, neither himself nor with the assistance of others; he to whom women were known as the causes of all sinful acts, he saw the true state of the world. . . .

He well saw that bondage comes through action. Whatever is sinful, the Venerable One left that undone: he consumed clean food.[9]

Knowing measure in eating and drinking, he was not desirous of delicious food, nor had he a longing for it. . . .

The Venerable One, exerting himself, did not seek sleep for the sake of pleasure; he waked up himself, and slept only a little, free from desires. . . .

Always well guarded, he bore the pains (caused by) grass, cold, fire, flies, and gnats; manifold pains.

He traveled in the pathless country of the Ladhas.[10] . . .

In Ladha natives attacked him; the dogs bit him, ran at him.

Few people kept off the attacking, biting dogs. . . .

Such were the inhabitants. Many other mendicants,[11] eating rough food . . . and carrying about a strong pole [to keep off the dogs], . . . lived there.

Even thus armed they were bitten by the dogs, torn by the dogs. It is difficult to travel in Ladha.

Ceasing to use the stick against living beings, abandoning the care of the body, the houseless, the Venerable One endures the thorns of the villages being perfectly enlightened.

---

3. How can a person sin ("come to the other") who does not "act on the motives of the world"?

4. The law of karma as understood by Jains.

5. The Mahavira.

6. Present and future.

7. The life of the Jain.

8. The Mahavira.

9. Food that did the absolute least amount of violence to sentient life in all of its forms.

10. Possibly western Bengal.

11. Wandering holy persons who beg for their food.

As an elephant at the head of the battle, so was Mahavira there victorious. . . .

The Venerable One was able to abstain from indulgence of the flesh. . . .

Purgatives and emetics, anointing of the body and bathing, shampooing and cleansing of the teeth do not behoove him, after he learned [that the body is something unclean]. . . .

In summer he exposes himself to the heat, he sits squatting in the sun; he lives on rough food: rice, pounded jujube, and beans. . . .

Sometimes the Venerable One did not drink for half a month or even for a month.

Or he did not drink for more than two months, or even six months, day and night, without desire for drink. Sometimes he ate stale food.

Sometimes he ate only the sixth meal, or the eighth, the tenth, the twelfth; without desires, persevering in meditation.

Having wisdom, Mahavira committed no sin himself, nor did he induce others to do so, nor did he consent to the sins of others.

Having entered a village or a town, he begged for food which had been prepared for somebody else. Having got clean food, he used it, restraining the impulses. . . . The Venerable One slowly wandered about, and, killing no creatures, he begged for his food.

Moist or dry or cold food, old beans, old pap, or bad grain, whether he did or did not get such food he was rich. . . .

Himself understanding the truth and restraining the impulses for the purification of the soul, finally liberated, and free from delusion, the Venerable One was well guarded during his whole life.

The Venerable Ascetic[12] Mahavira endowed with the highest knowledge and intuition taught the five great vows.

. . .

The first great vow, Sir, runs thus:

I renounce all killing of living beings, whether subtle or gross, whether movable or immovable. Nor shall I myself kill living beings, nor cause others to do it, nor consent to it. As long as I live, I confess and blame, repent and exempt myself of these sins, in the thrice threefold way,[13] in mind, speech, and body. . . .

The second great vow runs thus:

I renounce all vices of lying speech arising from anger or greed or fear or mirth. I shall neither myself speak lies, nor cause others to speak lies, nor consent to the speaking of lies by others. . . .

The third great vow runs thus:

I renounce all taking of anything not given, either in a village or a town or a wood, either of little or much, of small or great, of living or lifeless things. I shall neither take myself what is not given, nor cause others to take it, nor consent to their taking it.

The fourth great vow runs thus:

I renounce all sexual pleasures, either with gods or men or animals. I shall not give way to sensuality. . . .

The fifth great vow runs thus:

I renounce all attachments, whether little or much, small or great, living or lifeless; neither shall I myself form such attachments, nor cause others to do so, nor consent to their doing so.

---

12. A person who leads a life of rigorous self-denial for religious reasons.

13. Acting, commanding, consenting in mind, speech, or body, in the past, present, or future.

The Buddha

TWO SERMONS

Many parallels exist between the legendary lives of the Mahavira and the Buddha, and several of their teachings are strikingly similar. Each rejected the special sanctity of Vedic literature, and each denied the meaningfulness of caste distinctions and duties. Yet a close investigation of their doctrines reveals substantial differences.

Like the Mahavira, young Prince Gautama, shrinking in horror at the many manifestations of misery in this world, fled his comfortable life and eventually became an ascetic. Where the Mahavira found victory over karma in severe self-denial and total nonviolence, however, Prince Gautama found only severe disquiet. This life offered him no enlightenment as to how one might escape the sorrows of mortal existence. After abandoning extreme asceticism in favor of a more moderate life of self-restraint, Gautama achieved Enlightenment in a flash while meditating under a fig tree (the sacred Nyagrodha tree). He was now the Buddha.

Legend tells us he then proceeded to share Enlightenment by preaching a sermon in a deer park at Benares in northeastern India to five ascetics, who became his first disciples. Buddhists refer to that initial sermon as "Setting in Motion the Wheel of the Law," which means that the Buddha had embarked on a journey (turning the wheel) on behalf of the law of Righteousness (dharma).

A reconstruction of the first sermon and a second sermon, purported to have been delivered shortly after the first, follow. The second lesson introduces the Buddhist concept of Selflessness and is known as the "Discourse on Not Having Signs of the Self." Both texts date from at least several centuries after Siddhartha Gautama's death, but they contain the essence of the Buddha's original, fundamental principles.

Questions for Analysis

1. What is the Middle Path? Why is it the proper path to Enlightenment?
2. What are the Four Noble Truths?
3. Buddhists call the law or code taught by the Buddha *dharma*. How does Buddhist dharma differ from that of Hinduism?
4. How has the Buddha reached the point of escaping the cycle of rebirth?
5. How does one free oneself from this world?
6. In what ways have both the Mahavira and the Buddha rejected the caste system, especially the primacy of the brahmins? Why would Jainism and Buddhism possibly appeal to nonbrahmins?
7. Both the Buddha and the Mahavira came from the warrior caste. Do their respective doctrines hint at this fact in any way?
8. What elements do Hinduism, Jainism, and Buddhism share? Where do they differ? What are more significant, the similarities or the differences? Is it correct to call Hinduism, Jainism, and Buddhism "world-denying"?

And the Blessed One thus addressed the five Bhikkhus[1]: "There are two extremes, O Bhikkhus, which he who has given up the world, ought to avoid. What are these two extremes? A life given to pleasures, devoted to pleasures and lusts: this is degrading, sensual, vulgar, ignoble, and profitless; and a life given to mortifications: this is painful, ignoble, and profitless. By avoiding these two extremes, O Bhikkhus, the Tathagata[2] has gained the knowledge of the Middle Path which leads to insight, which leads to wisdom which conduces to calm, to knowledge, to the Sambodhi,[3] to Nirvana.[4]

"Which, O Bhikkhus, is this Middle Path the knowledge of which the Tathagata has gained, which leads to insight, which leads to wisdom, which conduces to calm, to knowledge, to the Sambodhi, to Nirvana? It is the holy eightfold Path, namely, Right Belief,[5] Right Aspiration,[6] Right Speech,[7] Right Conduct,[8] Right Means of Livelihood,[9] Right Endeavor,[10] Right Memory,[11] Right Meditation.[12] This, O Bhikkhus, is the Middle Path the knowledge of which the Tathagata has gained, which leads to insight, which leads to wisdom, which conduces to calm, to knowledge, to the Sambodhi, to Nirvana.

"This, O Bhikkhus, is the Noble Truth of Suffering: Birth is suffering; decay is suffering; illness is suffering; death is suffering. Presence of objects we hate, is suffering; Separation from objects we love, is suffering; not to obtain what we desire, is suffering. Briefly, . . . clinging to existence is suffering.

"This, O Bhikkhus, is the Noble Truth of the Cause of suffering: Thirst, that leads to re-birth, accompanied by pleasure and lust, finding its delight here and there. This thirst is threefold, namely, thirst for pleasure, thirst for existence, thirst for prosperity.

"This, O Bhikkhus, is the Noble Truth of the Cessation of suffering: it ceases with the complete cessation of this thirst, — a cessation which consists in the absence of every passion — with the abandoning of this thirst, with the doing away with it, with the deliverance from it, with the destruction of desire.

"This, O Bhikkhus, is the Noble Truth of the Path which leads to the cessation of suffering: that holy eightfold Path, that is to say, Right Belief, Right Aspiration, Right Speech, Right Conduct, Right Means of Livelihood, Right Endeavor, Right Memory, Right Meditation. . . .

"As long, O Bhikkhus, as I did not possess with perfect purity this true knowledge and insight into these four Noble Truths . . . so long, O Bhikkhus, I knew that I had not yet obtained the highest, absolute Sambodhi in the world of men and gods. . . .

---

1. Ascetics.

2. He who has arrived at the Truth. This is one of the Buddha's titles.

3. Total enlightenment.

4. The state of release from the limitations of existence and rebirth.

5. Understanding the truth about the universality of suffering and knowing the path leading to its extinction.

6. A mind free of ill will, sensuous desire, and cruelty.

7. Abstaining from lying, harsh language, and tale-bearing.

8. Avoiding killing, stealing, and unlawful sexual intercourse.

9. Avoiding any occupation that brings harm directly or indirectly to any other living being.

10. Avoiding unwholesome and evil things.

11. Awareness in contemplation.

12. Concentration that eventually reaches the level of trance.

"But since I possessed, O Bhikkhus, with perfect purity this true knowledge and insight into these four Noble Truths . . . then I knew, O Bhikkhus, that I had obtained the highest, universal Sambodhi. . . .

"And this knowledge and insight arose in my mind: "The emancipation of my mind cannot be lost; this is my last birth; hence I shall not be born again!"

. . .

And the Blessed One thus spoke to the five Bhikkhus: "The body, O Bhikkhus, is not the self. If the body, O Bhikkhus, were the self, the body would not be subject to disease, and we should be able to say: "Let my body be such and such a one, let my body not be such and such a one." But since the body, O Bhikkhus, is not the self, therefore the body is subject to disease, and we are not able to say: "Let my body be such and such a one, let my body not be such and such a one. . . .

"Now what do you think, O Bhikkhus, is the body permanent or perishable?"

"It is perishable, Lord."

"And that which is perishable, does that cause pain or joy?"

"It causes pain, Lord."

"And that which is perishable, painful, subject to change, is it possible to regard that in this way: 'This is mine, this am I, this is my self?'"

"That is impossible, Lord,". . .

"Therefore, O Bhikkhus, whatever body has been, will be, and is now, belonging or not belonging to sentient beings, gross or subtle, inferior or superior, distant or near, all that body is not mine, is not me, is not my self: thus it should be considered by right knowledge according to the truth. . . .

"Considering this, O Bhikkhus, a learned, noble hearer of the word becomes weary of body, weary of sensation, weary of perception . . . weary of consciousness. Becoming weary of all that, he divests himself of passion; by absence of passion he is made free; when he is free, he becomes aware that he is free; and he realizes that re-birth is exhausted; that holiness is completed; that duty is fulfilled; and that there is no further return to this world."

Thus the Blessed One spoke; the five Bhikkhus were delighted, and rejoiced at the words of the Blessed One. And when this exposition had been propounded, the minds of the five Bhikkhus became free from attachment to the world, and were released from the Asavas.[13]

At that time there were six Arahats[14] . . . in the world.

Persians, Israelites, and Their Gods of the Universe

By the sixth century B.C. two Middle Eastern peoples, the Hebrews and the Persians, had evolved separate visions of a single God of the universe who demanded wholehearted devotion and imposed an uncompromising code of moral behavior upon all

13. The cankers or sores of existence: sensual desire, desire for becoming, and ignorance.

14. Perfected disciples or, in this instance, totally enlightened persons (the Buddha and his five disciples).

believers. Both the Persian Ahura Mazda (Wise Lord) and the Hebrew Yahweh (I Am Who Am) were originally perceived as sky gods, existing among a multiplicity of other gods of nature; by the sixth century, however, their respective devotees worshiped each as the sole creator of the entire universe and envisioned each as transcending all material creation. This totally spiritual nature did not prevent either from also being a god of history. That is, each God used humans as agents to serve the Divine Will and thereby to assist in the realization of the Divine Plan for humanity. For both the Persians and Hebrews, human history had a purpose and a goal. By serving as agents in the working out of God's plan for creation, humans thus assumed a spiritual dignity and importance that they could otherwise never hope to attain.

Zarathustra

GATHAS

About the same time the Aryans were wandering into the Indian subcontinent, a closely related group of Indo-Europeans was settling the Iranian highlands. The religion and general culture of these people initially resembled that of the Vedic Aryans. For example, they celebrated the slaying of Verethra, the drought, by their war-god Indara. The parallel with Indra's striking down Vritra, the dragon of drought, is obvious. In time, however, these settlers, of what is today largely Iran and the southern Caucasus region of the Soviet Union, developed a civilization that differed radically from that of the Indo-Aryans. We call that ancient civilization Persian.

By the late sixth century B.C. the Persians possessed the largest empire the world had yet seen. For nearly two centuries they united the Middle East and portions of Central Asia, North Africa, and the Balkan region of Europe into a politically centralized yet culturally diverse entity. During the reign of Darius the Great (522–486 B.C.), who rightly styled himself King of Kings, the royal house of Persia officially adopted as its religion the teachings of a native son, Zarathustra. The highly ethical message of this Persian religious visionary appears to have been one of the major factors contributing to the empire's general policy of good government.

We know very little about the life of Zarathustra. Apparently he flourished in eastern Iran around 660 B.C. and taught his disciples to uphold, through ritual and moral conduct, the cause of Ahura Mazda, the sole deity of the universe. It is clear that Zarathustra claimed to be a prophet (a person speaking by divine inspiration, thereby revealing the will of God). Equally clear is that Zarathustra transmitted to his followers the message that Ahura Mazda required all humans to join in the cosmic struggle against Angra Mainyu (Enemy Spirit). Although in no way the equal of Ahura Mazda, Angra Mainyu, the Liar, afflicted human souls with evil and led them away from the path of righteousness.

Zarathustra's teachings took hold in Persia, evolving into a complex religion we call Zoroastrianism (after Zoroaster, the Greek version of "Zarathustra"). In the process, however, Zarathustra's strict monotheism was lost. From A.D. 224 to 651, Zoroastrianism was the official state religion of a revived Persian empire under the Sassanian house, but Zoroastrianism had by then lapsed into polytheism. Moreover, Angra Mainyu was now seen as coeternal and coequal with Ahura Mazda. Where one deity was the creator of all goodness, the other was the origin of all evil.

The *Avesta,* the Zoroastrian collection of holy scripture, was compiled only in the early Sassanian era and strongly reflects this later dualism. It also contains, however, a few short devotional hymns, known as *Gathas,* which date to the age of Zarathustra and probably owe their composition to him or an early disciple. Essentially our only reliable sources for the teachings of the Persian prophet, they serve to illustrate his vision and message.

Questions for Analysis

1. How are we able to infer that Zarathustra believed he had been called directly by Ahura Mazda to serve as a prophet?
2. What evidence indicates that Zarathustra saw Ahura Mazda as the sole creator of the universe?
3. Where and how does Zarathustra refer to Ahura Mazda's use of humanity and history to realize certain sacred purposes?
4. How does each person's life become a microcosm of the battle between Ahura Mazda and the Liar?
5. What is promised those who serve Ahura Mazda faithfully?
6. How do we know that Zarathustra believed Ahura Mazda would ultimately triumph over evil?
7. Does Zarathustra see his faith as only one of many paths to the truth, or is it the Truth?

Then shall I recognize thee as strong and holy, Mazda,[1] when by the hand in which thou thyself dost hold the destinies that thou wilt assign to the Liar and the Righteous . . . the might of Good Thought[2] shall come to me.

As the holy one I recognised thee, Mazda Ahura,[3] when I saw thee in the be-

1. Mazda means "wise" or "wisdom."

2. Zarathustra appears to have conceived of Good Thought, Piety, and other entities as angelic spirits and not simply abstract virtues.

3. Ahura means "lord."

ginning at the birth of Life, when thou madest actions and words to have their meed[4] — evil for the evil, a good Destiny for the good — through thy wisdom when creation shall reach its goal.

At which goal thou wilt come with thy holy Spirit, O Mazda, with Dominion, at the same with Good Thought, by whose action the settlements[5] will prosper through Right. Their judgments shall Piety proclaim, even those of thy wisdom which none can deceive.

As the holy one I recognized thee, Mazda Ahura, when Good Thought came to me and asked me, "Who art thou? to whom dost thou belong? By what sign wilt thou appoint the days for questioning about thy possessions and thyself?"

Then I said to him: "To the first (question), Zarathustra am I, a true foe to the Liar, to the utmost of my power, but a powerful support would I be to the Righteous, that I may attain the future things of the infinite Dominion, according as I praise and sing thee, Mazda.". . .

As the holy one I recognized thee, Mazda Ahura, when Good Thought came to me, when the still mind taught me to declare what is best: "Let not a man seek again and again to please the Liars, for they make all the righteous enemies."

And thus Zarathustra himself, O Ahura, chooses that spirit of thine that is holiest, Mazda. May Right be embodied, full of life and strength! May Piety abide in the Dominion where the sun shines! May Good Thought give destiny to men according to their works!

. . .

This I ask thee, tell me truly, Ahura. Who is by generation the Father of Right, at the first? Who determined the path of sun and stars? Who is it by whom the moon waxes and wanes again? This, O Mazda, and yet more, I am fain to know.

This I ask thee, tell me truly, Ahura. Who upheld the earth beneath and the firmament from falling? Who the waters and the plants? Who yoked swiftness to winds and clouds? Who is, O Mazda, creator of Good Thought?

This I ask thee, tell me truly, Ahura. What artist made light and darkness? What artist made sleep and waking? Who made morning, noon, and night, that call the understanding man to his duty?

This I ask thee, tell me truly, Ahura — whether what I shall proclaim is verily the truth. Will Right with its actions give aid (at the last)? Will Piety? Will Good Thought announce from thee the Dominion? For whom hast thou made the pregnant cow[6] that brings good luck?

This I ask thee, tell me truly, Ahura. Who created together with Dominion the precious Piety? Who made by wisdom the son obedient to his father? I strive to recognize by these things thee, O Mazda, creator of all things through the holy spirit. . . .

This I ask thee, tell me truly, Ahura. The Religion which is the best for (all) that are, which in union with Right should prosper all that is mine, will they duly observe it, the religion of my creed, with the words and action of Piety, in desire for thy (future) good things, O Mazda?

This I ask thee, tell me truly, Ahura — whether Piety will extend to those to whom thy Religion shall be proclaimed? I was ordained at the first by thee: all others I look upon with hatred of spirit.

4. Reward.

5. People who are settled or civilized.

6. A symbol of good fortune and earthly prosperity.

This I ask thee, tell me truly, Ahura. Who among those with whom I would speak is a righteous man, and who a liar? On which side is the enemy? (On this), or is he the enemy, the Liar who opposes thy blessings?[7] How shall it be with him? Is he not to be thought of as an enemy?

This I ask thee, tell me truly, Ahura — whether we shall drive the Lie away from us to those who being full of disobedience will not strive after fellowship with Right, nor trouble themselves with counsel of Good Thought. . . .

This I ask thee, tell me truly, Ahura — whether through you I shall attain my goal, O Mazda, even attachment unto you, and that my voice may be effectual, that Welfare and Immortality may be ready to unite according to that promise with him who joins himself with Right.

This I ask thee, tell me truly, Ahura — whether I shall indeed, O Right, earn that reward, even ten mares with a stallion and a camel,[8] which was promised to me, O Mazda, as well as through thee the future gift of Welfare and Immortality.

. . .

I will speak of that which Mazda Ahura, the all-knowing, revealed to me first in this (earthly) life. Those of you that put not in practice this word as I think and utter it, to them shall be woe at the end of life. . . .

I will speak of that which the Holiest declared to me as the word that is best for mortals to obey: he, Mazda Ahura (said), "They who at my bidding render him[9] obedience, shall all attain unto Welfare and Immortality by the actions of the Good Spirit.". . .

In immortality shall the soul of the righteous be joyful, in perpetuity shall be the torments of the Liars. All this doth Mazda Ahura appoint by his Dominion.

THE BOOK OF ISAIAH

As we saw in Chapter 2, around 1200 B.C. the Israelites moved into the land of Canaan, where they waged a continuing battle to retain their independence, cultural identity, and exclusive devotion to Yahweh. In the late eleventh century B.C., largely in response to Philistine pressure, the Israelites created a kingdom. Around 1020 B.C., their second king, David, captured Jerusalem and converted it into the religious and political capital of the Israelites.

The political stability of this kingdom was precarious at best. In 922 it was split into two independent entities: the larger kingdom of Israel in the north and the kingdom of Judah, centering on Jerusalem, in the south. In 722 the Assyrians obliterated Israel. The more compact and remote kingdom of Judah survived until 586 B.C., when finally a Semitic people from Mesopotamia known as the Chaldeans

7. Of future life.

8. Symbols of wealth on earth.

9. Zarathustra.

captured and destroyed Jerusalem and carried off most of Judah's upper classes into exile in Babylon, an episode known forever after as the Babylonian Captivity.

Cultural and religious stability was equally precarious. The cult of Yahweh was in many ways more suitable to the life of the desert herder than the settled farmer. As the Hebrews settled down, they adopted many of the religious practices of their Canaanite neighbors. This action occasioned angry protests from a group of religious reformers known as "the prophets." The prophets, who claimed inspiration from Yahweh, protested vehemently against debasement of the Mosaic religion, but in the process of their protest they broadened considerably the moral and theological scope of the worship of Yahweh.

One of the greatest and last of these prophets was a person we know only as Second Isaiah. He served as the voice of a new faith that was born out of the anguish of the Babylonian Captivity. We call that faith Judaism.

The original Prophet Isaiah had towered over the religious scene of Jerusalem from the middle to late eighth century B.C. and left behind a rich legacy of teaching on Yahweh's role as the God who controls the destinies of all people. Second Isaiah carried on this tradition. Consequently, the prophecies of this otherwise unknown person were appended to the writings of Isaiah and appear as chapters 40 through 55 in the Bible's Book of Isaiah.

The following passages were composed around 538 B.C., when Cyrus the Great, king of Persia and conqueror of the Chaldean (Neo-Babylonian) empire, released the Israelites from captivity. Here Second Isaiah metaphorically describes the people of Israel as Yahweh's "Suffering Servant" and delineates the historical role that Yahweh has decreed for this servant.

Questions for Analysis

1. In what manner has Yahweh's special relationship with the people of Israel remained unchanged since the days of Moses (Chapter 2)?
2. Consider Yahweh's relationship with King Cyrus and the Persians. Even though Cyrus does not know or honor Yahweh, Yahweh has chosen him as a servant. Why? In what way does this represent a departure from the Israelites' traditional views of their neighbors?
3. What does Second Isaiah mean by the prophecy that Israel will be "a light to the nations"? How does this represent a new self-image for the people of Israel?
4. Yahweh promises a new covenant. Will it differ from the covenant that Yahweh entered into with Moses and the Israelites at the time of the Exodus (Chapter 2)? If so, in what way? How will it complete the covenant Yahweh entered into with Noah (Chapter 2)?
5. What are the essential elements of Second Isaiah's vision of Yahweh and this deity's Chosen People?
6. How do Ahura Mazda and Yahweh differ from Brahman?
7. "In the Middle East religion became the means of transforming the world, not negating it." Please comment on this quotation.

The LORD says,
"Listen now, Israel,[1] my servant,
my chosen people, the descendants of
 Jacob.
I am the LORD who created you;
from the time you were born, I have
 helped you.
Do not be afraid; you are my servant,
my chosen people whom I love.

I will give water to the thirsty land
and make streams flow on the dry
 ground.
I will pour out my spirit on your children
and my blessing on your descendants.
They will thrive like well-watered grass,
like willows by streams of running water.

One by one, people will say, 'I am the
 LORD's.'
They will come to join the people of
 Israel.
Each one will mark the name of the LORD
 on his arm[2]
and call himself one of God's people."

The LORD, who rules and protects Israel,
the LORD Almighty, has this to say:
"I am the first, the last, the only God;
there is no other god but me. . . ."

The LORD says,
"Israel, remember this;
remember that you are my servant.
I created you to be my servant,
and I will never forget you.
I have swept your sins away like a cloud.
Come back to me; I am the one who
 saves you."

Shout for joy, you heavens!
Shout, deep places of the earth!
Shout for joy, mountains, and every tree
 of the forest!
The LORD has shown his greatness
by saving his people Israel. . . .

"I tell Jerusalem that people will live there
 again,
and the cities of Judah that they will be
 rebuilt.
Those cities will rise from the ruins.
With a word of command I dry up the
 ocean.
I say to Cyrus, 'You are the one who will
 rule for me;
you will do what I want you to do:
you will order that Jerusalem be rebuilt
and that the foundations of the Temple
 be laid.'". . .

The LORD has chosen Cyrus to be king.
He has appointed him to conquer
 nations;
he sends him to strip kings of their
 power;
the LORD will open the gates of cities for
 him.
To Cyrus the LORD says,
"I myself will prepare your way,
leveling mountains and hills.
I will break down bronze gates and
 smash their iron bars.
I will give you treasures from dark,
 secret places;
then you will know that I am the LORD
and that the God of Israel has called you
 by name.
I appoint you to help my servant Israel,
the people that I have chosen.
I have given you great honor,
although you do not know me.

1. This refers to all the people of Israel and should not be confused with the kingdom of Israel, which the Assyrians destroyed in 722 B.C.

2. Compare this instruction with Moses' command in the Book of Deuteronomy (p. 63) that the Israelites tie the law to their arms and wear it on their foreheads.

I am the LORD; there is no other god.
I will give you the strength you need,
although you do not know me.
I do this so that everyone from one end of the world to the other
may know that I am the LORD
and that there is no other god.
I create both light and darkness;
I bring both blessing and disaster.
I, the LORD, do all these things.

I will send victory from the sky like rain;
the earth will open to receive it
and will blossom with freedom and justice.
I, the LORD, will make this happen. . . .

I myself have stirred Cyrus to action
to fulfill my purpose and put things right.
I will straighten out every road that he travels.
He will rebuild my city, Jerusalem,
and set my captive people free.
No one has hired him or bribed him to do this."
The LORD Almighty has spoken. . . .

The LORD says,
"Come together, people of the nations,
all who survive the fall of the empire;[3]
present yourselves for the trial!
The people who parade with their idols of wood
and pray to gods that cannot save them —
those people know nothing at all!
Come and present your case in court;
let the defendants consult one another.
Who predicted long ago what would happen?
Was it not I, the LORD, the God who saves his people?
There is no other god.

Turn to me now and be saved,
people all over the world!
I am the only God there is.
My promise is true,
and it will not be changed.
I solemnly promise by all that I am:
Everyone will come and kneel before me
and vow to be loyal to me.

They will say that only through me
are victory and strength to be found;
but all who hate me will suffer disgrace.
I, the LORD, will rescue all the descendants of Jacob,
and they will give me praise. . . ."

The LORD says,
"Listen to me, Israel, the people I have called!
I am God, the first, the last, the only God!
My hands made the earth's foundations
and spread the heavens out.
When I summon earth and sky,
they come at once and present themselves.

Assemble and listen, all of you!
None of the gods could predict that the man I have chosen would attack Babylon;
he will do what I want him to do.
I am the one who spoke and called him;
I led him out and gave him success. . . ."

Go out from Babylon, go free!
Shout the news gladly; make it known everywhere;
"The LORD has saved his servant Israel!"
When the LORD led his people through a hot, dry desert,[4]
they did not suffer from thirst.
He made water come from a rock for them;

3. The Chaldean, or Neo-Babylonian empire.

4. A reference to the forty years of wandering in the desert in the time of Moses.

he split the rock open, and water flowed
 out. . . .

Listen to me, distant nations, you people
 who live far away!
Before I was born, the LORD chose me
and appointed me to be his servant.
He made my words as sharp as a sword.
With his own hand he protected me.
He made me like an arrow,
sharp and ready for use.
He said to me, "Israel, you are my
 servant;
because of you, people will praise
 me.". . .

The LORD said to me,
"I have a greater task for you, my
 servant.
Not only will you restore to greatness
the people of Israel who have survived,
but I will also make you a light to the
 nations —
so that all the world may be saved."
Israel's holy God and savior says
to the one who is deeply despised,
who is hated by the nations
and is the servant of rulers:
"Kings will see you released and will rise
 to show their respect;
princes also will see it,
and they will bow low to honor you."
This will happen because the LORD has
 chosen his servant;
the holy God of Israel keeps his promises.

The LORD says to his people,
"When the time comes to save you, I will
 show you favor
and answer your cries for help.
I will guard and protect you and through
 you make a covenant with all peoples.
I will let you settle once again in your
 land that is now laid waste.
I will say to the prisoners, 'Go free!'
and to those who are in darkness,
'Come out to the light!'
They will be like sheep that graze on the
 hills;
they will never be hungry or thirsty.
Sun and desert heat will not hurt them,
for they will be led by one who loves
 them.
He will lead them to springs of water."

C H A P T E R

4

Development of the Secular Traditions of China and Hellas, 600–200 B.C.

The Chinese and the Greeks, who inhabited the two territorial extremes of civilized Eurasia in the sixth century B.C., had their gods and modes of worship. But religion in its narrowest sense — reverence for a supernatural being — offered these peoples relatively little in the way of either intellectual stimulation or emotional outlet. While contemporary Indians and Middle Easterners were raising religious speculation to high levels of abstract thought, religion for the Chinese and Greeks remained, for the most part, a practical affair. One sacrificed to the gods and spirits in order to assure their benevolence. Religion was a form of magical insurance and not a relationship with Ultimate Reality.

At the same time, the social and psychic crises of the Age of Iron were just as real in China and Hellas as elsewhere. In fashioning responses to the questions occasioned by the dislocation of traditional ways of life, the Chinese and Greeks looked more toward this world than to the Beyond and created essentially *secular* (relating to the observable world of space and time) cultures. The family, the state, and nature became the objects of focus for the Chinese. For the Greeks, the individual, the city-state, and rational philosophy and science were the focus.

China: Three Ways of Thought

Ages of political and social unrest often prove to be periods of significant intellectual ferment, and this was certainly true of the era of Eastern Chou (770–256 B.C.). The collapse of the Western Chou monarchy in 771 signaled the end of real royal power in China and ushered in a 500-year period in which regional states held center stage. Chou kings continued to perform their traditional religious roles and received tokens of nominal obedience from the great feudal lords. True power, however, lay in the hands of the regional lords, who developed bureaucratic governments and strong standing armies. With each local prince essentially a sovereign, military and diplomatic maneuvering among their states became a constant fact of life. As disruptive as this was at times, it also proved to be a stimulus to intellectual activity. Both the demands of statecraft at the regional level and the occasional social dislocation that resulted from the conflicts among these states stimulated the development of political theory and social philosophy.

This was especially the case from the fifth century B.C. onward, as wars became more frequent and bitter. Chinese historians traditionally catalog the period from 403 to 221 B.C. as the Age of Warring States. The introduction of cavalry, iron weapons, and the crossbow combined to break the old superiority on the battlefield of the chariot aristocracy. Armies of foot and horse soldiers became larger and more deadly. Concomitantly, intellectual activity kept pace.

Between 260 and 221 B.C., Ch'in, the most aggressive and best organized of the warring states, conquered all its rival powers in China and established a new royal family, the short-lived but pivotal Ch'in Dynasty (221–206 B.C.). The triumph of the lord of Ch'in, the self-styled Ch'in Shih Huang Ti (the First Emperor of Ch'in, 221–210 B.C.), not only inaugurated China's first age of empire, it brought with it the victory of a political philosophy known as "legalism." In conforming to the principles of legalism, the Ch'in regime was ruthless and brutal in its drive for complete centralization of authority. Undone by the harshness of its laws and policies, the Ch'in Dynasty collapsed in early 206 in the midst of rebellion and civil war. Within four years, however, a commoner general, Liu Pang, reformulated the empire by establishing the successful and long-lived Han Dynasty (202 B.C.–A.D. 220).

Although the extreme measures of the Ch'in Dynasty discredited legalism as a philosophy, legalist-inspired organizational structures and administrative procedures served as the framework of a highly centralized Han empire. By the late second century B.C., however, the Han Dynasty adopted as its official ideology the gentler and more humane philosophy of Confucianism, which had also taken shape in the disturbing period of Eastern Chou.

Han imperial policies and institutions were, therefore, the products of a Confucian-legalist synthesis, but these were not the only modes of thought to play a prominent role both then and ever after in China. Taoism, an antirational and, in many ways, quite antisocial philosophy, had also emerged from the confusion of Eastern Chou and survived the hostility of Ch'in legalists.

These three schools of Chinese thought were not the only important intellectual currents in China in the age of Han, but they were to become the philosophical tripod of Chinese civilization. Although they emphasized different aspects of human life and presented some striking differences of perspective, they were not mutually exclusive; indeed, they have served for over 2,000 years as complementary and intertwined elements of Chinese civilization.

Lao Tzu

THE CLASSIC OF THE WAY AND OF VIRTUE

Winston Churchill once characterized the Soviet Union as "a riddle wrapped in a mystery inside an enigma." He could have said the same of Taoism — the philosophy of the Way (Tao). The opening lines of this school's greatest masterpiece, *The Classic of the Way and of Virtue (Tao-te Ching),* which is ascribed to the legendary Lao Tzu ("Venerable Master"), immediately confront the reader with Taoism's essential paradox: "The Way that may truly be regarded as the Way is other than a permanent way. The terms that may truly be regarded as terms are other than permanent terms." Here is a philosophy that seeks to understand Ultimate Reality but claims that reality transcends human understanding and definition. For many American students, this is difficult to comprehend, especially as Taoism is a philosophy that purports to teach *the* Way.

Like the Tao itself, Taoism has many origins and manifestations. No one knows when or where it originated, although it probably sprang, at least in part, out of archaic Chinese folk religion. Its greatest early sages are equally shadowy. According to tradition, Lao Tzu was an older contemporary of Confucius, living and writing in the early to mid-sixth century B.C. Yet it is not certain that Lao Tzu ever lived. Many scholars believe that the bulk of the language and ideas contained within this classic indicate an intellectual environment closer to 300 than to 600 B.C.

Whatever the date and circumstances of its composition, the *Tao-te Ching* is one of the most profound and beautiful works ever written in Chinese. This little work of only about 5,000 words has exercised an incalculable influence on Chinese life, thought, and art over the centuries. There is a good deal of truth to the cliché that traditional Chinese upper-class males were Confucians in public and Taoists in private.

Questions for Analysis

1. How does one define the Way? How permanent is it? How limited is it? Is there anything that the Way does not encompass?

2. Does the Way acknowledge absolute right and wrong?
3. How does a ruler who is in harmony with the Way govern?
4. How does Wu-wei function, and what are its consequences?
5. Why would Taoism appeal to certain individuals in the Age of Warring States?
6. Does Taoism adopt a rational or a mystical (that which is beyond reason and sense experience) approach to life and its problems? If it is mystical, can it simultaneously be secular?
7. Compare the Way with the Supreme Beings of India and the Middle East (Chapter 3). Does it share any common characteristics with Brahman, Ahura Mazda, or Yahweh? What are more significant, the similarities or the differences?
8. Compare Wu-wei with the teachings of the Mahavira and the Buddha (Chapter 3). Do you see any similarities? What are more significant, the similarities or the differences?

[*The Way*]

The Way that may truly be regarded as the Way is other than a permanent way.

The terms that may truly be regarded as terms are other than permanent terms.

The term Non-being indicates the beginning of the heaven and earth; the term Being indicates the mother of the ten thousand things.

For, indeed, it is through the constant alternation between Non-being and Being that the wonder of the one and the limitation of the other will be seen.

These two, having a common origin, are named with different terms.

What they have in common is called the Mystery, the Mystery of Mysteries, the Gate of all Wonders.[1]

. . .

Everybody in the world recognizes beauty as beauty, and thus ugliness (is known).

Everybody recognizes the good as good, and thus what is not good (is known).

For indeed:

Being and Non-being produce one another,

Hard and easy complete one another,

Long and short are relative to one another,

High and low are dependent on one another,

Tones and voice harmonize with one another,

First and last succeed one another.

. . .

The movement of the Way is: to reverse.

The method of the Way is: to be weak.

Heaven and earth and the ten thousand things are born out of Being; Being is born out of Non-being.

[*The Ideal State*]

Not exalting ability ensures that the people do not strive.

Not prizing goods that are difficult to obtain ensures that the people do not become robbers.

1. The Way.

Not showing them what they might desire ensures that the people do not feel disturbed in their hearts.

Therefore the Saint,[2] in the exercise of government, empties their hearts and fills their bellies, weakens their wills and strengthens their bones, thus constantly ensuring that the people are without knowledge and without desires and that those who have knowledge dare not act. He practices Non-action[3] and consequently there is nothing that is not well governed.

. . .

When the Empire has the Way, (even) coursers[4] will be stabled for the sake of their dung.[5]

When the Empire is without the Way, warhorses will be raised in the suburb.[6]

No guilt is greater than to approve of desire.

No disaster is greater than not to know what is enough.

No fault is greater than the desire to acquire.

For, to know that enough is enough is to have always enough.

. . .

Abolish saintliness and reject knowledge: the people will benefit a hundredfold.

Abolish humanity and reject justice: the people will return to filial piety and maternal affection.[7]

Abolish skill and reject profit:[8] thieves and robbers will disappear.

(Lest) these three be considered as (mere) words which are inadequate, let there be something to hold on to.

Display natural simplicity and cling to artlessness: decrease selfishness and diminish desires.

[*Nonaction (Wu-wei)*]

Do by not doing, act by non-action, taste the taste-less, regard small as great, much as little.

Plan what is difficult where it is easy; do what is great where it is minute.

The hardest things in the world begin with what is easy; the greatest things in the world begin with what is minute.

Therefore the Saint never does anything great and so is able to achieve the great.

Now, he who promises lightly, will have but little faith. He who finds much easy, will find much hard.

Therefore the Saint, while finding even (the easy) hard, will in the end have nothing that is hard.

. . .

The Way is constantly inactive and yet there is nothing that remains undone.

---

2. A person of perfect wisdom who understands and follows the Way and who thus possesses magical powers.

3. Wu-wei, the supreme form of action. See the final passage.

4. War-horses.

5. Used for agricultural purposes.

6. They will be raised on sacred ground that is reserved for altars and shrines.

7. These first two lines reject the Confucian values of wisdom (saintliness), knowledge, human-heartedness, and righteousness, all of which, according to the Confucians, will result in filial piety (proper devotion to one's parents and ancestors).

8. This seems to be a rejection of the pragmatic values of legalism.

Confucius

ANALECTS

The Chinese refer to the period of Eastern Chou as the age of "the Hundred Schools." Of the many schools of thought that flourished then, none has affected Chinese culture more deeply than Confucianism.

Unlike the case of Lao Tzu, we are certain there was a historical Confucius. According to tradition, he was born in 551 B.C. into the lower aristocratic family of the K'ung and given the name Ch'iu. Later in life he was accorded the elegant title K'ung fu-tzu (K'ung the Philosopher), which Western scholars have Latinized into Confucius. Tradition records that he died in 479, a decade before the birth of his great Greek counterpart Socrates (ca 469–399 B.C.). Somewhat like Socrates, who professed that if he were wise it was because he realized his own ignorance, Confucius claimed to possess no special genius or knowledge. He simply saw himself as someone who revered the old ways and followed them zealously.

Much of what Confucius taught was already part of Chinese culture, but he took such traditional values as filial piety (respect for one's parents and ancestors) and propriety (regard for proper decorum) and turned them into moral principles. He insisted that human beings are moral creatures with social obligations and are, by that fact, obliged to comport themselves humanely and with integrity. He also believed that humans, or at least males, are capable of perfecting themselves as upright individuals. His ideal moral agent was the gentleman who cultivated virtue through study and imitation of the Way of the past. This person, by knowing the good, would choose the good. What is more, he would act as an example to others, who would irresistibly follow the path he set along the Way of Goodness.

Confucius longed to hold a position of authority where he could put his ideas into practice, but this was ultimately denied him. He then turned to teaching, seeking out students who showed promise of rising to eminent posts in the various states of feudal China. In this way he hoped his philosophy of life and government — his moral Way — would transform Chinese society to the point where it returned to the values and practices of the age of Tan, Duke of Chou, a twelfth-century legislator and consolidator of the Chou Dynasty, whom Confucius deeply admired.

Confucius's pupils were few; we know the names of only about twenty. Although he appears to have been a widely respected sage, he was only one of many itinerant teachers of his age and probably not the most popular. There is reason to conclude he died believing himself a failure. Such failure should happen to us all. In time Confucianism would become virtually synonymous with Chinese culture, and it would play an almost equally important role in the evolution of Korean and Japanese thought.

As is true of so many great teachers whose words and example have placed a permanent stamp on a civilization, Confucius was not a productive writer. As far as we know, nothing he wrote or edited survives. Early Confucian disciples, however, transmitted to posterity a number of sayings ascribed to Confucius and his immediate pupils. In time these were gathered into a book known as *The Analects (Lun-yu)*. We do not know which of these maxims Confucius actually uttered, but collectively they provide us with the best available view of K'ung fu-tzu's teachings as remembered by those who knew and followed him.

Questions for Analysis

1. Confucius, like Lao Tzu, speaks of the Way and claims to teach it. How does his Way differ from that of Taoism? What do you think his attitude was to those who preached either the way of nonaction or the idea that there are no absolute standards of behavior?
2. What is Confucius's attitude toward spiritual questions?
3. What is a Confucian gentleman, and what role does he play in society?
4. What role, if any, do women play in Confucius's scheme?
5. How does Confucius's reverence for the virtue of filial piety fit into the whole fabric of his political and social philosophy?
6. What is Confucius's concept of the ideal state?

[*Filial Piety*]

Master Yu[1] said, Those who in private life behave well towards their parents and elder brothers, in public life seldom show a disposition to resist the authority of their superiors. And as for such men starting a revolution, no instance of it has ever occurred. It is upon the trunk[2] that a gentleman works. When that is firmly set up, the Way grows. And surely proper behavior towards parents and elder brothers is the trunk of Goodness. . . .

The Master said, In serving his father and mother a man may gently remonstrate with them. But if he sees that he has failed to change their opinion, he should resume an attitude of deference and not thwart them; may feel discouraged, but not resentful. . . .

The Master said, Behave in such a way that your father and mother have no anxiety about you, except concerning your health. . . .

The Master said, "Filial sons" nowadays are people who see to it that their parents get enough to eat. But even dogs and horses are cared for to that extent. If there is no feeling of respect, wherein lies the difference?

[*Propriety*]

The Master said, If a gentleman is frivolous, he will lose the respect of his inferiors and lack firm ground upon which to build up his education. First and foremost

1. One of Confucius's disciples. The following saying, although not ascribed to Confucius, sums up the Confucian virtue of filial piety.

2. Filial piety serves as the base or tree trunk of a gentleman's character.

he must learn to be faithful to his superiors, to keep promises, to refuse the friendship of all who are not like him.[3] And if he finds he has made a mistake, then he must not be afraid of admitting the fact and amending his ways. . . .

The Master said, The good man does not grieve that other people do not recognize his merits. His only anxiety is lest he should fail to recognize theirs. . . .

The Master said, The gentleman calls attention to the good points in others; he does not call attention to their defects. The small man does just the reverse of this. . . .

The Master said, If out of the three hundred *Songs*[4] I had to take one phrase to cover all my teaching, I would say "Let there be no evil in your thoughts."

[*Government*]

The Master said, He who rules by moral force is like the pole-star, which remains in its place while all the lesser stars do homage to it. . . .

The Master said, Govern the people by regulations, keep order among them by chastisements, and they will flee from you, and lose all self-respect. Govern them by moral force, keep order among them by ritual[5] and they will keep their self-respect and come to you of their own accord. . . .

Duke Ching of Ch'i[6] asked Master K'ung about government. Master K'ung replied saying, Let the prince be a prince, the minister a minister, the father a father and the son a son. . . .

Chi K'ang-tzu[7] asked Master K'ung about government, saying, Suppose I were to slay those who have not the Way in order to help those who have the Way, what would you think of it? Master K'ung replied saying, You are there to rule, not to slay. If you desire what is good, the people will at once be good. The essence of the gentleman is that of wind; the essence of small people is that of grass. And when a wind passes over the grass, it cannot choose but bend. . . .

The Master said, Only if the right sort of people had charge of a country for a hundred years would it become really possible to stop cruelty and do away with slaughter. How true the saying is! . . .

The Master said, Once a man has contrived to put himself aright, he will find no difficulty at all in filling any government post. But if he cannot put himself aright, how can he hope to succeed in putting others right? . . .

The Master said, To demand much from oneself and little from others is the way (for a ruler) to banish discontent.

[*The Gentleman*]

The Master said, A gentleman is not an implement.[8]

Tzu-kung[9] asked about the true gentleman. The Master said, He does not preach what he practices till he has practiced what he preaches.

---

3. Those who are not gentlemen because they seek profit rather than goodness.

4. The *Book of Songs* (Chapter 1).

5. Ritual (*li*) has two meanings here: proper performance of court and religious ceremonies, which bring the blessings of Heaven, and correct etiquette in all matters large and small. In this sense, it is leadership by example.

6. A powerful feudal lord who died in 490 B.C.

7. The lord of the state of Lu (died 469 B.C.), whom several of Confucius's disciples served.

8. A specialist, or technician.

9. A disciple whose diplomatic career spanned the period 495–468 B.C.

The Master said, A gentleman can see a question from all sides without bias. The small man is biased and can see a question only from one side. . . .

The Master said, A Divine Sage[10] I cannot hope ever to meet; the most I can hope for is to meet a true gentleman. The Master said, A faultless man I cannot hope ever to meet; the most I can hope for is to meet a man of fixed principles. Yet where all around I see Nothing pretending to be Something, Emptiness pretending to be Fullness, Penury pretending to be Affluence,[11] even a man of fixed principles will be none too easy to find.

Wealth and rank are what every man desires; but if they can only be retained to the detriment of the Way he professes, he must relinquish them. Poverty and obscurity are what every man detests; but if they can only be avoided to the detriment of the Way he professes, he must accept them. The gentleman who ever parts company with Goodness does not fulfill that name. Never for a moment does a gentleman quit the way of Goodness. He is never so harried but that he cleaves to this; never so tottering but that he cleaves to this. . . .

The Master said, A gentleman, in his plans, thinks of the Way; he does not think how he is going to make a living. Even farming sometimes entails times of shortage; and even learning may incidentally lead to high pay. But a gentleman's anxieties concern the progress of the Way; he has no anxiety concerning poverty.

[*Women*]

The Master said, Women and people of low birth are very hard to deal with. If you are friendly with them, they get out of hand, and if you keep your distance they resent it.

[*Goodness*]

The Master said, It is Goodness that gives to a neighborhood its beauty. One who is free to choose, yet does not prefer to dwell among the Good — how can he be accorded the name of wise? . . .

The Master said, I have never yet seen anyone whose desire to build up his moral power was as strong as sexual desire. . . .

Jan Jung[12] asked about Goodness. The Master said, Behave when away from home[13] as though you were in the presence of an important guest. Deal with the common people as though you were officiating at an important sacrifice. Do not do to others what you would not like yourself.[14] Then there will be no feelings of opposition to you, whether it is the affairs of a State that you are handling or the affairs of a Family.

[*The Spirits*]

Tzu-lu[15] asked how one should serve ghosts and spirits.[16] The Master said, Till you have learnt to serve men, how can you serve ghosts? Tzu-lu then ventured upon a question about the dead. The Master said, Till you know about the living, how are you to know about the dead? . . .

---

10. The Divine Sages were mythical, predynastic rulers of antiquity who possessed divine powers.

11. A reference to Taoist teachers.

12. A disciple.

13. When handling public affairs.

14. Compare this with the Judeo-Christian Golden Rule.

15. A disciple who predeceased Confucius in 480 B.C.

16. The spirits of ancestors.

Fan Ch'ih[17] asked about wisdom. The Master said, He who devotes himself to securing for his subjects what it is right they should have, who by respect for the Spirits keeps them at a distance,[18] may be termed wise. . . .

Someone asked for an explanation of the Ancestral Sacrifice.[19] The Master said, I do not know. Anyone who knew the explanation could deal with all things under Heaven as easily as I lay this here; and he laid his finger upon the palm of his hand.

Han Fei

THE WRITINGS OF MASTER HAN FEI

Taoism offered no active political program, whereas Confucius and his disciples preached a doctrine of benevolent reform based upon virtuous imitation of the past. A third school of thought that emerged in the chaos of the late Eastern Chou era was legalism, which rejected both the way of nature, as embraced by the Taoists, and Confucianism's emphasis on the primacy of the ways of antiquity. Legalist writers, to the contrary, emphasized law as government's formulative force and advocated a radical restructuring of society in ways that were totally rational and up-to-date.

Legalist thought and practice reached their apogee in the late third century B.C. in the writings of Han Fei and the policies of Emperor Ch'in Shih Huang Ti. Han Fei was a prince of the state of Han who defected to its chief rival, the state of Ch'in, but eventually ran afoul of Ch'in's chief minister, Li Ssu (d. 208 B.C.), and was forced to commit suicide in 233 B.C. Before he died, he composed a number of essays on how to construct a stable and peaceful state. The following selections present Han Fei's major principles of political philosophy.

Questions for Analysis

1. In Han Fei's ideal state, what is the supreme governing authority, the will of the ruler or the law?
2. What roles do individuality and private initiative play in Han Fei's ideal state?
3. What are the "Two Handles" and how important are they to a legalist state?

---

17. A disciple.

18. The Chinese have traditionally believed that every human possesses two kinds of soul, a *hun* and a *po*. The *hun* normally dissipates at death, but the *po* becomes a spirit, which, if properly cared for by its family, will probably do its descendants no harm and may even help them. If the *po* is neglected, it can, and most likely will, interfere in harmful ways in the lives of those guilty of this major breach of filial piety.

19. The ceremony of offering sacrifices to the spirits of one's ancestors.

4. Han Fei was educated as a Confucian. Can you discover any elements of Confucian thought in his legalist philosophy? On what points would he and Confucius agree? Where would they disagree?
5. Why do you think legalism appealed to some people?

Having Regulations

No country is permanently strong. Nor is any country permanently weak. If conformers to law are strong, the country is strong; if conformers to law are weak, the country is weak. . . .

Any ruler able to expel private crookedness and uphold public law, finds the people safe and the state in order; and any ruler able to expunge private action and act on public law, finds his army strong and his enemy weak. So, find out men following the discipline of laws and regulations, and place them above the body of officials. Then the sovereign cannot be deceived by anybody with fraud and falsehood. . . .

Therefore, the intelligent sovereign makes the law select men and makes no arbitrary promotion himself. He makes the law measure merits and makes no arbitrary regulation himself. In consequence, able men cannot be obscured, bad characters cannot be disguised; falsely praised fellows cannot be advanced, wrongly defamed people cannot be degraded. Accordingly, between ruler and minister distinction becomes clear and order is attained. Thus it suffices only if the sovereign can scrutinize laws. . . .

To govern the state by law is to praise the right and blame the wrong.

The law does not fawn on the noble; the string does not yield to the crooked. Whatever the law applies to, the wise cannot reject nor can the brave defy. Punishment for fault never skips ministers, reward for good never misses commoners. Therefore, to correct the faults of the high, to rebuke the vices of the low, to suppress disorders, to decide against mistakes, to subdue the arrogant, to straighten the crooked, and to unify the folkways of the masses, nothing could match the law. To warn the officials and overawe the people, to rebuke obscenity and danger, and to forbid falsehood and deceit, nothing could match penalty. If penalty is severe, the noble cannot discriminate against the humble. If law is definite, the superiors are esteemed and not violated. If the superiors are not violated, the sovereign will become strong and able to maintain the proper course of government. Such was the reason why the early kings esteemed legalism and handed it down to posterity. Should the lord of men discard law and practice selfishness, high and low would have no distinction.

The Two Handles

The means whereby the intelligent ruler controls his ministers are two handles only. The two handles are chastisement and commendation. What are meant by chastisement and commendation? To inflict death or torture upon culprits, is called chastisement; to bestow encouragements or rewards on men of merit, is called commendation.

Ministers are afraid of censure and punishment but fond of encouragement and reward. Therefore, if the lord of men uses the handles of chastisement and commendation, all ministers will dread his severity and turn to his liberality. The villainous ministers of the age are different. To men they hate they would by securing the handle of chastisement from the sovereign ascribe crimes; on men they love they would by securing the handle of commendation from the sovereign bestow rewards. Now supposing the lord of men placed the authority of punishment and the profit of reward not in his hands but let the ministers administer the affairs of reward and punishment instead, then everybody in the country would fear the ministers and slight the ruler, and turn to the ministers and away from the ruler. This is the calamity of the ruler's loss of the handles of chastisement and commendation.

Ssu-ma Ch'ien

RECORDS OF THE GRAND HISTORIAN

Born around 145 B.C., Ssu-ma Ch'ien was educated in the classics, served his emperor on a variety of missions, and in 107 succeeded his father, Ssu-ma Tan, as Grand Historian of the Han Court. Even before rising to this position, Ssu-ma Ch'ien avidly collected historical records during his travels on imperial service, and, upon his appointment as Grand Historian, he embarked on the initial project of collecting additional sources, especially from the imperial library, and verifying his facts. Only in 104 was he ready to begin composition, a labor that lasted until 91 B.C. The result was a history monumental in scope. In 130 chapters he traced the story of China from the age of the legendary Five Emperors, who preceded the Hsia and Shang dynasties, to his own day. In later years he made small additions and changes and probably continued to revise his masterpiece in minor ways until his death, which occurred at an unknown date.

The result was well worth the effort. The Chinese rightly consider the *Records of the Grand Historian* to be premodern China's greatest piece of historical writing. Ssu-ma Ch'ien aimed at telling the whole truth, insofar as he could discover it, and in pursuit of that truth he scoured all available archives. As he composed his work, he included verbatim many of the records he had discovered, thereby providing modern historians with a wealth of documentary evidence that would otherwise be lost, for many of the sources Ssu-ma Ch'ien quoted, paraphrased, and cited exist today only in his history.

In the first excerpt the Grand Historian describes a memorial that China's First Emperor, Ch'in Shih Huang Ti (221–210 B.C.), built to proclaim his accomplishments. The second selection tells of an edict of 213 that banned virtually all nonlegalist literature.

Questions for Analysis

1. Of what accomplishments does the emperor boast?
2. Why does this memorial place so much emphasis on the government's standardization of society?

3. What definition of good government does this memorial imply?
4. Does the inscription contain any claims Confucius would have applauded?
5. What would a Taoist think of the emperor's policies?
6. How and for what reason did Li Ssu reject Confucian principles?
7. Why do you think books on medicine, divination, and agriculture were exempted from the general prohibition?
8. Imagine a series of conversations among a Taoist, a Confucian, and a legalist. How would each react to the following issues?

    What is the purpose of good government?
    What role does morality play in formulating law?
    What are the qualities of a superior ruler?

The emperor had a tower built on Mount Langya and a stone inscription set up to praise the power of Ch'in and make clear his will. The inscription read:

In the twenty-eighth year of his reign[1]
A new age is inaugurated by the Emperor;
Rules and measures are rectified,
The myriad things set in order,
Human affairs are made clear
And there is harmony between fathers and sons.
The Emperor in his sagacity, benevolence and justice
Has made all laws and principles manifest.
He set forth to pacify the east,
To inspect officers and men;
This great task accomplished
He visited the coast.
Great are the Emperor's achievements,
Men attend diligently to basic tasks,
Farming is encouraged, secondary pursuits discouraged,
All the common people prosper;
All men under the sky
Toil with a single purpose;
Tools and measures are made uniform,
The written script is standardized;
Wherever the sun and moon shine,
Wherever one can go by boat or by carriage,
Men carry out their orders
And satisfy their desires;
For our Emperor in accordance with the time
Has regulated local customs,
Made waterways and divided up the land.
Caring for the common people,
He works day and night without rest;
He defines the laws, leaving nothing in doubt,
Making known what is forbidden.
The local officials have their duties,
Administration is smoothly carried out,
All is done correctly, all according to plan.
The Emperor in his wisdom
Inspects all four quarters of his realm;
High and low, noble and humble,
None dare overshoot the mark;
No evil or impropriety is allowed,
All strive to be good men and true,

1. Ch'in Shih Huang Ti had ruled the state of Ch'in as King Cheng since 247 B.C. (His reign as First Ch'in emperor dates from 221–210 B.C.)

And exert themselves in tasks great and small;
None dares to idle or ignore his duties,
But in far-off, remote places
Serious and decorous administrators
Work steadily, just and loyal.
Great is the virtue of our Emperor
Who pacifies all four corners of the earth,
Who punishes traitors, roots out evil men,
And with profitable measures brings prosperity.
Tasks are done at the proper season,
All things flourish and grow;
The common people know peace
And have laid aside weapons and armor;
Kinsmen care for each other,
There are no robbers or thieves;
Men delight in his rule,
All understanding the law and discipline.
The universe entire
Is our Emperor's realm,
Extending west to the Desert,
South to where the houses face north,
East to the East Ocean,
North to beyond Tahsia;
Wherever human life is found,
All acknowledge his suzerainty,
His achievements surpass those of the Five Emperors,[2]
His kindness reaches even the beasts of the field;
All creatures benefit from his virtue,
All live in peace at home.

. . .

Chunyu Yueh, a scholar of Chi . . . said, "I have yet to hear of anything able to endure that was not based on ancient precedents. . . ."

The emperor ordered his ministers to debate this question.

The prime minister Li Ssu said, "The Five Emperors did not emulate each other nor did the Three Dynasties[3] adopt each other's ways, yet all had good government. This is no paradox, because times had changed. Now Your Majesty has built up this great empire to endure for generations without end. Naturally this passes the comprehension of a foolish pedant. Chunyu Yueh spoke about the Three Dynasties, but they are hardly worth taking as examples. In times gone by different barons fought among themselves and gathered wandering scholars. Today, however, the empire is at peace, all laws and order come from one single source, the common people support themselves by farming and handicrafts, while students study the laws and prohibitions.

"Now these scholars learn only from the old, not from the new, and use their learning to oppose our rule and confuse the black-headed people.[4] As prime minister I must speak out on pain of death. In former times when the world, torn by chaos and disorder, could not be united, different states arose and argued from the past to condemn the present, using empty rhetoric to cover up and confuse the real issues, and employing their learning to oppose what was established by authority. Now Your Majesty has conquered the whole world, distinguished between black and white, set unified standards. Yet these opinionated scholars get together to slander the laws and judge each new decree according to their own school of thought, opposing it secretly in their hearts while discussing it openly in the streets. They brag to the sovereign to win fame, put forward strange arguments to

2. Five mythical emperors of predynastic China.

3. Hsia, Shang, and Chou.

4. The common people.

gain distinction, and incite the mob to spread rumors. If this is not prohibited, the sovereign's prestige will suffer and factions will be formed among his subjects. Far better put a stop to it!

"I humbly propose that all historical records but those of Ch'in be burned. If anyone who is not a court scholar dares to keep the ancient songs, historical records or writings of the hundred schools, these should be confiscated and burned by the provincial governor and army commander. Those who in conversation dare to quote the old songs and records[5] should be publicly executed; those who use old precedents to oppose the new order should have their families wiped out; and officers who know of such cases but fail to report them should be punished in the same way.

"If thirty days after the issuing of this order the owners of these books have still not had them destroyed, they should have their faces tattooed and be condemned to hard labor at the Great Wall.[6] The only books which need not be destroyed are those dealing with medicine, divination, and agriculture. Those who want to study the law can learn it from the officers." The emperor sanctioned this proposal.

Hellenic Civilization: A Rational Inquiry into Life

During the sixth century B.C., certain Greeks, beginning with a semilegendary figure known as Thales (ca 640–562 B.C.), started looking at the world as an objective phenomenon that could be studied in a rational, systematic manner. These thinkers, who sought to discover the physical underpinnings of the universe, are acknowledged as ancient Hellas's first philosophers and scientists and the persons who established the Greek intellectual tradition of rational inquiry into all aspects of the physical and moral world.

As important as reason was in the formation of Greek thought, it never threatened to displace totally myth, mysticism, and religion. We would very much misunderstand Greek civilization by concluding that rational inquiry dominated every element of Greek life from the sixth century onward. Indeed, the nonrational permeated Greek society. This fact should not be surprising nor should it cause us to underevaluate the achievements of Greek rationalists, whose modes of analysis became the hallmark of Greek civilization.

As we survey the development of Greek rationalism, it would be helpful to keep in mind the broad division of Greek history favored by historians. The period from about 750 B.C. to the death of Alexander the Great in 323 B.C. is known as the Hel-

5. A reference to the *Book of Songs* and the *Book of History* (Chapter 1).

6. The First Emperor began the process of linking frontier fortresses together to form the Great Wall. Labor on the Great Wall, which was tantamount to a death sentence, was a common penalty under Ch'in.

lenic Age, because the people we call Greeks referred to themselves as *Hellenes* and their land as *Hellas.* (It was the Romans who began the tradition of calling all Hellenes *Greeks.*) The period from 323 to 30 B.C. is known as the Hellenistic Age. In this case, Hellenist means a non-Hellene who adopted the Greek language and culture.

During the Hellenic Age the Greek world was very much a frontier society along the western periphery of the ancient civilized world. As a result, the Greeks were able to draw from the experiences of their more developed neighbors while simultaneously enjoying a certain amount of freedom to experiment culturally, especially in the areas of politics and thought. This age was characterized by general Greek independence from foreign domination, political decentralization, intense rivalry among Hellas's many city-states, and a deep-seated ethnocentrism and even contempt for the non-Greek world. It was the Hellenes who coined the term *barbarian* and used it to refer to all non-Greek speakers, even the most civilized, because their alien languages sounded to Greek ears like so much babble or "bar-bar-bar." The two characteristic and dominating events of this period were the Persian wars (499–450 B.C.) and the Peloponnesian War (431–404 B.C.). In the first, Greeks, under the leadership of Athens and Sparta, successfully withstood the threat of Persian domination. In the second, again under Athenian and Spartan leadership, the whole Greek world was embroiled in a bitter family bloodletting.

Under the leadership of King Philip and his son Alexander (336–323 B.C.), the Macedonians finally forced internal peace and unity on the Greeks. Alexander the Great's conquest of the Persian Empire and his penetration even into northwest India ushered in a new age for western Eurasia. Where the Hellenic world had been parochial, the Hellenistic world was cosmopolitan and culturally eclectic. The armies of Alexander and the state-builders who followed helped create a cultural amalgamation of Middle Eastern, North African, and even some Indian elements, over which lay a deep layer of Greek language, thought, and artistic expression. What emerged was, to use a Greek word, a cultural *ecumene* (a unity of civilized peoples). This world culture stretched from Afghanistan and northwest India in the east to the regions of the central Mediterranean in the west, and much of it was Greek in form and inspiration. Although the Roman Empire later expanded the boundaries of this rich cultural ecumene into northwest Europe, it is convenient to date the end of the Hellenistic Age as 30 B.C., when Egypt, the last independent and arguably most brilliant of the Hellenistic kingdoms, passed into Roman hands.

Thucydides

HISTORY OF THE PELOPONNESIAN WAR

Before the age of Philip and Alexander of Macedon, Hellas was a shared civilization, not an empire or kingdom. It was divided into a number of competing city-states or *poleis* (the plural form of *polis*), which were organized along diverse political, social, and economic lines. Some were dictatorships, many were oligarchies (rule by the aristocratic few), and a few, like Athens, were democracies.

Between 461 and 429 B.C. Pericles (ca 495–429) presided over the final stages of the evolution of Athenian democracy, and in 431 he led Athens into the Peloponnesian War against the oligarchic polis of Sparta and its allies. The war dragged on for a generation, ending in 404 with a Spartan victory. In the early stages of the conflict, it had seemed as though there was no way Athens could lose the war. In 430 a confident Athens paused to honor those citizens who had fallen in battle during the first year of fighting and called upon Pericles, its unofficial First Citizen, to deliver the eulogy. Pericles used the occasion to praise the polis for which those citizens had lived and died.

Among those in attendance was Thucydides (ca 460–400 B.C.), an avid student of political affairs who participated fully in Athens's cultural environment. Later Thucydides would suffer exile from Athens because of his perceived failure as a military leader. He used his enforced retirement to study the war and write its history.

Thucydides admitted that the speeches in his *History* were not verbatim accounts, but he did attempt to preserve the sense of what was said. We can be fairly certain that his words convey the essence of Pericles' message, and that message tells us a good deal about Hellenic secular culture.

Just as telling is Thucydides' description of the plague that ravaged Athens in 430. Hippocrates of Cos (ca 460–377), the most celebrated physician of Greek antiquity, had recently taught his medical theories and clinical methods in Athens, where they became part of the city's intellectual atmosphere. The core of Hippocrates' teachings was that diseases are purely natural phenomena. If physicians could accumulate enough detailed notes on any disease, they would eventually be able to understand and treat it. Such a view of illness was a direct product of the intellectual revolution begun a century earlier.

Questions for Analysis

1. How does Pericles define Athenian democracy? According to him, what sort of citizens does this democracy breed? How does Athens help its citizens achieve their full potential? According to Pericles, what role should public affairs play in a citizen's life?
2. In his idealized portrait of Athens, Pericles contrasts Athens's spirit with that of Sparta. According to him, how do the Spartans live?
3. Why is Athens, in Pericles' words, "the school of Hellas"?
4. Pericles claims that Athenians respect authority and the laws. How, if at all, does this reverence for the rule of law differ from legalism?
5. How does Pericles' speech provide evidence of Hellenic secularism, particularly its preoccupation with the human individual, the life of the polis, and rational analysis?
6. How "scientific" is Thucydides' account of the plague and its social consequences?

7. How does Thucydides artfully demonstrate the fragility of Athens's social and political system?
8. Thucydides has been characterized as a hard-headed social scientist. Is this a fair description?

During the same winter, in accordance with an old national custom, the funeral of those who first fell in this war was celebrated by the Athenians at the public charge. . . . Over those who were the first buried Pericles was chosen to speak. At the fitting moment he advanced from the sepulchre to a lofty stage, which had been erected in order that he might be heard as far as possible by the multitude, and spoke as follows: . . .

"I will speak first of our ancestors, for it is right and becoming that now, when we are lamenting the dead, a tribute should be paid to their memory. There has never been a time when they did not inhabit this land, which by their valor they have handed down from generation to generation, and we have received from them a free state. But if they were worthy of praise, still more were our fathers, who added to their inheritance, and after many a struggle transmitted to us their sons this great empire. And we ourselves assembled here to-day, who are still most of us in the vigor of life, have chiefly done the work of improvement, and have richly endowed our city with all things, so that she is sufficient for herself both in peace and war. Of the military exploits by which our various possessions were acquired, or of the energy with which we or our fathers drove back the tide of war, Hellenic or Barbarian, I will not speak; for the tale would be long and is familiar to you. But before I praise the dead, I should like to point out by what principles of action we rose to power, and under what institutions and through what manner of life our empire became great. For I conceive that such thoughts are not unsuited to the occasion, and that this numerous assembly of citizens and strangers may profitably listen to them.

"Our form of government does not enter into rivalry with the institutions of others. We do not copy our neighbors, but are an example to them. It is true that we are called a democracy, for the administration is in the hands of the many and not of the few. But while the law secures equal justice to all alike in their private disputes, the claim of excellence is also recognized; and when a citizen is in any way distinguished, he is preferred to the public service, not as a matter of privilege, but as the reward of merit. Neither is poverty a bar, but a man may benefit his country whatever be the obscurity of his condition. There is no exclusiveness in our public life, and in our private intercourse we are not suspicious of one another, nor angry with our neighbor if he does what he likes; we do not put on sour looks at him which, though harmless, are not pleasant. While we are thus unconstrained in our private intercourse, a spirit of reverence pervades our public acts; we are prevented from doing wrong by respect for authority and for the laws, having an especial regard to those which are ordained for the protection of the injured as well as to those unwritten laws which bring upon the transgressor of them the reprobation of the general sentiment.

"And we have not forgotten to provide for our weary spirits many relaxations from toil; we have regular games and sacrifices throughout the year; at home the style of our life is refined; and the delight which we daily feel in all these things helps to banish melancholy. Because of the greatness of our city the fruits of the whole earth flow in upon us; so that we enjoy the goods of other countries as freely as of our own.

"Then, again, our military training is in many respects superior to that of our adversaries. Our city is thrown open to the world, and we never expel a foreigner or prevent him from seeing or learning anything of which the secret if revealed to an enemy might profit him. We rely not upon management or trickery, but upon our own hearts and hands. And in the matter of education, whereas they from early youth are always undergoing laborious exercises which are to make them brave, we live at ease, and yet are equally ready to face the perils which they face. . . .

"If then we prefer to meet danger with a light heart but without laborious training, and with a courage which is gained by habit and not enforced by law, are we not greatly the gainers? Since we do not anticipate the pain, although, when the hour comes, we can be as brave as those who never allow themselves to rest; and thus too our city is equally admirable in peace and in war. For we are lovers of the beautiful, yet simple in our tastes, and we cultivate the mind without loss of manliness. Wealth we employ, not for talk and ostentation, but when there is a real use for it. To avow poverty with us is no disgrace; the true disgrace is in doing nothing to avoid it. An Athenian citizen does not neglect the state because he takes care of his own household; and even those of us who are engaged in business have a very fair idea of politics. We alone regard a man who takes no interest in public affairs, not as a harmless, but as a useless character; and if few of us are originators, we are all sound judges of a policy. The great impediment to action is, in our opinion, not discussion, but the want of that knowledge which is gained by discussion preparatory to action. For we have a peculiar power of thinking before we act and of acting too, whereas other men are courageous from ignorance but hesitate upon reflection. And they are surely to be esteemed the bravest spirits who, having the clearest sense both of the pains and pleasures of life, do not on that account shrink from danger. . . . To sum up: I say that Athens is the school of Hellas, and that the individual Athenian in his own person seems to have the power of adapting himself to the most varied forms of action with the utmost versatility and grace. This is no passing and idle word, but truth and fact; and the assertion is verified by the position to which these qualities have raised the state. For in the hour of trial Athens alone among her contemporaries is superior to the report of her. No enemy who comes against her is indignant at the reverses which he sustains at the hands of such a city; no subject complains that his masters are unworthy of him. And we shall assuredly not be without witnesses; there are mighty monuments of our power which will make us the wonder of this and of succeeding ages; we shall not need the praises of Homer or of any other panegyrist whose poetry may please for the moment, although his representation of the facts will not bear the light of day. For we have compelled every land and every sea to open a path for our valor, and have everywhere planted eternal memorials of our friendship and of our enmity. Such is the city for whose sake these men nobly fought and died; they could not bear the thought that she might be taken from them; and every one of us who survive should gladly toil on her behalf.

"I have dwelt upon the greatness of Athens because I want to show you that we are contending for a higher prize than those who enjoy none of these privileges, and to establish by manifest proof the merit of these men whom I am now commemorating. Their loftiest praise has been already spoken. For in magnifying the city I have magnified them, and men like them whose virtues made her glorious. . . ."

Such was the order of the funeral celebrated in this winter, with the end of which ended the first year of the Peloponnesian War. As soon as summer returned, the Peloponnesian[1] army, comprising as before two-thirds of the force of each confederate state, under the command of the Lacedaemonian[2] king Archidamus, the son of Zeuxidamus, invaded Attica,[3] where they established themselves and ravaged the country. They had not been there many days when the plague broke out at Athens for the first time. A similar disorder is said to have previously smitten many places, particularly Lemnos,[4] but there is no record of such a pestilence occurring elsewhere, or of so great a destruction of human life. For a while physicians, in ignorance of the nature of the disease, sought to apply remedies; but it was in vain, and they themselves were among the first victims, because they oftenest came into contact with it. No human art was of any avail, and as to supplications in temples, enquiries of oracles, and the like, they were utterly useless, and at last men were overpowered by the calamity and gave them all up.

The disease is said to have begun south of Egypt in Aethiopia; thence it descended[5] into Egypt and Libya, and after spreading over the greater part of the Persian empire, suddenly fell upon Athens. It first attacked the inhabitants of the Piraeus,[6] and it was supposed that the Peloponnesians had poisoned the cisterns, no conduits having as yet been made there. It afterwards reached the upper city, and then the mortality became far greater. As to its probable origin or the causes which might or could have produced such a disturbance of nature, every man, whether a physician or not, will give his own opinion. But I shall describe its actual course, and the symptoms by which any one who knows them beforehand may recognize the disorder should it ever reappear. For I was myself attacked and witnessed the sufferings of others.

The season was admitted to have been remarkably free from ordinary sickness; and if anybody was already ill of any other disease, it was absorbed in this. Many who were in perfect health, all in a moment, and without any apparent reason, were seized with violent heats in the head and with redness and inflammation of the eyes. Internally the throat and the tongue were quickly suffused with blood, and the breath became unnatural and fetid. There followed sneezing and hoarseness; in a short time the disorder, accompanied by a violent cough, reached the chest; then fastening lower down, it would move the stomach and bring on all the vomits of bile to which physicians have ever given names; and they were very distressing. An ineffectual retching

---

1. The Spartans and their allies. Sparta was located in the Peloponnesus, the southern peninsula of the Greek mainland.

2. Lacedaemonia was the region of the Peloponnesus in which Sparta was situated.

3. The peninsula on which Athens was located.

4. An Aegean island.

5. Since the Nile flows northward, one "descends" from south to north.

6. Athens's port.

producing violent convulsions attacked most of the sufferers; some as soon as the previous symptoms had abated, others not until long afterwards. The body externally was not so very hot to the touch, nor yet pale; it was of a livid color inclining to red, and breaking out in pustules and ulcers. But the internal fever was intense; the sufferers could not bear to have on them even the finest linen garment; they insisted on being naked, and there was nothing which they longed for more eagerly than to throw themselves into cold water. And many of those who had no one to look after them actually plunged into the cisterns, for they were tormented by unceasing thirst, which was not in the least assuaged whether they drank little or much. They could not sleep; a restlessness which was intolerable never left them. While the disease was at its height the body, instead of wasting away, held out amid these sufferings in a marvelous manner, and either they died on the seventh or ninth day, not of weakness, for their strength was not exhausted, but of internal fever, which was the end of most; or, if they survived, then the disease descended into the bowels and there produced violent ulceration; severe diarrhoea at the same time set in, and at a later stage caused exhaustion, which finally with few exceptions carried them off. For the disorder which had originally settled in the head passed gradually through the whole body, and, if a person got over the worst, would often seize the extremities and leave its mark, attacking the privy parts and the fingers and the toes, and some escaped with the loss of these, some with the loss of their eyes. Some again had no sooner recovered than they were seized with a forgetfulness of all things and knew neither themselves nor their friends.

The malady took a form not to be described, and the fury with which it fastened upon each sufferer was too much for human nature to endure. There was one circumstance in particular which distinguished it from ordinary diseases. The birds and animals which feed on human flesh, although so many bodies were lying unburied, either never came near them, or died if they touched them. This was proved by a remarkable disappearance of the birds of prey, who were not to be seen either about the bodies or anywhere else; while in the case of the dogs the fact was even more obvious, because they live with man.

Such was the general nature of the disease: I omit many strange peculiarities which characterized individual cases. None of the ordinary sicknesses attacked any one while it lasted, or, if they did, they ended in the plague. Some of the sufferers died from want of care, others equally who were receiving the greatest attention. No single remedy could be deemed a specific; for that which did good to one did harm to another. No constitution was of itself strong enough to resist or weak enough to escape the attacks; the disease carried off all alike and defied every mode of treatment. Most appalling was the despondency which seized upon any one who felt himself sickening; for he instantly abandoned his mind to despair and, instead of holding out, absolutely threw away his chance of life. Appalling too was the rapidity with which men caught the infection; dying like sheep if they attended on one another; and this was the principal cause of mortality. When they were afraid to visit one another, the sufferers died in their solitude, so that many houses were empty because there had been no one left to take care of the sick; or if they ventured they perished, especially those who aspired to heroism. For they went to see their friends without thought of themselves and were ashamed to leave them, even at a time when the very relations of the dying were at last growing weary and ceased to make lamentations, overwhelmed by the vastness of the calamity. But whatever instances there may have been of such devotion, more often the sick and the dying were tended by the pitying care of those who had recovered, because they knew the course of the disease and were themselves free from apprehension. For no one was ever attacked a second time, or not with a fatal result. All men congratulated them, and they themselves, in the excess of their joy at the moment, had an innocent fancy that they could not die of any other sickness.

The crowding of the people out of the country into the city aggravated the misery; and the newly-arrived suffered most. For, having no houses of their own, but inhabiting in the height of summer stifling huts, the mortality among them was dreadful, and they perished in wild disorder. The dead lay as they had died, one upon another, while others hardly alive wallowed in the streets and crawled about every fountain craving for water. The temples in which they lodged were full of the corpses of those who died in them; for the violence of the calamity was such that men, not knowing where to turn, grew reckless of all law, human and divine. The customs which had hitherto been observed at funerals were universally violated, and they buried their dead each one as best he could. Many, having no proper appliances, because the deaths in their household had been so frequent, made no scruple of using the burial-place of others. When one man had raised a funeral pile, others would come, and throwing on their dead first, set fire to it; or when some other corpse was already burning, before they could be stopped would throw their own dead upon it and depart.

There were other and worse forms of lawlessness which the plague introduced at Athens. Men who had hitherto concealed their indulgence in pleasure now grew bolder. For, seeing the sudden change, — how the rich died in a moment, and those who had nothing immediately inherited their property, — they reflected that life and riches were alike transitory, and they resolved to enjoy themselves while they could, and to think only of pleasure. Who would be willing to sacrifice himself to the law of honor when he knew not whether he would ever live to be held in honor? The pleasure of the moment and any sort of thing which conduced to it took the place both of honor and of expediency. No fear of God or law of man deterred a criminal. Those who saw all perishing alike, thought that the worship or neglect of the Gods made no difference. For offences against human law no punishment was to be feared; no one would live long enough to be called to account. Already a far heavier sentence had been passed and was hanging over a man's head; before that fell, why should he not take a little pleasure?

Euripides

MEDEA

Pericles concluded that Athens had become "the school of Hellas" because of the freedom its citizens enjoyed. As citizens with a vested interest in the polis, its people could develop independence and self-reliance easily and in many different directions. There is likely much truth to Pericles' conclusion, and undoubtedly this freedom contributed substantially to Athens's vitality as an intellectual and artistic center. Yet we must remember that in Pericles' day the benefits of citizenship were restricted to a minority of the population — free, native-born, male adults. Moreover, a number of Hellenic rationalists, including some Athenians, found the atmosphere of city-states that were dictatorships and oligarchies more attractive or less threatening than the often tumultuous democracy of Athens. One notable expatriate from Athens was the playwright Euripides (ca 480–406 B.C.).

While Hippocrates studied the clinical course of physical diseases, Euripides specialized in diagnosing emotional disorders and mental breakdowns, especially those brought on by social ills. Deep compassion underlay his dissections of tortured human psyches. Although he sought more to understand than to judge, his extant plays show him to have been an outspoken critic of the indignities suffered by those whom Athenian society exploited: war victims, slaves, foreigners, and especially women.

Athenian women lived in a society that accorded them little status and less freedom. They dominate, however, most of Euripides' extant plays. His heroines differ among themselves in character and situation, but all share several qualities. Each is memorable and a powerful personality in her own right. Each also, in differing degrees, is a social victim and consequently displays the aberrant behavior of a person denied the full range of human expression.

Euripides possessed more than just a voice of indignation and a strong social conscience. He was able, through his art, to analyze rationally and coolly the terrible personal and social consequences of exploitation in works that his fellow citizens found fascinating but disturbing. His plays were always well attended, yet the playwright's more than ninety works, composed over a career of some fifty years, won only five first prizes, one of which was posthumous. Late in life the aged artist-psychologist was forced to leave Athens, probably because of his outspoken opposition to Athenian atrocities in the Peloponnesian War. Eventually he took up residence in the wilds of far-off Macedon.

A quarter of a century earlier, on the eve of the outbreak of the Peloponnesian War, Euripides produced *Medea,* ironically a play revolving around a mythical exile. The story tells how Medea, a "barbarian" woman from the region of the Black Sea, had fallen in love with the adventurer Jason and resolved to assist him in his quest for the Golden Fleece, no matter the price. The price was high. She killed her brother and betrayed her father. Eventually she, Jason, and their two children arrived at Corinth as refugees. Here Jason abandoned Medea and became engaged to King Creon's daughter. Creon, perceiving Medea and her children as a threat and embarrassment, orders them to leave Corinth.

Love and hate, emotions so clearly allied, soon become one and the same in Medea. Eventually she kills Creon, his daughter, and her own two children before magically escaping. Here, in the opening scene, Euripides establishes the play's theme and provides clear hints of the horrors to come.

Questions for Analysis

1. The play takes place within a mythic framework. How can we be certain that Euripides was commenting on contemporary social problems?
2. What does the evidence tell us specifically about the status of women and minors in Athenian society?
3. What does Medea's speech tell us about the status of foreigners and other noncitizens in Greek poleis?

The scene is **Corinth,** *in front of* **Medea's** *house.*

Enter aged **Nurse,** *who accompanied* **Medea** *from Colchis and now serves as nurse of* **Medea's** *children*

Nurse. How I wish that the ship Argo[1] had never flown between the blue Clashing Rocks to Colchis,[2] that the pine had never been cut down to make oars for the hands of those princes who sought the Golden Fleece for Pelias![3] For then my mistress would never have fallen in love with Jason and sailed with him to the towers of Iolchus,[4] she would never have persuaded the daughters of Pelias to kill their father;[5] she would never have come to live in this land of Corinth[6] with her husband and children.

To be sure, the people here were pleased when she came. She helped Jason in every way. They never had arguments, and it's a happy home when husband and wife agree. But now love has sickened, and everything is hatred between them. Jason has betrayed his children and my mistress. He is taking to his bed the royal princess, and wretched Medea, outraged, cries aloud the promises he gave her, their right hands clasped in loyalty to each other, the greatest pledge there is, and summons the gods to witness how Jason repays all she did for him. She lies without food, her body smitten with grief, wasting away all the time in tears, brooding over the wrong done her by her husband. She doesn't lift her face from the floor, she's like a rock or a wave of the sea, deaf to her friends' advice, turning away from them as she moans for her father, her native land, and the home she deserted to follow a man who has now dishonored her.

Yes, poor woman, she has learned from disaster what it is to lose one's country. She even hates her children, they give her no joy when she looks at them. I'm afraid she has something terrible in mind, for in her sullen fury she won't put up with being insulted. I know her! What will she

---

1. The ship Jason captained in his search for the Golden Fleece.

2. Medea's homeland along the eastern shores of the Black Sea.

3. Jason's uncle, who sent Jason to Colchis to secure the Golden Fleece.

4. Jason's homeland in Thessaly, northern Greece.

5. Medea was a witch and dispatched the evil Pelias by duping his daughters through her magical arts.

6. Because of Pelias's death, Jason, Medea, and their children sought refuge in Corinth, which is in the Peloponnesus.

do? Will she go silently into a bedroom and drive a dagger through someone's heart? Or will she kill the King and the bridegroom and then pay for it with even greater suffering? A terrible woman she is, and no one will easily harm her and sing a song of triumph.

But here come the children, through with their morning sport. How little they know of their mother's troubles, for the mind of the young does not take to grief.

Enter **Children** *and* **Attendant.**

Medea *(within the house).* O God!
Wretched am I and full of woe,
How I wish I were dead!

Nurse. Do you hear that, dearest children? Your mother's
Heart is racked, her fury full.
Hasten quickly inside the house,
And don't approach within her sight,
Don't go near her, but guard against
The savage nature and raging hate
Of her self-willed heart.
Come now, go in as fast as you can.
For a cloud has arisen above the earth,
A cloud which will quickly burst into flame
With rising fury. What will she do,
That heart, proud and hard to control,
That spirit stung by injustice?

Medea *(within).* How I have suffered, suffered things
Full of agony! O cursed children
Of a hated mother, I wish you were dead!
May your father and our home perish!

Nurse. O God, O God, you pitiful woman!
What part have the children in their father's sin?
Why do you hate them? O my dears,
How I fear lest you will suffer!
For terrible are the moods of princes,
Ruled in few things, controlling many,
They find it hard to govern their wrath.
To learn to live as an equal with equals
Is better. In modest and quiet ways
May I come to life's end securely.
Best is the middle road. To use it
Is good for mortals, but any excess
Brings no advantage whatever to people.
Greater ruin, when he becomes outraged,
A god brings on prosperous homes.

As she finishes speaking, the **Chorus** *of women of Corinth, with their* **Leader,** *enter.*

Leader. I heard the voice, I heard the cry
Of the wretched
Woman of Colchis, savage still.
Tell me, old woman, why is she wailing
Within her home? I am unhappy
At the pain she suffers, for this home
I have come to regard with devotion.

Nurse. It's a home no more, all that is gone.
He has a bed in the royal palace,
She wastes her life away in her room.
My mistress allows herself no comfort
In words that her friends would offer.

Medea *(within).* O God,
Through my brain let a lightning bolt from heaven
Smite. What's the gain of living longer?
If only death would give me release
And I could leave hated life behind!

Chorus. Do you hear, Zeus, Earth, and Light,
What a cry the unfortunate wife
Utters of woe?
Why, wretched one, long for the last
Bed on which all of us once must lie?
Death will hasten all too soon,
Do not beg for it.
If your husband
Rejoices in a new marriage
That is common. Do not be agonized,
Zeus will befriend you. Do not so bitterly

Waste away grieving over your husband.

Medea *(within).* O great Themis[7] and Lady Artemis,[8]
You see what I suffer, after I bound
That cursed husband to me with great oaths.
Now may I see him and his bride
Crumble to dust in their new home,
They who dared wrong me without cause.
O father, O city, which I fled from
After I shamelessly slew my brother!

Nurse. Do you hear what she says, and how she calls
On Themis and Zeus with her entreaties,
Zeus the trusted steward of promises?
Certainly no mild revenge
Will satisfy my lady's anger.

Chorus. If only she would let us see her,
Let us soothe her with comforting words,
Then she might lessen her fierce rage
And her frenzy of spirit.
I would never be alien to my friends.
So go to her,
Bring her forth from the house,
Tell her friends are here.
Hurry before she harms those within,
For great grief journeys fast.

Nurse. I will do it, but I am afraid
I can never persuade my mistress.
Yet I will do this labor of love.
Like a lioness with her brood
She glares at us servants, whenever one
Approaches her with soothing words. . . .

Exit **Nurse** *into the house.*

Chorus. I heard the cry weighted with woe
Of the woman grieving over betrayal
By the husband who forsook her bed,
And she calls on the gods to avenge the injustice,
On Themis, keeper of oaths for Zeus,
Who led her to Hellas over the sea,
The sea to the north, through the endless gate
Of the Hellespont.[9]

Medea *enters.*

Medea. Women of Corinth, I have come out of the house so that you will not blame me for keeping to myself. For I know that many people are too reserved toward others; they stay at home too much or are not friendly in company, and some by sheer laziness get the reputation of not caring for their neighbors. But it isn't fair to judge and dislike at first sight people who have done no wrong, without understanding them. A foreigner must be especially careful to conform to the customs of the city, but even a Greek who lives entirely to himself is criticized for it and becomes unpopular, because people do not know him.

As for me, you must be tolerant, because a totally unexpected blow has fallen on me and ruined my life. I go about with all joy in life gone, friends, wishing only

7. The handmaiden of the gods, who presides over justice and order and serves as Zeus's counselor. She was the protector of the oppressed and goddess of the rights of hospitality.

8. Daughter of Zeus and Apollo's twin, she punished the wicked and impious with her arrows.

9. The narrow strait separating Europe from Asia Minor, it connects the Aegean with the Sea of Marmara. Its modern name is the Dardanelles.

to die. The man in whom all my happiness rested has turned out to be the basest of all men — my husband.

Of all things that live upon the earth and have intelligence we women are certainly the most wretched. First we must get a great amount of money to buy a husband, and then it's a master of our bodies that we take. Not to succeed in getting one brings even greater unhappiness. Then comes the greatest gamble of all — will he be kind or cruel to us? You know how hard it is for women to get a divorce, and it's impossible to reject a husband. So then, entering among new ways of life and customs, a bride must be a seer — she never learned those things at home — to get on well with this man who sleeps beside her. If by working our hardest we bring it about that our husbands stay with us without fretting, life is enviable, but if we fail we were better dead. When a man finds life unbearable at home he goes out to visit some friend, or to his club, and gets relief, but we have no one to look to but him. Then they say we lead a sheltered life at home, avoiding danger, while they go out to fight, but I say that's absurd. I'd sooner go three times into battle than bear one child.

But beyond these things we share in common, my situation is different from yours. You have this city and your father's homes, security, and the company of your friends. I am alone, without a city, and now I am outraged by the man who dragged me from a foreign country. I have no mother, no brother, no kin to take refuge with from this disaster.

There is only one thing I shall ask of you. If I find some way of repaying my husband for the way he has treated me, keep quiet about it. For you know that a woman is timid in other things, and is a coward in looking on cold steel, but whenever she is wronged in her marriage there is no heart so murderous as hers.

Plato

APOLOGIA

The *Dialogues* of Plato (427–348 B.C.) are the major source for the life and teachings of Socrates of Athens (ca 469–399 B.C.). Although Socrates left behind only a small number of students and no writings, he served a pivotal role in the development of Greek philosophy. Indeed, modern students of ancient philosophy generally divide Greek thought into the pre- and post-Socratic periods.

Socrates' ultimate contribution was his refusal to accept easy answers as he searched after wisdom and virtue, which to him were the same. Like Confucius, Socrates had an implicit faith in the proposition that action inevitably follows knowledge. The moral person, for Socrates, was the one who knew the good and acted accordingly. Unlike Confucius, however, Socrates refused to accept the answers of tradition and the way of the past as infallible guides to wisdom and moral behavior.

Socrates' uncompromising search for truth and goodness of soul earned him a number of enemies, and he finally fell victim to the mood of bitter recrimination that followed Athens's defeat in the Peloponnesian War. In 399, a conservative politician brought charges of impiety against the gods and corruption of youth against Socrates. On trial for his life, the seventy-year-old philosopher refused to defend himself against the charges, choosing, instead, to offer a justification of his life and methods of inquiry. He was found guilty and condemned to death by a jury that fully expected him to flee the city. Socrates, faithful to the end to his sense of morality, refused to avoid the sentence and went serenely to his death.

The best account of Socrates' *apologia,* or defense, at his trial comes to us from Plato, Socrates' brilliant pupil and, arguably, the most original of all of Hellas's great thinkers. It is impossible to say exactly where Socrates' ideas end and Plato's begin in the many philosophical dialogues Plato composed and in which his former master serves as hero. It is likely, however, that the *Apologia* is faithful to the concepts, if not the actual words, that Socrates presented in his defense of philosophy.

Following the death of his teacher, Plato withdrew from his native Athens and did not return for twelve years. Upon his return, he founded his own school of philosophy, the Academy, which he presided over for nearly forty years, although later he again left Athens, this time for six years. When he returned, he again took up residence in the Academy and there, for the rest of his life, instructed the men and women who attended in large numbers. The Academy continued to be a center of Greek rational philosophy until the Christian emperor Justinian ordered its closing in A.D. 529. For over 900 years, the Academy served the cause of the unfettered pursuit of wisdom that Socrates so ably defended and for which he died.

Questions for Analysis

1. What defense does Socrates offer against the charges of impiety and corruption of Athens's youth?
2. How was it possible for persons to perceive him as guilty of those charges?
3. What god compels Socrates to seek the truth?
4. According to Socrates, what necessary social function does he fulfill?
5. What wisdom does Socrates claim to have?
6. What does he teach and what is his method of instruction? Can you hazard a guess as to what is the "Socratic method"?
7. According to Socrates, what is a human being's highest function and greatest responsibility?
8. How does Socrates' definition of virtue parallel that of Confucius?

Men of Athens, do not interrupt me with noise, even if I seem to you to be boasting; for the word which I speak is not mine, but the speaker to whom I shall refer it is a person of weight. For of my wisdom — if it is wisdom at all — and of its nature, I will offer you the god of Delphi[1] as a witness. You know Chaerephon, I

1. The oracle, or prophetess, of Apollo at Delphi.

fancy. He was my comrade from a youth and the comrade of your democratic party. . . . Well, once he went to Delphi and made so bold as to ask the oracle this question; and, gentlemen, don't make a disturbance at what I say; for he asked if there were anyone wiser than I. Now the Pythia[2] replied that there was no one wiser. And about these things his brother here will bear you witness, since Chaerephon is dead.

But see why I say these things; for I am going to tell you whence the prejudice against me has arisen. For when I heard this, I thought to myself: "What in the world does the god mean, and what riddle is he propounding? For I am conscious that I am not wise either much or little. What then does he mean by declaring that I am the wisest? He certainly cannot be lying, for that is not possible for him." And for a long time I was at a loss as to what he meant; then with great reluctance I proceeded to investigate him somewhat as follows.

I went to one of those who had a reputation for wisdom, thinking that there, if anywhere, I should prove the utterance wrong and should show the oracle "This man is wiser than I, but you said I was wisest." So examining this man — for I need not call him by name, but it was one of the public men with regard to whom I had this kind of experience, men of Athens — and conversing with him, this man seemed to me to seem to be wise to many other people and especially to himself, but not to be so; and then I tried to show him that he thought he was wise, but was not. As a result, I became hateful to him and to many of those present; and so, as I went away, I thought to myself, "I am wiser than this man; for neither of us really knows anything fine and good, but this man thinks he knows something when he does not, whereas I, as I do not know anything, do not think I do either. I seem, then, in just this little thing to be wiser than this man at any rate, that what I do not know I do not think I know either." From him I went to another of those who were reputed to be wiser than he, and these same things seemed to me to be true; and there I became hateful both to him and to many others. . . .

Now from this investigation, men of Athens, many enmities have arisen against me, and such as are most harsh and grievous, so that many prejudices have resulted from them and I am called a wise man. For on each occasion those who are present think I am wise in the matters in which I confute someone else; but the fact is, gentlemen, it is likely that the god is really wise and by his oracle means this: "Human wisdom is of little or no value." And it appears that he does not really say this of Socrates, but merely uses my name, and makes me an example, as if he were to say: "This one of you, O human beings, is wisest, who, like Socrates, recognises that he is in truth of no account in respect to wisdom."

Therefore I am still even now going about and searching and investigating at the god's behest anyone, whether citizen or foreigner, who I think is wise; and when he does not seem so to me, I give aid to the god and show that he is not wise. And by reason of this occupation I have no leisure to attend to any of the affairs of the state worth mentioning, or of my own, but am in vast poverty on account of my service to the god.

2. The priestess who acted as the vehicle for the sacred serpent spirit (the python), who was believed to be the actual soothsayer at Delphi.

And in addition to these things, the young men who have the most leisure, the sons of the richest men, accompany me of their own accord, find pleasure in hearing people being examined, and often imitate me themselves, and then they undertake to examine others; and then, I fancy, they find a great plenty of people who think they know something, but know little or nothing. As a result, therefore, those who are examined by them are angry with me, instead of being angry with themselves, and say that "Socrates is a most abominable person and is corrupting the youth."

And when anyone asks them "by doing or teaching what?" they have nothing to say, but they do not know, and that they may not seem to be at a loss, they say these things that are handy to say against all the philosophers, "the things in the air and the things beneath the earth" and "not to believe in the gods" and "to make the weaker argument the stronger." For they would not, I fancy, care to say the truth, that it is being made very clear that they pretend to know, but know nothing. . . . If you should say to me . . . : "Socrates, this time we will not do as Anytus[3] says, but we will let you go, on this condition, however, that you no longer spend your time in this investigation or in philosophy, and if you are caught doing so again you shall die"; if you should let me go on this condition which I have mentioned, I should say to you, "Men of Athens, I respect and love you, but I shall obey the god rather than you, and while I live and am able to continue, I shall never give up philosophy or stop exhorting you and pointing out the truth to any one of you whom I may meet, saying in my accustomed way: "Most excellent man, are you who are a citizen of Athens, the greatest of cities and the most famous for wisdom and power, not ashamed to care for the acquisition of wealth and for reputation and honor, when you neither care nor take thought for wisdom and truth and the perfection of your soul?" And if any of you argues the point, and says he does care, I shall not let him go at once, nor shall I go away, but I shall question and examine and cross-examine him, and if I find that he does not possess virtue, but says he does, I shall rebuke him for scorning the things that are of most importance and caring more for what is of less worth. This I shall do to whomever I meet, young and old, foreigner and citizen, but most to the citizens, inasmuch as you are more nearly related to me. For know that the god commands me to do this, and I believe that no greater good ever came to pass in the city than my service to the god. For I go about doing nothing else than urging you, young and old, not to care for your persons or your property more than for the perfection of your souls, or even so much; and I tell you that virtue does not come from money, but from virtue comes money and all other good things to man, both to the individual and to the state. If by saying these things I corrupt the youth, these things must be injurious; but if anyone asserts that I say other things than these, he says what is untrue. Therefore I say to you, men of Athens, either do as Anytus tells you, or not, and either acquit me, or not, knowing that I shall not change my conduct even if I am to die many times over. . . .

For know that if you kill me, I being such a man as I say I am, you will not injure me so much as yourselves. . . . And

---

3. The person who introduced charges against Socrates.

so, men of Athens, I am now making my defence not for my own sake, as one might imagine, but far more for yours, that you may not by condemning me err in your treatment of the gift the god gave you. For if you put me to death, you will not easily find another, who, to use a rather absurd figure, attaches himself to the city as a gadfly to a horse, which, though large and well bred, is sluggish on account of his size and needs to be aroused by stinging. I think the god fastened me upon the city in some such capacity, and I go about arousing, and urging and reproaching each one of you, constantly alighting upon you everywhere the whole day long. Such another is not likely to come to you, gentlemen; but if you take my advice, you will spare me. But you, perhaps, might be angry, like people awakened from a nap, and might slap me, as Anytus advises, and easily kill me; then you would pass the rest of your lives in slumber, unless God, in his care for you, should send someone else to sting you. And that I am, as I say, a kind of gift from the god, you might understand from this; for I have neglected all my own affairs and have been enduring the neglect of my concerns all these years, but I am always busy in your interest, coming to each one of you individually like a father or an elder brother and urging you to care for virtue; now that is not like human conduct. If I derived any profit from this and received pay for these exhortations, there would be some sense in it; but now you yourselves see that my accusers, though they accuse me of everything else in such a shameless way, have not been able to work themselves up to such a pitch of shamelessness as to produce a witness to testify that I ever exacted or asked pay of anyone. For I think I have a sufficient witness that I speak the truth, namely, my poverty. . . .

I was never any one's teacher. If any one, whether young or old, wishes to hear me speaking and pursuing my mission, I have never objected, nor do I converse only when I am paid and not otherwise, but I offer myself alike to rich and poor; I ask questions, and whoever wishes may answer and hear what I say. And whether any of them turns out well or ill, I should not justly be held responsible, since I never promised or gave any instruction to any of them; but if any man says that he ever learned or heard anything privately from me, which all the others did not, be assured that he is lying.

But why then do some people love to spend much of their time with me? You have heard the reason, men of Athens; for I told you the whole truth; it is because they like to listen when those are examined who think they are wise and are not so; for it is amusing.

Diogenes Laertius

THE LIVES AND OPINIONS OF EMINENT PHILOSOPHERS

The multicultural world Alexander and his generals created was complex, exciting, and bewildering. For Greeks, the comfortable and friendly confines of the polis, which defined and gave meaning to the life of each citizen, had given way to the *cosmopolis* — the city of the world — in which individuals felt insignificant and unimportant. The resultant anxiety helped foster the growing popularity of a number of different religions and schools of philosophy, all of which, in some manner or other, offered an answer to this stress. Of the new schools of moral philosophy, three proved in the long run to be the most important: Stoicism, Epicureanism, and Cynicism.

Stoics believed in an absolute moral standard that could be deduced from the material laws governing the universe. The wise person and, therefore, the person at peace internally was one who understood these laws and this moral code and acted accordingly. If Stoics had been given to slogans, their motto would have been, "Duty above all else." Epicureans, on the other hand, believed life to be ultimately meaningless and, moreover, filled with pain rooted in activity in the world. Hence the wise person avoided activity and sought the enlightenment and moderate pleasures of simple living. The most one could hope for in life was to avoid pain, largely by fleeing a hostile and empty world. The Cynics offered a third approach to the dilemmas facing people in the overlarge and competitive Hellenistic world. As our selection illustrates, the spirit of Cynicism attracted a number of discontented intellectuals who could embrace neither Stoicism's self-confident sense of truth and involvement in the world nor Epicureanism's pessimistic message of emptiness and noninvolvement.

Diogenes the Cynic, the movement's most influential figure, predated the Hellenistic Age, having been born before 400 B.C. at Sinope in Asia Minor and dying around 323 at Corinth. As a youth he emigrated to Athens, where he took up philosophy. In Athens, Diogenes often crossed verbal swords with Plato, who characterized him as "a Socrates gone mad" and a "dog" (*kynos* in Greek). The latter appellation stuck. Diogenes proudly bore the title throughout his public life, and those who later patterned their lives upon his likewise called themselves dogs (Cynics).

The Hellenistic Cynics who claimed spiritual descent from Diogenes and his teacher, Antisthenes (ca 450–366 B.C.), were a mixed lot, yet they shared a general attitude toward life. Whereas the Stoics accepted an ordered world with inflexible laws, the Cynics generally defied convention, which they saw as soul-corrupting, and advocated return to a simple, natural life of self-sufficiency. Cynics prided themselves in being happily out of step with society and often with one another, but the life and legend of Diogenes, their patron saint, served as a common source of inspiration. They relished and embellished the stories that told how this fourth-century contrarian exposed the hypocrisies of civilization.

The chief source for the life and teachings of Diogenes the Cynic is a collection of biographies of Greek rationalists commonly ascribed to another Diogenes — Diogenes Laertius. Laertius, about whom we know virtually nothing, probably composed his work in the early decades of the third century A.D., or over 500 years after Diogenes the Cynic's death. Although undoubtedly a good deal of error crept into Laertius's biographies, one of the collection's strengths is that the author drew on and quoted from large numbers of ancient sources now lost in their original form. Laertius thus preserved the flavor of Hellenistic Cynicism's memory of Diogenes the Dog.

Questions for Analysis

1. What does the word "cynical" mean in common English parlance? Was Diogenes cynical in the modern sense of the word?
2. Was Diogenes a rationalist? If so, what sort?
3. If he rejected such studies as geometry, astronomy, and music, what form of wisdom did Diogenes pursue?
4. Diogenes has been characterized as a misanthrope. Did he truly hate humankind or was he a person who loved humanity but was constantly disappointed by humans?
5. Why would Plato characterize Diogenes as "a Socrates gone mad"? Was Plato correct?
6. Did Diogenes reject the notion of an underlying order in the world that the human mind can know?
7. Why would Cynicism have attracted certain thinkers during the Hellenistic Age?
8. Can you find any parallels between Taoism and Cynicism? Any essential differences?
9. How does Greek rationalism compare with Chinese rationalism?

Diogenes was a native of Sinope, son of Hicesius, a banker. Diocles relates that he went into exile because his father was entrusted with the money of the state and adulterated the coinage. But Eubulides in his book on Diogenes says that Diogenes himself did this and was forced to leave home along with his father. Moreover Diogenes himself actually confesses in his *Pordalus* that he adulterated the coinage. . . .

On reaching Athens he fell in with Antisthenes. Being repulsed by him, because he never welcomed pupils, by sheer persistence Diogenes wore him out. Once when he stretched out his staff against him, the pupil offered his head with the words, "Strike, for you will find no wood hard enough to keep me away from you, so long as I think you've something to say." From that time forward he was his pupil, and, exile as he was, set out upon a simple life. . . .

He [Diogenes] was great at pouring scorn on his contemporaries. . . . He used also to say that when he saw physicians, philosophers and pilots[1] at their work, he deemed man the most intelligent of all animals; but when again he saw interpreters of dreams and diviners and those who at-

1. Of ships.

tended to them, or those who were puffed up with conceit of wealth, he thought no animal more silly. He would continually say that for the conduct of life we need right reason or a halter. . . .

When one day he was gravely discoursing and nobody attended to him, he began whistling, and as people clustered about him, he reproached them with coming in all seriousness to hear nonsense, but slowly and contemptuously when the theme was serious. He would say that men strive in digging[2] and kicking to outdo one another, but no one strives to become a good man and true. . . . He was moved to anger that men should sacrifice to the gods to ensure health and in the midst of the sacrifice should feast to the detriment of health. . . . He used to say, moreover, that we ought to stretch out our hands to our friends with fingers open and not closed. . . .

One day, observing a child drinking out of his hands, he cast away the cup from his wallet with the words, "A child has beaten me in plainness of living." He also threw away his bowl when in like manner he saw a child who had broken his plate taking up his lentils with the hollow part of a morsel of bread. He used also to reason thus: "All things belong to the gods. The wise are friends of the gods, and friends hold things in common. Therefore all things belong to the wise.". . . He claimed that to fortune he could oppose courage, to convention nature, to passion reason. . . . Plato had defined Man as an animal, biped and featherless, and was applauded. Diogenes plucked a fowl and brought it into the lecture-room with the words, "Here is Plato's man.". . . To one who asked what was the proper time for lunch, he said, "If a rich man, when you will; if a poor man, when you can."

At Megara he saw the sheep protected by leather jackets, while the children went bare. "It's better," said he, "to be a Megarian's ram than his son.". . . He lit a lamp in broad daylight and said, as he went about, "I am looking for a man.". . . He would often insist loudly that the gods had given to men the means of living easily, but this had been put out of sight, because we require honeyed cakes, unguents and the like. Hence to a man whose shoes were being put on by his servant, he said, "You have not attained to full felicity, unless he wipes your nose as well; and that will come, when you have lost the use of your hands."

At a feast certain people kept throwing all the bones to him as they would have done to a dog. Thereupon he played a dog's trick and drenched them.

He once begged alms of a statue, and, when asked why he did so, replied, "To get practice in being refused." In asking alms — as he did at first by reason of his poverty — he used this form: "If you have already given to anyone else, give to me also; if not, begin with me.". . .

When some one declared that life is an evil, he corrected him: "Not life itself, but living ill."

Alexander [the Great] once came and stood opposite him and said, "I am Alexander the great king." "And I," said he, "am Diogenes the Cynic." Being asked what he had done to be called a hound, he said, "I fawn on those who give me

---

2. Competition in digging trenches was part of the physical training athletes underwent in preparation for the Olympic games.

anything, I yelp at those who refuse, and I set my teeth in rascals.". . .

Being asked what was the most beautiful thing in the world, he replied, "Freedom of speech.". . . It was his habit to do everything in public, the works of Demeter[3] and of Aphrodite[4] alike. He used to draw out the following arguments. "If to breakfast be not absurd, neither is it absurd in the market-place[5] but to breakfast is not absurd, therefore it is not absurd to breakfast in the market-place." Behaving indecently in public[6] he wished "it were as easy to banish hunger by rubbing the belly.". . . He held that we should neglect music, geometry, astronomy, and the like studies, as useless and unnecessary.

Diogenes is said to have been nearly ninety years old when he died. Regarding his death there are several different accounts. One is that he was seized with colic after eating an octopus raw and so met his end. Another is that he died voluntarily by holding his breath.

---

3. The goddess of the fruits of the earth.

4. The goddess of love.

5. Greek society considered it unbecoming to eat in public.

6. Masturbating.

C H A P T E R

5

Regional Empires and Eurasian Unification, 300 B.C.–A.D. 500

Eurasia's four major cultural traditions were in place by 300 B.C., and for the next several centuries these religious, philosophical, and social systems expanded geographically, often as a consequence of political and military action. The most dramatic early example of this phenomenon was the Hellenistic amalgamation brought about by Alexander the Great and his Macedonian generals. By the end of the first century B.C., four regional empires linked the cultural traditions of India, the Middle East, China, and Hellas in a chain of civilization from the Pacific to the Atlantic. Han China dominated East Asia and reached deeply into Central Asia. India, which was not politically united, was joined to Central Asia by the Kushana Empire in its northern regions. The Parthian Empire controlled the lands of Iran and Mesopotamia and aggressively neighbored the Roman Empire, which was centered on the Mediterranean.

Land and sea routes now joined these civilized regions, creating Eurasia's first age of unification. Very few Mediterranean people traveled all the way to China, and fewer Chinese ventured even to the borders of the Roman Empire. Instead, merchant intermediaries speeded along the silk, cotton, spices, gold, ideas, and even diseases that traveled from one end of Eurasia to the other.

Africa shared in this unification to the extent that its northern regions were an integral part of the Roman Empire and portions of its eastern coast were linked by trade with Arabia, India, and Southeast Asia.

This age of grand-scale linkage began to break down around A.D. 200, when both China and the Roman Empire entered periods of severe crisis, and by 500 it was mostly a dim memory. While it existed, however, this age witnessed the flourishing of some brilliant civilizations and empires. Indeed, this was a period when several of Eurasia's classical civilizations reached the fullness of their cultural flowering.

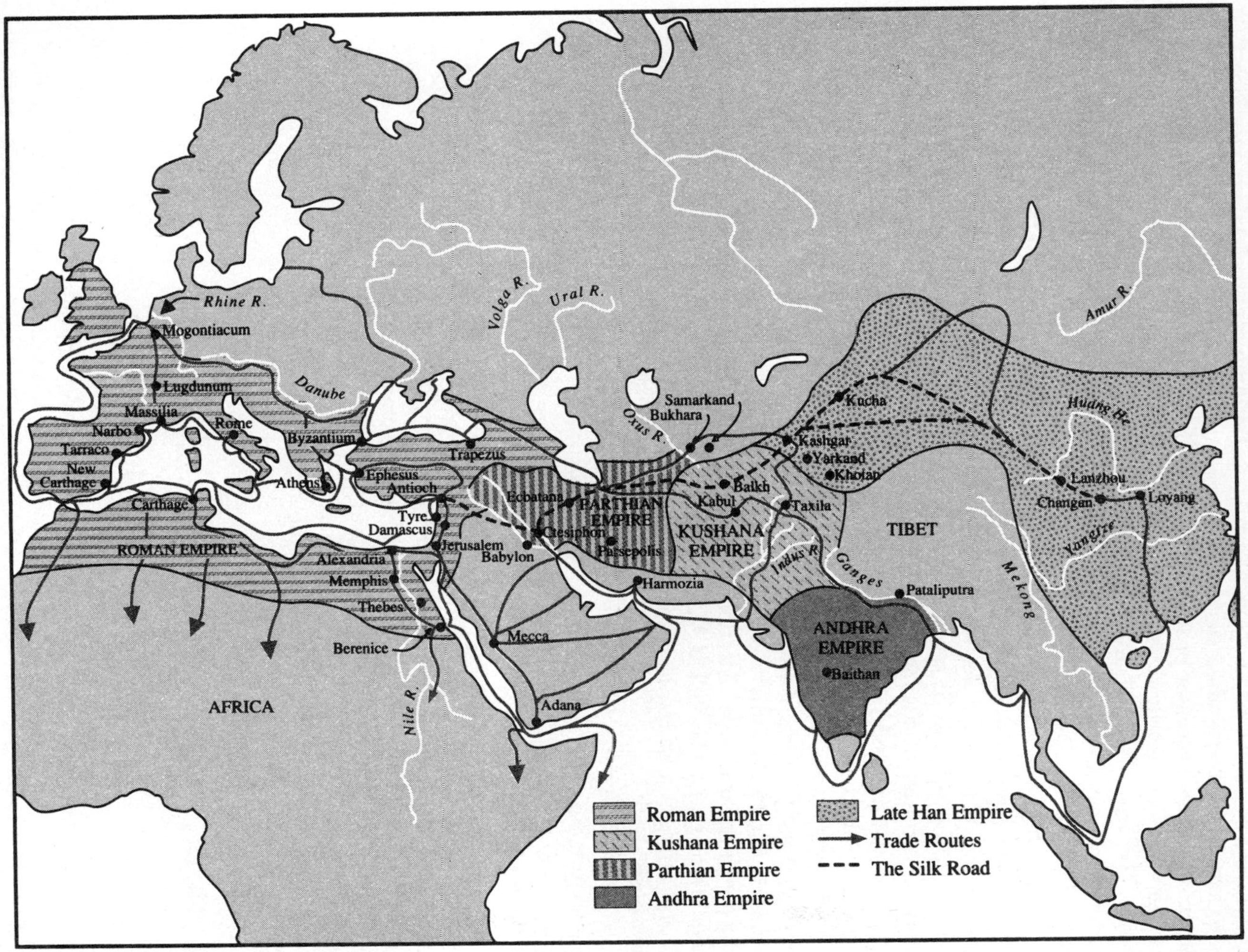

Map 1 The First Afro-Eurasian Ecumene

The Greco-Roman World

Alexander the Great died in Babylon in 323 B.C. Tradition says that, when questioned as to whom he bequeathed his world empire, he replied, "To the strongest." No single, would-be successor proved strong enough to seize the entire empire. Rather, rival generals eventually divided the Hellenistic world into a number of successor states. The two mightiest and most brilliant were the kingdom of the Seleucids, centered in Asia Minor, Mesopotamia, and Syria, and the kingdom of Egypt, which fell to the family of Ptolemy, one of Alexander's younger Macedonian generals.

Ptolemy and his successors lavished money on their capital, Alexandria, transforming this new city, located in Egypt's northern delta region, into the most impressive cosmopolitan setting in the Hellenistic world. The city's twin crowning glories, at least in the opinion of scholars and scientists, were the Museum, which functioned as a center of advanced research, and the Library, which represented an attempt to gather under one roof the entire Hellenistic world's store of written knowledge and contained perhaps as many as 500,000 separate scrolls.

Both institutions enjoyed the continuous generous patronage of these Macedonian Greek god-kings of Egypt and served as focal points for scientific and literary studies that were Greek in form and substance but cosmopolitan in scope and clientele. Educated Persians, Jews, Mesopotamians, Syrians, Italians, and members of many other ethnic groups flocked to Alexandria, where they formed a community of scholars and artists whose common tongue and intellectual perspective were as Greek as their hosts'.

In 30 B.C. Cleopatra VII, the last Ptolemaic ruler of Egypt, died in Alexandria by her own hand, and Egypt came under the direct control of a rising imperial power — Rome. By this time Rome had already seized control of Italy, Greece, major portions of Asia Minor, Syria, most of North Africa, all the major Mediterranean islands, Spain, and the area north of the Alps known as Gaul. The Mediterranean had become Rome's *Mare Nostrum* ("Our Sea"), and the Roman Empire now controlled a large portion of the Hellenistic world. Rome would disseminate a Greco-Roman form of Hellenistic culture throughout the western Mediterranean, as well as among various "barbarian" people living in European lands far beyond the Mediterranean coastline. Within a century, Roman legions would erect Greek-style temples to the Persian god Mithras along the Rhine and in the British Isles.

Strabo

Geography

The life and work of the late Hellenistic historian and geographer Strabo (ca 64 B.C.–A.D. 25) reflect the hybrid nature of Hellenistic civilization and its wide horizons. By descent Strabo was part Asiatic and part Greek. He was born in Amaseia in northeastern Asia Minor but spent significant periods of time studying and working in Rome and Alexandria. He admired the Romans and their empire but composed his historical and geographical works in Greek, the common language of educated Hellenistic people.

His only work to survive is the *Geography*. Its seventeen books are chiefly a compilation of information (and misinformation) garnered from accounts and studies by earlier Hellenistic travelers and geographers of the known lands of Europe, Asia (up to and including India), and Africa. Because most of Strabo's sources were lost when the Library of Alexandria was destroyed in late Roman times, the *Geography* is our main source of information on the Hellenistic world's geographical knowledge and lore. In this selection Strabo discusses his evidence and the state of his society's knowledge of the world.

Questions for Analysis

1. Using the map of Strabo's World, trace that portion of the inhabited world that Strabo knew from firsthand experience.
2. What sort of sources did Strabo use for his *Geography?*
3. Why does he prefer the accounts of contemporary to past writers and travelers, and what does this suggest about travel in his own day?
4. What sort of contact did Strabo's society have with India? How did it compare with earlier exchanges in the age of the Ptolemies?
5. Consider the map and Strabo's account of Asia. What does he know about lands to the east of India, and what does this suggest about direct Greco-Roman knowledge of China?
6. What does Strabo tell us about the physical and human geography of North Africa? What does he know about Africa's interior? What do you infer about Hellenistic knowledge of Africa?

Now I shall tell what part of the land and sea I have myself visited and concerning what part I have trusted to accounts given by others by word of mouth or in writing. I have travelled westward from Armenia as far as the regions of Tyrrhenia[1] opposite Sardinia, and southward from the Euxine Sea[2] as far as the frontiers of Ethiopia.[3] And you could not find another person among the writers on geography who has travelled over much more of the distances just mentioned than I; indeed, those who have travelled more than I in the western regions have not covered as much ground in the east, and those who have travelled more in the eastern countries are behind me in the western; and the same holds true in regard to the regions towards the south and north. However, the greater part of our material both

1. North-central Italy.
2. The Black Sea.
3. All the land of southeast Africa. See the map of Strabo's World.

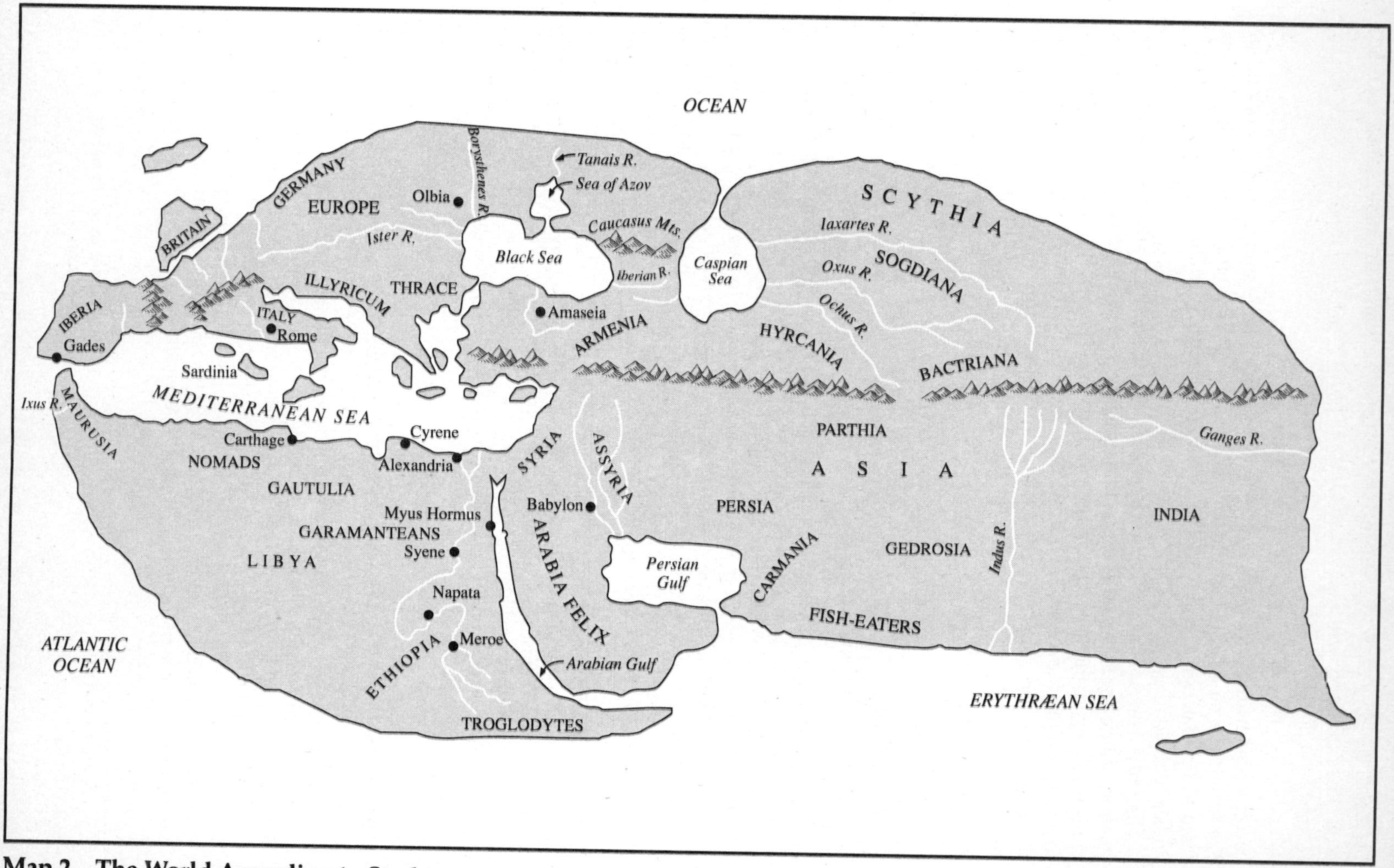

Map 2 The World According to Strabo

they and I receive by hearsay and then form our ideas. . . . And men who are eager to learn proceed in just that way: they trust as organs of sense those who have seen or wandered over any region, no matter what, some in this and some in that part of the earth, and they form in one diagram their mental image of the whole inhabited world. . . . And he who claims that only those have knowledge who have actually seen abolishes the criterion of the sense of hearing, though this sense is much more important than sight for the purposes of science.

In particular the writers of the present time can give a better account of the Britons, the Germans, the peoples both north and south of the Ister, the Getans, the Tyregetans, the Bastarnians,[4] and, furthermore, the peoples in the regions of the Caucasus, such as the Albanians and the Iberians.[5] Information has been given us also concerning Hyrcania and Bactriana by the writers of Parthian histories (Apollodorus of Artemita[6] and his school), in which they marked off those countries more definitely than many other writers. Again, since the Romans have recently invaded Arabia Felix with an army, of which Aelius Gallus,[7] my friend and companion, was the commander, and since the merchants of Alexandria are already sailing with fleets by way of the Nile and of the Arabian Gulf as far as India, these regions also have become far better known to us of to-day than to our predecessors. At any rate, when Gallus was prefect of Egypt, I accompanied him and ascended[8] the Nile as far as Syene and the frontiers of Ethiopia, and I learned that as many as one hundred and twenty vessels were sailing from Myos Hormos[9] to India, whereas formerly, under the Ptolemies, only a very few ventured to undertake the voyage and to carry on traffic in Indian merchandise. . . .

And Libya[10] is — as the others show, and indeed as Cnaeus Piso,[11] who was once the prefect of that country, told me — like a leopard's skin; for it is spotted with inhabited places that are surrounded by waterless and desert land. The Egyptians call such inhabited places "auases."[12] But though Libya is thus peculiar, it has some other peculiarities, which give it a threefold division. In the first place, most of its coastline that lies opposite to us[13] is extremely fertile, and especially Cyrenaea and the country about Carthage up to Maurusia and to the Pillars of Heracles[14]; secondly, even its coastline on the ocean affords only moderate sustenance; and thirdly, its interior region, which produces silphium,[15] affords only a wretched sustenance, being, for the most part, a rocky and sandy desert; and the same is also

4. Tribes wandering through the Balkans, especially in Thrace.

5. These are the *eastern* Iberians, who resided in the region between the Black and Caspian seas. The western Iberians inhabited the land that is today Spain and Portugal.

6. A second-century B.C. geographer of Alexandria and Athens.

7. A Roman prefect of Egypt who led a disastrous two-year-expedition into southern Arabia in 25–24 B.C.

8. Sailed south.

9. An African port on the Red Sea.

10. Libya here means all of Africa.

11. Proconsul of the North African province of Africa in the early years following the birth of Christ.

12. Oases.

13. The coast of North Africa.

14. The Strait of Gibraltar.

15. An aromatic plant grown for export in Cyrene, on Africa's northeast coast; its resin was a popular medicine.

true of the straight prolongation of this region through Ethiopia, the Troglodyte Country,[16] Arabia, and Gedrosia where the Fish-Eaters live. The most of the peoples of Libya are unknown to us; for not much of it is visited by armies, nor yet by men of outside tribes; and not only do very few of the natives from far inland ever visit us, but what they tell is not trustworthy or complete either. But still the following is based on what they say. They call the most southerly peoples Ethiopians; those who live next north of the Ethiopians they call, in the main, Garamantians, Pharusians, and Nigritans; those who live still north of these latter, Gaetulans; those who live near the sea, or even on the seacoast, next to Egypt and as far as Cyrenaea, Marmaridans; while they call those beyond Cyrenaea and the Syrtes, Psyllians, Nasamonians, and certain of the Gaetulans, and then Asbystians and Byzacians, whose territory reaches to that of Carthage. The territory of Carthage is large, and beyond it comes that of the Nomads[17], the best known of these are called, some of them, Masylians, and others Masaesylians. And last of all come the Maurusians. The whole country from Carthage to the Pillars is fertile, though full of wild beasts, as is also the whole of the interior of Libya. So it is not unlikely that some of these peoples were also called Nomads for the reason that in early times they were not able to cultivate the soil on account of the multitude of wild animals. But the Nomads of today not only excel in the skill of hunting (and the Romans take a hand in this with them because of their fondness for fights with wild animals), but they have mastered farming as well as the chase. This, then, is what I have to say about the continents.

Caesar Augustus

The Accomplishments of the Deified Augustus

Following its total victory over Carthage in the Second Punic War (218–201 B.C.), the Roman Republic was the major power in the Mediterranean and an empire in fact if not in name. Rome's acquisition of an empire had major repercussions at home, and the resultant strains triggered more than a century of unrest, discord, and civil war. The civil war ended in 30 B.C., when Octavian, the great-nephew and adopted son of Julius Caesar (ca 100–44 B.C.), defeated Mark Antony and became sole master of the Roman world. In 27 B.C. the Senate accorded him the honorific title *Augustus* ("revered one"). Posterity remembers him as Caesar Augustus (63 B.C.–A.D. 14), the man who created and presided over the *Pax Romana*, the Roman Peace.

Augustus maintained the forms of oligarchic republicanism while creating a political entity effectively ruled by one person — himself. The system he established, known as the Principate (from one of his favorite titles, *Princeps* or "First Citizen"), worked fairly well for close to two centuries.

16. A Stone Age people of sub-Saharan Africa.

17. The Berber inhabitants of the North African Roman province of Numidia.

. . . Here before us is their general, here his army; behind are the tribute, the mines and all the other whips to scourge slaves. Whether you are to endure these for ever or take summary vengeance, this field must decide. On, then, into action and, as you go, think of those that went before you and of those that shall come after."

Ammianus Marcellinus

History

Great empires were not only predators, they were also prey to their civilized neighbors and to less civilized fringe people. Between A.D. 230 and 285 both the Sassanian Persians and a variety of seminomads battered the Roman Empire, which, by the late third century, shored up its frontier defenses and, through drastic measures, secured an additional century of relative stability. Toward the end of the fourth century, however, the old pressures were again becoming intolerable.

Just as Tacitus chronicled the early years of the empire, another great historian appeared to record the troubles of the late fourth century. Ammianus Marcellinus (ca 330–390), a Greek soldier from Antioch, in Syria, picked up Rome's story where Tacitus had left off (in A.D. 98) and brought it down to his own day. His history fittingly ended with the events of 378, which included the Visigoths' victory over a Roman army at Adrianople and the death of Emperor Valens. Although Ammianus surely could not have known it, this disaster presaged events that would engulf and ultimately transform the Greco-Roman world over the next several centuries, ending forever the Roman Peace.

In the following selection, Ammianus describes the Huns, a Turkic people from the steppes of Central and East Asia whose fourth-century migration westward was pushing a number of border tribes, such as the Visigoths, into the Roman Empire. Although Ammianus had earlier campaigned in Persia, he appears to have had no first-hand knowledge of these Asiatic nomads. Rather, his account is a mixture of rumor and stereotype, and it tells us as much about late Greco-Roman views of the "barbarians" on the frontiers as about Hunnish culture.

Questions for Analysis

1. According to Ammianus, what qualities make the Huns such formidable foes?
2. What does Ammianus's description of the Huns tell us about the attitudes of a member of the Greco-Roman ecumene toward these nomads from the steppes?
3. What aspects of this description seem to ring truest? Why?

The seed-bed and origin of all this destruction[1] and of the various calamities inflicted by the wrath of Mars,[2] which raged everywhere with unusual fury, I find to be this. The people of the Huns, who are mentioned only cursorily in ancient writers and who dwell beyond the Sea of Azov[3] near the frozen ocean,[4] are quite abnormally savage. From the moment of birth they make deep gashes in their children's cheeks, so that when in due course hair appears its growth is checked by the wrinkled scars; as they grow older this gives them the unlovely appearance of beardless eunuchs. They have squat bodies, strong limbs, and thick necks, and are so prodigiously ugly and bent that they might be two-legged animals, or the figures crudely carved from stumps which are seen on the parapets of bridges.[5] Still, their shape, however disagreeable, is human; but their way of life is so rough that they have no use for fire or seasoned food, but live on the roots of wild plants and the half-raw flesh of any sort of animal, which they warm a little by placing it between their thighs and the backs of their horses.[6] They have no buildings to shelter them, but avoid anything of the kind as carefully as we avoid living in the neighborhood of tombs; not so much as a hut thatched with reeds is to be found among them. They roam at large over mountains and forests, and are inured from the cradle to cold, hunger, and thirst. On foreign soil only extreme necessity can persuade them to come under a roof, since they believe that it is not safe for them to do so. They wear garments of linen or of the skins of field-mice stitched together, and there is no difference between their clothing whether they are at home or abroad. Once they have put their necks into some dingy shirt they never take it off or change it till it rots and falls to pieces from incessant wear. They have round caps of fur on their heads, and protect their hairy legs with goatskins. Their shapeless shoes are not made on a last and make it hard to walk easily. In consequence they are ill-fitted to fight on foot, and remain glued to their horses, hardy but ugly beasts, on which they sometimes sit like women to perform their everyday business. Buying or selling, eating or drinking, are all done by day or night on horseback,[7] and they even bow forward over their beasts' narrow necks to enjoy a deep and dreamy sleep. When they need to debate some important matter they conduct their conference in the same posture. They are not subject to the authority of any king, but break through any obstacle in their path under the improvised command of their chief men.

They sometimes fight by challenging their foes to single combat, but when they join battle they advance in packs, uttering their various war cries. Being lightly equipped and very sudden in their movements they can deliberately scatter and gallop about at random, inflicting tremen-

1. The disaster at Adrianople.

2. The Roman god of war.

3. The northern arm of the Black Sea.

4. If Ammianus means the Arctic, his sense of geography is poor.

5. Ammianus's description of the Huns' size, bandy legs, and hairless faces conforms with many other accounts.

6. No evidence exists to support the popular notion of ancient authors that the nomads of the steppes "cooked" their meat this way. Modern beef tartar, a concoction of raw ground beef, a raw egg, and various condiments, perpetuates this myth.

7. Other accounts also emphasize how the Huns and other steppe peoples lived on horseback.

dous slaughter; their extreme nimbleness enables them to force a rampart or pillage an enemy's camp before one catches sight of them. What makes them the most formidable of all warriors is that they shoot from a distance arrows tipped with sharp splinters of bone instead of the usual heads; these are joined to the shafts with wonderful skill. At close quarters they fight without regard for their lives, and while their opponents are guarding against sword-thrusts they catch their limbs in lassos of twisted cloth which make it impossible for them to ride or walk. None of them ploughs or ever touches a plough-handle. They have no fixed abode, no home or law or settled manner of life, but wander like refugees with the wagons in which they live. In these their wives weave their filthy clothing, mate with their husbands, give birth to their children, and rear them to the age of puberty. No one if asked can tell where he comes from, having been conceived in one place, born somewhere else, and reared even further off. You cannot make a truce with them, because they are quite unreliable and easily swayed by any breath of rumor which promises advantage; like unreasoning beasts they are entirely at the mercy of the maddest impulses. They are totally ignorant of the distinction between right and wrong, their speech is shifty and obscure, and they are under no restraint from religion or superstition. Their greed for gold is prodigious, and they are so fickle and prone to anger that often in a single day they will quarrel with their allies without any provocation, and then make it up again without anyone attempting to reconcile them.

This wild race, moving without encumbrances and consumed by a savage passion to pillage the property of others, advanced robbing and slaughtering over the lands of their neighbors.

Han China

In A.D. 2 an imperial census counted 12,233,062 families, or approximately 60 million persons, residing in China. As we have seen, Rome's census of A.D. 14 recorded 4,937,000 Roman citizens. Full-fledged citizens of Rome probably constituted less than 10 percent of the empire's total population at that time, so it is reasonable to conclude that the Roman Empire contained between 50 and 60 million people in the early decades of the first century A.D. Therefore, as we look at Eurasia around the turn of the millennium, we see two massive empires of about the same size and population at either end of this great land mass. For the next two centuries Han China and Rome dominated their respective regions and, although each experienced periods of crisis, each also offered its subjects fairly stable government and a degree of prosperity.

A measure of Rome's and China's greatness can be seen in their powerful mythic influence on those who followed. Well into the modern period, European emperors and kings claimed to be legitimate heirs of Roman authority. As late as the early twentieth century, German and Russian monarchs styled themselves Kaiser and

Tsar, variations on the title Caesar. In China today, all ethnic Chinese — 97 percent of the population of the People's Republic — proudly call themselves Han.

The Han Dynasty reigned during one of China's golden ages, creating a political and social order based on a synthesis of legalist and Confucian principles. It expanded China's influence into Korea, Vietnam, and across the reaches of Central Asia, presided over a general economic upswing, and witnessed a period of rich cultural productivity. Han China flourished for nearly four centuries, but in the end, like the Roman Empire, the dynasty and its empire collapsed due to internal instabilities and invasions.

The age of Han was not one period but two. Between 202 B.C. and A.D. 9 the Former Han ruled China, and its most powerful and important emperor was Han Wu-ti, the Martial Emperor of Han, who reigned from 141 to 87 B.C. His domestic and foreign policies provided his successors for the next 2,000 years with *the* model of aggressive imperial greatness. Following an interlude in which Wang Mang (A.D. 9–23) wrested the imperial throne temporarily from the Han family, the dynasty returned to power as the Later, or Eastern, Han (A.D. 25–220). After the first century, however, domestic and frontier conditions deteriorated. From A.D. 88 onward, a series of ineffective rulers plagued the family.

By 220, when the Han Dynasty formally came to an end, local lords and invaders from the steppes ruled China. The stability of the earlier Han was only a memory as China plunged into a social, economic, and political chaos that would last for almost four centuries. This period has often been compared with the so-called Dark Ages that ensued after the disintegration of Roman imperial unity in the West, although the differences between the two are more significant than any superficial parallels.

Ssu-ma Ch'ien

Records of the Grand Historian

During its short existence the Ch'in Dynasty had experimented with various recruitment procedures for filling bureaucratic offices with competent and loyal officials. The early emperors of Former Han and their chief ministers continued the search for rational ways of discovering persons of ability. In 124 B.C. Emperor Han Wu-ti established an important precedent when he decreed that proven knowledge of one of the Confucian classics would be a basis for promotion into the imperial civil service and created a rudimentary imperial academy for educating aspiring scholar-officials in the various fields of Confucian learning. By this act he set in motion a process whereby centuries later Confucianism became the ideological framework of the empire.

What began modestly as an academy designed to educate fifty young men became an institution that numbered upward of 30,000 students in the last days of Later Han. Relatively few of these scholars, however, were called to the emperor's service, and the examinations Han Wu-ti initiated were irregularly held under his Han successors. Government office was still largely the privilege of the landed aristocracy, but a regular system of civil service examinations did emerge in the age of the T'ang Dynasty (618–907), when the imperial court successfully sought to break the power of the old landed aristocracy by creating a new class of salaried imperial officials. By the end of the T'ang era education in all the Confucian classics was virtually the only route to civil office. China had not only established the world's first known civil service examination system, it had also, for the most part, restricted civil governance to a class of people who shared a common education and philosophy. This class of Confucian *literarchs*, or "literary rulers," would, more often than not, control China into the twentieth century.

In the following selection, Ssu-ma Ch'ien, China's "Grand Historian" (Chapter 4) and one of Former Han's greatest Confucian scholars, traces the vicissitudes of Confucianism as a practiced political doctrine from the days of Master K'ung to the time of the contemporary emperor, Han Wu-ti.

Questions for Analysis

1. Can you infer from this account why Confucians considered a knowledge of literature, music, and the proper performance of rituals (rites) necessary for good government and a well-ordered society? Why would a mastery of these subjects make a person worthy of holding an important civil post?
2. How were students selected for the academy, and what sort of person was admitted? What do these standards for admission tell us of the values and purposes of Confucian education in the era of Han Wu-ti?
3. Consider what Confucius says in the *Analects* about government and gentlemen (Chapter 4). How do you think he would respond to this academy, its students, curriculum, and purpose for existence?
4. By approving this proposal, how has Han Wu-ti joined Confucianism with legalism?

After the death of Confucius, his band of seventy disciples broke up and scattered among the feudal lords, the more important ones becoming tutors and high ministers to the rulers, the lesser ones acting as friends and teachers to the lower officials, while some went into retirement and were never seen again. . . . Among the feudal lords, however, only Marquis Wen of Wei had any fondness for literature. Conditions continued to deteriorate until the time of the First Emperor of the Ch'in; the empire was divided among a number of states, all warring with each other, and no one had any use for the arts of the Confucians. Only in Ch'i and Lu[1] did scholars appear to carry on the teachings and save them from oblivion. During the reigns of Kings Wei and Hsüan of Ch'i (378–323 B.C.), Mencius[2] and Hsün Ch'ing[3] and their respective groups both honored the doctrines of the Master and worked to expand and enrich them, winning prominence among the men of the time by their learning.

Then followed the twilight[4] days of the Ch'in emperor, who burned the *Odes* and *Documents* and buried the scholars alive,[5] and from this time on the texts of the Six Classics[6] of the Confucians were damaged and incomplete. . . .

Later, when Kao-tsu[7] had defeated Hsiang Yu,[8] he marched north and surrounded the state of Lu with his troops, but the Confucian scholars of Lu went on as always, reciting and discussing their books, practicing rites and music, and never allowing the sound of strings and voices to die out. Is it not because of the teachings and influence which the Sage left behind him that the state of Lu[9] loves rites and music so? Thus, when Confucius was in Ch'en he said, "Let me return! Let me return to Lu! The little children of my school are ambitious and too hasty. They are accomplished and complete so far, but they do not know how to restrict and shape themselves."

Since ancient times the people of the region of Ch'i and Lu have had a natural talent for literature. And when the Han came to power, these scholars were at last

---

1. Two of the seven Warring States.

2. Mencius (the Latinized form of Meng Tzu or Master Meng), lived from around 372 to about 289 B.C. and, after Confucius, was the single most important thinker in the evolution of Confucian ideology. His basic doctrines were that humans are innately good and that each person has the potential for becoming a sage. From these two principles he evolved a political philosophy of benevolent government.

3. Master Hsün (ca 300–235 B.C.) was the last great philosopher in the formative age of Confucian classical thought. Unlike Confucius and Mencius, he set his ideas down systematically in a detailed book. Although he may have been the most original and systematic of the three great Confucian sages, the Chinese valued his teachings far less than those of Confucius and Mencius, because he was too much of a free thinker, rejecting the existence of spirits, and because he doubted that humans are innately good.

4. Twilight because, in Han Confucian eyes, this brief and evil reign was more the last stage of Chou than a full-fledged dynasty itself. It had not followed the classic pattern, established in the first three dynasties, of vigorous growth, maturity, and decay.

5. See Chapter 4.

6. The *Book of Songs* (Odes), the *Book of History* (Documents), the *Analects*, the *Book of Changes*, the *Book of Rites*, the *Spring and Autumn Annals*. Excerpts from the first three appear in Chapters 1 and 4. The *Book of Changes*, or *I Ching*, is a work on divination that enjoys popularity today among Western readers; the *Book of Rites* is a compilation of proper rituals. See note 18 for a description of the *Spring and Autumn Annals*. Although the *Analects* always remained a revered book of Confucian wisdom, the other five classics assumed greater importance during the age of Later Han and collectively emerged as the *wu-ching* — the core of the Confucian canon.

7. Formerly called Liu Pang, Han Kao-tsu reigned as the first Han Emperor from 202 to 195 B.C.

8. The brilliant but erratic noble whom the commoner Liu Pang defeated in contest for the empire after the fall of Ch'in.

9. Confucius's native land in northeast China.

allowed to study and teach their Classics freely and to demonstrate the proper rituals. . . .

Shu-sun T'ung[10] drew up the ceremonial for the Han court and was rewarded with the post of master of ritual, while all the other scholars who assisted him were likewise given preferential treatment in the government. The emperor sighed over the neglected state of learning and would have done more to encourage its revival, but at the time there was still considerable turmoil within the empire and the region within the four seas had not yet been set at peace. Likewise, during the reigns of Emperor Hui[11] and Empress Lü[12] there was still no leisure to attend to the matter of government schools. Moreover, the high officials at this time were all military men who had won their distinction in battle.

With the accession of Emperor Wen,[13] Confucian scholars began little by little to be summoned and employed in the government, although Emperor Wen himself rather favored the Legalist teachings on personnel organization and control. Emperor Ching[14] made no effort to employ Confucian scholars, and his mother, Empress Dowager Tou,[15] was an advocate of the teachings of the Yellow Emperor[16] and Lao Tzu. Thus various scholars were appointed to fill the posts of court erudit and to answer questions, but they had no prospects of advancement.

When the present emperor came to the throne there were a number of enlightened Confucian scholars . . . at court. The emperor was much attracted by their ideas and accordingly sent out a summons for scholars of moral worth and literary ability to take service in the government.

After Empress Dowager Tou passed away, the marquis of Wu-an, T'ien Fen,[17] became chancellor. He rejected the doctrines of the Taoists, the Legalists, and the other philosophical schools, and invited several hundred Confucian scholars and literary men to take service in the government. Among them was Kung-sun Hung who, because of his knowledge of the *Spring and Autumn Annals*,[18] advanced from the rank of commoner to that of one of the three highest ministers in the government and was enfeoffed as marquis of P'ing-chin. Scholars throughout the

---

10. A Confucian scholar who served both the Ch'in and early Han rulers.

11. Known as the Filial Emperor, he reigned from 195 to 188 B.C., but his mother, the Empress Dowager Lü, held all real power. See the next note.

12. The widow of Kao-tsu, she ruled China as the power behind the throne between 195 and 180 B.C.

13. Wen the Filial (180–157 B.C.), the fourth son of Kao-tsu and the first strong emperor since his father's death fifteen years earlier.

14. Wen's successor, who ruled from 157 to 141 B.C.

15. This powerful woman, who died in 135 B.C., sponsored the study of Taoist teachings at the courts of her husband and son.

16. Huang-ti (the Yellow Emperor) was a legendary predynastic ruler who supposedly reigned during the mid-third millennium B.C. He was believed to be, along with Lao Tzu, the founder of Taoism.

17. Maternal uncle of Han Wu-ti.

18. A terse chronicle of events covering the period 722 to 481 B.C. and written from the perspective of the state of Lu; this Confucian classic was believed to be authored by the Great Master. There is no reason to believe Confucius had a hand in composing it, but apparently he did study and admire the work.

empire saw which way the wind was blowing and did all they could to follow his example.

As a scholar official, Kung-sun Hung, who held the post of imperial secretary, was disturbed that the teachings of Confucius were being neglected and not put into greater practice and he therefore submitted the following memorial:

> The chancellor and the imperial secretary wish to make this statement. Your Majesty has issued an edict which reads:
>
> "I have heard that the people are to be guided by rites and led to the practice of virtue through music, and that the institution of marriage is the basis of the family. Yet at the present time rites have fallen into disuse and music has declined, a fact which grieves me deeply. Therefore I have invited men of outstanding moral worth and wide learning from all over the empire to come and take service at court. Let the officials in charge of ritual encourage learning, hold discussions, and gather all the information they can to encourage the revival of rites in order to act as leaders of the empire. Let the master of ritual consult with the erudites and their students on how to promote the spread of virtue in the countryside and open the way for men of outstanding talent."
>
> In accordance with this edict we have respectfully discussed the matter with the master of ritual K'ung Tsang, the erudit P'ing, and others, and they have told us that, according to their information, it was the custom under the Three Dynasties of antiquity to set up schools for instruction in the villages. In the Hsia dynasty these were called *hsiao*, in the Shang dynasty *hsü*, and in the Chou dynasty *hsiang*. These schools encouraged goodness by making it known to the court and censured evil by applying punishments. Thus it was the officials of the capital who took the initiative in instructing and educating the people, and virtue spread from the court outwards to the provinces.
>
> Now Your Majesty, manifesting supreme virtue and displaying a profound intelligence worthy to rank with that of heaven and earth, has sought to rectify human relations, encourage learning, revive the former rites, promote instruction in goodness, and open the way for men of worth so that the people of the four directions may be swayed to virtue. This is indeed the way to lay the foundations for an era of great peace.
>
> In earlier times, however, the instruction provided by the government was incomplete and the rites were not fully carried out. We therefore beg that the previous official system be utilized to increase the spread of instruction. In order to fill the offices of erudit we suggest that fifty additional students be selected and declared exempt from the usual labor services. The master of ritual shall be charged with the selection of these students from among men of the people who are eighteen years of age or older and who are of good character and upright behavior. In order to supply candidates for the selection, the governors, prime ministers, heads, and magistrates of the various provinces, kingdoms, districts, marches,[19] and feudal cities shall recommend to the two thousand picul officials[20] in their respective regions any men who are fond of learning, show respect for their superiors, adhere to the teachings of the government, and honor the customs of their village, and whose actions in no way reflect discredit upon their reputations. The two thousand picul officials shall in turn make a careful examination of the men recommended; those found worthy shall then be sent in com-

19. Frontier regions.

20. A picul was about a bushel of grain. Every office was graded according to its annual salary, most ranging between 2,000 and 100 piculs a year, although the emperor's chief counselor received 10,000 piculs. Salaries were paid partly in grain and partly in silk and cash equivalents.

pany with the local accounting officials when the latter come to the capital to make their reports, and shall there be presented to the master of ritual. They shall then receive instruction in the same manner as the regular students of the erudits.

At the end of a year, all of them shall be examined. Those who have mastered one or more of the Classics shall be assigned to fill vacancies among the scholar officials in the provinces or among the officers . . . who serve under the master of ritual. If there are any outstanding students who qualify for the post of palace attendant, the master of ritual shall present their names to the throne. In this way men of exceptional talent and ability will be brought at once to the attention of the ruler. If, on the contrary, there are any who have not applied themselves to their studies, whose ability is inferior, or who have failed to master even one Classic, they shall be summarily dismissed. In addition, if there are any among the recommending officials who have failed to carry out their duties properly, we suggest that they be punished. . . .

The emperor signified his approval of this proposal, and from this time on the number of literary men who held positions as ministers and high officials in the government increased remarkably.

Pan Chao

Lessons for Women

Education in the Confucian classics increasingly became one of several avenues to a position of social and political power in Han China. Confucian doctrine, however, did not accord women a status equal to that of men, and they generally were regarded as unworthy or incapable of a literary education. The Confucian classics themselves say little about women, which shows how little they mattered in the scheme of Confucian values. Most Confucians accepted the subservience of women to men as natural and proper. In their view, failure to maintain a proper relationship between two such obviously unequal persons as husband and wife or brother and sister would result in social disharmony and a breakdown of all the rules of propriety.

Yet this was only part of the traditional Chinese view of women. Both Confucian doctrine and Chinese society at large accorded women, as both mothers and mothers-in-law, a good deal of honor, and with that honor came power within the family structure. In every age there were, moreover, a handful of extraordinary women who acquired literary educations or otherwise achieved positions of far-ranging influence and authority despite social constraints. The foremost female Confucian in the age of Han was Pan Chao (ca A.D. 45–116), younger sister of the court historian Pan Ku (32–92). Upon Ku's death, Chao served as imperial historian under Emperor Han Ho-ti (88–105) and completed her brother's *Book of Han,* a history of the Former Han Dynasty, which is generally regarded as second only to the historical work of Ssu-ma Ch'ien. Pan Chao also served as an adviser on state matters to the Empress Teng, who assumed power as regent for her infant son in 106.

Madame Pan was the daughter of the widely respected writer and administrator Pan Piao (A.D. 3–54) and received her elementary education from her literate mother while still a child in her father's house. Otherwise her early life appears to have been quite conventional. She married at the age of fourteen, thereby becoming the lowest-ranking member of her husband's family, and bore children. Although her husband died young, Pan Chao never remarried, devoting herself instead to literary pursuits and acquiring a reputation for scholarship and compositional grace that eventually brought her to the imperial court.

Among her many literary works, Pan Chao composed a commentary on the popular *Lives of Admirable Women* by Liu Hsiang (ca 77–6 B.C.) and later in life produced her most famous work, the *Nu Chieh*, or *Lessons for Women*, which purports to be an instructional manual on feminine behavior and virtue for her daughters. In fact, she intended it for a much wider audience. Realizing that Confucian texts contained little in the way of specific and practical guidelines for a woman's everyday life, Pan Chao sought to fill that void with a coherent set of rules for women, especially young women.

Questions for Analysis

1. What does Pan Chao tell us about the status of daughters-in-law?
2. How has she escaped the fears of servitude?
3. What do her claims to lack of intelligence suggest?
4. Why are we able to infer that her daughters also received at least a rudimentary education in Confucian literature?
5. What does Pan Chao consider the principal duty of a husband? Of a wife? How and why are they complementary parts of the natural order of the universe?
6. According to Pan Chao, what rules of propriety should govern a marriage?
7. How and why does Pan Chao advocate a departure from tradition?
8. What sort of education does she advocate for women, and what is its purpose?
9. Why was Pan Chao's essay so highly regarded by Confucian scholars over the following centuries?
10. Is it correct to call Pan Chao a feminist?

I, the unworthy writer, am unsophisticated, unenlightened, and by nature unintelligent, but I am fortunate both to have received not a little favor from my scholarly father, and to have had a (cultured) mother and instructresses upon whom to rely for a literary education as well as for training in good manners. More than forty years have passed since at the age of fourteen I took up the dustpan and the broom in the Ts'ao family.[1] During this time with trembling heart I feared con-

1. The family into which she married.

stantly that I might disgrace my parents, and that I might multiply difficulties for both the women and the men (of my husband's family). Day and night I was distressed in heart, (but) I labored without confessing weariness. Now and hereafter, however, I know how to escape (from such fears).

Being careless, and by nature stupid, I taught and trained (my children) without system. Consequently I fear that my son Ku may bring disgrace upon the Imperial Dynasty by whose Holy Grace he has unprecedentedly received the extraordinary privilege of wearing the Gold and the Purple, a privilege for the attainment of which (by my son, I) a humble subject never even hoped. Nevertheless, now that he is a man and able to plan his own life, I need not again have concern for him. But I do grieve that you, my daughters, just now at the age for marriage, have not at this time had gradual training and advice; that you still have not learned the proper customs for married women. I fear that by failure in good manners in other families you will humiliate both your ancestors and your clan. I am now seriously ill, life is uncertain. As I have thought of you all in so untrained a state, I have been uneasy many a time for you. At hours of leisure I have composed . . . these instructions under the title, "Lessons for Women." In order that you may have something wherewith to benefit your persons, I wish every one of you, my daughters, each to write out a copy for yourself.

From this time on every one of you strive to practice these (lessons).

Humility

On the third day after the birth of a girl the ancients observed three customs: (first) to place the baby below the bed; (second) to give her a potsherd[2] with which to play; and (third) to announce her birth to her ancestors by an offering. Now to lay the baby below the bed plainly indicated that she is lowly and weak, and should regard it as her primary duty to humble herself before others. To give her potsherds with which to play indubitably signified that she should practice labor and consider it her primary duty to be industrious. To announce her birth before her ancestors clearly meant that she ought to esteem as her primary duty the continuation of the observance of worship in the home.

These three ancient customs epitomize a woman's ordinary way of life and the teachings of the traditional ceremonial rites and regulations. Let a woman modestly yield to others; let her respect others; let her put others first, herself last. Should she do something good, let her not mention it; should she do something bad, let her not deny it. Let her bear disgrace; let her even endure when others speak or do evil to her. Always let her seem to tremble and to fear. (When a woman follows such maxims as these,) then she may be said to humble herself before others.

Let a woman retire late to bed, but rise early to duties; let her not dread tasks by day or by night. Let her not refuse to perform domestic duties whether easy or difficult. That which must be done, let her finish completely, tidily, and systematically. (When a woman follows such rules as these,) then she may be said to be industrious.

Let a woman be correct in manner and upright in character in order to serve her husband. Let her live in purity and quietness (of spirit), and attend to her own affairs. Let her love not gossip and silly

2. A piece of broken pottery.

laughter. Let her cleanse and purify and arrange in order the wine and the food for the offerings to the ancestors. (When a woman observes such principles as these,) then she may be said to continue ancestral worship.

No woman who observes these three (fundamentals of life) has ever had a bad reputation or has fallen into disgrace. If a woman fail to observe them, how can her name be honored; how can she but bring disgrace upon herself?

Husband and Wife

The Way of husband and wife is intimately connected with *Yin* and *Yang*,[3] and relates the individual to gods and ancestors. Truly it is the great principle of Heaven and Earth, and the great basis of human relationships. Therefore the "Rites"[4] honor union of man and woman; and in the "Book of Poetry"[5] the "First Ode" manifests the principle of marriage. For these reasons the relationship cannot but be an important one.

If a husband be unworthy then he possesses nothing by which to control his wife. If a wife be unworthy, then she possesses nothing with which to serve her husband. If a husband does not control his wife, then the rules of conduct manifesting his authority are abandoned and broken. If a wife does not serve her husband, then the proper relationship (between men and women) and the natural order of things are neglected and destroyed. As a matter of fact the purpose of these two (the controlling of women by men, and the serving of men by women) is the same.

Now examine the gentlemen of the present age. They only know that wives must be controlled, and that the husband's rules of conduct manifesting his authority must be established. They therefore teach their boys to read books and (study) histories. But they do not in the least understand that husbands and masters must (also) be served, and that the proper relationship and the rites should be maintained.

Yet only to teach men and not to teach women — is that not ignoring the essential relation between them? According to the "Rites," it is the rule to begin to teach children to read at the age of eight years, and by the age of fifteen years they ought then to be ready for cultural training. Only why should it not be (that girls' education as well as boys' be) according to this principle?

Respect and Caution

As *Yin* and *Yang* are not of the same nature, so man and woman have different characteristics. The distinctive quality of the *Yang* is rigidity; the function of the *Yin* is yielding. Man is honored for strength; a woman is beautiful on account of her gentleness. Hence there arose the common saying: "A man though born like a wolf may, it is feared, become a weak monstrosity; a woman though born like a mouse may, it is feared, become a tiger."

Now for self-culture nothing equals respect for others. To counteract firmness

---

3. According to Chinese cosmology these were the two basic elements of the universe: *Yin*, the soft, yielding, feminine element, and *Yang*, the hard, aggressive, male element. Every substance contains both elements in varying proportions. As one element increases within a substance or being, the other decreases, but neither is ever eliminated.

4. The *Book of Rites* (page 146, note 6).

5. The *Book of Songs* (Chapter 1).

nothing equals compliance. Consequently it can be said that the Way of respect and acquiescence is woman's most important principle of conduct. So respect may be defined as nothing other than holding on to that which is permanent; and acquiescence nothing other than being liberal and generous. Those who are steadfast in devotion know that they should stay in their proper places; those who are liberal and generous esteem others, and honor and serve (them).

If husband and wife have the habit of staying together, never leaving one another, and following each other around within the limited space of their own rooms, then they will lust after and take liberties with one another. From such action improper language will arise between the two. This kind of discussion may lead to licentiousness. Out of licentiousness will be born a heart of disrespect to the husband. Such a result comes from not knowing that one should stay in one's proper place.

Furthermore, affairs may be either crooked or straight; words may be either right or wrong. Straightforwardness cannot but lead to quarreling; crookedness cannot but lead to accusation. If there are really accusations and quarrels, then undoubtedly there will be angry affairs. Such a result comes from not esteeming others, and not honoring and serving (them).

(If wives) suppress not contempt for husbands, then it follows (that such wives) rebuke and scold (their husbands). (If husbands) stop not short of anger, then they are certain to beat (their wives). The correct relationship between husband and wife is based upon harmony and intimacy, and (conjugal) love is grounded in proper union. Should actual blows be dealt, how could matrimonial relationship be preserved? Should sharp words be spoken, how could (conjugal) love exist? If love and proper relationship both be destroyed, then husband and wife are divided.

Womanly Qualifications

A woman (ought to) have four qualifications: (1) womanly virtue; (2) womanly words; (3) womanly bearing; and (4) womanly work. Now what is called womanly virtue need not be brilliant ability, exceptionally different from others. Womanly words need be neither clever in debate nor keen in conversation. Womanly appearance requires neither a pretty nor a perfect face and form. Womanly work need not be work done more skillfully than that of others.

To guard carefully her chastity; to control circumspectly her behavior; in every motion to exhibit modesty; and to model each act on the best usage, this is womanly virtue.

To choose her words with care; to avoid vulgar language; to speak at appropriate times; and not to weary others (with much conversation), may be called the characteristics of womanly words.

To wash and scrub filth away; to keep clothes and ornaments fresh and clean; to wash the head and bathe the body regularly, and to keep the person free from disgraceful filth, may be called the characteristics of womanly bearing.

With whole-hearted devotion to sew and to weave; to love not gossip and silly laughter; in cleanliness and order (to prepare) the wine and food for serving guests, may be called the characteristics of womanly work.

These four qualifications characterize the greatest virtue of a woman. No woman can afford to be without them. In fact they are very easy to possess if a woman only treasure them in her heart. The ancients had a saying: "Is Love afar off? If I desire love, then love is at hand!" So can it be said of these qualifications. . . .

Implicit Obedience

Whenever the mother-in-law says, "Do not do that," and if what she says is right, unquestionably the daughter-in-law obeys. Whenever the mother-in-law says, "Do that," even if what she says is wrong, still the daughter-in-law submits unfailingly to the command.

Let a woman not act contrary to the wishes and the opinions of parents-in-law about right and wrong; let her not dispute with them what is straight and what is crooked. Such (docility) may be called obedience which sacrifices personal opinion. Therefore the ancient book, "A Pattern for Women," says: "If a daughter-in-law (who follows the wishes of her parents-in-law) is like an echo and a shadow, how could she not be praised?"

India in the Age of Empires

More often than not in its long history, India has been divided into political fragments, and modern study of its past has consequently centered far more on its cultural developments than on its transitory political structures, which are so confusing to Western observers. During these centuries, however, India witnessed the creation of two significant native empires that command our attention.

First there was the mighty Mauryan Empire (ca 315–183 B.C.), which controlled all but the most southern portions of the subcontinent. Centuries later there was the Gupta Empire (A.D. 320–ca 550), which was centered on the Ganges River in the northeast but which exercised authority over most of northern and central India. Although even the Mauryan Empire never equaled the Han and Roman empires in size, military power, and longevity, both Indian empires provided peace and a general prosperity based in part on energetic administration and benign social intervention. At the height of the Gupta Empire under Chandragupta II (ca A.D. 376–415), India may well have been the most prosperous and peaceful society in all of Eurasia. China was then immersed in its interdynastic time of troubles; Greco-Roman civilization was undergoing severe stresses at every level; and the mighty Sassanian Empire of Persia was embroiled in internal religious turmoil and wars on its frontiers.

Between these two home-bred imperial periods, India underwent a series of invasions from the northwest, which resulted in portions of northern India falling under the domination of alien rulers and being joined to important Central Asian kingdoms and empires. The first of these invaders were Greeks from Bactria, essentially a region of today's northern Afghanistan, who came in the early second century B.C. and established a number of competing kingdoms. The Greco-Bactrians did not remain in India long, soon giving way to various nomadic invaders from East Asia, who were forced to move westward by the emergence of Chinese imperialism in the late third and second centuries B.C.

The most significant of the new invaders were the Yueh-Chih, who created the

Kushana Empire toward the end of the first century B.C. The Kushana, whose imperial focus was always Central Asia, lasted into the third century A.D., and during their reign they provided India with connections to the Middle East and China. Much of that interaction involved the peaceful exchange of goods and ideas, but Chinese annals also tell how General Pan Ch'ao, brother of the historians Ku and Chao, destroyed a Yueh-Chih army in A.D. 90 when the Kushana emperor launched a retaliatory strike against the Chinese after he was refused the hand of a Han princess.

All these important political developments should not, however, blind us to the fact that the most significant developments taking place in India during the period 300 B.C.–A.D. 500 were cultural. The Gupta era is especially important in this regard and is rightly acknowledged as one of traditional India's golden ages.

Asoka

Rock and Pillar Edicts

As Alexander the Great and his Macedonian generals pulled out of northwest India, a local lord, Chandragupta Maurya (ca 315–281 B.C.), began carving out what would become the greatest of India's ancient empires, the Mauryan. Under the founder and his son Bindusara, the empire expanded and functioned with brutal efficiency. Around 269 B.C. Bindusara's son Asoka (ca 269–232) inherited the throne and initially continued his family's tradition of imperial aggression.

In the eighth year following his consecration as emperor, however, he underwent a spiritual conversion when he beheld the bloodshed and misery that resulted from his conquest of the land of Kalinga, along India's southeast flank. As a consequence, Asoka embraced the teachings of the Buddha and embarked on a new policy of government. Inspired probably by the public monuments of the kings of Persia, Asoka publicized his change of heart and new imperial policies in a series of engraved rock and pillar inscriptions scattered throughout his lands.

Questions for Analysis

1. What does Asoka mean by "Righteousness"?
2. What evidence is there that Asoka attempted to export Buddhist teachings to his western neighbors?
3. What does Asoka consider as the "True Conquest"?
4. Does Asoka totally reject the use of imperial force?
5. What is, in Asoka's mind, the essential message of all sects?
6. What was Asoka's attitude and policy toward all other religions, especially Hinduism?

7. Compare Asoka's understanding of the essential message of Buddhism with the Buddha's two sermons in Chapter 3. Do you see any elements in Asoka's Buddhism that the Buddha's message lacks? What does this suggest about the development of Buddhism by Asoka's day?
8. What duties did Asoka assume to be his?
9. In what ways did Asoka attempt to further Righteousness?

[*Asoka's Conversion*]

When the king, Beloved of the Gods and of Gracious Mien, had been consecrated eight years Kalinga was conquered, 150,000 people were deported, 100,000 were killed, and many times that number died. But after the conquest of Kalinga, the Beloved of the Gods began to follow Righteousness (Dharma), to love Righteousness, and to give instruction in Righteousness. Now the Beloved of the Gods regrets the conquest of Kalinga, for when an independent country is conquered people are killed, they die, or are deported, and that the Beloved of the Gods finds very painful and grievous. And this he finds even more grievous — that all the inhabitants — brahmins, ascetics, and other sectarians, and householders who are obedient to superiors, parents, and elders, who treat friends, acquaintances, companions, relatives, slaves, and servants with respect, and are firm in their faith — all suffer violence, murder, and separation from their loved ones. Even those who are fortunate enough not to have lost those near and dear to them are afflicted at the misfortunes of friends, acquaintances, companions, and relatives. The participation of all men in common suffering is grievous to the Beloved of the Gods. Moreover there is no land, except that of the Greeks, where groups of brahmins and ascetics are not found, or where men are not members of one sect or another. So now, even if the number of those killed and captured in the conquest of Kalinga had been a hundred or a thousand times less, it would be grievous to the Beloved of the Gods. The Beloved of the Gods will forgive as far as he can, and he even conciliates the forest tribes[1] of his dominions; but he warns them that there is power even in the remorse of the Beloved of the Gods, and he tells them to reform, lest they be killed.

For all beings the Beloved of the Gods desires security, self-control, calm of mind, and gentleness. The Beloved of the Gods considers that the greatest victory is the victory of Righteousness; and this he has won here (in India) and even five hundred leagues[2] beyond his frontiers in the realm of the Greek king Antiochus,[3] and beyond Antiochus among the four kings Ptolemy, Antigonus, Magas, and Alexander.[4] Even where the envoys of the Beloved of the Gods have not been sent men hear of the way in which he follows

1. The primitive, largely uncivilized folk of the southern jungle.

2. A league is generally reckoned as equal to three miles.

3. Antiochus II, or Antiochus Theos, Seleucid King of Syria.

4. Ptolemy II, or Ptolemy Philadelphus of Egypt; Antigonos Gonatas of Macedonia; Magos of Cyrene in North Africa; Alexander of Epirus in the northwest region of Greece.

and teaches Righteousness, and they too follow it and will follow it. Thus he achieves a universal conquest, and conquest always gives a feeling of pleasure; yet it is but a slight pleasure, for the Beloved of the Gods only looks on that which concerns the next life as of great importance.

I have had this inscription of Righteousness engraved that all my sons and grandsons may not seek to gain new victories, that in whatever victories they may gain they may prefer forgiveness and light punishment, that they may consider the only (valid) victory the victory of Righteousness, which is of value both in this world and the next, and that all their pleasure may be in Righteousness. . . .

[*Other Religions*]

The Beloved of the Gods . . . honors members of all sects, whether ascetics or householders, by gifts and various honors. But he does not consider gifts and honors as important as the furtherance of the essential message of all sects. This essential message varies from sect to sect, but it has one common basis, that one should so control one's tongue as not to honor one's own sect or disparage another's on the wrong occasions; for on certain occasions one should do so only mildly, and indeed on other occasions one should honor other men's sects. By doing this one strengthens one's own sect and helps the others, while by doing otherwise one harms one's own sect and does a disservice to the others. Whoever honors his own sect and disparages another man's, whether from blind loyalty or with the intention of showing his own sect in a favorable light, does his own sect the greatest possible harm. Concord is best, with each hearing and respecting the other's teachings. It is the wish of the Beloved of the Gods that members of all sects should be learned and should teach virtue. . . . Many officials are busied in this matter . . . and the result is the progress of my own sect and the illumination of Righteousness.

[*Hindu Ceremonies*]

People perform various ceremonies, at the marriage of sons and daughters, at the birth of children, when going on a journey . . . or on other occasions. . . . On such occasions women especially perform many ceremonies which are various, futile, and useless. Even when they have to be done (to conform to custom and keep up appearances) such ceremonies are of little use. But the ceremonies of Righteousness are of great profit — these are the good treatment of slaves and servants, respect for elders, self-mastery in one's relations with living beings, gifts to brahmins and ascetics, and so on. But for their success everyone — fathers, mothers, brothers, masters, friends, acquaintances, and neighbors — must agree — "These are good! These are the ceremonies that we should perform for success in our undertakings . . . and when we have succeeded we will perform them again!" Other ceremonies are of doubtful utility — one may achieve one's end through them or one may not. Moreover they are only of value in this world, while the value of the ceremonies of Righteousness is eternal, for even if one does not achieve one's end in this world one stores up boundless merit in the other, while if one achieves one's end in this world the gain is double.

[*Asoka's Duty*]

I am not satisfied simply with hard work or carrying out the affairs of state, for I consider my work to be the welfare of the whole world, of which hard work and the carrying out of affairs are merely the basis. There is no better deed than to work for the welfare of the whole world, and all my efforts are made that I may clear my debt to all beings. I make them happy here and now that they may attain heaven in the life to come. . . . But it is difficult without great effort. . . .

Everywhere in the empire of the Beloved of the Gods, and even beyond his frontiers in the lands of the Cholas, Pandyas, Satyaputras, Keralaputras[5] and as far as Ceylon, and in the kingdoms of Antiochus the Greek king and the kings who are his neighbors, the Beloved of the Gods has provided medicines for man and beast. Wherever medicinal plants have not been found they have been sent there and planted. Roots and fruits have also been sent where they did not grow, and have been planted. Wells have been dug along the roads for the use of man and beast. . . .

In the past kings sought to make the people progress in Righteousness, but they did not progress. . . . And I asked myself how I might uplift them through progress in Righteousness. . . . Thus I decided to have them instructed in Righteousness, and to issue ordinances of Righteousness, so that by hearing them the people might conform, advance in the progress of Righteousness, and themselves make great progress. . . . For that purpose many officials are employed among the people to instruct them in Righteousness and to explain it to them. . . .

All the good deeds that I have done have been accepted and followed by the people. And so obedience to mother and father, obedience to teachers, respect for the aged, kindliness to brahmins and ascetics, to the poor and weak, and to slaves and servants, have increased and will continue to increase. . . . And this progress of Righteousness among men has taken place in two manners, by enforcing conformity to Righteousness, and by exhortation. I have enforced the law against killing certain animals and many others, but the greatest progress of Righteousness among men comes from exhortation in favor of noninjury to life and abstention from killing living beings.

I have done this that it may endure . . . as long as the moon and sun, and that my sons and my great-grandsons may support it; for by supporting it they will gain both this world and the next.

Laws of Manu

Despite Asoka's promotion of the Buddhist principle of *dharma*, or the Law of Righteousness, the majority of classical India's population seems to have remained true to more traditional Hindu ways and beliefs, which included acceptance of the caste system and the concept that dharma defined one's caste duties. Hindus, like Buddhists, believed that dharma was the moral law of the universe and the highest good upon which all reality was founded. Yet for Hindus dharma was not an abstract, impersonal code of righteousness, it was Sacred Law and, as such, governed all of a

5. Tamil kingdoms in the southern tip of India.

person's social and religious activities. For most Hindus, dharma became concrete in the innumerable rituals Asoka found so useless and in Hindu civilization's numerous forms of mandated social behavior. Faith, worship, and social duty all sprang from dharma.

The earliest extant codification of the Sacred Law of dharma is the *Laws of Manu,* which was compiled between the first century B.C. and the second or third century A.D. In Hindu mythology, Manu was the primeval human being, the father of humanity and its first king. In the Vedas he appears as the founder of all human social order and the original teacher of dharma, having been instructed in the Sacred Law by Brahman. Tradition also regarded him as an Indian Utnapishtim, or Noah, the sole survivor of a catastrophic flood, after which he created a woman, through whom he generated the human species. The anonymous compilers of the *Laws of Manu* claimed that the rules and regulations contained in this code were universal and timeless. Each law was a manifestation of dharma, passed down uncorrupted from Manu. In reality, these laws had evolved over the past 2,500 years as Indian society took shape.

The selections illustrate the two major determinants of classical Indian society: caste and sex. As far as we can ascertain, sex distinctions of one sort or another were common to all ancient civilizations, but the Hindu caste system was unique to India. The English word *caste* is derived from the Portuguese *casta,* which means "pure." Hindus use two different Sanskrit words for caste, *varna* ("color") and *jati* ("birth"). Varna refers only to the four major social-religious divisions that "The Hymn to Purusha" (Chapter 2) enumerated: Brahmins (priests), Kshatriyas (warriors), Vaisyas (farmers, artisans, and merchants), and Sudras (workers). These classifications of Indian society clearly resulted from the Aryans' attempt to separate themselves from the darker-skinned natives they had conquered. The jati system, which today includes over 3,000 identifiable groupings, was not fully developed until around the Gupta period, long after the Aryans had disappeared into India's general population. Jatis are hereditary occupations, each with its own dharma. Hindus generally classify jatis as subdivisions of the varna system and steps in the ladder of reincarnation.

Questions for Analysis

1. What relationship do Sudras have to members of the other three castes? Why are they excluded from the vedic ceremonies?
2. Can you see from this evidence why the Portuguese concluded that "purity" was the essential component of the varna and jati systems? What forms of purity are most important?
3. The lowest-ranking jatis are composed of people known as "untouchables." Why are they called that, and what manner of life do they lead? Why do other Hindus find their occupations so offensive?

4. Under what circumstances might a person engage in work appropriate to a lower varna? How far may one go in this regard, and what are the consequences? May one legitimately assume the duties of a higher varna?
5. Each varna and jati has its own dharma. Is there also a universal dharma, common to all Hindus?
6. How might the caste system make political and social unification difficult, if not impossible?
7. Why are women denied access to ceremonies where the vedic texts are recited? Notwithstanding this prohibition, do women perform any necessary religious functions? If so, what are they, and what do these functions tell us about the status of women?
8. Why are women protected and honored? What are the duties of their fathers and husbands?
9. What constraints are placed on women, and why? What freedoms, if any, does a woman enjoy?
10. Compare the legal status of Hindu women with that of women in Han China (see Pan Chao, *Lessons for Women*). Are their positions comparable, or does one seem to enjoy greater freedom and power? Is one better protected than the other?

[*Varna*]

The Brahmin, the Kshatriya, and the Vaisya castes (varna) are the twice-born ones,[1] but the fourth, the Sudra, has one birth only; there is no fifth caste. . . .

To Brahmins he[2] assigned teaching and studying (the Veda), sacrificing for their own benefit and for others, giving and accepting of alms.

The Kshatriya he commanded to protect the people, to bestow gifts, to offer sacrifices, to study the Veda, and to abstain from attaching himself to sensual pleasures;

The Vaisya to tend cattle, to bestow gifts, to offer sacrifices, to study the Veda, to trade, to lend money, and to cultivate land.

One occupation only the lord prescribed to the Sudra, to serve meekly even these other three castes.

[*Jatis*]

From a [male] Sudra are born an Ayogava, a Kshattri, and a Kandala, the lowest of men, by Vaisya, Kshatriya, and Brahmin females [respectively], sons who owe their origin to a confusion of the castes. . . .

Killing fish to Nishadas; carpenters' work to the Ayogava; to Medas, Andhras, Kunkus, and Madgus, the slaughter of wild animals. . . .

But the dwellings of Kandalas . . . shall be outside the village. . . .

Their dress shall be the garments of the dead, they shall eat their food from broken dishes, black iron shall be their orna-

1. One's second birth was initiation into the recitation of the Vedas. Only men could be "twice-born."

2. Brahman.

ments, and they must always wander from place to place.

A man who fulfills a religious duty, shall not seek intercourse with them; their [Kandala] transactions shall be among themselves, and their marriages with their equals. . . .

[A]t night they shall not walk about in villages and in towns.

By day they may go about for the purpose of their work, distinguished by marks at the king's command, and they shall carry out the corpses of persons who have no relatives; that is a settled rule.

By the king's order they shall always execute the criminals, in accordance with the law, and they shall take for themselves the clothes, the beds, and the ornaments of such criminals.

[*Dharma*]

A king who knows the sacred law, must inquire into the laws of castes [jatis], of districts, of guilds, and of families, and settle the peculiar law of each. . . .

Among the several occupations the most commendable are, teaching the Veda for a Brahmin, protecting the people for a Kshatriya, and trade for a Vaisya.

But a Brahmin, unable to subsist by his peculiar occupations just mentioned, may live according to the law applicable to Kshatriyas; for the latter is next to him in rank. . . .

A man of low caste [varna] who through covetousness lives by the occupations of a higher one, the king shall deprive of his property and banish.

It is better to discharge one's own duty incompletely than to perform completely that of another; for he who lives according to the law of another caste is instantly excluded from his own.

A Vaisya who is unable to subsist by his own duties, may even maintain himself by a Sudra's mode of life, avoiding however acts forbidden to him, and he should give it up, when he is able to do so. . . .

Abstention from injuring creatures, veracity, abstention from unlawfully appropriating the goods of others, purity, and control of the organs,[3] Manu has declared to be the summary of the law for the four castes.

[*The Nature of Women*]

It is the nature of women to seduce men in this world; for that reason the wise are never unguarded in the company of females. . . .

For women no rite is performed with sacred texts, thus the law is settled; women who are destitute of strength and destitute of the knowledge of Vedic texts, are as impure as falsehood itself, that is a fixed rule.

[*Honoring Women*]

Where women are honored, there the gods are pleased; but where they are not honored, no sacred rite yields rewards.

Where the female relations live in grief, the family soon wholly perishes; but that family where they are not unhappy ever prospers.

[*Female Property Rights*]

A wife, a son, and a slave, these three are declared to have no property; the wealth which they earn is acquired for him to whom they belong. . . .

What was given before the nuptial fire, what was given on the bridal procession,

3. Control of all the senses and especially one's sexual drives.

what was given in token of love, and what was received from her brother, mother, or father, that is called the six-fold property of a woman.

Such property, as well as a gift subsequent and what was given to her by her affectionate husband, shall go to her offspring, even if she dies in the lifetime of her husband. . . .

But when the mother has died, all the uterine[4] brothers and the uterine sisters shall equally divide the mother's estate.

[*A Woman's Dependence*]

In childhood a female must be subject to her father, in youth to her husband, when her lord is dead to her sons; a woman must never be independent.

She must not seek to separate herself from her father, husband, or sons; by leaving them she would make both (her own and her husband's) families contemptible. . . .

Him to whom her father may give her, or her brother with the father's permission, she shall obey as long as he lives, and when he is dead, she must not insult his memory.

[*Betrothal*]

No father who knows the law must take even the smallest gratuity for his daughter; for a man who, through avarice, takes a gratuity, is a seller of his offspring. . . .

Three years let a damsel wait,[5] though she be marriageable[6]; but after that time let her choose for herself a bridegroom of equal caste and rank.

If, being not given in marriage, she herself seeks a husband, she incurs no guilt, nor does he whom she weds.

[*Marriage and Its Duties*]

To be mothers were women created, and to be fathers men; religious rites, therefore, are ordained in the Veda to be performed by the husband together with the wife. . . .

No sacrifice, no vow, no fast must be performed by women apart from their husbands; if a wife obeys her husband, she will for that reason alone be exalted in heaven. . . .

By violating her duty towards her husband, a wife is disgraced in this world, after death she enters the womb of a jackal, and is tormented by diseases (the punishment of) her sin. . . .

Let the husband employ his wife in the collection and expenditure of his wealth, in keeping everything clean, in the fulfilment of religious duties, in the preparation of his food, and in looking after the household utensils. . . .

Drinking spirituous liquor, associating with wicked people, separation from the husband, rambling abroad, sleeping at unseasonable hours, and dwelling in other men's houses, are the six causes of the ruin of women. . . .

Offspring, religious rites, faithful service, highest conjugal happiness and heavenly bliss for the ancestors and oneself, depend on one's wife alone. . . .

"Let mutual fidelity continue until death," . . . may be considered as the

4. All natural siblings (born from her uterus).

5. To be offered in marriage by her father or brother.

6. Twelve was a common age of marriage for women; men tended to wait until their twenties.

summary of the highest law for husband and wife.

Let man and woman, united in marriage, constantly exert themselves, that they may not be disunited and may not violate their mutual fidelity.

[Divorce]

For one year let a husband bear with a wife who hates him; but after a year let him deprive her of her property and cease to cohabit with her. . . .

But she who shows aversion towards a mad or outcaste[7] husband, a eunuch,[8] one destitute of manly strength, or one afflicted with such diseases as punish crimes,[9] shall neither be cast off nor be deprived of her property. . . .

A barren[10] wife may be superseded[11] in the eighth year, she whose children all die in the tenth, she who bears only daughters in the eleventh, but she who is quarrelsome without delay.

But a sick wife who is kind to her husband and virtuous in her conduct, may be superseded only with her own consent and must never be disgraced.

Fa-hsien

Travels in India and Ceylon

During the Later, or Eastern, Han Dynasty (A.D. 25–220), Buddhist missionaries traveled to China along the overland routes of Central Asia and the oceanic trade routes of Southeast Asia. As China underwent increasing stresses during the last stages of the Han empire, a form of salvationist Buddhism known as the Mahayana doctrine became particularly popular. In the post-Han period of disunity, it provided many Chinese with a comforting refuge from the evils of the world.

As Buddhism expanded in China, devotees of the new religion, particularly monks, avidly sought to add to the available body of Buddhist literature, which often meant locating various Buddhist holy books in their original homeland, India, and translating them into Chinese. This search for a complete and authentic library of Buddhist scripture, together with the desire of many Chinese Buddhists to make pilgrimages to sites sacred to the Buddha, meant that Chinese travel to India for

7. One who has so egregiously violated the dharma of his caste (varna) that he has been made an outcaste. For example, a Brahmin who knowingly receives food or a gift from a Kandala or other "unclean" person.

8. Sexually impotent.

9. A disease incurred by reason of a sin in a previous incarnation (the law of karma). Hindu society evolved complex and lengthy lists of diseases and their corresponding sins.

10. Childless.

11. Replaced as primary wife by a second wife.

religious purposes became common practice during India's Gupta age and thereafter.

The earliest known Chinese pilgrim to travel to India and return with sacred books was the monk Fa-hsien. Between 399 and 413, he journeyed overland from North China to visit all of Buddhism's holy shrines in India. From India, he sailed to the island of Ceylon (modern Sri Lanka), which, according to tradition, had received Buddhism through the efforts of Asoka and his missionary son Mahendra. From there Fa-hsien traveled to Java and eventually reached home, where he spent the rest of his days translating the texts he had obtained in India.

In addition to these translations, Fa-hsien left behind a record of his travels, in which he described Indian society in the reign of Chandragupta II (ca 376–415). Although this Chinese monk was much more concerned with pilgrimage sites and holy books than with providing detailed descriptions of Indian culture, his travelogue is important, because it provides an outsider's view of India at the height of Gupta prosperity.

Questions for Analysis

1. According to Fa-hsien, how strong was Buddhism in northern India in his day?
2. How did Buddhist principles influence the various social practices and values of Gupta India?
3. To what extent does Fa-hsien's account of the life led by members of the Kandala jati agree with the evidence from the *Laws of Manu?*
4. How has the Buddha's original teaching, which denied the existence of spirits, the soul, and gods, and rejected all ritual, merged with folk beliefs and customs?
5. How well or poorly do the Hindu and Buddhist communities interact?
6. How prosperous and well governed do the land and its people appear to be?
7. How intensively governed and restricted were the subjects of the Gupta Empire?
8. In describing Indian society, Fa-hsien indirectly tells us a lot about China. What can we reasonably infer about Chinese culture from this account?

From this place they[1] traveled southeast, passing by a succession of very many monasteries, with a multitude of monks, who might be counted by myriads. After passing all these places, they came to a country named Ma-t'aou-lo.[2] They still followed the course of the P'oo-na river, on the banks of which, left and right, there were twenty monasteries, which might contain three thousand monks; and (here) the Law of Buddha was still more flourishing. Everywhere, from the Sandy Desert, in all the countries of India, the kings had been firm believers in that Law. When

1. Fa-hsien and his fellow pilgrims.

2. Muthra, in north-central India.

they make their offerings to a community of monks, they take off their royal caps, and along with their relatives and ministers, supply them with food with their own hands. That done, (the king) has a carpet spread for himself on the ground, and sits down on it in front of the chairman; — they dare not presume to sit on couches in front of the community. The laws and ways, according to which the kings presented their offerings when Buddha was in the world, have been handed down to the present day.

All south from this is named the Middle Kingdom. In it the cold and heat are finely tempered, and there is neither hoarfrost nor snow. The people are numerous and happy; they have not to register their households, or attend to any magistrates and their rules; only those who cultivate the royal land have to pay (a portion of) the gain from it. If they want to go, they go; if they want to stay on, they stay. The king governs without decapitation or (other) corporal punishments. Criminals are simply fined, lightly or heavily, according to the circumstances (of each case). Even in cases of repeated attempts at wicked rebellion, they only have their right hands cut off. The king's bodyguards and attendants all have salaries. Throughout the whole country the people do not kill any living creature, nor drink intoxicating liquor, nor eat onions or garlic. The only exception is that of the Chandalas[3]. That is the name for those who are (held to be) wicked men, and live apart from others. When they enter the gate of a city or a market-place, they strike a piece of wood to make themselves known, so that men know and avoid them, and do not come into contact with them. In that country they do not keep pigs and fowls, and do not sell live cattle; in the markets there are no butchers' shops and no dealers in intoxicating drink. . . . Only the Chandalas are fishermen and hunters, and sell flesh meat.

After Buddha attained to pari-nirvana[4] the kings of the various countries and the heads of the Vaisyas[5] built viharas[6] for the priests,[7] and endowed them with fields, houses, gardens, and orchards, along with the resident populations and their cattle, the grants being engraved on plates of metal, so that afterwards they were handed down from king to king, without any one daring to annul them, and they remain even to the present time.

The regular business of the monks is to perform acts of meritorious virtue, and to recite their Sutras[8] and sit wrapt in meditation. When stranger monks arrive (at any monastery), the old residents meet and receive them, carry for them their clothes and alms-bowl, give them water to wash their feet, oil with which to anoint them, and the liquid food permitted out of the regular hours.[9] When (the stranger) has enjoyed a very brief rest, they further ask the number of years that he has been a monk, after which he receives a sleeping apartment with its appurtenances, according to his regular order, and everything is done for him which the rules prescribe.

Where a community of monks resides,

---

3. Kandalas. See the *Laws of Manu*.

4. The Buddha's release from life.

5. The merchant and prosperous farmer caste. See the *Laws of Manu*.

6. A hermitage for a recluse or a little house built for a holy person.

7. A better translation would be "monks," or "disciples."

8. Sacred texts.

9. Solid food was prohibited between sunrise and noon.

they erect topes[10] to Sariputtra, to Mahamaudgalyayana, and to Ananda,[11] and also topes (in honor) of the Abhidharma, the Vinaya, and the Sutras.[12] A month after the (annual season of) rest, the families which are looking out for blessing stimulate one another to make offerings to the monks, and send round to them the liquid food which may be taken out of the ordinary hours. All the monks come together in a great assembly, and preach the Law; after which offerings are presented at the tope of Sariputtra, with all kinds of flowers and incense. All through the night lamps are kept burning, and skillful musicians are employed to perform. . . .

Having crossed the river, and descended south . . . (the travelers) came to the town of Pataliputtra,[13] in the kingdom of Magadha, the city where king Asoka ruled. . . .

By the side of the tope of Asoka, there has been made a mahayana monastery, very grand and beautiful; there is also a hinayana[14] one; the two together containing six hundred or seven hundred monks. The rules of demeanor and the scholastic arrangements in them are worthy of observation.

Shamans[15] of the highest virtue from all quarters, and students, inquirers wishing to find out truth and the grounds of it, all resort to these monasteries. There also resides in this monastery a Brahmin teacher, whose name also is Manjusri, whom the Shamans of greatest virtue in the kingdom, and the mahayana Bhikshus[16] honor and look up to.

The cities and towns of this country are the greatest of all in the Middle Kingdom. The inhabitants are rich and prosperous, and vie with one another in the practice of benevolence and righteousness. Every year on the eighth day of the second month they celebrate a procession of images. They make a four-wheeled car, and on it erect a structure of five stories by means of bamboos tied together. This is supported by a king-post, with poles and lances slanting from it, and is rather more than twenty cubits high, having the shape of a tope. White and silk-like cloth of hair is wrapped all round it, which is then painted in various colors. They make figures of devas,[17] with gold, silver, and lapis lazuli grandly blended and having silken streamers and canopies hung out over them. On the four sides are niches, with a Buddha seated in each, and a Bodhisattva[18] standing in attendance on him. There may be twenty cars, all grand and imposing, but each one different from the others. On the day mentioned, the monks and laity within the borders all

10. Usually known as stupas. A stupa, or tope, was a large domed structure built to house some relic of the Buddha or one of his early disciples. Asoka had commissioned the construction of a large number of these holy sites throughout his empire, and they continued to be built and refined architecturally long after the collapse of the Mauryan Empire. See the illustration on page 127.

11. Three of the Buddha's principal disciples.

12. The three major collections of Buddhist sacred literature.

13. Modern Patna.

14. The Hinayana (Small Vehicle) or, more correctly, Theravada school, was the second of Buddhism's two major sects at this time. Both it and the Mahayana (Great Vehicle) school are treated in Chapter 6.

15. Possibly the author means Hindu yogis and other holy persons.

16. Buddhist monks.

17. Gods and goddesses.

18. A saint who voluntarily postpones Buddhahood, or escape from this world, in order to work for the salvation of others. See Chapter 6.

come together; they have singers and skillful musicians; they pay their devotions with flowers and incense. The Brahmins come and invite the Buddhas to enter the city. These do so in order, and remain two nights in it. All through the night they keep lamps burning, have skillful music, and present offerings. This is the practice in all the other kingdoms as well. The heads of the Vaisya families in them establish in the cities houses for dispensing charity and medicines. All the poor and destitute in the country, orphans, widowers, and childless men, maimed people and cripples, and all who are diseased, go to those houses, and are provided with every kind of help, and doctors examine their diseases. They get the food and medicines which their cases require, and are made to feel at ease; and when they are better, they go away of themselves.

Images of Sacred Authority

The most visible manifestation of this age of Afro-Eurasian interchange was the manner in which artistic motifs and styles traveled across the four major cultural pools, especially from west to east. As these ideas and forms moved from one region to another, they were reshaped and merged with native elements to produce striking examples of hybrid art. The four selections that appear here illustrate the way in which a Greco-Roman sculptural style traveled from the Mediterranean to China between the late first century B.C. and the fifth century A.D. and, in the process, how it was changed by the various cultures that adopted it.

Caesar Augustus as Chief Priest

Every human society seeks to express in its art the force of sacred authority. In this sculpture, crafted by an unknown eastern Mediterranean artist around 20 B.C., Caesar Augustus is portrayed in the fullness of his civil and religious power. As head of the Roman state, Augustus held the office of *Pontifex Maximus* (Chief Priest) and was responsible for presiding over Rome's major religious ceremonies. His very title, Augustus ("Revered One"), imparted an aura of sanctity to him, and throughout the empire temples were erected for the worship of his divine spirit even while he lived.

This work is typical of late Hellenistic sculpture in its idealized naturalism, evocative use of drapery, and sense of drama and mystery. At the same time, its stolidity, restraint, and soberness mark it as Roman. Augustus's appearance, especially his attire, pose, and facial expression, conform to accepted Hellenistic norms for portraying deities, priests, and other sacred persons.

Questions for Analysis

1. Consider Augustus's expression, posture, and dress. How has the sculptor evoked a sense of sacred authority?

Caesar Augustus

2. Compare this sculpture with Harappan India's *Bearded Man* (Chapter 1). In what ways do he and Augustus share certain "priestly" attributes?

A Parthian Noblewoman

In 171 B.C. the Parthians, an Iranian steppe people, replaced the Macedonian Seleucids as masters of Persia and Mesopotamia and established an empire that lasted to A.D. 226. Although creative in military and administrative matters, the Parthians

Parthian Noblewoman

seem to have been content to be inheritors rather than innovators in the fine arts. As a result, their rise did not result in any immediate repudiation of the Hellenistic forms of artistic expression that had been part of the fabric of Persian civilization since the late fourth century B.C. The Parthian Empire, however, was where the Middle East met Central Asia. As a result, its culture was a rich combination of many elements, of which Mediterranean Hellenism was only one.

The sculpture represented here of a woman in Iranian dress dates from the late second or early third century A.D. and illustrates a typical Parthian blend of Greco-Roman and Iranian components. It is one of over a hundred similar votive statues discovered at the many shrines of the city of Hatra in northern Mesopotamia. The unknown noblewoman whom it portrays offered it in devotion to an equally unknown deity. The statue, which is over six feet high, affirms the importance of this woman, who stands with her hand raised in reverence.

Questions for Analysis

1. Consider the woman's expression, posture, and dress. How has the sculptor evoked a sense of her authority?
2. Compare this statue with that of Caesar Augustus. What common elements do you find in each? Do you perceive any differences? Which are more significant?

A Gandharan Buddha

Early Buddhists believed it was wrong to depict the Buddha artistically in human form, since he had broken the chains of matter and had achieved Nirvana. For over 500 years, Buddhist artists used such symbols as a wheel, a pipal tree, a throne, a footprint, and a stupa to symbolize his last earthly body. Toward the end of the first century A.D., artists in the Kushana province of Gandhara, which today comprises Afghanistan and northwest Pakistan, began representing the Buddha as a human. The sculpture of the standing Buddha that appears here is typical of the many carvings that have survived from this period and place. The setting is the Buddha's first sermon on the Law of Dharma (Chapter 3).

Many of the features are distinctively Buddhist. The knot on the top of the Buddha's head is known as the *ushnisha* and represents his cosmic consciousness; the garment he wears is the *sanghati,* or monk's robe. His missing right hand probably was raised palm outward in the gesture of blessing. It is interesting to compare this statue with the preceding Roman and Parthian sculptures. Scholars claim that the style and majesty of the Roman imperial sculpture from the workshops of the eastern Mediterranean deeply influenced the creators of the early Gandharan statues of the Buddha.

Gandharan Buddha

Questions for Analysis

1. Consider the Buddha's expression, posture, and dress. How has the sculptor evoked a sense of his authority?
2. Compare this statue with those of Caesar Augustus and the Parthian noblewoman. What common elements do you find in all three pieces of art? Do you perceive any differences? Which are more significant?
3. Consider this statue in light of the Buddha's sermon on the body (Chapter 3). What do you think he would have said about this sculpture?

A Chinese Buddha

During the age of Later Han and for several centuries thereafter, Buddhism made deep inroads into China through the Silk Route, a pathway of trade linking western China with the eastern Mediterranean coast (Chapter 6). Here we have an early northern Chinese relief sculpture of the Buddha dating to around A.D. 500. This work, which deals with the same theme and setting as the Gandharan Buddha, has been characterized as an example of a fully developed Chinese style of Buddhist art.

Questions for Analysis

1. Consider the Buddha's expression and posture. What responses does the sculptor seem to hope to elicit from the viewer?
2. Compare this Buddha with the Gandharan Buddha. In what ways are they similar, and how do they differ? What are more significant — the similarities or the differences? Which of the two seems to be closer to the message of the Buddha's sermons in Chapter 3?
3. Compare this Buddha with the statues of Caesar Augustus and the Parthian noblewoman. What styles and motifs has the sculptor borrowed from the Hellenistic West? In what ways does this Buddha differ from these Greco-Roman and Parthian prototypes? What seem to be more important to the sculptor's message — these borrowed elements or the differences?

Chinese Buddha

PART II

Faith, Devotion, and Salvation: Great World Religions to A.D. 1500

By about 200 B.C. two overarching religious traditions had taken shape in Eurasia. Indian civilization produced Buddhism and Hinduism, each of which denied the reality of this world and sought release from it. In the Middle East, two monotheistic faiths emerged — Judaism and Zoroastrianism — whose believers saw themselves as agents in the transformation of this world according to precepts decreed by their God.

During the next 1,500 years these four religions underwent significant evolution. Zoroastrianism virtually disappeared after the ninth century A.D., but Judaism survived, continued to develop, and served as a source for the world's two most aggressive and expansionistic faiths: Christianity and Islam. Meanwhile, one school of Buddhist thought, the Mahayana sect, gradually became a salvific faith. Mainstream Hinduism never developed this doctrine of heavenly salvation, as it is understood in Middle Eastern tradition, but it did produce a form of worship centered on an intensely personal and deeply emotional devotion to a single, select deity.

Three of these five faiths — Buddhism, Christianity, and Islam — became universal religions. That is, they found homes in a wide variety of cultural settings and claimed to offer salvation to all humanity. Of the three, Buddhism was the most regional, confined largely to the vast and heavily populated regions of East and South Asia. Islam was the most global. Muslim communities dominated the east coast of Africa and the trading empires of interior West Africa. Islam stretched across the entire breadth of North Africa, the Middle East, and the northern and central portions of India. It spread throughout much of Central Asia, the island and coastal regions of Southeast Asia, and even touched many parts of China. Christianity in its various forms could be found in Ethiopia, in the ancient lands that bordered the eastern rim of the Mediterranean, among the Slavs of Eastern and Central Europe, and throughout Western Europe. In addition, groups of Christians inhabited portions of Central Asia and even the western shores of India. With the new age of European transoceanic explorations that was getting under way by 1500, Westerners would plant their version of the Cross throughout the Americas and in various parts of East and South Asia. Meanwhile, although Judaism and Hinduism also expanded beyond the confines of their ethnic and geographic origins, they remained far less universal in scope or appeal.

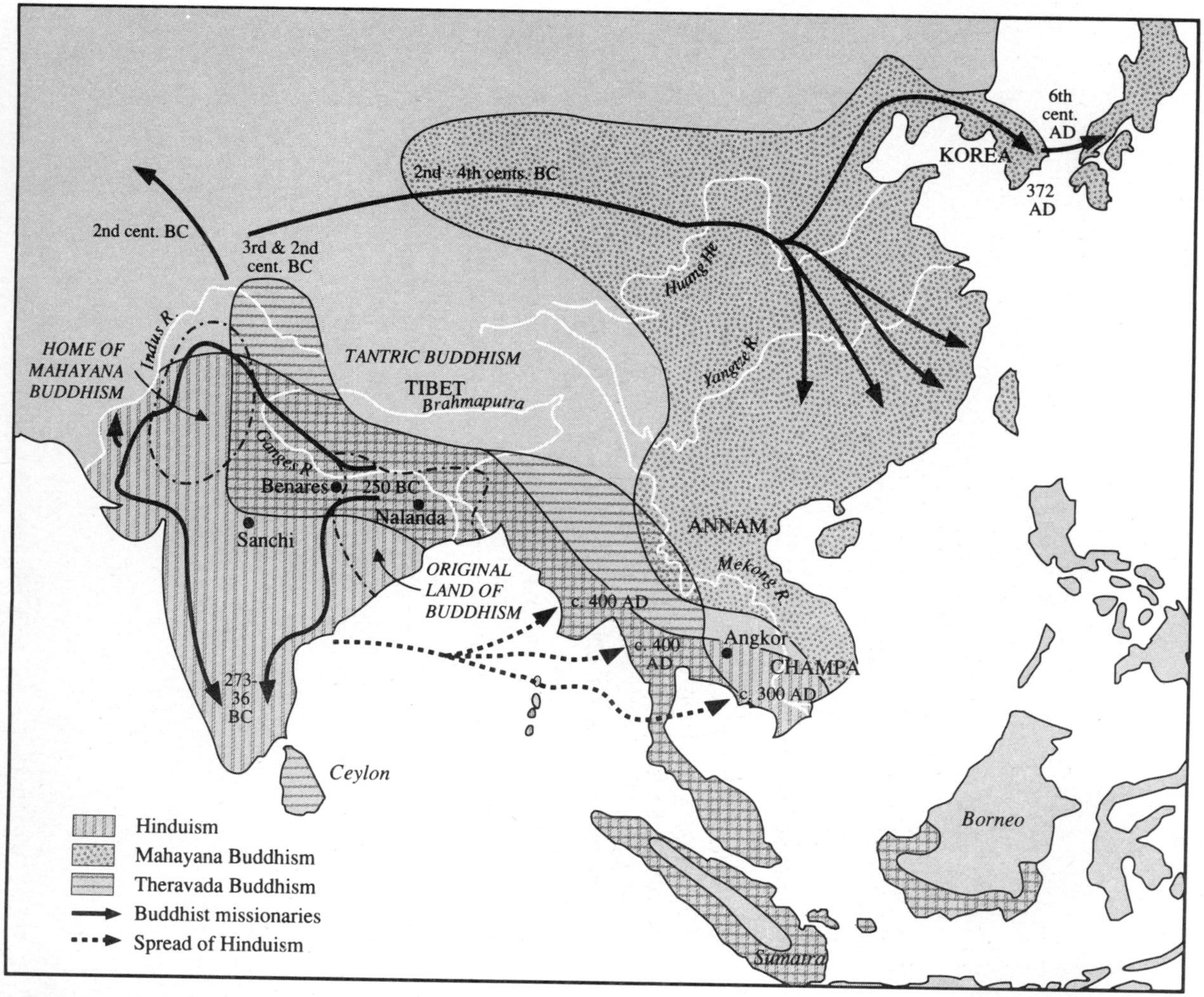

Map 3 Hinduism and Buddhism Around 1200

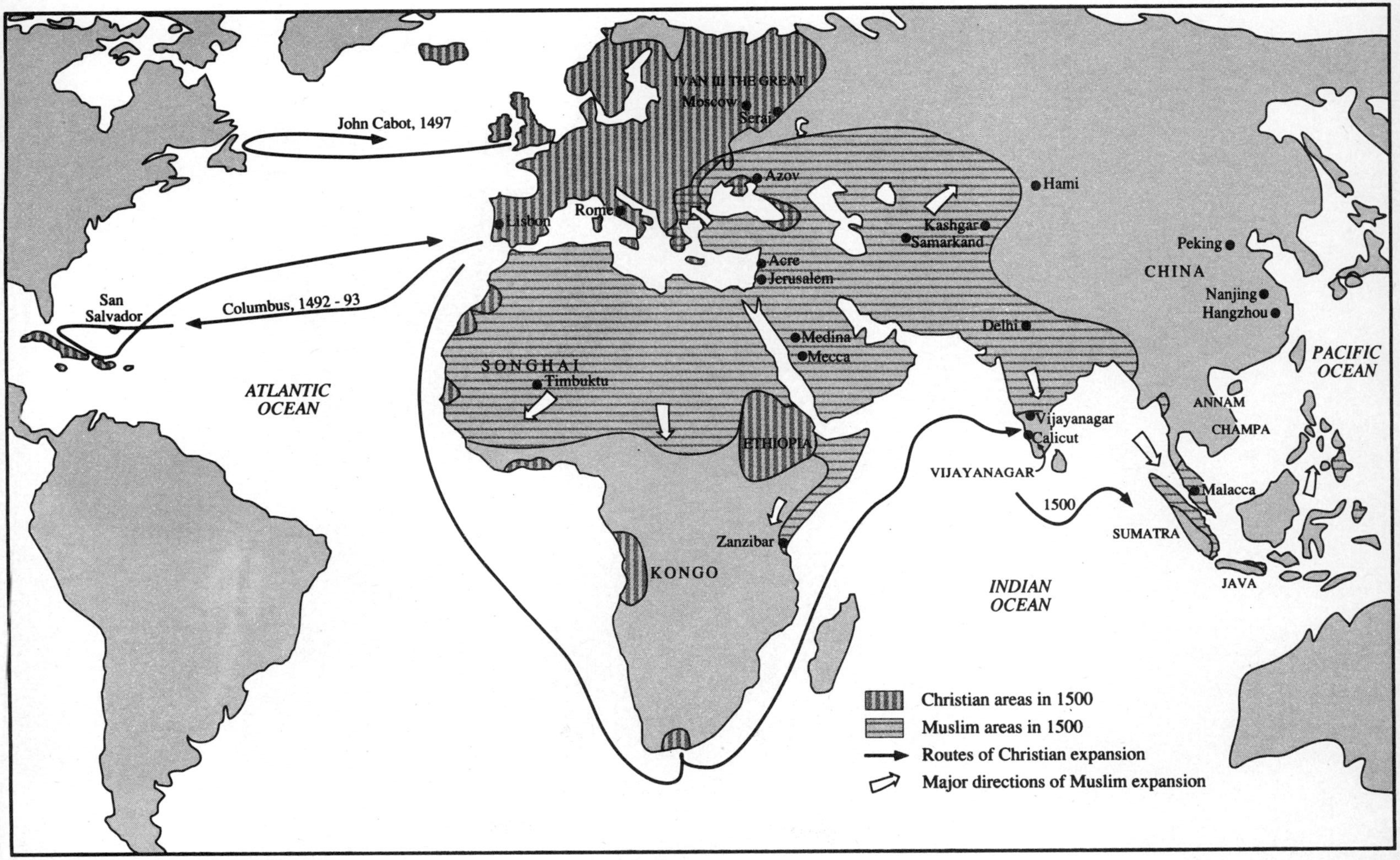

Map 4 Christianity and Islam Around 1500

C H A P T E R

6

New Developments in Three Ancient Religions

During the first age of Afro-Eurasian interchange (Chapter 5), Hinduism, Judaism, and Buddhism all experienced important changes that profoundly affected their historical development. Within Hinduism a new movement known as *bhakti,* or the Way of Devotion, challenged the caste system without actually rejecting it. At the same time, it was this new form of Hindu religion, not the caste system, that Indian merchants brought to the emerging civilizations of Southeast Asia in the early centuries A.D. Without the Way of Devotion, Hinduism would probably not have spread significantly beyond the Indian subcontinent.

Hinduism and Judaism have historically been "family" religions, because each has been largely confined to the heirs of a single civilization. Normally their adherents are born into these religious-social complexes and are not converts. At the same time, both religions have occasionally reached out beyond their cultural matrices. This was particularly so in the case of Judaism because of the Diaspora, or Great Dispersion, which scattered Jewish communities all over the Afro-Eurasian ecumene. While Jews remained conscious of being a people apart from their gentile (non-Jewish) neighbors, Jewish communities could not totally avoid cultural interchange with the societies among whom they settled.

Cultural exchange also contributed substantially to the development of a new form of Buddhist belief and devotion — the Mahayana sect. This school moved radically away from the Buddha's original teachings, which rejected all notions of God and personal immortality, by offering the promise of salvation. This message attracted many people suffering from the chaos of the breakdown of the first age of Afro-Eurasian linkage. As early as the first century A.D., Mahayana Buddhist ideas were entering China, and in the centuries that followed Buddhism in its many different forms swept through East Asia.

Hinduism: The Way of Devotion

In the *Bhagavad Gita* the hero-god Krishna (Vishnu) teaches Arjuna that bhakti, or unconditional devotion to a god, is one of several ways a person can win release (*moksha*) from the cycle of rebirth. Such an approach to liberation appealed to many low-caste and casteless persons, including women, who found strict and selfless conformity to the laws of dharma (the Way of Works) unattractive. It also appealed to persons who lacked the temperament or leisure to attain release from the shackles of matter through asceticism, study of the sacred scriptures, and meditation (the Way of Knowledge). The Way of Devotion, in which one passionately adored a savior god, offered a promise of immediate liberation to everyone.

In the Gupta period and thereafter, many Hindus tended to reduce the myriad divine personifications of Brahman, the One, to three: Brahma the Creator, Vishnu the Preserver, and Shiva the Destroyer. Of this trinity, Brahma (not to be confused with Brahman) was the least widely worshiped, because he was perceived as a remote kingly god who, after completing the process of creation, had retired from concerning himself with worldly affairs. Hindus widely adored Vishnu and Shiva, however, and they became two of the great gods of Asia. The cult of Shiva was especially popular in Southeast Asia, where he merged with several local deities.

Hindus who concentrated their worship on Vishnu or Shiva did not deny the existence of the many other divine and semidivine personalities who were part of the traditional pantheon. They chose Shiva or Vishnu as gods of special devotion because each, in his way, was a loving personification of the totality of Divine Reality. Vishnu's worshipers, for example, believed he had selflessly blessed and taught humanity on a number of critical occasions in descents (avataras) from heaven. On each occasion he took on either human or animal form and intervened on behalf of the forces of goodness to redress the equilibrium between good and evil. In fact, Vishnu's worshipers regarded the Buddha as one of Vishnu's nine chief avataras. Among his various descents, or incarnations, however, the warriors Krishna and Rama enjoyed the widest devotional popularity. As Lord Krishna exemplified in the *Bhagavad Gita,* Vishnu's emergence into this world provided humanity with a model of divine perfection. By offering such a god exclusive and unqualified devotion, a worshiper hoped to share in that perfection.

The religious development of bhakti, which met so many needs of the members of Hindu India's lower social levels, helped Hinduism to counter successfully the challenges of Buddhism, especially that of the Mahayana school. Indeed, Hinduism was more than able to hold its own against that faith, and by A.D. 1500 Buddhism had largely disappeared from the land of its origin.

VISHNU PURANA

Between approximately A.D. 300 and 1000 a new sacred literature known as the *Puranas* ("stories of ancient times") developed to give voice to bhakti. Composed for popular consumption, each of the eighteen major Puranas was a long, rambling collection of myth and folklore that brought to its largely unsophisticated audience the central message that a particular god — Brahma, Vishnu, or Shiva — deserved worship without reservation. The following selection comes from the closing lines of the *Vishnu Purana*.

Questions for Analysis

1. What power does the very name of Vishnu have?
2. What traditional avenues to liberation does this passage refer to, and how does worship of Vishnu allow one to by-pass or transcend them?
3. How does Vishnu encompass all the powers of the Hindu trinity? How is he equated with Brahman, the World Soul? Was the author of this passage a monotheist?
4. How does the theological message of this Purana represent a departure from the spirit that pervades the *Laws of Manu* (Chapter 5)?

I have related to you this Purana, which is equal to the Vedas in sanctity, and by hearing which all faults and sins whatever are expiated. . . .

By hearing this, all sins are at once obliterated. In this also the glorious Hari[1] has been revealed, the cause of the creation, preservation, and destruction of the world; the soul of all things, and himself all things: by the repetition of whose name man is undoubtedly liberated from all sins, which fly like wolves that are frightened by a lion. The repetition of his name with devout faith is the best remover of all sins, destroying them as fire purifies the metal from the dross. The stain of the Kali age,[2] which ensures to men sharp punishments in hell,[3] is at once effaced by a single invocation of Hari. He who is all that is, the whole egg of

1. Another name for Vishnu.

2. The last of a cycle of four repetitive ages, the Kali age is 360,000 years of evil. Following Kali's dissolution, a period of new birth and virtue will commence again. The authors of the Puranas assumed they were living in a Kali age.

3. There are many hells (one purana enumerates twenty-one) where the servants of Yama, god of death, punish persons for their social sins, especially sins against caste restrictions. This punishment is not eternal; eventually each soul is reborn into a lower caste, or life form, depending on the weight of one's karma.

Brahma[4]. . . . he who is all things, who knoweth all things, who is the form of all things, being without form himself, and of whom whatever is, from mount Meru[5] to an atom, all consists — he, the glorious Vishnu, the destroyer of all sin — is described in this Purana. By hearing this Purana an equal recompense is obtained to that which is derived from the performance of an Asvamedha sacrifice,[6] or from fasting at the holy places. . . . This Purana is the best of all preservatives for those who are afraid of worldly existence, a certain alleviation of the sufferings of men, and remover of all imperfections. . . . Whoever hears this great mystery, which removes the contamination of the Kali, shall be freed from all his sins. He who hears this every day acquits himself of his daily obligations to ancestors, gods and men. . . . What marvel therefore is it that the sins of one who repeats the name of Achyuta[7] should be wiped away? Should not that Hari be heard of, whom those devoted to acts[8] worship with sacrifices continually as the god of sacrifice; whom those devoted to meditation[9] contemplate . . . , who, as the gods, accepts the offerings addressed to them; the glorious being who is without beginning or end; . . . who is the abode of all spiritual power; in whom the limits of finite things cannot be measured; and who, when he enters the ear, destroys all sin?

I adore him, that first of gods, Purushottama,[10] who is without end and without beginning, without growth, without decay, without death; who is substance that knows not change. I adore that ever inexhaustible spirit, who assumed sensible qualities;[11] who, though one, became many; who, though pure, became as if impure, by appearing in many and various shapes; who is endowed with divine wisdom, and is the author of the preservation of all creatures. I adore him, who is the one conjoined essence and object of both meditative wisdom and active virtue; who is watchful in providing for human enjoyments; who is one with the three qualities;[12] who, without undergoing change, is the cause of the evolution of the world; who exists of his own essence, ever exempt from decay. I constantly adore him, who is entitled heaven, air, fire, water, earth, and ether; who is the bestower of all the objects which give gratification to the senses; who benefits mankind with the instruments of fruition; who is perceptible, who is subtle, who is imperceptible. May that unborn, eternal Hari, whose form is manifold, and whose essence is composed of both nature and spirit, bestow upon all mankind that blessed state which knows neither birth nor decay!

4. All creation.

5. The polar or central mountain of the earth and the home of the gods.

6. A horse sacrifice, which was a carryover from Aryan times.

7. "The unfallen one," another of Vishnu's titles.

8. Those who seek moksha (release) through the Way or Yoga (discipline) of Works.

9. Those who seek release through the Way or Yoga of Knowledge.

10. Another name for Vishnu — the sacrificial substance from which the world was created (see pages 50–51).

11. Who had many incarnations or avataras, such as Krishna.

12. Creation, preservation, destruction.

SHIVA NATARAJA

A Westerner might find it hard to accept the fact that a god whose primary function is destruction and death is regarded as a loving deity. The name Shiva, in fact, means "auspicious" and, among his many functions, the god serves as the patron of ascetics and other holy persons.

The illustration is of a bronze statue of Shiva Nataraja (Lord of the Dance) from the Chola Kingdom of southern India (ca 850–1250) and represents the god engaged in an ecstatic cosmic dance. The symbols in this statue offer numerous clues as to how Shiva's worshipers perceived him. Here he is dancing within a circle of fire. His hair is piled up into a crownlike style; flowing from the sides of his head are strands of hair intertwined with flowers and forming the shape of wings. His upper left hand holds a devouring flame; his upper right hand clasps a drum for beating out the rhythm of the universe. A cobra entwines his lower right arm, but his hand is raised in the silent "fear not" gesture (compare this with the Buddha's right hand in the illustrations in Chapter 5). His lower left hand points to his raised left foot as a sign of "release." His other foot is planted firmly on the writhing body of Apasamara, the demon of ignorance and heedlessness.

Questions for Analysis

1. Keeping in mind that Shiva uses the drum to beat out the rhythm of the universe, what do you think the circle of fire represents?
2. How would you characterize Shiva's facial expression, and what does it suggest about this god?
3. What double message does Shiva give through his "body language"?
4. Consider the demon of ignorance. How would an "ignorant" person regard death? What do you think Shiva's triumph over this demon represents?
5. We saw in the preceding selection that Vishnu's devotees believed their savior god exercised all the primary functions of the Godhead — creation, destruction, regeneration, preservation, and release (moksha). Can you find the appropriate symbols in this statue that illustrate a similar belief on the part of Shiva's followers?

Shiva Nataraja

Diaspora Judaism

In A.D. 66 Palestine broke out in general rebellion against Roman occupation, and it took the Roman armies seven bloody years to root out the last vestiges of insurgency. In the process, Jerusalem and its Temple were destroyed in A.D. 70. Long before the destruction of the Temple, Jews had established prosperous communities throughout the Greco-Roman, Persian, and Arabic worlds. After this unsuccessful rebellion, however, the Jewish flight from Palestine reached the proportions of a folk migration. The Great Dispersion, or Diaspora, was under way. For 1,900 years, Jews would be strangers in a variety of foreign lands — a people without a homeland.

In spite of these travails, Judaism survived as a living faith and culture, because wherever Jews settled, they remained faithful to the memory of their special covenant with God and their Promised Land. Furthermore, despite its innate conservatism, born of a need to maintain contact with the ways of the past, Judaism continued to be a flexible religious and social entity. Jews proved adaptable to a variety of alien settings, and over the centuries Judaism continued its historical development in response to the needs of its various scattered communities.

Benjamin of Tudela

BOOK OF TRAVELS

Rabbi Benjamin Ben Jonah of Tudela provides the best eyewitness account of twelfth-century Jewish life in Europe, Asia, and North Africa. This scholar and traveler, whose birth and death dates are unknown, departed his native Spain around 1159 and spent the next thirteen or fourteen years visiting several hundred Jewish communities from the Mediterranean to possibly as far east as India (see the map on page 344). The purpose of his journey seems to have been to establish contact with the scattered remnants of Israel (which he tells us were flourishing even in China) and to report on the state of Judaism throughout the world.

In the following excerpt, he describes the quality of life for Jews under Muslim rule in Baghdad on the Tigris (in modern Iraq). As we shall see in Chapter 8, the Abbasid caliphs (750–1258), who ruled over Baghdad and much of the Middle East, claimed (but never exercised) authority over all Islam.

Questions for Analysis

1. Who was Daniel the son of Hisdai, and what function did he serve under the caliph?

2. What was the status of Jews within the lands ruled by the caliph, and how would you characterize Muslim-Jewish relations in the reign of al-Abbasi?

Bagdad [is] . . . the royal residence of the Caliph Emir al Muminin al Abbasi[1] of the family of Muhammad.[2] He is at the head of the Muslim religion, and all the kings of Islam obey him; he occupies a similar position to that held by the Pope over the Christians.[3] He has a palace in Bagdad three miles in extent, wherein is a great park with all varieties of trees, fruit-bearing and otherwise, and all manner of animals. . . . There the great king, Al Abbasi the Caliph holds his court, and he is kind unto Israel, and many belonging to the people of Israel are his attendants; he knows all languages, and is well versed in the law of Israel. He reads and writes the holy language (Hebrew). . . . He is truthful and trusty, speaking peace to all men. . . .

In Bagdad there are about 40,000 Jews, and they dwell in security, prosperity and honor under the great Caliph, and amongst them are great sages, the heads of Academies engaged in the study of the law. In this city there are ten Academies.[4]. . . And at the head of them all is Daniel the son of Hisdai, who is styled "Our Lord the Head of the Captivity of all Israel." He possesses a book of pedigrees going back as far as David, King of Israel.[5] The Jews call him "Our Lord, Head of the Captivity," and the Muslims call him "Saidna ben Daoud,"[6] and he has been invested with authority over all the congregations of Israel at the hands of the Emir al Muminin, the Lord of Islam. For thus Muhammad[7] commanded concerning him and his descendants; and he granted him a seal of office over all the congregations that dwell under his rule, and ordered that every one, whether Muslim or Jew, or belonging to any other nation in his dominion, should rise up before him and salute him, and that any one who should refuse to rise up should receive one hundred stripes.

And every fifth day when he goes to pay a visit to the great Caliph, horsemen, Gentiles as well as Jews, escort him, and heralds proclaim in advance, "Make way before our Lord, the son of David, as is due unto him," the Arabic words being "Amilu tarik la Saidna ben Daud." He is mounted on a horse, and is attired in robes of silk and embroidery with a large turban on his head. . . . Then he appears before the Caliph and kisses his hand, and the Caliph rises and places him on a throne which Muhammad had ordered to be made for him, and all the Muslim princes who attend the court of the Caliph rise up before him. And the Head of the Captivity is seated on his throne opposite to the Caliph, in compliance with the command of Muhammad. . . . The authority of the Head of the Captivity extends over

1. Also known as al-Mustanjid (A.D. 1160–1170).

2. The Prophet of Islam. See Chapter 8.

3. See Chapter 7.

4. Academies for the study of scripture and postbiblical law (the Talmud). These scholars served as the chief teachers and judges of their community.

5. King of Israel around 1000 B.C.

6. "The Lord son of David."

7. Not the Prophet Muhammad but possibly al-Abbasi's predecessor Muhammad el-Moktafi.

all the communities of Shinar,[8] Persia, Khurasan[9] and Sheba which is El-Yemen,[10] and Diyar Kalach[11] and the land of Aram Naharaim[12], and over the dwellers in the mountains of Ararat[13] and the land of the Alans,[14] which is a land surrounded by mountains and has no outlet except by the iron gates which Alexander[15] made, but which were afterwards broken. Here are the people called Alani. His authority extends also over the land of Siberia, and the communities in the land of the Togarmim[16] unto the mountains of Asveh and the land of Gurgan, the inhabitants of which are called Gurganim who dwell by the river Gihon, and these are the Girgashites who follow the Christian religion.[17] Further it extends to the gates of Samarkand,[18] the land of Tibet, and the land of India. In respect of all these countries the Head of the Captivity gives the communities power to appoint Rabbis and Ministers who come unto him to be consecrated and to receive his authority. They bring him offerings and gifts from the ends of the earth. He owns hospices, gardens and plantations in Babylon,[19] and much land inherited from his fathers, and no one can take his possessions from him by force. He has a fixed weekly revenue arising from the hospices of the Jews, the markets and the merchants, apart from that which is brought to him from far-off lands. The man is very rich, and wise in the Scriptures as well as in the Talmud,[20] and many Israelites dine at his table every day.

At his installation, the Head of the Captivity gives much money to the Caliph, to the Princes and the Ministers. On the day that the Caliph performs the ceremony of investing him with authority, he rides in the second of the royal equipages, and is escorted from the palace of the Caliph to his own house with timbrels and fifes. The Exilarch[21] appoints the Chiefs of the Academies by placing his hand upon their heads, thus installing them in their office. The Jews of the city are learned men and very rich.

In Bagdad there are twenty-eight Jewish Synagogues, situated either in the city itself or in Al-Karkh on the other side of the Tigris; for the river divides the metropolis into two parts. The great synagogue of the Head of the Captivity has columns of marble of various colors overlaid with silver and gold, and on these

8. Southern Mesopotamia (ancient Sumer and Akkad).

9. Northeastern Iran (ancient Bactria).

10. Southern Arabia.

11. Asia Minor or Anatolia (modern Turkey).

12. Northern Mesopotamia (modern north Syria).

13. Armenia.

14. An Indo-European people inhabiting the Caucasus Mountain region of Georgia.

15. Alexander the Great (336–323 B.C.).

16. One of a number of people of the central Euphrates in biblical times (*Genesis:* 10).

17. Apparently the author means the African Christian civilizations of the Sudan (Kush) and Ethiopia. Gihon was one of the four biblical rivers of the Garden of Eden and usually refers to the Nile. The Girgashites were one of the seven people who inhabited Canaan before its conquest by the Hebrews under Joshua.

18. In Turkestan.

19. The region around Baghdad.

20. Collections of legal opinions touching every aspect of Jewish life that scholars compiled in Palestine and Mesopotamia between approximately A.D. 100 and 500. Diaspora Jews generally regarded the Talmud as the highest source of legal authority after the Torah (the first five books of the Bible).

21. The "ruler of the exile" — Daniel the son of Hisdai.

columns are sentences of the Psalms in golden letters. And in front of the ark are about ten steps of marble; on the topmost step are the seats of the Head of the Captivity and of the Princes of the House of David. The city of Bagdad is twenty miles in circumference, situated in a land of palms, garden and plantations, the like of which is not to be found in the whole land of Shinar.

Moses Ben Maimon

SELECTED WRITINGS

As Rabbi Benjamin bears witness, many medieval Jewish congregations, located in Muslim and Christian lands, enjoyed varying degrees of self-government in local affairs. Two of the most notable examples of prosperous, semiautonomous Jewish communities were the twelfth-century Jews of Baghdad and of Cairo in Egypt. Under the tolerant rule of the Caliph of Baghdad and the Sultan of Egypt, the Jews of both cities achieved a deserved reputation for piety and scholarship. Even when Jews lived under less benign rulers, as most did, their communities generally fostered scholarship, especially in theological and legal studies. Jewish biblical scholars of twelfth-century Paris, for example, played an important role in upgrading the level of understanding of the ancient biblical texts among their Christian counterparts, until the Jews were expelled from France in 1182.

In discussion of medieval Jewish scholarship, one name inevitably arises: Rabbi Moses Ben Maimon (1135–1204), known in the West as Maimonides. Maimonides had the most comprehensive and original intellect of medieval Jewry and composed works that deeply influenced Jewish, Muslim, and Christian contemporaries. His scholarship was immense: he composed works in Arabic and Hebrew on such topics as the Bible, astronomy, mathematics, jurisprudence, medicine, ethics, and metaphysics. Born in Cordova, Spain, Maimonides and his family fled to Morocco in North Africa while he was a teenager. At the age of thirty, he again had to take flight, from potential persecution in Morocco, and landed in Palestine, then the scene of the crusades. Finding the Promised Land bitterly disappointing, he emigrated the following year to the tolerant land of Muslim Egypt, where he became physician at the court of Sultan Saladin (1138–1193) and spent the rest of his life in a ceaseless round of duties that would have destroyed a lesser person. He was one of the most popular and widely published physicians of his day. For thirty years he served as head of the Jewish congregation of Cairo and in this capacity enjoyed wide prestige among Jewish communities throughout the Middle East and carried on an extensive correspondence in which he answered questions on a wide variety of issues. Impelled by his own inner drives, he wrote voluminous treatises on every imaginable topic of Jewish religion and law. The sheer volume, scope, and depth of his writings have earned him the sobriquet the "Great Eagle."

The following selections from Rabbi Moses, all written in response to burning late twelfth-century issues, reveal Judaism's dual sense of universality and exclusivity.

Questions for Analysis

1. How are Jews to treat one another?
2. According to Maimonides, why were Jews persecuted, and how were they to respond to that persecution? How would those persecutions affect Judaism?
3. Does Rabbi Moses consider a convert to Judaism to be fully a Jew? Why or why not?
4. What does the World-to-Come appear to be, and who will enjoy it?
5. What place does the Promised Land hold in a Jew's life?
6. Will King Messiah be a spiritual or political leader? What will be the consequences of the Messiah's coming?
7. Does Rabbi Moses agree with Second Isaiah that, as a Chosen People, the Jews have a special role to play in human history (Chapter 3)? If so, what is that role?
8. According to Rabbi Moses, was the Jewish community a spiritual or a political entity?
9. Can you perceive any tensions or apparent contradictions in Rabbi Moses' description of what it means to be a Jew?
10. Can you discover any evidence provided by Rabbis Benjamin and Moses that suggests why Jews were able to maintain their cultural identity despite their dispersal?

[*Relations Among Jews*]

It is incumbent on every one to love each individual Israelite as himself, as it is said, "Thou shalt love thy neighbor as thyself." Hence a person ought to speak in praise of his neighbor and be careful of his neighbor's property as he is careful of his own property and solicitous about his own honor. Whoever glorifies himself by humiliating another person, will have no portion in the world to come. . . .

The house of Israel that bears the name of Jacob[1] and upholds the religion of Moses our teacher, must be one united community. Nothing whatsoever should create dissension. You are wise and understanding people and you must know how serious are the consequences of discord and to what misfortunes it leads.

[*Why Are Jews Persecuted?*]

The antagonism of the nations toward us is due to our unique position as a people of faith. This is why their kings oppress us

1. Jacob was the son of Isaac, who in turn was the son of Abraham, the father of the Hebrews. Yahweh blessed Jacob, changed his name to Israel, and promised that he would be "the father of nations."

and visit upon us hatred and hostility. But the Creator endowed us with confidence, so that whenever the fury of persecution arises against Israel, it will surely be endured. The power of the kings presses down upon us and they exercise a hard rule over us; they persecute and torment us with oppressive decrees, but they cannot destroy us or wipe out our name. . . .

Therefore, brethren, be strong and of good courage. If persecutions arise, let them not disconcert you. Let not the mighty hand of the enemy and the weakness of our nation frighten you. These events are but trial and proof of your faith and your love. By holding firm to the law of truth in times like these, you prove that you belong to those of Jacob's seed who fear God and who are named "the remnant whom the Lord shall call."[2]

[*Converts*]

Thus says Moses the son of Rabbi Maimon, one of the exiles from Jerusalem, who lived in Spain.

I received the question of the master Obadiah, the wise and learned proselyte,[3] may the Lord reward him for his work, may a perfect recompense be bestowed upon him by the Lord of Israel, under whose wings he has sought cover.

You ask me if you, too, are allowed to say in the blessings and prayers you offer alone or in the congregation: "*Our* God" and "God of *our* Fathers," "Thou hast sanctified *us* through Thy commandments," "Thou has separated *us*," "Thou hast chosen *us*," "Thou hast inherited *us*," "Thou who hast brought *us* out of the land of Egypt," "Thou who hast worked miracles for *our* fathers," and more of this kind.

Yes, you may say all this in the described order and not change it in the least. In the same way as every Jew by birth says his blessing and prayer you, too, shall bless and pray alike, whether you are alone or pray in the congregation. The reason for this is, that Abraham, our father, taught the people, opened their minds, and revealed to them the truth, faith and the unity of God; he rejected the idols and abolished their adoration; he brought many children under the wings of the Divine Presence; he gave them counsel and advice, and ordered his sons and the members of his household after him to keep the ways of the Lord forever, as it is written. "For I have known him to the end that he may command his children and his household after him, that he may keep the way of the Lord, to do righteousness and justice." Ever since then whoever adopts Judaism and confesses the unity of the Divine Name, as it is prescribed in the Torah,[4] is counted among the disciples of Abraham, our father, peace be with him. These men are Abraham's household, and he it is who converted them to righteousness.

In the same way as he converted his contemporaries through his words and teaching, he converts future generations through the testament he left to his children and household after him. Thus, Abraham, our father, his pious posterity who kept his ways, is the father of his disciples and of all proselytes who adopt Judaism. . . .

For the Creator, may He be extolled, has indeed chosen you and separated you from the nations and given you the Torah. For the Torah has been given to us *and* to the proselytes.

---

2. Joel 2:32. This biblical prophet of the fifth or fourth century B.C. continued the theme of Second Isaiah and spoke of the coming Day of the Lord, when God would judge all humanity.

3. A convert.

4. The basic law of Judaism, comprising the first five books of the Bible.

[*Righteous Gentiles*]
As to your question about the nations, know that the Lord desires the heart, and that the intention of the heart is the measure of all things. That is why our sages say, "The pious men among the Gentiles have a share in the World-to-Come," namely, if they have acquired what can be acquired of the knowledge of God, and if they ennoble their souls with worthy qualities. There is no doubt that every man who ennobles his soul with excellent morals and wisdom based on the faith in God, certainly belongs to the men of the World-to-Come.

[*The Promised Land*]
At all times one should live in Palestine even in a place the majority of whose population is heathen, and not live outside Palestine even in a place the majority of whose population is Jewish. . . .

It is forbidden to emigrate from Palestine and go abroad, unless one goes to study the Law, or to marry a wife, or to rescue property from heathens and then returns to Palestine.[5] So, too, one may leave on business. . . . But though one is permitted to emigrate, if one does, the act is not in conformity with the law of saintliness. . . .

When the Temple was destroyed, the Sages of the time ruled that a Jew should not build a painted and wainscoted house, but daub it with clay, wash it with lime, and leave about the entrance a square cubit's spot unwashed. The Sages likewise ordained: Whoever sets his table for a feast should let something be missing on it, and should leave one place empty without the service plate that otherwise would have been put there. When a woman orders ornaments of silver or gold, she should omit one of the details so that it should not appear perfect. When a man takes a wife, he should strew hearth-ashes on his head. All this one should do in remembrance of Jerusalem. As it is said: "If I forget thee, O Jerusalem, let my right hand forget her cunning. Let my tongue cleave to the roof of my mouth if I remember thee not; if I set not Jerusalem above my chiefest joy."

[*The Messiah*]
King Messiah[6] will arise and restore the kingdom of David to its former state and original sovereignty. He will rebuild the sanctuary and gather the dispersed of Israel. All the ancient laws will be reinstated in his days. . . .

He who does not believe in the restoration or does not look forward to the coming of the Messiah denies not only the teachings of the Prophets but also those of the Law of Moses, our teacher, for Scripture affirms the rehabilitation of Israel, as it is said: "Then the Lord thy God will turn thy captivity, and have compassion upon thee, and will return and gather thee . . . if any of thine that are dispersed be in the uttermost parts of heaven . . . and the Lord thy God will bring thee unto the land which thy fathers possessed." These words stated in Scripture include all that the Prophets said. . . . The prophecy in that section bears upon the two Messiahs: the first, namely, David,[7] who

5. Rabbi Moses left Palestine for Egypt because he discovered, to his dismay, that it was intellectually and spiritually a wasteland, and in this age of the crusades and the Latin Kingdom of Jerusalem, there was no place for Jews in Judea. He never returned.

6. The Anointed One. The Messiah was the deliverer promised through the prophets. Christians believed Jesus Christ was the Messiah; Jews were still awaiting the deliverer's coming.

7. See page 186, note 5.

saved Israel from the hand of their enemies; and the later Messiah, a descendant of David, who will achieve the final salvation. . . .

The ultimate and perfect reward, the final bliss which will suffer neither interruption nor diminution is the life in the World-to-Come. The Messianic Era, on the other hand, will be realized in this world; which will continue in its normal course except that independent sovereignty will be restored to Israel. The ancient Sages already said, "The only difference between the present and the Messianic Era is that political oppression will then cease.". . .

Let no one think that in the days of the Messiah any of the laws of nature will be set aside, or any innovations be introduced into creation. The world will follow its normal course. The words of Isaiah: And the wolf shall dwell with the lamb, and the leopard shall lie down with the kid are to be understood figuratively, meaning that Israel will live securely among the wicked of the heathens who are likened to wolves and leopards. . . . They will all accept the true religion, and will neither plunder nor destroy, and together with Israel earn a comfortable living in a legitimate way.

Said the Rabbis: "The sole difference between the present and the Messianic days is deliverance from servitude to foreign powers.". . .

The Sages and Prophets did not long for the days of the Messiah that Israel might exercise dominion over the world, or rule over the heathens or be exalted by the nations, or that it might eat and drink and rejoice. Their aspiration was that Israel be free to devote itself to the Law and its wisdom, with no one to oppress or disturb it, and thus be worthy of the life of the world to come.

In that era will be neither famine nor war, neither jealousy nor strife. Blessings will be abundant, comforts within the reach of all. The one preoccupation of the whole world will be to know the Lord. Hence Israelites will be very wise; they will know the things that are now concealed, and will attain an understanding of their Creator to the utmost capacity of the human mind, as it is written: For the earth shall be full of the knowledge of the Lord as the waters cover the sea.[8]

Buddhism: A Religion of Infinite Compassion

Asoka's Buddhism (Chapter 5) was idealistic rather than ideological and, above all else, practical. Asoka endeavored to make the Law of Righteousness a living reality for his people. Withdrawal from the world to live the life of a mendicant (begging) monk who sought Nirvana through meditation was not for him. While he revered and patronized Buddhist monks, he practiced social activism based on his under-

8. Isaiah 11:9.

standing of Buddhist principles. In addition, by sending missionaries to neighboring and distant regions he affirmed his belief in Buddhism's universality. As his edicts indicate, Asoka also did not abandon belief in the gods or a heavenly hereafter.

All the qualities of Asoka's Buddhism became more pronounced in the generations that followed. Eventually they engendered a new interpretation of Buddhism known as the Mahayana, or Great Vehicle. The title is metaphorical: Mahayana sectarians picture their form of Buddhism as a great ferry, which, under the guidance of a pilot, carries large numbers of persons across the river of life to salvation on the opposite shore.

Conversely, Mahayanists term the older, more traditional form of Buddhism the Hinayana, or Small Vehicle. The image is of a one-person raft, since Hinayana Buddhism centers on the single *arahat,* or perfected disciple, who attains Nirvana through solitary meditation, usually within a monastic setting. Followers of this form of Buddhism, which today predominates in Sri Lanka and the countries of mainland Southeast Asia, especially Burma and Thailand, generally dislike the term Hinayana, because it implies inferiority, and call their sect Theravada (the Teaching of the Elders).

Evidence indicates that Mahayana Buddhism emerged in northwest India during the Kushana Empire (ca first century B.C.–third century A.D.), probably, in part, as a result of certain Middle Eastern influences, primarily the notion of a savior god. According to Mahayana belief, Gautama the Buddha is a divine being, worthy of adoration, who came to earth in a series of incarnations out of infinite compassion for suffering humanity. In his final incarnation as Gautama, he taught humans the way not to the Nirvana of nothingness but to salvation. What is more, there had been many Buddhas or enlightened ones before him and many after, and all of them assisted less-enlightened humans to achieve salvation. They generally did so in the form of a *Bodhisattva* (a Buddha in the making), who, out of compassion, delayed full Buddhahood in order to act as the pilot of the Great Vehicle, leading others of all walks of life to salvation.

Such a comforting, unexclusive doctrine was destined to become the basis of a world religion. As early as the reign of Emperor Han Ming-ti (A.D. 58–75), Buddhist ideas were entering China. At first Buddhism made little progress there, since its practices, especially monasticism, and such basic principles as its otherworldliness ran counter to two central Chinese qualities: the centrality of the family and preoccupation with this world. The few early inroads Buddhism made in China occurred because some Chinese initially were able to equate it with Taoism. In the time of troubles that followed the collapse of Later Han, however, Buddhism, especially in its Mahayana form, won a place alongside Taoism and Confucianism as a doctrine that offered comfort in the face of affliction.

Buddhism continued to grow at a rapid rate in China until the middle of the ninth century, when it suffered a severe setback. Although it would never regain its former strength, it did not die out and has remained an element of Chinese civilization to the present. At the same time, with their remarkable ability to adapt virtually all foreign elements to their own culture, the Chinese reshaped Buddhism, creating a variety of schools, most of which were deeply affected by Taoist principles.

From China, Buddhist ideas were introduced into Korea by the fourth century, into Japan by the sixth, and later into Tibet, Mongolia, and regions of Southeast Asia. Meanwhile, perhaps because Hinduism in all its various forms was proving able to meet so many different religious needs, Buddhism was in decline in India by the seventh century. Between the twelfth and fourteenth century zealous Muslim warriors administered the final blow to Buddhist monasticism and Buddhism essentially disappeared in India, save for a few scattered remnants, largely in the northeast.

Shantideva

A COMPENDIUM OF DOCTRINE

The seventh-century Indian poet-philosopher Shantideva compiled excerpts from over 100 early Mahayana works, many of which would otherwise have been lost, to create a summary of that sect's basic doctrines. One of the essential themes of his compendium is the superiority of the selfless Bodhisattva over the Theravadan monk. The following passages describe a Bodhisattva's attributes.

Questions for Analysis

1. Why is it incorrect to state that the Bodhisattva has virtues or acts virtuously?
2. Why does the Bodhisattva assume the burden of the sins of the world?
3. What are the consequences of the Bodhisattva's assumptions of this burden?
4. Compare the Bodhisattva with Second Isaiah's Suffering Servant (Chapter 3). What are their similarities? Their differences? Which are more significant, the similarities or the differences?

The bodhisattva is lonely, with no . . . companion, and he puts on the armor of supreme wisdom. He acts himself, and leaves nothing to others, working with a will steeled with courage and strength. He is strong in his own strength . . . and he resolves thus:

"Whatever all beings should obtain, I will help them to obtain. . . . The virtue of generosity is not my helper — I am the helper of generosity. Nor do the virtues of morality, patience, courage, meditation and wisdom help me — it is I who help them. The perfections of the bodhisattva do not support me — it is I who support them. . . . I alone, standing in this round and adamantine world, must subdue Mara,[1] with all his hosts and chariots, and develop supreme enlightenment with the wisdom of instantaneous insight! . . .

"All creatures are in pain," he resolves, "all suffer from bad and hindering karma . . . so that they cannot see the Buddhas or hear the Law of Righteousness or know the Order. . . . All that mass of pain and evil karma I take in my own body. . . . I take upon myself the burden of sorrow; I resolve to do so; I endure it all. I do not turn back or run away, I do not tremble . . . I am not afraid . . . nor do I despair. Assuredly I must bear the burdens of all beings . . . for I have resolved to save them all. I must set them all free, I must save the whole world from the forest of birth, old age, disease, and rebirth, from misfortune and sin, from the round of birth and death, from the toils of heresy. . . . For all beings are caught in the net of craving, encompassed by ignorance, held by the desire for existence; they are doomed to destruction, shut in a cage of pain . . . they are ignorant, untrustworthy, full of doubts, always at loggerheads one with another, always prone to see evil; they cannot find a refuge in the ocean of existence; they are all on the edge of the gulf of destruction.

"I work to establish the kingdom of perfect wisdom for all beings. I care not at all for my own deliverance. I must save all beings from the torrent of rebirth with the raft of my omniscient mind. I must pull them back from the great precipice. I must free them from all misfortune, ferry them over the stream of rebirth.

"For I have taken upon myself, by my own will, the whole of the pain of all things living. Thus I dare try every abode of pain, in . . . every part of the universe, for I must not defraud the world of the root of good. I resolve to dwell in each state of misfortune through countless ages . . . for the salvation of all beings . . . for it is better that I alone suffer than that all beings sink to the worlds of misfortune. There I shall give myself into bondage, to redeem all the world from the forest of purgatory, from rebirth as beasts, from the realm of death. I shall bear all grief and pain in my own body, for the good of all things living. I venture to stand surety for all beings, speaking the truth, trustworthy, not breaking my word. I shall not forsake them. . . . I must so bring to fruition the root of goodness that all beings find the utmost joy, unheard of joy, the joy of omniscience. I must be their charioteer. I must be their leader, I must be their torchbearer. I must be their guide to safety. . . . I must not wait for the help of another, nor must I lose my resolution and leave my tasks to another. I must not turn back in my efforts to save all beings nor cease to use my merit[2] for the destruction of all pain. And I must not be satisfied with small successes."

1. The lord of the realm of the senses; the Tempter, or Evil One.

2. The infinite merit the Bodhisattva has earned in numerous lives, which is sufficient to save all humanity.

Han Yu

MEMORIAL ON BUDDHISM

During the early stages of the T'ang Dynasty (618–907), when China regained both imperial unity and prosperity, Chinese Buddhism reached its high point of popularity and influence. Buddhist monastaries and sects proliferated, and the imperial court itself, more often than not, patronized Buddhism in one form or another. However, because so many aspects of Buddhism were at variance with the historically evolved culture of China, especially Confucian values, conflict was inevitable.

One of the most important figures in the Confucian counterattack on Buddhism was the classical prose stylist and poet Han Yu (768–824), who in 819 composed a vitriolic polemic attacking Buddhism. The emperor was so enraged that at first he wanted to execute Han Yu, but eventually he contented himself with banishing this impudent civil servant to a frontier outpost.

Later Confucians considered Han Yu a pioneer of a Confucian intellectual revival that culminated in the eleventh and twelfth centuries with the rise of Neo-Confucianism, a movement that wedded metaphysical speculation (concern with matters that transcend the senses) to traditional Confucian practicality. In so doing, the Neo-Confucians offered a metaphysical alternative to the otherworldliness of Taoism and Buddhism and undercut their popularity severely. Furthermore, Han Yu's essay foreshadowed by only a generation a nativist reaction against "foreign" religions.

Han Yu wished to suppress Taoism as well as Buddhism, yet, ironically, it was due to Taoist influence that Emperor Wu-tsung initiated a policy of state suppression of a number of foreign religious establishments between 841 and 845. Buddhist monasteries were hard hit by these events, and Chinese Buddhism consequently suffered a major reversal of fortune. Buddhism still remained strong at the popular level, where it increasingly merged with folk magic and other forms of religious Taoism, but from the mid-ninth century onward it declined rapidly as a powerful rival to Confucianism for the allegiance of China's ruling class.

Han Yu's *Memorial on Buddhism,* which he composed in protest over the emperor's devotion to a relic of the Buddha's finger bone, reveals why so many Chinese ultimately found Buddhism unacceptable.

Questions for Analysis

1. How does Han Yu imply that Buddhism is not Chinese?
2. How does he imply that those emperors who have espoused Buddhism have lost the Mandate of Heaven (Chapter 1)?
3. Keeping in mind the Chinese cult of ancestors, explain why a Confucian would find the practice of venerating the Buddha's finger bone especially disgusting.

4. In Han Yu's mind, what are the social and political dangers of Buddhism?
5. What aspect of Buddhism most repels Han Yu?

Your servant submits that Buddhism is but one of the practices of barbarians which has filtered into China since the Later Han. In ancient times there was no such thing. . . . In those times the empire was at peace, and the people, contented and happy, lived out their full complement of years. . . . The Buddhist doctrine had still not reached China, so this could not have been the result of serving the Buddha.

The Buddhist doctrine first appeared in the time of the Emperor Ming[1] of the Han Dynasty, and the Emperor Ming was a scant eighteen years on the throne. Afterwards followed a succession of disorders and revolutions, when dynasties did not long endure. From the time of the dynasties Sung, Ch'i, Liang, Ch'en, and Wei,[2] as they grew more zealous in the service of the Buddha, the reigns of kings became shorter. There was only the Emperor Wu of the Liang who was on the throne for forty-eight years. First and last, he thrice abandoned the world and dedicated himself to the service of the Buddha. He refused to use animals in the sacrifices in his own ancestral temple. His single meal a day was limited to fruits and vegetables. In the end he was driven out and died of hunger. His dynasty likewise came to an untimely end. In serving the Buddha he was seeking good fortune, but the disaster that overtook him was only the greater. Viewed in the light of this, it is obvious that the Buddha is not worth serving.

When Kao-tsu[3] first succeeded to the throne of the Sui,[4] he planned to do away with Buddhism, but his ministers and advisors were short-sighted men incapable of any real understanding of the Way of the Former Kings, or of what is fitting for past and present; they were unable to apply the Emperor's ideas so as to remedy this evil, and the matter subsequently came to naught — many the times your servant has regretted it. I venture to consider that Your Imperial Majesty, shrewd and wise in peace and war, with divine wisdom and heroic courage, is without an equal through the centuries. When first you came to the throne, you would not permit laymen to become monks or nuns or Taoist priests,[5] nor would you allow the founding of temples or cloisters. It constantly struck me that the intention of Kao-tsu was to be fulfilled by Your Majesty. Now even though it has not been possible to put it into effect immediately, it is surely not right to remove all restric-

1. Hang Ming-ti (A.D. 57–75).

2. Five fairly short-lived dynasties of the troubled fourth through sixth centuries.

3. "Great ancestor," an honorific title bestowed posthumously on a large number of Chinese emperors, especially the founders of dynasties. This great ancestor was Li Yuan (618–626), the first T'ang emperor.

4. The Sui Dynasty (581–618) reunited China in 589.

5. By the second century A.D. a polytheistic Taoist church that practiced congregational worship, preached immortality, and utilized drugs and magic had emerged.

tions and turn around and actively encourage them.

Now I hear that by Your Majesty's command a troupe of monks went to Feng-hsiang[6] to get the Buddha-bone, and that you viewed it from a tower as it was carried into the Imperial Palace; also that you have ordered that it be received and honored in all the temples in turn. Although your servant[7] is stupid, he cannot help knowing that Your Majesty is not misled by this Buddha, and that you do not perform these devotions to pray for good luck. But just because the harvest has been good and the people are happy, you are complying with the general desire by putting on for the citizens of the capital this extraordinary spectacle which is nothing more than a sort of theatrical amusement. How could a sublime intelligence like yours consent to believe in this sort of thing?

But the people are stupid and ignorant; they are easily deceived and with difficulty enlightened. If they see Your Majesty behaving in this fashion, they are going to think you serve the Buddha in all sincerity. All will say, "The Emperor is wisest of all, and yet he is a sincere believer. What are we common people that we still should grudge our lives?" Burning heads and searing fingers by the tens and hundreds, throwing away their clothes and scattering their money, from morning to night emulating one another and fearing only to be last, old and young rush about, abandoning their work and place; and if restrictions are not immediately imposed, they will increasingly make the rounds of temples and some will inevitably cut off their arms and slice their flesh in the way of offerings. Thus to violate decency and draw the ridicule of the whole world is no light matter.

Now the Buddha was of barbarian origin. His language differed from Chinese speech; his clothes were of a different cut; his mouth did not pronounce the prescribed words of the Former Kings, his body was not clad in the garments prescribed by the Former Kings. He did not recognize the relationship between prince and subject, nor the sentiments of father and son. Let us suppose him to be living today, and that he come to court at the capital as an emissary of his country. Your Majesty would receive him courteously. But only one interview in the audience chamber, one banquet in his honor, one gift of clothing, and he would be escorted under guard to the border that he might not mislead the masses.

How much the less, now that he has long been dead, is it fitting that his decayed and rotten bone, his ill-omened and filthy remains, should be allowed to enter in the forbidden precincts of the Palace? Confucius said, "Respect ghosts and spirits, but keep away from them." The feudal lords of ancient times, when they went to pay a visit of condolence in their states, made it their practice to have exorcists go before with rush-brooms and peachwood branches to dispel unlucky influences. Only after such precautions did they make their visit of condolence. Now without reason you have taken up an unclean thing and examined it in person when no exorcist had gone before, when neither rush-broom nor peachwood branch had been employed. But your ministers did not speak of the wrong nor did the censors call attention to the impropriety; I am in truth ashamed of them. I pray that Your Majesty will turn this bone over to the officials that it may be cast into water or fire, cutting off for all time the root and so dispelling the suspicions of the empire and preventing the befuddlement of later generations. Thereby men may know in what

6. A western city.

7. Han Yu.

manner a great sage acts who a million times surpasses ordinary men. Could this be anything but ground for prosperity? Could it be anything but a cause for rejoicing?

If the Buddha has supernatural power and can wreak harm and evil, may any blame or retribution fittingly fall on my person. Heaven be my witness: I will not regret it. Unbearably disturbed and with the utmost sincerity I respectfully present my petition that these things may be known.

Your servant is truly alarmed, truly afraid.

Dogen

ON LIFE AND DEATH

Ch'an (meditation) Buddhism emerged in China during the seventh century as a fusion of Buddhist and Taoist principles. For the Ch'an masters, meditation was not an avenue to insight; it *was* insight. Disdaining all learning and logic, Ch'an masters sought to lead their students to a state in which they suspended all normal forms of reasoning and intuitively grasped the Buddha-nature that lies within each person and thing. This Enlightenment, or Awakening, would be a blinding and unexpected flash that could be triggered by any nonrational activity or external stimulus: contemplating a rock or the jolt of a clap of thunder. To prepare their students for this moment of Awakening, Ch'an masters presented them with puzzles for meditation that had no logical answers. One of the classic conundrums Ch'an students wrestled with was "What is the sound of one hand clapping?"

Because Ch'an monks mostly remained aloof from imperial patronage in the early T'ang period, their sect suffered far less than others in the persecutions of the mid-ninth century. By the Sung Dynasty (960–1279), Ch'an was the only Buddhist school in China that still showed intellectual and artistic vitality, and it thus deeply influenced Sung art, literature, and philosophy. During the age of Sung, Ch'an also took root in Japan due to the efforts of two Japanese masters who had studied in China: Eisei (1141–1215) and Dogen (1200–1253). Characteristically, the Japanese converted this import, which they pronounced Zen, into something distinctly Japanese.

Zen's austerity and discipline, as well as its emphasis on intuitive action as opposed to logical thought, appealed to Japan's feudal warrior class, the emerging samurai. Many fused Zen philosophy to their military skills, attempting to break down the artificial and "logical" duality between warrior and weapon. For example, a form of archery in which the archer sought to become one with the bow and arrow became part of Zen training. The archer did not consciously aim; instead, the arrow projected itself from the bow into the target. In a similar manner, Zen profoundly influenced all other forms of Japanese culture, particularly its expressions of beauty. The tea ceremony became a moment of Zen meditation and a potential Awakening, as one intuited how this common herb and lump of clay are things of serene delicacy and comfort. Their Buddha-reality is revealed to the person open to receiving this insight.

One of the pioneers of the tea ceremony was Dogen, who, on a visit to China in 1222, brought with him a potter to study the art of Chinese porcelain. The potter later established a thriving center for the production of tea vessel ceramics in Japan. In the following sermon, Dogen talks not about tea but about life and death, important issues to a Zen master, but no more so than the proper preparation and drinking of tea. Here, Dogen addresses the issue of how life and death are equally expressions of Buddha-reality.

Questions for Analysis

1. What does Dogen mean when he states that one should neither renounce nor covet life and death?
2. What does he mean when he says that life and death must be regarded as identical to Nirvana?
3. Is Buddhahood something to be attained in another life? Is it something to be achieved?
4. Reread Lao Tzu in Chapter 4. Can you find any Taoist elements in Dogen's thought?
5. Why would the Zen approach to life and death be especially attractive to a warrior?
6. Can you see any germs of a code of warrior conduct in this philosophy?
7. Why would Dogen agree with the saying, "Do not anticipate, be"?

"Since there is Buddhahood in both life and death," says Kassan, "neither exists." Jozan says, "Since there is no Buddhahood in life or death, one is not led astray by either." So go the sayings of the enlightened masters, and he who wishes to free himself of the life-and-death bondage must grasp their seemingly contradictory sense.

To seek Buddhahood outside of life and death is to ride north to reach Southern Etsu or face south to glimpse the North Star. Not only are you traveling the wrong way on the road to emancipation, you are increasing the links in your karma-chain. To find release you must begin to regard life and death as identical to nirvana, neither loathing the former nor coveting the latter.

It is fallacious to think that you simply move from birth to death. Birth, from the Buddhist point of view, is a temporary point between the preceding and the succeeding; hence it can be called birthlessness. The same holds for death and deathlessness. In life there is nothing more than life, in death nothing more than death: we are being born and are dying at every moment.

Now, to conduct: in life identify yourself with life, at death with death. Abstain from yielding and craving. Life and death constitute the very being of Buddha. Thus, should you renounce life and death, you will lose; and you can expect no more if you cling to either. You must neither loathe, then, nor covet, neither think nor speak of these things. Forgetting body and mind, by placing them together in Buddha's hands and letting him lead you on, you will without design or effort gain freedom, attain Buddhahood.

There is an easy road to Buddhahood: avoid evil, do nothing about life-and-death, be merciful to all sentient things, respect superiors and sympathize with inferiors, have neither likes nor dislikes, and dismiss idle thoughts and worries. Only then will you become a Buddha.

KUAN-YIN

Avalokitesvara ("the lord who looks down on all in compassion") was the most widely worshiped figure in the vast Mahayana pantheon. Originally perceived as a male Bodhisattva in northwest India, Avalokitesvara underwent a sex change in China. Here his cult merged with that of an ancient local goddess of mercy known as Kuan-yin ("she who heeds the sound of anguish"), and in the process Kuan-yin became China's most beloved Bodhisattva. From there she migrated to Japan, where she proved to be equally popular under the name Kannon. In both male and female form, Avalokitesvara/Kuan-yin was the compassionate companion of Amitabha (A-mi-t'o-fo in China), the Buddha who presided over the Pure Land or Western Paradise, a way station of afterlife bliss on the road to Nirvana.

Statues of Kuan-yin were almost universal fixtures in China's temples and private homes from the twelfth century onward. The example that appears here was carved from wood and dates from late in the Sung Dynasty (960–1279). Kuan-yin, whose tiara bears an image of the Buddha Amitabha, is seated in the classic pose known as "royal ease."

As you analyze this statue, compare it with the sculpture on page 178. In this fourteenth-century work of art from the Southeast Asian island of Java, the Bodhisattva Arapacana wields the sword of knowledge, while clutching in his left hand the book of wisdom (*The Scripture of the Perfection of Insight*). He wears the tiered crown of a prince and has assumed a meditative pose. Surrounding him are four lesser Bodhisattvas, who serve as his constant companions.

Questions for Analysis

1. Note Kuan-yin's languid pose. What qualities does her effortless posture convey?
2. Many scholars maintain that representations of both Avalokitesvara and Kuan-yin are essentially asexual and devoid of erotic overtones — in fact, androgynous (having both male and female characteristics). Do you think that this stat-

Kuan-yin

uette supports their view? What does your answer suggest about the nature of the love that Kuan-yin offered her devotees?

3. Consider Kuan-yin in the light of Shantideva's description of a Bodhisattva's attributes (page 194). Which of these does she seem to possess? Are there any that she appears to lack?
4. What are Arapacana's apparent qualities? Compare these with Shantideva's description.
5. Compare Kuan-yin and Arapacana. In what ways are they similar? How do they differ? What does your answer suggest about Bodhisattvas?

C H A P T E R

7

The Growth of Christianity

Mainstream Jewish thought perceived no meaningful distinction between Church and State, because Judaism's special covenant with God bound it body and soul to the Lord of the universe. Jews therefore believed that, as God's people, they had been given a sanctified homeland. When they were dispossessed of that inheritance and scattered among the Gentiles, they believed it was because of their sins. Should they reform their ways and return to full observance of their special covenant with God, they would regain sovereign possession of Palestine. By right, this Holy Land and its Chosen People should be ruled strictly according to the laws given them by God through Moses and incorporated into the Torah (the first five books of the Bible).

Not all Jewish sects, however, accepted this interpretation of the covenant. One such dissident element was a small body of religious Jews who coalesced around a prophet from Nazareth called Jesus (ca 4 B.C.–A.D. 33). The heart of Jesus' message was that the promised messianic Kingdom of God was at hand. The Messiah, God's anointed deliverer whose coming the prophets had foretold, was generally expected to be a political and military leader who would reestablish Israel as a free state. Jesus, to the contrary, expanding upon certain themes in the teachings of Second Isaiah, preached that the Messiah would usher in a spiritual age of universal judgment and redemption, whereby God's holy reign would extend to all lands and peoples.

As his ministry developed, Jesus became convinced he was the Messiah. Although he claimed, "My kingdom is not of this earth," local Roman and Jewish authorities were disquieted by the threat to the establishment that Jesus and his followers seemed to offer, and they conspired successfully to execute him by crucifixion. Jesus' followers believed, however, that he rose from the dead, appeared to a number of his friends, and then ascended to heaven with the promise of returning soon to sit in judgment of all humanity. Believing that his resurrection proved Jesus' divinity, his disciples proceeded to spread the Gospel (Good News) of redemption.

At first these disciples preached only to fellow Jews. Within a short time, however, they spread the faith throughout the entire Roman Empire and beyond. Before the first century A.D. was over, Christians (so called because of Jesus' title *Christos,* which is Greek for Messiah, or " the anointed one") had established the faith in every major city of the Roman Empire and had penetrated the Persian Empire, sub-Saharan Africa, Arabia, and the west coast of India. In the early fourth century Christianity was adopted as the state religion of the Axumite Kingdom of Ethiopia, became the favored religion of the Roman Emperor Constantine I (306–337), and took root among a number of German tribes beyond the northeast frontiers of the Roman Empire. In the seventh century a group of dissident Christians known as Nestorians established themselves in western China (see Chapter 11). This otherworldly faith was conquering a fair portion of the world.

Despite Jesus' claim that the Kingdom of God was a purely spiritual entity, evidence shows that even the earliest Christians were ambivalent when it came to defining their relationship with the world. Some wanted to reach an accommodation with it; others wanted nothing to do with it. Out of this conflict within Christianity several different traditions emerged. One was the Western notion of separation of Church and State, which was still not fully delineated by 1500. Another was the Eastern Christian tradition that the Church is a community of all God's people, an indivisible entity ruled jointly by priests and lay officials, all of whom are subject to the Orthodox (right-believing) Emperor.

Between 330 and 1453 the Eastern branch of Christianity was centered on imperial Constantinople. The Western Church's center of gravity was Rome, which from A.D. 400 onward increasingly evolved into the spiritual capital of Europe. Despite growing differences, particularly in their visions of how to govern the Church, Eastern and Western Christians agreed on most basic doctrinal issues. They also shared the belief, inherited from their common Judaic origin, that they were members of the only true Church on earth and had a divine mission to battle the forces of unbelief and evil and to win over the world for Christ. Each branch of Christendom was active in spreading the faith and otherwise acting to help accomplish their understanding of the Divine Plan for humanity.

The Early Centuries

Christianity's first 500 years were filled with challenges and changes. First, and most basic, was the ministry of Jesus of Nazareth, whose call for spiritual perfection has been the foundation of the Christian faith for almost 2,000 years. Following Jesus' departure from the world, his followers had to grapple with many still unresolved questions: Who was Jesus? What was his relationship with God and humanity? What was the nature of the community he left behind? Among the teachers who tried to answer these questions, none was more influential than Paul of Tarsus. The next major developmental period in Christian history occurred when the Roman Empire adopted Christianity as its own in the fourth century. This new status forced Christians to face, more squarely than ever before, the issue of how they, as both individuals and a church, related to the world.

Never was there unanimity on any answer to any of these questions. By the year 500 Christianity was divided into a wide variety of often hostile sects and schools. At the same time, the essential outlines of medieval Christendom's two major traditions — the cultures of Constantinople and Rome — were in place.

THE GOSPEL OF SAINT MATTHEW

Tradition ascribes authorship of the Gospels, the four major accounts of Jesus of Nazareth's life and teachings, to authors known as Matthew, Mark, Luke, and John. The early Christian Church believed that Matthew had been one of Jesus' twelve apostles, or major companions, and accepted his Gospel (Good News) as authoritative. Modern scholarship dates the work, as we know it, to around A.D. 85, or approximately fifty years after Jesus' ministry. This late date does not preclude authorship by the Apostle Matthew or one of his disciples, since evidence strongly indicates that the Greek version of this Gospel, which is the only one extant today, is a translation, or even revision, of a long-lost Aramaic original. The author appears to have been a Palestinian Jewish Christian who had been trained in the rabbinical tradition of Jewish law and scripture and who was writing specifically for other Christian converts from Judaism.

The central theme of the Gospel of Matthew is that Jesus is the Messiah and the fulfillment of the promises made by God through Abraham, Moses, and the prophets. For Matthew, Second Isaiah was the greatest of those prophets, the one who most clearly foretold Jesus' mission of salvation. In the following selection Matthew presents what is commonly known as the Sermon on the Mount. Second Isaiah had preached that the universal reign of Yahweh was imminent. Jesus here instructs his followers on what the Kingdom of God requires of all its members. In all likelihood, what Matthew wrote is not a verbatim account of a specific sermon but a distillation of the essence of Jesus' moral and theological teachings.

Questions for Analysis

1. What does Jesus require of his followers? How easy is it to obey his demands?
2. In what ways does Jesus emphasize the personal, spiritual relationship of each believer in God?
3. How does Jesus regard Judaism and especially the Law of Moses?
4. What is Jesus' attitude toward the world and its riches?
5. What does Matthew mean that Jesus taught with authority and not like the teachers of the Law? What is the basis of Jesus' authority?
6. To whom would Jesus' message appear especially appealing?
7. Compare the message and spirit behind the Sermon on the Mount with that of the Buddha's First Sermon on the Law (Chapter 3). What strikes you as more significant, their differences or similarities?

Jesus saw the crowds and went up a hill, where he sat down. His disciples gathered around him, and he began to teach them:

"Happy are those who know they are spiritually poor;
the Kingdom of heaven belongs to them!
"Happy are those who mourn;
God will comfort them!
"Happy are those who are humble;
they will receive what God has promised!
"Happy are those whose greatest desire is to do what God requires;
God will satisfy them fully!
"Happy are those who are merciful to others;
God will be merciful to them!
"Happy are the pure in heart;
they will see God!
"Happy are those who work for peace;
God will call them his children!
"Happy are those who are persecuted because they do what God requires;
the Kingdom of heaven belongs to them!

"Happy are you when people insult you and persecute you and tell all kinds of evil lies against you because you are my followers. Be happy and glad, for a great reward is kept for you in heaven. This is how the prophets who lived before you were persecuted.

"Do not think that I have come to do away with the Law of Moses and the teachings of the prophets. I have not come to do away with them, but to make their teachings come true. Remember that as long as heaven and earth last, not the least point nor the smallest detail of the Law will be done away with — not until the end of all things. So then, whoever disobeys even the least important of the commandments and teaches others to do the same, will be least in the Kingdom of heaven. On the other hand, whoever obeys the Law and teaches others to do the same, will be great in the Kingdom of heaven. I tell you, then, that you will be able to enter the Kingdom of heaven only if you are more faithful than the teachers of the Law and the Pharisees[1] in doing what God requires.

"You have heard that people were told in the past, 'Do not commit murder; anyone who does will be brought to trial.' But now I tell you: whoever is angry with his brother will be brought to trial, whoever calls his brother 'You good-for-nothing!' will be brought before the Council,[2] and whoever calls his brother a worthless fool will be in danger of going to the fire of hell. So if you are about to offer your gift to God at the altar and there you remember that your brother has something against you, leave your gift there in front of the altar, go at once and make peace with your brother, and then come back and offer your gift to God. . . .

"You have heard that it was said, 'Love your friends, hate your enemies.' But now I tell you: love your enemies and pray for those who persecute you, so that you may become the sons of your Father in heaven. For he makes his sun to shine on bad and good people alike, and gives rain to those who do good and to those who do evil. Why should God reward you if you love only the people who love you? Even the tax collectors do that! And if you speak only to your friends, have you done anything out of the ordinary? Even the pagans do that! You must be perfect — just as your Father in heaven is perfect. . . .

"When you pray, do not be like the hypocrites! They love to stand up and pray in the houses of worship and on the street corners, so that everyone will see them. I assure you, they have already been paid in full. But when you pray, go to your room, close the door, and pray to your Father, who is unseen. And your Father, who sees what you do in private, will reward you.

"When you pray, do not use a lot of meaningless words, as the pagans do, who think that God will hear them because their prayers are long. Do not be like them. Your Father already knows what you need before you ask him. This, then, is how you should pray:

'Our Father in heaven;
May your holy name be honored;
may your Kingdom come;
may your will be done on earth as it is in heaven.
Give us today the food we need.
Forgive us the wrongs we have done,
as we forgive the wrongs that others have done to us.
Do not bring us to hard testing,
but keep us safe from the Evil One.'

"If you forgive others the wrongs they have done to you, your Father in heaven will also forgive you. But if you do not forgive others, then your Father will not forgive the wrongs you have done. . . .

"Do not store up riches for yourselves here on earth, where moths and rust destroy, and robbers break in and steal. Instead, store up riches for yourselves in heaven, where moths and rust cannot destroy, and robbers cannot break in and steal. For your heart will always be where your riches are. . . .

1. Religious teachers who stressed that the written Law of Moses and all the nonscriptural traditions of Judaism had to be equally and fully observed.

2. The Sanhedrin, Judaism's chief religious and judicial body.

"This is why I tell you: do not be worried about the food and drink you need in order to stay alive, or about clothes for your body. After all, isn't life worth more than food? And isn't the body worth more than clothes? Look at the birds: they do not plant seeds, gather a harvest and put it in barns; yet your Father in heaven takes care of them! Aren't you worth much more than birds? Can any of you live a bit longer by worrying about it? . . .

"So do not start worrying: 'Where will my food come from? or my drink? or my clothes?' (These are the things the pagans are always concerned about.) Your Father in heaven knows that you need all these things. Instead, be concerned above everything else with the Kingdom of God and with what he requires of you, and he will provide you with all these other things. So do not worry about tomorrow; it will have enough worries of its own. There is no need to add to the troubles each day brings. . . .

"Do not judge others, so that God will not judge you, for God will judge you in the same way you judge others, and he will apply to you the same rules you apply to others. Why, then, do you look at the speck in your brother's eye and pay no attention to the log in your own eye? How dare you say to your brother, 'Please, let me take that speck out of your eye,' when you have a log in your own eye? You hypocrite! First take the log out of your own eye, and then you will be able to see clearly to take the speck out of your brother's eye. . . .

"Go in through the narrow gate, because the gate to hell is wide and the road that leads to it is easy, and there are many who travel it. But the gate to life is narrow and the way that leads to it is hard, and there are few people who find it. . . ."

When Jesus finished saying these things, the crowd was amazed at the way he taught. He wasn't like the teachers of the Law; instead he taught with authority.

SAINT PAUL'S EPISTLE TO THE ROMANS

Saint Paul (ca 3 B.C.–A.D. 64), a Hellenized Jew from Tarsus in Asia Minor, has often been called "the second founder of Christianity." His was the leading voice opposing those conservatives who wished to keep Christianity within the boundaries of Judaism. From about A.D. 47 to his death in Rome sometime around 64, Paul was an indefatigable missionary, converting both Gentiles and Jews throughout the Mediterranean region. Most important of all, Paul transformed Jesus' messianic message into a faith that centered on Jesus as Lord and Savior.

Paul developed his distinctive theology in a series of letters, or *epistles,* which he sent to various Christian communities. Although each of these epistles was addressed to a specific group of Christians, they were revered as authoritative pronouncements of general interest for all believers. As a result, copies were circulated, and, in time, a number of the letters (as well as some Paul never composed but that were ascribed to him) were incorporated into the body of scriptural books known to Christians as the New Testament (the Old Testament being the pre-Christian, or Jewish, portion of the Bible).

Around A.D. 57, probably while residing in Corinth, Greece, Paul planned to establish a mission in Spain and decided to make Rome his base of operations. In preparation, he wrote to the Christians at Rome to inform them of his plans and to instruct them in the faith. The result was the Epistle to the Romans, the most fully articulated expression of Paul's theology of salvation.

Questions for Analysis

1. According to Paul, who was Jesus?
2. This epistle centers on the issue of how one is "put right" with God. What role does faith play in putting one right with God? Faith in what or whom? Can the Law of Moses or any other body of law put one right with God?
3. Like Second Isaiah (Chapter 3), Paul believes God has a master plan for all humanity. How does Paul's understanding of that plan differ from that of his sixth-century B.C. predecessor?
4. According to Paul, where have most Jews gone wrong, and why are Christians, whether they are former Gentiles or Jews, the new Chosen People?
5. Compare this epistle with the Sermon on the Mount. Do they agree, disagree, or complement one another?
6. For Paul, what two virtues or qualities must dominate a Christian's life?
7. What do you infer from this epistle about the role of women in the early Church?
8. What parallels can you discover between Christian devotion to Jesus, as taught by Paul, and similar contemporary forms of piety and belief in the Hindu and Buddhist traditions? In answering this question, consider the sources in Chapter 6.

From Paul, a servant of Christ Jesus and an apostle[1] chosen and called by God to preach his Good News.

The Good News was promised long ago by God through his prophets, as written in the Holy Scriptures. It is about his Son, our Lord Jesus Christ: as to his humanity, he was born a descendant of David;[2] as to his divine holiness, he was shown with great power to be the Son of God by being raised from death. Through him God gave me the privilege of being an apostle for the sake of Christ, in order to lead people of all nations to believe and obey. This also includes you who are in Rome, whom God has called to belong to Jesus Christ. . . .

I have complete confidence in the gospel; it is God's power to save all who believe, first the Jews and also the Gentiles.

1. Paul was not one of the original twelve apostles. He claimed apostolic status, because he believed he had been miraculously called and converted by the Risen Christ, who appeared to him in a vision.

2. The prophetic tradition maintained that the Messiah would be descended from King David's house, and Christian Jews stressed Jesus' Davidic lineage.

For the gospel reveals how God puts people right with himself: it is through faith from beginning to end. As the scripture says, "The person who is put right with God through faith shall live.". . . For we are the people he called, not only from among the Jews but also from among the Gentiles. . . .

So we say that the Gentiles, who were not trying to put themselves right with God, were put right with him through faith; while God's people, who were seeking a law[3] that would put them right with God, did not find it. And why not? Because they did not depend on faith but on what they did.[4]. . .

My brothers, how I wish with all my heart that my own people might be saved! How I pray to God for them! I can assure you that they are deeply devoted to God; but their devotion is not based on true knowledge. They have not known the way in which God puts people right with himself, and instead, they have tried to set up their own way, and so they did not submit themselves to God's way of putting people right. For Christ has brought the Law to an end, so that everyone who believes is put right with God. . . .

If you confess that Jesus is Lord and believe that God raised him from death, you will be saved. For it is by our faith that we are put right with God; it is by our confession that we are saved. . . .

So then, my brothers, because of God's great mercy to us I appeal to you: Offer yourselves as a living sacrifice to God, dedicated to his service and pleasing to him. This is the true worship that you should offer. Do not conform yourselves to the standards of this world, but let God transform you inwardly by a complete change of your mind. Then you will be able to know the will of God — what is good and is pleasing to him and is perfect. . . .

Be under obligation to no one — the only obligation you have is to love one another. Whoever does this has obeyed the Law. The commandments, "Do not commit adultery; do not commit murder; do not steal; do not desire what belongs to someone else" — all these, and any others besides, are summed up in the one command, "Love your neighbor as you love yourself." If you love someone, you will never do him wrong; to love, then, is to obey the whole Law. . . .

I recommend to you our sister Phoebe, who serves the church at Cenchreae.[5] Receive her in the Lord's name, as God's people should, and give her any help she may need from you; for she herself has been a good friend to many people and also to me.

I send greetings to Priscilla and Aquila,[6] my fellow workers in the service of Christ Jesus; they risked their lives for me. I am grateful to them — not only I, but all the Gentile churches as well. Greetings also to the church that meets in their house.

Greetings to my dear friend Epaenetus, who was the first man in the province of Asia to believe in Christ. Greetings to Mary, who has worked so hard for you. Greetings also to Andronicus and Junias, fellow Jews who were in prison with me; they are well known among the apostles, and they became Christians before I did.

---

3. The Law, or Torah, of Judaism.

4. That is, they followed the letter of the Law.

5. A community in the Greek Peloponnesus. The Greek text literally states that Phoebe was a deaconess. Deacons and deaconesses were assistants to the presbyters, or elders. Their duties consisted of baptizing, preaching, and dispensing charity.

6. A married couple of Jewish Christians from Asia Minor who figured prominently in the church of Rome. Priscilla was the wife, Aquila the husband.

THE THEODOSIAN CODE

Paul finally arrived in Rome, where he was martyred for his faith around A.D. 64. For the next two and a half centuries Roman authorities treated Christianity as an illegal religion. While persecutions were sporadic and localized until the middle of the third century, Christians lived and worshiped under a cloud and were all too often convenient scapegoats when crops failed or other disasters occurred. Life became increasingly precarious for Christians during the empire-wide crises of the third century, and between 303 and 311 the Church was rocked by a major assault known as the Great Persecution.

After 305 this persecution was largely confined to the eastern half of an empire that was now officially divided between two coemperors. In the West, a general named Constantine claimed the imperial crown in 306 and by 312 had secured control over that half of the empire. In 313 Constantine I (306–337) and his eastern colleague granted freedom of worship to all persons in the empire, Christians included. In the years that followed, Constantine became an increasingly enthusiastic patron of Christianity, especially from 324 onward, when he assumed control of the entire empire. In 330 he dedicated a new imperial capital, Constantinople, which was to serve as the seat for the new imperial-Christian order.

All Roman emperors from Constantine onward were baptized Christians, and most proved to be generous patrons of the Church. It was almost an anticlimax when Emperor Theodosius I (379–395) and his two coemperors declared Catholic Christianity to be the imperial state religion in 380.

The following documents are from *The Theodosian Code*, a collection of late imperial law gathered and published under the direction of Emperor Theodosius II (408–450) in 438. They provide us with a panorama of the first century of imperial Christianity.

Questions for Analysis

1. According to the edicts of February 380 and May 391, what is the status of heretical Christians, those who do not accept the orthodox (correctly taught) form of Christianity?
2. What do you think distinguished a heretic from an orthodox Catholic Christian in this imperial Church? What policies did the empire adopt in regard to heretics?
3. Compare the legal status of Jews and pagans by the end of the fourth century. Which group was tolerated? Can you infer why? How would you characterize this toleration?
4. Compare the legal treatment of Jews and heretics. Which group was better treated? Which group presented more of a perceived threat to imperial authority and the faith, and why?

5. How did the Christian emperors treat the Christian clergy? Can you think of any reasons for this policy?
6. Compare Asoka's edicts in favor of the Law of Rightousness (Chapter 5) with these laws. What are more significant, the similarities or the differences, and what do they tell us about these two societies?

[*The Imperial Church*]

[*February 28, 380*]

Edict to the people of the Constantinopolitan city.

All peoples, whom the moderation of our Clemency rules, we wish to be engaged in that religion, which the divine Peter,[1] the apostle, is declared — by the religion which has descended even to the present from him — to have transmitted to the Romans and which, it is clear the pontiff Damasus[2] and Peter,[3] bishop of Alexandria, a man of apostolic sanctity, follow: this is, that according to apostolic discipline[4] and evangelic doctrine[5] we should believe the sole Deity of the Father and of the Son and of the Holy Spirit under an equal Majesty[6] and under a pious Trinity.

We order those following this law to assume the name of Catholic[7] Christians, but the rest, since we judge them demented and insane, to sustain the infamy of heretical[8] dogma and their conventicles[9] not to take the name of churches, to be smitten first by divine vengeance, then also by the punishment of our authority, which we have claimed in accordance with the celestial will.

[*Heretics*]

[*May 11, 391*]

Those who shall have betrayed the holy faith and shall have profaned holy baptism[10] should be segregated from all

1. Saint Peter the apostle (d. ca A.D. 64).

2. Damasus I, bishop of Rome (366–384). By the end of the first century A.D., the office of bishop had changed from that of the earlier presbyter, or elder, and each bishop ruled over the Christian community of a particular city and its suburbs. See the following introduction to Pope Gelasius's letters for an explanation of the claims of the bishops of Rome.

3. Peter II (373–381). The bishop or patriarch of Alexandria was one of the most honored leaders in the Church by virtue of the importance of Alexandria. Like the bishop of Rome, he claimed the title of *papa* (father), or pope.

4. According to the practices of the apostles.

5. According to the faith as revealed in the Gospels.

6. Here Theodosius I and his coemperors reject the teaching of that group of Christians known as Arians. The Arians believed that Jesus was God only by adoption and was not, therefore, equal in majesty or nature to God the Father. The majority of the Church accepted the doctrine of the Holy Trinity, which recognizes three separate and equal divine persons in a single, indivisible God: God the Father, the Creator; God the Son (Jesus), the Redeemer; and God the Holy Spirit, the Sanctifier.

7. Catholic means "universal." Here it means the Church of the entire empire.

8. Heresy here means wrong Christian belief or dogma, e.g., that of the Arians.

9. A secret religious meeting place.

10. It is not clear if this condemnation extended to all heretics, who profaned their baptism (the rite through which they were initiated into the Church) by their heresy, or only those heretics who insisted on rebaptizing persons who had previously been baptized as orthodox, or Catholic Christians.

persons' association, should be debarred from testifying[11] should not have . . . the making of a will, should succeed to no one in an inheritance, should be written by no one as heirs.

And these also we should have commanded to be banished to a distance and to be removed rather far away, if it had not seemed to be a greater penalty for them to dwell among men and to lack men's approbation.

But they never shall return to their previous status, the shame of their conduct shall not be obliterated by penitence and shall not be concealed by any shade of elaborate defense or protection, since things which are fabricated and fashioned cannot protect indeed those who have polluted the faith which they had vowed to God and who, betraying the divine mystery,[12] have turned to profanations. And indeed for the lapsed[13] and the errant[14] there is help, but for the lost — that is, the profaners of holy baptism — there is no aid through any remedy of penitence, which is wont to be available for other crimes.

[*May 19, 391*]

We order the heretics' polluted contagions to be driven from cities, to be ejected from villages, and the communities not at all to be available for any meetings, lest in any place a sacrilegious company of such persons should be collected. Neither public meeting places to their perversity nor more hidden retreats to their errors should be granted.

[*Pagans*]

[*August 7, 395*]

We ordain that none may have the liberty of approaching any shrine or temple whatever or of performing abominable sacrifices at any place or time whatever.

[*Jews*]

[*May 29, 408*]

Governors of provinces should forbid Jews, in a certain ceremony of their festival Aman[15] for remembrance of a former punishment, to ignite and to burn for contempt of the Christian faith with sacrilegious mind a simulated appearance of the Holy Cross[16] lest they should connect our faith's sign with their sports; but they should retain their rites without contempt of the Christian law,[17] because without doubt they shall lose privileges previously permitted to them, unless they shall have abstained from illicit acts.

[*August 6, 412 or 418*]

No one, on the ground that he is a Jew, when he is innocent, should be

---

11. In a court of law.

12. The sacrament of baptism.

13. Those who no longer practice the faith but are not heretics.

14. Non-Christians.

15. The feast of Purim, which commemorates the deliverance of Persian Jews from the evil designs of Haman, a fifth-century B.C. Persian official.

16. Haman was hung for his machinations. In celebrating the feast, Jews burned his effigy suspended from a gallows that vaguely resembled a Cross.

17. The Christian religion.

condemned nor any religion whatsoever should cause a person to be exposed to contumely.[18]

Their synagogues or habitations should not be burned indiscriminately or should not be damaged wrongfully without any reason, since, moreover, even if anyone should be implicated in crimes, yet the vigor of the law-courts and the protection of the public law appear to have been established in our midst, lest anyone should have the power to venture on vengeance for himself.

But as we desire this to be provided for the persons of the Jews, so we decree also that the following warning ought to be made: that Jews perchance should not become insolent and, elated by their own security, should not commit anything rash against reverence for the Christian worship.

[*The Clergy*]

[*June 23, 318*]

Pursuant to his own duty a judge shall be bound to observe that, if there should be an appeal to an episcopal court,[19] silence should be applied[20] and that, if anyone shall have wished to transfer a matter to the Christian law and to observe that sort of court, he should be heard, even if the matter has been begun before the judge. . . .

[*October 21, 319*]

Whoever devote to divine worship the services of religion, that is, those who are called clergymen, should be excused entirely from all public services, lest through certain persons' sacrilegious malice they should be diverted from divine services.

Pope Gelasius I

WRITINGS

From the late third century onward Rome rapidly lost its position of political primacy and was replaced in the West by such new imperial centers as Milan and Ravenna in Italy and Trier in Germany. With Constantinople's dedication as the New Rome in 330, the center of imperial power shifted eastward. When the last Roman emperor in the West was forced to abdicate in 476, the emperor residing at Constantinople became the sole legitimate ruler of an empire whose Western regions were rapidly becoming fragmented, ungovernable by a single imperial authority, and quite un-Roman, as German tribes carved out kingdoms there.

While Rome was losing its political power, its spiritual authority was on the rise. The bishop who presided over Rome's Christian community held a unique position in the Church. His bishopric alone could claim the bodies and, therefore, the inherited powers of Saints Peter and Paul, the Church's two greatest apostles. From the fifth century onward, the bishops of Rome increasingly claimed to be the legal heirs

18. Abuse.

19. A bishop's court.

20. The civil judge cannot object.

of Saint Peter, whom they believed had received special powers of governance over the Church directly from Jesus. They thus assumed the title Pope or Father (*Papa* in Latin), thereby claiming the right to govern the Church with an authority analogous to the almost absolute power of a traditional Roman head of a household. At this time few persons were ready to accept or even acknowledge the implications of the claims of the bishops of Rome, but the foundations had been laid for what would become the medieval papacy.

One of the most important popes of the fifth century was Gelasius I (492–496), who in 494 wrote to Emperor Anastasius I (491–518) complaining of the emperor's interference in church affairs. Separated from the emperor at Constantinople by an ever widening gulf between the Eastern and Western portions of the empire and supported by a Germanic king of Italy known as Theodoric the Ostrogoth (ca 454–526), Gelasius felt confident to lecture Anastasius on the proper relationship between the imperial and priestly powers. The first excerpt contains Gelasius's definition of the respective powers and areas of responsibility of priests and emperors, as set out in his letter to Anastasius. Two years later Gelasius returned to the issue in a treatise entitled *On the Bond of Anathema* and more clearly spelled out the relationship between spiritual and worldly authority. This is the second excerpt.

Questions for Analysis

1. According to Gelasius, whose responsibilities and authority are the greater, the pope's or the emperor's? Why?
2. According to Gelasius, why are there two separate authorities within Christendom?
3. Consider the evidence relating to Caesar Augustus in Chapter 5. How does Gelasius's definition of the priestly and royal spheres of power represent a departure from the beliefs and practices of traditional Roman society?

Two there are, august emperor, by which this world is chiefly ruled, the sacred authority of the priesthood and the royal power. Of these the responsibility of the priests is more weighty in so far as they will answer for the kings of men themselves at the divine judgment. You know, most clement son, that, although you take precedence over all mankind in dignity, nevertheless you piously bow the neck to those who have charge of divine affairs and seek from them the means of your salvation, and hence you realize that, in the order of religion, in matters concerning the reception and right administration of the heavenly sacraments, you ought to submit yourself rather than rule, and that in these matters you should depend on their judgment rather than seek to bend them to your will. For if the bishops themselves, recognizing that the imperial office was conferred on you by divine disposition, obey your laws so far as the sphere of public order is concerned lest they seem to obstruct your decrees in mundane matters, with what zeal, I ask you, ought you to obey those who have been charged with administering the sacred mysteries? Moreover, just as no light risk attends pontiffs[1] who keep silent in matters concerning the service of God, so too no little danger threatens those who show scorn — which God forbid — when they ought to obey. And if the hearts of the faithful should be submitted to all priests in general who rightly administer divine things, how much more should assent be given to the bishop of that see[2] which the Most High wished to be preeminent over all priests, and which the devotion of the whole church has honored ever since.[3] As Your Piety is certainly well aware, no one can ever raise himself by purely human means to the privilege and place of him whom the voice of Christ has set before all, whom the church has always venerated and held in devotion as its primate.[4] The things which are established by divine judgment can be assailed by human presumption; they cannot be overthrown by anyone's power.

. . .

It happened before the coming of Christ that certain men, though still engaged in carnal activities,[5] were symbolically both kings and priests, and sacred history tells us that Melchisedek[6] was such a one. The Devil also imitated this among his own people, for he always strives in a spirit of tyranny to claim for himself what pertains to divine worship, and so pagan emperors were called supreme pontiffs.[7] But when He[8] came who was true king and true priest, the emperor no longer assumed the title of priest, nor did the priest claim the royal dignity — though the members of Him[9] who was true king and true priest, through participation in his nature, may be said to have received both qualities in their sacred nobility so that they constitute a race at once royal and priestly. For Christ, mindful of human frailty, regulated with an excellent disposition what pertained to the salvation of his people. Thus he distinguished between the offices of both powers according to their own proper activities and separate dignities, wanting his people to be saved by healthful humility and not carried away again by human pride, so that Christian emperors would need priests for attaining eternal life and priests would avail themselves of imperial regulations in the conduct of temporal affairs. In this fashion spiritual activity would be set apart from worldly encroachments and the "soldier of God"[10] would not be involved in secular affairs,[11]

---

1. High priests. As a Christian title, pontiff is reserved for bishops and popes.

2. A see, or seat, is a bishop's church (the city and region over which he presides).

3. The see, or bishopric, of Rome, which claims the authority of Saint Peter, prince of the apostles.

4. The chief bishop of a major region, in this case, the pope.

5. Activities of the flesh or worldly matters.

6. King of Salem (an unknown ancient city, possibly Jerusalem) and also its chief priest, Melchizedek blessed Abraham, father of the Hebrews (*Genesis* 14: 17–20).

7. See the statue of Caesar Augustus as *Pontifex Maximus* (Chief Priest) in Chapter 5. The bishops of Rome took the title as their own in the fourth century.

8. Jesus.

9. All Christians.

10. A priest.

11. Things that pertain to the world (*saeculum* in Latin).

while on the other hand he who was involved in secular affairs would not seem to preside over divine matters. Thus the humility of each order would be preserved, neither being exalted by the subservience of the other, and each profession would be especially fitted for its appropriate functions.

CHRIST TRIUMPHANT

Early Christian artists generally portrayed Jesus either as a lamb or as a youthful and beardless Good Shepherd. When Christianity became the emperor's religion, artists had to create new iconographical symbols in order to incorporate Christ into the imperial culture.

The following mosaic (a mural composed of pieces of colored stone, glass, and precious metal) dates from around 500 and is located in the archbishop's chapel at Ravenna, a city in northeast Italy that served as the western capital of the Roman Empire from 402 to 476 and continued to be Italy's most prominent political center into the eighth century. During the fifth century, the archbishops of Ravenna, often imperial appointees, rivaled the popes of Rome in power and prestige.

Here Christ is dressed as a conquering Roman emperor. He wears armor, a general's cloak, and military boots. He carries his cross, the means by which he triumphed over death and redeemed the world, in the careless manner of a soldier bearing a weapon. Underneath his feet are a lion and a snake, which represent two biblical quotations. The Book of Psalms declares, "You shall tread on the lion and the adder; the young lion and the dragon you shall trample under feet." In the Gospel of Luke, Jesus tells his disciples, "Behold, I have given you power to tread on snakes and scorpions and to overcome all the power of the Enemy." The open book, symbolizing the Gospels, reads, "I am the Way, the Truth, and Life."

Questions for Analysis

1. With whose interpretation of the emperor's role in the Church does the patron of the mosaic agree, Pope Gelasius's or that of the Christian emperors whose laws were preserved in *The Theodosian Code*?
2. Compare this mosaic with the sculpture of Arapacana (page 178; described on page 201). What common elements can you find in these two pieces of religious art? How do the scenes and central figures differ? What strike you as more significant, their similarities or differences in style and message? What does your answer to this question suggest about the two faiths?
3. Consider also the statue of Shiva Nataraja (page 184). What common triumph do these three savior deities claim, and what do their parallel victories suggest?

Christ Triumphant

Justinian

CODE OF CIVIL LAW

During the sixth century the Roman Empire underwent a metamorphosis. The western half was divided into a number of German kingdoms. Circumstances were causing it to sever most ties with the old Mediterranean ecumene and fall back on its own resources.

While the West was in the midst of this painful process of cultural transformation, the East was developing a new Hellenistic synthesis we call Byzantine civilization. Modern historians have coined the term Byzantine to refer to the Eastern Christian civilization centered at Constantinople, which was located on the site of the ancient Greek city of Byzantion. This new civilization resulted from the amalgamation of three key elements: the autocratic structure of the late Roman Empire, Eastern Orthodox Christianity, and the cultural heritage of the Hellenistic past.

In true Hellenistic fashion, the entire Byzantine world revolved around the Orthodox emperor, who in theory was answerable to no one on earth. As a Christian, he could not play the part of a Middle Eastern god-king, but he was the next best thing: the living image of God on earth, insofar as his imperial majesty was a pale reflection of the Glory of God. As such, the emperor was the link between the Chosen People and their God.

Justinian I (527–565) was the first great Byzantine emperor, even though he was the last emperor of Constantinople to speak Latin as his native tongue. It was in the reign of this man, who tried so hard to reimpose imperial control over the Western empire, that Byzantine civilization enjoyed its first golden age. The following excerpt comes from an imperial decree of 535 dealing with the consecration of bishops and other clerics and the general upkeep of churches.

Questions for Analysis

1. Like Gelasius, Justinian distinguishes between the functions of priests and emperors. Are there any areas in which he disagrees with Gelasius? How do you think Justinian would react if he were to receive a letter such as the one Gelasius sent Anastasius?
2. According to Justinian, who ultimately is responsible for the well-being of the priesthood and the maintenance of true doctrine?
3. Does Justinian believe that Church and State can and should be separated?

The greatest gifts which God in His heavenly clemency bestows upon men are the priesthood and the Imperial authority. The former ministers to Divine things, the latter presides and watches over human affairs; both proceed from one and the same source and together they are the ornaments of human life. Therefore nothing is so close to the hearts of Emperors as the moral well-being of the priesthood since priests have the task of perpetual prayer to God on behalf of Emperors themselves. For if the priesthood is in all matters free from vice and filled with faith in God, and if the Imperial authority with justice and efficiency sets in order the commonwealth committed to its charge, there shall be an ideal harmony to provide whatever is useful for the human race. We therefore have the greatest anxiety for the true doctrines of God and for the moral well-being of the priesthood by which, if it is preserved, we believe that the greatest gifts will be given to us by God and we shall preserve undisturbed those things which we have and in addition acquire benefits which are at present lacking to us. But all things are done rightly and efficiently if a beginning is made which is fitting and agreeable to God. We believe that this will come about if there is due care for the observance of the holy canons,[1] which the justly praised Apostles and venerated eyewitnesses and servants of the word of God handed down and which the holy Fathers preserved and interpreted.

THE SAYINGS OF THE DESERT ELDERS

During the fourth and fifth centuries many pious men and women sought escape from the new Christian-imperial order and what they perceived as a corrupt and decaying society by going into the wastelands of Egypt, Syria-Palestine, and Asia Minor. These desert elders included such colorful and unconventional characters as Abbot John the Dwarf, Abbot Moses the Black, and Saint Mary the Harlot. Despite their many differences, they shared a number of characteristics, chief of which was a desire to live the spirit of the Gospels in a totally uncompromising manner.

This flight to the desert was the foundation of Christian monasticism. The first desert elders were usually hermits (also known as *anchorites*), who elected to live solitary lives in their desert refuges. The desert oases could support only a limited number of hermitages, however, and in time many former hermits chose to join together into communities. Those who elected to live communally were known as *cenobites*. By the end of the sixth century, cenobitic communities became the Christian monastic norm, but they never totally displaced hermits. Moreover, the lives and legends of the first desert hermits continued to inspire Christian monasticism through the ages. Whether anchorite or cenobite, Christian monks of every variety have universally claimed that their ways of life continue the tradition of the flight to the desert.

The Sayings of the Desert Elders is an undatable collection of aphorisms and anecdotes revolving around the earliest desert hermits. Although many of these stories

1. Laws. Church law is called canon law.

were modified over time, they sprang out of an oral and literary tradition that had its origins in fourth-century Egypt and Palestine. The entries that appear here concern Macarius the Great (ca 300–390), one of fourth-century Egypt's most influential Christian holy men. The virtues and attitudes displayed in these stories have remained part of the Christian monastic ideal to the present day.

Questions for Analysis

1. How, if at all, do Macarius's words and actions reflect the message of the Sermon on the Mount?
2. Compare the ideal of desert monasticism with the reality of the new Christian-imperial tradition. Do you perceive any contradiction or tension?
3. Could any state support an entire population of people like Macarius?
4. Contrary to what one might expect, emperors and bishops generally tended to support and even venerate many of these monks and their way of life. Can you think of any reason why?
5. As these stories illustrate, many of the desert hermits had disciples, lived in close proximity to one another, visited among themselves, and even went to town on occasion. Can you infer why these hermits were not absolutely cut off from all human contact?

[*Charity*]

Abba Peter[1] said this about the holy Macarius: "One day he came to the cell of an anchorite who happened to be ill, and he asked him if he would take something to eat, though his cell was stripped bare. When the other replied, "some sherbet," that courageous man did not hesitate, but went as far as Alexandria to fetch some for the sick man. The astonishing thing is that no one knew about it.". . .

They said about Abba Macarius that when he visited the brethren he laid this rule upon himself, "If there is wine, drink some for the brethren's sake, but for each cup of wine, spend a day without drinking water." So the brothers would offer him some refreshment, and the old man would accept it joyfully to mortify himself; but when his disciple got to know about it he said to the brethren, "In the name of God, do not offer him any more, or he will go and kill himself in his cell." When they heard that, the brethren did not offer him wine any more. . . .

They said of Abba Macarius the Great that he became, as it is written, a god upon earth, because, just as God protects the world, so Abba Macarius would cover the faults which he saw, as though he did not see them; and those which he heard, as though he did not hear them.

---

1. *Abba* means "father" in Aramaic, the common tongue of Syria-Palestine, and was an honorific title accorded to certain elders whose reputations gave them a large measure of moral authority. Most of these hermits, like Peter, were layfolk, who held no position of formal authority in the Church. Many were poorly educated, if even literate, and came from the least powerful levels of society.

[Humility]

When Abba Macarius was returning from the marsh to his cell one day carrying some palm-leaves, he met the devil[2] on the road with a scythe. The latter struck at him as much as he pleased, but in vain, and he said to him, "What is your power, Macarius, that makes me powerless against you? All that you do, I do, too; you fast, so do I; you keep vigil, and I do not sleep at all; in one thing only do you beat me." Abba Macarius asked what that was. He said, "Your humility. Because of that I can do nothing against you.". . .

A brother came to see Abba Macarius the Egyptian, and said to him, "Abba, give me a word, that I may be saved." So the old man said, "Go to the cemetery and abuse the dead." The brother went there, abused them and threw stones at them; then he returned and told the old man about it. The latter said to him, "Didn't they say anything to you?" He replied "No." The old man said, "Go back tomorrow and praise them." So the brother went away and praised them, calling them, "Apostles, saints and righteous men." He returned to the old man and said to him, "I have complimented them." And the old man said to him, "Did they not answer you?" The brother said no. The old man said to him, "You know how you insulted them and they did not reply, and how you praised them and they did not speak; so you too if you wish to be saved must do the same and become a dead man. Like the dead, take no account of either the scorn of men or their praises, and you can be saved.". . .

Abba Isaiah questioned Abba Macarius saying, "Give me a word." The old man said to him, "Flee from men." Abba Isaiah said to him, "What does it mean to flee from men?" The old man said, "It means to sit in your cell and weep for your sins.". . .

They said of Abba Macarius that if a brother came to see him with fear, like someone coming to see a great and holy old man, he did not say anything to him. But if one of the brethren said to him, as though to humiliate him, "Abba, when you were a camel-driver, and stole nitre[3] and sold it again, did not the keepers beat you?" If someone talked to him like that he would talk to them with joy about whatever they asked him.

[Divine Providence]

It was said of Abba Macarius the Egyptian that one day when he was going up from Scetis[4] with a load of baskets,[5] he sat down, overcome with weariness and began to say to himself, "My God, you know very well that I cannot go any further," and immediately he found himself at the river.

[Prayer]

Abba Macarius was asked, "How should one pray?" The old man said, "There is no need at all to make long discourses; it is enough to stretch out one's hands and say, "Lord, as you will, and as you know, have mercy." And if the conflict grows fiercer say, "Lord, help!" He knows very well what we need and he shews us his mercy.". . .

2. Confrontations with a physical devil were common in the legends of these holy people.

3. Prior to becoming a hermit, Macarius supported himself as a camel driver and traded in saltpeter.

4. Scetis, or Scete, was an oasis west of the Nile delta that became one of the most densely populated centers of hermit life.

5. Many hermits supported themselves by making baskets or rope.

Abba Moses[6] said to Abba Macarius at Scetis, "I should like to live in quiet prayer and the brethren do not let me." Abba Macarius said to him, "I see that you are a sensitive man and incapable of sending a brother away. Well, if you want to live in peace, go to the interior desert, to Petra,[7] and there you will be at peace." And so he found peace.

[*The Golden Rule*]

Abba Paphnutius, the disciple of Abba Macarius, said, "I asked my father to say a word to me and he replied, 'Do no evil to anyone, and do not judge anyone. Observe this and you will be saved.'"

The Medieval Centuries

Western historians often refer to the period from about 500 to 1500 as the medieval era (from the Latin *Media Aeva* — the Middle Ages). Although the term is inappropriate for world history and misleading even when applied to Western Europe, there is good reason to view this era as Christianity's Middle Ages. By A.D. 500 Christianity was ready to play a major role in both Byzantium and Western Europe, and the thousand years that followed would be *the* Christian millennium for each. After 1500 the situation was different. The Byzantine world was, for the most part, swallowed up by Islam, while serious challenges to medieval forms of Christian expression and organization arose on several fronts in Western Europe.

One element of Western Europe's medieval Christian civilization that suffered severe diminution after 1500 was the Roman papacy. Between approximately 1050 and 1300, however, the papacy was at the height of its powers, and its aggressive claim to be the moral center of Christendom occasioned several significant shifts in Christian history during this period. Popes quarreled with emperors and kings over their respective powers and areas of authority, and two major consequences followed from those controversies. A bitter estrangement developed between the Churches of Rome and Constantinople, and that schism has persisted to our own day. Also, certain political thinkers in the West began to articulate the idea that it is necessary for the well-being of society to separate the functions of Church and State. This concept would become a reality and a hallmark of Western civilization centuries later.

---

6. Abba Moses, a black giant of a man and a former slave, had been a brigand before his conversion. He eventually became a priest and a hermit and earned a reputation for gentleness and charity.

7. A site in the desert of modern Jordan.

Gregory VII

THE POPE'S PROCLAMATION

The tradition of imperial governance of the Christian Church, which some historians term *caesropapism* (a Caesar acting as a pope), was not unique to Constantinople. When Pope Leo III (795–816) crowned Charlemagne (768–814) emperor on Christmas Day 800, the West once again had its own "Roman" emperor. Even before he became emperor, Charles controlled the churches within his lands and felt no hesitation in instructing even the pope on points of theology, a policy that he and his imperial successors continued after 800.

The Roman papacy at times acquiesced in and at other times resisted this imperial direction. When popes resisted, they did so on a variety of grounds but chiefly on the basis of their Petrine claim that they alone were the successors of Saint Peter, the Rock of the Church, to whom Christ had committed stewardship over all Christians. In Constantinople, while occasionally there were a few extraordinarily independent patriarchs (the chief priest of the Eastern Church), most were easily directed by an all too close and powerful imperial court.

By the late eleventh century the Roman papacy had achieved a level of independence and institutional strength whereby it could directly confront the Western emperor. The result was the Investiture Controversy (1075–1122), which began with Pope Gregory VII (1073–1085) and Henry IV (1056–1106). The controversy divided Western Europe for almost fifty years and was left to their successors to settle. When Henry V (1106–1125) and Pope Calixtus II (1119–1124) finally accepted the Concordat of Worms of 1122, they essentially agreed to continue to disagree on the still unresolved central issue: who is the God-appointed head of the community of Christians on earth, the pope or the emperor?

The following source provides a view of the Investiture Controversy from the papal court. This curious document, known as the *Dictatus Papae,* appears in the official collection of Pope Gregory's correspondence for March 1075 under the title "What Is the Power of the Roman Pontiffs?" It is clearly not a letter. The best-informed guess is that, in the normal course of events, each of the twenty-seven principles in this list would have been supported by citations from the Bible and other authoritative sources. It was, in other words, the outline of a church lawyer's uncompleted brief or, more correctly, a collection of canons. As sketchy as it is, the document provides a good insight into the program and mind set of the papal party.

Questions for Analysis

1. What powers does Gregory claim over other clerics?
2. What powers does Gregory claim over princes?

3. In Gregory's mind, is the Church simply a collection of priests and other clerics, or is it the whole body of Christians?
4. What does Gregory consider to be his position in the Church?
5. Is Gregory's vision of papal power consistent with Pope Gelasius's view?

1. That the Roman church was established by God alone.

2. That the Roman pontiff alone is rightly called universal.[1]

3. That he alone has the power to depose and reinstate bishops.

4. That his legate,[2] even if he be of lower ecclesiastical rank,[3] presides over bishops in council,[4] and has the power to give sentence of deposition against them.

5. That the pope has the power to depose those who are absent (i.e., without giving them a hearing).

6. That, among other things, we ought not to remain in the same house with those whom he has excommunicated.[5]

7. That he alone has the right, according to the necessity of the occasion, to make new laws, to create new bishoprics. . . .

8. That he alone may use the imperial insignia.[6]

9. That all princes shall kiss the foot of the pope alone.

10. That his name alone is to be recited in the churches.

11. That the name applied to him belongs to him alone.[7]

12. That he has the power to depose emperors.

13. That he has the right to transfer bishops from one see[8] to another when it becomes necessary.

14. That he has the right to ordain as a cleric anyone from any part of the church whatsoever.

15. That anyone ordained by him may rule (as bishop) over another church. . . .

16. That no general synod[9] may be called without his order.

---

1. The pope alone has universal authority over all churches.

2. A papal representative who carries delegated papal authority.

3. There were a number of clerical grades, of which bishop (the head of a diocese) was one of the most powerful.

4. A gathering of church leaders to discuss and decide on church policy.

5. Denied communion — banned from the spiritual and social activities of the Christian community.

6. This claim was based on an eighth-century forgery known as the *Donation of Constantine,* which claimed that Constantine, upon leaving for Constantinople, ceded to the pope and his successors dominion over Rome, Italy, and all the Western regions, as well as the prerogative of wearing all the imperial insignia.

7. He alone may bear the title "pope." The patriarch of Alexandria also claimed the title, however.

8. The official seat or center of a bishop's authority. For example, the pope's *see* is the city of Rome.

9. A council. A general, or ecumenical, council is a convocation of all the bishops of the Church.

17. That no action of a synod and no book shall be regarded as canonical[10] without his authority.

18. That his decree can be annulled by no one, and that he can annul the decrees of anyone.

19. That he can be judged by no one.

20. That no one shall dare to condemn a person who has appealed to the apostolic seat [to the pope].

21. That the important cases of any church whatsoever shall be referred to the Roman church (to the pope).

22. That the Roman church has never erred and will never err to all eternity, according to the testimony of the holy scriptures.

23. That the Roman pontiff who has been canonically ordained[11] is made holy by the merits of St. Peter. . . .

24. That by his command or permission subjects may accuse their rulers.

25. That he can depose and reinstate bishops without the calling of a synod.

26. That no one can be regarded as catholic who does not agree with the Roman church.

27. That he has the power to absolve subjects from their oath of fidelity to wicked rulers.

John of Paris

A TREATISE ON ROYAL AND PAPAL POWER

The Investiture Controversy was only the opening round of over two and a half centuries of conflict, as first popes and emperors, and later popes and kings of new nation-states, struggled with one another to control the lives of their Christian subjects. The fact that neither popes nor secular rulers were ever able to overwhelm the other resulted in a growing feeling among some observers that perhaps there were two powers, Church and State, which have legitimate but different claims upon a subject's loyalty. The clearest medieval articulator of this position was John of Paris, a French priest and scholar of the Dominican order of friars, who around 1302 composed *A Treatise on Royal and Papal Power*, in which he argued that civil government and the priesthood have separate roles to play in guiding human conduct.

Questions for Analysis

1. According to John of Paris, what are humanity's two ends or goals, and how is each attained?
2. Why is civil government natural and necessary?
3. Why is the priesthood higher in dignity than secular authority?

---

10. Legal.

11. Legally elected.

4. In what ways is secular authority greater than priestly authority?
5. Compare John of Paris's political theories with those of Popes Gelasius and Gregory. How do they agree or disagree?

First it should be known that kingship, properly understood, can be defined as the rule of one man over a perfect multitude so ordered as to promote the public good. . . . Such a government is based on natural law and the law of nations. For, since man is naturally a civil or political creature . . . it is essential for a man to live in a multitude and in such a multitude as is self-sufficient for life. The community of a household or village is not of this sort, but the community of a city or kingdom is, for in a household or village there is not found everything necessary for food, clothing and defense through a whole life as there is in a city or kingdom. But every multitude scatters and disintegrates as each man pursues his own ends unless it is ordered to the common good by some one man who has charge of this common good. . . .

Next it must be borne in mind that man is not ordered only to such a good as can be acquired by nature, which is to live virtuously, but is further ordered to a supernatural end which is eternal life, and the whole multitude of men living virtuously is ordered to this. Therefore it is necessary that there be some one man to direct the multitude to this end. If indeed this end could be attained by the power of human nature, it would necessarily pertain to the office of the human king to direct men to this end, for we call a human king him to whom is committed the highest duty of government in human affairs. But since man does not come to eternal life by human power but by divine . . . this kind of rule pertains to a king who is not only man but also God, namely Jesus Christ . . . and because Christ was to withdraw his corporal presence from the church it was necessary for him to institute others as ministers who would administer the sacraments to men, and these are called priests. . . . Hence priesthood may be defined in this fashion. Priesthood is a spiritual power of administering sacraments to the faithful conferred by Christ on ministers of the church. . . .

From the foregoing material it is easy to see which is first in dignity, the kingship or the priesthood. . . . A kingdom is ordered to this end, that an assembled multitude may live virtuously, as has been said, and it is further ordered to a higher end which is the enjoyment of God; and responsibility for this end belongs to Christ, whose ministers and vicars are the priests. Therefore the priestly power is of greater dignity than the secular and this is commonly conceded. . . .

But if the priest is greater in himself than the prince and is greater in dignity, it does not follow that he is greater in all respects. For the lesser secular power is not related to the greater spiritual power as having its origin from it or being derived from it as the power of a proconsul is related to that of the emperor, which is greater in all respects since the power of the former is derived from the latter. The relationship is rather like that of a head of a household to a general of armies, since one is not derived from the other but both from a superior power. And so the secular power is greater than the spiritual in some things, namely in temporal affairs, and in such affairs it is not subject to the spiritual power in any way because it does not have its origin from it but rather both have their origin immediately from the one supreme power, namely the divine. Accordingly the inferior power is not subject to the superior in all things but only in those where the supreme power has subordinated it to the greater. A teacher of literature or an instructor in morals directs the members of a household to a nobler end, namely the knowledge of truth, than a doctor who is concerned with a lower end, namely the health of bodies, but who would say therefore the doctor should be subjected to the teacher in preparing his medicines? For this is not fitting, since the head of the household who established both in his house did not subordinate the lesser to the greater in this respect. Therefore the priest is greater than the prince in spiritual affairs and, on the other hand, the prince is greater in temporal affairs.

TWO THIRTEENTH-CENTURY REPRESENTATIONS OF THE VIRGIN

By the thirteenth century, Eastern and Western Christians disagreed over many issues, but they equally regarded Mary, the mother of Jesus, as the most lovable and loving of all God's saints. Both Byzantine and Latin Christians revered Mary as the fully human yet sinless Mother of God who served as advocate for all humanity before her Son's throne.

The cult of Mary resulted in a massive volume of paintings and statues in East and West of the Virgin Mother, as she was also known. One of the more popular themes, especially in Byzantium, was the Dormition, or "Falling Asleep," of Mary. According to a tradition accepted in East and West, when Mary died, her incorruptible body was assumed into heaven. With body and soul reunited, she was crowned Queen of Heaven.

The following two illustrations represent typical thirteenth-century High Gothic (Western) and Late Byzantine renderings of the Dormition. The first is a carving at the Rhineland cathedral of Strasbourg, which today is located in eastern France, and dates from around 1230. The other is a wall painting from the Serbian church of Saint Mary Peribleptos, located in modern Yugoslavia, and dates to around 1295. During the thirteenth century, that region of the northwest Balkans known as Serbia was culturally part of Byzantine civilization.

Both pieces of art employ many of the same features. Mourning apostles surround a sleeping Virgin. Saint Peter is at the far left, at the head of the bed, and Saint Paul is at the far right, at the foot of the bed. Christ dominates the central background, where he tenderly holds his mother's winged soul in his arms. In the Strasbourg sculpture a kneeling Saint Mary Magdalene, one of Jesus' most important female disciples, grieves at the bedside, but she is absent in the Serbian painting. Just as these iconographic similarities suggest an essential theological agreement between

Dormition, Cathedral of Strasbourg

the two separated branches of Christendom, the differences in style may help us understand better the ways in which these two Christian civilizations had parted.

Questions for Analysis

1. Which scene seems more naturalistic? Why? Which scene seems to emphasize more the "mystery," or otherworldliness, of the faith?
2. In which scene do Mary and Christ appear more serenely detached from this world? Do they seem approachable? Do the figures in the other scene appear more "human"?
3. In which scene do the mourners appear more to be paying court than grieving? Compare it with the other scene. Which is more awe-inspiring? Why?
4. Judging from these scenes, which Christian tradition emphasized the cult of the Risen, glorified Christ? Which emphasized the suffering Jesus? Which tradition probably placed greater emphasis on the Nativity (Christmas)?
5. If each scene does represent a different devotional emphasis and a different way of perceiving humanity's relationship with the Divine, what can you say about the two Christian cultures that produced them?

Dormition, Church of Saint Mary Peribleptos

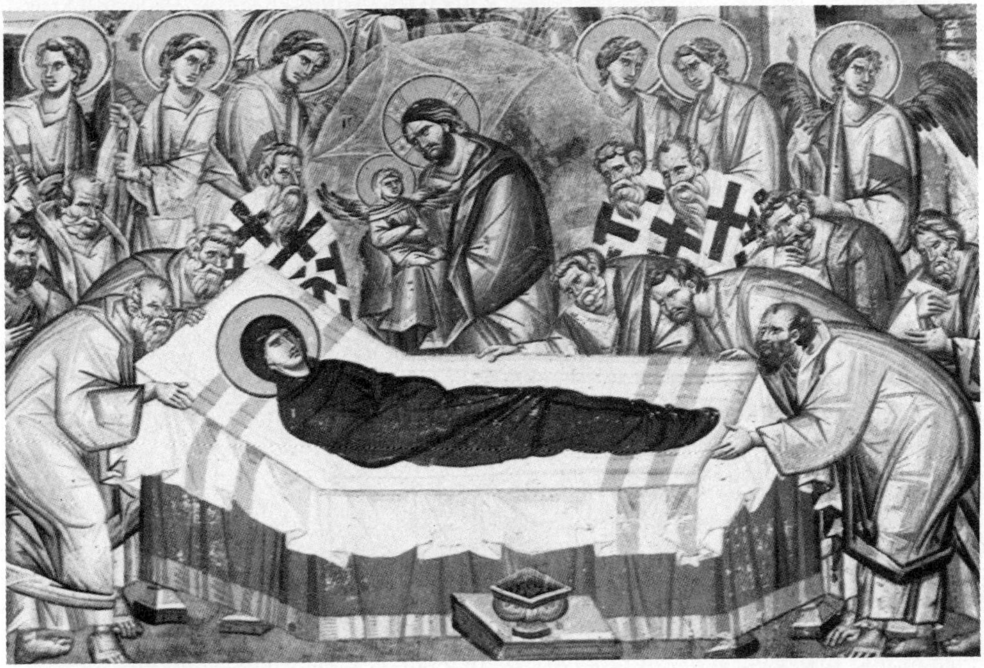

John Mandeville

TRAVELS

In 1054 the patriarch of Constantinople and several papal envoys to the Byzantine Empire laid bans of excommunication on one another in a mutual fit of wounded pride and xenophobia (fear of foreigners). Although this incident symbolized the growing estrangement between these two Christian cultures, it did not precipitate a sudden rupture between the two Churches. Mutual acknowledgment that a schism existed came only during the age of the crusades (1095–1291), as Byzantines and Western Europeans came into closer contact with one another, learned of their cultural differences, and clashed on the battlefield. By 1204, when the army of the Fourth Crusade captured and sacked Constantinople, Western (or Latin) and Byzantine (or Greek) Christians generally hated one another intensely.

One document illustrating that estrangement comes from a curious work ascribed to a largely unknown person named Sir John Mandeville. First appearing in Europe between 1356 and 1366, the *Travels* purported to be the firsthand account of an English knight's trans-Eurasian adventures between 1322 and 1356, in which he claimed to have served both the sultan of Egypt and the Mongol khan of China. There is good reason to believe this work is mostly a fictional tour de force by a gifted author whose travels were largely imaginative. Whatever the case, the book, written originally in French, was widely circulated and translated into virtually every European language by 1400. Indeed, it became late medieval Europe's most popular travelogue in an age noted for its fascination with world travel (Chapter 11), and, in many ways, it shaped Western Europeans' vision of the outside world. Even if Sir John (if that was his name) did not travel to all the regions he said he did, his work is historically important because it illustrates the manner in which Europeans of the fourteenth and fifteenth centuries viewed the lands and peoples beyond their frontiers.

In the following selection the author describes the faith and religious practices of the people of Constantinople (a city he does seem to have visited). His description of the ways in which Greek Christians differed from their Latin coreligionists is largely correct, but even his occasional errors reveal the depth of hostility and misunderstanding that divided Latins and Greeks by the fourteenth century.

Questions for Analysis

1. The differences that separated Latin and Byzantine Christians fell into three categories: doctrinal (basic articles of faith), cultural (modes of religious expression and practice), and institutional (the manner in which each Church was organized and led). Place each of the differences Sir John enumerates into its appropriate category. Which category is the largest? What does this suggest?
2. Of all the "errors" of the Greeks listed here, which seem the most serious and basic? Why?
3. Can you find any evidence indicating that Greeks and Latins misunderstand and dislike one another?

And although the Greeks are Christian, nevertheless they vary from our faith. For they say that the Holy Ghost proceeds not from the Son, but only from the Father;[1] and they are not in obedience to the Church of Rome, nor to the Pope. And they say that beyond the Greek Sea[2] their Patriarch has as much power as our

1. Reference to the so-called *Filioque* (Latin for "and from the Son") controversy. In saying the Creed of Faith, Eastern Christians stated, "The Holy Spirit proceeds from the Father." Since the tenth century, the Church of Rome added "and from the Son." The issue was largely semantic and cultural, but by the mid-eleventh century some Greeks and Latins believed it to be a major doctrinal difference.

2. The Ionian Sea.

Pope has on his side of it.[3] And therefore Pope John XXII[4] sent letters to them showing them that the Christian faith should be unified, and that all Christian men ought to obey a Pope, who is Christ's Vicar on earth and to whom God gave full power to bind and to loose; and therefore they ought to obey him. And they sent to him many answers; and, among others, they sent one saying . . . "We well believe your power is great over your subjects; we cannot support your great pride; we do not purpose to slake your great avarice. God be with you, for God is with us. Farewell." And other answer had he none of them. The Greeks also make the sacrament at the altar of leavened bread; for Our Lord made it of leavened bread when he held the Last Supper. And they say that we err in making the sacrament with unleavened bread.[5] And on Maundy Thursday[6] they make that bread as a token of Our Lord's Institution, and dry it in the sun, and keep it all year and give it to sick men instead of the consecrated Body of Christ. And they anoint only once when they christen children, and dip them but once at the font.[7] They do not anoint sick men; and they say there is no Purgatory,[8] and that souls shall have neither joy nor pain before the Day of Judgment.[9] They say also that fornication is not a deadly sin, but a natural one, and that men and women should only marry once; and, whoever marries more than once, their children are bastards and begotten in sin.[10] Their priests too are married.[11] And they say that usury is no deadly sin.[12] They sell benefices[13] of Holy Church, and so do men in other places; and that is a great scandal and disgrace. For now is simony[14] crowned like a king in Holy Church. God can amend it when it is His will. They say also that in Lent[15] men should not sing Mass except on Saturdays and Sundays. And they do not fast on

---

3. The Church of Constantinople claimed immediate authority over all bishops in the East, but no patriarch of Constantinople ever claimed powers equal to those claimed by Pope Gregory VII in the *Dictatus Papae*.

4. Reigned 1316–1334.

5. The Roman Church uses unleavened bread for the Eucharist (the sacrament of the altar), while the Byzantine Church uses leavened bread. Sir John errs here. Because Jesus' Last Supper was the Seder meal of Passover, he used unleavened bread.

6. Holy Thursday.

7. The Roman Church uses a triple anointment with water.

8. The Roman Church developed a belief in Purgatory as a place after death where the souls of persons who did not deserve hell but were not ready for heaven underwent purgation or cleansing through suffering.

9. The end of the world, when Christ will come to judge all humanity.

10. The Eastern Church did (and does) discourage multiple marriages, but it was (and is) more flexible in its attitude than this.

11. Most Byzantine priests were married; their bishops and monks, however, remained celibate.

12. According to the early medieval Roman Church, the sin of usury was charging interest on a loan. Because of changes in Europe's economy, Western theologians had largely modified the Church's teaching on this matter during the thirteenth century and allowed venture capitalists to charge interest. Because Constantinople always had enjoyed a complex commercial economy, interest charges for business transactions had never been considered sinful.

13. A source of income to support a cleric.

14. The sin of buying or selling anything holy, such as a clerical office and its attendant benefice. Many Western reformers believed this sin was rampant among the Roman Church's upper clergy.

15. The forty days preceding Easter.

Saturdays at any time of the year, unless it be Christmas or Easter Eve. They allow no man who comes from this side of the Greek Sea to celebrate at their altars; and if it so chance that any do, they wash the altar immediately with holy water.[16] And they say that there should be but one Mass sung at each altar each day.[17] Moreover, they say that Our Lord never ate bodily food, but made an appearance of eating, feigning that He had, showing sign of man's nature.[18] They say we commit a deadly sin in shaving our beards, for they say that the beard is a symbol of manhood and the gift of God.[19] And they who shave their beards do it only to appear well to the world and to please their wives. They say too that we commit deadly sin in eating animals that were forbidden in the Old Law, like pigs, hares and other beasts that do not chew the cud. And also they say we sin in eating meat on the three days before Ash Wednesday,[20] and also in eating meat on Wednesdays, and when we eat white meat on Fridays. And they curse all those who do not eat meat on Saturday. Also the Emperor of Constantinople appoints the patriarchs, archbishops, and bishops, and distributes all the dignities of Holy Church in that country; and he deprives of office and goods those who seem to him unworthy. And so he is their lord both temporal and spiritual.

---

16. Reports of this Byzantine practice date back to at least the mid-twelfth century.

17. The Latin practice was for every priest to celebrate mass daily. Therefore, multiple masses would be performed on an altar in the course of a day.

18. Untrue. The Byzantine Church had condemned this belief as a heresy.

19. While its clerics were bearded, the Eastern Church was more flexible than Sir John implies.

20. The first day of Lent.

C H A P T E R

8

Islam: Universal Submission to God

The last of the great monotheistic faiths to arise in the Middle East was Islam, which emerged in Arabia during the early seventh century. *Islam* means "submission" in Arabic, and a *Muslim* is one who submits to the Will of God.

The prophet of Islam was a retired merchant of Mecca called Muhammad (ca 571–632), who around 610 began to receive visions in which he was called by God (*Allah* in Arabic) to preach God's oneness, the imminence of the Resurrection of the dead, a divine Day of Judgment, an all-consuming hellfire for the unjust and unbelievers, and a paradise of bliss for the faithful. Muhammad believed that, just as Jews and Christians had their divine revelations from God, now the Arabs were receiving the full and final word of God through himself, the last and greatest of the prophets, but still only a man. Abraham, Moses, Jesus, and the other prophets had been earlier witnesses of God. Muhammad was the "seal" of these forerunners.

Muhammad's message initially failed to move most of Meccan society, so in 622 he journeyed to the city of Yathrib, where he established a theocratic (ruled by God) Muslim community. In his honor, the city was renamed Medina, "City of the Prophet." From Medina Muhammad and his followers initiated a war against Mecca, and in 630 Muslim forces captured the city. The Prophet of Allah was now the most powerful chieftain in Arabia, and the various tribes of the peninsula soon were united under his leadership. When Muhammad died, his closest friend, Abu Bakr, became caliph (*khalifa*), or deputy or successor to the Prophet. Under Abu Bakr (632–634) Islam remained a unified community ready to explode out of its homeland, which it did under the second caliph, Umar (634–644).

Both the Sassanian Persian and Byzantine empires had exhausted each other in a series of destructive wars that lasted from 503 to 627. In addition, the Byzantine Empire was rent by ethnic and religious dissension, especially in Syria-Palestine and Egypt, so, when Umar's Muslims began raiding these neighboring territories, they discovered lands ripe for conquest. Before Umar's death the Byzantines had lost all of Syria-Palestine and Egypt to the green flag of Islam, and the Arab conquest of the Persian Empire was virtually completed. By 750 Muslim territory reached from the Pyrenees and Atlantic coast in Spain to the Indus Valley of India and the far-western borders of the Chinese empire.

Originally the Arabs considered Islam their special revelation and had no intention of sharing the faith with their non-Arab subjects, but several factors combined to attract large numbers of converts. These included Islam's uncompromising monotheism and the straightforwardness of its other central doctrines; the psychic and social security offered by membership in a totally integrated Muslim community, where one's entire life is subject to God's Word; and desire to escape the second-class status of Islam's non-Muslim subjects. When the Abbasid caliphs (750–1258) established their court at Baghdad on the Tigris in 762, the "Shadow of God on Earth," as the caliph was now called, ruled over a multiethnic ecumene bound together by one of the most attractive and fastest-growing salvific religions in the history of humanity. The culture of this world community was a combination of many different elements, of which the most important were Arabic, Persian, and Hellenistic.

Later, other peoples, especially the Turks from the eleventh century onward, would convert to Islam and carry it farther afield, especially into the heart of India. Arab and East African merchants would transport the faith across the Indian Ocean to the ports of Southeast Asia, and Berbers from North Africa would introduce Islam into western sub-Saharan Africa. Today Islam remains a vibrant and still expanding religion. Approximately one out of seven individuals throughout the world is a Muslim, and Islam is the most rapidly expanding faith and culture of the late twentieth century.

The Foundations of Muslim Life

The Prophet seems to have been illiterate, and many of the Arabs to whom he preached were equally unlettered. Islam quickly became a religious culture centered on a body of sacred texts, however, and has remained so to the present. Islam's text without equal is the *Qur'an* ("the Recitations"), which Muslims believe contains, word for word, absolutely everything God revealed to Muhammad and nothing else. As the full and final revelation of God, the Qur'an encompasses all that any human needs to know. Its verses, each a proclamation from heaven, are both doctrine and law, governing almost every aspect of a Muslim's life.

A second source of guidance for most Muslims is *hadith* (literally, "news" or "tales"), a vast body of transmitted stories and sayings attributed to the Prophet and his Companions. Unlike the Qur'an, hadith does not consist of a single, absolutely accepted text. Instead, there are many collections of hadith, some more authoritative than others, some largely dismissed as spurious. The majority of Muslims believe that authentic hadith enshrines the *sunna* ("the beaten track"), or traditions of the first Muslim community, and thereby provides perfect models for behavior in all aspects of life, especially those not expressly covered in the precepts of the Qur'an.

THE QUR'AN

As long as the Prophet was alive, there was no compelling reason to set his messages down in some definitive form. Following Muhammad's sudden death in 632, however, Caliph Abu Bakr ordered one of the Prophet's secretaries, Zayd ibn Thabit, to collect from both oral and written sources all of Muhammad's inspired utterances. Subsequently, Caliph Uthman (644–656) promulgated these "Recitations" as an official collection and ordered all other versions destroyed.

This standard text became the basis for every pious Muslim's education. As Islam spread beyond Arab ethnic boundaries, Muslims all over the world continued to learn Arabic in order to study and recite (usually from memory) the sacred *surahs* ("verses") of this holy book. Because of the centrality of the book, Arabic literacy became the hallmark of Muslims from sub-Saharan West Africa to Southeast Asia.

The following excerpts illustrate several of Islam's major doctrinal and moral tenets and also provide an example of *Shari'a*, or Qur'anic law. Shari'a means "the Way" and should be understood in the sense of the true path of religion. For members of God's community on earth, there is no distinction between what one believes and the manner in which one lives and conducts one's affairs.

Questions for Analysis

1. What sort of moral behavior does God require of Muslims?
2. How do the Muslim ten commandments compare to those of the Judeo-Christian tradition?
3. Does the Qur'an teach that one should "turn the other cheek"?
4. How does Islam view itself in relation to Judaism and Christianity?
5. Why do Muslims regard Abraham and Jesus as having been Muslims?
6. How should Muslims treat Jews and Christians?

[*Moral Obligations*]

Who speaks in a finer way than someone who appeals to God, acts honorably and says: "I am a Muslim!"?

A good deed and an evil deed are not alike: repel [evil] with something (that is) finer, and notice how someone who is separated from you because of enmity will become a bosom friend!

. . .

SAY: "Come close, I will recite what your Lord has forbidden you:

I. Do not associate anything with Him:[1]

II. And (show) kindness towards both (your) parents.

III. Do not kill your children because of poverty; We shall provide for you as well as for them.

IV. Do not indulge in shocking acts which you may practice either openly or keep secret.

V. Do not kill any person whom God has forbidden, except through (due process of) law. He has instructed you in this so that you may use your reason.

VI. Do not approach an orphan's estate before he comes of age, except to improve it.

VII. Grant full measure and weight in all fairness. We do not assign any person to do more than he can cope with.

VIII. Whenever you speak, be just even though it concerns a close relative.

IX. Fulfill God's agreement. Thus has He instructed you so that you may bear it in mind.

X. This is My Straight Road, so follow it and do not follow (other) paths which will separate you from His path. Thus has He instructed you so that you may do your duty."

. . .

Show kindness to both (your) parents and with near relatives, orphans, the needy, the neighbor who is related (to you) as well as the neighbor who is a stranger, and your companion by your side and the wayfarer, and anyone else

---

1. Polytheism, or associating any other god with God, is the worst of all possible sins, according to Muslim belief.

under your control. God does not love someone who is conceited, boastful, nor those who are tight-fisted and order (other) people to be stingy, and hide anything that God has given them out of His bounty.

[*Jews and Christians*]

SAY: "We believe in God and what has been sent down to us, and what was sent down to Abraham, Ishmael,[2] Isaac, Jacob and their descendants, and what was given Moses, Jesus and the prophets by their Lord. We do not differentiate between any one of them, and we are committed to (live at) peace with Him."

. . .

SAY: "People of the Book,[3] (let us) rally to a common formula to be binding on both us and you, that we shall worship only God (Alone) and associate nothing else with Him, nor shall any of us take on others as lords instead of God." If they should turn away, then say: "Bear witness that we are Muslims."

People of the Book, why do you argue about Abraham when the Torah and the Gospel were not sent down until after him? Do you not use your reason? There you go, arguing on about someone you (actually) have some knowledge about! Yet why do you (then) argue about something you have no knowledge about? God knows while you do not know.

> Abraham was neither a Jew nor a Christian, but he was a Seeker [after Truth], a Muslim; he was no associator [of others with God].

The closest people to Abraham are those who follow him, as well as this Prophet and those who believe. God is the believers' Patron. A faction from the People of the Book would like to lead you (all) astray; yet they only lead themselves astray, even though they do not notice it. People of the Book, why do you disbelieve in God's signs while you watch them happen? People of the Book, why do you dress Truth up with falsehood and knowingly conceal the Truth?

. . .

If the People of the Book would only believe and do their duty, We would overlook their evil deeds for them and show them into gardens full of Bliss. If they had only kept up the Torah and the Gospel, and whatever was sent down to them by their Lord, they would have eaten anything above them and from beneath their feet. Some of them form a moderate community, while many of them act badly in anything they do.

. . .

God made a covenant with the Children of Israel, and We despatched twelve of them as captains. God said: "I shall be with you if you will keep up prayer and pay the welfare tax, and believe in My messengers and respect them, and advance God a handsome loan. I shall overlook your evil deeds for you and show you into gardens through which rivers flow. Anyone of you who disbelieves following that will have strayed from the Level Path."

---

2. Both Muslim and Jewish tradition see Ishmael, the son of Abraham and half brother of Isaac (from whom the Jews are descended), as the forefather of the Arabs.

3. Jews and Christians, who also have divinely revealed scriptures.

Since they broke their covenant, We have cursed them and planted a hard shell over their hearts. They lift words out of their context and have forgotten a portion of what they should have memorized. Except for a few of them, you will always catch some of them committing some act of treachery. Yet pardon them and overlook it; God loves those who act kindly.

We accepted their agreement from those who say: "We are Christians"; then they forgot a portion of what they had been reminded of, so We have stirred up enmity and jealousy among them until Resurrection Day. God will notify them about whatever they have been accomplishing. People of the Book, Our messenger has come to you to explain much of what you have been concealing out of the Book, and to dispense with much of it. Light and a Clear Book have been brought to you from God. God thereby guides anyone who seeks His approval along pathways of peace; He leads them out of darkness into Light by His permission, and guides them along a Straight Road.

Those who say: "God is Christ, the son of Mary," disbelieve.

SAY: "Who would control anything from God if He ever wanted to do away with Christ, the son of Mary and his mother, plus everyone on earth? God holds control over Heaven and Earth, as well as anything in between them. He creates anything He wishes. God is Capable of everything!"

Jews and Christians say: "We are God's children and His favorites."

SAY: "Then why does He punish you for your offences?" Rather you are human beings just like anyone else He has created. He forgives anyone He wishes and punishes anyone He wishes. God holds control over Heaven and Earth, and whatever lies between them. Towards Him lies the goal!" O People of the Book, Our messenger has come to explain (things) to you after an interval between the messengers, lest you say: "No herald nor any warner has ever come to us." A herald and a warner has indeed come to you! God is Capable of everything!

. . .

Those who say: "God is the third of three,"[4] have disbelieved! There is no deity except God Alone. If they do not stop saying what they say, painful torment will afflict those among them who disbelieve. Why do they not turn towards God and seek His forgiveness? God is Forgiving, Merciful.

Christ the son of Mary was only a messenger; messengers have passed away before him. His mother was sincere. They both ate food.

. . .

When God said: "Jesus, son of Mary, have you told people: 'Take me and my mother as two gods instead of God (Alone)?';" he said: "Glory be to You! It is not my place to say what I have no right to (say). If I had said it, You would have known it already: You know what is on my mind, while I do not know anything that is on Yours. You are the Knower of Unseen things. I have never told them anything except what You have ordered me to: 'Worship God as my Lord and your Lord.' I was a witness for them so long as I was among them. When You gathered me up, You became the Watcher over

4. The Christian Trinity (page 213, note 6).

them; You are a Witness for everything. If you should punish them, they are still Your servants; while if You should forgive them, surely You are Powerful, Wise."

. . .

Fight[5] the ones among those who were given the Book who do not believe in God nor the Last Day, nor forbid whatever God and His messenger have forbidden, nor profess the True Religion, until they pay the polltax[6] of their own accord and act submissive.

. . .

Do not drive away those who appeal to their Lord, wanting His presence in the early morning and the evening. You have nothing to do with their reckoning, while they have nothing to do with your reckoning. Should you drive them off, you would be a wrongdoer.

Imam Nawawi

GARDENS OF THE RIGHTEOUS

Although early Muslims, such as Malik ibn-Anas (d. 795), had collected stories about the Prophet, it was not until about two centuries after Muhammad's death that Muslim scholars began systematically to catalogue the traditions that circulated about the Prophet and his first followers. The most important individual in this effort was the Persian lawyer Ismail al-Bokhari (810–870), who reportedly collected some 600,000 tales (undoubtedly many were variations of common themes) and memorized more than 200,000 of them. From this vast body of material he identified a little over 7,000 tales as genuine, which he then preserved. The second great editor of hadith was Bokhari's younger contemporary Abul Husain Muslim (819–875), whose collection is almost identical to Bokhari's. Slightly less important than the work of these two scholarly giants were the collections of Abu Daud (d. 889), al-Tirmidhi (d. 892), Ibn Majah (d. 896), and al-Nisai (d. 915). The combined efforts of these six individuals are known as the *Sahih Sitta* (*The Six Authentic Compilations*).

The sheer bulk of these canonical texts, as well as the discrepancies among them and the existence of many other less universally accepted compendia of hadith, necessitated continued editing and digesting of Muslim tradition by legions of Islamic jurists and religious scholars in every generation. One of the most significant of these later scholars was the Syrian *imam* (religious teacher) Nawawi (1233–1278), whose *Gardens of the Righteous* provided an analytical digest of the spiritual values enshrined in *The Six Authentic Compilations* and several lesser collections of hadith.

5. See question 6 in the next reading.

6. The *jizya*, or tribute, exacted from all non-Muslim subjects as a token of their submission to Islam.

As the following texts show, Nawawi's method of exposition was generally to set out a relevant passage or series of passages from the Qur'an and then to list a number of variant stories and sayings, largely as remembered by the Prophet's Companions, that illustrate the spiritual message in that Qur'anic text.

Questions for Analysis

1. What gives hadith its authority, since, unlike the Qur'an, it is not the literal word of God?
2. "Hadith is a living commentary on the Qur'an, insofar as it makes explicit all that is implicit in that book." What does this statement mean?
3. How does hadith allow for diversity within the context of religious uniformity?
4. What virtues do these selections emphasize? Which are part of the Christian tradition?
5. What picture emerges of the place of women in Muslim society? Compare the status of Muslim women with that of Hindu women as illustrated in the *Laws of Manu* (Chapter 5). Which are more striking, the differences or the parallels?
6. The Arabic word used for "striving" in both the Qur'an and hadith is *jihad*, which is often translated as "holy war." Judging from these excerpts, does this translation seem correct and complete?

On Making Peace Between People

Allah, the Exalted, has said:

> Most of their conferrings together are devoid of good, except such as enjoin charity, or the promotion of public welfare or of public peace (4.115).
>
> Reconciliation is best (4.129).
>
> Be mindful of your duty to Allah and try to promote accord between yourselves (8.2).
>
> All believers are brothers; so make peace between your brothers (49.11).

Abu Hurairah relates that the Holy Prophet said: Charity is incumbent upon every human limb every day on which the sun rises. To bring about just reconciliation between two contestants is charity. Helping a person to mount his animal, or to load his baggage on to it is charity. A good word is charity. Every step taken towards the mosque for *salat*[1] is charity. To remove anything from the street that causes inconvenience is charity (Bokhari and Muslim).

Umm Kulthum relates that she heard the Holy Prophet say: He who brings about peace between people and attains good or says that which is good is not a liar (Bokhari and Muslim). Muslim's version adds: I did not hear him let people have a latitude in what they said except in three situations: war, making peace, and talk between husband and wife.

1. Ritual prayer. Muslims pray five times daily and on Friday attend community prayer services at a mosque.

On the Superiority of the Poor and Weak Among Muslims

Allah, the Exalted, has said:

> Continue thy companionship with those who call on their Lord, morning and evening, seeking His pleasure, and look not beyond them (18.29).

Haritha ibn Wahb relates that he heard the Holy Prophet say: Shall I tell you who are the dwellers of Paradise? It is every weak one who is accounted weak and is looked down upon, who if he takes an oath relying upon Allah He would fulfill it. Now shall I tell you who are the denizens of the Fire? It is every ignorant, impertinent, prideful and arrogant one (Bokhari and Muslim). . . .

Abu Sa'id Khudri relates that the Holy Prophet said: There was a contest between Paradise and the Fire. The Fire said: I shall compass the tyrants and the arrogant ones; and Paradise said: My dwellers will be the weak and the lowly. Allah decided between them, saying: Thou art Paradise, My mercy, through thee I shall have mercy on whomsoever I determine; and thou art the Fire. My torment, through thee I shall chastise whomsoever I determine. It is for Me to fill both of you (Muslim). . . .

Abu Hurairah relates that a dark-skinned woman (or perhaps young man) used to take care of the mosque. The Holy Prophet missed her (or him) and inquired about her (or him) and was told that she (or he) had died. He said: Why did you not let me know? as if they had not considered the matter of any importance. He then said: Show me the grave, and on being shown it he prayed over it and said: These graves cover those in them with darkness and Allah illumines them for the denizens in consequence of my prayers for them (Bokhari and Muslim). . . .

Usamah relates that the Holy Prophet said: I stood at the gate of Paradise and observed that the generality of those who entered it were the lowly. The wealthy had been held back from it. Then those condemned to the Fire were ordered to it and I stood at the gate of the Fire and observed that the generality of those who entered it were women (Bokhari and Muslim).

On Kind Treatment of Orphans, Girls, the Weak, the Poor, and the Lowly

Allah, the Exalted, has said:

> Continue to be kindly gracious towards the believers (15.89).
>
> Continue thy companionship with those who call on their Lord, morning and evening, seeking His pleasure, and look not beyond them, for if thou dost that thou wouldst be seeking the values of this life (18.29).
>
> Oppress not the orphan and chide not him who asks (93.10-11).
>
> Knowest thou him who rejects the faith? That is the one who drives away the orphan and urges not the feeding of the poor (107.2-4). . . .

Abu Hurairah relates that the Holy Prophet said: He who exerts himself on behalf of widows and the indigent is like one who strives[2] in the cause of Allah; and the narrator thinks he added: and like the guardian who never retreats, and like one who observes the fast and does not break it (Bokhari and Muslim). . . .

---

2. Jihad. See question 6.

Anas relates that the Holy Prophet said: He who brings up two girls through their childhood will appear on the Day of Judgment attached to me like two fingers of a hand (Muslim). . . .

Ayesha[3] relates: A poor woman came to me with her two daughters. I gave her three dates. She gave one to each girl and raised the third to her own mouth to eat. The girls asked her for it. So she broke it into two parts and gave one to each of the girls. I was much struck by her action and mentioned what she had done to the Holy Prophet. He said: Allah appointed Paradise for her in consequence of it; or he said: Allah freed her from the Fire on account of it.

Abu Shuraih Khuwailad ibn Amr Khuza'i relates that the Holy Prophet said: Allah, I declare sinful any failure to safeguard the rights of two weak ones; orphans and women (Nisai).

ON A HUSBAND'S RIGHT CONCERNING HIS WIFE

Allah, the Exalted, has said:

> Men are appointed guardians over women, because of that in respect of which Allah has made some of them excel others, and because the men spend their wealth. So virtuous women are obedient and safeguard, with Allah's help, matters the knowledge of which is shared by them with their husbands (4.35). . . .

Ibn Umar relates that the Holy Prophet said: Every one of you is a steward and is accountable for that which is committed to his charge. The ruler is a steward and is accountable for his charge, a man is a steward in respect of his household, a woman is a steward in respect of her husband's house and his children. Thus everyone of you is a steward and is accountable for that which is committed to his charge (Bokhari and Muslim).

Abu Ali Talq ibn Ali relates that the Holy Prophet said: When a man calls his wife for his need, she should go to him even if she is occupied in baking bread (Tirmidhi and Nisai). . . .

Umm Salamah relates that the Holy Prophet said: If a woman dies and her husband is pleased with her she will enter Paradise (Tirmidhi).

Mu'az ibn Jabal relates that the Holy Prophet said: Whenever a woman distresses her husband his mate from among the *houris*[4] of Paradise says to her: Allah ruin thee, do not cause him distress for he is only thy guest and will soon part from thee to come to us (Tirmidhi).

Usamah ibn Zaid relates that the Holy Prophet said: I am not leaving a more harmful trial for men than woman (Bokhari and Muslim).

ON STRIVING IN THE CAUSE OF ALLAH

Allah, the Exalted, has said:

> Fight the idolators all together, as they fight you all together, and know that Allah is with the righteous (9.36). . . .
>
> Allah has purchased of the believers their persons and their belongings in return for the promise that they shall have Paradise, for they fight in the cause of Allah and they slay the enemy or are themselves slain. This is a promise that He has made incumbent upon Himself as set out in the Torah, and the Gospel and the Qur'an; and who is more faithful to his promises than Allah? Rejoice, then, in the bargain that you have made with

3. One of the Prophet's wives and a chief source of hadith.

4. Beautiful virgins who serve the saved in Paradise.

> Him; that indeed is the supreme triumph (9.111). . . .
>
> O ye who believe, shall I guide you to a commerce that will deliver you from a painful chastisement? It is that you believe in Allah and His Messenger, and strive in the cause of Allah with your belongings and your persons, that is the better for you, did you but know. He will forgive you your sins and will admit you to gardens beneath which rivers flow, and to pure and pleasant dwellings in Gardens of Eternity. That is the supreme triumph (61.11–14). . . .

Anas relates that the Holy Prophet said: To be occupied in the cause of Allah a morning or evening is better than the world and all it contains (Bokhari and Muslim). . . .

Sahl ibn Sa'ad relates that the Holy Prophet said: Patroling the frontier for a day is better than the world and all it contains. Your being allotted a strip in Paradise no wider than your horse-whip is better than the world and all it contains. Being occupied with striving in the cause of Allah for a morning or an evening is better than the world and all it contains (Bokhari and Muslim). . . .

Fuzalah ibn Ubaid relates that the Holy Prophet said: Death puts an end to all action, except in the case of one who patrols the frontier in the cause of Allah, for his activity continues to grow till the Day of Judgment and he is shielded against the trials of the grave (Abu Daud and Tirmidhi).

Uthman relates that he heard the Holy Prophet say: Patroling the frontier for a day in the cause of Allah is better than a thousand days of other good works (Tirmidhi). . . .

Abu Bakr ibn Abu Musa Ash'ari relates that he heard his father say in the face of the enemy: The Holy Prophet said: The gates of Paradise are under the shadow of swords. Thereupon a man of lowly condition stood up and inquired: Abu Musa, did you indeed hear the Holy Prophet say that? He answered: Yes. The man then turned towards his companions and saluted them in farewell. He then broke the scabbard of his sword and threw it away and walked with his sword into the enemy ranks and fought till he was killed (Muslim).

Abdullah ibn Jubair relates that the Holy Prophet said: The Fire[5] will not touch one whose feet are covered with dust in striving for the cause of Allah (Bokhari). . . .

Anas relates that the Holy Prophet said: He who supplicates sincerely for martyrdom is granted it, even though he is not slain (Muslim).

Abu Hurairah relates that the Holy Prophet said: A martyr does not suffer when he is slain anymore than one of you suffers from being bitten by an ant (Tirmidhi). . . .

Abu Hurairah relates that the Holy Prophet said: He who observes the fast for a day in the cause of Allah will find that Allah has dug a moat between him and the Fire as wide as the distance between heaven and earth (Tirmidhi).

Abu Hurairah relates that the Holy Prophet said: He who dies without having fought in the cause of Allah and without having thought of it in his mind dies with one characteristic of hypocrisy within him (Muslim). . . .

Abu Hurairah relates that a man asked the Holy Prophet's permission to travel and he told him: The travel for my people is striving in the cause of Allah, the Lord of honor and glory (Abu Daud). . . .

Anas relates that the Holy Prophet said: Strive against the idolators with your belongings, your persons and your tongues (Abu Daud).

---

5. Hell.

Variety and Unity in Islam

Ideally, Islam is a single community united in its submission and service to God. In fact, however, it has been fragmented into a wide variety of sects and schools. Chief among these are the Sunni and Shi'ite traditions and various forms of Sufi mysticism.

Despite these divisions, Muslims have still maintained a degree of unity because of the centrality of the Qur'an in the life of every practicing Muslim, regardless of sect, and most Muslims' acceptance of certain fundamental religious obligations. Most basic of all are the Five Pillars of Islam: to say with absolute conviction, "There is no God but God, and Muhammad is the Prophet of God"; to offer prescribed prayers at five stipulated times during the day; to give alms in charity to poorer members of the Islamic community; to fast from sunrise to sunset during the month of Ramadan; and to make a pilgrimage to Mecca and Medina at least once in one's lifetime. Many Muslims would add a sixth pillar, jihad, which is understood in many different senses.

Ibn Babawayh al-Saduq

CREED CONCERNING THE IMAMS

The Six Authentic Compilations preserve traditions sacred to that majority group in Islam known as *Sunni* Muslims (those who follow the *sunna,* or practices of the Prophet and his Companions). Another major faction of Islam is the *Shi'at Ali,* or Party of Ali, which claims its own hadith as the authentic record of the Prophet's words and actions. Members of this group, known popularly as *Shi'ites,* today comprise almost all of Iran's population and can be found in parts of Iraq, Syria, Lebanon, and the Indian subcontinent.

The Shi'ite break with other Muslims dates back to the mid-seventh century, when partisans of Ali, Muhammad's cousin and son-in-law, managed his installation as fourth caliph (656–661) following the murder of Caliph Uthman. Many of Uthman's followers did not recognize Ali, however, and civil war ensued. The result was Ali's eventual assassination in 661, establishment of the rival Umayyad Dynasty as caliphs (661–750), and the martyrdom of Ali's son, al-Husayn, the Prophet's sole surviving grandson, in 680. Supporters of the family of Ali, who included many of the original Muslims of Medina, refused to accept the Umayyads as rightful successors of the Prophet. Following the patriarchal traditions of the desert, they claimed that only a member of Muhammad's family could succeed him as *imam,* or religious leader of Islam. The result was a schism in Islam, and to this day the annual commemoration of al-Husayn's martyrdom is the most sorrowful event in the Shi'ite religious calendar.

Over time, the Shi'ites, often persecuted as religious dissidents and driven underground, evolved a theology of history. They not only traced the rightful succession of leadership over the community of Islam from Ali through a number of subsequent imams, whom the Sunnis did not accept as legitimate, but they developed the notion of a messianic "hidden imam," or *Mahdi* ("the guided one"). According to this religious vision, the line of visible imams ended at an early point in time (here the various Shi'ite sects disagree on the identity of the last visible imam). The imamate, however, was not destroyed. Rather, the last visible imam had simply withdrawn from sight and would at some future time reappear to gather his faithful, persecuted followers around him, usher in a Muslim holy age, and herald the Last Judgment.

The largest of all Shi'ite sects is the Twelver Shia, which developed around A.D. 900. These Shi'ites, who predominate in Iran, accept a line of twelve infallible imams, divinely appointed from birth, and believe that the twelfth and last of these visible imams, Muhammad al-Qaim, disappeared in the late ninth century. The following selection from the creed of Muhammad ibn Ali ibn Babawayh, known as Sheik al-Saduq (d. 991), one of the greatest of the early Twelver theologians, illustrates several major Twelver beliefs.

Questions for Analysis

1. Shi'ites are said to see themselves as a persecuted, righteous remnant. Is there any evidence for such a conclusion in this document? What evidence is there that Twelvers were persecuted in the late tenth century and, like their twelfth imam, hid themselves?
2. What roles does martyrdom play in Twelver theology? Is the Twelver attitude toward martyrdom consistent with the teachings of the Qur'an?
3. How does al-Suduq view Sunnis? Can you find any evidence that Shi'ites believe they possess a secret religious truth denied Sunnis? What is the source of that truth?
4. What evidence is there of deep religious divisions among Shi'ites by the late tenth century?
5. Christians believe the end of time and the Final Judgment will be ushered in by Jesus' Second Coming in triumph. Is there reason to believe that there may have been Christian influences on the evolution of Shi'ite theology?

Our belief concerning the number of the prophets is that there have been one hundred and twenty-four thousand prophets and a like number of plenipotentiaries. Each prophet had a plenipotentiary to whom he gave instructions by the command of God. And concerning them we believe that they brought the truth from God and their word is the word of God, their command God's command, and obedience to them obedience to God. . . .

The leaders of the prophets are five (on whom all depends): Noah, Abraham,

Moses, Jesus, and Muhammad. Muhammad is their leader . . . he confirmed the (other) apostles.

It is necessary to believe that God did not create anything more excellent than Muhammad and the Imams. . . . After His prophet, the proofs of God for the people are the Twelve Imams. . . .

We believe that the Proof of Allah in His earth and His viceregent among His slaves in this age of ours is the Upholder [*al-Qa'im*] [of the law of God], the Expected One, Muhammad ibn al-Hasan al-'Askari.[1] He it is concerning whose name and descent the Prophet was informed by God, and he it is who WILL FILL THE EARTH WITH JUSTICE AND EQUITY JUST AS IT IS NOW FULL OF OPPRESSION AND WRONG. He it is whom God will make victorious over the whole world until from every place the call to prayer is heard and religion will belong entirely to God, exalted be He. He is the rightly guided *Mahdi* about whom the prophet gave information that when he appears, Jesus, son of Mary, will descend upon the earth and pray behind him. We believe there can be no other *Qa'im* than him; he may live in the state of occultation[2] (as long as he likes); were it the space of the existence of this world, there would be no *Qa'im* other than him.

Our belief concerning prophets, apostles, Imams and angels is that they are infallible . . . and do not commit any sin, minor or major . . . he who denies infallibility to them in any matter . . . is a *kafir*, an infidel.

Our belief concerning those who exceed the bounds of belief, the *ghulat*[3], and those who believe in delegation[4] is that they are . . . deniers of God. They are more wicked than the Jews, the Christians, the Fire Worshippers[5] . . . or any heretics; none have belittled God more. . . .

Our belief concerning the Prophet is that he was poisoned (by Jews) during the expedition to Khaybar. The poison continued to be noxious and (shortening his life) until he died of its effects.

I. Imam: And the Prince of Believers ('Ali), on whom be peace, was murdered by . . . Ibn Muljam al-Muradi, may God curse him, and was buried in Ghari.

II. Imam: Hasan ibn 'Ali,[6] on whom be peace, was poisoned by his wife Ja'da bint Ash'ath of Kinda, may God curse (her and her father).

III. Imam: Husayn ibn 'Ali[7] was slain at Karbala. His murderer was Sinan ibn-Anas al-Nakha'i, may God curse him and his father.

IV. Imam: 'Ali ibn Husayn, the Sayyid Zayn al-'Abidin,[8] was poisoned by al-Walid ibn 'Abd al-Malik,[9] God curse him.

V. Imam: Muhammad Baqir ibn 'Ali was poisoned by Ibrahim ibn al-Walid,[10] God curse him.

---

1. The twelfth imam. Al-Hasan al-Askari, the eleventh imam, died around January 1, 874. Twelvers believe he was succeeded by his young son Muhammad al-Qaim (the Upholder of God's law), who went into concealment around 878.

2. Invisible to earthly eyes.

3. Shi'ite heretics, such as those who ascribed divinity to Ali and the other imams.

4. The belief that after creating Muhammad and Ali, God rested and delegated control over all creation to them.

5. Zoroastrians.

6. Hasan, the son of (*ibn*) Ali, was Ali's elder son.

7. Al-Husayn, Ali's younger son.

8. Al-Abidin (d. ca 712) was the son of al-Husayn, and all subsequent Twelver imams are descended from him.

9. Al-Walid I was Umayyad caliph from 705 to 715.

10. The son of al-Walid, Ibrahim was caliph for a few months in 744.

VI. Imam: Ja'far al-Sadiq was poisoned by Abu Ja'far al-Mansur al-Dawaniqu,[11] may God curse him.

VII. Imam: Musa al-Kazim ibn Ja'far was poisoned by Harun al-Rashid,[12] may God curse him.

VIII. Imam: 'Ali al-Rida ibn Musa was poisoned by Ma'mun ibn Harun al-Rashid, may God curse him.

IX. Imam: Abu Ja'far Muhammad al-Taqi ibn 'Ali was poisoned by al-Mu'tasim, may God curse him.

X. Imam: 'Ali al-Naqi ibn Muhammad was poisoned by Mutawakkil, may God curse him.

XI. Imam: Hasan al-'Askari was poisoned by al-Mu'tamid, may God curse him. . . . And verily the Prophets and Imams, on whom be peace, had informed (people) that they would be murdered. He who says that they were not has given them the lie and has imputed falsehood to God the Mighty and Glorious.

Our belief concerning *taqiya* (permissible dissimulation of one's true beliefs) is that it is obligatory, and he who forsakes it is in the same position as he who forsakes prayer. . . . Now until the time when the Imam al-Qa'im appears, *taqiya* is obligatory and it is not permissible to dispense with it. He who does . . . has verily gone out of the religion of God. And God has described the showing of friendship to unbelievers as being (possible only) in the state of *taqiya*.

And the Imam Ja'far said, "Mix with enemies openly but oppose them inwardly, so long as the authority is a matter of question." He also said, "Diplomacy with a true believer is a form of polytheism, but with a (hypocrite) in his own house, it is worship." And he said "He who prays with hypocrites (i.e., Sunnis), standing in the first row, it is as though he prayed with the Prophet standing in the first row." And he said, "Visit their sick and attend their funerals and pray in their mosques."

Our belief concerning the (ancestors of the Prophet, contrary to the Sunnis) is that they were Muslims from Adam down to 'Abdallah, father of the Prophet. . . .

Our belief concerning the 'Alawiya (descendants of 'Ali) is that they are the progeny of the Messenger of God and devotion to them is obligatory (in) requital of his apostleship. . . .

Al-Mawardi

BOOK OF THE PRINCIPLES OF GOVERNMENT

In the Shi'ite tradition "imam" could be applied to either *the* infallible imam or any lesser but acknowledged religious leader. Sunnis generally accorded this title only to local religious leaders and, until the mid-thirteenth century, preferred to bestow the

11. Al-Mansur was the second Abbasid caliph (754–775). Although the Abbasids claimed descent from al-Abbas, the Prophet's uncle and the brother of Ali's father, most Shi'ites considered them no better than the Umayyads.

12. Harun al-Rashid (786–809) is generally considered the greatest of the Abbasid caliphs. As was true of his predecessors, his reign was filled with Shi'ite plots and rebellions. Ironically, his throne-name means "Harun (Aaron), the rightly-guided," and his father bore the throne-name al-Mahdi.

title of caliph, or successor, on the person who claimed earthly authority over all Islam. For Abu Bakr, the first caliph, the title simply meant he was Muhammad's successor in temporal matters and "first among equals" within the Muslim community. The Umayyads, however, altered the nature of the caliphate by using the title *khalifat Allah*, "God's Deputy." The implication was that whoever disobeyed them in any matter was an enemy of God and an unbeliever. The Abbasids expanded this policy, transforming the caliphate into a Persian-styled autocracy.

In the following document, al-Mawardi (d. 1058), a jurist and political philosopher who resided in eleventh-century Baghdad, describes the office and qualities of the ideal caliph. His use of the term *imam* for "caliph" stems from the fact that, beginning in the reign of Caliph al-Mahdi (775–785), the Abbasids asserted that the Prophet directly conferred the office of imam on their ancestor al-Abbas. This claim, as well as the caliph's assuming the throne-name al-Mahdi, was the Sunnis' attempt to counter the charismatic personality of their Shi'ite rivals.

Questions for Analysis

1. How does al-Mawardi describe the caliph's office? What are his most important attributes? What are his most important duties?
2. Does al-Mawardi lay emphasis on the caliph's duties or his powers and prerogatives?
3. What is the caliph's relationship, in theory, with the Muslim community at large?
4. How does the caliph's position compare with that of the orthodox Christian emperor residing at Constantinople (Chapter 7)?

The office of Iman was set up in order to replace the office of Prophet in the defense of the faith and the government of the world. By general consensus . . . the investiture of whichsoever member of the community exercises the functions of Imam is obligatory. But there is disagreement as to whether this obligation derives from reason or from Holy Law. One group says it derives from reason, since it is in the nature of reasonable men to submit to a leader who will prevent them from injuring one another and who will settle quarrels and disputes, for without rulers men would live in anarchy and heedlessness like benighted savages. . . .

Another group says that the obligation derives from the Holy Law and not from reason, since the Imam deals with matters of Holy Law to which, in reason, he would be allowed not to devote himself, since reason does not make them obligatory. All that reason requires is that a reasonable man should refrain from mutual injury and conflict with his neighbor and act equitably in mutual fairness and good relations, conducting himself in accordance with his own reason, and not with someone else's. But it is the Holy Law which intervenes to entrust these affairs to its religious representative. God said, "O you who believe, obey God, obey the Prophet, and obey those among you who are in authority"(Qur'an, iv, 62). He thus explicitly enjoined us to obey those among us who are in authority, and they are the Imams who hold sway over us. . . .

The conditions of eligibility for the Imamate are seven:

1. Rectitude in all respects.

2. The knowledge to exercise personal judgment in cases and decisions.

3. Soundness of hearing, sight, and tongue so that he may deal accurately with those matters which can only be attained by them.

4. Soundness of limb so that he has no defect which would prevent him from moving freely and rising quickly.

5. The discernment needed to govern the subjects and conduct public affairs.

6. The courage and vigor to defend the lands of Islam and to wage holy war against the enemy.

7. Descent, that is to say, he must be of the tribe of Quraysh,[1] as is prescribed by a text and accepted by consensus. . . .

The Imamate is conferred in two ways: one is by the choice of the electors, and the other is by the nomination of the previous Imam. . . .

When the electors meet, they scrutinize the qualified candidates and proceed to appoint that one among them who is the most worthy, who best meets the required conditions, and to whom the people are most willing to give obedience. They recognize him without delay. If the exercise of their judgment leads them to choose a particular person from the community, they offer him the Imamate. If he accepts, they swear allegiance to him, and the Imamate is vested in him by this procedure. Allegiance to him and obedience to him then become binding on the entire community. If he holds back and refuses the Imamate, it cannot be imposed upon him, since it is a contract by consent and choice and may not involve compulsion or constraint. In such case the Imamate is offered to another qualified candidate.

If two candidates are equally well qualified, the elder takes precedence in choice; however, seniority, where the parties are of age, is not a necessary condition, and if the younger is appointed, it is still valid. If one is wiser and the other braver, the choice should be determined by the needs of the time. If the need for courage is more urgent because of the disorder of the frontiers and the appearance of rebels, then the braver has a better claim. If the need for wisdom is more urgent because of the quiescence of the populace and the appearance of heretics, then it is the wiser who has a better claim.

If the choice falls on one of two candidates and they dispute the Imamate, some jurists hold that this is a flaw which disqualifies both of them and that the Imamate must be given to someone else. But the view of most scholars and jurists is that such a dispute does not disqualify and that seeking for the Imamate is not in itself reprehensible, since the members of Umar's committee competed for it and this did not disqualify any candidate or exclude any aspirant.

Jurists disagree on how to settle a dispute between two candidates who are equally qualified. One group says that lots should be cast and the winner preferred. Others say that the electors may choose freely and appoint whichever they prefer without drawing lots. . . .

1. Arabs of Mecca.

If at any time there is only one person possessing the necessary qualifications for the Imamate and no other person is equally qualified, the Imamate must be conferred upon him, and it is not lawful to set him aside in favor of another. But scholars disagree as to whether his Imamate is established and his authority inaugurated without contract and choice. Some jurists of Iraq consider that his authority is established and his Imamate inaugurated *ipso facto,* thus imposing on the community the duty of obeying him, even if the electors have not appointed him, since the purpose of the choice is to designate the one who is most fit to rule, and this one is designated as such by his attributes. The generality of jurists and theologians maintain that his appointment as Imam can only take place by consent and choice, but that the electors are bound to choose him as Imam. . . .

The duties of the Imam in the conduct of public affairs are ten:

1. To maintain the religion according to established principles and the consensus of the first generation of Muslims. If an innovator appears or if some dubious person deviates from it, the Imam must clarify the proofs of religion to him, expound that which is correct, and apply to him the proper rules and penalties so that religion may be protected from injury and the community safeguarded from error.

2. To execute judgments given between litigants and to settle disputes between contestants so that justice may prevail and so that none commit or suffer injustice.

3. To defend the lands of Islam and to protect them from intrusion so that people may earn their livelihood and travel at will without danger to life or property.

4. To enforce the legal penalties for the protection of God's commandments from violation and for the preservation of the rights of his servants from injury or destruction.

5. To maintain the frontier fortresses with adequate supplies and effective force for their defense so that the enemy may not take them by surprise, commit profanation there, or shed the blood, either of a Muslim or an ally.

6. To wage holy war (*jihad*) against those who, after having been invited to accept Islam, persist in rejecting it, until they either become Muslims or enter the Pact (*dhimma*)[2] so that God's truth may prevail over every religion.

7. To collect the booty and the alms in conformity with the prescriptions of the Holy Law, as defined by explicit texts and by independent judgment, and this without terror or oppression.

8. To determine the salaries and other sums due from the treasury, without extravagance and without parsimony, and to make payment at the proper time, neither in advance nor in arrears.

9. To employ capable and trustworthy men and appoint sincere men for the tasks which he delegates to them and for the money which he entrusts to them so that the tasks may be competently discharged and the money honestly safeguarded.

10. To concern himself directly with the supervision of affairs and the scrutiny of conditions so that he may personally govern the community, safeguard the faith,

---

2. A compact by which non-Muslims accept the rule of Islam and become, thereby, *dhimmis,* or protected subject people, and pay *jizyat,* or tribute.

and not resort to delegation in order to free himself either for pleasure or for worship, for even the trustworthy may betray and the sincere may deceive. God said, "O David,[3] we have made you our vicegerent (*khalifa*) on earth; therefore, judge justly among men and do not follow your caprice, which will lead you astray from God's path." (Qur'an, xxxviii, 25). In this, God was not content with delegation, but required a personal performance and did not excuse the following of passions, which, He says, lead astray from His path, and this, though He considered David worthy to judge in religion and to hold His vicegerency. This is one of the duties of government of any shepherd. The Prophet of God, may God bless and save him, said, "You are all shepherds, and you are all answerable for your flocks.". . .

The rules of the Imamate and its general jurisdiction over the interests of religion and the governance of the community, as we have described them, being established, and the investiture of an Imam being duly confirmed, the authority which comes from him to his deputies is of four kinds:

1. Those who have unlimited authority of unlimited scope. These are the viziers[4] for they are entrusted with all public affairs without specific attribution.

2. Those who have unlimited authority of limited scope. Such are the provincial and district governors, whose authority is unlimited within the specific areas assigned to them.

3. Those who have limited authority of unlimited scope. Such are the chief qadi,[5] the commander of the armies, the commandant of the frontier fortresses, the intendant of the land tax, and the collector of the alms, each of whom has unlimited authority in the specific functions assigned to him.

4. Those with limited authority of limited scope, such as the qadi of a town or district, the local intendant of the land tax, collector of tithes,[6] the frontier commandant, or the army commander, every one of whom has limited authority of limited scope.

Shaikh Sharaf ud-din Maneri

COLLECTED LETTERS

Islam reached the Indus region by A.D. 711 but did not press into the heartland of India until the early eleventh century, when Muslim Turks from Afghanistan established themselves in the Punjab, in north-central India. From here they launched a second wave of invasions toward the end of the twelfth century. The result was the

3. The king of Israel ca 1000 B.C.

4. Literally, "helper." The vizier was the chief official, a sort of prime minister, in the Abbasid empire.

5. A religious judge.

6. Almsgiving, or charity ("a loan to God"), is required of all Muslims. It became common practice for Muslim authorities to assess and collect these alms (*zakat*) from all believers and to distribute them.

Turkish sultanate of Delhi, which ruled all northern India from the Indus to the mouth of the Ganges by 1206.

The remnants of Indian Buddhism, which by the tenth century existed mainly in monasteries, could not survive the Turkish destruction and essentially passed away. Hinduism was another story. Some Hindu principalities survived as tributary states within the Turkish sultanate, and much of the population directly subject to the Turks retained their traditional Hindu ways despite the open hostility of Muslim zealots. In addition, the southern two-thirds of the subcontinent was outside Turkish control and remained firmly Hindu.

Notwithstanding Hinduism's resilience, Islam was on the ascent in thirteenth-century India. One factor that made Islam understandable and even palatable to many Indians was Muslim mysticism. Most simply defined, a mystic is a religious visionary who seeks union with the Divine while still remaining in this world. Normally mystics employ a variety of meditative exercises and forms of physical discipline in order to free and prepare the soul for this union. Within Islam such mystics are generally known as Sufis — those who clothe themselves in rough wool (*suf*).

Sufism had taken form in Syria and Iraq as early as the eighth century, partially influenced by the example of Christian monasticism. Even though most Sufis remained within the spectrum of Muslim orthodoxy, many legalists instinctively distrusted their approach to religion. Sufis, however, had a champion in Abu Hamid al-Ghazali (1058–1111), Islam's most brilliant and respected theologian. This Persian Sunni managed in both his life and writings to create a synthesis of Sufi devotion and Sunni tradition and intellectualism. As a result, Sufis became more acceptable to Islam's learned religious teachers.

Sufis were marvelous ambassadors of the faith, especially in India and Southeast Asia. In the following selections an Indian Sufi, Shaikh Sharaf un-din Maneri, who lived in the region of the Ganges around 1400, addresses a series of letters to a disciple.

Questions for Analysis

1. Why does asceticism play such an important role in Sufi devotion?
2. Why does the Sufi seek to be absolutely selfless?
3. Why is even heaven irrelevant to a Sufi?
4. What does Maneri mean when he states "intellect is a bondage"?
5. How does the Sufi serve God?
6. How do you imagine most Sufis understand the religious duty of jihad?
7. What are the four stages of Sufi spiritual development, and where do they lead?
8. Does Maneri reject the law and practices of orthodox Sunnism? If not, what role do traditional Muslim practices play in a Sufi's spiritual growth?
9. Does Maneri's ideal of mystical union with God call into question any of the

basic beliefs of Islam, such as the Oneness, Uniqueness, and Transcendance of God? Is Maneri, in other words, an orthodox Muslim?

10. Compare Maneri's teachings with the life of Saint Macarius in Chapter 7. Which are more striking, the similarities or the differences?
11. Compare Sufi teachings with both Hindu and Buddhist beliefs as illustrated in the *Upanishads* and the Buddha's sermons (Chapter 3). Are there any significant similarities? Any important differences? Why would an Indian mystic be sympathetic to Sufism?

SEEKING THE PATH

The aspiration of the Seeker should be such that, if offered this world with its pleasures, the next with its heaven, and the Universe with its sufferings, he should leave the world and its pleasures for the profane,[1] the next world and its heaven for the faithful,[2] and choose the sufferings for himself. He turns from the lawful in order to avoid heaven, in the same way that common people turn from the unlawful to avoid hell. He seeks the Master and His Vision in the same way that worldly men seek ease and wealth. The latter seek increase in all their works; he seeks the One alone in all. If given anything, he gives it away; if not given, he is content.

The marks of the Seeker are as follows. He is happy if he does not get the desired object, so that he may be liberated from all bonds; he opposes the desire-nature so much that he would not gratify its craving, even if it cried therefore for seventy years; he is so harmonized with God that ease and uneasiness, a boon and a curse, admission and rejection, are the same to him; he is too resigned to beg for anything either from God or from the world; his asceticism keeps him as fully satisfied with his little all — a garment or a blanket — as others might be with the whole world. . . . He vigilantly melts his desire-nature in the furnace of asceticism and does not think of anything save the True One. He sees Him on the right and on the left, sitting and standing. Such a Seeker is called the Divine Seer. He attaches no importance to the sovereignty of earth or of heaven. His body becomes emaciated by devotional aspirations, while his heart is cheered with Divine Blessedness. Thoughts of wife and children, of this world and the next, do not occupy his heart. Though his body be on earth, his soul is with God. Though here, he has already been there, reached the Goal, and seen the Beloved with his inner eye.

This stage can be reached only under the protection of a perfect teacher, the Path safely trodden under his supervision only. . . . it is indispensable for a disciple to put off his desires and protests, and place himself before the teacher as a dead body before the washer of the dead, so that He may deal with him as He likes.

RENUNCIATION

The first duty incumbent upon a Seeker is the practice of *Tajrid* and *Tafrid*. The one is to quit present possessions; the other, to

1. Those immersed in the nonsacred things of this world.

2. Muslims in general.

cease to care for the morrow. The second duty is seclusion, outer and inner. Outer seclusion consists in flying from the world and turning thy face to the wall in order that thou mayest give up thy life on the Divine threshold; inner seclusion consists in cleansing the heart of all thoughts connected with the non-God, whether the non-God be earth or heaven. . . .

Intellect is a bondage; faith, the liberator. The disciple should be stripped naked of everything in the universe in order to gaze at the beauty of faith. . . .

All attachments have dropped from the masters. Their garment is pure of all material stain. Their hands are too short to seize anything tainted with impermanence. Light has shone in their hearts enabling them to see God. Absorbed in His vision are they, so that they look not to their individualities, exist not for their individualities, have forgotten their individualities in the ecstasy of His existence, and have become completely His. They speak, yet do not speak; hear, yet do not hear; move, yet do not move; sit, yet do not sit. There is no individual being in their being, no speech in their speech, no hearing in their hearing. Speakers, they are dumb; hearers, they are deaf. They care little for material conditions, and think of the True One alone. Worldly men are not aware of their whereabouts. Physically with men, they are internally with God. They are a boon to the universe — not to themselves, for they are not themselves. . . .

The knowledge that accentuates personality is verily a hindrance. The knowledge that leads to God is alone true knowledge. The learned are confined in the prison of the senses, since they but gather their knowledge through sensuous objects. He that is bound by sense-limitations is barred from supersensuous knowledge. Real knowledge wells up from the Fountain of Life, and the student thereof need not resort to senses and gropings. The iron of human nature must be put into the melting-pot of discipline, hammered on the anvil of asceticism, and then handed over to the polishing agency of the Divine Love, so that the latter may cleanse it of all material impurities. It then becomes a mirror capable of reflecting the spiritual world, and may fitly be used by the King for the beholding of His Own Image.

The Steps of a Disciple

The first step is holy law (Shari'a). When the disciple has fully paid the demand of religion, and aspires to go beyond, the Path appears before him. It is the way to the heart. When he has fully observed the conditions of the Path, and aspires to soar higher, the veils of the heart are rent, and Truth shines therein. It is the way to the soul, and the goal of the seeker.

Broadly speaking, there are four stages: *Nasut, Malakut, Jabarut,* and *Lahut,* each leading to the next. *Nasut* is the animal nature, and functions through the five senses — e.g., eating, contacting, seeing, hearing, and the like. When the disciple controls the senses to the limit of bare necessity, and transcends the animal nature by purification and asceticism, he reaches *Malakut,* the region of the angels. The duties of this stage are prayers to God. When he is not proud of these, he transcends this stage and reaches *Jabarut,* the region of the soul. No one knows the soul but with the divine help; and truth, which is its mansion, baffles description and allusion. The duties of this stage are love, earnestness, joy, seeking, ecstasy, and insensibility. When the pilgrim transcends these by forgetting self altogether, he reaches *Lahut,* the unconditioned state. Here words fail.

The Final Stage

The fourth stage consists in the pouring forth of the Divine Light so profusely that it absorbs all individual existences in the eyes of the pilgrim. As in the case of the absorption of particles floating in the atmosphere in the light of the sun, the particles become invisible — they do not cease to exist, nor do they become the sun, but they are inevitably lost to sight in the overpowering glare of the sun — so, here, a creature does not become God, nor does it cease to exist. Ceasing to exist is one thing, invisibility is another. . . . When thou lookest through a mirror, thou dost not see the mirror, for thou mergest into the reflection of thy face, and yet thou canst not say that the mirror has ceased to exist, or that it has become the reflection, or that the reflection has become the mirror. Such is the vision of the Divine Energy in all beings without distinction. This state is called by the Sufis absorption in monotheism. Many have lost their balance here: no one can pass through this forest without the help of the Divine Grace and the guidance of a teacher, perfect, open-eyed, experienced in the elevations and depressions of the Path and inured to its blessings and sufferings. . . . Some pilgrims attain to this lofty state only for an hour a week, some for an hour a day, some for two hours a day, some remain absorbed for the greater portion of their time.

Mahmud Kati

THE CHRONICLE OF THE SEEKER

Despite their differences, all Muslims accept certain basic beliefs, such as the Oneness of God, and perform certain common religious obligations that serve as powerful forces for Islamic unification. Among these is the pilgrimage, or *hajj*, to Mecca. Every Muslim adult is expected, unless it is impossible, to travel once in a lifetime to Mecca, arriving during the sacred month of *Dhu-al-Hijja*, and join a vast multitude of other pilgrims in a mass celebration of devotional activities. Here Muslims of all sects, races, and social levels mingle without distinction and join in affirming the unity of the family of Islam.

The following document describes the famous pilgrimage that Mansa (King) Musa (Moses) of Mali (1312–1327) made to Mecca in 1324–1325. The sheer size of Musa's entourage and the generosity this king of sub-Saharan West Africa exhibited to Muslims along the route guaranteed that the memory of his pilgrimage would not be lost. Several written accounts exist. This particular record is ascribed to the family of Mahmud Kati (1468?–1593), a scholar and Islamic judge of Timbuktu. Kati, who according to tradition lived for 125 years, began to compose his history around 1519 and continued it until his death almost seventy-five years later. His sons and grandsons carried on his labors, bringing the story of Islam in black West Africa to 1655. Kati and his family composed the work in Arabic, as did all contemporary writers in that part of the world.

save him, to go with him to his country, so that the people of these parts might be blessed by the sight of them and by the blessing of their footsteps in these lands. But the shaykh refused, it being generally agreed that such things should be prevented and refused out of respect and regard for the noble blood of the *sharifs* and for fear lest one of them fall into the hands of the infidels and be lost or go astray. But he persisted in his request and urged them very strongly, until the shaykh said, "I will not do it, but I will neither command nor forbid it. If anyone wishes, let him follow you. His fate is in his own hands, I am not responsible."

The Malli-koy then sent a crier to the mosques to say, "Whoever wishes to have a thousand *mithqals*[13] of gold, let him follow me to my country, and the thousand is ready for him." Four men of the tribe of Quraysh came to him, but it is claimed that they were freedmen[14] of Quraysh and not real Qurayshis. He gave them 4,000, 1,000 each, and they followed him, with their families, when he returned to his country.

When the Malli-koy reached Timbuctoo on his way back, he collected ships and small boats on which he transported their families and luggage, together with his own women, as far as his country, for the riding animals were too exhausted to use. When the ships, carrying the *sharifs* from Mecca, reached the town of Kami, the Dienné-koy and the Kuran attacked the ships and plundered all that they contained. They took the *sharifs* ashore and revolted against the Malli-koy. But when the people of the ships told them about the *sharifs* and informed them of their high station, they attended them, and installed them in a nearby place called Shinshin. It is said that the *sharifs* of the town of Kay are descended from them.

This is the end of the story of the pilgrimage of the Malli-koy Kankan Musa. . . .

As for Malli, it is a vast region and an immense country, containing many towns and villages. The authority of the Sultan of Malli extends over all with force and might. We have heard the common people of our time say that there are four sultans in the world, not counting the supreme Sultan,[15] and they are the Sultan of Bagdad,[16] the Sultan of Egypt, the Sultan of Bornu,[17] and the Sultan of Malli.

13. A weight, that varied by region, of precious metal.

14. Freed former slaves.

15. The Ottoman sultan of Constantinople (Chapter 12).

16. The last caliph of Baghdad died in 1258.

17. The West African trading rival of Songhay located in the region of Lake Chad, along the border of modern Chad and Nigeria.

PART III

Continuity, Change, and Interchange, 500–1500

Hinduism, Buddhism, Confucianism, Greek rationalism, imperial systems of government and bureaucracy, Christianity, and many other major world traditions were firmly in place by 500 and, despite changes, they remained integral elements of global civilization for the next thousand years and beyond. The continuity of culture, especially in China and India, is one of the major features of the period 500–1500. A Chinese of the Han Dynasty would find much that was familiar in Ming China (1368–1644) and, while Islam was making an important impact on northern India after 1000, Hindu culture continued to flourish and develop along lines that reached back at least to Indo-Aryan antiquity. At the same time, this millennium witnessed radical changes from which even the essentially conservative societies of China and India were not immune.

Much of this change was due to the movement and interchange of people. Germans and other fringe groups infiltrated the western regions of the Roman Empire, thereby serving as a major factor in the radical transformation of society in Western Europe. The rise and spread of Islam in the seventh and eighth centuries created a new cultural bloc that stretched from western North Africa and Spain to Central Asia. The later movement of Turkish and Mongol nomads out of Central Asia resulted in empires that severely strained but also richly cross-pollinated virtually all of Eurasia's older civilized societies. Hindu, Chinese, and Arab merchants greatly influenced the development of civilization in Southeast Asia, their common meeting ground. It is almost impossible to exaggerate the impact China had on the development of Korean and Japanese cultures. The Byzantine world became the model and civilizer of the Eastern Slavs, most notably the Russians. Western Christian Europe expanded into Ireland, Scandinavia, Germany, the lands of the Baltic Sea, Poland, and Hungary. By 1500 Christianity, in both its Latin and Byzantine forms, provided spiritual direction to Europeans from Iceland to the Volga. Long before 1500, major portions of sub-Saharan Africa had become integral parts of the Muslim world, and toward the end of the fifteenth century Europeans were making their presence known along the African coast.

Of all Eurasia's civilizations, Western Europe underwent the most radical changes during this thousand-year period. Out of the chaos that ensued following the collapse of Roman society in the West, a new civilization emerged — Western Christian Europe. By 1100 it was an aggressive, expansionistic power, as the crusades bear witness. Despite a number of crises in the fourteenth century, which occasioned a momentary retrenchment, Western Europe never abandoned its spirit of expansion. In 1492 it was ready to resume explorations across the Atlantic. The eventual result was the virtual destruction of almost all Amerindian cultures and their absorption into the fabric of European civilization.

C H A P T E R

9

Asia

Asia was home to the world's oldest and most complex civilizations, and, as such, its deeply rooted cultures were the most tradition-bound. Even Asia's newer civilizations, such as Japan, exhibited an innate conservatism, in part because they had borrowed so heavily from their well-established neighbors.

Change, of course, comes to all societies, old and new, and Asia was no exception. Occasionally change arrived in dramatic fashion, as in the destruction of the Abbasid caliphate in 1258 or the establishment of the hated Mongol or Yüan Dynasty (1264–1368) in China. Usually, however, change arrived clothed in the guise of tradition. Even the Mongol Kublai Khan (1260–1294) adopted a Chinese name for his dynasty, performed the Confucian imperial rites, and tried to reestablish the civil service examination system. When Minamoto Yoritomo (1147–1199), established the supreme office of *shogun* (barbarian-subduing generalissimo), he left Japan's imperial court and structure in place and allowed local lords to retain a good measure of their old feudal autonomy.

A reverence for tradition did not mean a lack of dynamism. The great urban centers of Asia — Baghdad, Benares, Delhi, Hangchou, Nara, Kyoto — were prosperous and cosmopolitan. China in the eleventh century had several cities with populations of a million or more, and the volume of commerce in those urban centers eventually necessitated the creation of imperially guaranteed paper money. Economic prosperity also meant artistic patronage, and all the fine arts flourished from the Middle East to Japan. As European travelers learned, the riches of Asia were no empty fable.

Japan

It is not certain when civilization arose in Japan, but by about A.D. 400 Korean scribes were introducing the Chinese system of writing into the islands. In the mid-sixth century a Chinese form of Mahayana Buddhism made its way to Japan from Korea, and in 646 it was officially acknowledged as the religion of the aristocracy. The coming of Buddhism sharpened the desire of Japan's leaders to adopt Chinese culture, and during the seventh and eighth centuries the imperial court of Japan dispatched large numbers of students to China, where they could observe the T'ang (618–907) governmental system at first hand before returning home to assume important official positions. These scholars brought back with them not only the forms of Chinese government but also some of the spirit that infused Chinese culture. Confucianism and even Taoism became parts of the fabric of Japanese civilization during these centuries of tutelage.

Although the Japanese borrowed extensively from China, their separation from the mainland enabled them to absorb these foreign influences in a manner that did not destroy native culture. During the Heian period (794–1185), when the imperial court was located at Kyoto, Japanese civilization reached a level of mature independence it would never relinquish. The Japanese became more selective in their assimilation of things Chinese and increasingly discovered inspiration for creative expression in their own land and people. By the early eleventh century, Japan had developed a distinctive civilization that set it apart from its two ancient mentors — Korea and China.

CHRONICLES OF JAPAN

Glorification of martial values is common to all societies ruled by a warrior aristocracy, and Japan was no exception. In the late seventeenth century A.D. this ethic was codified in *bushido,* "the way of the warrior," a canon of moral conduct that has had significant impact on Japanese life and national conduct well into the twentieth century. Centuries before Japanese intellectuals transformed traditional military behavior into a code of ethical values, however, Japan's warrior class had celebrated its distinctive ways of life and death. One of the most popular recurring themes in Japanese history, legend, and art, from earliest recorded days to the present, is the warrior who triumphs in death.

Our source illustrating the warrior as hero is an excerpt from the *Nihongi,* or *Chronicles of Japan,* one of Japan's two oldest collections of legend and history. Composed in its final form in A.D. 720, the *Nihongi* traces the history of Japan to the mythological descent of the imperial family from the Sun Goddess in 660 B.C. By the time the *Nihongi* reaches the sixth century A.D., its narrative has, for the most part, left the realm of myth and become more reliable history.

The following document recounts the story of Yorodzu, a partisan of the Mononobe clan in its unsuccessful struggle against the Soga clan for power over the imperial court. The time is the late sixth century, just prior to the reign of Empress Suiko (592–628). During her reign, her nephew and regent Prince Shotoku (573–621), a member of the Soga clan, attempted, with limited success, to restructure Japan along Chinese lines.

Questions for Analysis

1. Consider Yorodzu's death. Why does he destroy his weapons and then commit suicide?
2. How does the chronicler treat Yorodzu's rebellion and death? Is he a rebel against the emperor? Is his death dishonorable?
3. What do your answers to the above questions suggest about the chronicler's attitude toward the conflict between the Soga and Mononobe chieftains? Is it a struggle between lawfully constituted authority and a rebel, or is it something else? If it is something else, what is it?
4. Japan had already had emperors and empresses for centuries. Judging from this account, who controlled the other — the emperor or the great clan chiefs?
5. What values does this account celebrate?

The Emperor Tachibana no Toyohi died in the second year of his reign [ca 587]. Summer, the 4th month. In the 5th month the army of the Mononobe no Ohomuraji[1] made a disturbance thrice. The Ohomuraji from the first wished to set aside the other Imperial Princes and to establish the Imperial Prince Anahobe[2] as Emperor. . . .

His plan is defeated when the Soga clan assassinates Prince Anahobe.

Autumn, 7th month. The Oho-omi,[3] Soga no Mumako no Sukune, incited the Imperial Princes and the Ministers to plot the destruction of the Ohomuraji, Mononobe no Moriya. . . .

1. Literally, the Great Deity Chief Mononobe. This was an hereditary office, second in power only to that of the Oho-omi, or Great Imperial Chief. As was true of all clan chieftains, the Great Deity Chiefs (Ohomuraji) traced their ancestry back to the gods of heaven and earth.

2. The emperor's half brother.

3. Soga, the Great Imperial Chief (Prime Minister). The office of Oho-omi was also hereditary. Imperial Chiefs were leaders of clans that claimed, like their emperor and empress cousins, descent from Jimmu Tenno, the First Emperor and great-grandson of the Sun Goddess.

These princes and ministers advance with their forces against the Mononobe clan.

The Ohomuraji [Mononobe], in personal command of the young men of his family and of a slave-army, built a rice-fort and gave battle. Then the Ohomuraji climbed up into the fork of an elm at Kisuri, from which he shot down arrows like rain. His troops were full of might. They filled the house and overflowed into the plain. The army of the Imperial Princes and the troops of the Ministers were timid and afraid, and fell back three times. At this time the Imperial Prince Mumayado [Shotoku], his hair being tied up on the temples,[4] . . . followed in the rear of the army. He pondered in his own mind, saying to himself: — "Are we not going to be beaten? Without prayer we cannot succeed." So he cut down a nuride tree, and swiftly fashioned images of the four Heavenly Kings.[5] Placing them on his top-knot,[6] he uttered a vow: — "If we are now made to gain the victory over the enemy, I promise faithfully to honor the four Heavenly Kings, guardians of the world, by erecting to them a temple with a pagoda." The Oho-omi Soga no Mumako also uttered a vow: — "Oh! all ye Heavenly Kings and great Spirit King, aid and protect us, and make us to gain the advantage. If this prayer is granted, I will erect a temple with a pagoda in honor of the Heavenly Kings and the great Spirit King, and will propagate everywhere the three precious things."[7] When they had made this vow, they urged their troops of all arms sternly forward to the attack. Now there was a man named Ichihi, Tomi no Obito, who shot down the Ohomuraji from his branch and killed him and his children. The Ohomuraji's troops accordingly gave way suddenly. Joining their forces, they every one put on black clothes[8] and going hunting[9] on the plain of Magari in Hirose, so dispersed. In this war some of the children and relatives of the Ohomuraji made their escape, and concealing themselves on the plain of Ashihara, changed their personal names and altered their titles, while others fled away nobody knew where. . . .

A dependant of the Ohomuraji Mononobe no Moriya named Yorodzu . . . in command of one hundred men, guarded the house at Naniha, but hearing of the Ohomuraji's downfall, he urged his horse into a gallop, and made his escape by night in the direction of the village of Arimaka in the district of Chinu, where, having passed his wife's house, he at length concealed himself among the hills. The Court took counsel together, saying: — "Yorodzu cherishes traitorous feelings, and therefore has concealed himself among these hills. Let his kindred be extirpated promptly, and no remissness shown." Yorodzu, in tattered and filthy raiment, and with a wretched countenance, came forth alone, of his own accord, bow in hand and girt with a sword. The officials sent several hundred guardsmen to surround him. Yorodzu, accord-

4. About the age of fourteen or fifteen, when adolescent men wore their hair in this style as a token of incipient manhood.

5. Buddhist guardian deities.

6. A knot of hair on the top of his head.

7. Buddhism's three treasures: the Buddha, the Law, and the monastic orders.

8. Servants wore black; therefore, they were assuming disguises.

9. They dropped the outward manifestations of war and pretended to be hunters.

ingly, was afraid, and hid himself in a bamboo thicket, where he tied cords to the bamboos and pulled them so as to shake the bamboos, and thus make the people to doubt where he had gone in. The guardsmen were deceived, and pointing to the quivering bamboos, ran forward, saying: — "Yorodzu is here!" Yorodzu forthwith shot his arrows, not one of which missed its mark, so that the guardsmen were afraid, and did not dare to approach. Yorodzu then unstrung his bow, and taking it under his arm, ran off towards the hills. The guardsmen accordingly pursued him, shooting their arrows at him from both sides of a river, but none of them were able to hit him. Hereupon one of the guardsmen ran on swiftly, and got before Yorodzu. Lying down by the river's side, he aimed at him, and hit him on the knee. Yorodzu forthwith pulled out the arrow, and stringing his bow, let fly his arrows. Then prostrating himself on the earth, he exclaimed aloud: — "A shield of the Emperor, Yorodzu would have devoted his valor to his service, but no examination was made, and, on the contrary, he has been hard pressed, and is now at an extremity. Let some one come forward and speak with me, for it is my desire to learn whether I am to be slain or to be made a prisoner." The guardsmen raced up and shot at Yorodzu, but he warded off the flying shafts, and slew more than thirty men. Then he took the sword which he wore, and cut his bow into three pieces, and bending back his sword, flung it into the midst of the water of the river. With a dagger which he had besides, he stabbed himself in the throat, and died. The Governor of Kahachi reported the circumstances of Yorodzu's death to the Court, which gave an order by a stamp that his body should be cut into eight pieces and disposed for exposure among the eight provinces. The Governor of Kahachi accordingly, in obedience to the purport of the stamped order, was about to dismember him for exposure, when thunder pealed, and a great rain fell. Now, there was a white dog which had been kept by Yorodzu. Looking up, and looking down, he went round, howling beside the corpse, and at last, taking up the head in his mouth, placed it on an ancient mound. He then lay down close by, and starved to death in front of it. The Governor of Kahachi, thinking that dog's conduct very strange, reported it to the Court. The Court could not bear to hear of it for pity, and issued a stamped order to this effect: — "The case of this dog is one that is rarely heard of in the world, and should be shown to after ages. Let Yorodzu's kindred be made to construct a tomb and bury their remains." The kindred of Yorodzu accordingly assembled together, and raised a tomb in the village of Arimaka, where they buried Yorodzu and his dog.

CHRONICLES OF JAPAN

The Soga-Mononobe factional struggle for control over the imperial court points out the dominance of the clans in sixth-century Japan. Despite the efforts of Prince Shotoku to introduce a centralized imperial system modeled on that of T'ang China, Japan entered the seventh century in much the same state as earlier, with most real power divided among the great clan chiefs and their warriors. Toward the middle of the century, however, a new reformer arose in Fujiwara Kamatari (also known as Nakatomi no Kamako no Muraji, since he was chief of the Nakatomi clan). Between 645 and 650 he and his hand-picked emperor, Kotoku Tenno (645–654), instituted a series of administrative and land reforms that are known collectively as the *Taika* (Great Transformation).

Questions for Analysis

1. Why did Nakatomi and Prince Naka plot Iruka's death?
2. Why did Prince Naka refuse the imperial throne in 645? What Confucian principle did he uphold by that action, and how does the chronicler make that particular principle a recurring theme throughout this account?
3. How does the oath taken by the imperial ministers sum up the essence of the Taika movement?
4. How did the Taika reforms represent the wish of Emperor Kotuku and Kamatari to institute in Japan a Confucian-legalist system modeled on that of T'ang China?
5. What do both this and the preceding selection tell us about the rising influence of Buddhism among Japan's aristocracy?

The Empress Ame[1] . . . was the great-granddaughter of the Emperor Nunakura. . . . This Empress conducted the government in conformity with the ancient path.

In the second year of the Emperor Okinaga . . . she was appointed Empress-consort. This Emperor died in the 10th month of the 13th year of his reign.

1st year,[2] Spring, 1st month, 15th day. The Empress-consort assumed the Imperial Dignity. Yemishi, Soga no Omi,[3] was made Oho-omi[4] as before. The Oho-omi's son, Iruka (also called Kuratsukuri), took into his own hands the reins of government, and his power was greater than his father's. Therefore thieves and robbers were in dread of him, and things dropped on the highways were not picked up. . . .

3rd year, Spring, 1st month, 1st day. Nakatomi no Kamako no Muraji[5] [Fujiwara Kamatari] was appointed Chief of the Shinto[6] religion. He declined the appointment several times, and would not

1. Also known as Kogyoku Tenno. She reigned from 642 to 645 and again from 655 to her death in 661.

2. Of her reign — 642.

3. Literally, Yemishi, Imperial Chief of the Soga clan.

4. See page 267, note 3.

5. Literally, Nakatomi, the Deity Chief of the Kamako clan. Deity chiefs (Muraji) were clan leaders who claimed descent from the ancestral gods of heaven and earth and were second in rank only to the imperial chiefs. Because deity chiefs were not directly descended from the Sun Goddess, however, they were not worthy of holding the imperial throne.

6. "The Way of the Gods" or Shinto, the ancient folk religion of Japan.

take it up. On the plea of ill-health he went away and lived at Mishima. . . .

Nakatomi no Kamako no Muraji was a man of an upright and loyal character and of a reforming disposition. He was indignant with Soga no Iruka for breaking down the order of Prince and Vassal, of Senior and Junior, and cherishing veiled designs upon the State. One after another he associated with the Princes of the Imperial line, trying them in order to discover a wise ruler who might establish a great reputation. He had accordingly fixed his mind on Naka no Ohoye, but for want of intimate relations with him he had been for so far unable to unfold his inner sentiments. Happening to be one of a football party in which Naka no Ohoye played at the foot of the keyaki tree of the Temple of Hokoji, he observed the (Prince's) leathern shoe fall off with the ball. Placing it on the palm of his hand, he knelt before the Prince and humbly offered it to him. Naka no Ohoye in his turn knelt down and respectfully received it. From this time they became mutual friends, and told each other all their thoughts. There was no longer any concealment between them. They feared, however, that jealous suspicions might be caused by their frequent meetings, and they both took in their hands yellow rolls,[7] and studied personally the doctrines of Chou[8] and Confucius. . . . Thus they at length while on their way there and back, walking shoulder to shoulder, secretly prepared their plans. On all points they were agreed. . . .

Prince Naka and Nakatomi succeed in assassinating Iruka in 645.

In the fourth year, the sixth month, and the fourteenth day of her reign,[9] the Empress Ame . . . wished to transfer the Dignity to Naka no Ohoye, and made order, saying — "etc., etc." Naka no Ohoye, when he retired (from her presence), informed Nakatomi, Kamako no Muraji, who advised him, saying: — "Furubito no Ohoye is Your Highness's elder brother: the Imperial Prince Karu is Your Highness's maternal uncle. If at present, during the lifetime of Furubito no Ohoye, Your Highness should ascend to the Imperial Dignity, it would be a transgression against the sentiment of respect and obedience due from younger brothers. Would it not, therefore, be better to raise your maternal uncle to the throne, and so respond to the expectations of the people?" Upon this Naka no Ohoye was profoundly pleased with this advice and reported it privately to the Empress. The Empress Ame . . . granted the Imperial Seal and resigned the Dignity to the Imperial Prince Karu, and made a rescript, saying: — "Thou, the Imperial Prince Karu, etc., etc." The Imperial Prince Karu declined firmly and repeatedly in favor of Furubito no Ohoye . . . saying: — "Ohoye no Mikoto is the offspring of the former Emperor, and he is of mature age, for both which reasons it is fit that he should occupy the Celestial Dignity." Upon this, Furubito no Ohoye left his seat, and, retiring to a distance, folded his arms and excused himself, saying: — "Let us comply with the sage will of the Empress. Why shouldst thou take the trouble to transfer it to thy servant? It is my desire to renounce the world, and to go to Yoshino, there to devote myself to the practice of the Law of Buddha, and thus render sup-

7. Chinese books.

8. The semilegendary Duke of Chou, one of the architects of the Western Chou regime and one of the statesmen most admired by Confucius.

9. Two days after the assassination.

port to the Emperor." When he had concluded his refusal, he ungirt the sword which he had on, and flung it to the ground. Moreover he gave orders to all his household to ungird their swords. That same day he went to the Temple of Hokoji, and there, between the Hall of Buddha and the pagoda, he shaved off his beard and hair, and put on the kesa.[10] In consequence the Imperial Prince Karu was unable to persist in his refusal, and, ascending the throne, assumed the Dignity.[11] . . .

The Emperor, the Empress Dowager,[12] and the Prince Imperial [Prince Naka] summoned together the Ministers . . . and made an oath appealing to the Gods of Heaven and Earth, and saying: —

> Heaven covers us: Earth upbears us: the Imperial way is but one. But in this last degenerate age, the order of Lord and Vassal was destroyed, until Supreme Heaven by Our hands put to death the traitors. Now, from this time forward, both parties shedding their heart's blood, the Lord will eschew double methods of government, and the Vassal will avoid duplicity in his service of the sovereign! On him who breaks this oath, Heaven will send a curse and earth a plague, demons will slay them, and men will smite them. This is as manifest as the sun and moon.

The style 4th year of the Empress Ame . . . was altered to Daikwa[13] 1st year. . . .

2nd year, Spring, 1st month, 1st day. As soon as the ceremonies of the new year's congratulations were over, the Emperor promulgated an edict of reforms, as follows: —

> The capital is for the first time to be regulated, and Governors appointed for the Home provinces and districts. Let barriers, outposts, guards, and post-horses, both special and ordinary, be provided . . . and mountains and rivers regulated.[14] . . .

For each ward in the capital let there be appointed one alderman, and for four wards one chief alderman, who shall be charged with the superintendence of the population, and the examination of criminal matters. For appointment as chief aldermen of wards let men be taken belonging to the wards, of unblemished character, firm and upright, so that they may fitly sustain the duties of the time. For appointments as aldermen, whether of rural townships or of city wards, let ordinary subjects be taken belonging to the township or ward, of good character and solid capacity. If such men are not to be found in the township or ward in question, it is permitted to select and employ men of the adjoining township or ward. . . .

Let men of solid capacity and intelligence who are skilled in writing and arithmetic be appointed assistants and clerks. . . .

Let there now be provided for the first time registers of population, books of account and a system of the receipt and regranting of distribution-land.

---

10. The monastic robe.

11. The former Imperial Prince Karu reigned from 645 to 654 as Emperor (Tenno) Kotuku. Prince Naka succeeded to the throne as Emperor Tenchi in 662 and reigned to 671.

12. The former Empress Ame.

13. Or Taika. Daikwa (Taika) means both Great Civilization and Great Transformation.

14. By providing guards at ferries and passes.

Murasaki Shikibu

DIARY

The centralized administrative system established in the Great Transformation failed to function as intended, and by the mid-ninth century true power in the provinces rested in the hands of local clan chiefs and a new element, Buddhist monasteries. Each of these powers based its independence on large landed estates and armies of private retainers known as *samurai* (one who serves). At the same time, the basic structure of Taika government remained in place, even though most provincial governors resided at the imperial court, which became an increasingly elegant setting for emperors and empresses, who remained living gods on earth and theoretically stood at the summit of all power. The elaborate ceremony that surrounded this living god, who claimed to rule the world, masked the fact that effective power lay elsewhere.

While the court at Kyoto was increasingly losing touch with the center of political authority, a group of aristocratic women at court were developing Japan's first native literature. Unlike many of Japan's Confucian scholars, who continued to study the Chinese classics along fairly rigid lines established a millennium earlier in a foreign land, these court women gave free play in their prose and poetry to their imaginations, emotions, and powers of analysis.

Japan's greatest literary artist of the Heian period was Murasaki Shikibu (978-after 1010), a lady-in-waiting at the court of Second Empress Akiko. Her masterpiece is the massive *The Tale of Genji*, a romance whose psychological insights and realistic portraits of life have earned it universal recognition as the single greatest piece of classical Japanese literature and one of the world's immortal novels. Like many other imperial ladies-in-waiting, Madame Murasaki kept a diary in which she recorded, with the same level of insight and narrative ability she displayed in *The Tale of Genji*, her observations on court life and her deepest reflections.

Questions for Analysis

1. What was expected of court women? How did male aristocrats look upon and treat women of their class? As equals? As servants? As ornaments? As something else?
2. Would Madame Murasaki ever think of herself as "liberated"? Would she understand such a concept? What seems to be her view of women in general and herself in particular? Compare her vision of what it means to be a woman with that of Madame Pan Chao (Chapter 5).
3. How "Confucian" was Murasaki Shikibu in her values and way of life? Does the diary contain any non-Confucian tones?

4. What did this aristocratic society think of literary accomplishment? How important was Chinese literature to Japanese literary artists?
5. What does this diary tell us about the level of refinement and sophistication among Japan's aristocracy?

As the autumn season approaches the Tsuchimikado[1] becomes inexpressibly smile-giving. The tree-tops near the pond, the bushes near the stream, are dyed in varying tints whose colors grow deeper in the mellow light of evening. The murmuring sound of waters mingles all the night through with the never-ceasing recitation of sutras[2] which appeal more to one's heart as the breezes grow cooler.

The ladies waiting upon her honored presence are talking idly. The Queen hears them; she must find them annoying, but she conceals it calmly. Her beauty needs no words of mine to praise it, but I cannot help feeling that to be near so beautiful a queen will be the only relief from my sorrow.[3] So in spite of my better desires (for a religious life) I am here. Nothing else dispels my grief — it is wonderful! . . .

I can see the garden from my room beside the entrance to the gallery. The air is misty, the dew is still on the leaves. The Lord Prime Minister is walking there; he orders his men to cleanse the brook. He breaks off a stalk of omenaishi (flower maiden) which is in full bloom by the south end of the bridge. He peeps in over my screen! His noble appearance embarrasses us, and I am ashamed of my morning (not yet painted and powdered) face. He says, "Your poem on this! If you delay so much the fun is gone!" and I seize the chance to run away to the writing-box, hiding my face —

Flower-maiden in bloom —
Even more beautiful for the bright dew,
Which is partial, and never favors me.

"So prompt!" said he, smiling, and ordered a writing-box to be brought (for himself).

His answer:

The silver dew is never partial.
From her heart
The flower-maiden's beauty.

One wet and calm evening I was talking with Lady Saisho. The young Lord[4] of the Third Rank sat with the misu[5] partly rolled up. He seemed maturer than his age and was very graceful. Even in light conversation such expressions as "Fair soul is rarer than fair face" come gently to his lips, covering us with confusion. It is a mistake to treat him like a young boy. He keeps his dignity among ladies, and I saw in him a much-sought-after romantic hero

1. The residence of Prime Minister Fujiwara Michinaga, father of Second Empress Akiko, who has returned to her father's home to give birth to Prince Atsusada.

2. Buddhist texts.

3. Her husband, whom she had married in 999, had died in 1001. It is now 1007.

4. The prime minister's son Yorimichi, who was sixteen years old.

5. A bamboo curtain used to hide distinguished persons from view.

when once he walked off reciting to himself:

> Linger in the field where flower-maidens
> are blooming
> And your name will be tarnished with tales
> of gallantry.

Some such trifle as that sometimes lingers in my mind when really interesting things are soon forgotten — why? . . .

On the fifth night the Lord Prime Minister celebrated the birth.[6] The full moon on the fifteenth day was clear and beautiful. Torches were lighted under the trees and tables were put there with rice-balls on them. Even the uncouth humble servants who were walking about chattering seemed to enhance the joyful scene. All minor officials were there burning torches, making it as bright as day. Even the attendants of the nobles, who gathered behind the rocks and under the trees, talked of nothing but the new light which had come into the world, and were smiling and seemed happy as if their own private wishes had been fulfilled. . . .

This time, as they chose only the best-looking young ladies, the rest who used to tie their hair on ordinary occasions to serve the Queen's dinner wept bitterly; it was shocking to see them. . . .

To serve at the Queen's dinner eight ladies tied their hair with white cords, and in that dress brought in Her Majesty's dining-table. The chief lady-in-waiting for that night was Miya-no-Naishi. She was brilliantly dressed with great formality, and her hair was made more charming by the white cords which enhanced her beauty. I got a side glance of her when her face was not screened by her fan.[7] She wore a look of extreme purity. . . .

The court nobles rose from their seats and went to the steps (descending from the balcony). His Lordship the Prime Minister and others cast da.[8] It was shocking to see them quarreling about paper. Some [others] composed poems. A lady said, "What response shall we make if some one offers to drink saké with us?"[9] We tried to think of something.

Shijo-no-Dainagon is a man of varied accomplishments. No ladies can rival him in repartee, much less compete with him in poetry, so they were all afraid of him, but (this evening) he did not give a cup to any particular lady to make her compose poems. Perhaps that was because he had many things to do and it was getting late. . . .

The Great Adviser[10] is displeased to be received by ladies of low rank, so when he comes to the Queen's court to make some report and suitable ladies to receive him are not available, he goes away without seeing Her Majesty. Other court nobles, who often come to make reports, have each a favorite lady, and when that one is away they are displeased, and go away saying to other people, that the Queen's ladies are quite unsatisfactory. . . .

Lady Izumi Shikibu[11] corresponds charmingly, but her behavior is improper indeed. She writes with grace and ease and with a flashing wit. There is fragrance even in her smallest words. Her poems are attractive, but they are only improvisations which drop from her mouth spontaneously. Every one of them has some interesting point, and she is acquainted

6. Of his imperial grandson.

7. Women were expected to hide their faces behind fans.

8. A game of dice.

9. Thereby challenging the person to compose an impromptu poem.

10. Fujiwara Michitaka, the prime minister's brother.

11. One of Japan's greatest poets.

with ancient literature also, but she is not like a true artist who is filled with the genuine spirit of poetry. Yet I think even she cannot presume to pass judgment on the poems of others.

The wife of the Governor of Tamba Province is called by the Queen and Prime Minister Masa Hira Emon. Though she is not of noble birth, her poems are very satisfying. She does not compose and scatter them about on every occasion, but so far as we know them, even her miscellaneous poems shame us. Those who compose poems whose loins are all but broken, yet who are infinitely self-exalted and vain, deserve our contempt and pity.

Lady Seishonagon.[12] A very proud person. She values herself highly, and scatters her Chinese writings all about. Yet should we study her closely, we should find that she is still imperfect. She tries to be exceptional, but naturally persons of that sort give offense. She is piling up trouble for her future. One who is too richly gifted, who indulges too much in emotion, even when she ought to be reserved, and cannot turn aside from anything she is interested in, in spite of herself will lose self-control. How can such a vain and reckless person end her days happily!

(Here there is a sudden change from the Court to her own home.)

Having no excellence within myself, I have passed my days without making any special impression on any one. Especially the fact that I have no man who will look out for my future makes me comfortless. I do not wish to bury myself in dreariness. Is it because of my worldly mind that I feel lonely? On moonlight nights in autumn, when I am hopelessly sad, I often go out on the balcony and gaze dreamily at the moon. It makes me think of days gone by. People say that it is dangerous to look at the moon in solitude, but something impels me, and sitting a little withdrawn I muse there. In the wind-cooled evening I play on the koto,[13] though others may not care to hear it. I fear that my playing betrays the sorrow which becomes more intense, and I become disgusted with myself — so foolish and miserable am I. . . .

A pair of big bookcases have in them all the books they can hold. In one of them are placed old poems and romances. They are the homes of worms which come frightening us when we turn the pages, so none ever wish to read them. (Perhaps her own writings, she speaks so slightingly of them.) As to the other cabinet, since the person[14] who placed his own books (there) no hand has touched it. When I am bored to death I take out one or two of them; then my maids gather around me and say: "Your life will not be favored with old age if you do such a thing! Why do you read Chinese? Formerly even the reading of sutras was not encouraged for women." They rebuke me in the shade (i.e., behind my back). I have heard of it and have wished to say, "It is far from certain that he who does no forbidden thing enjoys a long life," but it would be a lack of reserve to say it (to the maids). Our deeds vary with our age and

12. One of the leading literary figures of her day and a rival of Murasaki Shikibu. Lady Seishonagon served at the court of the First Empress, who was a rival of her cousin, the Second Empress.

13. A stringed instrument.

14. Her deceased husband, who had been a scholar of Chinese literature.

deeds vary with the individual. Some are proud (to read books), others look over old cast-away writings because they are bored with having nothing to do. It would not be becoming for such a one to chatter away about religious thoughts, noisily shaking a rosary. I feel this, and before my women keep myself from doing what otherwise I could do easily. But after all, when I was among the ladies of the Court I did not say what I wanted to say either, for it is useless to talk with those who do not understand one and troublesome to talk with those who criticize from a feeling of superiority. Especially one-sided persons are troublesome. Few are accomplished in many arts and most cling narrowly to their own opinion.

China

The period 500–1500 witnessed a variety of momentous developments in China: renewed imperial greatness, philosophical and technological innovation, economic expansion and a rapidly growing population, new modes of artistic expression, conquest by Mongol invaders, and eventual recovery and retrenchment. Through it all, Chinese civilization kept its basic institutions and way of life intact.

The Time of Troubles that followed the fall of the House of Han was over by the end of the sixth century, and under the T'ang (618–907) China was again a great imperial power, with a Confucian civil service solidly in power. At the end of the seventh century, China's borders reached to the Aral Sea in the western regions of Central Asia, Korea, and Manchuria in the northeast, and Vietnam to the south. T'ang was also an age of artistic brilliance. Sculptural art, particularly the representation of magnificent horses, poetry, and painting, became T'ang hallmarks.

Fifty-three years of disunity followed T'ang's collapse. The Sung (960–1279) finally reunited most of the Chinese heartland, but geographically and militarily Sung China was a truncated shadow of former T'ang greatness. Despite its external weakness, China under the Sung achieved levels of political stability, economic prosperity, technological advancement, and cultural maturity that were unequaled anywhere else on earth at that time. By the mid-eleventh century the production of printed books had become such an important industry that artisans were experimenting with movable type — 400 years before the introduction of a similar printing process in Europe. The thousands of books and millions of pages printed in Sung China are evidence that a remarkably high degree of its population was literate. In addition to this dramatic rise in basic literacy, there were significant developments in advanced philosophy. Intellectuals reinvigorated Confucian thought by injecting into it metaphysical concepts borrowed from Buddhism and Taoism. This new "Study of the Way," or Neo-Confucianism, provided fresh philosophical insights clothed in traditional forms and enabled Confucianism to topple Buddhism from its position of intellectual preeminence.

The fine arts also reached new levels of achievement. Landscape painting, particularly during the period known as Southern Sung (1127–1279), expressed in two dimensions the mystical visions of Taoism and Chan Buddhism. The craft of porcelain-making became a high art, and large numbers of exquisitely delicate pieces of fine "China" were traded from Japan to Mesopotamia.

Advanced ships and navigational aids enabled Chinese traders to take to the sea in unprecedented numbers, especially in the direction of Southeast Asia, thus transforming their homeland into the world's greatest merchant marine power of its day. Rapid-maturing strains of rice were introduced from Champa in Indochina, making it possible to feed a population that exceeded 100 million, about double that of the Age of T'ang. Although most of this massive population engaged in traditional, labor-intensive agriculture, some Chinese worked in industries, such as mining, iron and steel production, and textile manufacture, whose advanced technologies were unequaled anywhere else in the world.

Sung's age of greatness was brought to a close by Mongol invaders, who by 1279 had joined all China to the largest land empire in world history. Mongol rule during what is known as the Yüan Dynasty (1264–1368) was unmitigated military occupation, and the Mongols and the many foreigners whom they admitted into their service exploited and oppressed the Chinese. While the Mongols encouraged agriculture and trade, few Chinese benefited from a prosperity that was largely confined to a small circle of landlords.

By the mid-fourteenth century China was in rebellion, and in 1368 a commoner, Chu Yüan-chang, reestablished native rule in the form of the Ming Dynasty (1368–1644). This new imperial family restored Chinese prestige and influence in East Asia to levels enjoyed under T'ang and provided China with stability and prosperity well beyond 1500. Under the Ming, traditional Chinese civilization attained full maturity. Toward the middle of the Age of Ming, China reluctantly established relations with seaborne western European merchants and missionaries, and the consequent challenge of the West would result, centuries later, in major transformations in Chinese life.

Tu Fu

POEMS

The Chinese consider the eighth century their golden age of classical poetry. Among the century's many poetic geniuses, three are universally recognized as preeminent: the Buddhist Wang Wei (699–759), the Taoist Li Po (701–762), and the Confucian Tu Fu (712–770). Despite their differences in personality and perspective, they knew and deeply respected one another. Of the three, the Chinese most esteem Tu Fu, primarily for the tone of compassion for the downtrodden that pervades his poetry.

Tu Fu himself knew adversity. Despite his extraordinary erudition, he was denied a position of public responsibility and spent much of his adult life as an impoverished wanderer and farmer. He lived to see one of his children die of starvation and suffered through the destruction of General An Lu-shan's rebellion (755–763), a civil war from which the T'ang regime never recovered. Despite these adversities, Tu Fu never lost his love for humanity or his belief in the innate goodness of the common person.

Questions for Analysis

1. According to Tu Fu, what costs have the Chinese paid for their empire? Has it been worth it?
2. What does Tu Fu think of military glory?
3. What do the second and third poems tell you about the economic and social consequences of An Lu-shan's rebellion?
4. From a Confucian perspective, what is wrong with eighth-century China?

BALLAD OF THE WAR CHARIOTS

The jingle of war chariots,
Horses neighing, men marching,
Bows and arrows slung over hips;
Beside them stumbling, running
The mass of parents, wives and children
Clogging up the road, their rising dust
Obscuring the great bridge at Hsienyang;
Stamping their feet, weeping
In utter desperation with cries
That seem to reach the clouds;

Ask a soldier: Why do you go?
Would simply bring the answer:
Today men are conscripted often;
Fifteen-year-olds sent up the Yellow River
To fight; men of forty marched away
To colonize the western frontier;
Village elders take young boys,
Do up their hair like adults
To get them off; if they return
It will be white with age, but even then
They may be sent off to the frontier again;
Frontiers on which enough blood has
flowed
To make a sea, yet our Emperor still
would
Expand his authority! Have you not
heard
How east of Huashan[1] many counties
Are desolate with weeds and thorns?
The strongest women till the fields,
Yet crops come not as well as before;

Lads from around here are well known
For their bravery, but hate to be driven
Like dogs or chickens; only because
You kindly ask me do I dare give vent
To grievances; now for instance
With the men from the western frontier
Still not returned, the government
Demands immediate payment of taxes,
But how can we pay when so little
Has been produced?

Now, we peasants have learnt one thing:
To have a son is not so good as having

1. The land back home, east of the western frontier.

A daughter who can marry a neighbor
And still be near us, while a son
Will be taken away to die in some
Wild place, his bones joining those
That lie bleached white on the shores
Of Lake Kokonor,[2] where voices of new
 spirits
Join with the old, heard sadly through
The murmur of falling rain.

Thinking of Other Days

In those prosperous times
Of the period of Kai Yuan,[3]
Even a small county city
Would be crowded with the rich;
Rice flowed like oil and both
Public and private granaries
Were stuffed with grain; all
Through the nine provinces
There were no robbers on
The roads; traveling from home
Needless to pick an auspicious
Day to start; everywhere carriages
With folk wearing silk or brocade;
Farmers ploughed, women picked
Mulberries, nothing that did
Not run smoothly; in court
Was a good Emperor for whom
The finest music was played;
Friends were honest with each other
And for long there had been
No kind of disaster; great days with
Rites and songs, the best of other times,
Laws the most just; who could
Have dreamed that later a bolt
Of silk would cost ten thousand
Cash? Now the fields farmers
Tilled have become covered
With bloodshed; palaces at Loyang[4]
Are burnt, and temples to
The imperial ancestors are full
Of foxes and rabbit burrows!
Now I am too sad to ask
Questions of the old people,
Fearing to hear tales
Of horror and strife;
I am not able, but yet
The Emperor[5] has given me
A post, I hoping that he
Can make the country
Rise again like King Hsuan
Of Chou,[6] though for myself
I simply grieve that now age
And sickness take their toll.

On Asking Mr. Wu for the Second Time

Do please let your neighbor
Who lives to the west of you
Pick up the dates in front of
Your home; for she is a woman
Without food or children; only
Her condition brings her to
This necessity; surely she
Ought not to fear you, because
You are not a local man, yet
It would be good of you to try
And help her, and save her
Feelings; so do not fence off
Your fruit; heavy taxation is
The cause of her misery; the
Effect of war on the helpless
Brings us unending sorrow.

2. A lake west of the Great Wall.

3. A title of Emperor Hsüan-tsung (712–756), also known as Ming-huang or Brilliant Monarch. He was the last effective T'ang emperor. An Lu-shan's rebellion broke out at the end of his forty-four-year reign.

4. The auxiliary capital and one of China's most sacred and ancient cities.

5. Hsüan-tsung's son and successor.

6. The last effective king of the Western Chou Dynasty, he spent most of his reign (827–781 B.C.) fighting defensive wars against non-Chinese to the north.

Ch'en P'u

THE CRAFT OF FARMING

China has continually faced the problem of producing sufficient food to meet the needs of an expanding population. During the Sung era the Chinese met this challenge with reasonable success despite a dramatic increase in numbers. The following selections from a popular treatise written in 1149 by the otherwise unknown Ch'en P'u provide insights into some of the factors contributing to that agrarian success.

Questions for Analysis

1. In what way is this treatise a combination of agricultural science and Confucian learning? Can you find any Taoist elements or influences in the essay?
2. According to Ch'en P'u, what qualities set the superior farmer apart from all others?
3. Traditional Chinese agriculture has often been characterized as market gardening rather than farming. What do you think this means, and does this treatise support such a conclusion?
4. What does Ch'en P'u assume is more scarce and thus more valuable, labor or land?
5. Ch'en P'u focuses on several key elements that contributed to Sung China's success in feeding its people. What were they?

Finance and Labor

All those who engage in business should do so in accordance with their own capacity. They should refrain from careless investment and excessive greed, lest in the end they achieve nothing. . . . In the farming business, which is the most difficult business to manage, how can you afford not to calculate your financial and labor capacities carefully? Only when you are certain that you have sufficient funds and labor to assure success should you launch an enterprise. Anyone who covets more than he can manage is likely to fall into carelessness and irresponsibility . . . Thus, to procure more land is to increase trouble, not profit.

On the other hand, anyone who plans carefully, begins with good methods, and continues in the same way can reasonably expect success and does not have to rely on luck. The proverb says, "Owning a great deal of emptiness is less desirable than reaping from a narrow patch of land.". . . For the farmer who is engaged in the management of fields, the secret lies not in expanding the farmland, but in balancing finance and labor. If the farmer can achieve that, he can expect prosperity and abundance. . . .

Plowing

Early and late plowing both have their advantages. For the early rice crop, as soon as the reaping is completed, immediately plow the fields and expose the stalks to glaring sunlight. Then add manure and bury the stalks to nourish the soil. Next, plant beans, wheat, and vegetables to ripen and fertilize the soil so as to minimize the next year's labor. In addition, when the harvest is good, these extra crops can add to the yearly income. For late crops, however, do not plow until spring. Because the rice stalks are soft but tough, it is necessary to wait until they have fully decayed to plow satisfactorily. . . .

The Six Kinds of Crops

There is an order to the planting of different crops. Anyone who knows the right timing and follows the order can cultivate one thing after another, and use one to assist the others. Then there will not be a day without planting, nor a month without harvest, and money will be coming in throughout the year. How can there then be any worry about cold, hunger, or lack of funds?

Plant the nettle-hemp in the first month. Apply manure in intervals of ten days and by the fifth or sixth month it will be time for reaping. The women should take charge of knotting and spinning cloth out of the hemp.

Plant millet in the second month. It is necessary to sow the seeds sparsely and then roll cart wheels over the soil to firm it up; this will make the millet grow luxuriantly, its stalks long and its grains full. In the seventh month the millet will be harvested, easing any temporary financial difficulties.

There are two crops of oil-hemp. The early crop is planted in the third month. Rake the field to spread out the seedlings. Repeat the raking process three times a month and the hemp will grow well. It can be harvested in the seventh or the eighth month.

In the fourth month plant beans. Rake as with hemp. They will be ripe by the seventh month.

In mid-fifth month plant the late oil-hemp. Proceed as with the early crop. The ninth month will be reaping time.

After the 7th day of the seventh month, plant radishes and cabbage.

In the eighth month, before the autumn sacrifice to the god of the earth, wheat can be planted. It is advisable to apply manure and remove weeds frequently. When wheat grows from the autumn through the spring sacrifices to the god of the earth, the harvest will double and the grains will be full and solid.

The *Book of Poetry* says, "The tenth month is the time to harvest crops." You will have a large variety of crops, including millet, rice, beans, hemp, and wheat and will lack nothing needed through the year. Will you ever be concerned for want of resources? . . .

Fertilizer

At the side of the farm house, erect a compost hut. Make the eaves low to prevent the wind and rain from entering it, for when the compost is exposed to the moon and the stars, it will lose its fertility. In this hut, dig a deep pit and line it with bricks to prevent leakage. Collect waste, ashes, chaff, broken stalks, and fallen leaves and burn them in the pit; then pour manure over them to make them fertile. In this way considerable quantities of compost are acquired over time. Then, whenever sowing is to be done, sieve and discard stones and tiles, mix the fine compost with the seeds, and plant them sparsely in pinches. When the seedlings have grown tall, again sprinkle the compost and bank it up against the roots. These methods will ensure a double yield.

Some people say that when the soil is exhausted, grass and trees will not grow;

that when the *ch'i* (material force) is weak, all living things will be stunted; and that after three to five years of continuous planting, the soil of any field will be exhausted. This theory is erroneous because it fails to recognize one factor: by adding new, fertile soil, enriched with compost, the land can be reinforced in strength. If this is so, where can the alleged exhaustion come from?

WEEDING

The *Book of Poetry* says, "Root out the weeds. Where the weeds decay, there the grains will grow luxuriantly." The author of the *Record of Ritual* also remarks, "The months of mid-summer are advantageous for weeding. Weeds can fertilize the fields and improve the land." Modern farmers, ignorant of these principles, throw the weeds away. They do not know that, if mixed with soil and buried deep under the roots of rice seedlings, the weeds will eventually decay and the soil will be enriched; the harvest, as a result, will be abundant and of superior quality. . . .

CONCENTRATION

If something is thought out carefully, it will succeed; if not, it will fail; this is a universal truth. It is very rare that a person works and yet gains nothing. On the other hand, there is never any harm in trying too hard.

In farming it is especially appropriate to be concerned about what you are doing. Mencius said, "Will a farmer discard his plow when he leaves his land?" Ordinary people will become idle if they have leisure and prosperity. Only those who love farming, who behave in harmony with it, who take pleasure in talking about it and think about it all the time will manage it without a moment's negligence. For these people a day's work results in a day's gain, a year's work in a year's gain. How can they escape affluence?

A RECORD OF MUSINGS ON THE EASTERN CAPITAL

When Jurchen steppe-people overran all of northern China in the early twelfth century and established the rival Chin Dynasty (1115–1234) with its capital at Peking (modern Beijing), the Sung imperial court moved to the port city of Hang-chou, just south of the Yangtze River. From here the Sung ruled over the southern remnants of their mutilated empire until Mongols captured the city in 1276.

Southern Sung (1127–1279) presided over territory that in the age of T'ang had been a pestilential borderland. By the twelfth century, however, it was China's most densely populated region and the newest hub of Chinese culture. Its heart was Hang-chou, which was more than merely an administrative center. In the thirteenth century it was home to well over one million people, who inhabited an area of seven to eight square miles, making it the largest and richest city in the world.

The following account, composed anonymously in 1235, describes the city and its residents.

Questions for Analysis

1. Compare life in Hang-chou with that in a modern metropolis, such as New York or Los Angeles. What would a modern urban dweller recognize as familiar in this thirteenth-century city?
2. How prosperous and varied does the city's economy appear to be?
3. How can we infer that Hang-chou was often confusing for visitors?

Markets

During the morning hours, markets extend from Tranquility Gate of the palace all the way to the north and south sides of the New Boulevard. Here we find pearl, jade, talismans, exotic plants and fruits, seasonal catches from the sea, wild game — all the rarities of the world seem to be gathered here. The food and commodity markets at the Heavenly-View Gate, River Market Place, Central Square, Pa Creek, the end of Superior Lane, Tent Place, and Universal Peace Bridge are all crowded and full of traffic.

In the evening, with the exception of the square in front of the palace, the markets are as busy as during the day. The most attractive one is at Central Square, where all sorts of exquisite artifacts, instruments, containers, and hundreds of varieties of goods are for sale. In other marketplaces, sales, auctions, and exchanges go on constantly. In the wine shops and inns business also thrives. Only after the fourth drum[1] does the city gradually quiet down, but by the fifth drum, court officials already start preparing for audiences and merchants are getting ready for the morning market again. This cycle goes on all year round without respite. . . .

On the lot in front of the wall of the city building, there are always various acting troupes performing, and this usually attracts a large crowd. The same kind of activity is seen in almost any vacant lot, including those at the meat market of the Great Common, the herb market at Charcoal Bridge, the book market at the Orange Grove, the vegetable market on the east side of the city, and the rice market on the north side. There are many more interesting markets, such as the candy center at the Five Buildings, but I cannot name them all.

Commercial Establishments

In general, the capital attracts the greatest variety of goods and has the best craftsmen. For instance, the flower company at Superior Lane does a truly excellent job of flower arrangement, and its caps, hairpins, and collars are unsurpassed in craftsmanship. Some of the most famous specialties of the capital are the sweet-bean soup at the Miscellaneous Market, the pickled dates of the Ko family, the thick soup of the Kuang family at Superior Lane, the fruit at the Great Commons marketplace, the cooked meats in front of Eternal Mercy Temple, Sister Sung's fish broth at Penny Pond Gate, the juicy lungs at Flowing Gold Gate, the "lamb rice" of the Chih family at Central Square, the

1. The night was divided into five "watches," each of which was signaled by a drumbeat.

boots of the P'eng family, the fine clothing of the Hsüan family at Southern Commons, the sticky rice pastry of the Chang family, the flutes made by Ku the Fourth, and the Ch'iu family's Tatar whistles at the Great Commons.

Wine Shops

Among the various kinds of wine shops, the tea-and-food shops sell not only wine, but also various foods to go with it. However, to get seasonal delicacies not available in these shops, one should go to the inns, for they also have a menu from which one can make selections. The pastry-and-wine shops sell pastries with duckling and goose fillings, various fixings of pig tripe, intestines and blood, fish fat and spawn; but they are rather expensive. The mansion-style inns are either decorated in the same way as officials' mansions or are actually remodeled from such mansions. The garden-style inns are often located in the suburbs, though some are also situated in town. Their decoration is usually an imitation of a studio-garden combination. Among other kinds of wine shops are the straight ones which do not sell food. There are also the small retail wine shops which sell house wine as well as wine from other stores. Instead of the common emblem — a painted branching twig — used by all other winehouses, they have bamboo fences and canvas awnings. To go drinking in such a place is called "hitting the cup," meaning that a person drinks only one cup; it is therefore not the most respectable place and is unfit for polite company.

The "luxuriant inns" have prostitutes residing in them, and the wine chambers are equipped with beds. At the gate of such an inn, on top of the red gardenia lantern, there is always a cover made of bamboo leaves. Rain or shine, this cover is always present, serving as a trademark. In other inns, the girls only keep the guests company. If a guest has other wishes, he has to go to the girl's place. . . .

The expenses incurred on visiting an inn can vary widely. If you order food, but no drinks, it is called "having the lowly soup-and-stuff," and is quite inexpensive. If your order of wine and food falls within the range of 100–5000 cash,[2] it is called a small order. However, if you ask for female company, then it is most likely that the girls will order the most expensive delicacies. You are well advised to appear shrewd and experienced, so as not to be robbed. One trick, for instance, in ordering wines is to give a large order, of say, ten bottles, but open them one by one. In the end, you will probably have used only five or six bottles of the best. You can then return the rest. . . .

Teahouses

In large teahouses there are usually paintings and calligraphies by famous artists on display. In the old capital,[3] only restaurants had them, to enable their patrons to while away the time as the food was being prepared, but now it is customary for teahouses as well to display paintings and the like. . . .

Often many young men gather in teahouses to practice singing or playing

2. The basic unit of currency was the "cash," or minted coin with a square hole in the middle, which were strung together in groups of hundreds and thousands. By the late century, the government was circulating bank notes, backed by gold and silver, ranging in value from 1,000 to 100,000 cash coins.

3. Kaifeng, which was captured in 1126.

musical instruments. To give such amateur performances is called "getting posted."

A "social teahouse" is more of a community gathering place than a mere place that sells tea. Often tea-drinking is but an excuse, and people are rather generous when it comes to the tips.

There is a special kind of teahouse where pimps and gigolos hang out. Another kind is occupied by people from various trades and crafts who use them as places to hire help, buy apprentices, and conduct business. These teahouses are called "trade heads."

"Water teahouses" are in fact pleasure houses, the tea being a cover. Some youths are quite willing to spend their money there, which is called "dry tea money.". . .

Specialty Stores

The commercial area of the capital extends from the old Ch'ing River Market to the Southern Commons on the south and to the border on the north. It includes the Central Square, which is also called the Center of Five Flowers. From the north side of the Five Buildings to South Imperial Boulevard, there are more than one hundred gold, silver, and money exchanges. On the short walls in front of these stores, there are piles of gold, silver, and copper cash: these are called "the money that watches over the store." Around these exchanges there are also numerous gold and silversmiths. The pearl marts are situated between the north side of Cordial Marketplace and Southtown Marketplace. Most deals made here involve over 10,000 cash. A score of pawnshops are scattered in between, all owned by very wealthy people and dealing only in the most valuable objects.

Some famous fabric stores sell exquisite brocade and fine silk which are unsurpassed elsewhere in the country. Along the river, close to the Peaceful Ford Bridge, there are numerous fabric stores, fan shops, and lacquerware and porcelain shops. Most other cities can only boast of one special product; what makes the capital unique is that it gathers goods from all places. Furthermore, because of the large population and busy commercial traffic, there is a demand for everything. There are even shops that deal exclusively in used paper or in feathers, for instance.

Warehouses

In Liu Yung's (ca 1045) poem on Ch'ien-t'ang, we read that there were about ten thousand families residing here; but that was before the Yüan-feng reign (1078–1085). Today, having been the "temporary capital" for more than a hundred years,[4] the city has over a million households. The suburbs extend to the south, west, and north; all are densely populated and prosperous in commerce as well as in agriculture. The size of the suburbs is comparable to a small county or prefecture, and it takes several days to travel through them. This again reflects the prosperity of the capital.

In the middle of the city, enclosed by the Northern Pass Dam, is White Ocean Lake. Its water spreads over several tens of *li*. Wealthy families have built scores of warehouse complexes along this waterfront. Each of these consists of several hundred to over a thousand rooms for the

---

4. The Sung emperors never gave up hope of recovering Kaifeng and the northern part of the empire. Kaifeng thus remained the official capital, and Hang-chou was designated only "temporary capital."

storage needs of the various businesses in the capital and of traveling merchants. Because these warehouses are surrounded by water, they are not endangered by fires or thieves, and therefore they offer a special convenience.

Hustlers

Some of these hustlers are students who failed to achieve any literary distinction. Though able to read and write, and play musical instruments and chess, they are not highly skilled in any art. They end up being a kind of guide for young men from wealthy families, accompanying them in their pleasure-seeking activities. Some also serve as guides or assistants to officials on business from other parts of the country. The lowliest of these people actually engage themselves in writing and delivering invitation cards and the like for brothels. . . .

There are also professional go-betweens, nicknamed "water-treaders," whose principal targets are pleasure houses, where they flatter the wealthy young patrons, run errands for them, and help make business deals. Some gather at brothels or scenic attractions and accost the visitors. They beg for donations for "religious purposes," but in fact use the money to make a living for themselves and their families. If you pay attention to them, they will become greedy; if you ignore them, they will force themselves on you and will not stop until you give in. It requires art to deal with these people appropriately.

India

Invasions from Central Asia by a nomadic people known as the Hunas, or White Huns, precipitated the collapse of the Gupta Empire around the middle of the sixth century. Northern India was again politically fragmented, but Hindu culture, which reached maturity in the Gupta period, continued to develop vigorously. Indeed, the history of classical India is mostly the story of cultural continuity and evolution, in which political events and their chronology have little relevance. The one significant exception to this rule in the period 500–1500 was the coming of Islam, whose impact was profound and permanent.

Early in the eighth century Arabs conquered the northwest corner of the Indian subcontinent — a region known as Sind — but advanced no farther. While Hindu civilization moved to its own rhythms, its Arab neighbors traded with it and freely borrowed whatever they found useful and nonthreatening to their Islamic faith, which included India's decimal mathematics and the misnamed "Arabic" system of numeration.

Islam did not make a significant impact on Indian life until the appearance of the Turks. These recent converts to the faith, whose origins lay in Central Asia, conducted a series of raids out of Afghanistan between 986 and 1030. After a respite of about 150 years, they turned to conquest. In 1192 the army of Muhammad of Ghor crushed a coalition of Indian princes, and the whole Ganges basin lay defenseless before his generals. By 1206 the Turkish sultanate of Delhi dominated all of northern India, and by 1327 it had extended its power over virtually the entire peninsula. Although these Turkish sultans lost the south to the native Hindu state of Vijayanagar (1336–1565), they controlled India's northern and central regions until the arrival of other Muslim conquerors: first, Timur the Lame's plundering horde (from the Turkish word *ordu,* which means "camp") in 1398; then Babur, who established the great Mughal Dynasty (1526–1857), which ruled most of India until the mid-eighteenth century.

As the modern Muslim states of Pakistan and Bangladesh bear witness, Islam became an important element in Indian society, but Hinduism has prevailed as the way of life for the Indian subcontinent's majority. The coming and going of armies destroyed the vital remnants of Buddhist monasticism in mainland India, but nothing could root out the hold the many varieties of Hindu faith and practice had upon Indian life.

Dandin

TALES OF THE TEN PRINCES

India's earliest known novels date from the sixth and seventh centuries, and the first acknowledged master of this art form was Dandin, who lived around 600. His *Tales of the Ten Princes* is an ingenious interweaving of numerous subplots and stories around the central theme of the adventures of Prince Rajavahana. All these stories celebrate the three possessions Dandin believed all people hold most dear in this life: virtue, wealth, and love. As such, they illustrate the other side of the Hindu vision of the physical world. Although Hindus view all material existence as transitory and "unreal," they accept *kama,* or delight in the sensual pleasures of life, and *artha,* pursuit of riches and power, as valid human responses to the attractions of this world. Like many of the stories in this novel, the following vignette sheds light on everyday life and values.

Questions for Analysis

1. What qualities does the ideal wife possess?
2. What does a man expect to receive in an ideal marriage? What is he expected to give in return?
3. Compare this story with the view of women provided by the *Laws of Manu* (Chapter 5). Are they similar or different? Together what do they tell us about the role and status of women in Hindu society?

"In the land of the Dravidians[1] is a city called Kanci. Therein dwelt the very wealthy son of a merchant, by name Saktikumara. When he was nearly eighteen he thought: 'There's no pleasure in living without a wife or with one of bad character. Now how can I find a really good one?' So, dubious of his chance of finding wedded bliss with a woman taken at the word of others, he became a fortune-teller, and roamed the land with a measure of unhusked rice tied in the skirts of his robe; and parents, taking him for an interpreter of birthmarks, showed their daughters to him. Whenever he saw a girl of his own class, whatever her birthmarks, he would say to her: 'My dear girl, can you cook me a good meal from this measure of rice?' And so, ridiculed and rejected, he wandered from house to house.

"One day in the land of the Sibis, in a city on the banks of the Kaveri, he examined a girl who was shown to him by her nurse. She wore little jewelry, for her parents had spent their fortune, and had nothing left but their dilapidated mansion. As soon as he set eyes on her he thought: 'This girl is shapely and smooth in all her members. Not one limb is too fat or too thin, too short or too long. Her fingers are pink; her hands are marked with auspicious lines — the barleycorn, the fish, the lotus and the vase; her ankles are shapely; her feet are plump and the veins are not prominent; her thighs curve smoothly; her knees can barely be seen, for they merge into her rounded thighs; her buttocks are dimpled and round as chariot wheels; her naval is small, flat and deep; her stomach is adorned with three lines; the nipples stand out from her large breasts, which cover her whole chest; her palms are marked with signs which promise corn, wealth and sons; her nails are smooth and polished like jewels; her fingers are straight and tapering and pink; her arms curve sweetly from the shoulder, and are smoothly jointed; her slender neck is curved like a conch-shell; her lips are rounded and of even red; her pretty chin does not recede; her cheeks are round, full and firm; her eyebrows do not join above her nose, and are curved, dark and even; her nose is like a half-blown sesamum flower; her wide eyes are large and gentle and flash with three colors, black, white and brown; her brow is fair as the new moon; her curls are lovely as a mine of sapphires; her long ears are adorned doubly, with earrings and charming lotuses, hanging limply; her abundant hair is not brown, even at the tips, but long, smooth, glossy and fragrant. The character of such a girl cannot but correspond to her appearance, and my heart is fixed upon her, so I'll test her and marry her. For one regret after another is sure to fall on the heads of people who don't take precautions!' So, looking at her affectionately, he said, 'Dear girl, can you cook a good meal for me with this measure of rice?'

"Then the girl glanced at her old servant, who took the measure of rice from his hand and seated him on the veranda, which had been well sprinkled and swept, giving him water to cool his feet. Meanwhile the girl bruised the fragrant rice, dried it a little at a time in the sun, turned it repeatedly, and beat it with a hollow cane on a firm flat spot, very gently, so as to separate the grain without crushing the husk. Then she said to the nurse, 'Mother, goldsmiths can make

1. The dark-skinned people of the south, whose language differs radically from that of the northerners.

good use of these husks for polishing jewelry. Take them, and, with the coppers you get for them, buy some firewood, not too green and not too dry, a small cooking pot, and two earthen dishes.'

"When this was done she put the grains of rice in a shallow wide-mouthed, round-bellied mortar, and took a long and heavy pestle of acacia-wood, its head shod with a plate of iron. . . . With skill and grace she exerted her arms, as the grains jumped up and down in the mortar. Repeatedly she stirred them and pressed them down with her fingers; then she shook the grains in a winnowing basket to remove the beard, rinsed them several times, worshiped the hearth, and placed them in water which had been five times brought to the boil. When the rice softened, bubbled and swelled, she drew the embers of the fire together, put a lid on the cooking pot, and strained off the gruel. Then she patted the rice with a ladle and scooped it out a little at a time; and when she found that it was thoroughly cooked she put the cooking pot on one side, mouth downward. Next she damped down those sticks which were not burnt through, and when the fire was quite out she sent them to the dealers to be sold as charcoal, saying, 'With the coppers that you get for them, buy as much as you can of green vegetables, ghee,[2] curds, sesamum oil, myrobalans and tamarind.'

"When this was done she offered him a few savories. Next she put the rice-gruel in a new dish immersed in damp sand, and cooled it with the soft breeze of a palm-leaf fan. She added a little salt, and flavored it with the scent of the embers; she ground the myrobalans to a smooth powder, until they smelt like a lotus; and then, by the lips of the nurse, she invited him to take a bath. This he did, and when she too had bathed she gave him oil and myrobalans (as an unguent).

"After he had bathed he sat on a bench in the paved courtyard, which had been thoroughly sprinkled and swept. She stirred the gruel in the two dishes, which she set before him on a piece of pale green plantain leaf, cut from a tree in the courtyard. He drank it and felt rested and happy, relaxed in every limb. Next she gave him two ladlefuls of the boiled rice, served with a little ghee and condiments. She served the rest of the rice with curds, three spices (mace, cardamom and cinnamon), and fragrant and refreshing buttermilk and gruel. He enjoyed the meal to the last mouthful.

"When he asked for a drink she poured him water in a steady stream from the spout of a new pitcher — it was fragrant with incense, and smelt of fresh trumpet-flowers and the perfume of full-blown lotuses. He put the bowl to his lips, and his eyelashes sparkled with rosy drops as cool as snow; his ears delighted in the sound of the trickling water; his rough cheeks thrilled and tingled at its pleasant contact; his nostrils opened wide at its sweet fragrance; and his tongue delighted in its lovely flavor, as he drank the pure water in great gulps. Then, at his nod, the girl gave him a mouthwash in another bowl. The old woman took away the remains of his meal, and he slept awhile in his ragged cloak, on the pavement plastered with fresh cowdung.

"Wholly pleased with the girl, he married her with due rites, and took her home. Later he neglected her awhile and

2. Clarified butter.

took a mistress, but the wife treated her as a dear friend. She served her husband indefatigably, as she would a god, and never neglected her household duties; and she won the loyalty of her servants by her great kindness. In the end her husband was so enslaved by her goodness that he put the whole household in her charge, made her sole mistress of his life and person, and enjoyed the three aims of life — virtue, wealth and love. So I maintain that virtuous wives make their lords happy and virtuous."

VIKRAMA'S ADVENTURES

Early English visitors to India mistakenly believed that *sati* ("a virtuous woman"), which they mistakenly termed "suttee," referred to the practice of a widow's self-immolation on her late husband's funeral pyre rather than to the woman herself. By tradition, a widow could not remarry, for this would break her marriage vow and endanger her husband's spiritual welfare. She was expected to live out her life in severe austerity, shunned by all but her children, in the hope of remarrying her husband in some future incarnation. It seemed logical to many that a woman in such circumstances would prefer to join her deceased husband sooner rather than later and end her present life on his funeral day. Undoubtedly many satis committed suicide willingly, but probably far greater numbers were forced by their husbands' relatives to perform this final act of loyalty. Whatever their motivation, satis were common in traditional Hindu society until the British suppressed the custom during the last century.

Our text comes from an anonymous collection of stories recounting the adventures and wisdom of the semilegendary King Vikrama or Vikramaditya, who may have lived around 58 B.C. The stories were probably collected between the eleventh and thirteenth centuries.

Questions for Analysis

1. Can a widow who refuses to immolate herself achieve moksha (release)?
2. What proprietary interest do the families to which the sati belongs have in her sacrifice?
3. What impact does her act have on her husband's soul? On her own?
4. What social and psychological factors make suicide appear so attractive?
5. Compare this story with Dandin's *Tales of the Ten Princes.* Do they complement or contradict each other?

Once King Vikrama, attended by all his vassal princes, had ascended his throne. At this time a certain magician came in, and blessing him with the words "Live forever!" said: "Sire, you are skilled in all the arts; many magicians have come into your presence and exhibited their tricks. So today be so good as to behold an exhibition of my dexterity." The king said: "I have not time now; it is the time to bathe and eat. Tomorrow I will behold it." So on the morrow the juggler came into the king's assembly as a stately man, with a mighty beard and glorious countenance, holding a sword in his hand, and accompanied by a lovely woman; and he bowed to the king. Then the ministers who were present, seeing the stately man, were astonished, and asked: "O hero, who are you, and whence do you come?" He said: "I am a servant of Great Indra; I was cursed once by my lord, and was cast down to earth; and now I dwell here. And this is my wife. Today a great battle has begun between the gods and the Daityas (demons), so I am going thither. This King Vikramaditya treats other men's wives as his sisters, so before going to the battle I wish to leave my wife with him." Hearing this the king also was greatly amazed. And the man left his wife with the king and delivered her over to him, and sword in hand flew up into heaven. Then a great and terrible shouting was heard in the sky: "Ho there, kill them, kill them, smite them, smite them!" were the words they heard. And all the people who sat in the court, with upturned faces, gazed in amazement. After this, when a moment had passed by, one of the man's arms, holding his sword and stained with blood, fell from the sky into the king's assembly. Then all the people, seeing it, said: "Ah, this great hero has been killed in battle by his opponents; his sword and one arm have fallen." While the people who sat in the court were even saying this, again his head fell also; and then his trunk fell too. And seeing this his wife said: "Sire, my husband, fighting on the field of battle, has been slain by the enemy. His head, his arm, his sword, and his trunk have fallen down here. So, that this my beloved may not be wooed by the heavenly nymphs, I will go to where he is. Let fire be provided for me." Hearing her words the king said: "My daughter, why will you enter the fire? I will guard you even as my own daughter; preserve your body." She said: "Sire, what is this you say? My lord, for whom this body of mine exists, has been slain on the battlefield by his foes. Now for whose sake shall I preserve this body? Moreover, you should not say this, since even fools know that wives should follow their husbands. For thus it is said:

> **1.** Moonlight goes with the moon, the lightning clings to the cloud, and women follow their husbands; even fools know this.

And so, as the learned tradition has it:

> **2.** The wife who enters into the fire when her husband dies, imitating Arundhati (a star, regarded as the wife of one of the 'Seven Rishis' [the Dipper], and as a typical faithful spouse) in her behavior, enjoys bliss in heaven.
>
> **3.** Until a wife burns herself in the fire after the death of her husband, so long that woman can in no way be (permanently) freed from the body.
>
> **4.** A woman who follows after her husband shall surely purify three families: her mother's, her father's, and that into which she was given (in marriage).

And so:

> **5.** Three and a half crores (a crore is 10,000,000) is the number of the hairs on

the human body; so many years shall a wife who follows her husband dwell in heaven.

6. As a snake-charmer powerfully draws a snake out of a hole, so a wife draws her husband upward (by burning herself) and enjoys bliss with him.

7. A wife who abides by the law of righteousness (in burning herself) saves her husband, whether he be good or wicked; yes, even if he be guilty of all crimes.

Furthermore, O king, a woman who is bereft of her husband has no use for her life. And it is said:

8. What profit is there in the life of a wretched woman who has lost her husband? Her body is as useless as a banyan tree in a cemetery.

9. Surely father, brother, and son measure their gifts; what woman would not honor her husband, who gives without measure?

Moreover:

10. Though a woman be surrounded by kinsfolk, though she have many sons, and be endowed with excellent qualities, she is miserable, poor wretched creature, when deprived of her husband.

And so:

11. What shall a widow do with perfumes, garlands, and incense, or with manifold ornaments, or garments and couches of ease?

12. A lute does not sound without strings, a wagon does not go without wheels, and a wife does not obtain happiness without her husband, not even with a hundred kinsfolk.

13. Woman's highest refuge is her husband, even if he be poor, vicious, old, infirm, crippled, outcast, and stingy.

14. There is no kinsman, no friend, no protector, no refuge for a woman like her husband.

15. There is no other misery for women like widowhood. Happy is she among women who dies before her husband.

Thus speaking she fell at the king's feet, begging that a fire be provided for her. And when the king heard her words, his heart being tender with genuine compassion, he caused a pyre to be erected of sandalwood and the like, and gave her leave. So she took leave of the king, and in his presence entered the fire together with her husband's body.

THE DEEDS OF SULTAN FIRUZ SHAH

Firuz Shah Tughluq, who reigned from 1351 to 1388, enjoyed a reputation as the most humane and generous of the sultans of Delhi. Toward the end of his life he prepared an account of those accomplishments in which he took the greatest pride. This sincere and pious ruler little realized he had presided over the sultanate's last period of prosperity. Ten years to the day after Firuz Shah's death, Timur the Lame was encamped on the Indus, preparing to invade the heartland of India.

Questions for Analysis

1. What did Firuz Shah see as his responsibilities toward Muslims?
2. What did he see as his responsibility to his Hindu subjects?
3. What did he believe were his greatest responsibilities and achievements?
4. Compare Firuz Shah's policies with those of Asoka (Chapter 5). On what points would they agree and disagree?

Praises without end, and infinite thanks to that merciful Creator who gave to me his poor abject creature Firuz. . . . His impulse for the maintenance of the laws of His religion, for the repression of heresy, the prevention of crime, and the prohibition of things forbidden; who gave me also a disposition for discharging my lawful duties and my moral obligations. My desire is that, to the best of my human power, I should recount and pay my thanks for the many blessings He has bestowed upon me, so that I may be found among the number of His grateful servants. First I would praise Him because when irreligion and sins opposed to the Law prevailed in Hindustan,[1] and mens' habits and dispositions were inclined towards them, and were averse to the restraints of religion, He inspired me His humble servant with an earnest desire to repress irreligion and wickedness, so that I was able to labor diligently until with His blessing the vanities of the world, and things repugnant to religion, were set aside, and the true was distinguished from the false.

In the reigns of former kings[2] the blood of many Muslims had been shed, and many varieties of torture employed. Amputation of hands and feet, ears and noses; tearing out the eyes, pouring molten lead into the throat, crushing the bones of the hands and feet with mallets, burning the body with fire, driving iron nails into the hands, feet, and bosom, cutting the sinews, sawing men asunder; these and many similar tortures were practiced. The great and merciful God made me, His servant, hope and seek for His mercy by devoting myself to prevent the unlawful killing of Muslims, and the infliction of any kind of torture upon them or upon any men. . . .

By God's help I determined that the lives of Muslims and true believers should be in perfect immunity, and whoever transgressed the Law should receive the punishment prescribed by the book[3] and the decrees of judges. . . .

The sect of Shi'as . . . had endeavored to make proselytes.[4] They wrote treatises and books, and gave instruction and lectures upon the tenets of their sect, and traduced and reviled the first chiefs of our religion (on whom be the peace of God!). I seized them all and I convicted them of their errors and perversions. On the most

1. The north-central region of India inhabited largely by Hindus.

2. Muhammad ben Tughluq (1325–1351), his predecessor, had been noted for his cruelty.

3. The Qur'an.

4. Converts.

zealous I inflicted punishment, and the rest I visited with censure and threats of public punishment. Their books I burnt in public, and so by the grace of God the influence of this sect was entirely suppressed. . . .

The Hindus and idol-worshipers had agreed to pay the money for toleration, and had consented to the poll tax,[5] in return for which they and their families enjoyed security. These people now erected new idol temples[6] in the city and the environs in opposition to the Law of the Prophet which declares that such temples are not to be tolerated. Under Divine guidance I destroyed these edifices, and I killed those leaders of infidelity who seduced others into error, and the lower orders I subjected to stripes and chastisement, until this abuse was entirely abolished. . . . I forbad the infliction of any severe punishment on the Hindus in general, but I destroyed their idol temples, and instead thereof raised mosques. . . . Where infidels and idolaters worshiped idols, Muslims now, by God's mercy, perform their devotions to the true God. Praises of God and the summons to prayer are now heard there, and that place which was formerly the home of infidels has become the habitation of the faithful, who there repeat their creed and offer up their praises to God. . . .

In former times it had been the custom to wear ornamented garments, and men received robes as tokens of honor from kings' courts. Figures and devices were painted and displayed on saddles, bridles, and collars, on censers, on goblets and cups, and flagons, on dishes and ewers, in tents, on curtains and on chairs, and upon all articles and utensils. Under Divine guidance and favor I ordered all pictures and portraits to be removed from these things, and that such articles only should be made as are approved and recognized by the Law. Those pictures and portraits which were painted on the doors and walls of palaces I ordered to be effaced.[7]

Formerly the garments of great men were generally made of silk and gold brocades, beautiful but unlawful. Under Divine guidance I ordered that such garments should be worn as are approved by the Law of the Prophet, and that choice should be made of such trimmings of gold brocade, embroidery, or braiding as did not exceed four inches in breadth. Whatever was unlawful and forbidden by, or opposed to, the Law was set aside.

Among the gifts which God bestowed upon me, His humble servant, was a desire to erect public buildings. So I built many mosques and colleges and monasteries, that the learned and the elders, the devout and the holy, might worship God in these edifices, and aid the kind builder with their prayers. The digging of canals, the planting of trees, and the endowing with lands are in accordance with the directions of the Law. The learned doctors of the Law of Islam have many troubles; of this there is no doubt. I settled allowances upon them in proportion to their necessary expenses, so that they might regularly receive the income. . . .

For the benefit of travelers and pilgrims resorting to the tombs of illustrious kings and celebrated saints, and for providing the things necessary in these holy places, I confirmed and gave effect to the grants

5. The jizya, a tax paid by all subject non-Muslims as a token of their submission.

6. Presumably, previously constructed non-Muslim places of worship were tolerated.

7. Most Muslims regard the representation of human or animal figures as blasphemy.

of villages, lands, and other endowments which had been conferred upon them in olden times. In those cases where no endowment or provision has been settled, I made an endowment, so that these establishments might for ever be secure of an income, to afford comfort to travelers and wayfarers, to holy men and learned men. May they remember those (ancient benefactors) and me in their prayers.

I was enabled by God's help to build a . . . Hospital, for the benefit of every one of high or low degree, who was suddenly attacked by illness and overcome by suffering. Physicians attend there to ascertain the disease, to look after the cure, to regulate the diet, and to administer medicine. The cost of the medicines and the food is defrayed from my endowments. All sick persons, residents and travelers, gentle and simple, bond and free, resort thither; their maladies are treated, and, under God's blessing, they are cured. . . .

I encouraged my infidel subjects to embrace the religion of the prophet, and I proclaimed that every one who repeated the creed[8] and became a Muslim should be exempt from the jizya, or poll-tax. Information of this came to the ears of the people at large, and great numbers of Hindus presented themselves, and were admitted to the honor of Islam. Thus they came forward day by day from every quarter, and, adopting the faith, were exonerated from the jizya, and were favored with presents and honors. . . .

Whenever a person had completed the natural term of life and had become full of years, after providing for his support, I advised and admonished him to direct his thoughts to making preparation for the life to come, and to repent of all things which he had done contrary to the Law and religion in his youth; to wean his affections from this world, and to fix them on the next. . . .

My object in writing this book has been to express my gratitude to the All-bountiful God for the many and various blessings He has bestowed upon me. Secondly, that men who desire to be good and prosperous may read this and learn what is the proper course. There is this concise maxim, by observing which, a man may obtain God's guidance: Men will be judged according to their works, and rewarded for the good that they have done.

The Middle East

The Middle East stretches westward from the mountainous northwestern border of India, through Persia, Mesopotamia, Syria-Palestine, and the Arabian and Anatolian peninsulas to Egypt in the northeastern corner of Africa. It largely encompasses that area loosely defined as Southwest Asia.

Of all the significant developments that took place in the Middle East during this thousand-year period, the two most important were the rise and spread of Islam and

8. "There is no God but God, and Muhammad is the Prophet of God."

the arrival of various invaders after A.D. 1000. By approximately A.D. 750 Islam was firmly in control of the entire Middle East, except for the Anatolian peninsula, which remained the heart of the East Roman or Byzantine Empire until late in the eleventh century, when Muslim Turkish forces began to transform this land into Turkey. Seljuk and Ottoman Turks, European crusaders, Mongols, and the armies of Timur the Lame would invade and contest the Middle East for much of the period from 1000 to 1500.

Around the early sixteenth century a clear pattern emerged. Most of Europe's Christian crusaders had been expelled from the Levant (the eastern Mediterranean), and the Mongol empire was only a fading memory. Two Turkish Muslim empires dominated the entire Middle East — the Shi'ite Safavids of Persia and the Sunni Ottomans, who ruled everywhere else and were even driving deeply into Europe's Balkan region. Although these two empires would quarrel viciously for control of Islam, and Sunnis and Shi'ites would continue to shed one another's blood, a Turkish-dominated Middle East was secure for the foreseeable future. European attempts to counter the Turkish menace by launching new crusades in the eastern Mediterranean generally proved feeble, and the Ottomans' and Safavids' pastoral cousins on the steppes of Central Asia finally ceased to be a major threat to the stability of Eurasia's civilizations.

Al-Yaqubi

BOOK OF COUNTRIES

In 762 the Abbasid caliph al-Mansur shifted the capital of Islam east from Damascus in Syria to Baghdad in Iraq. The site was advantageous, because it lay on a navigable point of the Tigris River and was close to a canal leading to the Euphrates. Although Ummayad loyalists in Spain, as well as most Shi'ites and other sectarians, refused to acknowledge the leadership of Baghdad's caliphs, this previously minor Christian village soon became one of Asia's great metropolises and the focal point of an Islamic world that stretched from North Africa to the borders of China and India. Its official name was *Madinat as-Salam* — City of Peace.

In the following selection the ninth-century Arab-Egyptian historian and geographer al-Yaqubi (d. 897) describes the city's foundation.

Questions for Analysis

1. Why was Baghdad so prosperous in the ninth century?
2. What factors influenced al-Mansur to locate his capital in Baghdad? Can you discover a hint in this account of any political reason behind his decision?

3. How does the selection of Baghdad reflect Islam's new position as a world religion and culture?
4. Consider Benjamin of Tudela's account of Baghdad (Chapter 6). Although he and al-Yaqubi lived in different centuries and viewed the city from two different cultural perspectives, how do their descriptions of the city complement and support one another?

I begin with Iraq only because it is the center of this world, the navel of the earth, and I mention Baghdad first because it is the center of Iraq, the greatest city, which has no peer in the east or the west of the world in extent, size, prosperity, abundance of water, or health of climate, and because it is inhabited by all kinds of people, town-dwellers and country-dwellers. To it they come from all countries, far and near, and people from every side have preferred Baghdad to their own homelands. There is no country, the peoples of which have not their own quarter and their own trading and financial arrangements. In it there is gathered that which does not exist in any other city in the world. On its flanks flow two great rivers, the Tigris and the Euphrates, and thus goods and foodstuffs come to it by land and by water with the greatest ease, so that every kind of merchandise is completely available, from east and west, from Muslim and non-Muslim lands. Goods are brought from India, Sind,[1] China, Tibet, the lands of the Turks, the Daylam,[2] the Khazars,[3] the Ethiopians,[4] and others to such an extent that the products of the countries are more plentiful in Baghdad than in the countries from which they come. They can be procured so readily and so certainly that it is as if all the good things of the world are sent there, all the treasures of the earth assembled there, and all the blessings of creation perfected there.

Furthermore, Baghdad is the city of the Hashimites,[5] the home of their reign, the seat of their sovereignty, where no one appeared before them and no kings but they have dwelt. Also, my own forbears have lived there, and one of them was governor of the city.

Its name is famous, and its fame widespread. Iraq is indeed the center of the world, for in accordance with the consensus of the astronomers recorded in the writings of ancient scholars, it is in the fourth climate, which is the middle climate where the temperature is regular at all times and seasons. It is very hot in the summer, very cold in the winter, and temperate in autumn and in spring. The passage from autumn to winter and from

1. The Indus Valley.

2. A region north of Iraq along the western shores of the Caspian Sea.

3. A Turkic people who had a kingdom in the region just north of the Black Sea from about 600 to around 1200.

4. A people of east Africa.

5. Muhammad's clan of Hashim, to which the Abbasids traced their lineage.

spring to summer is gradual and imperceptible, and the succession of the seasons is regular. So, the weather is temperate, the soil is rich, the water is sweet, the trees are thriving, the fruit luscious, the seeds are fertile, good things are abundant, and springs are easily found. Because of the temperate weather and rich soil and sweet water, the character of the inhabitants is good, their faces bright, and their minds untrammeled. The people excel in knowledge, understanding, letters, manners, insight, discernment, skill in commerce and crafts, cleverness in every argument, proficiency in every calling, and mastery of every craft. There is none more learned than their scholars, better informed than their traditionists, more cogent than their theologians, more perspicuous than their grammarians, more accurate than their readers, more skillful than their physicians, more melodious than their singers, more delicate than their craftsmen, more literate than their scribes, more lucid than their logicians, more devoted than their worshipers, more pious than their ascetics, more juridical than their judges, more eloquent than their preachers, more poetic than their poets, and more reckless than their rakes.

In ancient days, that is to say in the time of the Chosroes[6] and the Persians, Baghdad was not a city, but only a village. . . . At that time there was nothing in Baghdad but a convent situated at a place called Qarn al-Sarat, at the confluence of the Sarat and the Tigris. This convent is called al-Dayr al-'Atiq (the ancient convent) and is still standing at the present time. It is the residence of the Catholicos, the head of the Nestorian Christians.[7]

Nor does Baghdad figure in the wars of the Arabs at the time of the advent of Islam, since the Arabs founded Basra and Kufa.[8]. . . The Arabs settled down in these two places, but the important people, the notables, and the rich merchants moved to Baghdad.

The Umayyads lived in Syria and did not stay in Iraq.[9]. . .

Then the Caliphate came to the descendants of the paternal uncle of the Apostle of God, may God bless and save him and also his family, the line of 'Abbas ibn 'Abd al-Muttalib. Thanks to clear discernment, sound intelligence, and perfect judgment, they saw the merits of Iraq, its magnificence, spaciousness, and central situation. They saw that it was not like Syria, with its pestilential air, narrow houses, rugged soil, constant diseases, and uncouth people; nor was it like Egypt, with changeable weather and many plagues, situated between a damp and fetid river, full of unhealthy mists that engender disease and spoil food, and the dry, bare mountains, so dry and salty and bad that no plant can grow nor any spring appear; nor like Ifriqiya,[10] far from the peninsula of Islam and from the holy house of God, with uncouth people and many foes; nor like Armenia,[11] remote, cold and icy, barren, and surrounded by enemies; nor like the districts of the Jabal, harsh, rough, and snow-

6. Chosroes, or Khusro I and II, two sixth- and seventh-century monarchs of Sassanid Persia.

7. See Chapter 11, pages 345-352.

8. Originally as fortified outposts.

9. The Umayyads (661–750) ruled from Damascus in Syria.

10. North Africa.

11. A region in the Caucasus Mountains between the Black and Caspian seas.

covered, the abode of the hard-hearted Kurds;[12] nor like the land of Khurasan,[13] stretching to the east, surrounded on every side by rabid and war-like enemies; nor like the Hijaz[14] where life is hard and means are few and the people's food comes from elsewhere, as Almighty God warned us in His book, through His friend Ibrahim, who said, "O Lord, I have given to my descendants as dwelling a valley without tillage" (Qur'an, xiv, 40); nor like Tibet, where, because of the foul air and food, the people are discolored, with stunted bodies and tufty hair.

When they understood that Iraq was the best of countries, the 'Abbasids decided to settle there. In the first instance the Commander of the Faithful, Abu'l-'Abbas,[15]. . . stayed in Kufa. Then he moved to Anbar and built a city on the banks of the Euphrates which he called Hashimiyya.[16] Abu'l-'Abbas, may God be pleased with him, died before the building of the city was completed.

Then, when Abu Ja'far al-Mansur[17] succeeded to the Caliphate, he founded a new city between Kufa and Hira, which he also called Hashimiyya. He stayed there for a while, until the time when he decided to send his son, Muhammad al-Mahdi,[18] to fight the Slavs in the year 140 (757–758). He then came to Baghdad and stopped there, and asked, "What is the name of this place?" They answered, "Baghdad." "By God," said the Caliph, "this is indeed the city which my father Muhammad ibn 'Ali told me I must build, in which I must live, and in which my descendants after me will live. Kings were unaware of it before and since Islam, until God's plans for me and orders to me are accomplished. Thus, the traditions will be verified and the signs and proofs be manifest. Indeed, this island between the Tigris in the east and the Euphrates in the west is a marketplace for the world. All the ships that come up the Tigris . . . will anchor here; wares brought on ships down the Tigris from Mosul,[19] Diyar-Rabi'a,[20] Adharbayjan,[21] and Armenia, and along the Euphrates from Diyar-Mudar,[22] Raqqa,[23] Syria, the border marches, Egypt, and North Africa, will be brought and unloaded here. It will be the highway for the people of the Jabal, Isfahan,[24] and the districts of Khurasan. Praise be to God who preserved it for me and caused all those who came before me to neglect it. By God, I shall build it. Then I shall dwell in it as long as I live, and my descendants shall dwell in it after me. It will surely be the most flourishing city in the world."

---

12. A fiercely independent Indo-European people who inhabit the Jabal — literally "the mountains" — the region of modern eastern Turkey and western Iraq.

13. A region east of the Caspian Sea.

14. The western region of Arabia where Mecca and Medina are located.

15. Caliph from 750 to 754.

16. The city of the Hashimites. It was more of a camp than a city.

17. Caliph from 754 to 775.

18. Caliph from 775 to 785.

19. Al-Mawsil, a city on the Tigris to the northwest of Baghdad.

20. The province in which Mosul, or al-Mawsil, is located.

21. Modern Azerbaidzhan, a republic in the Soviet Union along the southwest shores of the Caspian Sea.

22. A province in Mesopotamia on the Euphrates.

23. A city in northwest Iraq.

24. A city in Iran, therefore east of Baghdad.

Al-Jahiz

THE MERITS OF THE TURKS AND OF THE IMPERIAL ARMY AS A WHOLE

By the mid-ninth century Turkish officers were playing an important role in the selection of caliphs. From that point on, the caliphs and their ministers became increasingly dependent on various Turkish elements in the army, and it was almost an anticlimax when the leader of the Seljuk Turks, Tughril-Beg, entered Baghdad on December 19, 1055, to be recognized formally as *sultan* (governor) and have his name mentioned in Friday prayers after that of the caliph. Civil and military authority was now in the hands of Turkish sultans, and the caliph retained only religious and ceremonial functions. Under the Seljuks, Islam quickly expanded into Byzantine Anatolia, precipitating a Western Christian response — the crusades.

Two centuries earlier al-Jahiz of Basra in Persia (776–869), one of the most popular and gifted essayists of his day and a person of basically African lineage, wrote a study of the Turks in which he attempted to place these recent converts to Islam in a favorable light. Many cultivated Arabs and Persians despised these "barbarians" from Central Asia and resented their power. Al-Jahiz, always a voice of reason and moderation and a man who seems to have suffered some prejudice himself because of his dark skin, attempted to counter those attitudes.

Questions for Analysis

1. What does al-Jahiz's essay tell us about the equestrian and military qualities of the Turks and, by extension, of other pastoral people from Inner Asia? Does this portrait help explain the role played in Eurasian history by the horse nomads?
2. Compare this account with Ammianus Marcellinus's fourth-century description of the Huns (Chapter 5). Are the similarities or differences more striking? What conclusions do you draw from your answer?
3. How, according to al-Jahiz, do the Turks resemble the Arabs of the Prophet's day?
4. What special value do the Turks offer Muslim society?
5. Does al-Jahiz believe the Turks are capable of being "civilized" and becoming more than just warriors?
6. How does this essay reveal the cosmopolitan perspective of ninth-century Persia?

The Turk as a Horseman

A Kharijite[1] at close quarters relies entirely on his lance. But the Turks are as good as the Kharijites with the lance, and in addition, if a thousand of their horsemen are hard-pressed they will loose all their arrows in a single volley and bring down a thousand enemy horsemen. No body of men can stand up against such a test.

Neither the Kharijites nor the Bedouins[2] are famous for their prowess as mounted bowmen. But the Turk will hit from his saddle an animal, a bird, a target, a man, a couching animal, a marker post or a bird of prey stooping on its quarry. His horse may be exhausted from being galloped and reined in, wheeled to right and left, and mounted and dismounted: but he himself goes on shooting, loosing ten arrows before the Kharijite has let fly one. He gallops his horse up a hillside or down a gully faster than the Kharijite can make his go on the flat.

The Turk has two pairs of eyes, one at the front and the other at the back of his head. . . .

They train their horsemen to carry two or even three bows, and spare bowstrings in proportion. Thus in the hour of battle the Turk has on him everything needful for himself, his weapon and the care of his steed. As for their ability to stand trotting, sustained galloping, long night rides and cross-country journeys, it is truly extraordinary. In the first place the Kharijite's horse has not the staying-power of the Turk's pony; and the Kharijite has no more than a horseman's knowledge of how to look after his mount. The Turk, however, is more experienced than a professional farrier,[3] and better than a trainer at getting what he wants from his pony. For it was he who brought it into the world and reared it from a foal; it comes when he calls it, and follows behind him when he runs. . . .

If the Turk's daily life were to be reckoned up in detail, he would be found to spend more time in the saddle than on the ground.

The Turk sometimes rides a stallion, sometimes a brood mare. Whether he is going to war, on a journey, out hunting or on any other errand, the brood mare follows behind with her foals. If he gets tired of hunting the enemy he hunts waterfowl. If he gets hungry, jogging up and down in the saddle, he has only to lay hands on one of his animals. If he gets thirsty, he milks one of his brood mares. If he needs to rest his mount, he vaults on to another without so much as putting his feet to the ground.

Of all living creatures he is the only one whose body can adapt itself to eating nothing but meat. As for his steed, leaves and shoots are all it needs; he gives it no shelter from the sun and no covering against the cold.

As regards ability to stand trotting, if the stamina of the border fighters, the posthorse outriders, the Kharijites and the eunuchs were all combined in one man, they would not equal a Turk.

The Turk demands so much of his mount that only the toughest of his horses is equal to the task; even one that he had ridden to exhaustion, so as to be useless for his expeditions, would outdo a Kharijite's horse in staying-power, and no Tukhari pony could compare with it.

The Turk is at one and the same time

---

1. The earliest Muslim sect to break off from the main body of Islam, the Kharijites were noted as fierce warriors.

2. Arab nomads of Arabia, North Africa, and the Levant.

3. A blacksmith.

herdsman, groom, trainer, horse-dealer, farrier and rider: in short, a one-man team.

When the Turk travels with horsemen of other races, he covers twenty miles to their ten, leaving them and circling around to right and left, up on to the high ground and down to the bottom of the gullies, and shooting all the while at anything that runs, crawls, flies or stands still. The Turk never travels like the rest of the band, and never rides straight ahead. On a long, hard ride, when it is noon and the halting-place is still afar off, all are silent, oppressed with fatigue and overwhelmed with weariness. Their misery leaves no room for conversation. Everything round them crackles in the intense heat, or perhaps is frozen hard. As the journey drags on, even the toughest and most resolute begin to wish that the ground would open under their feet. At the sight of a mirage or a marker post on a ridge they are transported with joy, supposing it to be the halting-place. When at last they reach it, the horsemen all drop from the saddle and stagger about bandy-legged like children who have been given an enema, groaning like sick men, yawning to refresh themselves and stretching luxuriously to overcome their stiffness. But your Turk, though he has covered twice the distance and dislocated his shoulders with shooting, has only to catch sight of a gazelle or an onager near the halting-place, or put up a fox or a hare, and he is off again at a gallop as though he had only just mounted. It might have been someone else who had done that long ride and endured all that weariness.

At a gully the band bunches together at the bridge or the best crossing-place; but the Turk, digging his heels into his pony, is already going up the other side like a shooting star. If there is a steep rise, he leaves the track and scrambles straight up the hillside, going where even the ibex[4] cannot go. To see him scaling such slopes anyone would think he was recklessly risking his life: but if that were so he would not last long, for he is always doing it. . . .

National Characteristics

Know that every nation, people, generation or tribe that shows itself outstanding in craftsmanship or pre-eminent in eloquence, the various branches of learning, the establishment of empires or the art of war, only attains the peak of perfection because God has steered it in that direction and given it the means and the special aptitudes appropriate to those activities. Peoples of varying habits of thought, different opinions and dissimilar characters cannot attain perfection unless they fulfill the conditions needed to carry on an activity, and have a natural aptitude for it. Good examples are the Chinese in craftsmanship, the Greeks in philosophy and literature, the Arabs in fields that we mean to deal with in their proper place . . . and the Turks in the art of war. . . .

The Chinese for their part are specialists in smelting, casting and metalworking, in fine colors, in sculpture, weaving and drawing; they are very skillful with their hands, whatever the medium, the technique or the cost of the materials. The Greeks are theoreticians rather than practitioners, while the Chinese are practitioners rather than theoreticians; the former are thinkers, the latter doers.

The Arabs, again, were not merchants, artisans, physicians, farmers — for that would have degraded them —, mathematicians or fruit-farmers — for they wished

4. An Asiatic mountain goat.

to escape the humiliation of the tax; nor were they out to earn or amass money, hoard possessions or lay hands on other people's; they were not of those who make their living with a pair of scales . . . they were not poor enough to be indifferent to learning, pursued neither wealth, that breeds foolishness, nor good fortune, that begets apathy, and never tolerated humiliation, which was dishonor and death to their souls. They dwelt in the plains, and grew up in contemplation of the desert. They knew neither damp nor rising mist, neither fog nor foul air, nor a horizon bounded by walls. When these keen minds and clear brains turned to poetry, fine language, eloquence and oratory, to physiognomy and astrology, genealogy, navigation by the stars and by marks on the ground . . . to horse-breeding, weaponry and engines of war, to memorizing all that they heard, pondering on everything that caught their attention and discriminating between the glories and the shames of their tribes, they achieved perfection beyond the wildest dreams. Certain of these activities broadened their minds and exalted their aspirations, so that of all nations they are now the most glorious and the most given to recalling their past splendors.

It is the same with the Turks who dwell in tents in the desert and keep herds: they are the Bedouins of the non-Arabs. . . . Uninterested in craftsmanship or commerce, medicine, geometry, fruit-farming, building, digging canals or collecting taxes, they care only about raiding, hunting, horsemanship, skirmishing with rival chieftains, taking booty and invading other countries. Their efforts are all directed towards these activities, and they devote all their energies to these occupations. In this way they have acquired a mastery of these skills, which for them take the place of craftsmanship and commerce and constitute their only pleasure, their glory and the subject of all their conversation. Thus have they become in the realm of warfare what the Greeks are in philosophy, the Chinese in craftsmanship, and the Arabs in the fields we have enumerated.

C H A P T E R

10

Western Europe

The story of the birth of a new civilization on the frontiers of western Eurasia — a civilization variously termed "the Medieval West," or "the First Europe" — begins at the close of the fourth century A.D., when Rome, by then a Christian state, still ruled an empire stretching from the Atlantic Ocean to Mesopotamia, from the Scottish Lowlands to the Sahara. In the centuries that immediately followed, this Mediterranean-centered ecumene underwent a transformation. Like several civilizations to the east, most notably Gupta India and Han China, the Roman Empire entered a time of troubles. Unlike those Eastern cultures, the Roman world changed irrevocably. Centuries of upheaval, caused by internal weaknesses and invasions by various fringe peoples, resulted in radical mutations of its political, social, and cultural forms. By about A.D. 700 the empire and its civilization had passed away, succeeded by three heirs — Byzantine Christendom, Islam, and Latin-Christian Europe.

Of the three, the Latin West seemed the least promising. It had been the civilization most severely beset by late antiquity's economic and political problems and was fast becoming a society whose apparent weakness and low level of culture stood in stark contrast to the magnificence of Byzantium and Islam. While its two more powerful siblings jockeyed for power in the Mediterranean, Latin Christendom had to look northward, beyond the Alps, to still untamed lands and recently converted peoples. The eighth-century marriage of convenience between the Roman Church and the Franks, who received official recognition from Europe's leading spiritual power in return for offering the papacy military protection, shows that the West was following a path of historical development that differed radically from those of its eastern coheirs.

Yet, as backward as this society appears to have been during the Early Middle Ages (500–1000), these centuries were proving to be the formative period of a tenacious and revolutionary civilization, whose technology, ideas, and institutions would, in time, transform the world. All of this lay in the distant future, but by the eleventh century Christian Europe was ready to take its place as a major power in western Eurasia. A dramatic turnaround in Europe's economy, a rise in its general level of political stability, and a new religious vitality provided the necessary impetus for the Age of the Crusades. This first period of Western European overseas expansion resulted in crusader colonial states in the Holy Land by 1100.

The twelfth and thirteenth centuries were a period of overall growth and prosperity for Latin Europe. Among other developments, this age witnessed the emergence of numerous new towns and cities, which served as centers of trade, industry, learning, and religious change. Those who dwelt in these urban settings, the bourgeoisie, proved to be one of the West's major dynamic forces, despite their relatively small numbers. As towns of about 3,000 to 6,000 inhabitants and cities of perhaps five times that size on average sprang up throughout Europe, often in areas that had recently been forest or marginal land, churches and civic buildings proliferated. Toward the end of the twelfth century a new form of urban ecclesiastical architecture developed in the region around Paris that symbolized the new importance of Europe's urban centers and the many forces that drove this new civilization. This was the Gothic cathedral.

The essence of Gothic construction is the opposition of contrary forces to create a soaring edifice that seems to defy gravity. Thrust and counterthrust, particularly through use of a serendipitous architectural device known as the flying buttress, result in a complex structure whose sheer beauty and size reflect the faith of the society that created it. Such an achievement is fitting for a civilization that itself was the product of many creative tensions, and it is these tensions that explain the revolutionary changes taking place in Europe and Europeans' great adaptability for change.

Tension lay at the heart of Europe's new dynamism. There was the tension of political pluralism. Not only was Europe divided into a number of separate states, but within these states different orders competed for supremacy or independence. Nobility struggled with monarchy, and townspeople sought freedom from feudal constraints. One result was the drafting of *Magna Carta*, the "Great Charter" of English liberties, in 1215. Another was the emergence of powerful urban centers, such as Milan and Paris. There were the tensions between Church and State, as both popes and kings vied for control over one another and the loyalties of all Europeans, Christian and non-Christian. Because neither priests nor secular rulers were ever able to dominate the other totally, their subjects' opportunities for choice and freedom multiplied substantially. In the field of human inquiry and knowledge there was a similar fruitful stand-off. As heirs of both the mystical religious traditions of the Middle East and Hellenic philosophy, the West's teachers, intellectuals, and visionaries had to seek a balance between faith and reason.

On a more mundane level, Western Europeans had to accommodate their warrior ethic and spirit of adventure to an increasingly complex society's need for internal peace and stability. One answer was to export violence in the forms of crusades and frontier expansion. As Eurasia's "Wild West," Europe was a frontier society, and its people struggled against an often hostile environment. The drive to clear forests, drain swamps, and "civilize" the fringe peoples on their borders by converting them to Christianity left Europeans with the notion that the world is a place for humans to tame, settle, and remake in their own image. Because this European frontier was land-rich and people-poor, Europeans became fascinated by technology and every form of labor-saving device. Tools developed in China and elsewhere, particularly the stirrup and horse collar, water and windmills, the compass, gunpowder, and the printing press, often became instruments of radical change in the hands of Westerners.

Europe's first great age of cultural flowering is known as the High Middle Ages (1000–1300). Without ever losing their adaptability and readiness for change, Europeans fashioned in these three centuries a "Gothic" equilibrium out of their society's many contradictory forces. By 1300, however, this synthesis appeared to be in danger of total disintegration. Internal stresses, such as war, rebellion, and religious dissent, combined with natural disasters like climatic change and the Black Death (1347–1350), produced an age of crisis in the fourteenth and fifteenth centuries.

European civilization, however, was neither destroyed nor fundamentally transformed during these centuries. Most of medieval Europe's core ideas and institutions turned out to be amazingly resilient, and those that were decaying, such as the ideal of a united Christian commonwealth, were giving way to creative new forces. The simultaneous vitality of traditional and new forms of expression in art, literature, and philosophy have given these two centuries a dual identity: as the Later Middle Ages and as the Early Renaissance (1300–1500). By the end of this period, Europe was ready for another age of expansion, and in the last decade of the fifteenth century European sailors reached the shores of East Africa, the Americas, and India.

Establishing a New Order

With the passing of Roman imperial order, Western Europeans were thrown back on their own resources and forced to create new social and political structures and a new civilization. In fashioning this new society, Westerners melded three elements: the vestiges of Roman civilization, the moral and organizational leadership of the Roman Catholic Church, and the vigor and culture of the various fringe peoples who carved out kingdoms in Europe from the fifth century onward. The single act most vividly symbolizing the new order that emerged from this fusion was Pope Leo III's crowning of Charlemagne as "Roman emperor" on Christmas Day, 800.

Charles the Great's empire was short-lived, and Europe was again thrown on the defensive as it was invaded by new fringe peoples during the ninth and tenth centuries. As serious as these new challenges were, Europe's emerging civilization did not collapse. Instead, its people produced a variety of military and political expedients that allowed them to get on with the task of building a new society. One of the most important of these was a system known as *feudalism*, in which a class of heavily armed cavalry, or knights, dominated a fair portion of the continent and British Isles.

Feudal warriors were one of Europe's many tension-producing factors, because they were forces for both anarchy and order. This paradox was not lost on medieval Westerners, who, toward the end of the eleventh century, had achieved a sufficiently stable level of society to export some of this feudal violence in the form of crusades. At home, feudalism proved a fruitful element in fashioning new political structures, but feudal government was not medieval Europe's only answer to instability. From the eleventh century onward towns and cities proliferated, offering Europeans opportunities not only for survival but prosperity.

Einhard

THE LIFE OF CHARLES THE GREAT

Charles the Great (768–814), or Charlemagne, king of the Franks and Lombards and emperor in the West, ruled a major portion of continental Europe for close to half a century. During his lifetime, his herculean efforts to expand the boundaries of Christendom and impose an order based on his understanding of Christian principles won him a reputation that extended all the way to the court of Caliph Harun al-Rashid in Baghdad. Within a few years of his death, Westerners fondly looked back on Charles's reign as a golden age.

Between 829 and 836, a Frankish scholar and monk named Einhard (d. 840) composed in excellent classical Latin a biography of his late emperor, patron, and friend, which he modeled on the *Lives of the Twelve Caesars* by the Roman historian Suetonius (ca 69–140). For Einhard, Charlemagne had been more than the equal of these earliest exemplars of Roman imperial greatness. The main purpose of Einhard's masterpiece appears to have been to instruct Charles's son and successor, Louis the Pious (813–840), on what a Christian-Frankish emperor should be.

Unfortunately for Louis, times had changed, and the empire he had inherited was already showing signs of collapse. While the *Carolingian* (that which pertains to the family of Charles) Empire was breaking up in the mid-ninth century, the memory of Charles's greatness persisted and his legend grew. Since that time, Europeans have continued to revere Charlemagne as the "Father of Europe." In the following selection, Einhard describes Charles's imperial coronation, the reasons he deserved that singular honor, and his son's coronation in 813.

Questions for Analysis

1. How did Charles demonstrate his devotion to Christianity?
2. In what ways did he act like a Christian emperor even before his coronation in 800?
3. Einhard's statement that Charles initially had an aversion to the imperial title has long puzzled historians. On December 25, 800, Pope Leo, perhaps unexpectedly, placed a crown on Charles's head, and the assembled people in St. Peter's basilica acclaimed Charles emperor. Compare this ceremony with the manner in which Louis the Pious was made emperor. Can you think of any possible reason why Charles was displeased thirteen years earlier? Note that Charles never returned to Rome after 800.

He cherished with the greatest fervor and devotion the principles of the Christian religion, which had been instilled into him from infancy. Hence it was that he built the beautiful basilica at Aix-la-Chapelle,[1] which he adorned with gold and silver and lamps, and with rails and doors of solid brass. He had the columns and marbles for this structure brought from Rome and Ravenna,[2] for he could not find such as were suitable elsewhere. He was a constant worshiper at this church as long as his health permitted, going morning and evening, even after nightfall, besides attending mass; and he took care that all the services there conducted should be administered with the utmost possible propriety, very often

1. The modern German city of Aachen. Charles's church exists today as a chapel in the cathedral of Aachen.

2. A northeastern Italian city.

warning the sextons[3] not to let any improper or unclean thing be brought into the building, or remain in it. He provided it with a great number of sacred vessels of gold and silver, and with such a quantity of clerical robes that not even the door-keepers, who fill the humblest office in the church, were obliged to wear their everyday clothes when in the exercise of their duties. He was at great pains to improve the church reading and psalmody, for he was well skilled in both, although he neither read in public nor sang, except in a low tone and with others.

He was very forward in succoring the poor, and in that gratuitous generosity which the Greeks call alms, so much so that he not only made a point of giving in his own country and his own kingdom, but when he discovered that there were Christians living in poverty in Syria, Egypt, and Africa, at Jerusalem, Alexandria, and Carthage, he had compassion on their wants, and used to send money over the seas to them. The reason that he zealously strove to make friends with the kings beyond seas was that he might get help and relief to the Christians living under their rule.[4] He cherished the Church of St. Peter the Apostle at Rome above all other holy and sacred places, and heaped its treasury with a vast wealth of gold, silver, and precious stones. He sent great and countless gifts to the popes; and throughout his whole reign the wish that he had nearest at heart was to re-establish the ancient authority of the city of Rome under his care and by his influence, and to defend and protect the Church of St. Peter, and to beautify and enrich it out of his own store above all other churches. Although he held it in such veneration, he only repaired to Rome to pay his vows and make his supplications four times[5] during the whole forty-seven[6] years that he reigned.

When he made his last journey thither, he had also other ends in view. The Romans had inflicted many injuries upon the Pontiff Leo,[7] tearing out his eyes and cutting out his tongue, so that he had been compelled to call upon the King for help. Charles accordingly went to Rome,[8] to set in order the affairs of the Church, which were in great confusion, and passed the whole winter there. It was then that he received the titles of Emperor and Augustus, to which he at first had such an aversion that he declared that he would not have set foot in the Church the day that they were conferred, although it was a great feast-day, if he could have foreseen the design of the Pope. He bore very patiently with the jealousy which the Roman emperors[9] showed upon his assuming these titles, for they took this step very ill; and by dint of frequent embassies and letters, in which he addressed them

---

3. Persons charged with the maintenance of a church.

4. In 799 Charles sent an ambassador to Jerusalem to inquire after the state of Christians there. During the first decade of the ninth century Charles exchanged several embassies with Caliph Harun al-Rashid, presumably because of his interest in the well-being of Christians living under Harun's rule.

5. 774, 781, 787, and 800.

6. 768–814.

7. Pope Leo III (795–816) was attacked on April 25, 799. Although an attempt was made to blind him and cut out his tongue, the attackers failed.

8. Charles arrived on November 24, 799.

9. In Constantinople.

as brothers, he made their haughtiness yield to his magnanimity,[10] a quality in which he was unquestionably much their superior. . . .

Towards the close of his life,[11] when he was broken by ill-health and old age, he summoned Lewis, King of Aquitania,[12] his only surviving son by Hildegard, and gathered together all the chief men of the whole kingdom of the Franks in a solemn assembly. He appointed Lewis, with their unanimous consent,[13] to rule with himself over the whole kingdom, and constituted him heir to the imperial name; then, placing the diadem upon his son's head, he bade him be proclaimed Emperor and Augustus. This step was hailed by all present with great favor, for it really seemed as if God had prompted him to it for the kingdom's good; it increased the King's[14] dignity, and struck no little terror into foreign nations.

THE SONG OF ROLAND

By 1000, warrior-landholders in northern France and the Low Countries had evolved a system of governance that modern historians term feudalism. Like Japan's *samurai*, the feudal *vassal* (both terms essentially mean "one who serves") served a "lord" as a fighter and enjoyed a variety of political, social, and economic benefits. One of the major reasons a soldier became a vassal was to receive a *fief* (*feudum* in Latin, hence the term feudalism) as payment for services rendered. Originally, this fief, or *fee*, was anything of value, but increasingly it became a grant of land over which the vassal ruled in the lord's name. During the eleventh century these fiefs usually became hereditary, passing to the vassal's oldest surviving heir. Feudal soldiers thus became landed nobles and in the process articulated a set of shared values that became known as the Code of Chivalry. Ideally, these principles and customs governed the life and conduct of the *chevalier*, or mounted knight.

One of the earliest and most popular literary expressions of the chivalric code is the anonymous *Song of Roland*, an epic *chanson de geste*, or "song of heroic deeds." This French narrative poem, which dates from the eleventh century, relates the legendary last battle of Count Roland and his companions. The story is loosely based on a minor disaster Charlemagne suffered in 778. While his army was returning from an expedition in northern Spain, Christian Basques ambushed and wiped out his baggage train and rear guard in the mountain pass of Roncesvalles. Among the fallen was Roland, duke of the Breton frontier. We know little else about this skir-

10. In 812 Emperor Michael I (811–813) recognized Charles's imperial title in exchange for Venice and some territory in the Balkans.

11. 813.

12. A region in modern southwest France.

13. Frankish kingship was still elective in theory, and the consent of all leading Frankish nobles was needed in order to ratify a royal succession.

14. Louis.

mish or the historical Roland, but when he reemerges several centuries later, he has been transformed into Charlemagne's nephew and the greatest champion in the emperor's holy war against Islam, and the Basque bandits have become an enormous Muslim army. Charles, who was only around thirty-six at the time of the ambush and twenty-two years shy of his eventual coronation as emperor, has been metamorphosized into a Moses-like patriarch more than 200 years old, who rules as God's sole agent on earth over a united Christian world. He, his nephew, and his nephew's companions are now Frenchmen, even though there had been no France or French culture in Charlemagne's day. Furthermore, feudalism was in its infancy when Charles the Great's Frankish kingdom served as western Christendom's focal point, yet *The Song of Roland* assumes a society pervaded by feudal relationships and values.

The story revolves around the themes of feudal loyalty and honor. Roland has unwittingly offended his stepfather, Ganelon, who in revenge enters into a conspiracy with the Saracen (Muslim) king Marsilion to deliver up Roland and the rest of the flower of French knighthood. Ganelon then arranges for Roland to command the emperor's rear guard, knowing that the Saracens plan to ambush it and that Roland will be too proud to sound the horn for reinforcements. Such is the case. Despite the entreaties of Oliver, his closest friend, Roland does not sound the horn until the battle is lost and 20,000 Christian soldiers lie dead. The emperor returns too late to prevent his nephew's death but exacts revenge by destroying all Muslim forces in Spain and consigning Ganelon to death by torture. Our selection describes the opening and final stages of Roland's last fight.

Questions for Analysis

1. Why does Roland refuse to sound his horn?
2. Why does Oliver initially urge Roland to blow the horn but later tell him that it would be shameful to do so?
3. How does Roland define a vassal's duty? Would Oliver remove or add anything to that list?
4. Which of these two knights seems to have the poet's deeper sympathy, and which seems, in the poet's estimation, the better vassal?
5. Consider the words and actions of Roland, Oliver, and Turpin, and from them draw up a list of the Code of Chivalry's components. Do you see any potentially contradictory values or practices?
6. How does the author express the salvation of Roland's soul in feudal terms?
7. Why do the warriors give names to their weapons, and why does Roland attempt to destroy Durendal before he dies?
8. Students often confuse feudal vassals with serfs, the semifree tenant farmers who worked the estates of Europe's landed nobility. What evidence is there in this poem to indicate that, by the mid-eleventh century, feudal vassals were enjoying a status far higher than that of peasants?

9. Compare this poem with the *Nihongi*'s account of the conflict between the Mononobe and Soga clans and the death of Yorodzu (Chapter 9). What values do these two warrior societies share? Can you discern any significant differences between the two? What role does religion play in each?

The paynims[1] arm themselves with Saracen hauberks[2]. . . ; they lace on helms[3] of right good Saracen work, and gird on swords of Viennese steel, fair are their shields, and their lances are of Valencia,[4] tipped with gonfanons[5] white and blue and scarlet. They leave behind them the mules and palfries,[6] and mounting their war-horses, ride forth in close ranks. Fair was the day and bright the sun, and all their harness glistens in the light. And for the more joy they let sound a thousand trumpets; so great is the noise thereof that the Franks hear it. Then saith Oliver: "Sir comrade, me thinks we shall have ado with the Saracens." "Now God grant it be as thou sayest," Roland answers him, "for to make stand here for our King is to do as good men ought to do. Verily for his liege[7] a man well ought to suffer pain and woe, and endure both great heat and great cold, and should hold him ready to lose both hide and hair in his lord's service. Now let each have a care that he strikes good blows and great, that no man may mis-say us in his songs. These misbelieving men are in the wrong, and right is with the Christians, and for my part I will give ye no ill example." . . .

"Great is the host of the heathen," saith Oliver, "and few is our fellowship. Roland, fair comrade, I pray thee sound thy horn of ivory that Charles may hear it and return again with all his host." "That were but folly," quoth Roland, "and thereby would I lose all fame in sweet France. Rather will I strike good blows and great with Durendal,[8] that the blade thereof shall be blooded even unto the hilt. Woe worth the paynims that they came into the passes! I pledge thee my faith short life shall be theirs."

"Roland, comrade, blow now thy horn of ivory, and Charles shall hear it, and bring hither his army again, and the King and his barons shall succor us." But Roland answers him, saying: "Now God forfend that through me my kinsman be brought to shame, or aught of dishonor befall fair France. But first I will lay on with Durendal, the good sword that is girded here at my side, and thou shalt see the blade thereof all reddened. Woe worth the paynims when they gathered their hosts! I pledge me they shall all be given over to death." . . .

Saith Oliver, "I see no shame herein. I have seen the Saracens of Spain, they

1. Pagans (i.e., Muslims).

2. A knee-length garment of interconnected iron rings (chain mail) that protected the torso and thighs.

3. Helmets.

4. A region in eastern Spain.

5. A streamer attached to the shaft of a lance just below the point.

6. Mules bore their armor and other gear; palfries were small, comfortable riding horses. Knights would normally mount their massive war horses only prior to battle.

7. A feudal lord to whom a vassal swore allegiance.

8. The name of Roland's sword.

cover the hills and the valleys, the heaths and the plains. Great are the hosts of this hostile folk, and ours is but a little fellowship." And Roland makes answer: "My desire is the greater thereby. May God and His most holy angels forfend that France should lose aught of worship through me. Liefer[9] had I die than bring dishonor upon me. The Emperor loves us for dealing stout blows."

Roland is brave, and Oliver is wise, and both are good men of their hands; once armed and a-horseback, rather would they die than flee the battle. . . .

Nigh at hand is Archbishop Turpin;[10] he now spurs his horse to the crest of a knoll, and speaks to the Franks, and this is his sermon: "Lords, barons, Charles left us here, and it is a man's devoir[11] to die for his King. Now help ye to uphold Christianity. Certes,[12] ye shall have a battle, for here before you are the Saracens. Confess your sins and pray God's mercy, and that your souls may be saved I will absolve you. If ye are slain ye will be holy martyrs, and ye shall have seats in the higher Paradise." The Franks light off their horses and kneel down, and the Archbishop blesses them, and for a penance[13] bids them that they lay on with their swords.

Despite a valiant stand, the rear guard is overwhelmed.

When Count Roland is aware of the great slaughter of his men, he turns to Oliver, saying: "Sir comrade, as God may save thee, see how many a good man of arms lies on the ground; we may well have pity on sweet France, the fair, that must now be desolate of such barons. Ah, King and friend, would thou wert here! Oliver, my brother, what shall we do? How shall we send him tidings?" "Nay, I know not how to seek him," saith Oliver; "but liefer had I die than bring dishonor upon me."

Then saith Roland: "I will sound my horn of ivory, and Charles, as he passes the mountains, will hear it; and I pledge thee my faith the Franks will return again." Then saith Oliver: "Therein would be great shame for thee, and dishonor for all thy kindred, a reproach that would last all the days of their life. Thou wouldst not sound it when I bid thee, and now thou shalt not by my counsel." . . .

Then saith Roland: "Wherefore art thou wroth with me?" And Oliver answers him, saying: "Comrade, thou thyself art to blame. Wise courage is not madness, and measure is better than rashness. Through thy folly these Franks have come to their death; nevermore shall Charles the King have service at our hands. Hadst thou taken my counsel, my liege lord had been here, and this battle had been ended, and King Marsila[14] had been taken or slain. Woe worth thy prowess, Roland! Henceforth Charles shall get no help of thee;

9. More willingly.

10. Archbishop of the church of Reims and, along with Roland and Oliver, one of the Twelve Peers of France. Peer means "equal"; these twelve champions were socially the emperor's equals by virtue of their birth, prowess, and worth to him. Although a priest, Turpin is also a fighter.

11. Duty.

12. Certainly.

13. After receiving absolution of one's sins from God through the agency of a priest, the penitent was required by the priest to perform some penitential act as a token of contrition. Depending on the severity of the sins forgiven, the act could range from simple prayers to a pilgrimage to the Holy Land.

14. Marsilion.

never till God's Judgment Day shall there be such another man; but thou must die, and France shall be shamed thereby. And this day our loyal fellowship shall have an end; before this evening grievously shall we be parted."

The Archbishop, hearing them dispute together, spurs his horse with his spurs of pure gold, and comes unto them, and rebukes them, saying: "Sir Roland, and thou, Sir Oliver, in God's name I pray ye, let be this strife. Little help shall we now have of thy horn; and yet it were better to sound it; if the King come, he will revenge us, and the paynims shall not go hence rejoicing. Our Franks will light off their horses, and find us dead and maimed, and they will lay us on biers, on the backs of sumpters,[15] and will weep for us with dole[16] and pity; and they will bury us in the courts of churches, that our bones may not be eaten by wolves and swine and dogs." "Sir, thou speakest well and truly," quoth Roland.

And therewith he sets his ivory horn to his lips, grasps it well and blows it with all the might he hath. High are the hills, and the sound echoes far, and for thirty full leagues they hear it resound. Charles and all his host hear it, and the King saith: "Our men are at battle." . . .

With dolor and pain, and in sore torment, Count Roland blows his horn of ivory, that the bright blood springs out of his mouth, and the temples of his brain are broken. . . .

Now Roland feels that his sight is gone from him. With much striving he gets upon his feet; the color has gone from his face; before him lies a brown stone, and in his sorrow and wrath he smites ten blows upon it. The sword grates upon the rock, but neither breaks nor splinters; and the Count saith: "Holy Mary, help me now! Ah Durendal, alas for your goodness! Now am I near to death, and have no more need of you. Many a fight in the field have I won with you, many a wide land have I conquered with you, lands now ruled by Charles with the white beard. May the man who would flee before another, never possess you. For many a day have you been held by a right good lord, never will there be such another in France the free. . . . Many lands and countries have I won with thee, lands which Charles of the white beard rules. And now am I heavy of heart because of this my sword; rather would I die than that it should fall into the hands of the paynims. Lord God our Father, let not this shame fall upon France."

And again Roland smote upon the brown stone and beyond all telling shattered it; the sword grates, but springs back again into the air and is neither dinted nor broken. And when the Count sees he may in no wise break it, he laments, saying: "O Durendal, how fair and holy a thing thou art! In thy golden hilt is many a relic,[17] — a tooth of Saint Peter, and some of the blood of Saint Basil, and hairs from the head of my lord, Saint Denis,[18] and a bit of the raiment[19] of the Virgin Mary. It is not meet[20] that thou fall into the hands of the paynims, only Chris-

15. Pack mules.

16. Sorrow.

17. Literally, something left behind. Here it means things left behind on earth by saints who now enjoy the presence of God. Possession of these relics assures the favor of those holy advocates.

18. The patron saint of the French royal house.

19. Clothing.

20. Proper.

tians should wield thee. May no coward ever possess thee! Many wide lands have I conquered with thee, lands which Charles of the white beard rules; and thereby is the Emperor great and mighty." . . .

Roland lies on a high peak looking towards Spain; he feels that his time is spent, and with one hand he beats upon his breast: "O God, I have sinned; forgive me through thy might the wrongs, both great and small, which I have done from the day I was born even to this day on which I was smitten." With his right hand he holds out his glove to God; and lo, the angels of heaven come down to him.

Count Roland lay under the pine tree; he has turned his face towards Spain, and he begins to call many things to remembrance, — all the lands he had won by his valor, and sweet France, and the men of his lineage, and Charles, his liege lord, who had brought him up in his household; and he cannot help but weep. But he would not wholly forget himself, and again he confesses his sins and begs forgiveness of God: "Our Father, who art truth, who raised up Lazarus[21] from the dead, and who defended Daniel[22] from the lions, save thou my soul from the perils to which it is brought through the sins I wrought in my life days." With his right hand he offers his glove to God, and Saint Gabriel[23] has taken it from his hand. Then his head sinks on his arm, and with clasped hands he hath gone to his end. And God sent him his cherubim,[24] and Saint Michael of the Seas,[25] and with them went Saint Gabriel, and they carried the soul of the Count into Paradise.

Fulcher of Chartres

HISTORY OF THE EXPEDITION TO JERUSALEM

In 1095 Pope Urban II (1088–1099) attempted to harness the martial values of feudalism to the Church's service by calling for a holy war against Islam. The expedition he set in motion is known as the First Crusade (1096–1099), and it inaugurated close to 500 years of Western Christian involvement in the ancient lands of the eastern Mediterranean. The crusades launched Western Europe on its first great age of overseas colonization. The later transoceanic voyages of Columbus, da Gama, and those who followed were in many ways a continuation of the crusade tradition.

The Church's immediate enemies in the First Crusade were the Seljuk Turks, a new Muslim power in the Middle East (Chapter 9). In 1071 the Seljuks destroyed a Byzantine army at the Battle of Manzikert, and soon the Seljuk Empire encompassed

---

21. A friend whom Jesus raised from the dead.

22. A Jewish prophet protected by God while in a lion den.

23. An archangel and messenger of God.

24. An order of angels.

25. St. Michael the Archangel, a warrior saint. The island monastery of Mont-Saint-Michel off the Breton coast is dedicated to St. Michael.

Persia, Iraq, Syria-Palestine, and most of Asia Minor. When Emperor Alexius I Comnenus of Constantinople (1081–1118) appealed to Urban II for help, the pope issued an impassioned call for Western military action.

In the following selection, Fulcher (ca 1059–1127), a priest of the cathedral of Chartres near Paris, presents his version of Pope Urban's inaugural call to arms, which the Roman pontiff delivered on November 27, 1095, at the close of a church council at Clermont in France. A number of contemporary accounts of Urban's speech exist, but none is a verbatim transcription. Since Fulcher was at Clermont on that fateful day and began composing his memoirs of the First Crusade as early as 1101, we can assume his version of the speech does justice to most of the major points Urban raised.

Questions for Analysis

1. What reasons does Urban give for going to war with the Turks? What sort of war does he expect?
2. What incentives does the pope offer those who choose to fight the Turks? What do these incentives tell us about crusader motives and the type of war that was fought in the Holy Land?
3. What is Urban hoping to accomplish by this crusade for the Church, for Europe, for individual crusaders, and for the Christians of the East?
4. Consider Urban's speech in light of the testimony provided by Sir John Mandeville (Chapter 7). Does it seem the pope considered the Greek Christians of the East as separate from the Church of Rome?
5. Reread *The Song of Roland* in the light of Pope Urban's appeal. What evidence in the poem indicates it was a product of the Age of Crusades?

Since, oh sons of God, you have promised the Lord more earnestly than heretofore to maintain peace in your midst and faithfully to sustain the laws of the Church,[1] there remains for you, newly fortified by the correction of the Lord, to show the strength of your integrity in a certain other duty, which is not less your concern than the Lord's. For you must carry succor to your brethren dwelling in the East, and needing your aid, which they have so often demanded. For the Turks, a Persian people, have attacked them, as many of you know, and have advanced into the territory of Romania[2] as far as that part of the Mediterranean

1. The Council of Clermont had attempted to lower the level of feudal violence in Europe by declaring the Truce of God, which prohibited all fighting from Wednesday evening to Monday morning and during all church festival periods.

2. The Byzantine Empire. The Byzantines called themselves "Romans."

which is called the Arm of St. George;[3] and occupying more and more the lands of those Christians, have already seven times conquered them in battle, have killed and captured many, have destroyed the churches and devastated the kingdom of God. If you permit them to remain for a time unmolested, they will extend their sway more widely over many faithful servants of the Lord.

Wherefore, I pray and exhort, nay not I, but the Lord prays and exhorts you, as heralds of Christ, by frequent exhortation, to urge men of all ranks, knights and foot-soldiers, rich and poor, to hasten to exterminate this vile race from the lands of our brethren, and to bear timely aid to the worshipers of Christ. I speak to those who are present, I proclaim it to the absent, but Christ commands. Moreover, the sins of those who set out thither, if they lose their lives on the journey, by land or sea, or in fighting against the heathen, shall be remitted in that hour; this I grant to all who go, through the power of God vested in me.

Oh, what a disgrace if a race so despised, degenerate, and slave of the demons, should thus conquer a people fortified with faith in omnipotent God and resplendent with the name of Christ! Oh, how many reproaches will be heaped upon you by the Lord Himself if you do not aid those who like yourselves are counted of the Christian faith! Let those who have formerly been accustomed to contend wickedly in private warfare against the faithful, fight against the infidel[4] and bring to a victorious end the war which ought long since to have been begun. Let those who have hitherto been robbers now become soldiers of Christ. Let those who have formerly contended against their brothers and relatives now fight as they ought against the barbarians. Let those who have formerly been mercenaries at low wages, now gain eternal rewards. Let those who have been striving to the detriment both of body and soul, now labor for a two-fold reward. What shall I add? On this side will be the sorrowful and poor, on the other the joyful and the rich;[5] here the enemies of the Lord, there His friends. Let not those who are going delay their journey, but having arranged their affairs and collected the money necessary for their expenses, when the winter ends and the spring comes, let them with alacrity start on their journey under the guidance of the Lord.

MAGNA CARTA

The essence of the feudal bond between lord and vassal was the principle of reciprocal obligations and rights. Just as the vassal was expected to serve the lord faithfully, even unto death, the lord incurred an obligation to protect every vassal's honor, status, and well-being. A lord's failure to honor such commitments justified

3. The Hellespont, where Asia and Europe meet.

4. Unbelievers. Ironically, Muslims call all non-Muslims "infidels."

5. Urban meant this in both senses: spiritually wealthy and rich in the things of this world.

a vassal's rebellion and defiance of that lord. This built-in tension within feudalism often resulted in violence between parties who, rightly or wrongly, believed themselves aggrieved. It also gave rise to some interesting constitutional developments in England and elsewhere.

Following his conquest of England in 1066, William I (1066–1087) strengthened the English monarchy by emphasizing the feudal obligations all the lords and knights of the realm directly owed the monarch. Several generations later the kings of France and Germany would use similar means to expand their power. As fruitful as this strategy was for decreasing the level of "feudal anarchy" and increasing the range of royal authority, it carried with it certain dangers for those kings.

Early in the thirteenth century, many of the great lords of England believed that King John (1199–1216) was abusing his feudal privileges and generally treating all his subjects, especially the nobles, in a shoddy manner. The result was a baronial revolt in which the rebels sought not to depose or injure John, their liege lord, but to force him to acknowledge that he was equally subject to all the customs and laws of England, even though he was the source of justice and law. With the aid of the burghers of London, who also were disenchanted with the king's heavy-handedness, the rebels forced John in 1215 to agree to a list of reforms that eventually became known as *Magna Carta*.

Beginning with Henry III (1216–1272) in 1216, 1217, and 1225, subsequent English kings were required to reissue the Great Charter in return for baronial support and financial assistance. As a result, *Magna Carta* remained a living reminder of the limits of royal power.

Questions for Analysis

1. Judging from the guarantees John was forced to give, in what ways had he abused his royal and feudal rights?
2. How did the barons propose to prevent John from extorting uncustomary or unreasonable sums of money from them in the future?
3. What did the burghers of London get for their support of the rebellion?
4. Can you guess what institution this common council of the kingdom evolved into?
5. Some historians have characterized the Great Charter as a document that reflects only the narrow class interests of the baronage. What do you think of this judgment?
6. Which of the charter's clauses seem most familiar to you? Why?

John, by the grace of God, king of England, lord of Ireland, duke of Normandy and Aquitaine, count of Anjou, to the archbishops, bishops, abbots, earls, barons, justiciars, foresters, sheriffs, reeves, servants, and all bailiffs and his faithful people greeting.

1. In the first place we have granted to God, and by this our present charter confirmed, for us and our heirs forever, that the English church shall be free, and shall hold its rights entire and its liberties uninjured. . . .

We have granted moreover to all free men of our kingdom for us and our heirs forever all the liberties written below, to be had and holden by themselves and their heirs from us and our heirs.

2. If any of our earls or barons, or others holding from us in chief[1] by military service shall have died, and when he has died his heir shall be of full age and owe relief,[2] he shall have his inheritance by the ancient relief; that is to say, the heir or heirs of an earl for the whole barony of an earl a hundred pounds; the heir or heirs of a baron for a whole barony a hundred pounds; the heir or heirs of a knight, for a whole knight's fee, a hundred shillings at most; and who owes less let him give less according to the ancient custom of fiefs.

3. If moreover the heir of any one of such shall be under age, and shall be in wardship,[3] when he comes of age he shall have his inheritance without relief and without a fine.

4. The custodian of the land of such a minor heir shall not take from the land of the heir any except reasonable products, reasonable customary payments, and reasonable services, and this without destruction or waste of men or of property; and if we shall have committed the custody of the land of any such a one to the sheriff or to any other who is to be responsible to us for its proceeds, and that man shall have caused destruction or waste from his custody we will recover damages from him, and the land shall be committed to two legal and discreet men of that fief, who shall be responsible for its proceeds to us or to him to whom we have assigned them; and if we shall have given or sold to any one the custody of any such land, and he has caused destruction or waste there, he shall lose that custody, and it shall be handed over to two legal and discreet men of that fief who shall be in like manner responsible to us as is said above. . . .

7. A widow, after the death of her husband, shall have her marriage portion and her inheritance immediately and without obstruction, nor shall she give anything for her dowry or for her marriage portion, or for her inheritance which inheritance her husband and she held on the day of the death of her husband; and she may remain in the house of her husband for forty days after his death, within which time her dowry shall be assigned to her.

---

1. Any vassal who held a fief directly from the king, as opposed to a rear vassal, who was a vassal of a vassal.

2. The tax paid to a lord by anyone inheriting a fief.

3. The lord had the right and responsibility to act as guardian for any underaged heir or heiress of a deceased vassal. During the period of wardship, the lord was expected to protect the rights and status of the child but was also allowed to dispose of the income from the fief as he saw fit. When the child came of age, the lord was expected to pass on the complete and unspoiled fief to this new vassal without charging any relief.

8. No widow shall be compelled to marry so long as she prefers to live without a husband, provided she gives security that she will not marry without our consent, if she holds from us, or without the consent of her lord from whom she holds, if she holds from another.[4] . . .

12. No scutage[5] or aid[6] shall be imposed in our kingdom except by the common council of our kingdom,[7] except for the ransoming of our body, for the making of our oldest son a knight, and for once marrying our oldest daughter, and for these purposes it shall be only a reasonable aid; in the same way it shall be done concerning the aids of the city of London.

13. And the city of London shall have all its ancient liberties and free customs, as well by land as by water. Moreover, we will and grant that all other cities and boroughs and villages and ports shall have all their liberties and free customs.[8]

14. And for holding a common council of the kingdoms concerning the assessment of an aid otherwise than in the three cases mentioned above, or concerning the assessment of a scutage we shall cause to be summoned the archbishops, bishops, abbots, earls, and greater barons by our letters under seal; and besides we shall cause to be summoned generally, by our sheriffs and bailiffs all those who hold from us in chief, for a certain day, that is at the end of forty days at least, and for a certain place; and in all the letters of that summons, we will express the cause of the summons, and when the summons has thus been given the business shall proceed on the appointed day, on the advice of those who shall be present, even if not all of those who were summoned have come. . . .

20. A free man shall not be fined for a small offense, except in proportion to the measure of the offense; and for a great offense he shall be fined in proportion to the magnitude of the offense, saving his freehold; and a merchant in the same way, saving his merchandise; and the villain shall be fined in the same way, saving his wainage,[9] if he shall be at our mercy; and none of the above fines shall be imposed except by the oaths of honest men of the neighborhood.

21. Earls and barons shall only be fined by their peers,[10] and only in proportion to their offense. . . .

28. No constable or other bailiff of ours shall take anyone's grain or other chattels, without immediately paying for them in

---

4. A lord had the right to deny a vassal's widow permission to marry a specific person if he believed the marriage would place an enemy or other undesirable person in charge of the deceased vassal's fief. As the widow's guardian, he always faced the temptation to marry her and her late husband's fief off to the highest bidder or some lackey.

5. Money paid in place of required military service. Generally, John preferred to collect scutage so he could hire mercenaries, and his vassals preferred to meet their obligations by going into the field.

6. Any levy paid by vassals to a lord.

7. The feudal council of all his tenants-in-chief.

8. Customs and privileges that have been secured by royal charter.

9. Here villain means an unfree peasant or serf. Wainage was that portion of the harvest the serf was allowed to keep for food and seed.

10. Their equals, that is, other vassals. Every vassal had the right to trial by the lord's council of vassals.

money, unless he is able to obtain a postponement at the good-will of the seller. . . .

39. No free man shall be taken or imprisoned or dispossessed, or outlawed, or banished, or in any way destroyed, nor will we go upon him, nor send upon him, except by the legal judgment of his peers or by the law of the land.[11]

40. To no one will we sell, to no one will we deny, or delay right or justice.

41. All merchants shall be safe and secure in going out from England and coming into England and in remaining and going through England, as well by land as by water, for buying and selling, free from all evil tolls, by the ancient and rightful customs, except in time of war, and if they are of a land at war with us; and if such are found in our land at the beginning of war, they shall be attached without injury to their bodies or goods, until it shall be known from us or from our principal justiciar in what way the merchants of our land are treated who shall be then found in the country which is at war with us; and if ours are safe there, the others shall be safe in our land. . . .

60. Moreover, all those customs and franchises mentioned above which we have conceded in our kingdom, and which are to be fulfilled, as far as pertains to us, in respect to our men; all men of our kingdom as well clergy as laymen, shall observe as far as pertains to them, in respect to their men.

John of Viterbo

BOOK ON THE GOVERNMENT OF CITIES

Western Europe's feudal nobility never totally dominated medieval society and did not even enjoy a military monopoly. All too often mercenary foot soldiers proved more than a match for mounted knights, and even urban militias were capable of defeating feudal levies, as Emperor Frederick I (1152–1190) discovered in Italy and King Philip IV of France (1285–1314) learned in Flanders. Moreover, townspeople frequently served as royal officials and enjoyed the privilege of administering their own urban governments.

Overall, towns and townspeople served as effective counterweights to the feudal nobility. While early medieval society usually saw its members engaged in three primary tasks — prayer, fighting, and agricultural labor — Europe from the eleventh century onward embraced an emerging class of urban men and women who, unhampered by the servile bonds of serfdom, were employed in commerce and production. These bourgeoisie were not only personally free but also enjoyed a large measure of self-government. At the very least, a town would secure a charter of

11. Feudal vassals have the right to trial by their peers; everyone else will be tried according to the customs and laws governing his or her group and the alleged offense.

liberties that limited the extent to which the local lord could intervene in its fiscal, political, and judicial affairs. Some towns and cities, especially in northern Italy, went further and became independent of all outside control. While Sung China's prosperous and far more numerous urban dwellers also possessed personal freedom, their cities were not self-governing but centers of imperial administration. It was only in far less developed Europe that cities and towns, of modest size by Asiatic standards, achieved a degree of corporate independence, thereby challenging successfully the landed nobility's dominance.

If townsfolk were to govern themselves, they needed to understand the nature and functions of government. Consequently, schools of law proliferated from the late eleventh century onward, and jurists composed a number of treatises on the theory and practice of good government. One of the more famous is the thirteenth-century *Book on the Government of Cities* by the Italian lawyer John of Viterbo. We know little about the author, and even the date of the work's composition is uncertain. Some scholars have dated it as early as 1228 and others as late as sometime after 1261.

In the following excerpts John, quoting from Roman law, explains why cities exist and defines the role of the *podesta*, the chief municipal official in many northern Italian city-states of the thirteenth century. Podestas were often professional, salaried magistrates brought in from outside and given a one-year contract, generally renewable upon review, to govern the city. Because many cities suffered from family and class conflicts, they often recruited foreign chief executives. The theory was that only an outsider could treat all persons and groups in an evenhanded manner.

Questions for Analysis

1. The word *bourg*, from which we derive such terms for townspeople as *burgher* and *bourgeoisie*, originally meant a fortified site. Consider what John tells us about the primary function of a city. What does this suggest about medieval towns?
2. Are the podesta's powers absolute or limited? Compare his oath with *Magna Carta*. Can you discover any parallels between his office and that of King John? What do these parallels suggest?
3. John refers to the inhabitants of a city as "citizens." Why is that significant?
4. Is there any evidence that merchants played a prominent role in creating and governing these urban centers?
5. According to John, "Matters that touch all must be approved by all." What does he mean by this? Does he envision the ideal commune as a democracy? If not, what is his understanding of a commune's constitution and reason for existence?
6. Can you find any evidence for the judgment that thirteenth-century Italian cities tended to employ foreign-born podestas because they alone seemed to promise evenhanded governance?

The Meaning of "City"

A city, indeed, is said to be the liberty of its citizens or the defense of its inhabitants, as is said of a fortified town, for its walls are constructed to serve as a bulwark for those dwelling within. This word *civitas* [city] is syncopated, and so its aforementioned meaning comes from the three syllables that *civitas* contains within itself: namely, *ci, vi,* and *tas. Ci* stands for *citra* [apart from]; *vi* stands for *vim* [oppression]; *tas* stands for *habitas* [you dwell]. It follows that *civitas* means "you dwell apart from oppression." One resides there without oppression, because the governor of the city will protect men of more humble station so that they do not suffer injury at the hands of more powerful men (for, "We cannot be the equals of the more powerful").[1] Likewise, "it is not right for anyone to be oppressed by his adversary's might; if this is the case, it certainly reflects the ill-will of the person governing the province." Likewise, because everyone's house is his most secure refuge and place of shelter, no one ought to drag him from there against his will, nor is it natural that anyone in a city be constrained by violent fear, etc. Likewise, one speaks correctly of immunity, because inhabitants are made immune by the walls and towers of their city and are protected within it from hostile foreigners and personal enemies.

The Creation of Cities

Cities, indeed, were created or founded for a particular purpose. I do not speak of the holy, celestial city of Jerusalem, called "the Great City," the city of our God, whose explanation I leave to theologians and prophets, because it is not my intention to consider heaven. Rather, I speak of cities in this world, which have been founded so that anyone may hold on to his possessions and his guardianship of his belongings will not be disturbed. . . .

The Podesta's Oath

The podesta's oath is, in fact, normally administered by a judge: "You, Lord B., shall swear on the Holy Gospels, which you hold in your hands, to administer the affairs and business of this city pertaining to your office and to rule, unite, govern, maintain, and hold safe this city, its surrounding countryside and district, and all people and every person, the small as well as the great, foot soldiers as well as knights,[2] and to maintain and protect their rights and to preserve and assure the observance of the established law regarding minors and adults, especially little children, orphans, widows, and other people worthy of pity, and everyone else who will come to petition or answer charges under your jurisdiction and that of your judges. Likewise, to defend, preserve, and maintain churches, shrines, hospitals, and other revered places, roads, pilgrims, and merchants; to keep inviolate the constitution of this city, on which you are swearing with a sound and pure conscience, saving exceptions, if any exceptions have been made, putting aside hatred, love, fraud, favor, and every sort of deceit, according to our sound and pure common understanding, from the next

1. This and the following quotation come from the *Digest* of Justinian's code of Roman civil law (see Chapter 7).

2. Only the well-to-do could afford a knight's armor, weapons, and trained horses. Poorer citizens served their city as infantry.

Kalends of January[3] for one year and the whole day of the Kalends of January." Having said these words, let him who has administered the oath say, "Just as I have administered, so you, Lord B., will swear; and you promise to respect the commune of Florence,[4] and you will honor it in good faith and without fraud, guile, and any sort of deceit. So may God and these holy Gospels of God aid you." Following this, the judges, notaries, chamberlains, the podesta's knight or knights, and even his squires[5] swear oaths. . . .

The Podesta's Consultation with the Council on Complex Issues

To be sure, in those situations that are complex or serious or pertain to the essential interests of the city, he ought to confer with the council,[6] once it has been assembled, and should do so again and again if the nature of the matter demands it. . . . For then the podesta can act decisively with the knowledge and advice of the city council. . . . If the gravity of the situation requires greater counsel, others from among the wiser element of the citizenry should be summoned to render advice, after they have been elected by the city at large. To wit: representatives of the judges and those experienced in the law, representatives from the consuls of merchants and bankers[7] and from the priors of the trades,[8] and other appropriate persons. . . . For matters that touch all should be approved by all, and let unanimous agreement determine what benefits everyone.

Mind and Spirit

As religious cultures based on books of divine revelation, Judaism, Christianity, and Islam have all had to wrestle with the issue of the proper relationship of faith to reason. What legitimate role, if any, does human reason have in shedding light upon God's revealed truths and the mysteries of the faith? Is it illicit for a believer to pursue secular scholarship and science? If rational studies and religious doctrine seem to contradict each other, which is to be preferred?

---

3. January 1.

4. A commune was a self-governing town or city that possessed a charter defining its legal status. Florence, an industrial and commerical city in the north Italian province of Tuscany, had been a commune since at least 1200.

5. Podestas generally brought with them a large retinue of their own trained assistants, who would be given responsible positions within the commune during the podesta's term of office. These included notaries (legal secretaries), chamberlains (financial officers), knights (the podesta's bodyguard), and squires (personal attendants).

6. City councils, composed of aristocrats and rich merchants, were the usual governing bodies of Italy's early communes. During the thirteenth century many of these councils found it necessary to surrender their executive power to podestas.

7. The elected heads of merchant-banker associations or guilds.

8. The elected heads of other trade and artisan guilds.

From the middle of the twelfth century onward, European schoolmasters and students avidly collected and studied Latin translations of all the available works of the Greek scientist and philosopher Aristotle (384–322 B.C.) and several of his recent Muslim commentators. This swift influx of Greek rationalism, particularly the more advanced levels of Aristotelian logic, revolutionized education and had a profound effect on Latin Christianity's approach to theology. Europe's schoolmasters inaugurated an exciting period of intellectual flowering historians term the "Renaissance of the Twelfth Century."

The work of thirteenth-century intellectuals was no less impressive. Not only did they carry forward the breakthroughs of the twelfth century, but the best of them constructed encyclopedic syntheses in various fields, especially theology and law. Early twelfth-century scholars for the most part had been wandering students and teachers, but thirteenth-century academicians gravitated toward Europe's newest intellectual arenas — the universities. Although these universities attracted thinkers representing many schools of thought and approaches to learning, their means of investigation and instruction were refined variations on the methods of rational analysis championed by so many twelfth-century predecessors.

During the fourteenth century Europe dramatically shifted its intellectual and spiritual orientation, largely in response to a series of catastrophes that seemed to threaten its very survival. Famine, international war, civil discord and rebellion, and plague racked the West. To many, it seemed as though the last days of the world were at hand. These blows had a profound impact on the psyches of Western Europeans. Large numbers of Christians increasingly turned to more mystical and emotional forms of expression for solace, and death and decay became favorite artistic and literary themes.

Western civilization, however, did not decay or die. Its foundations had been firmly built over the previous thousand years, and by the end of the fourteenth century Europe was already beginning to show signs of recovery. The resiliency of Western European civilization was probably best expressed in new forms of literature and art that appeared toward the end of the century. By the fifteenth century, European artists were producing works that again breathed an optimistic view of humanity's place in the cosmos. Europe had entered another "Renaissance."

Peter Abelard

YES AND NO

One of the foremost pioneers of the Twelfth-Century Renaissance was Peter Abelard (1079–1142), a teacher of logic and theology at Paris. His brilliance and personality made him Christian Europe's most influential thinker of the time, and his approach to religious studies, which emphasized the use of logical analysis to illuminate divine truths, became the standard method of scholarship in the schools and universities of Europe.

The following selection comes from the preface to a textbook Abelard compiled sometime after 1120. Entitled *Sic et Non* (*Yes and No*), it presented Abelard's students with 156 theological issues, such as "Christ alone is the foundation of the Church," followed by groups of apparently conflicting texts culled from the Bible and other authoritative sources that seemed either to support (*sic*) or deny (*non*) the proposition under consideration. Abelard expected his students to apply the rules of logic and reason to resolve these quandaries. As any good teacher would, he provided his students with sufficient hints on how to deal successfully with these problems by laying down a series of general rules for textual analysis.

Questions for Analysis

1. How does Abelard regard the Bible? Does he believe its authors could have erred? How does he explain the apparent contradictions and errors that appear in portions of the Bible?
2. According to Abelard, what factors can contribute to one's misunderstanding of a text from scripture or the Church Fathers?
3. Does Abelard accept all texts as equally authoritative? If not, what order of priority has he established?
4. Is Abelard a religious skeptic, or does he believe there is an absolute standard of religious truth humans can know?
5. Abelard has been termed a "Christian rationalist" and a "Christian humanist." What do you think historians mean by those titles, and do you think them appropriate?

Among the multitudinous words of the holy Fathers[1] some sayings seem not only to differ from one another but even to contradict one another. Hence it is not presumptuous to judge concerning those by whom the world itself will be judged. . . . We do not presume to rebuke as untruthful or to denounce as erroneous those to whom the Lord said, "He who hears you hears me; he who despises you despises me" (Luke 10:16). Bearing in mind our foolishness we believe that our understanding is defective rather than the writing of those to whom the Truth Himself said, "It is not you who speak but the spirit of your Father who speaks in you"

1. The Fathers of the Church were early Christian authors whose writings were regarded as especially authoritative.

(Matthew 10:20). Why should it seem surprising if we, lacking the guidance of the Holy Spirit through whom those things were written and spoken, the Spirit impressing them on the writers, fail to understand them? Our achievement of full understanding is impeded especially by unusual modes of expression and by the different significances that can be attached to one and the same word, as a word is used now in one sense, now in another. Just as there are many meanings so there are many words. Tully[2] says that sameness is the mother of satiety in all things, that is to say it gives rise to fastidious distaste, and so it is appropriate to use a variety of words in discussing the same thing and not to express everything in common and vulgar words. . . .

We must also take special care that we are not deceived by corruptions of the text or by false attributions when sayings of the Fathers are quoted that seem to differ from the truth or to be contrary to it; for many apocryphal writings[3] are set down under names of saints to enhance their authority, and even the texts of divine Scripture are corrupted by the errors of scribes. That most faithful writer and true interpreter, Jerome,[4] accordingly warned us, "Beware of apocryphal writings. . . ." Again, on the title of Psalm 77 which is "An Instruction of Asaph," he commented, "It is written according to Matthew that when the Lord had spoken in parables and they did not understand, he said, 'These things are done that it might be fulfilled which was written by the prophet Isaias, *I will open my mouth in parables.*' The Gospels still have it so. Yet it is not Isaias who says this but Asaph." Again, let us explain simply why in Matthew and John it is written that the Lord was crucified at the third hour but in Mark at the sixth hour. There was a scribal error, and in Mark too the sixth hour was mentioned, but many read the Greek *epismo* as *gamma*. So too there was a scribal error where "Isaias" was set down for "Asaph." We know that many churches were gathered together from among ignorant gentiles. When they read in the Gospel, "That it might be fulfilled which was written by the prophet Asaph," the one who first wrote down the Gospel began to say, "Who is this prophet Asaph?" for he was not known among the people. And what did he do? In seeking to amend an error he made an error. We would say the same of another text in Matthew. "He took," it says, "the thirty pieces of silver, the price of him that was prized, as was written by the prophet Jeremias."[5] But we do not find this in Jeremias at all. Rather it is in Zacharias.[6] You see then that here, as before, there was an error. If in the Gospels themselves some things are corrupted by the ignorance of scribes, we should not be surprised that the same thing has sometimes happened in the writings of later Fathers who are of much less authority. . . .

It is no less important in my opinion to ascertain whether texts quoted from the Fathers may be ones that they themselves have retracted and corrected after they

---

2. Marcus Tullius Cicero (106–43 B.C.).

3. Counterfeit texts or works wrongly ascribed to a certain author.

4. Saint Jerome (345–420) was honored as one of the four major "Fathers of the Western Church" (as opposed to the Fathers of the Eastern Church).

5. A Hebrew prophet of the seventh and sixth centuries B.C.

6. A prophet of the late sixth century B.C.

came to a better understanding of the truth as the blessed Augustine did on many occasions; or whether they are giving the opinion of another rather than their own opinion . . . or whether, in inquiring into certain matters, they left them open to question rather than settled them with a definitive solution. . . .

In order that the way be not blocked and posterity deprived of the healthy labor of treating and debating difficult questions of language and style, a distinction must be drawn between the work of later authors and the supreme canonical authority of the Old and New Testaments. If, in Scripture, anything seems absurd you are not permitted to say, "The author of this book did not hold the truth" — but rather that the codex[7] is defective or that the interpreter erred or that you do not understand. But if anything seems contrary to truth in the works of later authors,[8] which are contained in innumerable books, the reader or auditor is free to judge, so that he may approve what is pleasing and reject what gives offense, unless the matter is established by certain reason or by canonical authority (of the Scriptures). . . .

In view of these considerations we have undertaken to collect various sayings of the Fathers that give rise to questioning because of their apparent contradictions as they occur to our memory. This questioning excites young readers to the maximum of effort in inquiring into the truth, and such inquiry sharpens their minds. Assiduous and frequent questioning is indeed the first key to wisdom. Aristotle, that most perspicacious of all philosophers, exhorted the studious to practice it eagerly, saying, "Perhaps it is difficult to express oneself with confidence on such matters if they have not been much discussed. To entertain doubts on particular points will not be unprofitable." For by doubting we come to inquiry; through inquiring we perceive the truth. . . .

Raymond Lull

A TREATISE ON THE STUDY OF ORIENTAL LANGUAGES

Sometime during the twelfth century, the world's first universities, as we know them today, took shape in Italy and France, and within the next several centuries others appeared in England, Spain, Germany, and elsewhere in Christian Europe. Of all the branches of learning taught at these universities, none was more prestigious or demanding than theology, and of all the schools of theology, Paris was preeminent. After about 1150, whenever medieval Christian Europe was confronted with a weighty religious issue it usually turned to the professors of theology at Paris for guidance.

One of Europe's pressing issues in the late thirteenth century was how to relate to

7. The manuscript.

8. The Church Fathers and other religious writers.

an expanding world. Two centuries of often disappointing crusades and the new Mongol menace in the east (Chapter 11) caused a number of European leaders to realize that armed force alone was not the answer to the problem of how to dutifully further God's plan for humanity by transforming the world into a single Christian body. One such person was the Spanish scholar, poet, and mystic Raymond Lull (ca 1232–1316).

Lull, who had studied Arabic and been influenced by Sufism, dedicated his life to the spiritual unification of all humanity, especially the conversion of all Muslims and Mongols to Roman Catholicism. A theorist and an activist, Lull served as a professor at three universities and worked as a missionary in Spain and North Africa. In 1298 or 1299, he sent the following letter to the University of Paris in the hope of persuading its masters to establish chairs of Eastern languages for missionary purposes. His call met with success in 1312, when Pope Clement V (1305–1314) ordered the universities of Paris, Bologna, Salamanca, and Oxford to provide instruction in Hebrew, Greek, Arabic, and Syriac.

Questions for Analysis

1. Why does Lull believe it is especially important to convert the Mongols?
2. Why does Lull believe it is a Christian's duty to work for the conversion of the world?
3. Does Lull offer any reasons, other than missionary work, for studying Arabaic and Greek? What do you infer from your answer?

Faithful to God is he and burning with supreme charity who in the knowledge and enjoyment of supreme wisdom and love directing the ignorant, illuminating the blind, leading back the dead to the way of life, fears not perils of his own adversity and bodily death for the testament of God. Who shall tell his glory and great splendor? Who shall number the generations of infidels who today know not God? Who shall estimate how many from the blindness of error slip into the shadows of hell? Alas! the devout Christian people of the faithful justly laments so great evils. O fount of science supernal,[1] that at Paris hast intoxicated marvelous doctrine so many professors of so great authority, extend thy torrents to the lands of the infidels, and irrigate the totally arid hearts of the erring with dew celestial, and drive away darkness, open to them the rays of light eternal. Ah, when shall all nations walk in thy light and every man walking in the splendor of thy sun see the salvation of God? With desire have I, Raymond Lull, desired this which is supremely desirable for all faithful Christians and obtainable by those whose

1. The heavenly science, i.e., theology.

intellects the supreme wisdom has divinely illuminated. Happy is that university which bears so many defenders of the faith, and happy that city whose soldiers armed with the wisdom and devotion of Christ can subdue barbarous nations to the supreme king. When shall all the earth adore Thee, God, hymn and bless Thy name, and every tribe and tongue serve Thee? . . .

Because as I know, since I speak from experience, there are many philosophers of the Arabs who strive to pervert Christians to the perfidy of Mahomet[2] and the sons of unbelievers pester us saying, Where is their God? And further, the Jews and Saracens to the best of their ability try to bring the Tartars[3] into their sects. And if it happens, which God forbid, that the Tartars become Jews or Saracens or constitute a sect by themselves, it is to be feared that this will result in incomparable detriment to all Christendom, just as happened from the sect of Mahomet at whose foundation the Saracens invaded us and about a third part of Christendom was lost.[4] Innumerable is that generation of Tartars, in a short time indeed it has subjugated many kingdoms and principalities by warlike hand.

You, reverend fathers and masters, see peril threaten the entire church of God, and unless your wisdom and devotion, by which all Christendom is sustained, opposes the shield of salvation to the perfidy of the Saracens, and if it neglects to restrain the impetuous torrent of Tartars — I will not say more — but think what may happen! And strange it is that there are more adversaries of God than defenders, and more men vituperate than praise Him; and God was made man for men and died that they might live; and many, too, have now declined from the unity of the church, like the Greeks and many other schismatics.[5] Consider how great evil is returned for good to God and how great opprobrium by those who were created to praise God, and how great persecution threatens us faithful, and what question we must answer to God at the last judgment, when He requires from us the death of those who should have enjoyed life eternal from our preaching and example.

Here the prick of conscience stings me and compels me to come to you, whose high discretion and wisdom it behooves to act in such a matter, so pious, so meritorious, in a service so grateful to God and useful to the entire world, namely, that here at Paris, where the fountain of divine wisdom rises, where the light of truth shines on Christian peoples, there should be founded study of Arabic, Tartar and Greek, that we, having learned the languages of the adversaries of God and ourselves, by preaching to and teaching them may overcome their errors in the sword of truth and render the people acceptable unto God and convert enemies into friends. If this be done and it please God that it so be, Christendom will receive the greatest exaltation and extension. And of this so inestimable thing you will be the foundation, and thou, university of Paris, will by no means be least among thy doctors, for from thee will come light to all peoples, and thou wilt offer testimony to the truth, and masters and disciples will

2. Muhammad.

3. The Mongols.

4. Islam conquered Syria-Palestine, North Africa, and Spain in the seventh and eighth centuries.

5. A schismatic is someone who has broken away from the main body of a church or religion but usually not for doctrinal reasons. Schismatics generally reject the authority rather than the beliefs of the main body.

flock to thee, and all shall hear all sciences from thee. What of good will the Greeks and Arabs have in their volumes that will not be known to thee, when thou shalt understand their tongues without an interpreter? Who will estimate how great praise, how great honor to God, how great compassion of charity towards poor sinners, and how great good would result in and from this place? And this can easily be done, if you direct your prayers to the illustrious king of France,[6] that he, who is noblest among the kings of earth, see fit to bestow his well-merited alms on this noblest of all undertakings, namely, to found and endow the said study or studies. And he will listen to you, I believe, after he has understood the importance of this undertaking.

Jean de Venette

CHRONICLE

Jean de Venette (ca 1307–1368), priest, master of theology at Paris, and head of the French province of the order of Carmelite Friars, composed a graphic account of French history covering the years 1340 to 1368 and concentrating on the disasters and devastations that seemed to characterize his age. Of peasant origin himself, he displayed genuine concern for the sufferings of France's lower classes, who bore a disproportionate amount of the pain. Our selections deal with the famine of 1315–1317 and the onslaught of the Black Death in 1348–1349.

Questions for Analysis

1. What is Venette's attitude toward visions, prophecies, and other supernatural phenomena?
2. Consider his treatment of the presumed causes of the Black Death. What does his analysis tell you about his methods of analysis and world-view? How does Venette's account of the plague compare with Thucydides' description of the Athenian epidemic of 430 B.C. (Chapter 4) as a "scientific" attempt to understand the cause, course, and consequences of this pestilence?
3. What does the flagellant movement suggest about the psychological effects of the plague? Compare it with the age's persecution of the Jews. Were they connected in any way?
4. What does the attitude of the masters of theology at Paris, the pope, and Venette toward the flagellants suggest?
5. According to Venette, what were the most serious consequences of the plague? What does this tell us about the man and the purpose behind his history?

---

6. Philip IV (1285–1314).

6. Was Jean de Venette a rationalist? If so, what sort?
7. What is the general tone of this history, and what does it tell us about the fourteenth century?

Let anyone who wishes to be reminded of most of the noteworthy events which happened in the kingdom of France from 1340 on read this present work in which I, a friar[1] at Paris, have written them down briefly, in great measure as I have seen and heard them. I shall begin with some hitherto unknown prognostications or prophecies which have come to hand. What they mean is not altogether known. Whether they speak truth or not I do not say but leave to the decision of the reader. This is one such. A priest of the diocese of Tours, freed in A.D. 1309 from the hands of the Saracens, who had held him captive for the space of thirteen years and three months, was saying mass in Bethlehem where the Lord was born. While he was praying for all Christian people . . . there appeared to him letters of gold written in this wise:

> In the year of the Lord 1315, on the fifteenth day of the month of March, shall begin so great a famine on earth that the people of low degree shall strive and struggle against the mighty and rich of this world. Also the wreath of the mightiest boxer shall fall to the ground very quickly afterwards. Also its flowers and its branches shall be broken and crushed. Also a noble and free city shall be seized and taken by slaves. Also strangers shall dwell there. Also the Church shall totter and the line of Saint Peter shall be execrated. Also the blood of many shall be poured out on the ground. Also a red cross shall appear and shall be lifted up. Therefore, good Christians, watch.

These are the words of this vision, but what they mean is not known.

Yet you must know that I, at the age of seven or eight, saw this great and mighty famine begin the very year foretold, 1315. It was so severe in France that most of the population died of hunger and want. And this famine lasted two years and more, for it began in 1315 and ceased in 1318. . . . Now, as I promised, I come to some of the noteworthy events, though not to all, which took place in the kingdom of France, and to a few which took place elsewhere, about A.D. 1340 and thereafter. I shall narrate them truthfully, as I saw them or heard about them. . . .

In A.D. 1348, the people of France and of almost the whole world were struck by a blow other than war. For in addition to the famine which I described in the beginning and to the wars which I described in the course of this narrative, pestilence and its attendant tribulations appeared again in various parts of the world. In the month of August, 1348, after Vespers[2] when the sun was beginning to set, a big and very bright star appeared above Paris,

1. Literally, a "brother." The Roman Church had four major orders of mendicant, or begging, friars who ministered to the spiritual needs of urban populations: the Franciscans, the Dominicans, the Augustinians, and the Carmelites.

2. A time of day set aside for prayer in the late afternoon or early evening.

toward the west. It did not seem, as stars usually do, to be very high above our hemisphere but rather near. As the sun set and night came on, this star did not seem to me or to many other friars who were watching it to move from one place. At length, when night had come, this big star, to the amazement of all of us who were watching, broke into many different rays and, as it shed these rays over Paris toward the east, totally disappeared and was completely annihilated. Whether it was a comet or not, whether it was composed of airy exhalations and was finally resolved into vapor, I leave to the decision of astronomers. It is, however, possible that it was a presage of the amazing pestilence to come, which, in fact, followed very shortly in Paris and throughout France and elsewhere, as I shall tell. All this year and the next, the mortality of men and women, of the young even more than of the old, in Paris and in the kingdom of France, and also, it is said, in other parts of the world, was so great that it was almost impossible to bury the dead. People lay ill little more than two or three days and died suddenly, as it were in full health. He who was well one day was dead the next and being carried to his grave. Swellings appeared suddenly in the armpit or in the groin — in many cases both — and they were infallible signs of death. This sickness or pestilence was called an epidemic by the doctors. Nothing like the great numbers who died in the years 1348 and 1349 has been heard of or seen or read of in times past. This plague and disease came from . . . association and contagion, for if a well man visited the sick he only rarely evaded the risk of death. Wherefore in many towns timid priests withdrew, leaving the exercise of their ministry to such of the religious as were more daring. In many places not two out of twenty remained alive. So high was the mortality at the Hôtel-Dieu[3] in Paris that for a long time, more than five hundred dead were carried daily with great devotion in carts to the cemetery of the Holy Innocents in Paris for burial. A very great number of the saintly sisters of the Hôtel-Dieu who, not fearing to die, nursed the sick in all sweetness and humility, with no thought of honor, a number too often renewed by death, rest in peace with Christ, as we may piously believe. . . .

Some said that this pestilence was caused by infection of the air and waters, since there was at this time no famine nor lack of food supplies, but on the contrary great abundance. As a result of this theory of infected water and air as the source of the plague the Jews were suddenly and violently charged with infecting wells and water and corrupting the air. The whole world rose up against them cruelly on this account. In Germany and other parts of the world where Jews lived, they were massacred and slaughtered by Christians, and many thousands were burned everywhere, indiscriminately. The unshaken, if fatuous, constancy of the men and their wives was remarkable. For mothers hurled their children first into the fire that they might not be baptized and then leaped in after them to burn with their husbands and children. It is said that many bad Christians were found who in a like manner put poison into wells. But in truth, such poisonings, . . . [if] . . . they actually were perpetrated, could not have caused so great a plague nor have infected

3. "The House of God" — Paris's largest hospital.

so many people. There were other causes; for example, the will of God and the corrupt humors and evil inherent in air and earth.[4] Perhaps the poisonings, if they actually took place in some localities, reinforced these causes. The plague lasted in France for the greater part of the years 1348 and 1349 and then ceased. Many country villages and many houses in good towns remained empty and deserted.

After the cessation of the epidemic, pestilence, or plague, the men and women who survived married each other. There was no sterility among the women, but on the contrary fertility beyond the ordinary. Pregnant women were seen on every side. Many twins were born and even three children at once. But the most surprising fact is that children born after the plague, when they became of an age for teeth, had only twenty or twenty-two teeth, though before that time men commonly had thirty-two in their upper and lower jaws together. What this diminution in the number of teeth signified I wonder greatly, unless it be a new era resulting from the destruction of one human generation by the plague and its replacement by another. But woe is me! the world was not changed for the better but for the worse by this renewal of population. For men were more avaricious and grasping than before, even though they had far greater possessions. They were more covetous and disturbed each other more frequently with suits, brawls, disputes, and pleas. Nor by the mortality resulting from this terrible plague inflicted by God was peace between kings and lords established. On the contrary, the enemies of the king of France and of the Church were stronger and wickeder than before and stirred up wars on sea and on land. Greater evils than before populated everywhere in the world. And this fact was very remarkable. Although there was an abundance of all goods, yet everything was twice as dear, whether it were utensils, victuals, or merchandise, hired helpers or peasants and serfs, except for some hereditary domains which remained abundantly stocked with everything. Charity began to cool, and iniquity with ignorance and sin to abound, for few could be found in the good towns and castles who knew how or were willing to instruct children in the rudiments of grammar. . . .

In the year 1349, while the plague was still active and spreading from town to town, men in Germany, Flanders, Hainaut, and Lorraine[5] uprose and began a new sect on their own authority. Stripped to the waist, they gathered in large groups and bands and marched in procession through the crossroads and squares of cities and good towns. There they formed circles and beat upon their backs with weighted scourges, rejoicing as they did so in loud voices and singing hymns suitable to their rite and newly composed for it. Thus for thirty-three days[6] they marched through many towns doing their penance and affording a great spectacle to the wondering people. They flogged their shoulders and arms with scourges tipped with iron points so zealously as to draw blood. But they did not come to Paris nor

---

4. Until the triumph of the germ theory in the late nineteenth century, one widely held explanation for disease was that it originated from *miasma*, the poisonous atmosphere arising from swamps and other putrifying matter.

5. Regions in modern Belgium, northwest Germany, eastern France, and Luxemburg.

6. Medieval Christians believed Jesus had lived on earth for thirty-three years.

to any part of France, for they were forbidden to do so by the king of France, who did not want them. He acted on the advice of the masters of theology of the University of Paris, who said that this new sect had been formed contrary to the will of God, to the rites of Holy Mother Church, and to the salvation of all their souls. That indeed this was and is true appeared shortly. For Pope Clement VI was fully informed concerning this fatuous new rite by the masters of Paris through emissaries reverently sent to him and, on the grounds that it had been damnably formed, contrary to law, he forbade the Flagellants under threat of anathema[7] to practice in the future the public penance which they had so presumptuously undertaken. His prohibition was just, for the Flagellants, supported by certain fatuous priests and monks, were enunciating doctrines and opinions which were beyond measure evil, erroneous, and fallacious. For example, they said that their blood thus drawn by the scourge and poured out was mingled with the blood of Christ. Their many errors showed how little they knew of the Catholic faith. Wherefore, as they had begun fatuously of themselves and not of God, so in a short time they were reduced to nothing. On being warned, they desisted and humbly received absolution and penance at the hands of their prelates as the pope's representatives. Many honorable women and devout matrons, it must be added, had done this penance with scourges, marching and singing through towns and churches like the men, but after a little like the others they desisted.

VISIONS OF DEATH AND LIFE

These two pieces of art illustrate the dual vision of the Later Middle Ages. The first, a 5 3/4-inch ivory figurine by an unknown French sculptor, dates from around 1450 and is entitled *Vanity: Allegory on the Transitoriness of Life*. The second, *The Adoration of the Shepherds*, was painted by the Alsatian German artist Martin Schongauer (ca 1430/1445–1491) between 1475 and 1480.

Questions for Analysis

1. What can we infer about the age and status of the woman in the French sculpture? What does she represent?
2. Consider the skeleton. What does it represent, and what is it saying to the woman by its posture and gestures?

(Questions continued on page 340.)

7. Excommunication.

Vanity: Allegory on the Transitoriness of Life

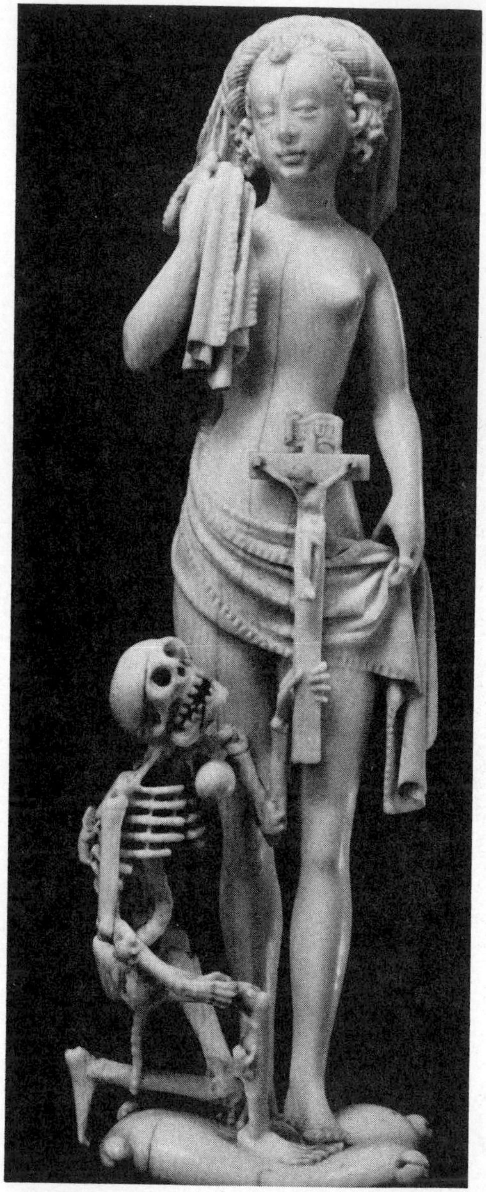

The Adoration of the Shepherds

3. What choices do you think the woman is contemplating?
4. What is the message of this work of art?
5. Compare Mary, the mother of Jesus, and the shepherds in Schongauer's nativity scene with the woman and skeleton in the French sculpture. What are the similarities? The differences? Which are more significant? Why?
6. What is the message of Schongauer's work?
7. Consider the manner in which both artists portray the human body and other natural phenomena. What might we infer from this?
8. How do these two masterpieces represent two complementary visions of life?

CHAPTER

11

Migrants, Merchants, and Missionaries: The Exchange and Clash of Cultures

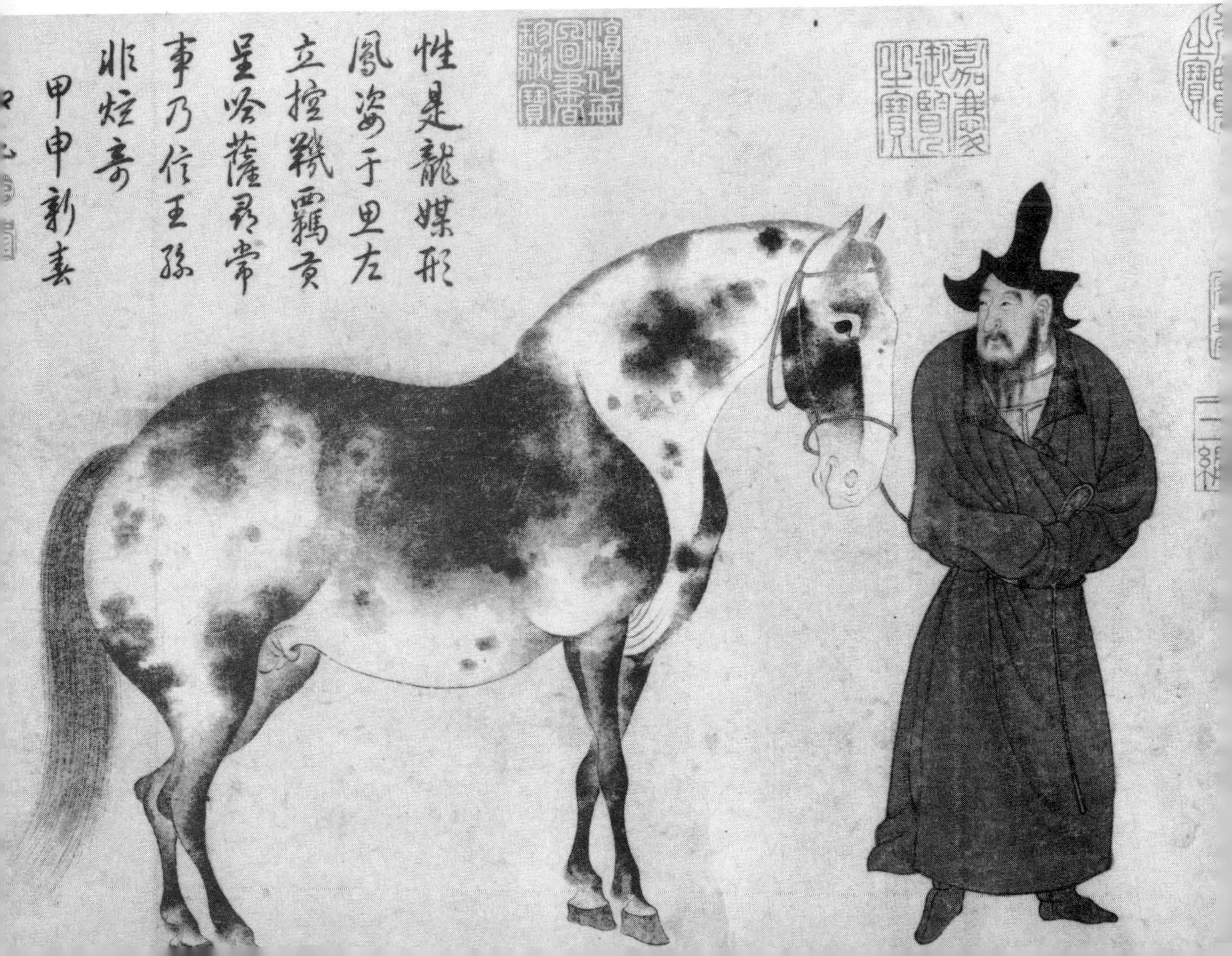

Although Europe's late-fifteenth-century transoceanic explorations inaugurated a new stage of global interconnectedness by virtue of Columbus's discovery of the Americas, in many respects the events of 1492 and following were a continuation of a process of long-range cultural exchange that had been gaining momentum throughout Eurasia and Africa since around A.D. 1000. This was due in part to the impetus provided by such peoples as the Turks, Vikings, and Mongols. Many of their travels and conquests were filled with wholesale destruction, yet these adventurers and empire builders created new pathways for the transmission of cultures between approximately 1000 and 1500.

As we have already seen (Chapter 9), Turkish converts to Islam spread their Muslim faith and culture into India, Anatolia (modern Turkey), the Balkan region of southeast Europe, and deeper into Central Asia as they carved out and expanded a variety of states. In less dramatic fashion, Scandinavian (also called Norse and Viking) seafarers established colonies in Iceland, Greenland, and even faraway "Vinland," somewhere along the northeast shore of North America. Norse who had settled in France in the tenth century and become Norman French expanded the boundaries of European Christendom in the Mediterranean. During the last half of the eleventh century, Norman adventurers conquered southern Italy from the Byzantine Empire and took Sicily from its Muslim overlords. These same Normans assaulted the Balkan possessions of the emperor at Constantinople and became an integral part of medieval Western Europe's most energetic and protracted overseas colonial adventure — the crusades in the Levant. Of all these migrant catalysts of cultural exchange, the most explosive and impressive were the Mongols. In the course of the thirteenth century, they created a Eurasian land empire that reached from the Pacific to the Ukraine. After the initial shock of their conquests, they established a *Pax Mongolica* (Mongol Peace) that opened up lines of direct communication between East Asia and Western Europe. For about a century, people, goods, ideas, and diseases traveled fairly quickly from one end of the Eurasian land mass to the other.

As important as the conquerors and state builders were, it was the largely anonymous men and women traveling as merchants, pilgrims, missionaries, and curiosity seekers who played the most significant roles in this half millennium of long-distance travel and cultural interchange. Indian and

Chinese merchants traveled into Southeast Asia, where they influenced the evolution of a hybrid culture that has been termed "Indo-Chinese." Arabs in camel caravans trekked south across the Sahara to trade salt and manufactured goods for gold, slaves, and ivory. Italian merchants established bases in the Black Sea on the western edge of Central Asia. Pilgrims of many different faiths often traveled great distances to worship at their holy sites. Muslim and Christian missionaries, motivated by devotion and love, labored among foreign people whom they believed would be damned to hell without spiritual guidance. African, Arab, Indian, Southeast Asian, and Chinese sailors shared the waters of the Indian Ocean. Long before Columbus and da Gama, the globe was on its way toward becoming the home of an interconnected human community.

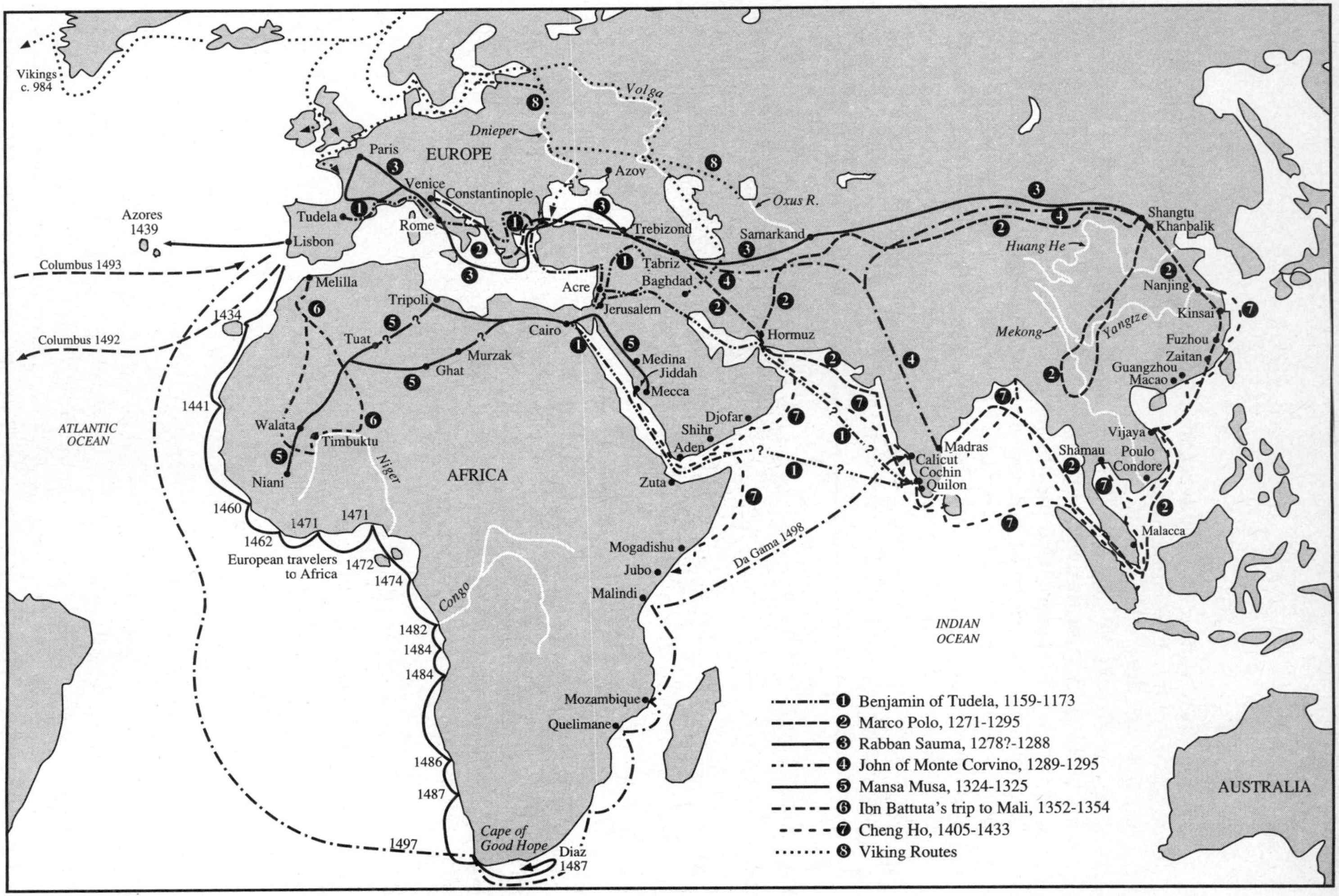

Map 5 Afro-Eurasian Travelers, 1000–1500

Travel in the Age of the *Pax Mongolica*

Temujin (ca 1162–1227), the Mongol lord who assumed the title Chingis (Ghengis) Khan, or "ruler from sea to sea," in 1206, believed he had a divine destiny to rule the world, and he and his immediate successors, particularly his grandson Kublai (ca 1214–1294), did come close to controlling all Eurasia. Although the Mongols were stopped in Syria, in Southeast Asia, at the borders of India and Arabia, in Eastern Europe, and in the waters off Japan, by 1279 they had still managed to create the largest land empire in history.

Beginning around the time of the rule of Kublai Khan (1260–1294) and extending for over half a century after his death, the Mongols governed their enormous empire in relative peace and good order. Mongol discipline and organization made it possible to travel from Eastern Europe to China with a reasonable degree of safety and speed. Brother William of Rubruck, for example, a Franciscan emissary to the Great Khan Mangu, left Constantinople on May 7, 1253, and arrived without serious incident at the khan's court at Karakorum in Mongolia on December 27 of that same year. William's experiences were far from unique. Large numbers of merchants, ambassadors, fortune seekers, missionaries, and other travelers journeyed in all directions across the Mongol Empire. This steppe land bridge between East Asia and Western Europe was severed after 1350, however, as the Mongol Empire broke up and the opportunity for normal direct contact between the eastern and western extremities of Eurasia was lost for a century and a half.

Rabban Sauma

TRAVELS IN THE WEST

Beginning in 1245, the Roman papacy initiated a series of embassies to various Mongol khans to discover their designs toward Western Europe and to convert them to Catholic Christianity. The hope was that if the Mongols became Christians they would join the West in crushing Islam in a final, glorious crusade. This double dream of conversion and crusade never became a reality, but at least one Mongol leader seriously thought about it. In 1287 Arghun, il-khan (a subordinate khan) of Persia (1284–1291) and a nephew of Kublai, the khan of khans, sent a Nestorian Christian monk, Rabban (Master) Sauma (ca 1230–1294), to the West with letters for the pope, the kings of France and England, and the emperor of Constantinople in which the Mongol prince offered to become a Christian in return for an alliance against the Muslims of Syria-Palestine. Arghun died before he or anyone else could act on this proposal, however, and in 1295 his successor embraced Islam, thus ending any threat of a Mongol-European crusade in the Holy Land.

Early in the fourteenth century an unknown author wrote a biography in Syriac of Mar ("Reverend") Yaballaha III (1281–1317), the patriarch, or head, of the Nestorian Church and Sauma's friend and former disciple. In it he included an abbreviated version of the monk's account of his travels in the West. The original, which Rabban Sauma wrote in Persian, is lost.

Sauma was born in the Mongol capital of Khanbalik (modern Beijing) into a Nestorian Christian family of Uighurs, a Turkic people from the steppes that lay west of China. Toward midlife he set out for Jerusalem. Because of troubles in the Holy Land, he had to abandon his pilgrimage in Baghdad, where he did have the satisfaction of seeing his traveling companion Markos installed as Yaballaha III, the spiritual leader of all Nestorians from Syria to China. Several years later Sauma accepted the il-khan's commission to travel to the Christian rulers of the West with a proposal for a holy alliance against Islam.

In the following selection this Turkic Christian from northern China tells of his experiences at the court of Pope Nicholas IV (1288–1292) during Lent and Easter of 1288. Rabban Sauma arrived in Rome in 1287, only to discover the papal throne vacant and the cardinal electors deeply divided. While waiting for them to elect a new pope, Sauma visited King Philip IV in Paris and Edward I of England, who was in the French province of Gascony. Then Sauma returned to Italy to winter at Genoa.

As you read this account, remember that Nestorianism, which had made inroads among the peoples of Central Asia and western China during the seventh and eighth centuries, had developed essentially in isolation from the Churches of Rome and Constantinople. Nestorian Christians differed from Roman Catholics on the issue of papal authority and on the question of how Jesus's human nature was related to his divinity.

Questions for Analysis

1. How did the pope and Rabban Sauma act toward one another? Is there any evidence that Nicholas or Rabban Sauma were aware of the differences that divided their Churches? If they were, did they have any reason to overlook those differences?
2. How do you interpret Pope Nicholas's "appointing" Mar Yaballaha to an office he had already held for quite a few years? Why do you think the pope made Rabban Sauma "Visitator over all Christians"? Why would Sauma accept such an office, especially since he was already the Nestorian patriarch's Visitator-General?
3. What is the general tone of this account?

At the end of the winter there came from the country of Almadan[1] a distinguished man who was the Visitator[2] of the Reverend Pope, going to Rome. And when he heard that Rabban Sauma was there, he came to greet him. And when he entered, they exchanged greetings and kissed one another in Christian love. And he said to Rabban Sauma: "I have come to see thee, for I have heard of thee that thou art a good and wise man, and also that thou desirest to go to Rome." Rabban Sauma said to him: "What can I say to thee, honored friend? For I have come on an embassy from King Arghon and the Catholicus[3] of the East in behalf of Jerusalem to the Reverend Pope, and it is a full year that I have been here, and a Pope is not seated. What shall I go and say and answer to the Mongols? They, whose heart is harder than rock, desire to take the Holy City,[4] while those whose business it is do not resolve upon it, even do not think of the thing at all. We know not what we shall go and say." The Visitator said to him: "Thy words are true. I will go myself, and all the words thou hast spoken I will tell literally to the Cardinals,[5] and I will constrain them to elect a Pope."

And the Visitator departed and came to Rome, and told it to the King,[6] and he to the Reverend Pope. On that same day he sent a messenger to them, that the party of Rabban Sauma should come. And they on the arrival of the messenger diligently set out for Rome, and they reached it in fifteen days. And they asked: "Who is this Pope they have elected?" They answered him: "It is the bishop who conversed with you, when you came here first, his name is Nicholas." And they rejoiced greatly. When they arrived, the Reverend Pope sent people to meet them, the Metropolitan[7] along with many others. And Rabban Sauma went in at once to the Reverend Pope. And he was seated on his throne. And he (Bar Sauma) presented himself with homage and kissed his feet and hands. And he retired backwards with his hands clasped. And he said to the Reverend Pope: "May thy throne be established, O Father, forever, and blessed may it be above all kings and peoples, and may peace reign in thy days in the whole Church to the ends of the earth! Now that I have seen thy face it has brightened my eyes that I do not come heartbroken to the lands. I acknowledge the grace of God that He has counted me

1. Germany (Allemand).

2. A personal representative bearing delegated power from a higher authority.

3. Another of Yaballaha's titles. *Catholicus* is a Greek word meaning "universal." Therefore, a catholicus claimed authority over an entire Church.

4. Jerusalem.

5. The cardinals were the pope's chief advisers and headed the different bureaucratic offices within the papacy. They also enjoyed the exclusive right of electing the pope.

6. He is mistaken; there was no king to visit. Because the Nestorian Church had a tradition of deferring to secular authority (Yaballaha was only consecrated patriarch after receiving Arghon's approval), either Rabban Sauma or the anonymous author assumed the pope was answerable to some king.

7. A metropolitan (also called an archbishop) exercised ecclesiastical authority over a number of subordinate, or *suffragan*, bishops within a large area known as a *province*. The metropolitan's cathedral, or seat of power, was located in the provincial capital, or *metropolis*. Apparently this metropolitan was the visitator whom Sauma met coming from Germany.

worthy of the sight of thee." And he presented to him the gift of King Arghon along with his letters and also the gift of Mar Yaballaha the Catholicus, that is, "the blessing," and his letters. And the Reverend Pope was glad and rejoiced, and he honored Rabban Sauma more than was wont. And he said to him: "It will be well if thou celebrate the season with us and see our custom," — for that day was the middle of the Dominical Fast (Lent). He replied: "Your command is high and lofty." And the Reverend Pope assigned an abode for his sojourn, and appointed attendants to give him all he desired.

And after some days Rabban Sauma said to the Reverend Pope: "I desire to consecrate (the Eucharist) that you too may see our custom." And he bade him to consecrate, as he requested. And on that day a great congregation assembled to see how the ambassador of the Mongols consecrates. And when they saw, they rejoiced and said: "The language is different, but the rite is one." . . .

And when Sunday came again, that is, Hosanna Sunday (Palm Sunday), there assembled in the morning thousands and tens of thousands without number before the throne (of the Pope), and they brought olive branches. . . . And he consecrated the Mysteries.[8] And he gave Rabban Sauma the Communion first, after he had confessed his sinfulness. And he absolved him from his faults and sins and those of his ancestors. And he rejoiced greatly to receive Communion from the hand of the Reverend Pope, and he received the Communion with tears and weeping, acknowledging the grace of God and thinking upon the mercy poured out upon him. . . .

Rabban Sauma now describes the various rituals he witnessed during the week preceding Easter Sunday.

And when all this had taken place, he desired of the Reverend Pope permission to depart. But he said to him: "It is our desire that thou remain with us, and thou shalt be in our company, and we will keep thee as the apple of our eye." But Rabban Sauma replied: "I, O Father, have come on an embassy to do you service. If my coming were of my own desire, in the outer gate of your monastery would I accomplish the days of this my life of vanity in your service. But when I return I will declare to the Kings there the favors you have done to my weakness. I think it will be a great satisfaction to the Christians. But I desire of your Holiness that you give me an alms of some of the relics you have." The Reverend Pope said: "If it were our custom to give everyone these relics, although they were mountains high, they would soon be finished off by the myriads. But since thou hast come from a far country, we will give thee a few." And he gave him a small relic from the garment of Our Lord Christ, and from the . . . bonnet of the Lady Mary, and small relics of the saints there. And he sent to Mar Yaballaha a crown of pure gold for his head, adorned with very precious stones, and clothing for the vestments of his function, red and embroidered with gold, and shoes sewn with small pearls, and boots, and also a ring from his own finger; and letters patent[9] which contained authorization of his Patriarchate over all the Orientals. And to

8. Celebrated mass.

9. An official grant.

Rabban Sauma he gave letters patent as Visitator over all Christians.[10] And he blessed him. And he allotted to him for the expenses of his journey 1500 pounds of red gold. And to King Arghon he sent some gifts. And he embraced and kissed Rabban Sauma and dismissed him. And Rabban Sauma rendered thanks to Our Lord that He had deemed him worthy of such boons.

John of Monte Corvino

LETTER

In response to Rabban Sauma's visit to Rome, in 1289 Pope Nicholas IV dispatched a Franciscan friar, John of Monte Corvino (1247–ca 1328), to the Mongols with letters for Arghun in Persia and other khans farther to the east, including the Great Khan, Kublai. Civil war among the Mongols delayed Friar John's journey across Central Asia, and he arrived at Khanbalik in northern China only in 1295, a year after Kublai's death. Making the best of his situation, John decided to remain as a missionary in the Mongol capital.

During his long stay in Asia, Friar John wrote three letters to his fellow Franciscans back home asking for their support. In response, Pope Clement V (1305–1314) appointed him archbishop of Khanbalik in 1307 and sent off several assistant missionaries. Although the new archbishop remained at his post until his death and Pope Benedict XII (1334–1342) sent a replacement, the Roman Catholic mission in China barely limped along. When the Ming Dynasty finally expelled the Mongols in 1368, European missionary activity in China ended and would not be revived until the coming of the Jesuits in the sixteenth century (Chapter 12). The following document is one of the letters sent westward by Friar John.

Questions for Analysis

1. What problems has Friar John encountered?
2. How does he seem to have gained most of his converts? Does he seem to have won most of them from the Nestorian Christians or the non-Christian Mongols and Chinese? What do you infer from this?
3. Compare the tone of this letter with that of Rabban Sauma's account. To what do you ascribe the difference?

---

10. Rabban Sauma had held the office of Visitator General of the Nestorian Church since 1280 and had visited Rome in that capacity.

I, Friar John of Monte Corvino, of the order of Minor Friars,[1] departed from Tauris, a city of the Persians,[2] in the year of the Lord 1291, and proceeded to India. And I remained in the country of India, wherein stands the church of St. Thomas the Apostle,[3] for thirteen months, and in that region baptized in different places about one hundred persons. The companion of my journey was Friar Nicholas of Pistoia, of the order of Preachers,[4] who died there, and was buried in the church aforesaid.

I proceeded on my further journey and made my way to Cathay,[5] the realm of the Emperor of the Tatars[6] who is called the Grand Cham.[7] To him I presented the letter of our Lord the Pope, and invited him to adopt the Catholic Faith of our Lord Jesus Christ, but he had grown too old in idolatry. However he bestows many kindnesses upon the Christians, and these two years past I am abiding with him.

The Nestorians, a certain body who profess to bear the Christian name, but who deviate sadly from the Christian religion, have grown so powerful in those parts that they will not allow a Christian of another ritual to have ever so small a chapel, or to publish any doctrine different from their own.

To these regions there never came anyone of the Apostles, nor yet of the Disciples.[8] And so the Nestorians aforesaid, either directly or through others whom they bribed, have brought on me persecutions of the sharpest. For they got up stories that I was not sent by our lord the Pope, but was a great spy and impostor; and after a while they produced false witnesses who declared that there was indeed an envoy sent with presents of immense value for the emperor, but that I had murdered him in India, and stolen what he had in charge. And these intrigues and calumnies went on for some five years. And thus it came to pass that many a time I was dragged before the judgment seat with ignominy and threats of death. At last, by God's providence, the emperor, through the confessions of a certain individual, came to know my innocence and the malice of my adversaries; and he banished them with their wives and children.

In this mission I abode alone and without any associate for eleven years; but it is now going on for two years since I was joined by Friar Arnold, a German of the province of Cologne.

I have built a church in the city of Cambaliech,[9] in which the king has his

1. The "lesser brethren," the official name of the Franciscans.

2. Tauris (modern Tabriz, Iran) was the capital city of the il-khan of Persia.

3. Missionaries (according to tradition, led by Saint Thomas the Apostle) established a small Christian community on the west coast of India in the late first century that continued to exist throughout the centuries that followed.

4. Also known as the Dominicans.

5. Northern China. So called because of the Khitan people, who had a kingdom centered on Beijing from 916 to 1125.

6. Timur (1294–1307). Although Western visitors used the names Tatar (or, incorrectly, Tartar) and Mongol interchangeably, the Tatars, who spoke a Turkic language, were not Mongols. There was, however, a fair amount of intermarriage among these various steppe nomads. For example, the Turkish warlord Timur the Lame (1336–1405) had some Mongol ancestry.

7. More often spelled "khan."

8. In other words, Christianity was not introduced into China until centuries after the Apostolic Age of the first century A.D.

9. Khanbalik.

chief residence. This I completed six years ago; and I have built a belltower to it, and put three bells in it. I have baptized there, as well as I can estimate, up to this time some 6,000 persons; and if those charges against me of which I have spoken had not been made, I should have baptized more than 30,000. And I am often still engaged in baptizing.

Also I have gradually bought one hundred and fifty boys, the children of pagan parents, and of ages varying from seven to eleven, who had never learned any religion. These boys I have baptized, and I have taught them Greek and Latin after our manner. Also I have written out Psalters for them, with thirty Hymnaries and two Breviaries.[10] By help of these, eleven of the boys already know our service, and form a choir and take their weekly turn of duty as they do in convents, whether I am there or not. Many of the boys are also employed in writing out Psalters and other things suitable. His Majesty the Emperor moreover delights much to hear them chanting. I have the bells rung at all the canonical hours, and with my congregation of babes and sucklings I perform divine service, and the chanting we do by ear because I have no service book with the notes.

A certain king of this part of the world, by name George, belonging to the sect of Nestorian Christians, and of the illustrious family of that great king who was called Prester John[11] of India, in the first year of my arrival here attached himself to me, and being converted by me to the truth of the Catholic faith, took the lesser orders,[12] and when I celebrated mass he used to attend me wearing his royal robes. Certain others of the Nestorians on this account accused him of apostasy, but he brought over a great part of his people with him to the true Catholic faith, and built a church on a scale of royal magnificence in honor of our God, of the Holy Trinity, and of our lord the Pope, giving it the name of the *Roman Church*.

This King George six years ago departed to the Lord a true Christian, leaving as his heir a son scarcely out of the cradle, and who is now nine years old. And after King George's death his brothers, perfidious followers of the errors of Nestorius, perverted again all those whom he had brought over to the church, and carried them back to their original schismatical creed. And being all alone, and not able to leave his Majesty the Cham, I could not go to visit the church above-mentioned, which is twenty days' journey distant.

Yet, if I could but get some good fellow-workers to help me, I trust in God that all this might be retrieved, for I still possess the grant which was made in our favor by the late King George before mentioned. So I say again that if it had not been for the slanderous charges which I have spoken of, the harvest reaped by this time would have been great!

Indeed if I had had but two or three comrades to aid me 'tis possible that the Emperor Cham would have been baptized by this time! I ask then for such brethren

---

10. Various prayer books.

11. A mythic Christian king of the East, who supposedly sought reunion with the West. His kingdom was variously located in Ethiopia, India, and Central Asia, all of which had Christian communities long separated from the West.

12. He was admitted to the four lesser clerical offices below those of priest, deacon, and subdeacon.

to come, if any are willing to come, such I mean as will make it their great business to lead exemplary lives. . . .

As for the road hither I may tell you that the way through the land of the Goths,[13] subject to the Emperor of the Northern Tatars, is the shortest and safest; and by it the friars might come, along with the letter-carriers, in five or six months. The other route again is very long and very dangerous, involving two sea-voyages; the first of which is about as long as that from Acre to the province of Provence,[14] whilst the second is as long as from Acre to England. And it is possible that it might take more than two years to accomplish the journey that way. But, on the other hand, the first-mentioned route has not been open for a considerable time, on account of wars that have been going on.

It is twelve years since I have had any news of the Papal court, or of our Order, or of the state of affairs generally in the west. Two years ago indeed there came hither a certain Lombard . . . chirurgeon,[15] who spread abroad in these parts the most incredible blasphemies about the court of Rome and our Order[16] and the state of things in the west, and on this account I exceedingly desire to obtain true intelligence. I pray the brethren whom this letter may reach to do their possible to bring its contents to the knowledge of our lord the Pope and the Cardinals, and the agents of the Order at the court of Rome. . . .

I have myself grown old and grey, more with toil and trouble than with years; for I am not more than fifty-eight. I have got a competent knowledge of the language and character which is most generally used by the Tatars. And I have already translated into that language and character the New Testament and the Psalter, and have caused them to be written out in the fairest penmanship they have; and so by writing, reading, and preaching, I bear open and public testimony to the Law of Christ. And I had been in treaty with the late King George, if he had lived, to translate the whole Latin ritual, that it might be sung throughout the whole extent of his territory; and whilst he was alive I used to celebrate mass in his church, according to the Latin ritual, reading in the before-mentioned language and character the words of both the preface and the Canon.[17]

And the son of the king before-mentioned is called after my name, John; and I hope in God that he will walk in his father's steps.

As far as I ever saw or heard tell, I do not believe that any king or prince in the world can be compared to his majesty the Cham in respect of the extent of his dominions, the vastness of their population, or the amount of his wealth. Here I stop.

Dated at the city of Cambalec in the kingdom of Cathay, in the year of the Lord 1305, and on the 8th day of January.

---

13. He probably means the Alans, a Christian, Iranian people who dwelt on the northern shores of the Black Sea. Undoubtedly he is telling them to take the overland route across the steppes.

14. From Israel to southern France.

15. A surgeon.

16. A bitter conflict existed between Pope Boniface VIII (1294–1303) and a radical splinter sect known as the Spiritual Franciscans.

17. The opening prayers (Preface) and Offertory, Consecration, and Communion (the Canon) of the mass. In other words, he celebrated the Latin rite mass in the language of King George's people.

Marco Polo

DESCRIPTION OF THE WORLD

No chapter on trans-Eurasian travel in the Mongol Age would be complete without a selection from Marco Polo (ca 1253–1324), a Venetian who spent twenty years in East Asia, most of it in the service of Kublai Khan. Around 1260 Marco's father and uncle, Niccolò and Maffeo, both merchants from Venice, set sail for the Black Sea and from there made an overland trek to Khanbalik and the court of Kublai. When they were preparing to return home, the Great Khan requested them to visit the pope and ask him to send 100 missionary-scholars to Cathay. The Polos arrived at the crusader port of Acre (in modern Israel) in 1269 and in 1271 received a commission from Pope Gregory X (1271–1276) to return to China with two Dominican friars. The two friars quickly abandoned the expedition, afraid of the dangers that awaited them, but Niccolò's seventeen-year-old son, Marco, was made of sterner stuff. The brothers Polo, accompanied by young Marco, returned to Khanbalik. Here Marco entered the khan's service and for close to two decades traveled extensively over much of Kublai's empire as one of the many foreign officials serving the Mongol, or Yüan, Dynasty (1264–1368).

In 1292 the three men set sail for the West by way of the Indian Ocean and arrived home in Venice in 1295. In 1298 Marco was captured in a war with Genoa and, while in prison, related his adventures to a writer of romances known as Rustichello of Pisa. Together they produced a rambling, often disjointed account of the sites, peoples, personalities, and events Marco had encountered in Asia.

Despite its literary flaws, the book was widely translated and distributed throughout late medieval Europe. Its popularity was due in part to Marco's eye for ethnographic detail, as the book abounds with stories of customs that Westerners found fascinatingly different. In the following selections Polo tells of certain sexual customs regarding women within several different Asian cultures.

Questions for Analysis

1. Why do you think the people of Kamul practiced their particular form of hospitality? Why would a Mongol such as Mangu Khan find this custom so offensive? How were the people of Kamul able to prevail on the khan to allow them to continue this practice? What does Mangu's eventual permission suggest about Mongol rule?
2. Compare the practices of the people of Kamul with the customs of Tibet. What strikes you as more significant, the similarities or the differences? Why?
3. Why do you think the people of Kardandan placed the husband in bed for forty days with his new child? Was this practice "liberating" for his wife?

4. Does any one of these groups of women appear to have greater power or status than the others? Which one? Why?
5. Despite differences in customs and attitudes, do you perceive any common elements shared by these four groups of women?

[*The Women of Kamul*]

Kamul is a district situated within the great province of Tanguth, subject to the grand khan, and contains many towns and castles, of which the principal city is also named Kamul.[1] This district lies in the intermediate space between two deserts. . . . The men are addicted to pleasure, and attend to little else than playing upon instruments, singing, dancing, reading, writing, according to the practice of the country, and the pursuit, in short, of every kind of amusement. When strangers arrive, and desire to have lodging and accommodation at their houses, it affords them the highest gratification. They give positive orders to their wives, daughters, sisters, and other female relations, to indulge their guests in every wish, whilst they themselves leave their homes, and retire into the city, and the stranger lives in the house with the females as if they were his own wives, and they send whatever necessaries may be wanted; but for which, it is to be understood, they expect payment: nor do they return to their houses so long as the strangers remain in them. This abandonment of the females of their family to accidental guests, who assume the same privileges and meet with the same indulgences as if they were their own wives, is regarded by these people as doing them honor and adding to their reputation; considering the hospitable reception of strangers, who (after the perils and fatigues of a long journey) stand in need of relaxation, as an action agreeable to their deities, calculated to draw down the blessing of increase upon their families, to augment their substance, and to procure them safety from all dangers, as well as a successful issue to all their undertakings. The women are in truth very handsome, very sensual, and fully disposed to conform in this respect to the injunction of their husbands. It happened at the time when Mangu Khan[2] held his court in this province, that the above scandalous custom coming to his knowledge, he issued an edict strictly commanding the people of Kamul to relinquish a practice so disgraceful to them, and forbidding individuals to furnish lodging to strangers, who should be obliged to accommodate themselves at a house of public resort or *caravanserai*.[3] In grief and sadness the inhabitants obeyed for about three years the command of their master; but finding at length that the earth ceased to yield the accustomed fruits, and that many unfortunate events occurred in their families, they resolved to dispatch a deputation to the grand khan, in their names, to be-

1. The modern city of Hami, located on the edge of the Gobi Desert in western China's Xinjiang Uighur Autonomous Region.

2. Kublai's older brother, he was Great Khan from 1251 to 1259.

3. A resting place for caravans.

seech him that he should be pleased to suffer them to resume the observance of a custom that had been solemnly handed down to them by their fathers, from their ancestors in the remotest times; and especially as since they had failed in the exercise of these offices of hospitality and gratification to strangers, the interests of their families had gone progressively to ruin. The grand khan, having listened to this application, replied: — "Since you appear so anxious to persist in your own shame and ignominy, let it be granted as you desire. Go, live according to your base customs and manners, and let your wives continue to receive the beggarly wages of their prostitution." With this answer the deputies returned home, to the great delight of all the people, who, to the present day, observe their ancient practice.

[*Mongol Women*]

Now that I have begun speaking of the Tatars,[4] I will tell you more about them. . . . The women it is who attend to their trading concerns, who buy and sell, and provide everything necessary for their husbands and their families; the time of the men being entirely devoted to hunting and hawking, and matters that relate to the military life. . . . Their women are not excelled in the world for chastity and decency of conduct, nor for love and duty to their husbands. Infidelity to the marriage bed is regarded by them as a vice not merely dishonorable, but of the most infamous nature, whilst on the other hand it is admirable to observe the loyalty of the husbands towards their wives, amongst whom, although there are perhaps ten or twenty, there prevails a degree of quiet and union that is highly laudable. No offensive language is ever heard, their attention being fully occupied with their traffic (as already mentioned) and their several domestic employments, such as the provision of necessary food for the family, the management of the servants, and the care of the children, which are amongst them a common concern. And the more praiseworthy are the virtues of modesty and chastity in the wives, because the men are allowed the indulgence of taking as many as they choose. Their expense to the husband is not great, and on the other hand the benefit he derives from their trading, and from the occupations in which they are constantly engaged, is considerable; on which account it is, that when he receives a young woman in marriage, he pays a dower to her parent. The wife who is the first espoused has the privilege of superior attention, and is held to be the most legitimate, which extends also to the children borne by her. In consequence of this unlimited number of wives, the offspring is more numerous than amongst any other people. Upon the death of the father, the son may take to himself the wives he leaves behind, with the exception of his own mother. They cannot take their sisters to wife, but upon the death of their brothers they can marry their sisters-in-law. Every marriage is solemnized with great ceremony.

[*The Women of Tibet*]

A scandalous custom, which could only proceed from the blindness of idolatry,

4. He means the Mongols. See note 6 to John of Monte Corvino's "Letter."

prevails amongst the people of these parts, who are disinclined to marry young women so long as they are in their virgin state, but require, on the contrary, that they should have had previous commerce with many of the other sex; and this, they assert, is pleasing to their deities, and that a woman who has not had the company of men is worthless. Accordingly, upon the arrival of a caravan of merchants, and as soon as they have set up their tents for the night, those mothers who have marriageable daughters conduct them to the place, and each, contending for a preference, entreats the strangers to accept of her daughter and enjoy her society so long as they remain in the neighborhood. Such as have most beauty to recommend them are of course chosen, and the others return home disappointed and chagrined, whilst the former continue with the travelers until the period of their departure. They then restore them to their mothers, and never attempt to carry them away. It is expected, however, that the merchants should make them presents of trinkets, rings, or other complimentary tokens of regard, which the young women take home with them. When, afterwards, they are designed for marriage, they wear all these ornaments about the neck or other part of the body, and she who exhibits the greatest number of them is considered to have attracted the attention of the greatest number of men, and is on that account in the higher estimation with the young men who are looking out for wives; nor can she bring to her husband a more acceptable portion than a quantity of such gifts. At the solemnization of her nuptials, she accordingly makes a display of them to the assembly, and he regards them as a proof that their idols have rendered her lovely in the eyes of men. From thenceforward no person can dare to meddle with her who has become the wife of another, and this rule is never infringed.

[*The Women of Southwestern China*]

Proceeding five days' journey in a westerly direction from Karazan, you enter the province of Kardandan,[5] belonging to the dominion of the grand khan. . . . [The men] pay little attention to anything but horsemanship, the sports of the chase, and whatever belongs to the use of arms and a military life; leaving the entire management of their domestic concerns to their wives, who are assisted in their duties by slaves, either purchased or made prisoners in war.

These people have the following singular usage. As soon as a woman has been delivered of a child, and, rising from her bed, has washed and swathed the infant, her husband immediately takes the place she has left, has the child laid beside him, and nurses it for forty days. In the meantime, the friends and relations of the family pay to him their visits of congratulation; whilst the woman attends to the business of the house, carries victuals and drink to the husband in his bed, and suckles the infant at his side.

5. Modern Yunnan Province, which borders Burma, Laos, and Vietnam.

Chou Ta-kuan

RECOLLECTIONS OF THE CUSTOMS OF CAMBODIA

The Yüan emperors of China used foreign-born officials, such as Marco Polo, because of the high degree of mutual distrust and antipathy that existed between the old Confucian governing class and their new Mongol lords, but many Chinese did serve the Mongols faithfully. Among them was Chou Ta-kuan (d. after 1346), who spent nearly a year in the Khmer kingdom of Cambodia as a high-ranking member of an embassy sent by Kublai Khan to secure the Cambodians' recognition of his overlordship.

When the successful legation returned home in 1297, Chou Ta-kuan set down his impressions of this land and its people. Although he modestly noted, "It goes without saying that the customs and the activities of the country cannot be completely known in so short a time," he was still able to provide posterity with the single best contemporary account of Khmer society at the height of its cultural brilliance. In the following selections Chou describes the land's cultural divisions, its economic activities, and the ceremony that attended the Khmer king.

Questions for Analysis

1. According to Chou, what kinds of hill people inhabited the regions outside Cambodia's centers of civilization, and what was their relationship with town and village dwellers?
2. What other divisions existed within Khmer society?
3. What sort of market economy did Cambodia have? What were its major items of export and import? How would you characterize its trade with China?
4. What does the evidence allow you to infer about Cambodia's overall relations with China?
5. Based on Chou's description of royal ceremony, how would you characterize Khmer kingship?
6. From Chou's perspective, why did Cambodia seem so "barbarous and strange"?
7. Overall, what picture emerges of late-thirteenth-century Cambodia from these selections?

The Savages

There are two kinds of savages: those who know the language and are sold as slaves; the other are those who do not understand the language and could not adapt themselves to civilization. The latter have no permanent dwelling places, but, followed by their families, wander in the mountains carrying their few provisions in clay jars on their heads. If they find a wild animal, they will kill it with spears or bows and arrows, make a fire by striking stones together, cook the animal, eat it in common, and continue their wandering. Ferocious by nature, they use deadly poisons. Within their own band, they often kill one another. In recent times a few have started cultivating cardamom and cotton and weaving a cloth that is coarse and irregularly patterned.

Slaves

Savages are brought to do the work of servants. When they are young and strong, they fetch a hundred pieces of cloth; old and weak, from thirty to forty. Wealthy families may have more than a hundred; even those of modest means have ten or twenty; only the poor have none at all. The savages inhabit the wild mountains and belong to a different race; they are called *chuangs*, thieves. If, in a quarrel, a man calls another a *chuang*, it is a deadly insult, so despised are the savages, who are considered to be subhuman. Brought to the city, they never dare appear on the street. They are forced to live in the space under the houses which are built on stilts and when they come up into the house to do their work, they must first kneel and make the proper obeisance, prostrating themselves before they can advance. They call their owners "father" and "mother." If they make a mistake, they are beaten. They take their punishment with bent head and without making the slightest movement.

The Language

This country has its own language. Even though the sounds are fairly similar, the people of Champa[1] and of Siam[2] do not understand it. . . . The officials have an official style for their deliberations; the scholars[3] speak in a literary manner; the Buddhist monks and Taoist priests[4] have their own language; and different villages speak differently. It is absolutely the same as in China.

Products

Many strange trees are found in the mountains and in the clearings, herds of rhinoceros and elephants live, rare birds and many unusual animals are to be found. The most precious articles are the feathers of the kingfisher (valued in Canton to ornament gold jewelry), ivory, rhinoceros horn, and beeswax; cardamom and other forest products are more common.

The kingfisher is quite difficult to catch. In the thick woods are ponds and in the ponds are fish. The kingfisher leaves the forest to catch fish. Hidden under the leaves, by the side of the water, the Cambodian crouches. In a cage he has a female bird to attract the male and in his hand a small net. He waits until the bird comes and then catches him in his net. Some days he can catch as many as five; other days he waits vainly for a kingfisher.

Ivory is collected by the hill people. From a dead elephant one secures two tusks. Formerly it was thought that the elephant shed his tusks every year; this is not true. The ivory taken from an animal killed by a spear is the best. Then comes that which is found shortly after the animal has died a natural death; the least valued is that which is found in the mountains years after the death of the elephant.

Beeswax is found in rotted trees standing in the villages. It is produced by

1. Central Vietnam.

2. Thailand.

3. These so-called scholars were probably Brahmin priests.

4. Probably priests of Shiva and not Taoists.

winged insects that have thin antlike waists. The Cambodians take it away from the insects; a boatload can carry from two to three thousand honeycombs.

Rhinoceros horn that is white and veined is the most valued; the black variety is of inferior quality.

Cardamom is cultivated in the mountains by the savages. Pepper is also found occasionally. It climbs up bushes and entwines itself like a common weed. The green-blue variety is the most bitter.

Trade

In Cambodia, women attend to trade. Even a Chinese who arrives there and takes a woman will profit greatly from her trading abilities. They do not have permanent stores, but simply spread a piece of mat on the ground. Everyone has her own spot. I have heard that they pay an official for the right to a location. In small transactions, one pays in rice, grain, Chinese goods, and, lastly, fabrics; in large transactions they use gold and silver.

In a general way, the country people are very naïve. When they see a Chinese, they address him timidly, respectfully, calling him Fo — Buddha. As soon as they catch sight of him, they throw themselves on the ground and prostrate themselves. Lately some of them have cheated the Chinese and harmed them. This has happened to numbers of those who have gone into the villages.

Chinese Merchandise Desired in Cambodia

I do not think that Cambodia produces either gold or silver; and what the Cambodians value most is Chinese silver and gold, then silks, lightly patterned in two-toned threads. After these items comes the pewter of Chen-chou, lacquerware from Wen-chou, the blue porcelain of Ch'üan-chou, mercury, vermilion, paper, sulphur, saltpeter, sandalwood, irisroot, musk, hemp cloth, umbrellas, iron pots, copper platters, sieves, wood combs, and needles. That which they desire most of all is beans and wheat — but their exportation is forbidden.

The Army

The troops go naked and barefoot. They hold a lance in their right hand and a shield in their left. The Cambodians have neither bows nor arrows, war machines nor bullets, helmets nor armor. It is said that in the war against the Siamese everyone was obliged to fight, but they had no knowledge of tactics or strategy.

The Prince's Appearances in Public

When the king leaves the palace, first comes the cavalry, leading his escort, followed by an array of standards, banners, and music. Next comes a troupe of palace girls, anywhere from three to five hundred, dressed in flowered material, their heads garlanded with flowers and holding large candles lighted even in broad daylight. After them come more palace girls bearing the royal utensils of gold and silver and an assortment of all kinds of ornaments whose usage I don't understand. Then come the palace girls who, armed with lance and shield, form the king's private bodyguard; they, too, form a troupe. They are followed by carriages ornamented in gold and drawn by goats and horses. Ministers and nobles mounted on elephants look straight ahead, while clustered around them are their many, many red parasols of rank. After them in palanquins, carriages, and on elephants come the king's wives and concubines; they have more than a hundred parasols decorated in gold. Behind them comes the king. Holding the precious sword, he stands on the royal elephant, whose tusks are encased in gold. More than twenty white parasols, gold-trimmed and with golden handles, surround him. A great many elephants form a cordon around the king and the cavalry guards him. . . .

Twice each day the king holds an audience to conduct the affairs of government. There is no set procedure. Whoever desires to see the king — either officials or any private person — sits on the ground and awaits him. After a little while, one hears, far off in the palace, distant music; outside they blow on conchs to announce his approach. I have heard that he uses only a gold palanquin and does not come from very far away. An instant later, two palace girls lift the curtain on the Golden Window and the king, sword in his hand, appears. All those present — ministers and people — clasp their hands together and beat their foreheads on the ground. As the sound of the conchs ceases, they can raise their heads. At the king's pleasure, they may approach and sit down on a lion skin, which is considered a royal object. When all matters are disposed of, the king retires, the two palace girls let the curtain fall; everyone rises. Thus one sees that, though this country is barbarous and strange, they do not fail to know what it is to be a king.

Francesco Pegolotti

THE BOOK OF DESCRIPTIONS OF COUNTRIES

Around 1340 Francesco Balducci Pegolotti, an otherwise unknown agent of the Florentine banking house of the Bardi, compiled a handbook of practical advice for merchants. Pegolotti, who had served the Bardi family's interests from London to Cyprus, drew upon his years of mercantile experience to produce a work filled with lists of facts and figures on such items as local business customs, the taxes and tariffs of various localities, and the relative values of different standards of weights, measures, and coinage. In other words, the book contained just about everything a prudent merchant would want to know before entering a new market. In addition to these catalogues of useful data, Pegolotti included a short essay of advice for merchants bound for China.

Questions for Analysis

1. What evidence is there that Pegolotti himself had not traveled the steppe route to Cathay? Considering that his advice is not based on firsthand experience, how knowledgeable does he appear to be on the subject, and what does this suggest?
2. Consider Pegolotti's advice regarding the types of interpreters the merchant will need. What language skills suffice to carry on this trans-Eurasian business enterprise? What does this suggest about the markets of northern China?

3. When and where could the trip be especially hazardous? What does this suggest about the *Pax Mongolica*?
4. What overall impression does Pegolotti give of this journey and its rewards?

Things Needful for Merchants Who Desire to Make the Journey to Cathay

In the first place, you must let your beard grow long and not shave. And at Tana[1] you should furnish yourself with a dragoman.[2] And you must not try to save money in the matter of dragomen by taking a bad one instead of a good one. For the additional wages of the good one will not cost you so much as you will save by having him. And besides the dragoman it will be well to take at least two good menservants, who are acquainted with the Cumanian[3] tongue. And if the merchant likes to take a woman with him from Tana, he can do so; if he does not like to take one there is no obligation, only if he does take one he will be kept much more comfortably than if he does not take one. Howbeit, if he does take one, it will be well that she be acquainted with the Cumanian tongue as well as the men.

And from Tana traveling to Gittarchan[4] you should take with you twenty-five days' provisions, that is to say, flour and salt fish, for as to meat you will find enough of it at all the places along the road. And so also at all the chief stations noted in going from one country to another in the route, according to the number of days set down above, you should furnish yourself with flour and salt fish; other things you will find in sufficiency, and especially meat.

The road you travel from Tana to Cathay is perfectly safe, whether by day or by night, according to what the merchants say who have used it. Only if the merchant, in going or coming, should die upon the road, everything belonging to him will become the perquisite of the lord of the country in which he dies, and the officers of the lord will take possession of all. And in like manner if he die in Cathay. But if his brother be with him, or an intimate friend and comrade calling himself his brother, then to such a one they will surrender the property of the deceased, and so it will be rescued.

And there is another danger: this is when the lord of the country dies, and before the new lord who is to have the lordship is proclaimed; during such intervals there have sometimes been irregularities practiced on the Franks, and other foreigners. (They call "Franks" all the Christians of these parts from Romania[5] westward.) And neither will the roads be safe to travel until the other lord be proclaimed who is to reign in room of him who is deceased.

Cathay is a province which contains a

1. The modern Soviet city of Azov on the northeast coast of the Sea of Azov, which itself is an extension of the Black Sea. Tana was the farthest eastern point to which a person could sail from the Mediterranean.

2. An interpreter fluent in Arabic, Persian, or Turkish.

3. A Turkic people inhabiting the middle Volga.

4. Modern Astrakhan, a Soviet city in the Volga delta, just north of the Caspian Sea.

5. The European term for the Byzantine Empire.

multitude of cities and towns. Among others there is one in particular, that is to say the capital city, to which is great resort of merchants, and in which there is a vast amount of trade; and this city is called Cambalec.[6] And the said city hath a circuit of one hundred miles, and is all full of people and houses and of dwellers in the said city. . . .

You may reckon also that from Tana to Sara[7] the road is less safe than on any other part of the journey; and yet even when this part of the road is at its worst, if you are some sixty men in the company you will go as safely as if you were in your own house.

Anyone from Genoa or from Venice, wishing to go to the places above-named, and to make the journey to Cathay, should carry linens with him, and if he visit Organci[8] he will dispose of these well. In Organci he should purchase sommi of silver,[9] and with these he should proceed without making any further investment, unless it be some bales of the very finest stuffs which go in small bulk, and cost no more for carriage than coarser stuffs would do.

Merchants who travel this road can ride on horseback or on asses, or mounted in any way that they choose to be mounted.

Whatever silver the merchants may carry with them as far as Cathay the lord of Cathay will take from them and put into his treasury. And to merchants who thus bring silver they give that paper money of theirs in exchange. This is of yellow paper, stamped with the seal of the lord aforesaid. And this money is called balishi; and with this money you can readily buy silk and all other merchandise that you have a desire to buy. And all the people of the country are bound to receive it. And yet you shall not pay a higher price for your goods because your money is of paper. And of the said paper money there are three kinds, one being worth more than another, according to the value which has been established for each by that lord.

Travel Beyond the Mongol Ecumene

Important as the Mongol Peace was in facilitating movement and trade across Eurasia, it was not the sole contributing factor to the upsurge of long-distance travel and cultural exchange after 1000. As the travels of Ibn Battuta demonstrate, the very nature of the community of Islam encouraged travel. Educated Muslims, no matter what their ethnic origins or native tongues, shared a sacred language — Arabic —

6. Khanbalik.

7. Sarai on the Volga, the capital of the il-khans of Kipchak (also known as the Golden Horde), who ruled Russia and Kazakhstan.

8. Urgench on the Oxus River in modern Soviet Central Asia.

9. Sommi were weights of silver. Each sommo was equivalent to five golden florins, the standard coin of Florence. Pegolotti calculated that the average merchant would carry merchandise worth about 25,000 florins, and the expenses for the merchant, interpreter, and two personal servants would amount to a combined sixty to eighty sommi, or 300 to 400 florins.

and could communicate with one another. They also shared an obligation to make a pilgrimage at least once in a lifetime to Mecca and Medina. The pilgrimage routes that enabled African, Indian, and East Asian Muslims to travel to these holy sites were also important avenues of cultural and material exchange. Moreover, merchants spread Islam to such faraway regions as sub-Saharan Africa and the coastal lands of Southeast Asia. Once the faith had taken root, there was even more reason to maintain contact with these societies, many of which were so distant from Islam's Middle Eastern birthplace.

The breakup of the Mongol Empire around the middle of the fourteenth century did not end long-distance travel for the non-Muslim peoples of Eurasia. China and Europe had taken to the seas long before the rise of the Mongols and continued their interests in seafaring and naval technology throughout the thirteenth and fourteenth centuries and beyond. Early in the fifteenth century, Ming China sent seven massive naval expeditions into the Indian Ocean, and portions of several of those fleets reached the shores of East Africa. Also in the fifteenth century, Western Europe, finding the overland roads to Cathay mostly blocked by a resurgent Islam, began to seek alternate sea routes to the Indies. The consequences of those explorations were astounding. Before the century was over Europeans had sailed to East Africa, India, and the Americas.

Ibn Battuta

A DONATION TO THOSE INTERESTED IN CURIOSITIES

The life and world travels of Abu Abdallah Muhammad ibn Battuta (1304–1369) provide eloquent testimony to the international cosmopolitanism of fourteenth-century Islam. Ibn Battuta was born into the religious upper class of Tangier, Morocco, where he received an education in Muslim law and Arabic literature. In 1325 he left home to make the first of six pilgrimages to Mecca. During the next thirty years he visited Constantinople, Mesopotamia, Persia, India, where he resided and worked for seven years, Sumatra, Spain, Mali, and probably southern China. In all, his travels covered about 75,000 miles, and most of his stops along the way were within the cultural confines of *Dar al Islam* ("the Abode of Islam"), where the sacred law of the Qur'an prevailed. In 1354 he returned to Morocco to stay and almost immediately began to narrate his experiences and observations to Ibn Jazayy, a professional scribe who fashioned them into a *rihla*, or book of travels, one of the most popular forms of literature in the Muslim world.

In the following selection Ibn Battuta describes the land and the people of that area known to the Arabs as *Bilad as-Sudan* ("the country of the blacks"), the sub-Saharan grasslands that stretch across the breadth of Africa. In early 1352 he embarked on what was to be his last great adventure, a trip by camel caravan to the

West African kingdom of Mali in the Niger River region. Almost two years later he arrived home with marvelous tales of this Malinke-speaking land of gold, whose leaders had converted to Islam in the early thirteenth century.

Questions for Analysis

1. In what ways were the cultures of the people Ibn Batutta's encountered a mixture of native African and Muslim elements?
2. What does Ibn Battuta admire most about these people? What does he find hardest to accept? Why?
3. Does Ibn Battuta understand fully all he encountered? Can you find any evidence of cultural or racial tension?
4. Compare Ibn Battuta's cultural biases with those of Chou Ta-kuan and Marco Polo. Are you struck more by the similarities or dissimilarities? Why?
5. How organized and controlled does the state of Mali appear to be?

Then we reached the town of Iwalatan . . . after a journey . . . of two whole months. It is the first district of the Sudan and the sultan's[1] deputy there is Farba Husayn. *Farba* means "deputy." When we arrived there the merchants[2] placed their belongings in an open space, where the Sudan[3] took over the guard of them while they went to the *farba*. He was sitting on a carpet under a *saqif*[4] with his assistants in front of him with lances and bows in their hands and the chief men of the Masufa[5] behind him. The merchants stood before him while he addressed them, in spite of their proximity to him, through an interpreter, out of contempt for them. At this I repented at having come to their country because of their ill manners and their contempt for white men.[6] I made for the house of Ibn Badda', a respectable man of Sala to whom I had written to rent a house for me. He had done so. Then the *mushrif*[7] (of Iwalatan), who is called (the) *manshaju*, invited those who had come with the caravan to (receive) his reception-gift (*diyafa*). I declined to go but my companions entreated me urgently, so I went with those who went. Then the *diyafa* was brought. It was *anili*[8] meal mixed with a little honey and yogurt which they had placed in half a gourd made into a kind of bowl. Those present drank and went away. I said to them: "Was it to this that the black man invited us?" They said: "Yes, for them this is a great banquet." Then I knew for certain that no good was to be expected from them and I wished to depart with the pilgrims of Iwalatan. But then I thought it better to go to see the seat of their king.

My stay in Iwalatan lasted about 50 days. Its inhabitants did me honor and made me their guest. Among them was

1. The sultan or king of Mali, for whom this was an outlying province.
2. North Africans and Arabs.
3. Local blacks.
4. A colonnade.
5. A Berber people of the western Sahara.
6. North Africans and Arabs.
7. The sultan's overseer of the town's markets.
8. Millet.

the qadi[9] of the place Muhammad b. 'Abd Allah b. Yanumur and his brother the faqih[10] and teacher Yahya. The town of Iwalatan is extremely hot. There are a few little palm trees there in the shade of which they sow watermelons. . . . Mutton is abundant there and the people's clothes are of Egyptian cloth of good quality. Most of the inhabitants there belong to the Masufa, whose women are of surpassing beauty and have a higher status than the men.

THE MASUFA LIVING IN IWALATAN

These people have remarkable and strange ways. As for their men, they feel no jealousy. None of them traces his descent through his father, but from his maternal uncle, and a man's heirs are the sons of his sister only, to the exclusion of his own sons. This is something that I have seen nowhere in the world except among the Indian infidels in the land of Mulaybar, whereas these are Muslims who observe the prayer and study fiqh[11] and memorize the Qur'an. As for their women, they have no modesty in the presence of men and do not veil themselves in spite of their assiduity in prayer. If anybody wishes to marry one of them he may do so, but they do not travel with the husband, and if one of them wished to do so her family would prevent her.

The women there have friends and companions among the foreign men, just as the men have companions from among the foreign women. One of them may enter his house and find his wife with her man friend without making any objection. . . .

One day I went into the presence of Abu Muhammad Yandakan al-Masufi in whose company we had come and found him sitting on a carpet. In the courtyard of his house there was a canopied couch with a woman on it conversing with a man seated. I said to him: "Who is this woman?" He said: "She is my wife." I said: "What connection has the man with her?" He replied: "He is her friend." I said to him: "Do you acquiesce in this when you have lived in our country and become acquainted with the precepts of the Shar?"[12] He replied: "The association of women with men is agreeable to us and a part of good conduct, to which no suspicion attaches. They are not like the women of your country." I was astonished at his laxity. I left him, and did not return thereafter. He invited me several times but I did not accept.

When I resolved to travel to Mali . . . I hired a guide from the Masufa, since there is no need to travel in company because of the security of that road, and set off with three of my companions. . . .

Then we . . . arrived at the River Sansara, which is about ten miles from the capital of Mali. It is their custom to prevent people from entering it except by authorization. I had written before this to the white community . . . to ask them to rent a house for me. When I reached the afore-mentioned river I crossed it by the ferry without anybody preventing me. I arrived at the town of Mali, the seat of the king of the Sudan. . . .

THE SULTAN OF MALI

He is the sultan Mansa Sulayman. *Mansa* means "sultan" and Sulayman is his name. He is a miserly king from whom no great donation is to be expected. It happened that I remained for this period without seeing him on account of my ill-

9. A religious judge.

10. A teacher of religion.

11. Religion.

12. Sharia or Muslim Sacred Law.

ness. Then he gave a memorial feast for our Lord Abu 'l-Hasan[13] (may God be content with him) and invited the emirs and faqihs and the qadi and khatib,[14] and I went with them. They brought copies of the Qur'an and the Qur'an was recited in full. They prayed for our Lord Abu 'l-Hasan (may God have mercy on him) and prayed for Mansa Sulayman. When this was finished I advanced and greeted Mansa Sulayman and the qadi and the khatib and Ibn al-Faqih told him who I was. He answered them in their language and they said to me: "The sultan says to you: 'I thank God.'" I replied: "Praise and thanks be to God in every circumstance."

Their Trivial Reception Gift and Their Respect for It

When I departed the reception gift was sent to me and dispatched to the qadi's house. The qadi sent it with his men to the house of Ibn al-Faqih. Ibn al-Faqih hastened out of his house barefooted and came in to me saying: "Come! The cloth and gift of the sultan have come to you!" I got up, thinking that it would be robes of honor and money, but behold! it was three loaves of bread and a piece of beef fried in *gharti*[15] and a gourd containing yogurt. When I saw it I laughed, and was long astonished at their feeble intellect and their respect for mean things.

My Speaking to the Sultan After This and His Kindness Towards Me

After this reception gift I remained for two months during which nothing was sent to me by the sultan and the month of Ramadan came in. Meanwhile I frequented the *mashwar* ["council-place"] and used to greet him and sit with the qadi and the khatib. I spoke with Dugha the interpreter, who said: "Speak with him, and I will express what you want to say in the proper fashion." So when he held a session at the beginning of Ramadan and I stood before him and said: "I have journeyed to the countries of the world and met their kings. I have been four months in your country without your giving me a reception gift or anything else. What shall I say of you in the presence of other sultans?" He replied: "I have not seen you nor known about you." The qadi and Ibn al-Faqih rose and replied to him saying: "He greeted you and you sent to him some food." Thereupon he ordered that a house be provided for me to stay in and an allowance to be allotted to me. Then, on the night of 27 Ramadan, he distributed among the qadi and the khatib and the faqihs a sum of money which they call *zakah*[16] and gave to me with them 33 1/3 mithqals.[17] When I departed he bestowed on me 100 mithqals of gold. . . .

The Self-debasement of the Sudan Before Their King and Their Scattering of Dust on Themselves Before Him and Other Peculiarities

The Sudan are the humblest of people before their king and the most submissive towards him. They swear by his name, saying: "*Mansa Sulayman ki.*" When he calls to one of them at his sessions in the

13. The late sultan of Morocco (1331–1351).

14. A public preacher at Friday mosque services.

15. A vegetable oil.

16. Alms distributed at the end of Ramadan.

17. A standard weight of gold (about 4.72 grams).

pavilion which we have mentioned the person called takes off his clothes and puts on ragged clothes, and removes his turban and puts on a dirty *shashiyya*[18] and goes in holding up his garments and trousers half-way up his leg, and advances with submissiveness and humility. He then beats the ground vigorously with his two elbows, and stands like one performing a *rak'a*[19] to listen to his words.

If one of them addresses the sultan and the latter replies he uncovers the clothes from his back and sprinkles dust on his head and back, like one washing himself with water. I used to marvel how their eyes did not become blinded. . . .

What I Approved of and What I Disapproved of Among the Acts of the Sudan

One of their good features is their lack of oppression. They are the farthest removed of people from it and their sultan does not permit anyone to practice it. Another is the security embracing the whole country, so that neither traveler there nor dweller has anything to fear from thief or usurper. Another is that they do not interfere with the wealth of any white man who dies among them, even though it be *qintar* upon *qintar*.[20] They simply leave it in the hands of a trustworthy white man until the one to whom it is due takes it. Another is their assiduity in prayer and their persistence in performing it in congregation and beating their children to make them perform it. If it is a Friday and a man does not go early to the mosque he will not find anywhere to pray because of the press of the people. It is their habit that every man sends his servant with his prayer-mat to spread it for him in a place which he thereby has a right to until he goes to the mosque. Their prayer-carpets are made from the fronds of the tree resembling the palm which has no fruit. Another of their good features is their dressing in fine white clothes on Friday. If any one of them possesses nothing but a ragged shirt he washes it and cleanses it and attends the Friday prayer in it. Another is their eagerness to memorize the great Qur'an. They place fetters on their children if there appears on their part a failure to memorize it and they are not undone until they memorize it.

I went into the house of the qadi on the day of the festival and his children were fettered so I said to him: "Aren't you going to let them go?" He replied: "I shan't do so until they've got the Qur'an by heart!" One day I passed by a youth of theirs, of good appearance and dressed in fine clothes, with a heavy fetter on his leg. I said to those who were with me: "What has this boy done? Has he killed somebody?" The lad understood what I had said and laughed, and they said to me: "He's only been fettered so that he'll learn the Qur'an!"

One of their disapproved acts is that their female servants and slave girls and little girls appear before men naked, with their privy parts uncovered. During Ramadan I saw many of them in this state, for it is the custom of the *farariyya*[21] to break their fast[22] in the house of the sultan, and each one brings his food carried

18. A skull cap.

19. A set sequence of utterances and gestures that form the *salah*, or obligatory ritual prayer, that Muslims must perform five times daily.

20. Weight upon weight, i.e., a large amount of wealth.

21. Emirs, or chief men.

22. The daily fast of the month of Ramadan ends at sunset.

by twenty or more of his slave girls, they all being naked. Another is that their women go into the sultan's presence naked and uncovered, and that his daughters go naked. On the night of 25 Ramadan I saw about 200 slave girls bringing out food from his palace naked, having with them two of his daughters with rounded breasts having no covering upon them. Another is their sprinkling dust and ashes on their heads out of good manners. . . . Another is that many of them eat carrion, and dogs, and donkeys.[23]

Ma Huan

THE OVERALL SURVEY OF THE OCEAN'S SHORES

Vigorous expansionism characterized the early Ming Dynasty (1368–1644), particularly during the reign of Yung-lo (1402–1424). Between 1405 and 1421 this emperor sent out a series of six great fleets under the command of China's most famous admiral, a Muslim eunuch of Mongolian ancestry named Cheng Ho (1371–1435). If we can believe the records, several fleets carried in excess of 27,000 sailors, soldiers, and officials. The first expedition of 1405–1407 reportedly consisted of 317 vessels, including 62 massive "treasure ships," some of which were 300 feet long, 150 feet wide (imagine a ship the size of a football field), and weighed around 3,100 tons. These armadas, as well as a seventh that went out in 1431 and returned in 1433, sailed through the waters of Southeast Asia and the Indian Ocean, visiting numerous ports of call in such places as India, East Africa, and the Arabian peninsula.

The main reason behind these voyages appears to have been the reassertion of Chinese prestige to the south and west. Like the expedition that Chou Ta-kuan joined a century earlier, these fleets were commissioned to accept the submission and tribute of the various "barbarian" rulers they encountered. A secondary purpose seems to have been to stimulate China's economy and strengthen its commercial position in South Asia, particularly as the armies of Timur the Lame had severed the old Silk Route.

Despite the psychological impact the fleets' show of strength had upon the people they visited (in one area of Thailand Cheng Ho was remembered as a god), China would never dominate the Indian Ocean. After Yung-lo's death, the imperial court did not follow through on what had begun so well for several reasons. The cost of mounting these expeditions was prohibitively high. Moreover, the Confucian literarchy, with its traditional contempt for commerce and foreign cultures, was on the ascendancy after Yung-lo's death. Although Cheng Ho was allowed to lead a seventh expedition westward, it was to be China's last moment of trans-oceanic great-

23. Unclean meat, according to Qur'anic law.

ness. The court called a halt to further overseas adventures; the fleet was allowed to decay; and China forgot much of the naval technology that had made it the world's greatest maritime power in the ages of Sung and early Ming.

The following account describes various sites visited in the course of three of Cheng Ho's expeditions in western waters. Its author, Ma Huan (ca 1380–after 1451), a Chinese Muslim, joined the fourth voyage (1413–1415) as an Arabic translator and on his return transcribed his notes into book form. He later sailed on the sixth (1421–1422) and seventh (1431–1433) expeditions and amended his record accordingly, eventually publishing it in 1451.

Questions for Analysis

1. What evidence is there that the emperor saw these expeditions as a way of extending Chinese influence abroad?
2. How did Cheng Ho use both diplomacy and military force to achieve this objective?
3. What evidence is there that these expeditions also served commercial purposes?
4. What evidence is there of a high level of international commerce in the Indian Ocean long before the coming of Cheng Ho's fleets?

THE COUNTRY OF MAN-LA-CHIA[1] (MALACCA)

From Chan City[2] you go due south, and after traveling for eight days with a fair wind the ship comes to Lung ya strait,[3] after entering the strait you travel west; (and) you can reach (this place) in two days.

Formerly this place was not designated a "country"; (and) because the sea (hereabouts) was named "Five Islands," (the place) was in consequence named "Five Islands." There was no king of the country; (and) it was controlled only by a chief. This territory was subordinate to the jurisdiction of Hsien Lo,[4] it paid an annual tribute of forty *liang*[5] of gold; (and) if it were not (to pay), then Hsien Lo would send men to attack it.

In the seventh year of the Yung-lo (period)[6] (the cyclic year) *chi-ch'ou*, the Emperor ordered the principal envoy the grand eunuch Cheng Ho and others to assume command (of the treasure-ships), and to take the imperial edicts and to bestow upon this chief two silver seals, a hat, a girdle and a robe. (Cheng Ho) set up a stone tablet and raised (the place) to a city; (and) it was subsequently called the "country of Man-la-chia." Thereafter Hsien Lo did not dare to invade it.

The chief, having received the favor of

---

1. Malacca, a port on the west coast of the Malay peninsula.

2. Champa (central Vietnam).

3. Singapore Strait.

4. Thailand.

5. About 48 ounces.

6. 1409. This would be the third expedition, of 1409–1411.

being made king, conducted his wife and son, and went to the court at the capital[7] to return thanks and to present tribute of local products. The court also granted him a sea-going ship, so that he might return to his country and protect his land. . . .

Whenever the treasure-ships of the Central Country[8] arrived there, they at once erected a line of stockading, like a city-wall, and set up towers for the watch-drums at four gates; at night they had patrols of police carrying bells; inside, again, they erected a second stockade, like a small city-wall, (within which) they constructed warehouses and granaries; (and) all the money and provisions were stored in them. The ships which had gone to various countries[9] returned to this place and assembled; they marshaled the foreign goods and loaded them in the ships; (then) waited till the south wind was perfectly favorable. In the middle decade of the fifth moon they put to sea and returned home.[10]

Moreover, the king of the country made a selection of local products, conducted his wife and son, brought his chiefs, boarded a ship and followed the treasure-ships; (and) he attended at court (and) presented tribute. . . .

The Country of Su-men-ta-la[11] *(Semudera, Lho Seumawe)*

The country of Su-men-ta-la is exactly the same country as that formerly (named) Hsu-wen-ta-na. This place is indeed the principal centre for the Western Ocean. . . .

The king of the country of Su-men-ta-la had previously been raided by the "tattooed-face king" of Na-ku-erh; (and) in the fighting he received a poisoned arrow in the body and died. He had one son, who was young and unable to avenge his father's death. The king's wife made a vow before the people, saying "If there is anyone who can avenge my husband's death and recover his land, I am willing to marry him and to share with him the management of the country's affairs." When she finished speaking, a fisherman belonging to the place was fired with determination, and said "I can avenge him."

Thereupon he took command of an army and at once put the "tattooed-face king" to flight in battle; (and) later he avenged the (former king's death) when the "tattooed-face king" was killed. The people of the (latter) submitted and did not dare to carry on hostilities.

Whereupon the wife of (the former) king, failing not (to carry out) her previous vow, forthwith married the fisherman. He was styled "the old king," and in such things as (the affairs of the royal) household and the taxation of the land, everybody accepted the old king's decisions. In the seventh year of the Yung-lo (period)[12] the old king, in fulfillment of his duty, brought tribute of local products,[13] and was enriched by the kindness of Heaven;[14] (and) in the tenth year of the

---

7. Nanking, the Ming capital at this time.

8. China, the Middle Kingdom.

9. This is evidence that elements were detached from the main fleet and sent off on special missions.

10. 1433, the last expedition.

11. Semudera, on the north coast of the island of Sumatra and across the Strait of Malacca from Malaysia.

12. 1409.

13. To the Ming court at Nanking.

14. The emperor.

Yung-lo (period)[15] he returned to his country.

When the son of the former king had grown up, he secretly plotted with the chiefs, murdered his adoptive father the fisherman, usurped his position, and ruled the kingdom.

The fisherman had a son by his principal wife; his name was Su-kan-la; he took command of his people, and they fled away, taking their families; (and), after erecting a stockade in the neighboring mountains, from time to time he led his men in incursions to take revenge on his father's enemies. In the thirteenth year of the Yung-lo (period)[16] the principal envoy the grand eunuch Cheng Ho and others, commanding a large fleet of treasure-ships, arrived there; they dispatched soldiers who captured Su-kan-la; (and) he went to the capital;[17] and was publicly executed. The king's son was grateful for the imperial kindness, and constantly presented tribute of local products to the court. . . .

At this place there are foreign[18] ships going and coming in large numbers, hence all kinds of foreign goods are sold in great quantities in the country.

In this country they use gold coins and tin coins. The foreign name for the gold coin is *ti-na-erh;*[19] they use pale gold, seventy percent pure, for casting it. . . . The foreign name for the tin coin is *chia-shih;*[20] (and) in all their trading they regularly use tin coins. . . .

The Country of Ku-li[21] *(Calicut)*

(This is) the great country of the Western Ocean. . . .

In the fifth year of the Yung-lo (period) the court ordered the principal envoy, the grand eunuch Cheng Ho, and others to deliver an imperial mandate to the king[22] of this country and to bestow on him a patent conferring a title of honor, and the grant of a silver seal, (also) to promote all the chiefs and award them hats and girdles of various grades.

(So Cheng Ho) went there in command of a large fleet of treasure-ships, and he erected a tablet with a pavilion over it and set up a stone which said "Though the journey from this country to the Central Country is more than a hundred thousand *li,*[23] yet the people are very similar, happy and prosperous, with identical customs. We have here engraved a stone, a perpetual declaration for ten thousand ages."

The king of the country is a Nan-k'un[24] man; he is a firm believer in the Buddhist religion;[25] (and) he venerates the elephant and the ox.

The population of the country includes

15. 1412.

16. 1415.

17. Presumably Nanking.

18. Non-Chinese.

19. From the Arabic *dinar*.

20. The English would later transliterate this local word as "cash."

21. Calicut on India's southwest coast (not to be confused with Calcutta in the northeast).

22. 1407. This was the second expedition (1407–1409). While Cheng Ho was its nominal commander, he did not accompany it.

23. A *li* is a bit more than a third of a mile.

24. Upper class. He probably means a member of the Kshatriya, or warrior, caste.

25. This is wrong. He was Hindu.

five classes, the Muslim people, the Nan-k'un people, the Che-ti people, the Ko-ling people, and the Mu-kua[26] people. . . .

The king has two great chiefs who administer the affairs of the country; both are Muslims. . . .

The people are very honest and trustworthy. Their appearance is smart, fine, and distinguished.

Their two great chiefs received promotion and awards from the court of the Central Country.

If a treasure-ship goes there, it is left entirely to the two men to superintend the buying and selling; the king sends a chief and a Che-ti Wei-no-chi[27] to examine the account books in the official bureau; a broker comes and joins them; (and) a high officer who commands the ships discusses the choice of a certain date for fixing prices. When the day arrives, they first of all take the silk embroideries and the open-work silks, and other such goods which have been brought there, and discuss the price of them one by one; (and) when (the price) has been fixed, they write out an agreement stating the amount of the price; (this agreement) is retained by these persons. . . .

THE COUNTRY OF HU-LU-MO-SSU[28] (HORMUZ)

Setting sail from the country of Ku-li, you go towards the north-west; (and) you can reach (this place) after traveling with a fair wind for twenty-five days. The capital lies beside the sea and up against the mountains.

Foreign ships from every place and foreign merchants traveling by land all come to this country to attend the market and trade; hence the people of the country are all rich. . . .

The king of this country, too, took a ship and loaded it with lions, *ch'i-lin*,[29] horses, pearls, precious stones, and other things, also a memorial to the throne (written on) a golden leaf; (and) he sent his chiefs and other men, who accompanied the treasure-ships dispatched by the Emperor, which were returning from the Western Ocean; (and) they went to the capital and presented tribute.[30]

Gomes Eannes de Azurara

CHRONICLE OF GUINEA

At the same time Cheng Ho's fleets were sailing majestically through the western seas and Muslim sailors dominated the coastal traffic of virtually every inhabited land washed by the Indian Ocean (except Australia), the Portuguese were tentatively inching down the west coast of Africa. From 1419 onward, Prince Henry (1394–

26. These would be the four castes.

27. Probably an accountant.

28. Hormuz, an island off the coast of Iran and at the mouth of the Persian Gulf.

29. A giraffe.

30. This probably took place at the end of the seventh expedition.

1460), third son of King John I (1385–1433), almost annually sent out a ship or two in an attempt to push farther toward the sub-Saharan land the Portuguese called Guinea, but only in 1434 did one of his caravels manage to round the feared Cape Bojador, along the western Sahara coast. Once this psychological barrier had been broken, the pace of exploration quickened. By 1460 Portuguese sailors had ventured as far south as modern Sierra Leone, an advance of about 1,500 miles in twenty-six years. Finally Bartholomeu Dias rounded the southern tip of Africa in early 1488, and Vasco da Gama, seeking, in his words, "Christians and spices," dropped anchor off Calicut on May 20, 1498. Although da Gama lost two of his four ships and many of his crew in this enterprise, Portugal was now in the Indian Ocean to stay.

Portugal's commercial empire was still over half a century in the future when Gomes Eannes de Azurara (ca 1400–after 1472) in 1452 began to write a history of the life and work of Prince Henry "the Navigator," in so many ways the parent of an empire-to-be. Azurara's history details Portuguese explorations along the West African coast until 1448. He promised a sequel, since Henry was still alive and actively promoting voyages to West Africa when Azurara completed *The Chronicle of Guinea* in 1453. His other duties apparently intervened, and he never returned to the topic. Still, the chronicle he has given us is a revealing picture of the spirit behind Portugal's first generation of oceanic exploration and colonialism.

In the following excerpts Azurara explains why Prince Henry sponsored the expeditions and defends the consequent enslavement of black West Africans. Trade in Guinean slaves, which became an integral part of Portugal's commercial imperialism, began in 1441 with the capture of ten Africans, and Azurara estimated that 927 West African slaves had come into Portugal by 1448. This humane man, who was disturbed by many of the unsavory aspects of this exploitation, could not foresee that between 1450 and 1500 about 150,000 more Africans would enter Portugal as slaves and that over the next four centuries untold millions of "heathens" would be transported out of Africa by European and Euro-American slavers.

Questions for Analysis

1. What were Henry's motives? What seems to have been foremost in his mind — commercial, political, or religious gain or simple curiosity?
2. It has been said that Henry was a fifteenth-century crusader. From the evidence, does this seem a fair judgment?
3. Compare this document with Christopher Columbus's letter of 1493 (see the Prologue). Do they seem to share a common spirit? If so, what is it?
4. Compare the purposes behind the Portuguese and Spanish explorations with those of Cheng Ho's expeditions. In what ways do they differ, and to what do you ascribe those differences?
5. How does the author justify the enslavement of Africans?

We imagine that we know a matter when we are acquainted with the doer of it and the end for which he did it. And since in former chapters we have set forth the Lord Infant[1] as the chief actor in these things, giving as clear an understanding of him as we could, it is meet that in this present chapter we should know his purpose in doing them. And you should note well that the noble spirit of this Prince, by a sort of natural constraint, was ever urging him both to begin and to carry out very great deeds. For which reason, after the taking of Ceuta[2] he always kept ships well armed against the Infidel, both for war, and because he had also a wish to know the land that lay beyond the isles of Canary and that Cape called Bojador, for that up to his time, neither by writings, nor by the memory of man, was known with any certainty the nature of the land beyond that Cape. Some said indeed that Saint Brandan[3] had passed that way; and there was another tale of two galleys rounding the Cape, which never returned. But this doth not appear at all likely to be true, for it is not to be presumed that if the said galleys went there, some other ships would not have endeavored to learn what voyage they had made. And because the said Lord Infant wished to know the truth of this — since it seemed to him that if he or some other lord did not endeavor to gain that knowledge, no mariners or merchants would ever dare to attempt it — (for it is clear that none of them ever trouble themselves to sail to a place where there is not a sure and certain hope of profit) — and seeing also that no other prince took any pains in this matter, he sent out his own ships against those parts, to have manifest certainty of them all. And to this he was stirred up by his zeal for the service of God and of the King Edward his Lord and brother,[4] who then reigned. And this was the first reason of his action.

The second reason was that if there chanced to be in those lands some population of Christians, or some havens, into which it would be possible to sail without peril, many kinds of merchandise might be brought to this realm, which would find a ready market, and reasonably so, because no other people of these parts traded with them, nor yet people of any other that were known; and also the products of this realm might be taken there, which traffic would bring great profit to our countrymen.

The third reason was that, as it was said that the power of the Moors in that land of Africa was very much greater than was commonly supposed, and that there were no Christians among them, nor any other race of men; and because every wise man is obliged by natural prudence to wish for a knowledge of the power of his enemy; therefore the said Lord Infant exerted himself to cause this to be fully discovered, and to make it known determinately how far the power of those infidels extended.

The fourth reason was because during the one and thirty years that he had warred against the Moors, he had never found a Christian king, nor a lord outside this land, who for the love of our Lord Jesus Christ would aid him in the said war. Therefore he sought to know if there

1. Prince Henry. An *infante* (fem. *infanta*) was any son of a Portuguese or Spanish monarch who was not an heir to the Crown.

2. A Muslim naval base in Morocco that Portugal captured in 1415.

3. A wandering Irish monk of the sixth century.

4. King Duarte (1433–1438).

were in those parts any Christian princes, in whom the charity and the love of Christ was so ingrained that they would aid him against those enemies of the faith.

The fifth reason was his great desire to make increase in the faith of our Lord Jesus Christ and to bring to him all the souls that should be saved, — understanding that all the mystery of the Incarnation, Death, and Passion of our Lord Jesus Christ was for this sole end — namely the salvation of lost souls — whom the said Lord Infant by his travail and spending would fain bring into the true path. For he perceived that no better offering could be made unto the Lord than this; for if God promised to return one hundred goods for one, we may justly believe that for such great benefits, that is to say for so many souls as were saved by the efforts of this Lord, he will have so many hundreds of guerdons[5] in the kingdom of God, by which his spirit may be glorified after this life in the celestial realm. For I that wrote this history saw so many men and women of those parts turned to the holy faith, that even if the Infant had been a heathen, their prayers would have been enough to have obtained his salvation. And not only did I see the first captives,[6] but their children and grandchildren as true Christians as if the Divine grace breathed in them and imparted to them a clear knowledge of itself.

---

5. Rewards.

6. West African slaves who had been captured and transported to Portugal by licensed slave hunters.

PART IV

A World of Change, 1500–1700

For many of the world's societies, the period from 1500 to 1700 was a time of significant change. In Japan, a century of civil war ended around 1600, when a new regime under the leadership of the Tokugawa clan brought an end to disorder and established a political system that maintained internal harmony for almost three centuries. In China, the Ming Dynasty, which had ruled the Middle Kingdom since 1368, was toppled and replaced by invading Manchus in 1644, who established the Ch'ing Dynasty (1644–1912). For the first century and a half, the Ch'ing gave China good government and strong leadership. The Russians, having ended their subservience to the "Tatar Yoke" of the Mongols in the late 1400s, struggled to establish a stable political order and initiated a campaign of eastward expansion that brought Russian settlers all the way to the shores of the Pacific. The Ottoman Turks consolidated and expanded an empire that included Asia Minor, the Arabian peninsula, the lands of Syria-Palestine, North Africa, southeastern Europe, and parts of the Ukraine. To their east, Ismail Safavi, through a series of lightning conquests, in 1502 established the Safavid Empire in the region of modern Iran and Iraq. The last important upheaval took place in northern India, where the conquests of Babur laid the foundations of the Mughal Empire, the third great Islamic empire of the Middle East and South Asia.

As important as these events and movements were, none matched the eventual historical significance of Europe's transoceanic expansion. In the fifteenth century, ships sailing the flag of the small kingdom of Portugal began to probe the waters of Africa's west coast in the hope of reaching the source of Muslim North Africa's sub-Saharan trade and of contacting Prester John, a legendary Christian king believed by some to live in Africa. Although the Portuguese finally made contact with the ancient Christian civilization of Ethiopia, they failed to convert it to Catholicism, and their missionaries were expelled in 1633. Portuguese commercial ventures in Africa and beyond proved to be enormously lucrative, however. Having reached India in 1498, the Malay coast in 1511, and China in 1513, Portuguese sailors were soon bringing back to Europe spices, silks, dyes, and other exotic items and reaping huge profits. Given the competitive nature of the European state system, before long other European nations sought to emulate the Portuguese success by seeking new ocean routes to Asia. Columbus's voyage of 1492 was only the first of dozens of Spanish enterprises that established Spain as the dominant power, not in Asia, as hoped, but in the Americas. The nations of northern Europe also joined in. The French, Dutch, English, Danes, and Swedes claimed lands in the western hemisphere, and the French, Dutch, and English successfully challenged the early Portuguese monopoly in African and Asian trade. By 1600, European empire-building across the globe had begun in earnest.

This initial burst of European expansion had little effect on the ancient centers of civilization in South and East Asia, whose rulers tolerated a limited amount of trade but were strong enough to prevent the Europeans from undermining their political power or the cultural traditions of their subjects. In contrast, the Amerindian civilizations of Central and South America were all but obliterated by Spanish military conquests, economic exploitation, and the introduction of deadly new diseases. The Amerindians of North America faced similar threats only after 1600, when the French and English arrived in substantial numbers. Here the Native Americans' loss of territory and identity was not so sudden, but the process was no less painful and, in the end, the results were largely the same. In Africa, Europeans were unable to topple native rulers or impose their language and religion on most indigenous communities. They remained on the coast, relying on Africans to bring them commodities for trade. Tragically, in addition to gold, ivory, and palm oil, these commodities included human slaves, who at first were shipped to Europe and then, in ever greater numbers, to the plantations of the New World. Before it ended in the nineteenth century, the European slave trade destabilized West African society, warped the region's economic development, and robbed millions of human beings of their freedom, dignity, and lives.

Meanwhile, European society continued to transform itself in the sixteenth and seventeenth centuries. New wealth from overseas trade, mines, and plantations fueled further economic development, facilitated the consolidation of nation-states, and strengthened the position of the business class at the expense of the traditional landed aristocracy. Knowledge of new lands and cultures added to the intellectual ferment already initiated by the Renaissance, the Prostestant Reformation, and the early Scientific Revolution. Europe by the end of the seventeenth century was far different from the Europe of 1500, and its continuing capacity for change made it the leading revolutionary element among the world's civilizations.

C H A P T E R

12

Europe's Expansion: Consequences and Counterattacks

Western Europe had begun to expand its frontiers as early as the eighth century, when Charlemagne campaigned against the pagan Saxons of northeast Germany, and its first great age of overseas colonialism began with the establishment of crusader states in the eastern Mediterranean in the late eleventh and twelfth centuries. Earlier, Scandinavians had advanced into the North Atlantic, setting up colonies in Iceland, Greenland, and, for a short while, North America by A.D. 1000.

Although aggressive expansion had already been part of the dynamics of European civilization for over 700 years, its transoceanic explorations from the late fifteenth century onward mark a turning point in the history not only of the West but of the entire world. Europe's push across wide expanses of ocean eventually became the single most important factor in the breakdown of regional isolation around the world and the creation of a true global community.

The story is not simple. By 1700 Europeans had culturally and demographically altered forever vast areas of the Americas, but they had yet to visit other parts of those two great continents. The major civilizations of East Asia were still successfully resisting most unwanted European influences, and European penetration of India's interior had hardly begun. At the end of the seventeenth century, Western exploration and direct exploitation of the regions of Africa beyond the coasts was even less advanced. Moreover, although it is easy from a contemporary perspective to see in its early transoceanic ventures the origins of Europe's eventual dominance of the world, such a phenomenon would not have been apparent to most people living during these two centuries. For every area into which Europeans were expanding their influence, there was another in which they were retreating or being rebuffed. For example, sixteenth- and seventeenth-century Europeans fearfully witnessed the advancing menace of the Ottoman Turks.

Under Sultan Suleiman II (1520–1566), the Ottoman Empire became a major player in European power politics. In 1522 Suleiman's armies established control over the eastern Mediterranean by seizing the island of Rhodes. In 1526 the Turks destroyed a Hungarian army and within two decades controlled most of that Christian kingdom. By the autumn of 1529 Turkish forces stood at the gates of Vienna but were forced to withdraw. The Ottoman Turks remained Europe's greatest challenger for the next two centuries, and many believed that the next time Turkish soldiers advanced on

Vienna they would not be stopped. Indeed, the siege of 1683 failed only by the slightest margin.

Equally impressive was the expansion of Chinese borders, especially during the reign of Emperor K'ang-hsi (1661–1722), when China took control of the island of Formosa (modern Taiwan), incorporated Tibet into its empire, finally turned the nomads of Mongolia into quiescent vassals, and entered into a border treaty with imperial Russia that inaugurated a long period of Sino-Russian peace. On its part, Russia carved out the largest land empire of its day through a steady process of exploration and colonization across eastern forests and steppes. In 1637 Russian pioneers reached the Pacific, and colonists were not far behind. Given this state of affairs, Western Europeans did not see expansion as a one-way street nor did they see themselves as aggressors and the rest of the world as their victim.

Europeans in the Americas

The first contacts between Europeans and Native Americans posed immediate problems for each group. The Amerindians had to decide whether to cooperate with the new arrivals or to resist them. The Europeans needed to balance the often conflicting religious, commercial, and imperialist aspirations that inspired colonization of the Americas. Should they treat Native Americans as "savages," to be worked as slaves, deprived of their lands, ruled with an iron hand, and killed? Or should they respect their customs and make honest efforts to "civilize" and protect them from exploitation?

As the following documents illustrate, neither the Amerindians nor the newcomers easily resolved these problem during the first two centuries of European presence in the "New World." In the end, however, European greed won out over altruism, and European diseases and firepower broke the back of Amerindian resistance. Native Americans lost their lands, self-determination, and much of their culture. Indeed, their numbers dramatically plummeted. By the early seventeenth century, the Native American populations of the Caribbean and Central and South America had been reduced by as much as 80 to 90 percent from preconquest levels.

Bernardino de Sahagun

GENERAL HISTORY OF THE THINGS OF NEW SPAIN

Bernardino de Sahagun (ca 1499–1590) was one of the earliest Franciscan missionaries in Mexico, arriving from Spain in 1529. In addition to piety, he possessed a thorough knowledge of the Aztec language, a love of the Mexican people among whom he worked, and a scientific curiosity. Around 1545 he began a systematic collection of oral and pictorial sources for the culture of the Mexican people, which became the basis for his *General History of the Things of New Spain.* This history is rightly regarded as the first significant ethnographic work on an Amerindian society and remains today a principal source for the study of Mexican culture at the time of the Spanish conquest.

In his own day, many Spaniards opposed Sahagun's work, because they saw his efforts to preserve native culture as a threat to their policy of transforming this land and its people into a new Spain. Sahagun consequently suffered the indignity of seeing his studies and notes confiscated by royal decree in 1578, and anthropologists and historians had to wait until the nineteenth century to rediscover them.

The following selection comes from the twelfth and last book of the *General History.* Relying on the tales of people who had experienced the conquest less than three decades earlier and on Aztec picture narratives that elderly storytellers interpreted for him, Sahagun vividly portrays initial native reactions to Cortes's arrival in Mexico in 1519. The excerpt begins with the Aztec ruler Moctezuma (Montezuma) nervously awaiting news of the arrival from the sea of what he believes may be Topiltzin-Quetzalcoatl, a legendary fair-skinned, bearded god-king prophesied to reappear after five centuries in 1519.

Questions for Analysis

1. What do we learn about Aztec religious beliefs and practices from this source? For example, what were two reasons for the practice of human sacrifice?
2. What leads the Spaniards to think the natives of Mexico are "savages"?
3. Why do the Aztecs believe the Spaniards are gods?
4. How do the Spaniards use native enmities to their advantage?
5. The Spanish expeditionary force is quite small, yet a number of factors favor it. How many can you discover in this excerpt?

Meanwhile Moctezuma had been unable to rest, to sleep, to eat. He would speak to no one. He seemed to be in great torment. He sighed. He felt weak. He could enjoy nothing. . . .

Then the five emissaries arrived. "Even if he is asleep," they told the guards, "wake him. Tell him that those he sent to the sea have returned."

But Moctezuma said, "I shall not hear them in this place. Have them go to the Coacalli building." Further he commanded, "Have two captives covered with chalk."[1]

So the messengers went to the Coacalli, the house of snakes.[2]

Moctezuma came later. In front of the messengers, the captives were killed — their hearts torn out, their blood sprinkled over the messengers; for they had gone into great danger; they had looked into the very faces of the gods; they had even spoken to them.

After this they reported to Moctezuma all the wonders they had seen, and they showed him samples of the food the Spaniards ate.

Moctezuma was shocked, terrified by what he heard. He was much puzzled by their food, but what made him almost faint away was the telling of how the great lombard gun,[3] at the Spaniards' command, expelled the shot which thundered as it went off. The noise weakened one, dizzied one. Something like a stone came out of it in a shower of fire and sparks. The smoke was foul; it had a sickening, fetid smell. And the shot, which struck a mountain, knocked it to bits — dissolved it. It reduced a tree to sawdust — the tree disappeared as if they had blown it away.

1. Slaves and captives were covered with chalk and feathers prior to sacrifice.

2. A reception hall for visiting dignitaries.

3. A ship deck gun, or cannon.

And as to their war gear, it was all iron. They were iron. Their head pieces were of iron. Their swords, their crossbows, their shields, their lances were of iron.

The animals they rode — they looked like deer — were as high as roof tops.

They covered their bodies completely, all except their faces.

They were very white. Their eyes were like chalk. Their hair — on some it was yellow, on some it was black. They wore long beards; they were yellow, too. And there were some black-skinned ones with kinky hair.

What they ate was like what Aztecs ate during periods of fasting: it was large, it was white, it was lighter than tortillas; it was spongy like the inside of corn stalks; it tasted as if it had been made of a flour of corn stalks; it was sweetish.

Their dogs were huge. Their ears were folded over; their jowls dragged; their eyes blazed yellow, fiery yellow. They were thin — their ribs showed. They were big. They were restless, moving about panting, tongues hanging. They were spotted or varicolored like jaguars.

When Moctezuma was told all this, he was terror-struck. He felt faint. His heart failed him.

Nevertheless, Moctezuma then again sent emissaries, this time all the doers of evil he could gather — magicians, wizards, sorcerers, soothsayers. With them he sent the old men and the warriors necessary to requisition all the food the Spaniards would need, the turkeys, the eggs, the best white tortillas, everything necessary. The elders and fighting men were to care well for them.

Likewise he sent a contingent of captives, so that his men might be prepared in case the supposed gods required human blood to drink. And the emissaries indeed so thought, themselves. But the sacrifice nauseated the Spaniards. They shut their eyes tight; they shook their heads. For Moctezuma's men had soaked the food in blood before offering it to them; it revolted them, sickened them, so much did it reek of blood.

But Moctezuma had provided for this because, as he assumed them to be gods, he was worshiping them as gods. So were the Mexicans.[4] They called these Spaniards "gods come from the heavens"; the Mexicans thought they were all gods, including the black ones, whom they called the dusky gods. . . .

As for the magicians, wizards, sorcerers, and soothsayers, Moctezuma had sent them just in case they might size up the Spaniards differently and be able to use their arts against them — cast a spell over them, blow them away, enchant them, throw stones at them, with wizards' words say an incantation over them — anything that might sicken them, kill them, or turn them back. They fulfilled their charge; they tried their skill on the Spaniards; but what they did had no effect whatsoever. They were powerless.

These men then returned to report to Moctezuma. "We are not as strong as they," was what they said as they described the Spaniards to him. "We are nothing compared to them.". . .

Moctezuma could only wait for the Spaniards, could only show resolution. He quieted, he controlled himself; he made himself submit to whatever was in store for him. So he left his proper dwelling, the great palace, so that the gods — the Spaniards — could occupy it, and moved to the palace he had originally occupied as a prince.

The Spaniards, pressing inland mean-

---

4. That is, the Aztecs.

while to go through the city of Cempoalla, had with them a previously captured man known to have been a high warrior. He was now interpreting for them and guiding them, since he knew the roads and could keep them on the right ones.

Thus they came to reach a place called Tecoac, held by people of the Otomí tribe subject to the city of Tlaxcalla.[5] Here the men of Tecoac resisted; they came out with their weapons. But the Spaniards completely routed them. They trampled them down; they shot them down with their guns; they riddled them with the bolts of their crossbows. They annihilated them, not just a few but a great many.

When Tecoac perished, the news made the Tlaxcallans beside themselves with fear. They lost courage; they gave way to wonder, to terror, until they gathered themselves together and, at a meeting of the rulers, took counsel, weighed the news among themselves, and discussed what to do.

"How shall we act?" some asked. "Shall we meet with them?"

Others said, "The Otomís are great warriors, great fighters, yet the Spaniards thought nothing of them. They were as nothing. In no time, with but the batting of an eyelash, they annihilated our vassals."

"The only thing to do," advised still others, "is to submit to these men, to befriend them, to reconcile ourselves to them. Otherwise, sad would be the fate of the common folk."

This argument prevailed. The rulers of Tlaxcalla went to meet the Spaniards with food offerings of turkey, eggs, fine white tortillas — the tortillas of lords.

"You have tired yourselves, O our lords," they said.

The Spaniards asked, "Where is your home? Where are you from?"

"We are Tlaxcallans," they answered. "You have tired yourselves. You have come to your poor home, Quauhtlaxcalla.". . .

The Tlaxcallans led the Spaniards to the city, to their palace. They made much of them, gave them whatever they needed, waited upon them, and comforted them with their daughters.

The Spaniards, however, kept asking them "Where is Mexico? What is it like? Is it far?"

"From here it is not far," was the answer; "it is a matter of perhaps only three days' march. It is a very splendid place; the Mexicans are strong, brave, conquering people. You find them everywhere."

Now the Tlaxcallans had long been enemies of the people of Cholula.[6] They disliked, hated, detested them; they would have nothing to do with them. Hoping to do them harm, they inflamed the Spaniards against them, saying, "They are very evil, these enemies of ours. Cholula is as powerful as Mexico. Cholula is friendly to Mexico."

Therefore the Spaniards at once went to Cholula, taking the Tlaxcallans and the Cempoallans with them all in war array. They arrived; they entered Cholula. Then there arose from the Spaniards a cry summoning all the noblemen, lords, war leaders, warriors, and common folk; and when they had crowded into the temple courtyard, then the Spaniards and their allies blocked the entrances and every exit.

There followed a butchery of stabbing, beating, killing of the unsuspecting Cholulans armed with no bows and arrows, protected by no shields, unable to contend against the Spaniards. So with no

5. Tlaxcalla was an independent state in the mountains east of the Aztec capital of Tenochtitlán.

6. A city allied with the Aztecs, some fifty miles east of Tenochtitlán.

warning they were treacherously, deceitfully slain. The Tlaxcallans had induced the Spaniards to do this.

What had happened was reported quickly to Moctezuma: his messengers, who had just arrived, departed fleeing back to him. They did not remain long to learn all the details. The effect upon the people of Mexico, however, was immediate; they often rose in tumults, alarmed as by an earthquake, as if there were a constant reeling of the face of the earth. They were terrified.

After death came to Cholula, the Spaniards resumed their marching order to advance upon Mexico. They assembled in their accustomed groups, a multitude, raising a great dust. The iron of their lances and their halberds glistened from afar; the shimmer of their swords was as of a sinuous water course. Their iron breast and back pieces, their helmets clanked. Some came completely encased in iron — as if turned to iron, gleaming, resounding from afar. And ahead of them, preceding them, ran their dogs, panting, with foam continually dripping from their muzzles.

All this stunned the people, terrified them, filled them with fear, with dread.

THE LAWS OF BURGOS

Many of Christopher Columbus's dreams and promises for the lands he explored were never realized, but his vision that their inhabitants could be easily enslaved proved all too correct. Queen Isabella was, by most accounts, disquieted by the idea of an Amerindian slave trade, but forced labor came to the new Spanish colonies nevertheless. The first major vehicle for forced labor in New Spain (the Caribbean) was the *encomienda,* whose major purpose was to ensure the colonists a reliable supply of cheap labor, while allowing them to avoid all of the legal and moral restrictions on slavery. The encomienda system, which had long existed in those areas of Spain conquered from the Moors, allocated to leading settlers the right to compel groups of natives to serve as laborers and personal servants. Throughout New Spain in the sixteenth century, various governors and captains gave villages wholesale to Spanish colonists as tributary fiefs, and the natives of these villages became, in effect, serfs — semifree persons bound to the soil and owing labor service to a lord.

In 1510 a group of Dominican priests arrived in New Spain to serve the spiritual needs of both colonists and natives. Shocked to discover what they perceived as the colonists' brutal callousness toward their native laborers, the priests launched a campaign to stir the Crown to eradicate these abuses. The result was a code of laws promulgated at Burgos, Spain, on December 27, 1512, with a supplement of four amendments added the following July. Altogether, the code comprises thirty-nine articles, which became the fundamental law governing Spanish-Amerindian relations for the next three decades. The laws are invaluable for the modern historian, because they reveal actual conditions in New Spain and early Spanish attitudes toward the natives.

Questions for Analysis

1. How does the Spanish royal court justify the encomienda system, and what does its justification tell us about official Spanish attitudes toward the natives?
2. What do these laws tell us about what was happening to native Amerindian culture in New Spain?
3. Does the royal court see the encomienda as a permanent system or an intermediate step? If intermediate, what is the professed goal?
4. What specific abuses are the Laws of Burgos aimed at eradicating, and what protections do they theoretically afford the natives?
5. Even if a landowner were to follow these laws to the letter, what would be the status of the natives on the plantation or in the mines?

Whereas, the King, my Lord and Father, and the Queen, my Mistress and Mother (may she rest in glory!),[1] always desired that the chiefs and Indians of the Island of Española[2] be brought to a knowledge of our Holy Catholic Faith. . . .

Whereas, it has become evident through long experience that nothing has sufficed to bring the said chiefs and Indians to a knowledge of our Faith (necessary for their salvation), since by nature they are inclined to idleness and vice, and have no manner of virtue or doctrine, . . . and that the principal obstacle in the way of correcting their vices and having them profit by and impressing them with a doctrine is that their dwellings are remote from the settlements of the Spaniards . . . because, although at the time the Indians go to serve them they are indoctrinated in and taught the things of our Faith, after serving they return to their dwellings where, because of the distance and their own evil inclinations, they immediately forget what they have been taught and go back to their customary idleness and vice, and when they come to serve again they are as new in the doctrine as they were at the beginning. . . .

Whereas, it is our duty to seek a remedy for it in every way possible, it was considered by the King, my Lord and Father, and by several members of my Council and by persons of good life, letters, and conscience . . . that the most beneficial thing that could be done at present would be to remove the said chiefs and Indians to the vicinity of the villages and communities of the Spaniards . . . and thus, by continual association with them, as well as by attendance at church on feast days to hear Mass . . . and by observing the conduct of the Spaniards, as well as the preparation and care that the Spaniards will display in demonstrating and teaching them, while they are together, the things of our Holy Catholic Faith, it is clear that they will the sooner learn them

1. These laws were granted in the name of Queen Joanna of Castile, daughter of Isabella and Ferdinand. Queen Isabella of Castile had died in 1504, but because Joanna was considered insane, her father Ferdinand, king of Aragon, served as regent of Castile and its colonial possessions in the New World.

2. New Spain.

and, having learned them, will not forget them as they do now. And if some Indian should fall sick he will be quickly succored and treated, and thus the lives of many, with the help of Our Lord, will be saved who now die because no one knows they are sick; and all will be spared the hardship of coming and going, which will be a great relief to them, because their dwellings are now so remote from the Spanish communities, so that those who now die from sickness and hunger on the journey, and who do not receive the sacraments which as Christians they are obligated to receive, will not die [without the sacraments], because they will be given the sacraments in the said communities as soon as they fall sick; and infants will be baptized at birth; and all will serve with less hardship to themselves and with greater profit to the Spaniards, because they will be with them more continually. . . .

I

First, since it is our determination to remove the said Indians and have them dwell near the Spaniards, we order and command that the persons to whom the said Indians are given, or shall be given, in encomienda, shall at once and forthwith build, for every fifty Indians, four lodges of thirty by fifteen feet, and have the Indians plant 5,000 hillocks (3,000 in cassava[3] and 2,000 in yams), 250 pepper plants, and 50 cotton plants . . . and as soon as the Indians are brought to the estates they shall be given all the aforesaid as their own property; and the person whom you[4] send for this purpose shall tell them it is for their own use and that it is given them in exchange for what they are leaving behind, to enjoy as their own property. And we command that the persons to whom they are given in encomienda shall keep it for them so that they may enjoy it as their own; and we command that this property shall not be sold or taken from them by any person to whom they may be given in encomienda, or by anyone else, but that it shall belong to the said Indians to whom it is assigned and to their descendants, even though this said person sell the estate in which they are, or the said Indians be removed from him; and we declare and command that the person to whom the said Indians are given in encomienda may utilize the goods that the said Indians abandon when they are brought to the estates of the Spaniards, each according to the number of Indians he has, in order to maintain them with such goods; and after the said persons have removed the said goods I command you, our said Admiral and judges and officers, to have the lodges of the said villages burned, since the Indians will have no further use for them: this is so that they will have no reason to return whence they have been brought. . . .

III

Also, we order and command that the citizen to whom the said Indians are given in encomienda shall, upon the land that is assigned to him, be obliged to erect a structure to be used for a church, . . . and in this said church he shall place an image of Our Lady[5] and a bell with which to call the Indians to prayer; and the person who has them in encomienda shall be obliged to have them called by the bell at nightfall

3. A tropical American plant, with a starchy root.

4. The person addressed is Admiral Christopher Columbus, governor of New Spain.

5. The Virgin Mary.

and go with them to the said church, and have them cross themselves and bless themselves, and together recite the *Ave Maria*, the *Pater Noster*, the *Credo*, and the *Salve Regina*,[6] in such wise that all of them shall hear the said person, and the said person hear them, so that he may know who is performing well and who ill, and correct the one who is wrong. . . .

IX

Also, we order and command that whoever has fifty Indians or more in encomienda shall be obliged to have a boy (the one he considers most able) taught to read and write, and the things of our Faith, so that he may later teach the said Indians, because the Indians will more readily accept what he says than what the Spaniards and settlers tell them: and if the said person has a hundred Indians or more he shall have two boys taught as prescribed. . . .

XIII

Also, we order and command that, after the Indians have been brought to the estates, all the founding (of gold) that henceforth is done on the said Island shall be done in the manner prescribed below: that is, the said persons who have Indians in encomienda shall extract gold with them for five months in the year and, at the end of these five months, the said Indians shall rest forty days, and the day they cease their labor of extracting gold shall be noted on a certificate, which shall be given to the miners who go to the mines. . . . And we command that the Indians who thus leave the mines shall not, during the said forty days, be ordered to do anything whatever, save to plant the hillocks necessary for their subsistence that season; and the persons who have the said Indians in encomienda shall be obliged, during these forty days of rest, to indoctrinate them in the things of our Faith more than on the other days, because they will have the opportunity and means to do so. . . .

XVIII

Also, we order and command that no pregnant woman, after the fourth month, shall be sent to the mines, or made to plant hillocks, but shall be kept on the estates and utilized in household tasks, such as making bread, cooking, and weeding; and after she bears her child she shall nurse it until it is three years old, and in all this time she shall not be sent to the mines, or made to plant hillocks. . . .

XXIV

Also, we order and command that no person or persons shall dare to beat any Indian with sticks, or whip him, or call him dog,[7] or address him by any name other than his proper name alone; and if an Indian should deserve to be punished for something he has done, the said person having him in charge shall bring him to the visitor[8] for punishment, on pain that the person who violates this article shall pay, for every time he beats or whips an Indian or Indians, five pesos gold; and if he should call an Indian dog, or address him by any name other than his own, he shall pay one gold peso, to be distributed in the manner stated.

Amendments

The King, my Lord and Father, and I were informed that, although the said ordi-

6. Four prayers: the Hail Mary, the Lord's Prayer ("Our Father"), the Creed of Faith, and the Hail Holy Queen.

7. An especially degrading insult.

8. A supervisor appointed by the governor.

nances were very useful, profitable, and necessary, as well as fitting, it was said that some of them had need of further elucidation and modification. . . .

Therefore, having considered the said ordinances and listened to the religious who have knowledge of the affairs of the said Island and the conditions and habits of the said Indians, they, together with other prelates and members of our Council, amended and modified the said ordinances as follows.

I

First, we order and command that Indian women married to Indian men who have been given in encomienda shall not be forced to go and come and serve with their husbands, at the mines or elsewhere, unless it is by their own free will, or unless their husbands wish to take them; but the said wives shall be obliged to work on their own land or on that of their husbands, or on the lands of the Spaniards, who shall pay them the wages agreed upon with them or with their husbands. . . .

II

Also, we order and command that Indian children under fourteen years of age shall not be compelled to work at tasks (of adults) until they have attained the said age or more; but they shall be compelled to work at, and serve in, tasks proper to children, such as weeding the fields and the like, on their parents' estates (if they have parents); and those above the age of fourteen shall be under the authority of their parents until they are of age and married. . . .

IV

Also, we order and command that within two years (of the publication of this ordinance) the men and women shall go about clad. And whereas it may so happen that in the course of time, what with their indoctrination and association with Christians, the Indians will become so apt and ready to become Christians, and so civilized and educated, that they will be capable of governing themselves and leading the kind of life that the said Christians lead there, we declare and command and say that it is our will that those Indians who thus become competent to live by themselves and govern themselves, under the direction and control of our said judges of the said Island, present or future, shall be allowed to live by themselves and shall be obliged to serve (only) in those things in which our vassals in Spain are accustomed to serve, so that they may serve and pay the tribute which they (our vassals) are accustomed to pay to their princes.

David Pieterzen DeVries

VOYAGES FROM HOLLAND TO AMERICA

As a result of the efforts of Henry Hudson, who explored what is now New York Harbor and the Hudson River in 1609, the Dutch claimed New Netherlands, an area that included Long Island, eastern New York, and parts of New Jersey and Connecticut. To encourage colonization, the government granted wealthy Dutch colonists huge tracts of land, known as "patroonships," with the understanding that each patroon would settle at least fifty tenants on the land within four years. At first, relations with the Algonquins and Raritans in the area around New Amsterdam (modern New York City) were generally cordial, but they rapidly deteriorated after the arrival of the merchant Wilhelm Kieft as governor in 1642. He sought to tax the Algonquins to pay for the construction of a fort and attempted to force them off their land to create new patroonships, even though few existing patroonships had attracted the minimum number of tenants. When the Algonquins resisted, Kieft ordered the massacre described by David Pieterzen DeVries in the following excerpt from his 1655 work, *Voyages from Holland to America.* Born in Rochelle, France, in 1592 or 1593, DeVries spent most of his life as a merchant in the Netherlands, Mediterranean, Americas, and Southeast Asia before becoming a patroon in the Dutch colony in 1638.

Questions for Analysis

1. What are the main reasons DeVries opposes the governor's plan to attack the Algonquins? What does this suggest about DeVries's attitude toward Amerindians?
2. How did the Algonquins react immediately after the massacre? What does their behavior suggest about their early relations with the Dutch?
3. What was the long-term consequence of the massacre?

The 24th of February, sitting at a table with the Governor, he began to state his intentions, that he had a mind to *wipe the mouths* of the savages; that he had been dining at the house of Jan Claesen Damen, where Maryn Adriaensen and Jan Claesen Damen, together with Jacob Planck, had presented a petition to him to begin this work. I answered him that they were not wise to request this; that such work could not be done without the approbation of the Twelve Men;[1] that it could not take place without my assent, who was one of the Twelve Men; that moreover I was the first patroon, and no one else hitherto had risked there so many thousands and also his person, as I was the first to come from Holland or Zeeland to plant a colony; and that he should consider what profit he could derive from this business, as he well knew that on account of trifling with the Indians we had lost our colony in the South River at Swanendael, in the Hoere-kil, with thirty-two men, who were murdered in the year 1630; and that in the year 1640, the cause of my people being murdered on Staten Island was a difficulty which he had brought on with the Raritan Indians, where his soldiers had for some trifling thing killed some

1. The board of directors responsible for governing New Netherlands.

savages. . . . But it appeared that my speaking was of no avail. He had, with his co-murderers, determined to commit the murder, deeming it a Roman deed,[2] and to do it without warning the inhabitants in the open lands that each one might take care of himself against the retaliation of the savages, for he could not kill all the Indians. When I had expressed all these things in full, sitting at the table, and the meal was over, he told me he wished me to go to the large hall, which he had been lately adding in his house. Coming to it, there stood all his soldiers ready to cross the river to Pavonia to commit the murder. Then spoke I again to Governor Willem Kieft: "Let this work alone; you wish to break the mouths of the Indians, but you will also murder our own nation, for there are none of the settlers in the open country who are aware of it. My own dwelling, my people, cattle, corn, and tobacco will be lost." He answered me, assuring me that there would be no danger; that some soldiers should go to my house to protect it. But that was not done. So was this business begun between the 25th and 26th of February in the year 1643. I remained that night at the Governor's, sitting up. I went and sat by the kitchen fire, when about midnight I heard a great shrieking, and I ran to the ramparts of the fort, and looked over to Pavonia. Saw nothing but firing, and heard the shrieks of the savages murdered in their sleep. I returned again to the house by the fire. Having sat there awhile, there came an Indian with his squaw, whom I knew well, and who lived about an hour's walk from my house, and told me that they two had fled in a small skiff, which they had taken from the shore at Pavonia; that the Indians from Fort Orange had surprised them; and that they had come to conceal themselves in the fort. I told them that they must go away immediately; that this was no time for them to come to the fort to conceal themselves; that they who had killed their people at Pavonia were not Indians, but the Swannekens, as they call the Dutch, had done it. They then asked me how they should get out of the fort. I took them to the door, and there was no sentry there, and so they betook themselves to the woods. When it was day the soldiers returned to the fort, having massacred or murdered eighty Indians, and considering they had done a deed of Roman valor, in murdering so many in their sleep; where infants were torn from their mothers' breasts, and hacked to pieces in the presence of the parents, and the pieces thrown into the fire and in the water, and other sucklings, being bound to small boards, were cut, stuck, and pierced, and miserably massacred in a manner to move a heart of stone. Some were thrown into the river, and when the fathers and mothers endeavored to save them, the soldiers would not let them come on land but made both parents and children drown — children from five to six years of age, and also some old and decrepit persons. Those who fled from this onslaught, and concealed themselves in the neighboring sedge, and when it was morning, came out to beg a piece of bread, and to be permitted to warm themselves, were murdered in cold blood and tossed into the fire or the water. Some came to our people in the country with their hands, some with their legs cut off, and some holding their entrails in their arms, and others had such horrible cuts and gashes, that worse than they were could never happen. And these poor simple creatures, as also many of our own people, did not know any better than that

2. A glorious deed in the manner of the ancient Romans.

they had been attacked by a party of other Indians — the Maquas. After this exploit, the soldiers were rewarded for their services, and Director Kieft thanked them by taking them by the hand and congratulating them. At another place, on the same night, on Corler's Hook near Corler's plantation, forty Indians were in the same manner attacked in their sleep, and massacred there in the same manner. Did the Duke of Alva[3] in the Netherlands ever do anything more cruel? This is indeed a disgrace to our nation, who have so generous a governor in our Fatherland as the Prince of Orange,[4] who has always endeavored in his wars to spill as little blood as possible. As soon as the savages understood that the Swannekens had so treated them, all the men whom they could surprise on the farm-lands, they killed; but we have never heard that they have ever permitted women or children to be killed. They burned all the houses, farms, barns, grain, haystacks, and destroyed everything they could get hold of. So there was an open destructive war begun. They also burnt my farm, cattle, corn, barn, tobacco-house, and all the tobacco. My people saved themselves in the house where I alone lived, which was made with embrasures, through which they defended themselves. Whilst my people were in alarm the savage whom I had aided to escape from the fort in the night came there, and told the other Indians that I was a good chief, that I had helped him out of the fort, and that the killing of the Indians took place contrary to my wish. Then they all cried out together to my people that they would not shoot them; that if they had not destroyed my cattle they would not do it, nor burn my house; that they would let my little brewery stand, though they wished to get the copper kettle, in order to make darts for their arrows; but hearing now that it had been done contrary to my wish, they all went away, and left my house unbesieged. When now the Indians had destroyed so many farms and men in revenge for their people, I went to Governor Willem Kieft, and asked him if it was not as I had said it would be, that he would only effect the spilling of Christian blood. Who would now compensate us for our losses? But he gave me no answer. He said he wondered that no Indians came to the fort. I told him that I did not wonder at it; "why should the Indians come here where you have so treated them?"

The European Presence in Africa

Due mainly to a catastrophic decline of the native Amerindian population, the encomienda system of New Spain had collapsed by the end of the sixteenth century and Spanish colonists increasingly turned to African slaves for labor. Portugal, which had systematically begun to explore the west coast of Africa in 1418, was in

3. A general in the service of Philip II of Spain. Alva was responsible for carrying out harsh anti-Protestant measures in the Netherlands in the 1560s.

4. Frederick Henry, stadholder, or elected executive and military commander, of the Netherlands.

an especially advantageous position to supply this human chattel. During the 1480s the Portuguese established fortified posts along West Africa's Gold Coast, where it traded with such coastal kingdoms as Benin for gold, slaves, and ivory. By 1500 some 700 kilos of gold and approximately 10,000 slaves were arriving annually in Lisbon from West Africa. While engaging in this trade, the Portuguese were also pushing down the coast. Finally, in 1487–1488 Bartholomeu Dias rounded the Cape of Good Hope, opening the east coast of Africa to direct Portuguese contact. Under the leadership of Francisco de Almeida (ca 1450–1510), the Portuguese set up the East African trading colony of Mozambique and successfully challenged Arab hegemony over East African trade.

The Portuguese led the way, but other European maritime powers were not far behind in establishing their presence in Africa. While the Spanish concentrated on North Africa, capturing Tunis in 1535 and holding it until 1574, the English under John Hawkins instituted their own slave trade from West Africa to the New World between 1562 and 1568. In 1713, when England won the right of *asiento,* by which it was granted license to transport African slaves to the Spanish colonies in the Americas, the English became a major participant in the African slave trade. In 1595 the Dutch settled themselves on the Guinea coast, and in 1652 they founded Cape Town on the southern tip of the continent. The first French settlements in Africa appeared in 1626 on the island of Madagascar, which France annexed in 1686, and in 1637 the French were building numerous forts on West Africa's Gold Coast and exploring Senegal. Even the Prussians were building a West African settlement by 1683.

Slaves and gold were the two major attractions for all these European powers on the African coasts, and many Africans were quite willing to deal in these commodities with the outside world. Although the Europeans were becoming a major presence along the coasts, their penetration of the interior would have to wait for a later age. The general social and political strength of most African regional kingdoms, the wide variety of debilitating and often deadly African diseases, against which the Europeans had no immunities, and the absence of safe and fast inland transportation combined to block significant European thrust into the interior until the nineteenth century. The Europeans were thus forced to come largely as traders and not colonizers, and they had to negotiate with local African leaders for goods and slaves.

Nzinga Mbemba (Afonso I)

LETTERS TO THE KING OF PORTUGAL

The largest state in central West Africa by 1500 was the kingdom of Kongo, stretching along the estuary of the Congo River in territory that today lies within the nations of Angola and Zaire. In 1483 the Portuguese navigator Diogo Cão made contact with Kongo and several years later visited its inland capital. When he sailed home he brought with him Kongo emissaries, whom King Nzinga a Kuwu dispatched to

Lisbon to learn European ways. They returned in 1491, accompanied by Portuguese priests, artisans, and soldiers, who brought with them a wide variety of European goods, including a printing press. In the same year, the king and his son, Nzinga Mbemba, were baptized into the Catholic faith.

Around 1506 Nzinga Mbemba, whose Christian name was Afonso, succeeded his father and ruled until about 1543. Afonso promoted the introduction of European culture into his kingdom by adopting Christianity as the state religion (although most of his subjects, especially those in the hinterlands, remained followers of the ancient ways), imitating the etiquette of the Portuguese royal court, and using Portuguese as the language of state business. His son Henrique was educated in Portugal and returned to serve as West Africa's first black Roman Catholic bishop. European firearms, horses, and cattle, as well as new foods from the Americas, became common in Kongo, and Afonso dreamed of achieving a powerful and prosperous state through cooperation with the Europeans. By the time of his death, however, his kingdom was on the verge of disintegration, in no small measure because of the Portuguese. As many later African rulers were to discover, the introduction of European products and customs unsettled the people and caused widespread dissension. Worse, the unceasing Portuguese pursuit of slaves undermined Afonso's authority and made his subjects restive.

In 1526 King Afonso wrote the following three letters to King João III of Portugal. The three documents are part of a collection of twenty-four letters that Afonso and his Portuguese-educated native secretaries dispatched to two successive kings of Portugal on a variety of issues. This collection is our earliest extant source of African commentary on the European impact.

Questions for Analysis

1. According to King Afonso, how have the availability of Portuguese goods and the presence of slave traders affected Kongo society?
2. Does King Afonso see the Portuguese presence in his kingdom as a right or a privilege?
3. How has King Afonso attempted to control Portuguese activity?
4. How does King Afonso distinguish between legitimate and illegitimate trade in slaves?
5. What elements of Portuguese culture does he welcome? Why?
6. How would you characterize the general tone of these letters? What do they suggest about King Afonso's relations with the Portuguese?

Sir, Your Highness should know how our Kingdom is being lost in so many ways that it is convenient to provide for the necessary remedy, since this is caused by the excessive freedom given by your factors [agents] and officials to the men and merchants who are allowed to come to this Kingdom to set up shops with goods and many things which have been prohibited by us, and which they spread throughout our Kingdoms and Domains in such an abundance that many of our vassals, whom we had in obedience, do not comply because they have the things in greater abundance than we ourselves; and it was with these things that we had them content and subjected under our vassalage and jurisdiction, so it is doing a great harm not only to the service of God, but the security and peace of our Kingdoms and State as well.

And we cannot reckon how great the damage is, since the mentioned merchants are taking every day our natives, sons of the land and the sons of our noblemen and vassals and our relatives, because the thieves and men of bad conscience grab them wishing to have the things and wares of this Kingdom which they are ambitious of; they grab them and get them to be sold; and so great, Sir, is the corruption of licentiousness that our country is being completely depopulated, and Your Highness should not agree with this nor accept it as in your service. And to avoid it we need from those (your) Kingdoms no more than some priests and a few people to teach in schools, and no other goods, except wine and flour for the holy sacrament. That is why we beg of Your Highness to help and assist us in this matter, commanding your factors that they should not send here either merchants or wares, because it is *our will that in these Kingdoms there should not be any trade of slaves nor outlet for them.*[1] Concerning what is referred above, again we beg of Your Highness to agree with it, since otherwise we cannot remedy such an obvious damage. Pray Our Lord in His mercy to have Your Highness under His guard and let you do for ever the things of His service. . . .

The King. Dom Afonso.

. . .

Moreover, Sir, in our Kingdoms there is another great inconvenience which is of little service to God, and this is that many of our people, keenly desirous as they are of the wares and things of your Kingdoms, which are brought here by your people, and in order to satisfy their voracious appetite, seize many of our people, freed and exempt men; and very often it happens that they kidnap even noblemen and the sons of noblemen, and our relatives, and take them to be sold to the white men who are in our Kingdoms; and for this purpose they have concealed them; and others are brought during the night so that they might not be recognized.

And as soon as they are taken by the white men they are immediately ironed and branded with fire, and when they are carried to be embarked, if they are caught by our guards' men the whites allege that they have bought them but they cannot say from whom, so that it is our duty to do justice and to restore to the freemen their freedom, but it cannot be done if your subjects feel offended, as they claim to be.

And to avoid such a great evil we passed a law so that any white man living in our Kingdoms and wanting to purchase goods in any way should first inform three of our noblemen and officials of our court whom we rely upon in this matter, and these are Dom Pedro Manipanza and Dom Manuel Manissaba, our chief usher,

1. Emphasis appears in the original letter.

and Gonçalo Pires our chief freighter, who should investigate if the mentioned goods are captives or free men, and if cleared by them there will be no further doubt nor embargo for them to be taken and embarked. But if the white men do not comply with it they will lose the aforementioned goods. And if we do them this favor and concession it is for the part Your Highness has in it, since we know that it is in your service too that these goods are taken from our Kingdom, otherwise we should not consent to this.

. . .

Sir, Your Highness has been kind enough to write to us saying that we should ask in our letters for anything we need, and that we shall be provided with everything, and as the peace and the health of our Kingdom depend on us, and as there are among us old folks and people who have lived for many days, it happens that we have continuously many and different diseases which put us very often in such a weakness that we reach almost the last extreme; and the same happens to our children, relatives and natives owing to the lack in this country of physicians and surgeons who might know how to cure properly such diseases. And as we have got neither dispensaries nor drugs which might help us in this forlornness, many of those who had been already confirmed and instructed in the holy faith of Our Lord Jesus Christ perish and die; and the rest of the people in their majority cure themselves with herbs and breads and other ancient methods, so that they put all their faith in the mentioned herbs and ceremonies if they live, and believe that they are saved if they die; and this is not much in the service of God.

And to avoid such a great error and inconvenience, since it is from God in the first place and then from your Kingdoms and from Your Highness that all the good and drugs and medicines have come to save us, we beg of you to be agreeable and kind enough to send us two physicians and two apothecaries and one surgeon, so that they may come with their drug-stores and all the necessary things to stay in our kingdoms, because we are in extreme need of them all and each of them. We shall do them all good and shall benefit them by all means, since they are sent by Your Highness, whom we thank for your work in their coming. We beg of Your Highness as a great favor to do this for us, because besides being good in itself it is in the service of God as we have said above.

James Barbot

THE ABSTRACT OF A VOYAGE TO NEW CALABAR RIVER, OR RIO RIVER, IN THE YEAR 1699

The preceding document illustrates how an African king's attempt to control commerce between his subjects and the Portuguese was at least partially frustrated and how the slave trade had a number of unhappy consequences for African society. This source offers another perspective. James Barbot, a member of a late-seventeenth-century English slave-trading expedition to Ibani, describes trade negotiations with its king, William, in 1699. Ibani, or Bonny, as the English called it, was an island state off the Niger delta. By the late eighteenth century it would be known as the principal slave market of the entire Guinea coast. One English captain, who sailed to Bonny between 1786 and 1800, estimated that at least 20,000 slaves were bought and sold there annually. In this document we see how the trading system worked a century earlier.

Questions for Analysis

1. What is Barbot's attitude toward Ibani society?
2. How would you characterize trade at Bonny? Was it haphazard bartering? A well-developed system with specific currency? Something in between? What does this account tell about social arrangements in Ibani?
3. What benefit is there for the English in negotiating through the king?
4. What benefits does the king enjoy from this arrangement?
5. What do the prices of the other commodities purchased by the slavers say about the relative value of one slave?

June 30, 1699, being ashore, had a new conference which produced nothing. Then Pepprell [Pepple] the king's brother delivered a message from the king.

> He was sorry we would not accept his proposals. It was not his fault, since he had a great esteem and regard for the whites, who had greatly enriched him through trade. His insistence on thirteen bars[1] for male and ten for female slaves was due to the fact that the people of the country maintained a high price for slaves at their inland markets, seeing so many large ships coming to Bonny for them. However, to moderate matters and to encourage trade with us, he would be content with thirteen bars for males and nine bars and two brass rings for females, *etc.*

We offered thirteen bars for men and nine for women and proportionately for boys and girls, according to their ages. Following this we parted, without concluding anything further.

On July 1, the king sent for us to come ashore. We stayed there till four in the afternoon and concluded the trade on the terms offered them the day before. The king promised to come aboard the next day to regulate it and be paid his duties. . . .

The second [of July]. . . . At two o'clock we fetched the king from shore, attended by all his *Caboceiros*[2] and officers, in three large canoes. Entering the ship, he was saluted with seven guns. The king had on an old-fashioned scarlet coat, laced with gold and silver, very rusty, and a fine hat on his head, but bare-footed. All his attendants showed great respect to him and, since our arrival, none of the natives have dared to come aboard or sell the least thing, till the king adjusted trade matters.

We had again a long talk with the king and Pepprell, his brother, concerning the

1. Bars of iron.

2. A Portuguese term. Here it means chiefs and elders.

rates of our goods and his customs. This Pepprell was a sharp black and a mighty talking black, perpetually making objections against something or other and teasing us for this or that *dassy*[3] or present, as well as for drinks, etc. Would that such a one as he were out of the way, to facilitate trade. . . .

Thus, with much patience, all our affairs were settled equitably, after the fashion of a people who are not very scrupulous when it comes to finding excuses or objections for not keeping to the word of any verbal contract. For they do not have the art of reading and writing, and we therefore are forced to stand to their agreement, which often is no longer than they think fit to hold it themselves. The king ordered the public crier to proclaim permission to trade with us, with the noise of his trumpets . . . we paying sixteen brass rings to the fellow for his fee. The blacks objected against our wrought pewter and tankards, green beads and other goods, which they would not accept. . . .

We gave the usual presents to the king. . . . To Captain Forty, the king's general, Captain Pepprell, Captain Boileau, alderman Bougsby, my lord Willyby, duke of Monmouth, drunken Henry and some others[4] two firelocks, eight hats, nine narrow Guinea stuffs. We adjusted with them the reduction of our merchandise into bars of iron, as the standard coin, namely: one bunch of beads, one bar; four strings of rings, ten rings each, one ditto; four copper bars, one ditto. . . . And so on *pro rata* for every sort of goods. . . .

The price of provisions and wood was also regulated.

> Sixty king's yams, one bar; one hundred and sixty slave's yams, one bar; for fifty thousand yams to be delivered to us. A butt[5] of water, two rings. For the length of wood, seven bars, which is dear, but they were to deliver it ready cut into our boat. For one goat, one bar. A cow, ten or eight bars, according to its size. A hog, two bars. A calf, eight bars. A jar of palm oil, one bar and a quarter.

We also paid the king's duty in goods; five hundred slaves, to be purchased at two copper rings a head.

AN AFRO-PORTUGUESE SALTCELLAR

West African artists have excelled in the creation of sculpted human and animal effigies since at least the days of the Nok culture (Chapter 1). Using clay, wood, ivory, and bronze, they fashioned a wide variety of works of art that served a variety of cultural needs. In some regions bronze casting and ivory carving were royal monopolies carried on by highly trained professionals.

Such was the case in the coastal kingdom of Benin (modern Nigeria), when the Portuguese arrived in the fifteenth century. Impressed by the skills of the Benin ivory cutters, the Portuguese commissioned works such as condiment sets, utensils, and hunting horns. The ivory carving shown here was crafted in the sixteenth or

3. A trade term for "gift."

4. The king's chiefs and elders.

5. A large cask.

Saltcellar from Benin

seventeenth century and is usually identified as a *salerio* or saltcellar, even though it is unclear how its two chambers were actually used. It depicts two Portuguese officials flanked by two assistants. Above them is a Portuguese ship, with a man peering out of the crow's-nest.

Questions for Analysis

1. Notice what is hanging around the central standing figure's neck, what he holds in his hands, and his facial expression. What do you think the artist is telling us about this noble?
2. What might we infer from this work about Portuguese-African relations as perceived by the artist?

Chinese and Japanese Reactions to the West

Of all the regions Europeans reached during the sixteenth and seventeenth centuries, China and Japan were least affected. This was not for lack of European effort. Portuguese traders reached south China in 1513, opened trade at Canton in 1514, and established a permanent trading base in Macao in 1557. In 1542, the first Portuguese merchants reached Japan and soon were reaping healthy profits by carrying goods between China and Japan. Later in the century, the Dutch and English successfully entered these East Asian markets. Roman Catholic Europeans, especially the Portuguese, energetically supported missionary efforts in China and Japan, usually in cooperation with the newly founded Society of Jesus, more popularly known as the Jesuits. Francis Xavier and other Jesuits began preaching in Japan in 1549, and by the early 1600s they had won approximately 300,000 converts to Christianity. Catholic missionary activities in China began later, in 1583, and followed a somewhat different strategy: the Jesuits did less preaching to the common people and instead sought the support of Chinese intellectuals, government officials, and members of the imperial court. The Jesuits were moderately successful, because they impressed Confucian scholars with their erudition, especially in mathematics and science, and the Chinese appreciated the missionaries' willingness to understand and respect China's culture.

For all their efforts, the economic benefits and religious gains the Westerners obtained were meager. Although the Chinese tolerated learned Jesuit missionaries, they viewed European merchants as boorish, overly aggressive, and purveyors of shoddy goods. Preferring to deal with Arabs and other foreigners, they limited trade with Europeans to Canton and Macao and placed it under numerous restrictions. Missionary activity resulted in a few converts, but feuding among Catholic religious orders, staunch opposition from many Chinese officials, and the unwillingness of most Chinese, even converts, to abandon such ancient rites as ancestor worship weakened the enterprise. When in 1742 Pope Benedict XIV decreed that Chinese Catholics must abandon Confucianism, Emperor Ch'ien-lung expelled the missionaries and Chinese Christianity withered.

Although European efforts to trade and win souls had a more promising start in Japan, by the mid-seventeenth century the Japanese had suppressed Christianity and restricted European trade to only one Dutch ship a year. This turn of events resulted from attempts by Japanese leaders to bring stability to Japan after a century of civil war and rebellion. Convinced that European merchants and missionaries had contributed to Japan's disorder, the government outlawed Christianity and essentially closed Japan to the outside world.

Matteo Ricci

JOURNALS

The most celebrated of the Jesuit scholar-missionaries to work in China was the Italian Matteo Ricci (1552–1610), who arrived in 1583. Father Ricci dazzled the Chinese literarchy with clocks, maps, and various types of scientific equipment, much of which he constructed himself. A gifted linguist, he composed over twenty-five works in Chinese on mathematics, literature, ethics, geography, astronomy, and, above all else, religion. He so impressed Confucian scholars that they accorded him the title "Doctor from the Great West Ocean." In 1601 Emperor Wan-li summoned Ricci to his court at Peking (modern Beijing) and provided him with a subsidy to carry on his study of mathematics and astronomy. When Ricci died, the emperor donated a burial site outside the gates of the imperial city as a special token of honor.

During his twenty-seven years in China, Ricci kept a journal, with no thought of publishing it. Shortly after his death, however, a Jesuit colleague edited and published the journal, into which he incorporated a number of other, more official sources, and it became one of Europe's primary stores of information about China until the late eighteenth century, when accounts by European travelers to the Middle Kingdom became more common. In the following selection from that diary, Ricci tells of charges brought against certain Jesuits working at Nan-ch'ang. Here we can see some of the cultural barriers and attitudes that frustrated the Jesuits' efforts to accommodate Christianity to Chinese civilization.

Questions for Analysis

1. What most offended the Confucians who brought charges against the Jesuits and their religion? Compare these charges with Han Yu's *Memorial on Buddhism* (Chapter 6). Which are more striking, the similarities or the differences? What do you conclude from your answer?
2. The Jesuits' association with Father Ricci seems to have favored them in the

course of events. Why? What is there about Ricci that gives his fellow Jesuits an aura of legitimacy?

3. Does Ricci see the outcome of the hearing as a Christian victory? If so, why? Is there another way of interpreting the Chief Justice's decision and its consequences? How do you think one of the Jesuits' Confucian opponents might describe this confrontation and its resolution?
4. If the Chief Justice prepared a report on this case, what do you think he would write?

During 1606 and the year following, the progress of Christianity in Nancian[1] was in no wise retarded. . . . The number of neophytes[2] [increased] by more than two hundred, all of whom manifested an extraordinary piety in their religious devotions. As a result, the reputation of the Christian religion became known throughout the length and breadth of this metropolitan city. . . .

Through the efforts of Father Emanuele Dias another and a larger house was purchased, in August of 1607, at a price of a thousand gold pieces. This change was necessary, because the house he had was too small for his needs and was situated in a flood area. Just as the community was about to change from one house to the other, a sudden uprising broke out against them. . . .

At the beginning of each month, the Magistrates hold a public assembly . . . in the temple of their great Philosopher.[3] When the rites of the new-moon were completed in the temple, and these are civil rather than religious rites,[4] one of those present took advantage of the occasion to speak on behalf of the others, and to address the highest Magistrate present. . . . "We wish to warn you," he said, "that there are certain foreign priests in this royal city, who are preaching a law, hitherto unheard of in this kingdom,[5] and who are holding large gatherings of people in their house." Having said this, he referred them to their local Magistrate, . . . and he in turn ordered the plaintiffs to present their case in writing, assuring them that he would support it with all his authority, in an effort to have the foreign priests expelled. The complaint was written out that same day and signed with twenty-seven signatures. . . . The content of the document was somewhat as follows.

"Matthew Ricci, Giovanni Soerio, Emanuele Dias, and certain other foreigners from western kingdoms, men who are guilty of high treason against the throne, are scattered amongst us, in five different provinces. They are continually communicating with each other and are here and there practicing brigandage on the rivers, collecting money, and then distributing it

1. Nan-ch'ang in the southern province of Kiangsi.

2. Converts.

3. Confucius.

4. Ricci and his fellow Jesuits chose to regard all ceremonies of ancestor worship as purely "civil rites," thereby allowing their converts to continue to pay traditional devotion to deceased family members.

5. Ricci refers to China throughout his journal as a "kingdom," even though it had an emperor, not a king.

to the people, in order to curry favor with the multitudes. They are frequently visited by the Magistrates, by the high nobility and by the Military Prefects, with whom they have entered into a secret pact, binding unto death.

"These men teach that we should pay no respect to the images of our ancestors, a doctrine which is destined to extinguish the love of future generations for their forebears. Some of them break up the idols, leaving the temples empty and the gods to be pitied, without any patronage. In the beginning they lived in small houses, but by this time they have bought up large and magnificent residences. The doctrine they teach is something infernal. It attracts the ignorant into its fraudulent meshes, and great crowds of this class are continually assembled at their houses. Their doctrine gets beyond the city walls and spreads itself through the neighboring towns and villages and into the open country, and the people become so wrapt up in its falsity, that students are not following their courses, laborers are neglecting their work, farmers are not cultivating their acres, and even the women have no interest in their housework. The whole city has become disturbed, and, whereas in the beginning there were only a hundred or so professing their faith, now there are more than twenty thousand. These priests distribute pictures of some Tartar or Saracen,[6] who they say is God, who came down from heaven to redeem and to instruct all of humanity, and who alone, according to their doctrine, can give wealth and happiness; a doctrine by which the simple people are very easily deceived. These men are an abomination on the face of the earth, and there is just ground for fear that once they have erected their own temples, they will start a rebellion. . . . Wherefore, moved by their interest in the maintenance of the public good, in the conservation of the realm, and in the preservation, whole and entire, of their ancient laws, the petitioners are presenting this complaint and demanding, in the name of the entire province, that a rescript of it be forwarded to the King, asking that these foreigners be sentenced to death, or banished from the realm, to some deserted island in the sea.". . .

Each of the Magistrates to whom the indictment was presented asserted that the spread of Christianity should be prohibited, and that the foreign priests should be expelled from the city, if the Mayor saw fit, after hearing the case, and notifying the foreigners. . . . But the Fathers,[7] themselves, were not too greatly disturbed, placing their confidence in Divine Providence, which had always been present to assist them on other such dangerous occasions. . . .

Father Emanuele is summoned before the Chief Justice.

Father Emanuele, in his own defense, . . . gave a brief outline of the Christian doctrine. Then he showed that according to the divine law, the first to be honored, after God, were a man's parents. But the judge had no mind to hear or to accept any of this and he made it known that he thought it was all false. After that repulse, with things going from bad to worse, it looked as if they were on the verge of desperation, so much so, indeed, that they increased

6. The reference is to Jesus Christ.

7. The Jesuits.

their prayers, their sacrifices and their bodily penances, in petition for a favorable solution of their difficulty. Their adversaries appeared to be triumphantly victorious. They were already wrangling about the division of the furniture of the Mission residences, and to make results doubly certain, they stirred up the flames anew with added accusations and indictments. . . .

The Mayor, who was somewhat friendly with the Fathers, realizing that there was much in the accusation that was patently false, asked the Magistrate Director of the Schools,[8] if he knew whether or not this man Emanuele was a companion of Matthew Ricci, who was so highly respected at the royal court, and who was granted a subsidy from the royal treasury, because of the gifts he had presented to the King. Did he realize that the Fathers had lived in Nankin[9] for twelve years, and that no true complaint had ever been entered against them for having violated the laws. Then he asked him if he had really given full consideration as to what was to be proven in the present indictment. To this the Director of the Schools replied that he wished the Mayor to make a detailed investigation of the case and then to confer with him. The Chief Justice then ordered the same thing to be done. Fortunately, it was this same Justice who was in charge of city affairs when Father Ricci first arrived in Nancian. It was he who first gave the Fathers permission, with the authority of the Viceroy, to open a house there. . . .

After the Mayor had examined the charges of the plaintiffs and the reply of the defendants, he subjected the quasi-literati[10] to an examination in open court, and taking the Fathers under his patronage, he took it upon himself to refute the calumnies of their accusers. He said he was fully convinced that these strangers were honest men, and that he knew that there were only two of them in their local residence and not twenty, as had been asserted. To this they replied that the Chinese were becoming their disciples. To which the Justice in turn replied: "What of it? Why should we be afraid of our own people? Perhaps you are unaware of the fact that Matthew Ricci's company is cultivated by everyone in Pekin, and that he is being subsidized by the royal treasury. How dare the Magistrates who are living outside of the royal city expel men who have permission to live at the royal court? These men here have lived peacefully in Nankin for twelve years. I command," he added, "that they buy no more large houses, and that the people are not to follow their law.". . .

A few days later, the court decision was pronounced and written out. . . . [and] was then posted at the city gates as a public edict. The following is a summary of their declaration. Having examined the

---

8. The director of the local Confucian academy was one of the Jesuits' chief opponents.

9. Nanking, the southern auxiliary capital.

10. Ricci's term for the chief tormenters of the Jesuits in Nan-ch'ang. These were Confucian scholars who had passed the first and most basic of the three Confucian self-service examinations and were thereby known popularly as "cultivated talents." By passing the first examination level, these men earned recognition simply as competent students (quasi-literati). They were subject to periodic reexamination at that level and could lose their status and privileges. Only those who passed the second or provincial level examination and became "elevated men" attained a permanent rank and were eligible for appointment to one of the lower civil posts. Apparently these "cultivated talents" felt threatened by the Jesuits.

cause of Father Emanuele and his companions, it was found that these men had come here from the West because they had heard so much about the fame of the great Chinese Empire, and that they had already been living in the realm for some years, without any display of ill-will. Father Emanuele should be permitted to practice his own religion, but it was not considered to be the right thing for the common people, who are attracted by novelties, to adore the God of Heaven. For them to go over to the religion of foreigners would indeed be most unbecoming. . . . It would therefore seem to be . . . [in] . . . the best interests of the Kingdom, to . . . [warn] . . . everyone in a public edict not to abandon the sacrifices of their ancient religion by accepting the cult of foreigners. Such a movement might, indeed, result in calling together certain gatherings, detrimental to the public welfare, and harmful also to the foreigner, himself. Wherefore, the Governor of this district, by order of the high Magistrates, admonishes the said Father Emanuele to refrain from perverting the people, by inducing them to accept a foreign religion. The man who sold him the larger house is to restore his money and Emanuele is to buy a smaller place, sufficient for his needs, and to live there peaceably, as he has done, up to the present. Emanuele, himself, has agreed to these terms and the Military Prefects of the district have been ordered to make a search of the houses there and to confiscate the pictures of the God they speak of, wherever they find them. It is not permitted for any of the native people to go over to the religion of the foreigners, nor is it permitted to gather together for prayer meetings. Whoever does contrary to these prescriptions will be severely punished, and if the Military Prefects are remiss in enforcing them, they will be held to be guilty of the same crimes. To his part of the edict, the Director of the Schools added, that the common people were forbidden to accept the law of the foreigners, and that a sign should be posted above the door of the Father's residence, notifying the public that these men were forbidden to have frequent contact with the people.

The Fathers were not too disturbed by this pronouncement, because they were afraid that it was going to be much worse. In fact, everyone thought it was rather favorable, and that the injunction launched against the spread of the faith was a perfunctory order to make it appear that the literati were not wholly overlooked, since the Fathers were not banished from the city, as the literati had demanded. Moreover it was not considered a grave misdemeanor for the Chinese to change their religion, and it was not customary to inflict a serious punishment on those violating such an order. The neophytes, themselves, proved this when they continued, as formerly, to attend Mass.

Tokugawa Iemitsu

"CLOSED COUNTRY EDICT OF 1635" AND "EXCLUSION OF THE PORTUGUESE, 1639"

When the first Europeans reached Japan, they encountered a land plagued by civil war and rebellion. The authority of the *shoguns,* military commanders who had ruled

Japan on behalf of the emperor since the twelfth century, was in eclipse, as the *daimyo* (great lords) fought for power. Turbulence ended toward the close of the sixteenth century, when three military heroes, Oda Nobunaga (1534–1582), Toyotomi Hideyoshi (1536–1598), and Tokugawa Ieyasu (1543–1616), forced the daimyo to accept central authority. In 1603 the emperor recognized Tokugawa Ieyasu as shogun; the era of the Tokugawa Shogunate, which lasted to 1868, had begun.

Between 1624 and 1641, Iemitsu, grandson of Ieyasu and shogun from 1623 to 1651, issued edicts that closed Japan to virtually all foreigners. This was the culmination of policies begun under Toyotomi Hideyoshi, who had sought to limit contacts between Japanese and foreigners, especially Catholic missionaries. He and his successors viewed the missionaries' aggressive proselytizing as a disturbing factor in society and a potential political threat. The first document that follows, the most celebrated of Tokugawa Iemitsu's edicts, is directed to the two *bugyo*, or commissioners, of Nagasaki, a port city in southwest Japan and a center of Japanese Christianity; the second more specifically deals with the pro-Catholic activities of the Portuguese.

Questions for Analysis

1. To what extent is the edict of 1635 directed against the activities of foreigners?
2. Much of the 1635 edict deals with trade issues. What do the various provisions suggest about the shogun's attitude toward trade?
3. What can one infer about the reasons for the promulgation of the 1639 edict?

Closed Country Edict of 1635

1. Japanese ships are strictly forbidden to leave for foreign countries.

2. No Japanese is permitted to go abroad. If there is anyone who attempts to do so secretly, he must be executed. The ship so involved must be impounded and its owner arrested, and the matter must be reported to the higher authority.

3. If any Japanese returns from overseas after residing there, he must be put to death.

4. If there is any place where the teachings of padres[1] is practiced, the two of you must order a thorough investigation.

5. Any informer revealing the whereabouts of the followers of padres must be rewarded accordingly. If anyone reveals the whereabouts of a high ranking padre, he must be given one hundred pieces of silver. For those of lower ranks, depending on the deed, the reward must be set accordingly.

6. If a foreign ship has an objection (to the measures adopted) and it becomes

1. Fathers (Catholic priests).

necessary to report the matter to Edo,[2] you may ask the Ōmura[3] domain to provide ships to guard the foreign ship. . . .

7. If there are any Southern Barbarians[4] who propagate the teachings of padres, or otherwise commit crimes, they may be incarcerated in the prison. . . .

8. All incoming ships must be carefully searched for the followers of padres.

9. No single trading city shall be permitted to purchase all the merchandise brought by foreign ships.

10. Samurai are not permitted to purchase any goods originating from foreign ships directly from Chinese merchants in Nagasaki.

11. After a list of merchandise brought by foreign ships is sent to Edo, as before you may order that commercial dealings may take place without waiting for a reply from Edo.

12. After settling the price, all white yarns[5] brought by foreign ships shall be allocated to the five trading cities[6] and other quarters as stipulated.

13. After settling the price of white yarns, other merchandise (brought by foreign ships) may be traded freely between the (licensed) dealers. However, in view of the fact that Chinese ships are small and cannot bring large consignments, you may issue orders of sale at your discretion. Additionally, payment for goods purchased must be made within twenty days after the price is set.

14. The date of departure homeward of foreign ships shall not be later than the twentieth day of the ninth month. Any ships arriving in Japan later than usual shall depart within fifty days of their arrival. As to the departure of Chinese ships, you may use your discretion to order their departure after the departure of the Portuguese *galeota*.[7]

15. The goods brought by foreign ships which remained unsold may not be deposited or accepted for deposit.

16. The arrival in Nagasaki of representatives of the five trading cities shall not be later than the fifth day of the seventh month. Anyone arriving later than that date shall lose the quota assigned to his city.

17. Ships arriving in Hirado[8] must sell their raw silk at the price set in Nagasaki, and are not permitted to engage in business transactions until after the price is established in Nagasaki.

You are hereby required to act in accordance with the provisions set above. It is so ordered.

Exclusion of the Portuguese, 1639

1. The matter relating to the proscription of Christianity is known (to the Portuguese), However, heretofore they have secretly transported those who are going to propagate that religion.

2. If those who believe in that religion

---

2. Modern Tokyo, the seat of the Tokugawa government.

3. The area around Nagasaki.

4. Westerners.

5. Raw silk.

6. The cities of Kyoto, Edo, Osaka, Sakai, and Nagasaki.

7. A *galleon*, an oceangoing Portuguese ship.

8. A small island in the southwest, not far from Nagasaki.

band together in an attempt to do evil things, they must be subjected to punishment.

3. While those who believe in the preaching of padres are in hiding, there are incidents in which that country (Portugal) has sent gifts to them for their sustenance.

In view of the above, hereafter entry by the Portuguese *galeota* is forbidden. If they insist on coming (to Japan), the ships must be destroyed and anyone aboard those ships must be beheaded. We have received the above order and are thus transmitting it to you accordingly.

The above concerns our disposition with regard to the *galeota*.

Memorandum

With regard to those who believe in Christianity, you are aware that there is a proscription, and thus knowing, you are not permitted to let padres and those who believe in their preaching to come aboard your ships. If there is any violation, all of you who are aboard will be considered culpable. If there is anyone who hides the fact that he is a Christian and boards your ship, you may report it to us. A substantial reward will be given to you for this information.

This memorandum is to be given to those who come on Chinese ships. (A similar note to the Dutch ships.)

The Great Mughals and the West

Between 1526 and his death in 1530, the Turkish lord of Afghanistan, Babur, subdued north-central India with a small, well-equipped army that enjoyed the advantage of firearms received from the Ottoman Turks. This new Muslim lord of Hindustan, a direct descendant of the Mongol Ghenghis Khan and the Turk Timur the Lame, initiated India's Mughal (the Persian word for Mongol) Age and laid the base for the reign of his grandson Jalal ad-Din Akbar (1556–1605), known to history as simply Akbar ("the Great").

Akbar's empire encompassed only the northern half of the Indian subcontinent. His great-grandson Aurangzeb (1658–1707), the last effective Mughal emperor, reigned over twice that amount of land and people, holding all the subcontinent except its southern tip and the island of Ceylon (modern Sri Lanka). Nevertheless, Akbar fully deserved to be known as the "Great Mughal," a title awed European visitors to his court at Fatehpur-Sikri ("the City of Victory") bestowed on him. From this court Akbar forged a centralized empire that during his reign of over a half century enjoyed prosperity and a fair level of peace between Hindus and Muslims. Although the Portuguese had established three major bases along the west Indian coast by 1535, Akbar was secure enough in his power to keep them and other Europeans at arm's length throughout the last half of the sixteenth century.

In 1603, however, the English East India Company, chartered on December 31, 1600, the last day of the sixteenth century, sent its first envoy to Akbar's court. After defeating a Portuguese squadron in 1639, the English established their first trading station at Madras on India's east coast and in 1661 acquired Bombay on the west coast. As Portuguese influence in India declined, other European naval powers secured trading privileges in the Mughal Empire. The Dutch acquired several important sites on both coasts between 1640 and 1663; in 1664 France founded an East India Company and numerous French settlements followed. In time, the Dutch shifted their focus away from India to the Spice Islands (the modern Moluccas) of Southeast Asia, leaving the French and English to fight for control of the Indian markets.

Despite all these late-seventeenth-century incursions along India's coasts, Emperor Aurangzeb was able to hold the West and its merchants at bay for the most part, even dealing the English a major setback in the 1680s. In 1700 the directors of the English East India Company rejected as unrealistic the notion of acquiring additional territory or establishing colonies in India. The decline of Mughal authority in the eighteenth century changed the situation substantially, and toward mid-century the French and British were engaged in armed struggle for control of India.

Abul Fazl

AKBARNAMA

Assisting Akbar in formulating and carrying out his largely successful policies of state was Abul Fazl (1551–1602), the emperor's chief adviser and confidant from 1579 until his assassination at the instigation of Prince Salim, the future Emperor Jahangir (1605–1627). Abul Fazl's death cut short his composition of the *Akbarnama,* a gigantic, laudatory history of Akbar's distinguished ancestors and the emperor's own reign. Before he was murdered, Abul Fazl carried his history to Akbar's forty-sixth year, creating a work universally regarded as one of the masterpieces of Mughal literature.

These thousands of pages of elegant Persian prose and poetry provide surprisingly few references to Akbar's or even India's relations with Europeans or *Faringis* (Franks), as they were called at the Mughal court. This silence speaks eloquently of the level of early Mughal concern with these foreigners. The following excerpts constitute the work's major references to Europeans in India.

Questions for Analysis

1. What aspects of European culture most fascinated Akbar?
2. What did he and Abul Fazl believe they could gain from the *Faringis*?
3. What did they believe they could offer the Europeans?

4. How did Akbar and Abul Fazl regard the Portuguese coastal bases?
5. What does the discussion with Padre Radif (Father Rodolfo) tell us about Akbar and Abul Fazl's attitudes toward the teachings of Europe's Christian missionaries?
6. Jesuit missionaries to Akbar's court often believed they were on the verge of converting him to Catholic Christianity. What evidence strongly indicates there was never any chance Akbar would become a Christian?

One of the occurrences of the siege[1] was that a large number of Christians came from the port of Goa and its neighborhood to the foot of the sublime throne, and were rewarded by the bliss of an interview. Apparently they had come at the request of the besieged in order that the latter might make the fort over to them, and so convey themselves to the shore of safety. But when that crew saw the majesty of the imperial power, and had become cognizant of the largeness of the army, and of the extent of the siege-train they represented themselves as ambassadors and performed the *kornish*.[2] They produced many of the rarities of their country, and the appreciative Khedive[3] received each one of them with special favor and made inquiries about the wonders of Portugal and the manners and customs of Europe. It seemed as if he did this from a desire of knowledge, for his sacred heart is a storehouse of spiritual and physical sciences. But his . . . soul wished that these inquiries might be the means of civilizing this savage race.[4]

. . .

One of the occurrences was the dispatch of Haji Habibu-llah Kashi to Goa.[5] At the time when the country of Gujrat became included among the imperial dominions, and when many of the ports of the country came into possession, and the governors of the European ports became submissive,[6] many of the curiosities and rarities of the skilled craftsmen of that country became known to His Majesty. Accordingly the Haji,[7] who for his skill, right thinking and powers of observation was one of the good servants of the court, was appointed to take with him a large sum of money, and the choice articles of India to Goa, and to bring for His Majes-

---

1. The siege of the west coast port of Surat in 1573 during Akbar's campaign in Gujarat (note 6). This successful expedition gave Akbar access to the sea. Through his conquests, Akbar more than tripled the empire he had inherited.

2. The act of obeisance.

3. Akbar.

4. The Portuguese.

5. The chief Portuguese stronghold in India since 1510.

6. In 1573 Akbar conquered the northwest coastal region of Gujarat, where the Portuguese held the ports of Diu and Bassein. In theory, but not fact, these Portuguese bases were now under imperial control.

7. Haji Habibu-llah. He bore the title Haji since he had completed the hajj, or pilgrimage, to Mecca.

ty's delectation the wonderful things of that country. There were sent with him clever craftsmen, who to ability and skill added industry, in order that just as the wonderful productions of that country (Goa and Europe) were being brought away, so also might rare crafts be imported (into Akbar's dominions).

. . .

One of the occurrences was the arrival of Haji Habibullah. It has already been mentioned that he had been sent to the port of Goa with a large sum of money and skillful craftsmen in order that he might bring to his country the excellent arts and rarities of that place. On the 9th he came to do homage, attended by a large number of persons dressed up as Christians and playing European drums and clarions. He produced before His Majesty the choice articles of that territory. Craftsmen who had gone to acquire skill displayed the arts which they had learned and received praises in the critical place of testing. The musicians of that territory breathed fascination with the instruments of their country, especially with the organ. Ear and eye were delighted and so was the mind.

. . .

One night, the assembly in the 'Ibadatkhana[8] was increasing the light of truth. Padre Radif,[9] one of the Nazarene[10] sages, who was singular for his understanding and ability, was making points in that feast of intelligence. Some of the untruthful bigots[11] came forward in a blundering way to answer him. Owing to the calmness of the august assembly, and the increasing light of justice, it became clear that each of these was weaving a circle of old acquisitions, and was not following the highway of proof, and that the explanation of the riddle of truth was not present to their thoughts. The veil was nearly being stripped, once for all, from their procedure. They were ashamed, and abandoned such discourse, and applied themselves to perverting the words of the Gospels. But they could not silence their antagonist by such arguments. The Padre quietly and with an air of conviction said, "Alas, that such things should be thought to be true! In fact, if this faction have such an opinion of our Book, and regard the *Furqan* [the Qur'an] as the pure word of God, it is proper that a heaped fire be lighted. We shall take the Gospel in our hands, and the 'Ulama of that faith shall take their book, and then let us enter that testing-place of truth. The escape of any one will be a sign of his truthfulness." The liverless and black-hearted fellows wavered, and in reply to the challenge had recourse to bigotry and wrangling. This cowardice and effrontery displeased his (Akbar's) equitable soul, and the banquet of enlightenment was made resplendent by acute observations. Continually, in

8. The House of Worship, where Akbar held weekly Thursday-night discussions on theological issues with Muslim, Hindu, Zoroastrian, and Christian religious teachers.

9. Father Rodolfo Acquaviva, a Jesuit missionary.

10. Christian.

11. Conservative Muslim *ulama,* or religious teachers.

those day-like nights, glorious subtleties and profound words dropped from his pearl-filled mouth. Among them was this: "Most persons, from intimacy with those who adorn their outside, but are inwardly bad, think that outward semblance, and the letter of Islam, profit without internal conviction. Hence we by fear and force compelled many believers in the Brahman (i.e., Hindu) religion to adopt the faith of our ancestors. Now that the light of truth has taken possession of our soul, it has become clear that in this distressful place of contrarities (the world), where darkness of comprehension and conceit are heaped up, fold upon fold, a single step cannot be taken without the torch of proof, and that that creed is profitable which is adopted with the approval of wisdom. To repeat the creed, to remove a piece of skin (i.e., to become circumcised) and to place the end of one's bones on the ground (i.e., the head in adoration) from dread of the Sultan, is not seeking after God."

. . .

One of the occurrences was the appointing an army to capture the European ports.[12] Inasmuch as conquest is the great rule of princes, and by the observance of this glory-increasing practice, the distraction of plurality[13] places its foot in the peacefulness of unity, and the harassed world composes her countenance, the officers of the provinces of Gujarat and Malwa were appointed to this service under the leadership of Qutbu-d-din Khan on 18 Bahman, Divine month (February 1580). The rulers of the Deccan were also informed that the troops had been sent in that direction in order to remove the Faringis who were a stumbling-block in the way of the pilgrims to the Hijaz.[14]

Jean-Baptiste Tavernier

TRAVELS IN INDIA

The increasing volume of French trade with seventeenth-century Mughal India attracted Jean-Baptiste Tavernier (1605–after 1689), a Parisian gem merchant, who arrived in India in 1640 on the first of five trips to the empire of the Great Mughal. Following his last voyage to India, which ended in 1668, Tavernier was able to live in wealthy semiretirement thanks to his profitable Eastern ventures. In 1670 he purchased the title of baron of Aubonne and settled down to write his memoirs, probably from notes he had made during his career in the East.

12. The ports of Diu and Bassein (note 6). This expedition was unsuccessful, and Abul Fazl tells us nothing else about it.

13. That is, the distraction of multiple rulers.

14. Pilgrims to Mecca. Many Muslims complained that, when embarking at Portuguese ports, they were forced to accept letters of passage imprinted with images of Jesus and Mary. Orthodox Muslims consider such images blasphemous, and some Muslim teachers went so far as to argue that it was better to forgo the pilgrimage than to submit to such sacrilege.

His *Travels* covers a pivotal period in Mughal-European relations. French and English merchants were becoming increasingly important in India, even as cracks were beginning to appear in the Mughal Empire under Shah Jahan (1627–1658) and Aurangzeb (1658–1707), whose respective building programs (Shah Jahan constructed the Taj Mahal) and military campaigns placed severe strains on the economy and general well-being of Indian society. In the following selection, Tavernier details the manner in which the Mughal government attempted to control and profit from the Western merchants and the tactics some Europeans employed to circumvent these controls and raise their profit margins.

Questions for Analysis

1. Why do you think the English and Dutch East India companies paid a lower tariff on imported gold? What added to their costs of doing business in India, and why do you think they paid these extra expenses?
2. Did the European merchants take advantage of the Indian officials with whom they dealt? Did the Indian officials seem to resent or not want this business with the Europeans? What do your answers suggest?
3. Why do you think the officers of the Dutch and English East India companies were treated as described? Why did they refuse to engage in smuggling? What do your answers suggest about relations between the Mughal government and these trading companies?
4. What does the story of the roast pig suggest?

As soon as merchandise is landed at Surat[1] it has to be taken to the custom-house, which adjoins the fort. The officers are very strict and search persons with great care. Private individuals pay as much as 4 and 5 percent duty on all their goods; but as for the English and Dutch Companies, they pay less. But, on the other hand, I believe that, taking into account what it costs them in . . . presents, which they are obliged to make every year at court, the goods cost them nearly the same as they do private persons.

Gold and silver are charged 2 percent,[2] and as soon as they have been counted at the custom-house the Mintmaster removes them, and coins them into money of the country, which he hands over to the owner, in proportion to the amount and standard of the bullion. You settle with him, according to the nature of the amount, a day when he is to deliver the new coins, and for as many days as he delays to do so beyond the term agreed upon, he pays interest in proportion to the sum which he has received. The Indi-

1. A city on the west coast that served as India's main port of entry for Dutch, English, and French merchants and their goods at this time.

2. For the Dutch and English East India companies.

ans are cunning and exacting in reference to coin and payments; for when money has been coined for three or four years it has to lose ½ percent,[3] and it continues in the same proportion according to age, not being able, as they say, to pass through many hands without some diminution. . . .

As regards gold, the merchants who import it use so much cunning in order to conceal it, that but little of it comes to the knowledge of the customs' officers. The former do all they can to evade paying the customs, especially as they do not run so much risk as in the custom-houses of Europe. For in those of India, when anyone is detected in fraud, he is let off by paying double, 10 percent instead of 5, the Emperor comparing the venture of the merchant to a game of hazard, where one plays double or quits.[4] However, for some time back this has been somewhat changed, and it is today difficult to compound with the customs' officers upon that condition. The Emperor has conceded to the English Captains that they shall not be searched when they leave their vessels to go on shore; but one day an English Captain, when going to Tatta,[5] one of the largest towns of India, a little above Sindi,[6] which is at the mouth of the river Indus, as he was about to pass, was arrested by the customs' guards, from whom he could not defend himself, and they searched him in spite of anything he could say. They found gold upon him; he had in fact already conveyed some in sundry journeys which he had made between his vessel and the town; he was, however, let off on payment of the ordinary duty. The Englishman, vexed by this affront, resolved to have his revenge for it, and he took it in a funny manner. He ordered a suckling-pig to be roasted, and to be placed with the grease in a china plate, covered with a napkin, and gave it to a slave to carry with him to the town, anticipating exactly what would happen. As he passed in front of the custom-house, where the Governor of the town, the Shah-bandar,[7] and the Master of the Mint were seated in a divan, they did not fail to stop him, but the slave still advancing with his covered plate, they told his master that he must needs go to the custom-house, and that they must see what he carried. The more the Englishman protested that the slave carried nothing liable to duty, the less was he believed; and after a long discussion he himself took the plate from the hands of the slave, and proceeded to carry it to the custom-house. The Governor and the Shah-bandar thereupon asked him, in a sharp tone, why he refused to obey orders, and the Englishman, on his part, replied in a rage that what he carried was not liable to duty, and rudely threw the plate in front of them, so that the suckling-pig and the grease soiled the whole place, and splashed up on their garments. As the pig is an abomination to the Muslims, and by their Law they regard as defiled whatever is touched by it, they were compelled to

---

3. The Indians discounted these gold coins by 1/2 of 1 percent because of the metal that had been rubbed off.

4. Tavernier writes elsewhere that another reason the Mughals had such a lenient policy in regard to smuggling was because Qur'anic law forbids charging interest and tariffs, and they were troubled by the practice.

5. A city in modern Pakistan.

6. Better known as Sind, this harbor at the mouth of the Indus River gave its name to the whole northwest corner of India (today Pakistan).

7. The Mughal commissioner in charge of merchants.

change their garments, to remove the carpet from the divan, and to have the structure rebuilt, without daring to say anything to the Englishman, because the Shah-bandar and the Master of the Mint have to be careful with the Company,[8] from which the country derives so much profit. As for the Chiefs of the Companies, both English and Dutch, and their deputies, they are treated with so much respect that they are never searched when they come from their vessels; but they, on their part, do not attempt to convey gold in secret as the private merchants do, considering it beneath their dignity to do so. . . .

The English, seeing that the custom of searching them had been adopted, had recourse to little stratagems in order to pass the gold, and the fashion of wearing wigs having reached them from Europe, they bethought themselves of concealing . . . [gold coins] . . . in the nets of their wigs every time they left their vessels to go on shore.

8. The English East India Company.

C H A P T E R

13

Religious and Intellectual Ferment

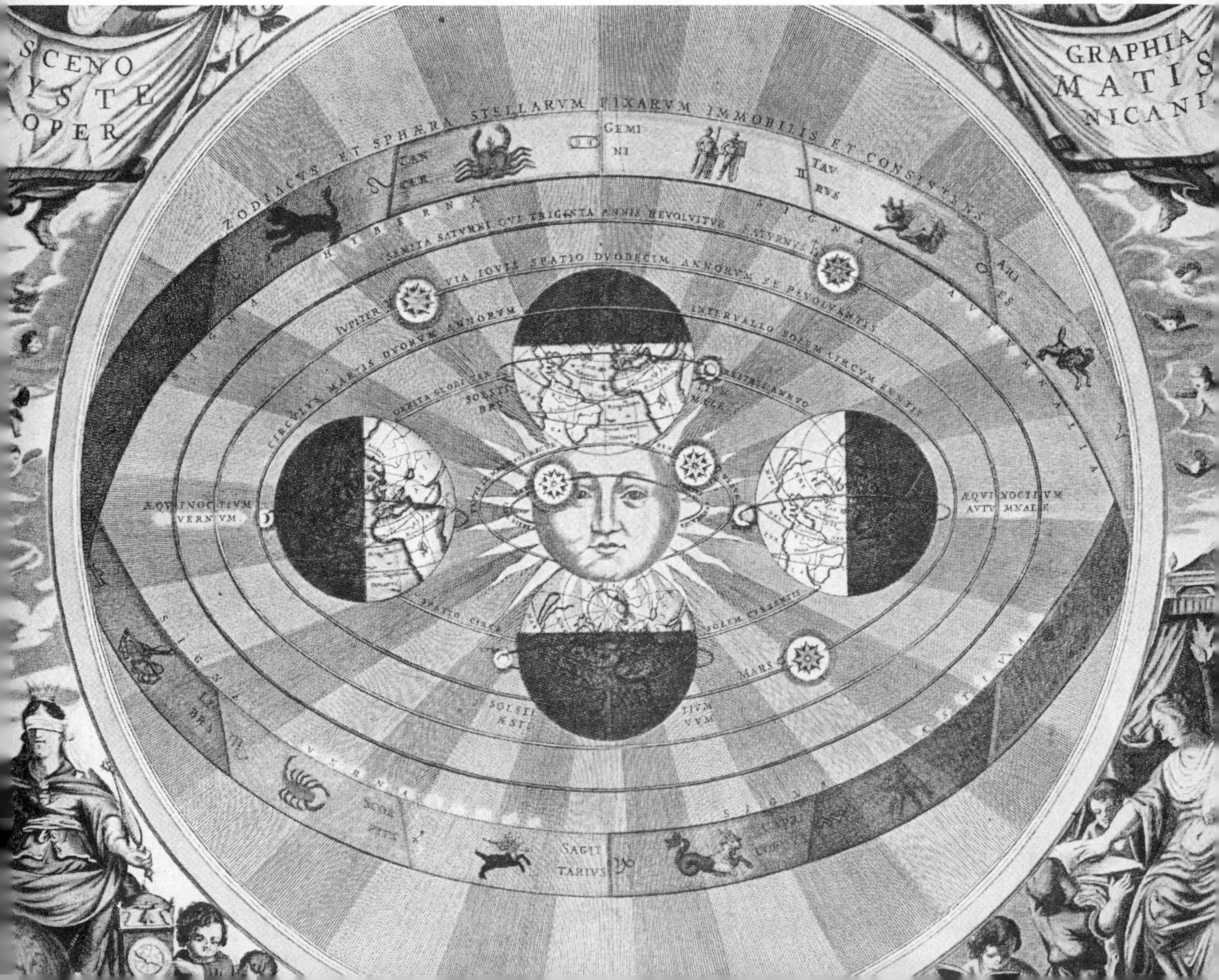

Historically, societies have feared change and resisted innovation, especially when their basic religious beliefs and intellectual values are involved. This fact alone makes the period 1500–1700 so interesting to historians. Despite the weight of tradition, these two centuries witnessed great change in the ways certain people perceived their place in the cosmos.

The most striking changes took place in Europe and the Americas. In Europe a renaissance in art, literature, and the study and practice of statecraft produced new modes of expression and aspiration. In the religious sphere, the Protestant Reformation, and the Catholic Counter Reformation it engendered, restructured and redefined Christianity for Protestants and Catholics alike. Most significant, Europe's Scientific Revolution redefined the physical world. The European impact on the thought processes and beliefs of Native Americans was probably even more profound than any changes taking place in Europe. Massive Amerindian depopulation from new diseases, which seemed to have little or no effect on the Spanish invaders, likely played a major role in convincing many natives of Central and South America that the god of the Spaniards was stronger than their own ancestral deities. This belief, combined with the missionary zeal of Spanish clerics, resulted in large numbers of conversions among the dispirited survivors.

India and Japan also experienced significant new directions in belief and thought. In India a new monotheistic faith called Sikhism arose. In Japan the Tokugawa shoguns adopted Chinese Neo-Confucianism, and *bushido,* "the way of the warrior," became a fully articulated code of behavior for the samurai class.

China, most of the Muslim world, and inland sub-Saharan Africa basically resisted change and continued to produce brilliant cultures along mainly traditional lines. None of these three societies had reason to alter substantially or even challenge what had worked so well for centuries and even millennia. Yet these societies did not stagnate. Rather, they had reached such levels of cultural stability that they were able to absorb internal modifications and even moderate amounts of stimuli from outside without undergoing transformation.

Europe

Sixteenth-century Europe saw the climax of the Renaissance, the explosion of the Protestant Reformation, and the beginnings of the Scientific Revolution. During the fourteenth and fifteenth centuries, a movement historians term *Renaissance humanism* emerged in Italy, and by the early 1500s it had migrated to northern Europe. Because the roots of this movement lay firmly in the soil of the Middle Ages, the accuracy of the term *Renaissance* (rebirth) is questionable. There is no denying, however, that a spirit of self-conscious rediscovery and renewed vitality united the persons we call Renaissance humanists. On their part, the Protestant Reformers rejected traditional Catholic doctrine concerning salvation, religious authority, and much else. By the mid-sixteenth century, at least 50 percent of all Europeans no longer considered themselves Roman Catholics and Europe's religious unity was shattered. Finally, during this century certain thinkers began to challenge the principles of ancient Greek science, a body of assumptions about nature and the universe that had served, with the Bible, as one of the two main foundations for most medieval philosophy and theology. By 1687, when Isaac Newton published his *Mathematical Principles of Natural Philosophy*, a new world-view had seized Europe's intellectuals. Together, these three movements — humanism, religious change, and scientific discovery — illustrate one of the most striking features of Western European civilization: its willingness to challenge, debate, and, at times, discard values inherited from the past.

Meanwhile, in Europe's most eastern region, Russia, Western ideas were beginning to challenge established beliefs and ways of life by the mid-seventeenth century. The immediate result was a schism in the Russian Orthodox Church between imperially supported Westernizers and conservative Old Believers, thereby prefiguring the violent upheaval that would result from the radical reforms of Tsar Peter I (1682–1725).

Niccolò Machiavelli

THE PRINCE

Niccolò Machiavelli (1469–1527), a contemporary of Botticelli, Leonardo da Vinci, and Michelangelo, lived at a time when the artistic and intellectual creativity of the Italian Renaissance was at its peak. With his love and knowledge of ancient history and literature, Michiavelli himself was a product of the Renaissance and became one of its most celebrated representatives. He also lived at a time when the states of Italy were engulfed in political turmoil and gradually succumbed to the control of France and Spain. The immediate cause of Italy's political troubles was its invasion by King

Charles VIII of France in 1494. As a diplomat in the service of the Florentine republic, Machiavelli was an active participant in the wars that followed and their victim. The Florentine republic was overthrown in 1512, and Machiavelli's political career was over. He retreated to his small country estate, read further in ancient history, and thought deeply about the reasons for Italy's political humiliation.

The first product of Machiavelli's rural exile was *The Prince,* which he essentially finished in 1514. *The Prince* represents Machiavelli's attempt to analyze, "from the wide experience of recent events and a constant reading of classical authors," the factors behind political success and failure and to reduce his findings to a series of general principles. This handbook on the art of successful government expresses views about the realities of political life that had never before been so unambiguously articulated by a Western commentator.

Questions for Analysis

1. Consider Machiavelli's discussion of Agathocles the Sicilian and Oliverotto of Fermo. What point is he trying to make?
2. How does Machiavelli attempt to convince his readers that his assertions about politics are correct?
3. According to Machiavelli, how does morality in politics differ from morality in private life?
4. How does he define "political virtue"? How does Machiavelli define "good government"? In Machiavelli's view, what are the characteristics of an ideal prince?
5. How does Machiavelli's view of human nature affect his political philosophy?
6. Compare John of Viterbo's thirteenth-century *podesta* (Chapter 10) with Machiavelli's prince. What strikes you as more significant, their similarities or differences? What does your answer suggest about the course of Italian political history from the thirteenth to the early sixteenth century?

VIII. Those Who Come to Power by Crime

Agathocles, the Sicilian, not only from the status of a private citizen but from the lowest, most abject condition of life, rose to become king of Syracuse.[1] At every stage of his career this man, the son of a potter, behaved like a criminal; nonetheless he accompanied his crimes with so much audacity and physical courage that when he joined the militia he rose through the ranks to become praetor[2] of Syracuse. After he had been appointed to this position, he determined to make himself prince and to possess by force and without obligation to others what had

1. Agathocles was tyrant of Syracuse, a Greek city on the east coast of Sicily, from 317 to 289 B.C.

2. A high-ranking elected magistrate of a city, who usually had judicial powers.

been voluntarily conceded to him. He reached an understanding about this ambition of his with Hamilcar the Carthaginian, who was campaigning with his armies in Sicily. Then one morning he assembled the people and Senate of Syracuse, as if he meant to raise matters which affected the republic; and at a prearranged signal he had all the senators, along with the richest citizens, killed by his soldiers; and when they were dead he seized and held the government of that city, without encountering any other internal opposition. . . .

In our own time, during the pontificate of Alexander VI,[3] there was Oliverotto of Fermo. Years before, he had been left fatherless as a small boy and was brought up by a maternal uncle called Giovanni Fogliani. In his early youth he was sent to serve as a soldier under Paulo Vitelli[4] so that he could win high command after being trained by him. When Paulo died, Oliverotto soldiered under Vitelozzo, his brother; and in a very short time, as he was intelligent, and a man of courage and audacity, he became Vitelozzo's chief commander. But he thought it was servile to take orders from others, and so he determined that, with the help of some citizens of Fermo[5] to whom the enslavement of their native city was more attractive than its liberty, and with the favor and help of the Vitelli, he would seize Fermo for himself. He wrote to Giovanni Fogliano saying that, having been many years away from home he wanted to come and see him and his city and to make some investigation into his own estate. He had worked for nothing else except honor, he went on, and in order that his fellow citizens might see that he had not spent his time in vain, he wanted to come honorably, with a mounted escort of a hundred companions and servants. He begged Giovanni to arrange a reception which would bring honor to Giovanni as well as to himself, as he was Giovanni's foster child. Giovanni failed in no duty of hospitality towards his nephew. He had him honorably welcomed by the citizens of Fermo and lodged him in his own mansion. There, after a few days had passed during which he waited in order to complete the secret arrangements for his future crime, Oliverotto prepared a formal banquet to which he invited Giovanni Fogliani and the leading citizens of Fermo. After they had finished eating and all the other entertainment usual at such banquets was done with, Oliverotto artfully started to touch on subjects of grave importance, talking of the greatness of Pope Alexander and of Cesare[6] his son, and of their enterprises. When Giovanni and the others began to discuss these subjects in turn, he got to his feet all of a sudden, saying that these were things to be spoken of somewhere more private, and he withdrew to another room, followed by Giovanni and all the other citizens. And no sooner were they seated than soldiers appeared from hidden recesses, and killed Giovanni and all the others. After this slaughter, Oliverotto mounted his horse, rode through the town, and laid siege to the palace of the governing council; consequently they were frightened

3. Alexander VI (Rodrigo Borgia), pope from 1492 to 1503.

4. An Italian mercenary leader.

5. A central Italian city.

6. Cesare Borgia (1475–1507), the son of Pope Alexander VI, had been duke of the Romagna, a region of central Italy; earlier in *The Prince,* Machiavelli praises Cesare for his political boldness and vision.

into obeying him and into setting up a government of which he made himself the prince. And having put to death all who, because they would resent his rule, might injure him, he strengthened his position by founding new civil and military institutions. . . .

One might well wonder how it was that Agathocles, and others like him, after countless treacheries and cruelties, could live securely in his own country and hold foreign enemies at bay, with never a conspiracy against him by his countrymen, inasmuch as many others, because of their cruel behavior, have not been able to maintain their rule even in peaceful times, let alone in the uncertain times of war. I believe that here it is a question of cruelty used well or badly. We can say that cruelty is used well (if it is permissible to talk in this way of what is evil) when it is employed once for all, and one's safety depends on it, and then it is not persisted in but as far as possible turned to the good of one's subjects. Cruelty badly used is that which, although infrequent to start with, as time goes on, rather than disappearing, grows in intensity. Those who use the first method can, with divine and human assistance, find some means of consolidating their position, as did Agathocles; the others cannot possibly stay in power. . . .

XV. The Things for Which Men, and Especially Princes, Are Praised or Blamed

It now remains for us to see how a prince must govern his conduct towards his subjects or his friends. I know that this has often been written about before, and so I hope it will not be thought presumptuous for me to do so, as, especially in discussing this subject, I draw up an original set of rules. But since my intention is to say something that will prove of practical use to the inquirer, I have thought it proper to represent things as they are in real truth, rather than as they are imagined. Many have dreamed up republics and principalities which have never in truth been known to exist; the gulf between how one should live and how one does live is so wide that a man who neglects what is actually done for what should be done learns the way to self-destruction rather than self-preservation. The fact is that a man who wants to act virtuously in every way necessarily comes to grief among so many who are not virtuous. Therefore if a prince wants to maintain his rule he must learn how not to be virtuous, and to make use of this or not according to need.

So leaving aside imaginary things, and referring only to those which truly exist, I say that whenever men are discussed (and especially princes, who are more exposed to view), they are noted for various qualities which earn them either praise or condemnation. Some, for example, are held to be generous, and others miserly. . . . Some are held to be benefactors, others are called grasping; some cruel, some compassionate; one man faithless, another faithful; one man effeminate and cowardly, another fierce and courageous; one man courteous, another proud; one man lascivious, another pure; one guileless, another crafty; one stubborn, another flexible; one grave, another frivolous; one religious, another sceptical; and so forth. I know everyone will agree that it would be most laudable if a prince possessed all the qualities deemed to be good among those I have enumerated. But, because of conditions in the world, princes cannot have those qualities, or observe them completely. So a prince has of necessity to be so prudent that he knows how to escape the evil reputation attached to those vices which could lose him his state, and how to avoid those vices which are not so dangerous if he possibly can; but, if he cannot, he need not worry so much about the latter. And then, he must not flinch from being blamed for vices which are necessary for safeguarding the state. This is because, taking everything into account, he will find that some of the things that appear to be virtues will, if he practices them, ruin him, and some of the things that appear to be vices will bring him security and prosperity. . . .

XVII. Cruelty and Compassion; and Whether It Is Better to Be Loved than Feared, or the Reverse

I say that a prince must want to have a reputation for compassion rather than for cruelty: nonetheless, he must be careful that he does not make bad use of compassion. Cesare Borgia was accounted cruel; nevertheless, this cruelty of his reformed the Romagna, brought it unity, and restored order and obedience. On reflection, it will be seen that there was more compassion in Cesare than in the Florentine people, who, to escape being called cruel, allowed Pistoia to be devastated.[7] So a prince must not worry if he incurs reproach for his cruelty so long as he keeps his subjects united and loyal. By making an example or two he will prove more compassionate than those who, being too compassionate, allow disorders which lead to murder and rapine. These nearly always harm the whole community, whereas executions ordered by a prince only affect individuals. . . .

From this arises the following question: whether it is better to be loved than feared, or the reverse. The answer is that one would like to be both the one and the other; but because it is difficult to combine them, it is far better to be feared than loved if you cannot be both. One can make this generalization about men: they are ungrateful, fickle, liars, and deceivers, they shun danger and are greedy for profit; while you treat them well, they are yours. They would shed their blood for you, risk their property, their lives, their children, so long, as I said above, as danger is remote; but when you are in danger they turn against you. Any prince who has come to depend entirely on promises and has taken no other precautions ensures his own ruin; friendship which is bought with money and not with greatness and nobility of mind is paid for, but it does not last and it yields nothing. Men worry less about doing an injury to one who makes himself loved than to one who makes himself feared. The bond of love is one which men, wretched creatures that they are, break when it is to their advantage to do so; but fear is strengthened by a dread of punishment which is always effective.

The prince must nonetheless make himself feared in such a way that, if he is not loved, at least he escapes being hated. For fear is quite compatible with an absence of hatred; and the prince can always avoid hatred if he abstains from the property of his subjects and citizens and from their women. If, even so, it proves necessary to execute someone, this is to be done only when there is proper justification and manifest reason for it. But above all a prince must abstain from the property of others; because men sooner forget the death of their father than the loss of their patrimony.

---

7. In 1501 Florence failed to act decisively in suppressing internal feuding in Pistoia, one of its subject cities.

Martin Luther

TABLE TALK

The Protestant Reformation had many voices, but its first prophet was Martin Luther (1483–1546), whose "Ninety-Five Theses" of 1517 initiated the great anti-Catholic rebellion. Born into the family of a German miner and educated at the University of Erfurt, Luther was preparing for a career in law when suddenly, in 1505, he changed course and entered a cloister of Augustinian friars.

Luther's intellect and religious intensity enabled him to rise quickly in the ranks of his religious order. After securing a doctorate, Father Luther became a professor of theology at the University of Wittenberg. Despite his apparent success, Luther experienced great anxiety and doubt about the life he was leading. He feared he could never merit salvation by living up to what he viewed as the impossibly high standards of selflessness, charity, and purity prescribed by the Bible and the Catholic Church, and he despaired of ever satisfying an angry God of Judgment, viewing with terror the prospect of his eternal damnation in hell.

His troubled soul finally found peace with his insight that salvation could in no way be "earned" by performing the traditional pious acts enjoined by the established Church. Instead, it came only through God-implanted faith in Jesus as Savior, and Luther's sole authority for this doctrine was the Bible, not the teachings of the Roman Church. From these two core principles — salvation by faith alone and the unique authority of sacred scripture — Luther evolved a theology that rejected the role of the Roman Catholic Church as the necessary intermediary between God and humanity. By 1521 Luther stood at the center of a German revolt against the authority of the medieval universal Church of Rome.

As the Reformation spread to other parts of Europe, leadership of the Protestant movement passed to younger persons, such as John Calvin and John Knox. Luther remained at Wittenberg, serving as a pastor and a university professor. He and his wife, Katharina, a former nun, made their home in the Augustinian convent where Luther had once been a friar. Here they raised a family and entertained scores of reformers and students, with whom the gregarious Luther loved to discourse on the issues of the day. Some of these guests recorded Luther's most notable utterances, as they remembered them, and from their journals we have what is known as Luther's *Tischreden*, or *Table Talk*.

Questions for Analysis

1. What does Luther mean by "idolatry"?
2. What can a Christian accomplish without God's grace?
3. According to Luther, what is the importance of the Bible in a Christian's life?

How had the Roman Catholic Church obscured the meaning and message of the Bible?

4. How does Luther define faith? Why is faith superior to external acts of devotion?
5. Compare Luther's theology of salvation with Saint Paul's statement about how one is "put right" with God (Chapter 7). What does your answer suggest?
6. What are Luther's main objections to the pope and other officials of the Roman Catholic Church?
7. Luther's message was spiritual, but many of his supporters found political and social implications in his teachings. How was that possible?
8. Do you see any parallels between *bhakti*, the Hindu Way of Devotion (Chapter 6), and Luther's theology?

[*The Majesty and Power of God*]

All the works of God are unsearchable and unspeakable, no human sense can find them out; faith only takes hold of them without human power or aid. No mortal creature can comprehend God in his majesty, and therefore did he come before us in the simplest manner, and was made man, ay, sin, death, and weakness.

In all things, in the least creatures, and in their members, God's almighty power and wonderful works clearly shine. For what man, how powerful, wise, and holy soever, can make out of one fig a fig-tree, or another fig? or, out of one cherry-stone, a cherry, or a cherry-tree? or what man can know how God creates and preserves all things, and makes them grow?

Neither can we conceive how the eye sees, or how intelligible words are spoken plainly, when only the tongue moves and stirs in the mouth; all which are natural things, daily seen and acted. How then should we be able to comprehend or understand the secret counsels of God's majesty, or search them out with our human sense, reason, or understanding. Should we then admire our own wisdom? I, for my part, admit myself a fool, and yield myself captive.

. . .

Forasmuch as the everlasting, merciful God, through his Word and Sacraments,[1] talks and deals with us, all other creatures excluded, not of temporal things which pertain to this vanishing life, and which in the beginning he provided richly for us, but as to where we shall go when we depart hence, and gives unto us his Son for a Savior, delivering us from sin and death, and purchasing for us everlasting righteousness, life, and salvation, therefore it is most certain that we do not die away like the beasts that have no understanding; but so many of us as sleep in Christ, shall through him be raised again to life everlasting at the last day, and the ungodly to everlasting destruction.

. . .

As lately I lay very sick, so sick that I thought I should have left this world,

1. Although he rejected most of the Catholic Church's sacraments and other "good works," Luther retained the sacraments of baptism and Holy Eucharist.

many cogitations and musings had I in my weakness. Ah! thought I, what may eternity be? What joys may it have? However, I know for certain, that this eternity is ours; through Christ it is given and prepared for us, if we can but believe. There it shall be opened and revealed; here we shall not know when a second creation of the world will be, seeing we understand not the first. If I had been with God Almighty before he created the world, I could not have advised him how out of nothing to make this globe, the firmament, and that glorious sun, which in its swift course gives light to the whole earth; how, in such manner, to create man and woman, etc., all which he did for us, without our counsel. Therefore ought we justly to give him the honor, and leave to his divine power and goodness the new creation of the life to come, and not presume to speculate thereon.

[*Faith Versus "Good Works"*]

He that goes from the gospel to the law, thinking to be saved by good works, falls as uneasily, as he who falls from the true service of God to idolatry; for, without Christ, all is idolatry and fictitious imaginings of God, whether of the Turkish Qur'an, of the pope's decrees, or Moses' laws; if a man think thereby to be justified[2] and saved before God, he is undone.

When a man will serve God, he must not look upon that which he does; not upon the work, but how it ought to be done, and whether God has commanded it or no; seeing, as Samuel[3] says, that "God hath more pleasure in obedience, than in burnt sacrifice."

Whoso hearkens not to God's voice is an idolater, though he perform the highest and most heavy service of God. 'Tis the very nature of idolatry not to make choice of that which is esteemed easy and light, but of that which is great and heavy, as we see in the friars and monks, who have been constantly devising new worshipings of God; but, forasmuch that God in his Word has not commanded these, they are idolatry, and blasphemy.

. . .

I have often been resolved to live uprightly, and to lead a true godly life, and to set everything aside that would hinder this, but it was far from being put in execution; even as it was with Peter,[4] when he swore he would lay down his life for Christ.

I will not lie or dissemble before my God, but will freely confess, I am not able to effect that good which I intend, but await the happy hour when God shall be pleased to meet me with his grace.

. . .

A Christian's worshiping is not the external, hypocritical mask that our spiritual friars wear, when they chastise their bodies, torment and make themselves faint, with ostentatious fasting, watching, singing, wearing hair shirts, scourging themselves, etc. Such worshiping God desires not.

. . .

2. Justification for Luther meant being made "righteous" in God's eyes, that is, acceptable to God and "saved." See Saint Paul, Chapter 7.

3. A Hebrew prophet and judge of the late eleventh century B.C., perhaps the author of the two biblical books named after him.

4. Peter was one of Jesus' twelve apostles; following Jesus' arrest, he three times denied any relationship with him, despite having vowed shortly before to lay down his life for his teacher. Eventually, Peter died a martyr's death in Rome.

The pope and his crew can in nowise endure the idea of reformation; the mere word creates more alarm at Rome than thunderbolts from heaven, or the day of judgment. A cardinal said the other day: Let them eat, and drink, and do what they will; but as to reforming us, we think that is a vain idea; we will not endure it. Neither will we protestants be satisfied, though they administer the sacrament in both kinds, and permit priests to marry;[5] we will also have the doctrine of the faith pure and unfalsified, and the righteousness that justifies and saves before God, and which expels and drives away all idolatry and false-worshiping; these gone and banished, the foundation on which Popedom is built falls also.

. . .

[*The Bible*]

Great is the strength of the divine Word. In the epistle to the Hebrews,[6] it is called "a two-edged sword." But we have neglected and contemned the pure and clear Word, and have drunk not of the fresh and cool spring; we are gone from the clear fountain to the foul puddle, and drunk its filthy water; that is, we have sedulously read old writers and teachers, who went about with speculative reasonings, like the monks and friars.

. . .

Like as in the world a child is an heir only because it is born to inherit, even so, faith only makes such to be God's children as are born of the Word, which is the womb wherein we are conceived, born, and nourished, as the prophet Isaiah says. Now, as through such a birth we become God's children, (wrought by God without our help or doing,) even so, we are also heirs, and being heirs, are freed from sin, death, and the devil, and shall inherit everlasting life.

. . .

I admonish every pious Christian that he take not offense at the plain, unvarnished manner of speech of the Bible. Let him reflect that what may seem trivial and vulgar to him, emanates from the high majesty, power, and wisdom of God. The Bible is the book that makes fools of the wise of this world; it is understood only by the plain and simple hearted. Esteem this book as the precious fountain that can never be exhausted. In it thou findest the swaddling-clothes and the manger whither the angels directed the poor, simple shepherds; they seem poor and mean, but dear and precious is the treasure that lies therein.

. . .

I did not learn my divinity at once, but was constrained by my temptations to search deeper and deeper; for no man, without trials and temptations, can attain a true understanding of the Holy Scriptures. St. Paul had a devil that beat him

---

5. Two of the many changes the Protestant reformers called for were allowing all Christians to receive the sacrament of the Eucharist in the forms of both bread and wine (in medieval Roman Catholic practice, only the priest drank the eucharistic wine) and allowing priests to marry. The principle behind both changes was Luther's teaching that all Christians are equally priests.

6. A letter addressed to Christian Hebrews and ascribed by the early Church to Saint Paul, it is contained in the Christian, or New, Testament of the Bible.

with fists, and with temptations drove him diligently to study the Holy Scripture. I had hanging on my neck the pope, the universities, all the deep-learned, and the devil; these hunted me into the Bible, wherein I sedulously read, and thereby, God be praised, at length attained a true understanding of it. Without such a devil, we are but only speculators of divinity, and according to our vain reasoning, dream that so and so it must be, as the monks and friars in monasteries do. The Holy Scripture of itself is certain and true: God grant me grace to catch hold of its just use.

[*The Pope and the Roman Church*]
Kings and princes coin money only out of metals, but the pope coins money out of everything — indulgences, ceremonies, dispensations, pardons; 'tis all fish comes to his net. 'Tis only baptism escapes him, for children came into the world without clothes to be stolen, or teeth to be drawn.

. . .

In Italy, the monasteries are very wealthy. There are but three or four monks to each; the surplus of their revenues goes to the pope and his cardinals.

The cuckoo takes the eggs out of the linnet's[7] nest, and puts her own in their place. When the young cuckoos grow big, they eat the linnet. The cuckoo, too, has a great antipathy towards the nightingale. The pope is a cuckoo; he robs the church of her true eggs, and substitutes in their place his greedy cardinals, who devour the mother that has nourished them. The pope, too, cannot abide that nightingale, the preaching and singing of the true doctrine.

. . .

'Tis wonderful how, in this our time, the majesty of the pope is fallen. Heretofore, all monarchs, emperors, kings, and princes feared the pope's power, who held them all at his nod; none durst so much as mutter a word against him. This great god is now fallen; his own creatures, the friars and monks, are his enemies, who, if they still continue with him, do so for the sake of gain; otherwise they would oppose him more fiercely than we do.

. . .

In Popedom they make priests, not to preach and teach God's Word, but only to celebrate mass, and to gad about with the sacrament. For, when a bishop ordains a man, he says: Take unto thee power to celebrate mass, and to offer for the living and the dead. But we ordain priests according to the command of Christ and St. Paul, namely, to preach the pure gospel and God's Word. The papists in their ordinations make no mention of preaching and teaching God's Word, therefore their consecrating and ordaining is false and unright, for all worshiping which is not ordained of God, or erected by God's Word and command, is nothing worth, yea, mere idolatry.

. . .

The pope places his cardinals in all kingdoms — peevish milk-sops, effeminate and unlearned blockheads, who lie

7. A small songbird of the finch family.

lolling in king's courts, among the ladies and women. The pope has invaded all countries with these and his bishops. Germany is taken captive by popish bishops, for I can count above forty bishoprics, besides abbeys and cathedrals, which are richer than the bishoprics. Now, there are in Germany but eight and twenty principalities, so that the popish bishops are far more rich and powerful than the princes of the empire.

Nicholas Copernicus

ON THE REVOLUTIONS OF THE HEAVENLY SPHERES

Renaissance humanist scholars concerned themselves for the most part with the study of literature, moral philosophy, history, and politics. What interested them primarily were human actions, not the motion of natural bodies. In many respects, Renaissance emphasis on the humanities was a reaction against what many intellectuals and artists regarded as the undue primacy of Aristotelian logic and science in the universities.

Since the twelfth century, Western European scholars had used Aristotle's system of logic as their primary tool for cataloguing and expanding knowledge. Aristotelian logic was to university studies of the High Middle Ages what the computer revolution is to late-twentieth-century education and research. In like manner, medieval scholars absorbed Aristotle's physics. Although a few medieval scientists questioned some basic tenets of Aristotle's scientific system, only in the mid-sixteenth century did the entire Western vision of the universe come under serious and sustained criticism.

This traditional view of the cosmos blended the physics of Aristotle (384–322 B.C), the astronomy of Ptolemy (second century A.D.), and the philosophy of Plato (429–347 B.C.) to create a universe centered on a stationary earth. Scholars saw all physical objects on earth as transitory compositions of the four basic elements — earth, air, fire, and water — and explained change as simply a shift in the ratio of elements within a particular body. They perceived celestial objects, to the contrary, as changeless, believing them to be composed of a pure, divine ether and traveling around the earth in circular orbits, because the circle is the perfect geometric form. All of this meant there were two sets of physical laws, one for the corruptible and constantly changing earth and one for the perfect and unchanging celestial spheres.

This scientific explanation of the universe fit comfortably into medieval Christian theology and Renaissance humanist scholarship. After all, Christians saw the earth as a corruptible place of sin but also as God's center stage, on which humans, through divine guidance and grace, could transcend the world of flesh and corruption and rise to the perfection of the heavens. Likewise, Platonic ideas that clearly distinguished between the heavenly world of Reality and the corporeal world of shadows deeply infused humanistic scholarship.

The first serious assault on this cosmology came in 1543 with the publication of *On the Revolutions of the Heavenly Spheres*. Its author, Nicholas Copernicus (1473–1543), a Polish Roman Catholic cleric, mathematically demonstrated that the earth revolves daily on its axis and completes an orbit of the sun annually. Many of his arguments and theories were wrong. He continued to believe, for example, that planets orbit in perfect circles and at constant velocities. Nonetheless, it is hard to exaggerate the importance of Copernicus's book. With justification, historians point to its publication date of 1543 as the beginning of the Scientific Revolution.

In the following selection, the book's preface and dedication to Pope Paul III (1534–1549), Copernicus describes the genesis of his new theories.

Questions for Analysis

1. Why did Copernicus delay the publication of his theories about the universe for so long?
2. Why had Copernicus become dissatisfied with contemporary models of the universe?
3. What kind of research did Copernicus do to arrive at his new theories? Is it "scientific" by modern standards?
4. What type of criticism does Copernicus anticipate, and how does he respond to it?

I can readily imagine, Holy Father, that as soon as some people hear that in this volume, which I have written about the revolutions of the spheres of the universe, I ascribe certain motions to the terrestrial globe, they will shout that I must be immediately repudiated together with this belief. For I am not so enamored of my own opinions that I disregard what others may think of them. I am aware that a philosopher's ideas are not subject to the judgment of ordinary persons, because it is his endeavor to seek the truth in all things, to the extent permitted to human reason by God. Yet I hold that completely erroneous views should be shunned. Those who know that the consensus of many centuries has sanctioned the conception that the earth remains at rest in the middle of the heaven as its center would, I reflected, regard it as an insane pronouncement if I made the opposite assertion that the earth moves. Therefore I debated with myself for a long time whether to publish the volume which I wrote to prove the earth's motion or rather to follow the example of the Pythagoreans[1] and certain others, who used to transmit philosophy's secrets only to kinsmen and friends, not in writing but by word of mouth. . . . When I weighed these considerations, the scorn which I

1. Followers of the Greek mathematician and philosopher Pythagoras (ca 580–500 B.C.); they comprised a closed community, jealously guarding their secret knowledge.

had reason to fear on account of the novelty and unconventionality of my opinion almost induced me to abandon completely the work which I had undertaken.

But while I hesitated for a long time and even resisted, my friends drew me back. . . . They exhorted me no longer to refuse, on account of the fear which I felt, to make my work available for the general use of students of astronomy. The crazier my doctrine of the earth's motion now appeared to most people, the argument ran, so much the more admiration and thanks would it gain after they saw the publication of my writings dispel the fog of absurdity by most luminous proofs. Influenced therefore by these persuasive men and by this hope, in the end I allowed my friends to bring out an edition of the volume, as they had long besought me to do.

I have . . . no desire to conceal from Your Holiness that I was impelled to consider a different system of deducing the motions of the universe's spheres for no other reason than the realization that astronomers do not agree among themselves in their investigations of this subject. For, in the first place, they are so uncertain about the motion of the sun and moon that they cannot establish and observe a constant length even for the tropical year. Secondly, in determining the motions not only of these bodies but also of the other five planets, they do not use the same principles, assumptions, and explanations of the apparent revolutions and motions. For while some employ only homocentrics, others utilize eccentrics and epicycles,[2] and yet they do not quite reach their goal. . . . On the contrary, their experience was just like someone taking from various places hands, feet, a head, and other pieces, very well depicted, it may be, but not for the representation of a single person; since these fragments would not belong to one another at all, a monster rather than a man would be put together from them. . . .

For a long time, then, I reflected on this confusion in the astronomical traditions concerning the derivation of the motions of the universe's spheres. I began to be annoyed that the movements of the world machine, created for our sake by the best and most systematic Artisan[3] of all, were not understood with greater certainty by the philosophers, who otherwise examined so precisely the most insignificant trifles of this world. For this reason I undertook the task of rereading the works of all the philosophers which I could obtain to learn whether anyone had ever proposed other motions of the universe's spheres than those expounded by the teachers of astronomy in the schools. And in fact first I found in Cicero that Hicetas supposed the earth to move.[4] Later I also discovered in Plutarch[5] that certain others

---

2. In Aristotle's original theory, the orbits of all celestial objects are "homocentric," that is, they all have the same center — the earth. By the fifteenth century, astronomers, in order to explain the apparently erratic motion of the planets, had postulated "eccentric" (out-of-center) orbits and epicycles. An eccentric orbit meant that a planet might have a "center" that was not its circular orbit's true geometrical center, or a planet might have two different "centers," one for calculating velocity and one for determining its circular orbit. An epicycle was a secondary orbital movement, a small circle, the center of which moved around the circumference of a larger circle, the center of which was the earth. Only by such tinkering could astronomers retain the basics of the ancient Greek celestial system.

3. A reference to God.

4. Cicero (106–43 B.C.) was a Roman orator and politician; Hicetas was a Pythagorean of the fourth century B.C.

5. Plutarch (ca A.D. 46–119) was a Greek moralist and biographer. The work cited by Copernicus, *Opinions of the Philosophers*, is no longer considered to be Plutarch's.

were of this opinion. I have decided to set his words down here, so that they may be available to everybody:

> Some think that the earth remains at rest. But Philolaus the Pythagorean believes that, like the sun and moon, it revolves around the fire in an oblique circle. Heraclides of Pontus and Ecphantus the Pythagorean make the earth move, not in a progressive motion, but like a wheel in a rotation from west to east about its own center.[6]

Therefore, having obtained the opportunity from these sources, I too began to consider the mobility of the earth. And even though the idea seemed absurd, nevertheless I knew that others before me had been granted the freedom to imagine any circles whatever for the purpose of explaining the heavenly phenomena. Hence I thought that I too would be readily permitted to ascertain whether explanations sounder than those of my predecessors could be found for the revolution of the celestial spheres on the assumption of some motion of the earth.

Having thus assumed the motions which I ascribe to the earth later on in the volume, by long and intense study I finally found that if the motions of the other planets are correlated with the orbiting of the earth, and are computed for the revolution of each planet, not only do their phenomena follow therefrom but also the order and size of all the planets and spheres, and heaven itself is so linked together that in no portion of it can anything be shifted without disrupting the remaining parts and the universe as a whole. . . .

Perhaps there will be babblers who claim to be judges of astronomy although completely ignorant of the subject and, badly distorting some passage of Scripture to their purpose, will dare to find fault with my undertaking and censure it. I disregard them even to the extent of despising their criticism as unfounded. For it is not unknown that Lactantius,[7] otherwise an illustrious writer but hardly an astronomer, speaks quite childishly about the earth's shape, when he mocks those who declared that the earth has the form of a globe. Hence scholars need not be surprised if any such persons will likewise ridicule me. Astronomy is written for astronomers.

Hans Holbein the Younger

THE FRENCH AMBASSADORS

The French Ambassadors appears to have been one of the favorite works of art of its creator, the German painter Hans Holbein the Younger (1497–1543). It is the only

6. Philolaus was a philosopher of the fifth century B.C. who is credited with the theory that the energy of the universe is provided by a great fire at its center. Heraclides of Pontus (b. ca 390 B.C.) suggested the idea that the earth rotates on its axis and that Venus and Mars revolve around the sun. Ecphantus, a fifth-century B.C. Pythagorean, is also thought to have believed the earth rotates on an axis.

7. Lactantius (A.D. 240–320), known as the "Christian Cicero" because of his elegant Latin style, wrote this in his *Divine Precepts*, an anti-pagan tract.

The French Ambassadors

painting on which he signed his full name. In 1533, while working at the court of Henry VIII (1509–1547) of England, Holbein painted a portrait of the French Crown's two ambassadors to England, Jean de Dinteville and Georges de Selve. Both men were ardent humanists, and Holbein presents them in a setting with examples of their wide-ranging intellectual, artistic, and spiritual interests. The open book is a hymnal containing Martin Luther's German translation of the medieval chant "Come, Holy Spirit," and the book to its left is a Bible, partially opened to reveal the Ten Commandments.

Questions for Analysis

1. Identify the other objects on the table. What do they tell us about the interests of these men? By extension, what do they suggest about some Renaissance humanists?
2. What do the objects tell us about the intellectual impact of Europe's recent voyages of exploration?
3. Consider this masterpiece in the context of Copernicus's publication of *On the Revolution of the Heavenly Spheres.* What does the painting suggest about the intellectual atmosphere in which Copernicus lived and worked?

Avvakum

AUTOBIOGRAPHY AND LETTERS

Much of Russian history has been determined by the fact that when the Russian people abandoned paganism for Christianity in the tenth century, they embraced the faith and traditions of Constantinople, not Rome. Russia's commitment to Eastern Orthodox religious culture substantially affected its art and learning, helped cut it off from Western Europe, and enhanced the authority of the Russian tsar, or emperor, who became, in keeping with the tradition of the Byzantine Empire, the living image of God on earth and the absolute ruler of the community of God's people. He was both Church and State. With the fall of Constantinople in 1453, the tsar and his subjects saw themselves as the only legitimate heirs of the imperial Christian system that Constantine had established in the early fourth century.

This essentially conservative vision did not preclude change and, therefore, conflict within the Russian Church, as Tsar Aleksei I (1645–1676) discovered. In 1652 he appointed a reforming priest named Nikon as patriarch of the Russian Church. One of Nikon's first actions was to propose changes in certain religious manuals and rituals in order to bring them closer to their original Greek models. Although the proposed changes, such as amending the spelling of Jesus's name and making the sign of the cross with three fingers instead of two, may seem minor today, they raised a storm of protest from clergy and laity, who were convinced the patriarch was defiling the Russian Orthodox way of life. Although Patriarch Nikon was eventually deposed, his proposed reforms were adopted, thus setting the stage for a major schism in the Russian Orthodox Church.

The opponents of reform were known as Old Believers. For the rest of the century they were associated with rebellions of every sort against tsarist authority and, in the face of government persecution, offered themselves up for martyrdom. Over 20,000 burned themselves to death in communal conflagrations rather than accept change. In the end, the Old Believers were outnumbered and lost their battle against religious innovation, even though large pockets of them persisted and millions can be found even today in the Soviet Union.

Archpriest Avvakum (ca 1620–1682) was the most eloquent and celebrated critic of Nikon's reforms. He, his wife, Anastasia, and their children suffered greatly for their zeal. After more than ten years of Siberian exile, Avvakum and his family were allowed to return to Moscow, but his and Anastasia's refusal to bend to the new order, or to be silent in their refusal, soon earned them additional persecution. The archpriest was incarcerated for fifteen years in an underground monastic dungeon, where he was allowed to write his life story and inspirational letters to his many followers. Because Avvakum was generally regarded as a living saint and enjoyed the protection of Tsar Aleksei, his life was spared until 1682, when he was burned at the stake as a heretic. The following excerpts come from works written in captivity. The first two are from his autobiography, the rest from his letters.

Questions for Analysis

1. How does Avvakum view all Christian churches other than the Russian?
2. Why is he especially hostile toward the Church of Constantinople, which introduced Christianity to Russia?
3. Why is it so important to him that the Russian Church retain its traditional ritual practices?
4. What were the core issues involved in this struggle, and what were the Old Believers ultimately resisting?

When they took me . . . to the Chudov monastery . . . in Moscow, they brought me before the ecumenical patriarchs, and all our (Nikonian churchmen) sat there like so many foxes. I spoke of many things in Holy Scripture with the patriarchs. God opened my sinful mouth and Christ put them to shame. The last word they spoke to me was this: "Why," said they, "do you remain stubborn? All our Christian lands, the Serbs and Albanians and Wallachians and Romans and Poles, all cross themselves with three fingers; you alone remain obstinate and cross yourself with five fingers;[1] it is not seemly." And I answered them for Christ this way: "O you teachers of Christendom! Rome fell long ago and lies prostrate, and the Poles perished with it,[2] being enemies of Christians to the end. And your own Orthodoxy has been tainted by the violence of the Turkish (sul-

1. Actually with two digits, but because of their position it was sometimes considered that all five digits were being used.

2. The Poles are Roman Catholics and follow the practices of papal Rome.

tan) Mohammed; and no wonder, for you have become impotent. And from now on it is you who should come to us to learn; for by the grace of God we are an autocratic (independent) realm. Before the time of Nikon, the apostate, in our Russia under our pious princes and tsars the Orthodox faith was pure and undefiled, and the church was free from turmoil. Nikon the wolf, together with the Devil, ordained that men should cross themselves with three fingers, but our first shepherds made the sign of the cross and blessed men with five fingers, according to the tradition of our holy fathers."

. . .

God will bless you: suffer tortures for the way you place your fingers, do not reason too much! And I am ready to die with you for this and for Christ. Even if I am a foolish man and without learning, yet this I know, that all the traditions of the church, handed down to us by the holy fathers, are holy and incorrupt, I will maintain them even unto death, as I received them. I will not alter the eternal rules that were laid down before our time; may they remain so unto ages of ages.

. . .

I know all your evil cunning, dogs, whores, metropolitans, archbishops, Nikonians, thieves, renegades, foreigners in Russian garb. You have changed the images of the saints and all the church canons and rituals: and a bitter thing it is for good Christians!

. . .

Alas and alack! These apostates have now extinguished the last great light, the great Russian church of old, which worked for the enlightenment of souls, shining throughout the world.

Oh you dogs! What do you have against the olden ways? Impious ones, thieves, sons of whores. . . . It does not befit us, the faithful, to speak much to you pagans. . . . And that you curse us with your devil: we laugh at that. Even a child would burst into laughter at your madness. If you curse us for (maintaining) the holy olden ways: then also should you curse your fathers and mothers, who died in our faith.

. . .

(Addressed by Avvakum to Tsar Aleksei Mikhailovich:) Take a good, old-fashioned breath, as in Stefan's[3] time and say in the Russian tongue: "Lord, forgive me, a sinner!" And be done with *Kyrie eleison;*[4] this is what the Hellenes[5] say: spit on them! For you are a Russian, (Aleksei) Mikhailovich, not a Greek. Speak in your native tongue; do not degrade it in church, or at home, or in sayings. It befits us to talk as Christ taught us. God loves us no less than the Greeks; he taught us to read and write in our tongue, through the holy Cyril and his brother.[6] What better can

3. Stefan Vonifatievich, Tsar Aleksei's spiritual adviser and chaplain, who was later exiled for his opposition to Nikon.

4. Greek for "Lord, have mercy."

5. Greeks.

6. Saints Cyril and Methodius were two ninth-century Greek missionaries who worked among the Balkan Slavs. These "Apostles to the Slavs" are credited with inventing the Cyrillic alphabet for their converts.

we want? . . . Stop tormenting us! Seize those heretics who destroy your soul, and burn them all, the filthy dogs, Latins and Jews; but release us, your countrymen. Truly, it will be good.

. . .

We, the true believers, follow the Sacred Scriptures and hold steadfastly to what the old printed books teach us about the Deity and about other dogmas; we seek integrity of mind in the old books printed in Moscow (in the reign) of former pious tsars.

. . .

And thenceforth for twenty-three years . . . to this day they burn and hang the confessors of Christ without ceasing. The Russians . . . poor dears — one may think them stupid, but they rejoice that the tormentor has come at last — brave the fire in hosts, for the love of Christ, the Son of God's Light. The Greeks, those sons of whores, are cunning; (their) patriarchs eat delicate viands from the same dish with the Turkish barbarians. Not so our dear Russians — they throw themselves into the fire, rather than betray the true faith! In Kazan the Nikonians burned thirty men, in Siberia the same number, in Vladimir six, in Borovsk fourteen men; while in Nizhnii[7] a most glorious thing took place: some were being burned by the heretics, while others, consumed with love and weeping for the true faith, did not wait to be condemned by the heretics, but themselves braved the fire, so that they might keep the true faith intact and pure; and having burned their bodies and committed their souls into God's hands, they rejoice with Christ unto ages of ages, martyrs by choice, slaves of Christ. May their memory live forever unto ages of ages! Theirs was a noble deed.

America and Asia

Western European modes of belief and thought were transforming a number of Amerindian cultures, particularly the major civilizations of Central and South America. Massive depopulation of the native people combined with generally sincere attempts to "save the souls" of the survivors by converting them to European forms of Christianity resulted in wide-scale acculturation. Yet, in spite of this European intrusion, Native Americans managed to resist total cultural absorption.

Elsewhere in the world conflicts between traditional and new ideas were either largely nonexistent or substantially less dramatic and far-reaching. Tradition and authority provided the framework for scholarship and artistic creativity throughout most of Islam. Even the Ottoman Empire, which spanned portions of three continents, and Mughal India, which had the example of the curious eclecticism of Akbar's court, ultimately resisted intellectual and religious challenges to Muslim

7. Modern Gorky.

orthodoxy. India, however, witnessed the rise of the religious vision of Sikhism, a noble but ultimately doomed attempt to end the bitter hostilities between Muslims and Hindus offered by a group of gurus (teachers). China under the Ming (1368–1644) and Ch'ing (1644–1912) dynasties remained anchored in the values of Confucian classicism, yet in Japan Chinese Neo-Confucianism provided intellectual support for the political and social changes of the Tokugawa Shogunate. The practical educational program the shoguns patronized emphasized social order and stability, but because of its focus on the utilitarian arts and technology, Japan's form of Neo-Confucianism created an atmosphere for potentially rapid change within the context of traditional values.

Christoval de Molina

AN ACCOUNT OF THE FABLES AND RITES OF THE INCAS

One often wonders about the depth of sixteenth-century Amerindian conversions to Christianity. In the following selection, Padre Christoval de Molina, a Spanish priest of Cuzco, Peru, who served in that city's hospital for natives, tells of certain conflicts between the old and new ways that occurred during the 1560s. The most serious was a millenarian movement known as the *taqui uncu* (the ritual song of the festival dress), which flared up in 1565. Inca belief held that life consists of thousand-year cycles, and the present Inca Age had begun in a year that computed to the Christian year 565. This meant that the arrival of the Spanish was the last act in the passing away of the Old Inca Age. Toward 1565 a number of Peruvian natives expectantly awaited a new age, which would begin with the overthrow of the Spaniards and their god.

Molina, a master of Quechua, the language of the Incas, interviewed large numbers of older natives in order to compile, sometime around 1575, his account of the folklore and religious practices of the Quechua people and their Inca lords. His avowed reason was "to root out these idolatries and follies." Despite the purpose of his research, without his work we would know far less about preconquest Inca culture and its resilient vitality under Spanish domination.

Questions for Analysis

1. Can you find in this account any mythic attempt to explain why natives suffered from Spanish diseases while the Spaniards remained largely immune?

2. How do the Quechua people explain their conquest by the Spaniards?
3. What must the people of the old gods do in order to win back their favor and usher in the new age?
4. How would the new age differ from the previous millennium?
5. How widespread was this movement? How and when was it finally suppressed?
6. Why do you think some natives committed suicide?
7. Molina claims that there are only a few Quechua wizards still functioning around 1575. Are there any reasons why we should suspect his testimony on this issue?
8. Compare Molina with Sahagun (Chapter 12). What are their respective strengths and weaknesses as reporters of Amerindian culture? Do you think one is less biased or better in some respect than the other? Why?

About ten years ago there was a joke among the Indians. They had a kind of song called *taqui uncu*. . . .

In the . . . diocese of Cuzco, . . . most of the Indians had fallen into the greatest apostasy,[1] departing from the Catholic Faith, which they had received, and returning to the idolatries which they practised in the time of their infidelity. It was not understood how this had come to pass; but it was suspected that the wizards,[2] whom the Incas[3] kept in Uiscacabamba,[4] were at the bottom of it. For in the year 1560, and not before, it was held and believed by the Indians, that an ointment from the bodies of the Indians had been sent for from Spain to cure a disease for which there was no medicine there. Hence it was that the Indians, at that time, were very shy of the Spaniards, and they would not bring fuel or grass or anything else to the house of a Spaniard, lest they should be taken in and killed, in order to extract this ointment. All this had originated from that villainy, with the object of causing enmity between the Indians and Spaniards. The Indians of the land had much respect for the things of the Inca, until the Lord Viceroy, Don Francisco de Toledo,[5] abolished and put an end to them, in which he greatly served God our Lord. The deception by which the Devil deceived these poor people was the belief that all the huacas[6] which the Christians had burnt and destroyed had been brought to life again; and that they had been divided into two parts, one of which was united with the huaca *Pachacama*,[7] and the other with the huaca *Titicaca*.[8] The story went on that they had formed in the air, in order of battle against God, and that they had conquered Him. But when the

1. Abandonment of one's faith.

2. Priests of the old faith.

3. Technically, only those Quechua people who were of royal blood and thereby descended from the gods were Incas.

4. An Inca stronghold that did not fall until 1572.

5. The king's deputy (viceroy) from 1568 to 1581.

6. Sacred images and gods.

7. The sun god and creator, the supreme deity in the Inca pantheon.

8. The sacred lake where the first Incas came to earth.

Marquis[9] entered this land, it was held that God had conquered the huacas, as the Spaniards had overcome the Indians. Now, however, it was believed that things were changed, that God and the Spaniards were conquered, all the Spaniards killed, and their cities destroyed, and that the sea would rise to drink them up, that they might be remembered no more. In this apostasy they believed that God our Lord had made the Spaniards, and Castille, and the animals and provisions of Castille; but that the huacas had made the Indians, and this land, and all the things they possessed before the Spaniards came. Thus they stripped our Lord of his omnipotence. Many preachers went forth from among the Indians, who preached as well in the desert places as in the villages, declaring the resurrection of the huacas, and saying that they now wandered in the air, thirsty and dying of hunger, because the Indians no longer sacrificed. . . . The huacas, it was announced, were enraged with all those who had been baptized, and it was declared that they would all be killed unless they returned to the old belief and renounced the Christian faith. Those who sought the friendship and grace of the huacas would, it was urged, pass a life of prosperity and health. Those who would return to the love of the huacas and live, were to fast for some days, not eating salt . . . nor colored maize, nor any Spanish thing, nor entering churches, nor obeying the call of the priests, nor using their Christian names. Henceforth the times of the Incas would be restored, and the huacas would not enter into stones or fountains to speak, but would be incorporated in men whom they would cause to speak: therefore the people were to have their houses prepared and ready, in case any huaca should desire to lodge in one of them. Thus it was that many Indians trembled and fell to the ground, and others tore themselves as if they were possessed, making faces; and when they presently became quiet, they said, when they were asked what they had felt, that such and such a huaca had entered into their bodies. Then the people took such a one in their arms, and carried him to a chosen spot, and there they made a lodging with straw and cloaks; and began to worship the huaca, offering sheep . . . and other things. Then they made a festival for two or three days, dancing and drinking, and invoking the huaca that was represented by the possessed man. Such persons, from time to time, preached to the people, threatening them, and telling them not to serve God, but the huacas; and to renounce all Christianity, with all Christian names, and the shirts, hats, and shoes of Christians. . . .

This evil was so widely credited that not only the Indians on the *Repartimientos*[10] but those who lived in the cities, among Spaniards, believed and performed the prescribed fasts. . . .

As they believed that God and the Spaniards were conquered, the Indians began to rise, as happened in the year 1565. . . .

There were several forms of apostasy in the different provinces. Some danced and gave out that they had the huaca in their bodies. Others trembled for the same reason. Others shut themselves up in their houses and shouted. Others flung them-

9. Francisco Pizarro (1470–1541).

10. Estates given to Spanish colonists in encomienda.

selves from rocks and were killed. Others jumped into the rivers, thus offering themselves to the huacas. At last our Lord, in his mercy, was pleased to enlighten these miserable people; and those who were left were led to see the nonsense that they had believed, that the Inca was dead[11] . . . and that nothing of what had been predicted had taken place, but the very opposite.

By reason of this devilish teaching, there are still some Indian sorcerers and witches, though their number is small. When any Indian is sick, these witches are called in to cure him, and to say whether he will live or die. . . . They . . . make him breathe on a little coca, and offer it to the Sun, praying for health; and the same to the Moon and Stars. Then, with a little gold and silver of little value in his hand, the sick man offers sacrifice to the Creator. Then the wizard commands him to give food to the dead, placing it on their tombs. . . . For the wizard gives the patient to understand that he is visited with this sickness because the dead are starving. If he is able to go on foot to some junction of two rivers, the wizard makes him go there and wash his body with water and flour of white maize, saying that he will there leave his illness. At the end of this ceremony the wizard tells him that, if he would free himself from his sickness, he must confess all his sins, without concealing any. They call this *hichoco*. These Indians are so simple that some of them readily, and with little persuasion, fall into this apostasy and error, though some afterwards repent and confess their sins.

There are also a very great number of Indian men and women who, understanding the offense against our Lord that they commit in doing this, will not permit any such acts, but rather accuse those who do them . . . , that they may be punished. If some exemplary punishment was inflicted on the wizards, I believe that this great evil would soon disappear, although, as I have said, there are now few wizards.

Nanak

ADI-GRANTH

Sikhism, one of the world's newest monotheistic faiths, grew out of Hinduism and Islam between 1500 and 1700. Sikhs (the word means disciples) believe their first guru, Nanak (1469–1539), received a revelation from God charging him with bringing the divided world to the worship of "the True Name." Nanak wandered through all India seeking disciples who would accept his message of love and reconciliation. He taught that such externals of religion as prilgrimages to Mecca (which he had made, disguised as a Muslim), bathing in the sacred Ganges River, and asceticism are worthless before God unless they are accompanied by inward sincerity and true morality. As a strict and uncompromising monotheist, he declared that love of God

11. As a result of this rebellion, the Inca Tupac Amaru was publicly beheaded in Cuzco in 1571.

alone suffices to free anyone of any caste from the law of karma, bringing an end to reincarnation and resulting in absorption into the One.

Although Nanak's sect began as a pacifistic religious movement that preached love and peace among all humans regardless of caste, religion, or race, the Sikhs evolved into a militant congregation in reaction to later Mughal persecution. The Sikhs turned their holiest shrine, the Golden Temple at Amritsar, into an armed camp. Under their tenth and last guru, Govind Singh (1675–1708), the practice began of conferring the surname Singh (Lion) on all male sect members and charging them to bear ever after a dagger. Sikhism's call to persons of all castes to be baptized by the sword was especially attractive to those from the lowest castes and untouchables. By 1700 the Sikhs were a military power to be reckoned with in the Punjab, and their subsequent history has been characterized by a tradition of military prowess and their often frustrated desire to carve out an independent Sikh state governed according to the democratic principle that all Sikhs are fully equal and the only ultimate authority is the *Adi-Granth*, their sacred book.

Compiled by Arjan (1563–1606), the fifth guru, the *Adi-Granth* (also known as the *Granth Sahid*) consists mostly of hymns and other religious poems composed by Nanak and other early gurus. It attained its final form in 1705–1706, when Gobind Singh added a number of hymns and declared that, from then on, the *Adi-Granth* itself, not any individual, was Sikhism's one true guru. The following poems are attributed to Nanak.

Questions for Analysis

1. What Muslim elements can you find in Nanak's message? What Hindu elements? Which religion seems to have had the stronger impact on Nanak's religious vision?
2. What Muslim and Hindu forms of devotion does Nanak reject?
3. Once established, Sikhism was persecuted by Hindu and Muslim authorities. Why would the religion of the Sikhs constitute such a serious challenge to both societies?
4. What parallels can you discover between Nanak's message and Martin Luther's? What differences are there?

There is one God,
Eternal Truth is His Name;
Maker of all things,
Fearing nothing and at enmity with nothing,
Timeless is His Image;
Not begotten, being of His own Being:
By the grace of the Guru, made known to men.

. . .

It is not through thought that He is to be comprehended
Though we strive to grasp Him a hundred thousand times;
Nor by outer silence and long deep meditation
Can the inner silence be reached;
Nor is man's hunger for God appeasable
By piling up world-loads of wealth.
All the innumerable devices of worldly wisdom
Leave a man disappointed; not one avails.

How then shall we know the Truth?
How shall we rend the veils of untruth away?
Abide thou by His Will, and make thine own,
His will, O Nanak, that is written in thy heart.

. . .

He cannot be installed like an idol,
Nor can man shape His likeness.
He made Himself and maintains Himself
On His heights unstained forever;
Honored are they in His shrine
Who meditate upon Him.

. . .

Those who have inner belief in the Name,
Always achieve their own liberation,
Their kith and kin are also saved.
Guided by the light of the Guru
The disciple steers safe himself,
And many more he saves;
Those enriched with inner belief
Do not wander begging.

Such is the power of His stainless Name,
He who truly believes in it, knows it.

. . .

There is no counting of men's prayers.
There is no counting their ways of adoration.
Thy lovers, O Lord, are numberless;
Numberless those who read aloud from the Vedas;
Numberless those Yogis[1] who are detached from the world;

---

1. Hindu holy people who have achieved occult powers through discipline of the body.

Numberless are Thy Saints contemplating,
Thy virtues and Thy wisdom;
Numberless are the benevolent, the lovers of their kind.

Numberless Thy heroes and martyrs[2]
Facing the steel of their enemies;
Numberless those who in silence
Fix their deepest thoughts upon Thee;

. . .

Pilgrimages, penances, compassion and almsgiving
Bring a little merit, the size of sesame seed.
But he who hears and believes and loves the Name
Shall bathe and be made clean
In a place of pilgrimage within him.

. . .

When in time, in what age, in what day of the month or week
In what season and in what month did'st Thou create the world?
The Pundits[3] do not know, or they would have written it in the Puranas;
The Qazis[4] do not know, or they would have recorded it in the Qur'an;
Nor do the Yogis know the moment of the day,
Nor the day of the month or the week, nor the month nor the season.
Only God Who made the world knows when He made it.

. . .

The Vedas proclaim Him,
So do the readers of the Puranas;
The learned speak of Him in many discourses;
Brahma and Indra speak of Him,
Sivas speak of Him, Siddhas[5] speak of Him,
The Buddhas He has created, proclaim Him.

. . .

Maya, the mythical goddess,[6]
Sprang from the One, and her womb brought forth

2. Muslim warriors.

3. Brahmins learned in Hindu religion and law.

4. Muslim judges.

5. A class of demigods.

6. A Hindu goddess of illusion who symbolizes material creation, because matter is the veil that covers the reality of the Spirit.

Three acceptable disciples of the One:
Brahma, Visnu and Siva.
Brahma, it is said bodies forth the world,
Visnu it is who sustains it;
Siva the destroyer who absorbs,
He controls death and judgment.

God makes them to work as He wills,
He sees them ever, they see Him not:
That of all is the greatest wonder.

. . .

I have described the realm of *dharma*,
Now I shall describe the realm of Knowledge;

How many are the winds, the fires, the waters,
How many are the Krishnas and Sivas,
How many are the Brahmas fashioning the worlds,
Of many kinds and shapes and colors;
How many worlds, like our own there are,
Where action produces the consequences. . . .
How many adepts, Buddhas and Yogis are there,
How many goddesses and how many the images of the goddesses;
How many gods and demons and how many sages;

How many hidden jewels in how many oceans,
How many the sources of life;
How many the modes and diversities of speech,
How many are the kings, the rulers and the guides of men;
How many the devoted there are, who pursue this divine knowledge,
His worshipers are numberless, saith Nanak.

Narushima Motonao and Yamazaki Ansai

TWO SEVENTEENTH-CENTURY NEO-CONFUCIAN TEXTS

The age of the Tokugawa Shogunate (1603–1867) marked a period of vigorous reorganization of Japanese society and laid the basis for Japan's active role in world affairs by the end of the nineteenth century. An integral element in that reorientation was education. Ieyasu, the first Tokugawa shogun (1603–1605), established a system of centralized feudalism, which he reinforced by patronizing Neo-Confucian studies.

Neo-Confucianism had been formulated in China during the age of the Sung Dynasty, and its greatest teacher had been Chu Hsi (1130–1200), whose voluminous writings were now avidly studied in Japan. The Neo-Confucians' basic message was that the world is real, not illusory as the Buddhists maintained, and that humans attain fulfillment by participating fully in society, not, as the Taoists believed, by remaining aloof. Neo-Confucians rejected all notions of immortality and spiritual salvation, concentrating instead on social and political reform. They believed that by applying reason to the study of natural and social phenomena, one could understand their underlying laws and thereby be able to act on the basis of sure knowledge. The single most important pathway to understanding government was the study of history.

The first source comes from an official chronicle account of Ieyasu's rule by Narushima Motonao that notes the shogun's promotion of learning through the medium of printing. Block printing had been known in Japan for centuries, having been introduced from China. The technique of printing by means of movable type had arrived around 1600 from Korea and the West. The second document is from the writings of Yamazaki Ansai (1619–1682), one of the mid-century's most prominent Neo-Confucian teachers. Here he is commenting on the regulations of Chu Hsi's White Deer Cave School, where a generation of twelfth-century Chinese students had gained instruction in the maxims of Neo-Confucianism.

Questions for Analysis

1. Despite his reputation as a person with a taste for elegant literature, Tokugawa Ieyasu actually preferred other types of books. What sort of books did he read, and what does his choice of reading matter tell us about his educational program and its objectives?
2. What elements of Japan's Neo-Confucian program were aimed at preserving order and stability in society?
3. What elements potentially prepared Japan for playing, at a later date, a major role in world affairs?
4. How do Ieyasu's concerns parallel those of Machiavelli?
5. In what ways was the Neo-Confucian program similar to that of Europe's Renaissance humanists?

Ieyasu's Rule

Having lived from boyhood to manhood in military encampments, and having suffered hardship after hardship in countless battles, large and small, His Lordship [Ieyasu] had little time to read or study. Although he had conquered the country on horseback, being a man of innate intelligence and wisdom, he fully appreciated the impossibility of governing the country on horseback. According to his judgment there could be no other way to govern the country than by a constant and deep faith in the sages and the scholars, and as a human being interested in the welfare of his fellow human beings, he patronized scholarship from the very beginning of his rule. Thus, he soon gained a reputation as a great devotee of letters and as one with a taste for elegant prose and poetry. On one occasion, Shimazu Yoshihisa, whose Buddhist name was Ryūhaku, took the trouble to arrange a poetry composition party in Ieyasu's honor, only to learn that His Lordship did not care at all for such a vain pastime. He listened again and again to discourses on the *Four Books*,[1] the *Records of the Historian* by Ssu-ma Ch'ien,[2] the *History of the Former Han Dynasty*,[3] and the *Precepts and Policies of T'ang T'ai-tsung*[4] as well as the *Six Tactics* and *Three Strategies*.[5] Among Japanese works he gave special attention to the *Institutes of Engi*, the *Mirror of the East*, and the *Kemmu Regulations*.[6] . . .

Whatever the subject, he was interested, not in the turn of a phrase or in literary embellishments, but only in discovering the key to government — how to govern oneself, the people, and the country. Ieyasu declared, "If we cannot clarify the principles of human relations, society and government will of itself become unstable and disorders will never cease. Books are the only means whereby these principles can be set forth and understood. Thus, the printing of books and their transmission to the public is the first concern of a benevolent government." For this reason steps were taken for the printing of various books.

Preface to the Collected Commentaries on Chu Hsi's Regulations for the White Deer Cave School

The philosopher Chu, styled Hui-an,[7] was conspicuously endowed with intellectual leadership. Following in the line of (the Sung philosophers) Chou Tun-i and the Ch'eng brothers, he advanced the cause of Confucianism in both elementary education and higher education. For the guidance of his students he established these regulations, but they failed to gain wide acceptance in his own time because of opposition from vile quarters. . . .

It would seem to me that the aim of education, elementary and advanced, is to clarify human relationships. In the elementary program of education the various human relationships are made clear, the essence of this education in human relationships being devotion to (or respect for) persons. The "investigation of things" in advanced studies (as set forth in *The Great Learning*)[8] simply carries to its ultimate conclusion what has already been learned from elementary instruction. . . .

Chu Hsi's school regulations list the Five Human Relationships as the curriculum, following an order of presentation

---

1. The Four Books of the Neo-Confucians were Confucius's *Analects*, the *Book of Mencius*, *The Great Learning*, and *The Doctrine of the Mean*. The last two books were short works dating from the age of China's Han Dynasty (202 B.C.–A.D. 220).

2. Ssu-ma Ch'ien (ca 145–87 B.C.) is generally regarded as China's greatest historian (Chapter 5).

3. The work of Pan Ku (A.D. 32–92) and his sister, Pan Chao (ca A.D. 45–114). As historians, they rank only slightly behind Ssu-ma Ch'ien in influence and reputation. Pan Chao was the preeminent female intellectual of the Han Dynasty (Chapter 5).

4. The T'ang Dynasty's first great emperor (626–649), who was noted for his military expansion of the empire, his capable administration, and his patronage of education. He was especially tolerant in religious and philosophical matters. Ieyasu admired T'ang T'ai-tsung and claimed him as a model.

5. Chinese works on the art of war.

6. The *Institutes of Engi* was a tenth-century compilation of government regulations; the *Mirror of the East* chronicled the Kamakura Shogunate from 1180 to 1266; the *Kemmu Regulations* was a fourteenth-century compilation of government regulations.

7. Chu Hsi.

8. See note 1.

which complements the curriculum of advanced education (as found in *The Great Learning*). Studying, questioning, deliberating and analyzing — these four correspond to the "investigation of things" and "extension of knowledge" in advanced education. The article dealing with conscientious action goes with the "cultivation of one's person." From the emperor to the common people, the cultivation of one's person is essential, including both "making the thoughts sincere" and "rectifying the mind." The "managing of affairs" and "social intercourse" (in Chu's Regulations) refer to "regulating the family," "governing the state" and "establishing peace" (in *The Great Learning*). These Regulations thus contain everything, and they should be used for instruction together with the *Book of Elementary Instruction* and the *Book of Advanced Education* (Great Learning). But so far they have gone almost unnoticed among the items in Chu's collected works, scarcely attracting any attention from scholars. I have taken the liberty, however, of bringing them out into the light of day by mounting and hanging them in my studio for constant reference and reflection. More recently I have found a detailed discussion of these regulations in *Some Reflections of Mine* by the Korean scholar Yi T'oege. It convinced me more than anything else that these Regulations are the true guide to education. . . .

(*Signed*) Yamazaki Ansai
Keian 3 (1650): Twelfth Month, 9th Day

Regulations for the School of the White Deer Cave

(*The Five Regulations*)

Between parent and child there is intimacy,

Between lord and minister there is duty.

Between husband and wife there is differentiation.

Between elder and junior there is precedence.

Between friend and friend there is fidelity.

These five articles of teaching are what (the sage-kings) Yao and Shun commanded Ch'i, the Minister of Education, solemnly to promulgate as the five subjects of teaching. All that the student should study is contained in these five regulations, but in studying them he should follow five steps, as given below:

Study widely.

Question thoroughly.

Deliberate carefully.

Analyze clearly.

Act conscientiously. . . .

In speech be loyal and true; in action be conscientious and reverent. Subdue ire and stifle passion. Change yourself for the better; do not hesitate to correct your errors. These things are essential to personal culture.

Do not do to others what you do not care for yourself. When action fails to get results, seek the reason for failure in yourself. These are important in social intercourse.

The aim of teaching and guidance given by ancient sages and scholars, it seems to me, is nothing more than to set forth moral principles, in order, first, to cultivate them in one's own person, and then to extend them to others. Simply to accumulate knowledge and learn to write well in order to gain fame and a well-paid position is far from being the true function of education. Nevertheless that is what most men pursue learning for today.

NOTES ON THE CHAPTER-OPENING ILLUSTRATIONS

Chapter 1

Akkadian seal-impression (2340–2180 B.C.) depicting Gilgamesh's journey beyond the guarded gates at the ends of the earth.

Chapter 2

Detail of relief from the palace of King Sancherib at Ninevah. The inhabitants of Lachish are shown being led off to Assyria to work on the palace's construction.

Chapter 3

Relief of the winged symbol of Ahura Mazda at Persepolis, the Persian capital.

Chapter 4

Rubbing from a Han Dynasty bas-relief illustrating a visit to Lao-tzu from Confucius, who offers a pheasant as a gift. From the Wu family tombs at Chia-hsiang, Shantung, 147 B.C.– A.D. 68. In *Chin-shih-so.*

Chapter 5

Relief showing Asoka's visit to the Ramagrama Stupa at Sanchi. From the south gate, Stupa 1 (the Great Stupa), Sanchi, first century B.C.

Chapter 6

Plaster cast of stone sculpture of Arapacana, East Java, A.D. 1343. The original has been missing since World War II.

Chapter 7

Mosaic of two fish flanking a basket of loaves from the floor of the Syrian Church of the Multiplication of the Loaves and Fishes. The present recent structure incorporated this mosaic floor from the original church built in the mid-fifth century.

Chapter 8

Side arch from the Great Mosque, Cordoba.

Chapter 9

Detail from *The Tale of Genji* scroll (Genji monogatari emaki) depicting Niou-no-miya and Prince Genji's sixth daughter on their wedding night. Text written by Lady Murasaki Shikibu ca A.D. 1000; artist unknown.

Chapter 10

Notre Dame, Paris. The device of flying buttresses and arches, which allowed cathedral builders to increase the height of nave vaults, was used for the first time around 1163, in the construction of the nave of Notre Dame.

Chapter 11

Yüan Dynasty painting of a Mongol groom leading a dappled horse. (In 1271 the Mongol Kublai Khan adopted the Chinese dynastic name of Yüan for his empire.)

Chapter 12

Wooden Incan beaker (ca 1650) illustrating Peru's new multiracial society. Shown in procession are an Amerindian, a Spaniard, and a black.

Chapter 13

Early seventeenth-century engraving of the Copernican system. The Polish astronomer Copernicus (1473–1543) proposed a heliocentric theory of the world: the sun is the center of the cosmos, and the earth is one of its planets.

SOURCES

Chapter 1

Pages 8–12: N. K. Sandars, tr., *The Epic of Gilgamesh* (London: Penguin Classics, 1972), 2nd rev. ed., pp. 91–93, 102, 106–114, 117–119. Copyright © N. K. Sandars, 1960, 1964, 1972. Reproduced by permission of Penguin Books Ltd. Pages 13–16, 18–19, 23–24, 25–26: James B. Pritchard, ed., *Ancient Near East in Pictures Relating to the Old Testament*, 2nd ed. with Supplement. Copyright 1954, © 1969 by Princeton University Press. Excerpts, pp. 32–33, 165–176, 365, 467, reprinted with permission of Princeton University Press. Pages 20–22: R. O. Faulkner, ed. and tr., "The Man Who Was Tired of Life," in William Kelly Simpson, ed., *The Literature of Ancient Egypt* (New Haven: Yale University Press, 1972), pp. 202–209. Translation slightly adapted from one that appeared in JEA 42 (1956). Original article copyright 1956. Book copyright 1972. Used by permission of Egypt Exploration Society and Yale University Press. Pages 28–29: *The Sacred Books of China: The Texts of Confucianism*, James Legge, trans., in F. Max Mueller, ed., *The Sacred Books of the East*, 50 vols. (Oxford: Clarendon Press, 1879–1910), Vol. 3, pp. 92–95. Pages 30–31, 32–33, 33–34: Arthur Waley, ed. and tr., *The Book of Songs* (London: Allen and Unwin, 1937), pp. 141–142, 318–319, 121, 67–68, 99, 86. Copyright 1937. Used by permission of Unwin Hyman. Page 36 (left): The Bettmann Archive. Page 36 (right): Courtesy, National Museum, Karachi. Page 37: Museum of Fine Arts, Boston. Gift of Mrs. W. Scott Fitz. Page 39: George Holton/Photo Researchers. Page 40: Courtesy, Hamlyn Publishing, London. Page 41: Werner Forman Archive. Page 43: Courtesy, Jos Museum, Nigeria.

Chapter 2

Pages 49–51: Ralph T. H. Griffith, trans., *The Hymns of the Rig Veda*, 4 vols. (Benares: E. J. Lazarus and Co., 1889–1892), Vol. 1, pp. 56–59; Vol. 4, pp. 289–293. Pages 53–55: Homer, *The Odyssey*, tr. by R. V. Rieu (London: Penguin Classics, 1946), pp. 173–174. Copyright © the Estate of E. V. Rieu, 1946. Reproduced by permission of Penguin Books Ltd. Pages 58–61, 62–64, 64–66: Scripture quotations are from the *Good News Bible* in Today's English Version. Copyright © American Bible Society 1966, 1971, 1976.

Chapter 3

Pages 71–73: *The Upanishads*, F. Max Mueller, trans., in Mueller, *The Sacred Books of the East*, Vol. 1, pp. 92, 104–105; Vol. 15, pp. 173, 175–177, 168–169, passim. Pages 74–76: *The Bhagavad Gita*, Kashinath Trimbak Telang, trans., in Mueller, *The Sacred Books of the East*, Vol. 8, pp. 43–46, 48–49, 51–52, 58–59, 126–128, passim. Pages 77–79: *Gaina Sutras*, Hermann Jacobi, trans., in Mueller, *The Sacred Books of the East*, Vol. 22, pp. 36, 81–87, 202–208, passim. Pages 81–82: *Vinaya Texts*, T. W. Rhys Davids and Hermann Oldenberg, trans., in Mueller, *The Sacred Books of the East*, Vol. 13, pp. 94–97, 100–102, passim. Pages 84–86: *Yasnas* 43, 44, 45 in James Hope Moulton, *Early Zoroastrianism* (London: Williams and Norgate, 1913), pp. 364–370, passim. Pages 88–90: Scripture quotations are from the *Good News Bible* in Today's English Version. Copyright © American Bible Society 1966, 1971, 1976.

Chapter 4

Pages 95–96: J. J. L. Duyvendak, tr., *Tao Te Ching* (London: John Murray [Publishers], 1954), pp. 17, 22, 96, 24, 105, 54, 135, 89. Copyright 1954. Used by permission of the publisher. Pages 98–101: Arthur Waley, tr., *The Analects of Confucius* (London: George Allen and Unwin, 1938), pp. 83, 105, 89, 87, 167, 88, 166, 168, 174, 196, 90–91, 128, 102, 199, 216–217, 102, 142, 162, 155, 120, 96. Copyright 1938. Used by permission of Unwin Hyman Limited. Pages 102–103: W. L. Liao, tr., *The Complete Works of Han Fei Tzu* (London: Arthur Probsthain, 1939), vol. 1, pp. 40, 45–47. Copyright 1939. Used by permission of Arthur Probsthain. Pages 104–106: Yang Hsien-yi and Gladys Yang, *Records of the Historian* (Hong Kong: Commercial Press, 1974), pp. 170–172, 177–178. Copyright 1974. Used by permission of Commercial Press (Hong Kong) Limited. Pages 109–113: B. Jowett, trans., *Thucydides Translated into English* (Oxford: Clarendon Press, 1881), Vol. 1, pp. 115–129, passim. Pages 115–118: Euripedes, *Medea*, ed. by Paul MacKendrick and Herbert M. Howe (Madison: University of Wisconsin Press, 1952). Copyright 1952. Used by permission of the publisher. Pages 119–122: F. J. Church, trans., *The Trial and Death of Socrates* (London: MacMillan, 1880). Pages 124–126: Reprinted by permission of the publishers and The Loeb Classical Library from Diogenes Laertius, Vol. II, translated by R. D. Hicks, Cambridge, Mass.: Harvard University Press, 1925. Pp. 23–25, 29, 31, 39, 41, 43, 47, 49, 51, 57, 71, 75, 79.

Chapter 5

Pages 131–134: Horace L. Jones, trans., *The Geography of Strabo*, 8 vols. (New York: G. P. Putnam's Sons, 1917), Vol. 1, pp. 451–455, 501–503, 377–385, passim. Pages 135–139: Naphtali Lewis and Meyer Reinhold, eds., *Roman Civilization*, vol. 2, pp. 9–19 passim. Copyright © 1951–55 Columbia University Press. Used by permission. Pages 140–141: Tacitus, *On Britain and Germany*,

H. Mattingly, trans. (Penguin Classics, 1958), p. 164. Pages 142–143: Ammianus Marcellinus, *The Later Roman Empire (A.D. 354–378)*, tr. by Walter Hamilton (London: Penguin Classics, 1986), pp. 411–412. Translation copyright © Walter Hamilton, 1986. Reproduced by permission of Penguin Books Ltd. Pages 145–149: Burton Watson, tr., *Records of the Grand Historian of China*, vol. 2, pp. 395–401 passim. Copyright © 1961 Columbia University Press. Used by permission. Pages 150–154: Pan Chao, "Lessons for Women," in Nancy Lee Swan, tr., *Pan Chao: Foremost Woman Scholar of China* (New York: Century, 1932), pp. 82–90. Used by permission of Gest Oriental Library and East Asian Collections, Princeton University. Pages 156–158: William Theodore de Bary et al., *Sources of Indian Tradition*, pp. 146–153 passim. Copyright © 1958 Columbia University Press. Used by permission. Pages 160–163: *The Laws of Manu*, G. Buehler, trans., in Mueller, *Sacred Books of the East*, Vol. 25, pp. 24, 69, 84–85, 195–197, 260, 326, 329–330, 343–344, 370–371, 402–404, 413–416, 420, 423, passim. Pages 164–167: James Legge, trans., *A Record of Buddhistic Kingdoms* (Oxford: Clarendon Press, 1886), pp. 42–45, 77–79. Page 168: Museo delle terme, Rome. Alinari/Art Resource, New York. Page 169: Courtesy, Iraq Museum, Baghdad. Page 171: Courtesy, Lahore Museum, Lahore, Pakistan. Page 173: Cleveland Museum of Art, Gift of Severance and Greta Millikin, 59.130.

Chapter 6

Pages 181–182: H. H. Wilson, tr., *The Vishnu Purana* (Calcutta: Punthi Pustak, 1961), 3rd ed., pp. 516–520 passim. Copyright 1961. Used by permission of the publisher. Page 184: National Museum, Madras. Lauros-Giraudon/Art Resource, New York. Pages 186–188: Benjamin Ben Jonah, *The Itinerary of Benjamin of Tudela*, Marcus N. Adler, trans. (London: H. Frowde, 1907), pp. 35–42, passim. Pages 189–192: Jacob S. Minkin, *The World of Moses Maimonides with Selections from His Writings* (New York: Thomas Yoseloff, 1957), pp. 371–373, 375–380, 398–399, 401. Copyright 1957. Used by permission of Associated University Presses. Pages 194–195: William Theodore de Bary et al., eds. and trs., *Sources of Indian Tradition*, pp. 163–165. Copyright © 1958 Columbia University Press. Used by permission. Pages 197–199: *Ennin's Travels in T'ang China*, Edwin O. Reischauer. Copyright © 1955, by the Ronald Press Company. Reprinted by permission of John Wiley & Sons Inc. Pp. 221–224. Pages 200–201: Lucian Stryk, *World of the Buddha: A Reader* (New York: Doubleday, 1968), pp. 364–365. © 1968 by Lucian Stryk. Used by permission of Grove Press, a division of Wheatland Corporation. Page 202: China, Seated Guanyin (Avolokitesvara). Jin dynasty (1115–1234), wood with polychromy and gilding, height 114.4 cm × 97.8 cm, Lucy Maud Buckingham Collection, 1923.921. © 1989 The Art Institute of Chicago. All Rights Reserved.

Chapter 7

Pages 207–209, 210–211: Scripture quotations are from the *Good News Bible* in Today's English Version. Copyright © American Bible Society 1966, 1971, 1976. Pages 213–215: P. R. Coleman-Norton, ed. and tr., *Roman State and Christian Church* (Reading, England: S. P. C. K., 1966), vol. 1, pp. 74, 76, 219, 254, 342, 354; vol. 2, pp. 387–388, 392–393, 436–437, 438, 452, 459, 510, 559–560. Copyright 1966. Used by permission of The Society for Promoting Christian Knowledge. Pages 216–218, 228–229: From the book, THE CRISIS OF CHURCH & STATE 1050–1300. By Brian Tierney © 1964. Used by permission of the publisher, Prentice-Hall, Inc., Englewood Cliffs, NJ. Pp. 13–15, 207–209. Page 219: Palazzo Arcivescorile, Ravenna. Alinari/Art Resource, New York. Pages 220–221: Sidney Z. Ehler and John B. Morrall, *Church and State Through the Centuries* (London: Burns and Oates, 1954), p. 10. Pages 222–224: Sr. Benedicta Ward SLG, ed. and tr., *The Sayings of the Desert Fathers* (Kalamazoo, Michigan: Cistercian Publications, 1975), pp. 109–113 passim. © Mowbray Publishing, a division of Cassell PLC. Used by permission of Mowbray. Pages 226–227: Oliver J. Thatcher and Edgar H. McNeal, *A Source Book for Mediaeval History* (New York: Charles Scribner's Sons, 1905), pp. 136–138. Page 230: Strasbourg Cathedral. Marburg/Art Resource, New York. Page 231: From *Art of the Byzantine World*, Christa Schug-Wille (Harry N. Abrams, Inc., 1975). Reproduced with permission. Pages 232–234: C. W. R. D. Moseley, tr., *The Travels of Sir John Mandeville* (London: Penguin Classics, 1983), translation copyright © C. W. R. D. Moseley, 1983, pp. 50–52. Reproduced by permission of Penguin Books Ltd.

Chapter 8

Pages 239–242: T. B. Irving, tr., *The Qur'an: The First American Version* (Brattleboro, Vt.: 1985), pp. 30–31, 55, 59, 62–63, 67, 74, 270. Copyright 1985. Used by permission of the publisher. Pages 243–246: Iman Nawawi, *Gardens of the Righteous*, tr. Muhammed Zafrulla Kahn (London: Curzon, 1975), pp. 60–63, 65–66, 68–69, 220–224, 226–228. Copyright 1975. Reprinted July, 1989. Used by permission of the publisher. Pages 248–250: A. A. A. Fyzec, ed. and tr., *A Shi'ite Creed* (New Delhi: Oxford, 1942). Copyright 1942. Used by permission of Oxford University Press, New Delhi. Pages 251–254: Bernard Lewis, ed. and tr., *Islam from the Prophet Muhammad to the Capture of Constantinople*, Volume I: Politics and War, pages 171–179, passim. Used by permission of Oxford University Press, New York. Pages 256–258: William Theodore de Bary et al., eds.

and trs., *Sources of Indian Tradition*, pp. 420–424. Copyright © 1958 Columbia University Press. Used by permission. Pages 259–261: Bernard Lewis, ed. and tr., *Islam from the Prophet Muhammad to the Capture of Constantinople*, Volume II: Religion and Society, pages 22–24, 26–27, passim. Used by permission of Oxford University Press, New York.

Chapter 9

Pages 267–269, 270–272: W. G. Aston, trans., *Nihongi. Chronicles of Japan from the Earliest Times to A.D. 697*, 2 vols. (London: Kegan, Paul, Trench, Truebner and Co., 1896), Vol. 2, pp. 112–117; Vol. 2, pp. 170, 184–185, 190–192, 194–198, 206–208, passim. Pages 274–277: Annie Shepley Omori and Kochi Doi, trans., *Diaries of Court Ladies of Old Japan* (Boston: Houghton Mifflin, 1920), pp. 71–73, 86–87, 89–90, 130–134. Pages 279–280: Tu Fu, *Selected Poems*, Rewi Alley, trans. (Beijing: Foreign Languages Press, 1964), pp. 12–13, 131–132, 163. Pages 281–283: Chen Pu, "On Farming," tr. by Clara Yu, pp. 109–112. Reprinted with permission of The Free Press, a Division of Macmillan, Inc. from CHINESE CIVILIZATION AND SOCIETY: A Sourcebook by Patricia Buckley Ebrey. Copyright © 1981 by The Free Press. Pages 284–287: Clara Yu, tr., "The Attractions of Farming," pp. 100–102, 104–105. Reprinted with permission of The Free Press, a Division of Macmillan, Inc. from CHINESE CIVILIZATION AND SOCIETY: A Sourcebook by Patrician Buckley Ebrey. Copyright © 1981 by The Free Press. Pages 289–291: Arthur L. Basham, *The Wonder That Was India* (London: Sidgwick & Jackson, 1954), pp. 444–446. Copyright 1954. Used by permission of the publisher. Pages 292–293: *Vikrama's Adventures* (Harvard Oriental Series, edited by Eugene Watson Burlingame). Copyright © 1926 by Harvard University Press. Reprinted by permission. Pages 294–296: H. M. Elliot and John Dowson, eds. and trans., *The History of India as Told by Its Own Historians*, 8 vols. (London: Truebner, 1867–1877), Vol. 3, pp. 374–388, passim. Pages 298–301: Bernard Lewis, ed. and tr., *Islam from the Prophet Muhammad to the Capture of Constantinople*, Vol. II: Religion and Society, pages 69–73. Used by permission of Oxford University Press, New York. Pages 302–304: Charles Pellat, *The Life and Words of Jahiz* (Berkeley: California, 1969), pp. 251, 257–258, 264–267. © 1969 The Regents of the University of California. Used by permission.

Chapter 10

Pages 310–312: Einhard, *The Life of Charlemagne*, trans. S. E. Turner (New York: Harper and Bros., 1880), pp. 62–66, 69. Pages 314–317: *The Song of Roland*, trans. by Isabel Butler (Cambridge, Mass.: Houghton Mifflin, 1904), pp. 35–36, 38–41, 63–66, 84–87, passim. Pages 318–319: Dana C. Munro, ed. and trans., *Urban and the Crusaders* (Philadelphia: University of Pennsylvania, 1896), pp. 4–5. Pages 320–323: "Magna Carta," trans. E. P. Cheyney, in *University of Pennsylvania Translations and Reprints* (Philadelphia: University of Pennsylvania, 1897), Vol. 1, no. 6, pp. 6–15, passim. Pages 325–326: *Liber de Regimine Civitatum*, ed. Gaietano Salvemini, trans. A. J. Andrea, in A. Gandenzi, ed., *Bibliotheca Juridica Medii Aevi*, 3 vols. (Bologna, 1888–1901), Vol. 3, pp. 218–219, 228–229, 260. Pages 328–330: Peter Abelard, *Sic et Non*, trans. Brian Tierney, in Brian Tierney, Donald Kagan, and L. Pearce Williams, eds., *Great Issues in Western Civilization*, 2nd ed. (New York: Random House, 1972), Vol. 1, pp. 412–414. Reprinted by permission of McGraw-Hill Publishing Company. Pages 331–333: Lynn Thorndike, ed. and tr., *University Records and Life in the Middle Ages*, pp. 125–127. Copyright © 1944 Columbia Unviersity Press. Used by permission. Pages 334–337: Richard A. Newhall, ed., and Jean Birdsall, tr., *The Chronicle of Jean de Venette* (New York: Columbia, 1953), pp. 31–32, 48–52 passim. Copyright 1953. Used by permission of Jane Lyons. Page 338: Bayerisches Nationalmuseum. Page 339: Gemäldegalerie Staatliche Museen Preussischer Kulturbesitz. Jörg P. Anders, photographer.

Chapter 11

Pages 347–349: James A. Montgomery, tr., *The History of Yaballaha III, Nestorian Patriarch, and of his Vicar Bar Sauma*, pp. 66–69, 72. Copyright © 1927 & 1958 Columbia University Press. Used by permission. Pages 350–352, 361–362: Henry Yule, ed. and tr., *Cathay and the Way Thither*, 2nd ed. revised by H. Cordier (London: Hakluyt, 1913–1916), vol. 3, pp. 45–51, 151–155. Copyright 1913–1916. Used by permission of the publisher. Pages 364–368: J. F. P. Hopkins, tr., and N. Levtzion and J. F. P. Hopkins, eds., *Corpus of Early Arabic Sources for West African History* (Cambridge, England: Cambridge, 1981), pp. 284–286, 288–291, 296–297. © University of Ghana, International Academic Union, Cambridge University Press 1981. Reprinted with the permission of Cambridge University Press. Pages 369–372: Ma Huan, *The Overall Survey of the Ocean's Shores* (London: Hakluyt, 1970), pp. 108–109, 113–117, 120, 137–140, 165, 172. Copyright 1970. Used by permission of the publisher. Pages 374–375: Gomes Eannes de Azurara, *The Chronicle of the Discovery and Conquest of Guinea*, trans. Charles Raymond Beazley and Edgar Prestage, 2 vols. (London: Hakluyt Society, 1896), Vol. 1, pp. 27–29, 83–85.

Chapter 12

Pages 382–385: Bernardino de Sahagun, *The War of Conquest: How It Was Waged Here in Mexico*, tr. by Arthur J.

O. Anderson and Charles E. Dibble (Salt Lake City: Utah, 1978), pp. 16–17, 19–23. Copyright 1976. Used by permission of the publisher. Pages 386–389: *The Laws of Burgos of 1512–1513: Royal Ordinances for the Good Government and Treatment of the Indians*, Lesley B. Simpson, trans. (San Francisco: John Howell, 1960), pp. 11–47, passim. Pages 390–392: David Pieterzen DeVries, *Voyages from Holland to New York* (New York: 1853), pp. 114–117. Pages 394–396: Extracts from Letters of King Afonso to King of Portugal, 1526. Translated and published in THE AFRICAN PAST by Basil Davidson. Copyright © Basil Davidson, 1964. Reproduced by permission of Curtis Brown Ltd, London. Pages 397–398: Awnsham and John Churchill, eds., *Collections of Voyages and Travels*, 3rd ed., 8 vols. (London: H. Lintot, 1744–1747), Vol. 5, p. 459. Modernized by A. J. Andrea. Page 399: Reproduced by Courtesy of the Trustees of the British Museum. Pages 402–405: From CHINA IN THE SIXTEENTH CENTURY: THE JOURNALS OF MATTHEW RICCI: 1583–1610, translated by Louis J. Gallagher, S.J. Copyright 1953 by Louis J. Gallagher, S.J. Reprinted by permission of Random House, Inc. Pages 406–408: David John Lu, ed. and tr., *Sources of Japanese History* (New York: McGraw-Hill, 1974), vol. 1, pp. 207–209. Copyright 1974. Used by permission of McGraw-Hill Publishing Company. Pages 410–412: *The Akbar Nama of Abu-1-Fazl*, trans. Henry Beveridge, 3 vols. (New Delhi: Ess Ess Publications, 1902–1939), Vol. 1, pp. 37, 207, 322–323, 368–370, 410–411. Pages 413–415: Jean-Baptiste Tavernier, *Travels in India*, ed. by William Ball, tr. by V. Ball (Oxford: Oxford, 1925), 2nd ed., pp. 7–11. Used by permission of the publisher.

Chapter 13

Pages 419–422: Niccolò Machiavelli, *The Prince*, tr. by George Bull (London: Penguin Classics, 1961), pp. 61–66, 90–99. Copyright © George Bull, 1961, 1975, 1981 (revised edition). Reproduced by permission of Penguin Books Ltd. Pages 424–428: William Hazlitt, ed. and trans., *The Tabletalk of Martin Luther* (London: H. G. Bohn, 1857), pp. 72–73, 117, 294, 28, 45, 54–55, 25–27, 198, 199, 205–206, 219, passim. Pages 429–431: Nicholas Copernicus, *On the Revolutions*, ed. by Jerry Dobrzycki, tr. by Edward Rosen (Baltimore: Johns Hopkins, 1978), pp. 3–6. Copyright 1978. Used by permission of Macmillan, London and Basingstoke. Page 432: Reproduced by courtesy of the Trustees, The National Gallery, London. pages 434–436: George Verdansky, *A Source Book for Russion History from Early Times to 1917* (New Haven: Yale, 1972), vol. 1, pp. 260–261. Copyright 1961. Used by permission of the publisher. Pages 438–440: Christoval de Molina, "The Fables and Rites of the Yncas," in Clements R. Markham, ed. and tr., *Narratives of the Rites and Laws of the Yncas* (London: Hakluyt, 1873), pp. 59–64. Used by permission of the publisher. Pages 441–444: Extract taken from THE SACRED WRITINGS OF THE SIKHS, translated by Kushwant Singh and others, reproduced by kind permission of Unwin Hyman Ltd. © George Allen & Unwin, 1960. Pages 445–447: Ryusaku Tsunoda, William Theodore de Bary, and Donald Keene, eds., *Sources of the Japanese Tradition*, pp. 340–342, 364–366. Copyright © 1927 & 1958 Columbia University Press. Used by permission.